34-ㄴ-36

# Fundamentals of Software Engineering

### Second Edition

**Carlo Ghezzi**
*Politecnico di Milano*

**Mehdi Jazayeri**
*Technische Universität Wien*

**Dino Mandrioli**
*Politecnico di Milano*

Pearson Education, Inc.
Upper Saddle River, New Jersey 07458

*Library of Congress Cataloging-in-Publication Data*
Ghezzi, Carlo.
    Fundamentals of software engineering / Carlo Ghezzi, Mehdi Jazayeri, and
Dino Mandrioli.--2nd ed.
      p. cm.
    Includes bibliographical references and index.
    ISBN 0-13-305699-6
     1. Software engineering. I. Jazayeri, Medhi. II. Mandrioli, Dino. III. Title.

QA76.758 .G47 2002
005.1--dc21.                                    2002072727

Vice President and Editorial Director, ECS: *Marcia J. Horton*
Senior Acquisitions Editor: *Petra Recter*
Editorial Assistant: *Renee Makras*
Vice President and Director of Production and Manufacturing, ESM: *David W. Riccardi*
Executive Managing Editor: *Vince O'Brien*
Managing Editor: *David A. George*
Production Editor: *Tami Savir*
Director of Creative Services: *Paul Belfanti*
Manager of Electronic Composition and Digital Content: *Jim Sullivan*
Creative Director: *Carole Anson*
Art Director: *Jayne Conte*
Art Editor: *Gregory Dulles*
Manufacturing Manager: *Trudy Pisciotti*
Manufacturing Buyer: *Lisa McDowell*
Marketing Manager: *Holly Stark*

© 2003 Pearson Education, Inc.
Upper Saddle River, New Jersey 07458

The author and publisher of this book have used their best efforts in preparing this book. These efforts include the development, research, and testing of the theories and programs to determine their effectiveness. The author and publisher make no warranty of any kind, expressed or implied, with regard to these programs or the documentation contained in this book. The author and publisher shall not be liable in any event for incidental or consequential damages in connection with, or arising out of, the furnishing, performance, or use of these programs.

Printed in the United States of America.

10 9 8 7 6 5 4 3 2 1

ISBN 0-13-305699-6

Pearson Education Ltd., *London*
Pearson Education Australia Pty. Ltd, *Sydney*
Pearson Education Singapore, Pte. Ltd.
Pearson Education North Asia Ltd., *Hong Kong*
Pearson Education Canada Inc., *Toronto*
Pearson Educación de Mexico, S.A. de C.V.
Pearson Education—Japan, *Tokyo*
Pearson Education Malaysia, Pte. Ltd.
Pearson Education, Inc., *Upper Saddle River, New Jersey*

*To our families, for their support and patience*

# Contents

# Preface to the Second Edition

The first edition of this book was published in 1991. Since then, there has been a lot of progress in computing technology and also in software engineering. Certainly the proliferation of the Internet has had a profound influence on education, research, development, business, and commerce. We decided to produce this second edition in order to bring the book up to date with respect to the advances in software engineering in the last 10 years.

We were pleased to find that the basic premise of the book—the durability and importance of principles—has been borne out by the passage of time: Even though the technology has improved, principles of software engineering have remained the same. We have therefore been able to update every chapter without changing the original structure of the book. The following is still the structure:

Introduction: Chapters 1 –3;

The product: Chapters 4 –6;

Process and management: Chapters 7 –8;

Tools and environments: Chapter 9.

The product-related chapters follow the sequence consisting of design (4), specification (5), and verification (6). This is different from the approach taken by other books, which cover specification before design. The reason for our choice follows from the principles-based approach of the book. All of these activities—design, specification, and verification—are basic activities that must be learned and applied throughout the software life cycle. For example, design is something we do not only with software architecture, but also with software specifications. The modular design approach helps us structure software and also the specification documents. Other books present specification first and then design, allegedly because—according to the traditional software processes—first we specify a software and then we design it. By contrast, we believe that learning about the design activity and approaches first, creates the needed motivation for the study of specification and provides the skills and techniques for structuring those specifications.

While all areas of software engineering have evolved since the first edition of the book was written, the area of tools and environments has changed substantially. Chapter 9, therefore, is revised considerably. Our approach in this chapter also is to present primarily principles rather than specific tools. We have seen over the years that tools change as technology evolves, and the choice of what particular tools to study depends on the student's environment and focus. We therefore cover a framework for studying and evaluating software tools without a detailed look at any particular tools.

Besides many minor improvements and changes, we have made the following major additions:

In Chapter 3, we have added two new case studies, one of a simple compiler and the other of the elevator system that we use throughout much of the book. The two case studies are complementary in that they deal with different application areas and pose different design challenges. They are presented in this chapter in a simple and intuitive way to get the student oriented towards thinking of system issues. They are intended to illustrate the use of general principles with concrete examples.

In Chapter 4, we have extended the treatment of object orientation, software architecture, components, and distributed systems.

In Chapter 5, we have added a treatment of Z and UML. A new section gives a more systematic treatment of requirements engineering.

In Chapter 6, we have added model checking and GQM as evaluation and verification techniques.

In Chapter 7, we have included a treatment of the unified process, the open-source process, and the synchronize-and-stabilize process. We have also added a new case study on requirements engineering.

In Chapter 8, we have added the capability maturity model and a description of the Nokia software factories.

In Chapter 9, we have added a treatment of the concurrent versioning system (CVS).

In Chapter 10, we have provided coverage of the Software Engineering Code of Ethics.

In the appendix, we have added a new case study on the use of formal methods in industry.

## THE ROLE OF OBJECT ORIENTATION

The book covers the principles of object orientation in a balanced way, rather than as the only way to do software engineering. Object-oriented analysis, design, and programming have certainly evolved and become a dominant approach to software engineering. We believe, however, that the principles underlying software engineering are deeper than objects. What the student should learn are principles and methods that can be used in different approaches. The student should learn how to choose between approaches and should be able to apply object orientation when it is the right choice. For example, the student should learn about information hiding before learning about objects and inheritance.

## THE PURPOSE OF CASE STUDIES

The case studies presented throughout the book and also in the appendix have two purposes. One is to present the issues discussed in a larger context, in order to give the student a broader view of why the principles or techniques are important. The second reason is to give those students who have not seen real projects a picture of realistic projects. The case studies are necessarily simplified to focus on important issues, but we have found that they are useful especially to less experienced students. The study of software engineering poses a challenge in a university setting because the typical student has not been exposed to the problems that software engineers face daily. These case studies attempt to overcome this challenge.

**INSTRUCTOR RESOURCES**

A companion CD, including solutions and sample course sylllabi is available to instructors. A companion Web site is available through the publisher to both students and instructors. You may contact the authors through the Web site. We welcome your feedback, comments, and suggestions.

CARLO GHEZZI
*Milan, Italy*

MEHDI JAZAYERI
*Palo Alto, California*

DINO MANDRIOLI
*Lugano, Switzerland*

# Preface to the First Edition

This is a textbook on *software engineering*. The theme underlying the book is the importance of rigor in the practice of software engineering. Traditional textbooks on the subject are based on the lifecycle model of software development—that is, requirements, specification, design, coding, maintenance—examining each phase in turn. In contrast, our presentation is based on important principles that can be applied independently of the lifecycle model and often in several phases of the lifecycle. Our emphasis is on identifying and applying fundamental principles that are applicable throughout the software lifecycle.

The general characteristics of the book are the following:

- *It deals with software engineering as opposed to programming.* Thus, we do not discuss any programming issues. For example, we omit any discussion of programming language constructs such as **goto**, loops, etc. We believe that the student of software engineering should have prior familiarity with these issues, which are more properly covered in textbooks on programming languages. On the other hand, we do discuss the issue of mapping software design constructs into specific programming languages. We concentrate on intermodule issues and assume as prerequisite the ability to program individual modules.

- *It emphasizes principles and techniques as opposed to specific tools (which may be used in examples).* Many companies are actively developing software engineering tools and environments today and we expect that better and more sophisticated tools will be invented as our knowledge of software engineering increases. Once the student understands the principles and techniques that the tool is based on, mastery of the tool will be easy. The principles and techniques are applicable across tools while mastering the use of any particular tool does not better prepare the student for the use of other tools. Further, use of tools without understanding their underlying principles is dangerous.

- *It presents engineering principles; it is not an engineering handbook.* Principles are general and are likely to remain applicable for many years while particular techniques will change due to technology, increased knowledge, etc. An engineering handbook may be consulted to learn *how* to apply a particular technique: it contains a set of prescriptions. This book, on the other hand, aims to enable the reader to understand *why* a particular technique should be used and, just as important, why it should *not* be. Even though we do show how a particular technique can be used to implement a given principle, our primary emphasis is on the understanding of the *why* question.

This book embodies our beliefs in the use of fundamental principles and the importance of theory in the practice of engineering. We have used the material in this book in both university and professional courses on various aspects of software engineering.

## AUDIENCE

This book is designed to be used as a textbook by students of software engineering either in a classroom or for self-study. Professional engineers and managers will find material here to convince them of the usefulness of modern practices of software engineering and the need to adopt them. It may be used by professionals who are willing to invest the time for serious study; it is not really appropriate for a cursory reading. In particular, wherever necessary, we have sacrificed breadth for depth. For the professional, the notes on further references will be especially helpful. An Instructor's Manual is available with ideas for course organizations and solutions to some of the exercises.

## PREREQUISITES

The book is designed for junior, senior, or beginning-graduate level students in computer science. The reader must have had a course in data structures and should be fluent in one or more programming languages. We assume that the reader is already proficient in programming. Analytical reasoning, although not strictly necessary, will greatly enhance the ability of the reader to appreciate the deeper concepts of the book. This skill is developed by mathematics courses such as calculus, discrete mathematics, or-even better-theoretical computer science. "Mathematical maturity" is necessary for the student of any engineering discipline.

## ORGANIZATION AND CONTENT

Software engineering is a large, multi-dimensional discipline. Organizing a textbook on the subject poses a challenge because a textbook should present material sequentially, but the many facets of software engineering are so interrelated that there is no optimal sequence of topics. We have organized this textbook based on the view that in software engineering:

> We are building a *product*: the software;
>
> We use a *process* to build that product; and
>
> We use *tools* in support of that process.

The book thus has three technical sections dealing in turn with the software product (Chapters 4 through 6), the software engineering process and management (Chapters 7 and 8), and the software engineering environment (Chapter 9). Chapters 1 through 3 form a general introduction to the field and the subsequent more technical sections of the book.

In Chapter 2, we discuss the many facets of software and common desirable characteristics for software. These characteristics impose constraints on the software builder and the process to be used. In Chapter 3, we present principles for building high-quality software. By studying principles rather than specific tools, the student gains knowledge that is independent of a particular technology and application environment. Because technology changes and environments evolve, the student should be armed with principles and techniques that can be utilized in different application areas. Chapters 4 through 8 present and discuss techniques for applying the principles of Chapter 3 to, respectively, design, specification, verification, engineering process, and engineering management. In Chapter 9, we discuss the use of computers themselves to help in the building of software. We postpone the discussion of any specific tools to this chapter.

While the material in the first two sections should withstand the passage of time, it is likely that the material in the third section will become outdated (we hope) because newer and better tools are being developed. Since programming languages are a fundamental tool of the software engineer, we use Chapter 9 as a bridge between the design issues of Chapter 4 and specific programming language constructs.

## EXERCISES

The book contains many exercises of three types:

- short, paper exercises, aimed at extending the knowledge gained from the book or applying the knowledge more deeply; these exercises are interspersed throughout the chapters.

- longer paper exercises at the end of each chapter, requiring integration of the material in the chapter.

- term-projects requiring the development of some substantial software system by a small team.

Solutions to some of the exercises are provided at the end of each chapter. More exercise solutions are given in the Instructor's Manual.

## CASE STUDIES

Several case studies are used in the text to demonstrate the integration of different concepts and to contrast different approaches in realistic situations. In addition, three case studies of real-life software engineering projects and their analyses are presented at the end of the book. These case studies may be read and studied at different times and for different purposes. From these case studies, the new student with little industrial experience can gain a quick view of the diversity of problems faced in industrial practice. The student with some experience perhaps will identify with certain aspects of these case studies and learn from others. The case studies may be read concurrently with the main text. Several exercises in the book refer to these case studies.

## LABORATORY COURSE

Many software engineering courses combine lectures and a laboratory project. To do this in a single semester is rather difficult. The teacher will find himself discussing organizational issues while the students are concentrating on their daily forays into debugging. We believe that software engineering must be taught as all other engineering disciplines by first providing the student with a solid foundation in the "theory." Only after this has been achieved will laboratory experience enhance the student's knowledge. This implies that the student project must start closer to the middle of the semester rather than at the beginning. In our view, a better approach is to spend one semester on the theory and a second semester on the laboratory. The Instructor's Manual offers several ideas for organizing a laboratory course based on this text.

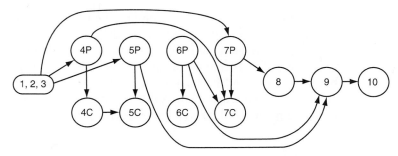

## READING GRAPH

The book may be read in different sequences and at different levels. Each of Chapters 4 through 7 contains material that may be skipped on the first reading or for a less detailed study. Chapters 1 through 3 are required reading for the subsequent chapters. The graph shows the dependencies among the chapters and the various paths through the book. The notation $n$P refers to a partial reading of Chapter $n$, skipping some sections; $n$C stands for a complete reading.

The Instructor's Manual discusses different course organizations based on the book. The conventional one-semester project software engineering course may follow the sequence: 1, 2, 3, 7P, 5P, 4P, 6P, 8, 9, 10. We ourselves prefer the sequence 1, 2, 3, 4P, 5P, 6P, 7P, 8, 9, 10. In either case, the students should start on the project after 5P.

## ACKNOWLEDGMENTS

We gratefully acknowledge reviews of earlier drafts provided by Reda A. Ammar of the University of Connecticut, Larry C. Christensen of Brigham Young University, William F. Decker of the University of Iowa, David A. Gustafson of Kansas State University, Richard A. Kemmerer of the University of California at Santa Barbara, John C. Knight of the University of Virginia, Seymour V. Pollack of Washington University, and K. C. Tai of North Carolina State University. We would also like to thank the following people who have provided valuable feedback on various drafts of the manuscript: Vincenzo Ambriola, Paola Bertaina, David Jacobson, and Milon Mackey.

Hewlett-Packard Laboratories and Politecnico di Milano made it possible to conceive this book by supporting a course offered by Mehdi Jazayeri at the Politecnico di Milano during the spring of 1988. Alfredo Scarfone and HP Italiana provided us with support in Italy. We would like to acknowledge the support of management at Hewlett-Packard Laboratories, especially John Wilkes, Dick Lampman, Bob Ritchie, and Frank Carrubba in Palo Alto, and Peter Porzer in Pisa. We would like to thank Bart Sears for his help with various systems, and John Wilkes for the use of his data base for managing references. We have also received support from Consiglio Nazionale delle Ricerche.

CARLO GHEZZI
*Milan, Italy*

MEHDI JAZAYERI
*Palo Alto, California*

DINO MANDRIOLI
*Pisa, Italy*

# CHAPTER 1

# Software Engineering: A Preview

Software engineering is the field of computer science that deals with the building of software systems that are so large or so complex that they are built by a team or teams of engineers. Usually, these systems exist in multiple versions and are in service for many years. During their lifetime, they undergo many changes: to fix defects, to enhance existing features, to add new features, to remove old features, or to be adapted to run in a new environment.

We may define software engineering as "the application of engineering to software." More precisely, the IEEE Std 610.12-1990's *Standard Glossary of Software Engineering Terminology (ANSI)* defines software engineering as the application of a systematic, disciplined, quantifiable approach to the development, operation, and maintenance of software.

Parnas [1978] defined software engineering as the "multi-person construction of multiversion software." This definition captures the essence of software engineering and highlights the differences between programming and software engineering. A programmer writes a complete program, while a software engineer writes a software component that will be combined with components written by other software engineers to build a system. The component written by one software engineer may be modified by other software engineers; it may be used by others to build different versions of the system long after the original engineer has left the project. Programming is primarily a personal activity, while software engineering is essentially a team activity.

Indeed, the term "software engineering" was invented in the late 1960s after the realization that all the lessons learned about how to program well were not helping to build better software systems. While the field of programming had made tremendous progress—through the systematic study of algorithms and data structures and the invention of "structured programming"—there were still major difficulties in building large software systems. The techniques that were used by a physicist to write a program to calculate the solution to a differential equation for an experiment were not adequate for a programmer working on a team that was trying to build an operating system or even an inventory-tracking system. What was needed in these complex cases was a classic engineering approach: Define clearly the problem you are trying to solve, and then use and develop standard tools and techniques for solving it.

To be sure, software engineering has made progress since the 1960s. There are standard techniques that are used in the field. Rather than being practiced as a craft, software engineering has moved closer to being practiced with more discipline that is traditionally associated with engineering. Yet, differences with traditional engineering disciplines still exist. In designing an electrical system, such as an amplifier, the electrical engineer can specify the system precisely. All parameters and tolerance levels are stated clearly and are understood by the customer and the engineer. Such parameters are still not known about software systems. We do not know what parameters to specify and how to specify them.

In classic engineering disciplines, the engineer has tools and mathematical training to specify the properties of the product separately from those of the design. For example, an electrical engineer relies on mathematical equations to verify that a design will not violate power requirements. In software engineering, such mathematical tools are not well developed, and their applicability is still under debate. The typical software engineer relies much more on experience and judgment rather than mathematical techniques. While experience and judgment are necessary, formal analysis tools also are essential in the practice of engineering.

This book presents software engineering as an engineering discipline. We offer certain principles that we believe are essential to the "multi-person construction of multi-version software." Such principles are much more important than any particular notation or methodology for building software. Principles enable the software engineer to evaluate different methodologies and apply them when they are appropriate. Chapter 3 presents these principles; the rest of the book can be viewed as showing their application to the various problems in software engineering.

In this chapter, we review the evolution of software engineering and its relationship to other disciplines. The goal of the chapter is to place the field of software engineering in perspective.

## 1.1 THE ROLE OF SOFTWARE ENGINEERING IN SYSTEM DESIGN

A software system is often a component of a much larger system. The software engineering activity is therefore a part of a much larger system design activity in which the requirements of the software are balanced against the requirements of other parts of the system being designed. For example, a telephone-switching system consists of computers, telephone lines and cables, telephones, other hardware such as satellites, and, finally, software to control the various components. It is the combination of all these components that is expected to meet the requirements of the whole system.

A requirement such as "the system must not be down for more than a second in 20 years" or "when a telephone receiver is taken off the hook, a dial tone is played within half a second" can be satisfied with a combination of hardware, software, and special devices. The decision of how best to meet the requirement involves many trade-offs. Power plant or traffic-monitoring systems, banking systems, and hospital administration systems are other examples of systems that exhibit the need to view the software as a component of a larger system.

Software is being increasingly embedded in diverse systems, from television sets to airplanes. Dealing with such systems requires the software engineer to take a broader look at the general problem of system engineering. It requires the software engineer to participate in developing the requirements for the whole system. It requires that the software engineer attempt to understand the application area before starting to think of what abstract interfaces the software must meet. For example, if the hardware device that is the interface to the user has primitive data-entry facilities, a sophisticated word processor will not be necessary in the system.

Considering software engineering as a part of system engineering makes us recognize the importance of compromise, which is the hallmark of any engineering discipline. A classic compromise concerns the choice of what should be done in software and what should be done in hardware. Software implementation offers flexibility, while hardware implementation offers performance. For example, in Chapter 2 we shall see an example of a coin-operated machine that could be built either with several coin slots, one for each type of coin, or a single slot, leaving it to software to recognize the different coins. An even more basic compromise involves the decision as to what should be automated and what should be done manually.

## 1.2    A SHORTENED HISTORY OF SOFTWARE ENGINEERING

The birth and evolution of software engineering as a discipline within computer science can be traced to the evolving and maturing view of the programming activity. In the early days of computing, the problem of programming was viewed essentially as how to place a sequence of instructions together to get the computer to do something useful. The problems being programmed were well understood—for example, how to solve a differential equation. The program was written by, say, a physicist to solve an equation of interest to him or her. The problem was just between the user and the computer; no other person was involved.

As computers became cheaper and more common, more and more people started using them. Higher level languages were invented in the late 1950s to make it easier to communicate with the machine. But still, the activity of getting the computer to do something useful was essentially performed by one person writing a program for a well-defined task.

It was at this time that "programming" attained the status of a profession: You could ask a *programmer* to write a program for you, instead of doing it yourself. This arrangement introduced a separation between the user and the computer: Now the user had to specify the task in a form other than the precise programming notation used before. The programmer then read this specification and translated it into a precise set of machine instructions. This, of course, sometimes resulted in the programmer misinterpreting the user's intentions, even in these usually small tasks.

Very few large software projects were being done at the time—the early 1960s— and these were undertaken by computer pioneers who were experts. For example, the CTSS operating system developed at MIT was indeed a large project, but it was done by highly knowledgeable and motivated individuals.

In the middle to late 1960s, truly large software systems were attempted to be built commercially. The best documented of these projects was the OS 360 operating system for the IBM 360 computer family. The people on these large projects quickly realized that building large software systems was significantly different from building smaller systems. There were fundamental difficulties in scaling up the techniques of small-program development to large software development. The term "software engineering" was invented around this time, and conferences were held to discuss the difficulties these projects were facing in delivering the promised products. Large software projects were universally over budget and behind schedule. Another term invented at the time was "software crisis."

It appeared that the problems seen in building large software systems were not a matter of putting computer instructions together. Rather, the problems being solved were not well understood, at least not by everyone involved in the project or by any single individual. People on the project had to spend a lot of time communicating with each other rather than writing code. People sometimes even left the project, and this affected not only the work they had been doing, but the work of the others who were depending on them. Replacing an individual required an extensive amount of training about the "folklore" of the project requirements and the system design. Any change in the original system requirements seemed to affect many parts of the project, further delaying delivery of the system. These kinds of problems just did not exist in the early "programming" days and seemed to call for a new approach.

Many solutions were proposed and tried. Some suggested that the solution lay in better management techniques. Others proposed different team organizations. Yet others argued for better programming languages and tools. Many called for organizationwide standards such as uniform coding conventions. A few called for the use of mathematical and formal approaches. There was no shortage of ideas. The final consensus was that the problem of building software should be approached in the same way that engineers had built other large complex systems, such as bridges, refineries, factories, ships, and airplanes. The point was to view the final software system as a complex product and the building of it as an engineering job. The engineering approach required management, organization, tools, theories, methodologies, and techniques. Thus was software engineering born.

In a classic paper in 1987, Brooks, paraphrasing Aristotle, argued that there are two kinds of challenges in software development: essential and accidental. The accidental difficulties are those which have to do with our current tools and technologies—for example, the syntactic problems arising from the programming language we are using. We can overcome such difficulties with better tools and technologies. The essential difficulties, on the other hand, are not helped substantially by new tools. Complex design problems—for example, creating and representing a model that can be useful for forecasting the weather or the economy—require intellectual effort, creativity, and time. Brooks argued that there is no magic—no "silver bullet"—for solving the essential problems faced by software engineers.

Brooks's argument exposes the false assumptions behind the term "software crisis." The term was invented because software projects were continually late and over budget. The conclusion was that the problem was temporary and could be fixed by better tools and management techniques. In reality, projects were late because the application was complex and poorly understood by both customers and developers and neither had any idea how to estimate the difficulty of the task and how long it would take to solve it. Although the term "software crisis" is still used sometimes, there is a general consensus that the inherent difficulties of software development are not short-term problems. New and complex application domains are inherently difficult to approach and are not subject to short-term, quick solutions.

The foregoing history emphasizes the growth of software engineering, starting from programming. Other technological trends have also played significant roles in the evolution of the field. The most important influence has been that of the change in the balance of hardware and software costs. Whereas the cost of a computerized system used to be determined largely by hardware costs, and software was an insignificant factor, today the software component is by far the dominant factor in a system's cost. The declining cost of hardware and the rising cost of software have tipped the balance further in the direction of software, accentuating the economical importance of software engineering.

Another evolutionary trend has been internal to the field itself. There has been a growing emphasis on viewing software engineering as dealing with more than just "coding." Instead, the software is seen as having an entire life cycle, starting from conception and continuing through design, development, deployment, maintenance, and evolution. The shift of emphasis away from coding has sparked the development of methodologies and sophisticated tools to support teams involved in the entire software life cycle.

We can expect the importance of software engineering to continue to grow for several reasons. First is economics: Worldwide expenditures in software have risen from $140 billion in 1985 to $800 billion in 2000. This fact alone ensures that software engineering will grow as a discipline. Second, software is permeating our society: More and more, software is used to control critical functions of various machines, such as aircraft and medical devices, and to support worldwide critical functions, such as electronic commerce. This fact ensures the growing interest of society in dependable software, to the extent of enacting legislation on specific standards, requirements, and certification procedures. No doubt, it will continue to be important to learn how to build better software better.

## 1.3    THE ROLE OF THE SOFTWARE ENGINEER

The evolution of the field has defined the role of the software engineer and the required experience and education. A software engineer must, of course, be a good programmer, be well versed in data structures and algorithms, and be fluent in one or more programming languages. These are requirements for "programming-in-the-small," roughly defined as building programs that can be written in their entirety by a single individual. But a software engineer is also involved in "programming-in-the-large," which requires more.

The software engineer must be familiar with several design approaches, be able to translate vague requirements and desires into precise specifications, and be able to converse with the user of a system in terms of the application rather than in "computerese." These capabilities in turn require the flexibility and openness to grasp and become conversant with the essentials of different application areas. The software engineer needs the ability to move among several levels of abstraction at different stages of the project, from specific application procedures and requirements, to abstractions for the software system, to a specific design for the system, and, finally, to the detailed coding level.

As in any other engineering field, the software engineer must develop skills that allow him or her to build a variety of models and to reason about those models in order to guide choices of the many trade-offs faced in the software development process. Different models are used in the requirements phase, in the design of the software architecture, and in the implementation phase. At some stage, the model might be used to answer questions about both the behavior of the system and its performance.

The software engineer is a member of a team and therefore needs communication skills and interpersonal skills. The software engineer also needs the ability to schedule work, both his or her own and that of others.

As already mentioned, a software engineer is responsible for many things. Often, many organizations divide the responsibilities among several specialists with different titles. For example, an analyst is responsible for deriving the requirements and for interacting with the customer and understanding the application area, while a performance analyst is responsible for analyzing the performance of the system. Sometimes the same engineer plays different roles in different phases of the project or in different projects.

## 1.4   THE SOFTWARE LIFE CYCLE

From the inception of an idea for a software system, until it is implemented and delivered to a customer, and even after that, the system undergoes gradual development and evolution. The software is said to have a *life cycle* composed of several phases. Each phase results in the development of either a part of the system or something associated with the system, such as a test plan or a user manual. In the traditional life cycle model, called the "waterfall model," each phase has well-defined starting and ending points, with clearly identifiable deliverables to the next phase. In practice, however, things are rarely so simple.

A sample waterfall life cycle model comprises the following phases:

- **Requirements analysis and specification.** Requirements analysis is usually the first phase of a large-scale software development project. It is undertaken after a *feasibility study* has been performed to define the precise costs and benefits of a software system. The purpose of this phase is to identify and document the exact requirements for the system. Such study may be performed by the customer, the developer, a marketing organization, or any combination of the three. In cases where the requirements are not clear (e.g., for a system that has never been done before), much interaction must take place between the user and the developer. The requirements at this stage should be in end-user terms, but often are not. Various software engineering methodologies advocate that this phase must also produce user manuals and even plans for the system test that will be performed eventually, before the system is delivered.

- **System design and specification.** Once the requirements for a system have been documented, software engineers design a software system to meet them. This phase is sometimes split into two subphases: *architectural* or *high-level design* and *detailed design*. Architectural design entails defining the overall organization of the system in terms of high-level components and interactions among them. As we move through increasingly detailed design levels, components are decomposed into lower level modules with precisely defined interfaces. All design levels are documented in specification documents that keep track of design decisions.

Separating the requirements analysis phase from the design phase is an instance of a fundamental "what-how" dichotomy that we encounter quite often in computer science. The general principle involves making a clear distinction between *what* the problem is and *how* to solve the problem. In this case, the requirements phase attempts to specify what the problem is. That is why we said that the requirements should be stated in terms of the needs of the end user. Usually, there are many ways to satisfy the requirements, sometimes including manual solutions that do not involve the use of computers at all. The purpose of the design phase is to specify a particular software system that will meet the stated requirements. Again, usually, there are many ways to build the specified system. In the coding phase, which follows the design phase, a particular system is coded to meet the design specification. We shall see many other instances of the what-how dichotomy throughout this book.

- **Coding and module testing.** In this phase, the engineer produces the actual code that will be delivered to the customer as the running system. The other phases of the life cycle may also develop code, such as that for prototypes, tests, and test drivers, but these are for use by the developers. Note that individual modules developed in the coding phase are tested before being delivered to the next phase.

- **Integration and system testing.** All the modules that have been developed before and tested individually are put together—integrated—in this phase and are tested as a whole system.

- **Delivery and maintenance.** Once the system passes all the tests, it is delivered to the customer and enters the maintenance phase. Any modifications made to the system after the initial delivery are usually attributed to this phase.

Figure 1.1 gives a graphical view of the software development life cycle and provides a visual explanation of the term "waterfall." Each phase yields results that "flow" into the next, and the process ideally proceeds in an orderly and linear fashion.

As presented here, the phases give a partial, simplified view of the conventional waterfall software life cycle. The process may be decomposed into a different set of phases, with different names, different purposes, and different granularity. Entirely different life cycle schemes may even be proposed, not based on a strictly phased waterfall development. For example, it is clear that if any tests uncover defects in the system, we have to go back at least to the coding phase and perhaps to the design phase to correct some mistakes. In general, any phase may uncover problems in previous phases, and when it does, that will necessitate going back to the previous phases and redoing some earlier work. For example, if the system design phase uncovers inconsistencies or ambiguities in the system requirements, the requirements analysis phase must be revisited to determine what requirements were really intended.

Another simplification in the preceding presentation is that it assumes that a phase is completed before the next one begins. In practice, it is often expedient to start

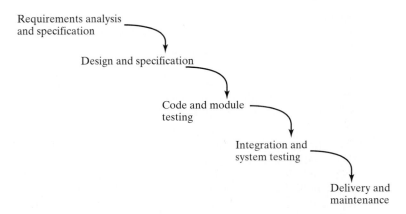

FIGURE 1.1

The waterfall model of the software life cycle.

a phase before a previous one is finished. This may happen, for example, if some data necessary for the completion of the requirements phase will not be available for some time. Or it might be necessary because the people ready to start the next phase are available and have nothing else to do. Or we may decide to do the next phase in order to reduce the product's time to market. *Concurrent engineering* is the term commonly used to refer to modern process organizations that try to achieve early delivery of products by introducing parallelism in the development steps of previously sequential processes. We postpone these and other issues related to the software life cycle until Chapter 7.

Many books on software engineering are organized according to the traditional software life cycle model, each section or chapter being devoted to one phase. Instead, we have organized this book according to principles. Once mastered, these principles can be applied by the software engineer in all phases of software development, as well as in life cycle models that are not based on phased development, as discussed earlier. Indeed, research and experience have shown that there is a variety of life cycle models and that no single one is appropriate for all software systems. In Chapter 7, we examine several different life cycle models.

## 1.5    THE RELATIONSHIP OF SOFTWARE ENGINEERING TO OTHER AREAS OF COMPUTER SCIENCE

Standing now on its own as a discipline, software engineering has emerged as an important field of computer science. Indeed, there is a synergistic relationship between it and many other areas in computer science: These areas both influence and are influenced by software engineering. In the subsections that follow, we explore the relationship between software engineering and some of the other important fields of computer science.

### 1.5.1   Programming Languages

The influence of software engineering on programming languages is evident: Programming languages are the central tools used in software development. As a result, they have a profound influence on how well we can achieve our software engineering goals. In turn, these goals influence the development of programming languages.

The most notable example of this influence on programming languages is the inclusion of *modularity* features, such as separate and independent compilation, and the separation of specification from implementation, in order to support team development of large software. Programming languages such as Ada 95 and Java, for example, support the development of "packages"—allowing the separation of the package interface from its implementation—and libraries of packages that can be used as components in the development of independent software systems. This is a step towards making it possible to build software by choosing from a catalog of available components and combining them, similarly to the way hardware is built. Another example is the introduction of *exception-handling* constructs in programming languages to allow for detecting and responding to any malfunction that may occur when the software is running. Such constructs support the engineer in building more reliable applications.

Conversely, programming languages have influenced software engineering. One example is the idea that requirements and design should be described precisely, possibly using a language as rigorous and machine-processible as a programming language. Another example is the treatment of the input to a software system as a program coded in some "programming" language. The commands that a user can type into a system are not just a random collection of characters; rather, they form a language used to communicate with the system. Designing an appropriate input language is a part of designing the system interface.

Old operating systems such as OS 360 had an intricate and cryptic interface—called job control language (JCL)—that was used to instruct the operating system. Later operating systems—UNIX in particular—introduced shell command languages designed to program the operating system. The language approach made the interface much easier to learn and use.

One result of viewing the software system interface as a programming language is that compiler development tools—which are quite well developed—can be used for general software development. For example, we can use grammars to specify the syntax of the interface and parser-generators to detect inconsistencies and ambiguities in the interface, and automatically generate the front end of the system.

User interfaces are an especially interesting case, because we also see an influence in the opposite direction: The software engineering issues revolving around graphical user interfaces have motivated programming language work in the area of *visual* languages. These languages attempt to capture the semantics of the windowing and interaction paradigms offered by graphical display devices.

Yet another influence of the programming language field on software engineering is through the implementation techniques that have been developed over the years for language processing. The generative approach to software engineering relies on the lesson learned in language processing that formalization leads to automation: Stating a formal grammar for a language allows a parser to be produced automatically. This technique is exploited in many software engineering areas for formal specification and automatic software generation.

### 1.5.2   Operating Systems

The influence of operating systems on software engineering is quite strong primarily because operating systems were the first really large software systems built, and therefore, they were the first instances of software that needed to be engineered. Many of the initial software design ideas originated from early attempts at building operating systems.

Virtual machines, levels of abstraction, and the separation of policy from mechanism are all concepts developed in the operating system field with general applicability to any large software system. For example, the idea of separating a policy that an operating system wants to impose, such as assuring fairness in task scheduling, from the mechanism used to accomplish concurrency, such as time slicing, is an instance of separating the "what" from the "how"—or the specification from the implementation—and the changeable parts from what remains fixed in a design. The idea of levels of abstraction is just another approach to modularizing the design of a system.

Examples of the influence of software engineering techniques on the *structure* of operating systems can be seen in portable operating systems and operating systems that are structured to contain a small "protected" microkernel that provides a minimum of functionality for interfacing with the hardware and a "nonprotected" part that provides the majority of the functionality previously associated with operating systems. For example, the nonprotected part may allow the user to control the paging scheme, which has traditionally been viewed as an integral part of the operating system.

Similarly, in early operating systems, the command language interpreter was an integral part of the operating system. Today, it is viewed as just another utility program that allows, for example, each user to have a personalized version of the interpreter. On many UNIX systems, there are at least three different such interpreters.

### 1.5.3   Databases

Databases represent another class of large software systems whose development has influenced software engineering through the discovery of new design techniques. Perhaps the most important influence of the database field on software engineering is through the notion of "data independence," which is yet another instance of the separation of specification from implementation. The database allows applications to be written that use data without worrying about the underlying representation of the data. Such independence allows the database to be changed in certain ways—for example, to increase the performance of the system—without any need to change the applications. This is an example of the benefit of abstraction and separation of concerns, two key software engineering principles, as we shall see in Chapter 3.

Another interesting impact of database technology on software engineering is that it allows database systems to be used as components of large software systems. Since databases have solved the many problems associated with the management of concurrent access to large amounts of information by multiple users, there is no need to reinvent these solutions when we are building a software system; we can simply use an existing database system as a component.

One interesting influence of software engineering on database technology has its roots in early attempts to use databases to support software development environments. This experience showed that traditional database technology was incapable of dealing with the problems posed by software engineering processes. For example, the following requirements are not handled well by traditional databases: storing large structured objects such as source programs or user manuals; storing large unstructured objects such as object code and executable code; maintaining different versions of the same object; and storing objects, such as a product, with many large structured and unstructured fields, such as source code, object code, and a user manual.

Another difficulty dealt with the length of *transactions*. Traditional databases support short transactions, such as a bank account deposit or withdrawal. Software engineers, on the other hand, need very long transactions: An engineer may require a long-running job to rebuild a multimodule system or may check out a program and work on it for weeks before checking it back in. The problem posed for the database is how to handle the locking of the code during those weeks. What if the engineer wants to work only on a small part of the program? Are all other programmers forbidden from accessing the program during this time?

These requirements have stimulated advances in the database area ranging from new models for databases and transactions to adapting current models.

## 1.5.4    Artificial Intelligence

Artificial intelligence is another field that has exerted an influence on software engineering. Many software systems built in the artificial-intelligence research community are large and complex systems. But they have been different from other software systems in significant ways. Many of them were built with only a vague notion of how the system was going to work. The term "exploratory development" has been used for the process followed in building these systems.

Exploratory development is the opposite of traditional software engineering, in which the designer goes through well-defined steps attempting to produce a complete design before proceeding to coding. Artificial intelligence has given rise to new techniques in dealing with specifications, verification, and reasoning in the presence of uncertainty. Other techniques advanced by artificial intelligence include the use of logic in both software specifications and programming languages.

Software engineering techniques have been used in those artificial-intelligence systems known as *expert systems*. These systems are modularized, with a clear separation between the facts "known" by the system and the rules used by the system for processing the facts—for example, a rule to decide on a course of action. This separation has enabled the building and commercial availability of "expert-system shells" that include the rules only. A user can apply the shell to an application of interest by supplying application-specific facts. The idea is that the expertise about the application is provided by the user and the general principles of how to apply expertise to any problem are provided by the shell.

Some researchers have been trying to apply artificial-intelligence techniques to improve software engineering tasks. For example, "programming assistants" have been developed to act as consultants to the programmer, watching for common programming idioms or the system requirements. Such "assistants" have also been developed to help in the testing activities of software development, to debug the software.

The problem of providing interfaces for nonexpert users—for example, through the use of natural language—was first attacked by artificial intelligence. Cognitive models were also used to model the user. These works have influenced the area of user-interface design in software engineering.

### 1.5.5   Theoretical Models

Theoretical computer science has developed a number of models that have become useful tools in software engineering. For example, finite-state machines have served both as the basis of techniques for software specifications and as models for software design and structure. Communication protocols and language analyzers use finite-state machines as their processing model.

Pushdown automata have also been used—for example, for operational specifications of systems and for building processors for such specifications. Interestingly, pushdown automata were themselves motivated by practical attempts to build parsers and compilers for programming languages.

Petri nets, which will be described in Chapter 5, are yet another contribution of the theoretical computer science field to software engineering. Petri nets were initially used to model hardware systems, but were later applied increasingly in the modeling of software. As another example, mathematical logic has been the basis for many specification languages.

Conversely, software engineering has affected theoretical computer science. Algebraic specifications and abstract data type theory are motivated by the needs of software engineering. Also in the area of specifications, software engineering has focused more attention on non-first-order theories of logic, such as temporal logic. Theoreticians used to pay more attention to first-order theories than higher order theories, because the two are equivalent in power, but first-order theories are more basic from a mathematical viewpoint. They are not as expressive as higher order theories, however. A software engineer, unlike a theoretician, is interested both in the power and the expressiveness of a theory. For example, temporal logic provides a more compact and natural style for specifying the requirements of a concurrent system than do first-order theories. The needs of software engineering, therefore, have ignited new interest by theoreticians in such higher order theories.

## 1.6    THE RELATIONSHIP OF SOFTWARE ENGINEERING TO OTHER DISCIPLINES

In the foregoing sections, we examined the relationship between software engineering and other fields of computer science. In this section, we explore how software engineering relates to fields outside of computer science.

Software engineering cannot be practiced in a vacuum. There are many problems that are not specific to software engineering and have been solved in other fields. Their solutions can be adapted to software engineering. Thus, there is no need to reinvent every solution. For example, cognitive science can help us develop better user interfaces and economic theory may help us in choosing among different development process models.

### 1.6.1    Management Science

Much of software engineering is involved with management issues. As in any kind of large, multiperson endeavor, we need to do project estimation, project scheduling, human resource planning, task decomposition and assignment, and project tracking. Additional personnel issues involve hiring personnel, motivating people, and assigning the right people to the right tasks.

Management science studies exactly these issues. Many models have been developed that can be applied in software engineering. By looking to management science, we can exploit the results of many decades of study.

In the opposite direction, software engineering has provided management science with a new domain in which to test management theories and models. The traditional management approaches to assembly-line production clearly do not apply to human-centered activities such as software engineering, giving rise to a search for more applicable approaches.

### 1.6.2    Systems Engineering

The field of systems engineering is concerned with studying complex systems. The underlying hypothesis is that certain laws govern the behavior of any complex system composed of many components with complex relationships. Systems engineering is useful when one is interested in concentrating on the system, as opposed to its individual components. Systems engineering tries to discover common themes that apply to diverse systems—for example, chemical plants, buildings, and bridges.

Software is often a component of a much larger system. For example, the software in a factory monitoring system or the flight software on an airplane are just components of more complicated systems. Systems engineering techniques can be applied to the study of such systems. We can also consider a software system consisting of thousands of modules as a candidate complex system subject to systems engineering laws.

On the other hand, system engineering has been enriched by expanding its set of analysis models—which were traditionally based on classical mathematics—to include discrete models that have been in use in software engineering.

### 1.7    CONCLUDING REMARKS

Software engineering is an evolving *engineering* discipline that deals with systematic approaches to building large software systems by teams of programmers. We have given a history of the evolution of the field, presented its relationship to other fields, and described the qualifications required of a software engineer. In this book, we shall study the principles that are essential to the engineering activity of building software.

## BIBLIOGRAPHIC NOTES

The definition of software engineering quoted at the beginning of the chapter is from Parnas [1978]. The distinction between programming in the small and programming in the large and the recognition that software engineering deals with programming in the large are due to DeRemer and Kron [1976].

The term "software engineering" was first used in a seminal NATO conference held in Garmisch, Germany, in 1968. A report on the conference appears in a book edited by Naur et al. [1976]. For standard terminology in the field, the reader may refer to the collection of standards published by IEEE [1999]. Boehm [1976] brought the field of software engineering and its challenges to the general attention.

The practical difficulties encountered in developing industrial software products are discussed in Brooks's classic book, *The Mythical Man-Month* [1975, 1995]. Brooks [1987] is the classic "silver bullet" paper. Boehm [1981, 2000] provides foundations for modeling and evaluating software costs.

The papers by Parnas [1985] and Brooks [1987] contain insightful discussions of the very nature of software and its inherent difficulties. A provocative view is contained in the debate reported in Denning [1989], which contains the text of an address by Dijkstra [1989] and rebuttals by many leading computer scientists.

For a discussion of the relationship between software engineering and programming languages, consult Ghezzi and Jazayeri [1998], which also provides a comprehensive view of programming languages, their concepts, and their evolution.

Much work in operating systems has influenced software design; in particular, we mention the early work of Dijkstra [1968a and b, and 1971], Hoare [1972, 1974, and 1985], and Brinch Hansen [1977]. The interaction between operating systems and software engineering is discussed by Browne [1980].

Data bases are studied by Ullman and Widom [1997] and Date [2000]. The specific database requirements of software engineering are reviewed by Dittrich et al. [2000].

The relationship between software engineering and artificial intelligence is analyzed in several papers, and the views are often controversial. For example, Simon [1986] and Tichy [1987] argue that software engineering should inherit methods and tools from artificial intelligence, while Parnas [1988] argues the opposite and provides a critical view of artificial intelligence. Some approaches to knowledge-based software engineering are described by Kant and Barstow [1981], the special issue of *IEEE Transactions on Software Engineering* edited by Mostow (TSE [1985]), Goldberg [1986], and Rich and Waters [1988].

A discussion of the relationship between theoretical computer science models and software development can be found in Mandrioli and Ghezzi [1987].

Boehm [2000] emphasizes the importance of the relationship between software engineering and systems engineering. Spector and Gifford [1986] discuss the relationship between software engineering and another engineering field, bridge design.

Neumann [1995] provides an alarmingly large list of documented risks to the public due to defective software, which raises the fundamental issue of the software engineer's social responsibility.

Boehm and Sullivan [2000] discusses the importance of economics in software engineering.

# CHAPTER 2

# Software: Its Nature and Qualities

The goal of any engineering activity is to build something—an artifact or a product. The civil engineer builds a bridge, the aerospace engineer builds an airplane, and the electrical engineer builds a circuit. The product of software engineering is a "software system." It is not as tangible as the other products, but it is a product nonetheless. It serves a function.

In some ways software products are similar to other engineering products, and in some ways they are very different. The characteristic that perhaps sets software apart from other engineering products the most is that software is *malleable*. We can modify the product itself—as opposed to its design—rather easily. This makes software quite different from other products, such as cars or ovens.

The malleability of software is often misused. Even though it is possible to modify a bridge or an airplane to satisfy some new need—for example, to make the bridge support more traffic or the airplane carry more cargo—such a modification is never taken lightly and certainly is not attempted without first making a design change and verifying the impact of the change extensively. Software engineers, on the other hand, are often asked to perform modifications of that nature on software. Software's malleability sometimes leads people to think that it can be changed easily. In practice, it cannot.

We may be able to change code easily with a text editor, but meeting the need for which the change was intended is not necessarily done so easily. Indeed, we need to treat software like other engineering products in this regard: A change in software must be viewed as a change in the design rather than in the code, which is just an instance of the product. We can exploit the malleability property, but we need to do it with discipline.

Another characteristic of software is that its creation is *human intensive*: It requires mostly engineering rather than manufacturing. In most other engineering disciplines, the manufacturing process determines the final cost of the product. Also, the process has to be managed closely to ensure that defects are not introduced into the product. The same considerations apply to computer hardware products. For software, on the other hand, "manufacturing" is a trivial process of duplication. The software production process deals with design and implementation, rather than manufacturing. This process has to meet certain criteria to ensure the production of high-quality software.

Any product is expected to fulfill some need and meet some acceptance standards that dictate the qualities it must have. A bridge performs the function of making it easier to travel from one point to another; one of the qualities it is expected to have is that it will not collapse when the first strong wind blows or when a convoy of trucks travels across it. In traditional engineering disciplines, the engineer has tools for describing the qualities of the product distinctly from the design of the product. In software engineering, the distinction is not so clear: The qualities of the software product are often intermixed in specifications with the qualities of the design.

In this chapter, we examine the qualities that are relevant in software products and software production processes. These qualities will become our goals in the practice of software engineering. In the next chapter, we will present software engineering principles that can be applied to achieve those goals. The presence of any quality will also have to be verified and measured. We introduce this topic in Section 2.4, and we study it in Chapter 6.

## 2.1    CLASSIFICATION OF SOFTWARE QUALITIES

There are many desirable software qualities. Some apply both to the product and to the process used to produce the product. The user wants the software product to be reliable, efficient, and easy to use. The producer of the software wants it to be verifiable, maintainable, portable, and extensible. The manager of the software project wants the process of software development to be productive, predictable and easy to control.

In this section, we consider two different classifications of software-related qualities: internal versus external and product versus process.

### 2.1.1    External versus Internal Qualities

We can divide software qualities into *external* and *internal* qualities. External qualities are visible to the users of the system; internal qualities concern the developers of the system. In general, users of software care only about external qualities, but it is the internal qualities—which deal largely with the structure of the software—that help developers achieve the external qualities. For example, the internal quality of verifiability is necessary for achieving the external quality of reliability. In many cases, however, the qualities are related closely, and the distinction between internal and external is not sharp.

### 2.1.2    Product and Process Qualities

We use a *process* to produce the software product. We can attribute some qualities to the process, although process qualities often are closely related to product qualities. For example, if the process requires careful planning of test data before any design and development of the system starts, product reliability will increase. When we discuss qualities, we have to distinguish between process and product qualities.

The word *product* usually refers to what is delivered to the customer. Even though this is an acceptable definition from the customer's perspective, it is not adequate for the developer who produces a number of intermediate "products" in the course of the software process. The customer-visible product consists perhaps of the executable code and the user manual, but the developers produce a number of other artifacts, such as the requirements and design documents, test data, etc. We refer to these intermediate products as work products or artifacts to distinguish them from the end product delivered to the customer. Work products are often subject to the same quality requirements as the end product. Given the existence of many work products, it is possible to deliver different subsets of them to different customers.

For example, a computer manufacturer might sell to a process control company the object code to be installed in the specialized hardware for an embedded application. It might sell the object code and the user's manual to software dealers. It might even sell the design and the source code to software vendors who modify them to build other products. In this case, the developers of the original system see one product, the salespersons in the same company see a set of related products, and the end user and the software vendor see still other, different products.

*Configuration management* is the part of the software production process that is concerned with maintaining and controlling the relationship between all the related work products of the various versions of a product. Configuration management tools allow the maintenance of families of products and their components. They help in controlling and managing changes to work products. We discuss configuration management in Chapter 7.

## 2.2    REPRESENTATIVE QUALITIES

In this section, we present the most important qualities of software products and processes. Where appropriate, we analyze a quality with respect to the classifications discussed in the previous section.

### 2.2.1    Correctness, Reliability, and Robustness

The terms "correctness," "reliability," and "robustness" are related and collectively characterize a quality of software which implies that the application performs its functions as expected. In this section, we define these three terms and discuss their relationships to one another.

#### 2.2.1.1  Correctness

A program is written to provide functions specified in its *functional requirements specifications*. Often, there are other requirements—such as performance and scalablity—that do not pertain to the functions of the system. We call these kinds of requirements *nonfunctional requirements*. A program is *functionally correct* if it behaves according to its stated functional specifications. It is common simply to use the term "correct" rather than "functionally correct"; similarly, in this context, the term "specifications" implies "functional requirements specifications." We shall follow this convention when the context is clear.

The definition of correctness assumes that specifications for the system are available and that it is possible to determine unambiguously whether a program meets the specifications. Such specifications rarely exist for most current software systems. If a specification does exist, it is usually written in an informal style using natural language. Therefore, it is likely to contain many ambiguities. Regardless of these difficulties with current specifications, however, the definition of correctness is useful because it captures a desirable goal for software systems.

Correctness is a mathematical property that establishes the equivalence between the software and its specification. Obviously, we can be more systematic and precise in assessing correctness, depending on how rigorous we are in specifying functional requirements. As we shall see in Chapter 6, we may assess the correctness of a program through a variety of methods, some based on an experimental approach (e.g., testing), others based on an analytic approach (e.g., inspections or formal verification of correctness). Correctness can be enhanced by using appropriate tools, such as high-level languages—particularly those supporting extensive static analysis. Likewise, correctness can be improved by using standard proven algorithms or libraries of standard modules, rather than inventing new ones. Finally, correctness can be enhanced by using proven methodologies and processes.

### 2.2.1.2 Reliability

Informally, software is reliable if the user can depend on it.[1] The specialized literature on software reliability defines reliability in terms of statistical behavior—the probability that the software will operate as expected over a specified time interval; we discuss this approach in Section 6.7.2. For the purpose of the current chapter, however, the informal definition is sufficient.

Correctness is an absolute quality: any deviation from its requirements makes a system incorrect, regardless of how minor or serious the consequence of the deviation is. The notion of reliability is, on the other hand, relative: If the consequence of a software error is not serious, the incorrect software may still be reliable.

Engineering products are *expected* to be reliable. Unreliable products, in general, disappear quickly from the marketplace. Unfortunately, software products have not achieved this enviable status yet. Software products are commonly released along with a list of "Known Bugs." Users of software take it for granted that "Release 1" of a product is "buggy." This is one of the most striking symptoms of the immaturity of the software engineering field as an engineering discipline.[2]

In classic engineering disciplines, a product is not released if it has "bugs." You do not expect to take delivery of an automobile along with a list of shortcomings or a bridge with a warning not to use the railing. Design errors are extremely rare and worthy of news headlines. A collapsed bridge may even cause the designers to be prosecuted in court.

---

[1] "Dependable" is a term frequently used as a synonym for "reliable."
[2] Dijkstra [1989] claims that even the sloppy term "bug," which is often used by software engineers, is a symptom of unprofessionalism.

By contrast, software design errors are generally treated as unavoidable. Far from being surprised when we find software errors, we *expect* them. Whereas with all other products the customer receives a guarantee of reliability, with software we get a disclaimer that the manufacturer is not responsible for any damages due to product errors. Software engineering can truly be called an engineering discipline only when we can achieve software reliability comparable to the reliability of other products.

Figure 2.1 illustrates the relationship between reliability and correctness, under the assumption that the functional requirements specification indeed captures all the desirable properties of the application and that no undesirable properties are erroneously specified in it. The figure shows that the set of all reliable programs includes the set of correct programs, but not vice versa. Unfortunately, things are different in practice. In fact, the specification is a model of what the user wants, but the model may or may not be an accurate statement of the user's actual requirements. All the software can do is meet the specified requirements of the model; it cannot assure the accuracy of the model.

Figure 2.1 represents an idealized situation wherein the requirements are themselves assumed to be correct; that is, they are a faithful representation of what the implementation must ensure in order to satisfy the needs of the expected users. As we shall discuss thoroughly in Chapter 7, there are often insurmountable obstacles to achieving this goal. The upshot is that we sometimes have correct applications designed for "incorrect" requirements, so that correctness of the software may not be sufficient to guarantee the user that the software behaves "as expected." This situation is discussed in the next subsection.

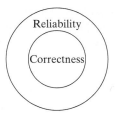

**FIGURE 2.1**

Relationship between correctness
and reliability in the ideal case.

### 2.2.1.3 Robustness

A program is robust if it behaves "reasonably," even in circumstances that were not anticipated in the requirements specification—for example, when it encounters incorrect input data or some hardware malfunction (say, a disk crash). A program that assumes perfect input and generates an unrecoverable run-time error as soon as the user inadvertently types an incorrect command is not robust. It might be correct, though, if the requirements specification does not state what the program should do in the face of incorrect input. Obviously, robustness is a difficult-to-define quality; after all, if we could state precisely what we should do to make an application robust, we would be able to specify its "reasonable" behavior completely. Thus, robustness would become equivalent to correctness (or reliability, in the sense of Figure 2.1).

Again, an analogy with bridges is instructive. Two bridges connecting two sides of the same river are both "correct" if they each satisfy the stated requirements. If, however, during an unexpected, unprecedented earthquake, one collapses and the other one does not, we can call the latter more robust than the former. Notice that the lesson learned from the collapse of the bridge will probably lead to more complete requirements for future bridges, establishing resistance to earthquakes as a correctness requirement. In other words, as the phenomenon under study becomes better known, we approach the ideal case shown in Figure 2.1, where specifications capture the expected requirements exactly.

The amount of code devoted to robustness depends on the application area. For example, a system written for novice computer users must be more prepared to deal with ill-formatted input than an embedded system that receives its input from a sensor. This, of course, does not imply that embedded systems do not need to be robust. On the contrary, embedded systems often control critical devices and require extra robustness.

In conclusion, we can see that robustness and correctness are strongly related, without a sharp dividing line between them. If we put a requirement in the specification, its accomplishment becomes an issue of correctness; if we leave the requirement out of the specification, it may become an issue of robustness. The border line between the two qualities is the specification of the system. Finally, reliability comes in because not all incorrect behaviors signify equally serious problems; that is, some incorrect behaviors may be tolerable.

We may also use the terms "correctness," "robustness," and "reliability" in relation to the software production process. A process is robust, for example, if it can accommodate unanticipated changes in the environment, such as a new release of the operating system or the sudden transfer of half the employees to another location. A process is reliable if it consistently leads to the production of high-quality products. In many engineering disciplines, considerable research is devoted to the discovery of reliable processes.

### 2.2.2 Performance

Any engineering product is expected to perform at a certain level. Unlike other disciplines, in software engineering we often equate performance with efficiency, but they are not the same. Efficiency is an internal quality and refers to how economically the software utilizes the resources of the computer. Performance, on the other hand, is an external quality based on user requirements. For example, a telephone switch may be required to be able to process 10,000 calls per hour. Efficiency affects, and often determines, the performance of a system.

Performance is important because it affects the usability of the system. If a software system is too slow, it reduces the productivity of the users, possibly to the point of not meeting their needs. If a software system uses too much disk space, it may be too expensive to run. If a software system uses too much memory, it may affect the other applications that are run on the same system, or it may run slowly while the operating system tries to balance the memory usage of the different applications.

Underlying all of these statements—and also what makes the determination of efficiency difficult—are the changing limits of efficiency as technology changes. Our view of what is "too expensive" is constantly changing as advances in technology extend the limits. The computers of today cost orders of magnitude less than computers of a few years ago, yet they provide orders of magnitude more power.

Performance is also important because it affects the scalability of a software system. An algorithm that is quadratic may work on small inputs, but not work at all on larger inputs. For example, a compiler that uses a register allocation algorithm whose running time is the square of the number of program variables will run more and more slowly as the length of the program being compiled increases.

There are several ways to *evaluate* the performance of a system. One method is to analyze the complexity of algorithms used in the software. An extensive theory exists for characterizing the average or worst case behavior of algorithms, in terms of significant resource requirements such as time and space, or—less traditionally—in terms of the number of message exchanges, in the case of distributed systems.

Analyzing the complexity of algorithms provides only average or worst case information, rather than specific information, about a particular implementation. For more specific information, we can use techniques of performance evaluation. The three basic approaches to evaluating the performance of a system are *measurement, analysis*, and *simulation*. We can measure the actual performance of a system by means of hardware and software monitors that collect data while the system is running and that thereby allow us to discover bottlenecks in the system. In this case, it is crucial to select input data that lead to representative executions of the system. The second approach is to build a model of the product and analyze it. The third approach is to build a model that simulates the product. Analytic models—often based on queuing theory—are usually easier to build, but are less accurate, while simulation models are more costly to build, but are more accurate. We can sometimes combine the two techniques: At the start of a large project, an analytic model can provide a general understanding of the performance-critical areas of the product, pointing out areas where more thorough study is required; then we can build simulation models of these particular areas.

In many software development projects, performance is addressed only after the initial version of the product is implemented. It is very difficult—sometimes even impossible—to achieve significant improvements in performance without redesigning the software. Even a simple model, however, is useful for predicting a system's performance and guiding design choices so as to minimize the need for redesign.

In some complex projects, in which the feasibility of the performance requirements is not clear, much effort is devoted to building performance models. Such projects start with a performance model and use it initially to answer feasibility questions and later in making design decisions. These models can help resolve issues such as whether a function should be provided by software or a special-purpose hardware device.

The preceding remarks apply in the large—that is, when the overall structure or architecture of the software is conceived. They often do not apply in the small, where individual programs may first be designed with an emphasis on correctness and then be locally modified to improve efficiency. For example, inner loops are obvious candidates for efficiency-improving modifications.

The notion of performance also applies to a development process, in which case we call it productivity. Productivity is important enough to be treated as an independent quality and is discussed in Section 2.2.10.

### 2.2.3  Usability

A software system is usable—or *user friendly*—if its human users find it easy to use. This definition reflects the subjective nature of usability. Properties that make an application user friendly to novices are different from those desired by expert users. For example, a novice user may appreciate verbose messages, while an experienced user will ignore them. Similarly, a nonprogrammer may appreciate the use of menus, while a programmer may be more comfortable with typing a textual command.

The *user interface* is an important component of user-friendliness. A software system that presents the novice user with a window interface and a mouse is friendlier than one that requires the user to enter a set of one-letter commands. On the other hand, an experienced user might prefer a set of commands that minimize the number of keystrokes, rather than a fancy window interface through which he has to navigate to get to the command that he knew all along he wanted to execute.

There is more to user-friendliness, however, than the user interface. For example, an embedded software system does not have a human user interface. Instead, it interacts with hardware and perhaps other software systems. In this case, user-friendliness is reflected in the ease with which the system can be configured and adapted to the hardware environment.

In general, the user-friendliness of a system depends on the consistency and predictability of its user and operator interfaces. Clearly, however, the other qualities mentioned—such as correctness and performance—also affect user-friendliness. A software system that produces wrong answers is not friendly, regardless of how fancy its user interface is. Also, a software system that produces answers more slowly than the user requires is not friendly, even if the answers are displayed in beautiful color.

User-friendliness is also discussed under the subject of human factors. *Human factors* and *usability engineering* play a major role in many engineering disciplines. For example, automobile manufacturers devote a significant effort to deciding the position of the various control knobs on the dashboard. Television manufacturers and microwave oven makers also try to make their products easy to use. User-interface decisions in these classical engineering fields are made after extensive study of user needs and attitudes by specialists in fields such as industrial design or psychology.

Ease of use in many engineering disciplines is achieved through standardization of the human interface. Once a user knows how to use one television set, he or she can operate almost any other television set.[3] There is a clear trend in software applications to more uniform and standard user interfaces, as seen, for example, in Web browsers.

### Exercise

**2.1**    Discuss the impact of the user interface on reliability.

---

[3] Although the standard interface for VCR programming seems to be uniformly confusing to all!

### 2.2.4    Verifiability

A software system is verifiable if its properties can be verified easily. For example, it is important to be able to verify the correctness or the performance of a software system. As we will see in Chapter 6, verification can be performed by formal and informal analysis methods or through testing. A common technique for improving verifiability is the use of "software monitors,"—that is, code inserted into the software to monitor various qualities such as performance or correctness. Modular design, disciplined coding practices, and the use of an appropriate programming language all contribute to verifiability.

Verifiability is usually an internal quality, although it sometimes becomes an external quality also. For example, in many security-critical applications, the customer requires the verifiability of certain properties. The highest level of the security standard for a trusted computer system requires the verifiability of the operating system kernel.

### 2.2.5    Maintainability

The term *software maintenance* is commonly used to refer to the modifications that are made to a software system after its initial release. Maintenance used to be viewed as merely "bug fixing," and it was distressing to discover that so much effort was being spent on fixing defects. Studies have shown, however, that the majority of time spent on maintenance is in fact spent on enhancing the product with features that were not in the original specifications or that were stated incorrectly there.

"Maintenance" is indeed not the proper word to use with software. First, as it is used today, the term covers a wide range of activities, all having to do with modifying an existing piece of software in order to make an improvement. A term that perhaps captures the essence of this process better is *software evolution*. Second, in other engineering products, such as computer hardware, automobiles, or washing machines, maintenance refers to the upkeep of the product in response to the gradual deterioration of parts due to extended use of the product. For example, transmissions are oiled and air filters are dusted and periodically changed. To use the word "maintenance" with software gives the wrong connotation, because software does not wear out. Unfortunately, the term is used so widely that we are practically obliged to continue using it here.

There is evidence that maintenance costs exceed 60 percent of the total costs of software. To analyze the factors that affect such costs, it is customary to divide software maintenance into three categories: *corrective, adaptive*, and *perfective*.

Corrective maintenance has to do with the removal of residual errors that are present in the product when it is delivered, as well as errors introduced into the software during its maintenance. Corrective maintenance accounts for about 20 percent of maintenance costs.

Adaptive and perfective maintenance are the real sources of change in software; they motivate the introduction of evolvability (defined shortly) as a fundamental software quality and anticipation of change (defined in Chapter 3) as a general principle to guide the software engineer. Adaptive maintenance accounts for nearly another 20 percent of maintenance costs, and perfective maintenance absorbs over 50 percent.

Adaptive maintenance involves adjusting the application to changes in the environment (e.g., a new release of the hardware or the operating system or a new database system). In other words, in adaptive maintenance, the need for software changes cannot be attributed to a feature in the software itself, such as the presence of residual errors or the inability to provide some functionality required by the user. Rather, the software must change because the environment in which it is embedded changes.

Finally, perfective maintenance involves changing the software to improve some of its qualities. Here, changes are due to the need to modify the functions offered by the application, add new functions, improve the performance of the application, make it easier to use, etc. The requests to perform perfective maintenance may come directly from the software engineer, in order to improve the status of the product on the market, or they may come from the customer, to meet some new requirements.

The term *legacy software* refers to software that already exists in an organization and usually embodies much of the organization's processes and knowledge. Therefore, such software holds considerable value for the organization, represents past investments, and may not be replaced easily. On the other hand, because of its age, it is usually written in older languages and uses older software engineering technology. Legacy software is, therefore, difficult to modify and maintain. For example, an old personnel system may embody an organization's operational procedures and personnel policies. Such legacy systems represent a challenge to software evolution. *Reverse engineering* and *reengineering* techniques and technologies are aimed at uncovering the structure of legacy software and restructuring or in some way improving it.

We shall view maintainability as two separate qualities: repairability and evolvability. Software is repairable if it allows the fixing of defects; it is evolvable if it allows changes that enable it to satisfy new requirements.

The distinction between repairability and evolvability is not always clear. For example, if the requirements specifications are vague, it may not be clear whether we are fixing a defect or satisfying a new requirement. We will discuss this point further in Chapter 7. In general, however, the distinction between the two qualities is useful.

### 2.2.5.1 Repairability

A software system is repairable if its defects can be corrected with a reasonable amount of work. In many engineering products, repairability is a major design goal. For example, automobile engines are built with the parts that are most likely to fail as the most accessible. In computer hardware engineering, there is a subspecialty called repairability, availability, and serviceability (RAS).

In other engineering fields, as the cost of a product decreases and the product assumes the status of a commodity, the need for repairability decreases: It is cheaper to replace the whole thing, or at least major parts of it, than to repair it. For example, in early television sets, you could replace a single vacuum tube. Today, a whole board has to be replaced.

In fact, a common technique for achieving repairability in such products is to use standard parts that can be replaced easily. For instance, personal computers were initially built from customized parts and proprietary interconnections. Today, personal computers are built out of standard parts connected through standard bus systems. This standardization has led to a proliferation of companies that specialize in producing certain parts. Through specialization, these companies can concentrate on improving reliability of the parts and reducing cost. As a result, the initial production of a computer is faster and cheaper, and a defect can be repaired by replacing a failing part. But software parts do not deteriorate. Thus, while the use of standard parts can reduce the time and cost of software *production*, the concept of replaceable parts does not seem to apply to software repairability. Such parts help in reducing design time, because the designer concentrates on combining well-known components, which he or she does not have to design.

Repairability is also affected by the *number* of parts in a product. For example, it is harder to repair a defect in a monolithic automobile body than it would be if the body were made of several regularly shaped parts. In the latter case, we could replace a single part more easily than the whole body. Of course, if the body consisted of too many parts, it would require too many connections among the parts, leading to the probability that the connections themselves might need repair.

An analogous situation applies to software: a software product that consists of well-designed modules is easier to analyze and repair than a monolithic one. Merely increasing the number of modules, however, does not make a more repairable product: We have to choose the right structure for the modules, with the right interfaces that avoid complex interconnections and interactions among modules. The right modularization promotes repairability by enabling the engineer to locate errors more easily. In Chapter 4, we examine several modularization techniques, including information hiding and abstract data types, in detail.

Repairability can be improved through the use of proper tools. For example, using a high-level language rather than an assembly language leads to better repairability. Tools such as debuggers can help in isolating and repairing errors.

A product's repairability affects its reliability. On the other hand, the need for repairability decreases as reliability increases.

### 2.2.5.2 *Evolvability*

Like other engineering products, software products are modified over time to provide new functions or to change existing functions. Indeed, the fact that software is so malleable makes modifications extremely easy to apply to an implementation. There is, however, a major difference between software modification and the modification of other engineering products. In the case of other engineering products, modifications start at the design level and then proceed to the implementation of the product. For example, if one decides to add a second story to a house, one must first do a feasibility study to check whether the addition can be done safely. Then one is required to do a design, based on the original design of the house. Then the design must be approved, after making sure that it does not violate the existing regulations. Finally, the construction of the new part may be commissioned.

Such an organized approach is often missing in software modifications. Even for radical changes in applications, people often skip the feasibility and design analysis phases and proceed immediately to the modification of the implementation. Still worse, after the change is accomplished, the modification is not even documented *a posteriori*; that is, the specifications are not updated to reflect the change. This makes future changes more and more difficult to apply.

On the other hand, successful software products are quite long lived. Their first release is the first of many releases, each successive release being a step in the evolution of the system. If the software is designed with evolution in mind, and if each modification is designed and applied carefully, then the software can evolve gracefully.

As the cost of software production and the complexity of applications grow, the evolvability of software assumes more and more importance. One reason for this is the need to leverage the investment made in the software as the hardware technology advances. Some of the earliest large systems developed in the 1960s are today taking advantage of new hardware, device, and network technologies. For example, the American Airlines SABRE reservation system, initially developed in the middle 1960s, has been evolving for decades to include increasingly rich functionality. This is an amazing feat, considering the increasing performance demands on the system.

Most software systems start out being evolvable, but after years of evolution they reach a state where any major modification runs the risk of "breaking" existing features. Evolvability is achieved by proper modularization, but unanticipated changes tend to reduce the modularity of the original system—even more if modifications are applied without carefully studying the original design and without describing precisely any changes in both the design and the requirements specification.

Indeed, studies of large software systems show that evolvability decreases with each release of a software product. Each release complicates the structure of the software, so that future modifications become more difficult to apply. To overcome this problem, the initial design of the product, as well as any succeeding changes, must be done with evolvability in mind. Evolvability is an important software quality because of its economic impact. Several of the principles we present in the next chapter help in achieving evolvability. In Chapter 4, we present special concepts, such as program and product families and software architecture, which are intended to foster evolvability. The product-family (also called product-line) approach in software architecture is aimed at finding a systematic way to achieve evolvability in software products.

## 2.2.6    Reusability

Reusability is akin to evolvability. In product evolution, we modify a product to build a new version of that same product; in product reuse, we use the product—perhaps with minor changes—to build another product. Reusability may be applied at different levels of granularity—from whole applications to individual routines—but it appears to be more applicable to software components than to whole products.

A good example of a reusable product is the UNIX shell, which is a command language interpreter; that is, it accepts user commands and executes them. But it is designed to be used both interactively and in "batch." The ability to start a new shell with a file containing a list of shell commands allows us to write programs—scripts— in the shell command language. We can view the program as a new product that uses the shell as a component. By encouraging standard interfaces, the UNIX environment in fact supports the reuse of any of its commands, as well as the shell, in building powerful utilities.

Numeric libraries were the first examples of reusable components. Several large FORTRAN libraries, now rewritten in C, C++, and other languages, have existed for many years. Users buy these libraries and use them to build their own products, without having to reinvent or recode well-known algorithms. Several companies are devoted to producing just such libraries. Nowadays, reusable libraries exist for different areas, such as graphical user interfaces, simulation, etc. One of the goals of reusability researchers is to increase the granularity of components that may be reused. One of the goals of object-oriented programming is to achieve both reusability and evolvability.

So far, we have discussed primarily the reusability of components, but the concept has broader applicability: It may occur at different levels and may affect both product and process. In general, any of the artifacts of the software process, such as the requirements specification, may be reused. Thus, the more modularly designed these artifacts are, the more likely it is that they, or parts of them, may be reused in the future. For example, a reusable requirements specification document allows parts of the results of problem analysis and understanding to be reused in several applications.

Reusability applies to the software process as well. Indeed, the various software methodologies can be viewed as attempts to reuse the same process for building different products. Life cycle models are also attempts at reusing higher level processes. We discuss these in Chapter 7.

Reusability of standard parts characterizes the maturity of an industrial field. We see high degrees of reuse in such mature areas as the automobile industry and consumer electronics. For example, a car is constructed by assembling together many components that are highly standardized and used across many models produced by the same industry. Certainly, the designs are routinely reused from model to model. Finally, the manufacturing process is often reused. The level of reuse is increasing in software, but it still is short of that of other established engineering disciplines.

## Exercises

**2.2**    Discuss how reusability may affect the reliability of products.

**2.3**    Reuse of a component may entail some adaptation of the component. Discuss how inheritance may be used in an object-oriented language such as Java or C++ to perform such adaptation.

### 2.2.7    Portability

Software is portable if it can run in different environments. The term "environment" may refer to a hardware platform or a software environment, such as a particular operating system. Portability is economically important because it helps amortize the investment in the software system across different environments and different generations of the same environment. Many applications are independent of the actual hardware platform, because the operating system provides portability across hardware platforms. These days, the applications' dependencies are on operating systems and other software systems, such as databases and user interface systems. Portability may be achieved by modularizing the software so that dependencies on the environment are isolated in only a few modules that must be modified to port the software to another environment. With the proliferation of networked systems, portability has taken on new importance because the execution environment is naturally heterogeneous, consisting of many different kinds of computers and operating systems. In addition, the delivery devices have become diverse. For example, Internet browsers need to be able to run not only on workstations and personal computers, but also on palmtops and even mobile phones.

Some software systems are inherently machine specific. For example, an operating system is written to control a specific computer, and a compiler produces code for a particular machine. Even in these cases, however, it is possible to achieve some level of portability. UNIX and its variant, Linux, are examples of an operating system that has been ported to many different hardware systems. Of course, the porting effort requires months of work. Still, we can call the software portable because writing the system from scratch for the new environment would require much more effort than porting it.

#### Exercises

**2.4**    Discuss portability as a special case of reusability.

**2.5**    We may apply portability to Web pages. Discuss what it means for a Web page to be portable.

### 2.2.8    Understandability

Some software systems are easier to understand than others. Of course, some tasks are inherently more complex than others. For example, a system that does weather forecasting, no matter how well it is written, will be harder to understand than one that prints a mailing list. Given tasks of inherently similar difficulty, we can follow certain guidelines to produce more understandable designs and to write more understandable programs. For example, abstraction and modularity enhance a system's understandability.

The activity of software maintenance is dominated by the subactivity of *program understanding*. Maintenance engineers spend most of their time trying to uncover the logic of the application and a smaller portion of their time applying changes to the application.

Understandability is an internal product quality, and it helps in achieving many of the other qualities, such as evolvability and verifiability. From an external point of view, the user considers a system understandable if it has predictable behavior. External understandability is a factor in a product's usability.

### 2.2.9    Interoperability

"Interoperability" refers to the ability of a system to coexist and cooperate with other systems—for example, a word processor's ability to incorporate a chart produced by a graphics package, the graphics package's ability to graph the data produced by a spreadsheet, or the spreadsheet's ability to process an image scanned by a scanner.

Interoperability abounds in other engineering products. For example, stereo systems from various manufacturers work together and can be connected to television sets and video recorders. In fact, stereo systems produced decades ago accommodate new technologies such as compact discs! In contrast, early operating systems had to be modified—sometimes significantly—before they could work with new devices. The generation of plug-and-play operating systems attempts to solve this problem by automatically detecting and working with new devices.

The UNIX environment, with its standard interfaces, offers a limited example of interoperability within a single environment: UNIX encourages software engineers to design applications so that they have a simple, standard interface, which allows the output of one application to be used as the input to another. The UNIX standard interface is a primitive, character-oriented one. It falls short when one application needs to use structured data—say, a spreadsheet or an image—produced by another application.

With interoperability, a vendor can produce different products and allow the user to combine them if necessary. This makes it easier for the vendor to produce the products, and it gives the user more freedom in exactly what functions to pay for and to combine. Interoperability can be achieved through standardization of interfaces. An example of such interoperability is the Web browser application that provides plug-in interfaces for different applications. For example, a new audio player provided by one vendor may be added to the browser provided by another vendor.

A concept related to interoperability is that of an *open system*—an extensible collection of independently written applications that function as an integrated system. An open system allows the addition of new functionality by independent organizations, after the system is delivered. This can be achieved, for example, by releasing the system together with a specification of its "open" interfaces. Any application developer can then take advantage of these interfaces, some of which may be used for communication between different applications or systems. Open systems allow different applications, written by different organizations, to interoperate.

An interesting requirement of open systems is that new functionality may be added without taking the system down. An open system is analogous to a growing (social) organization that evolves over time, adapting to changes in the environment. The importance of interoperability has sparked a growing interest in open systems, producing some recent efforts at standardization in this area. For example, the CORBA standard defines interfaces that support the development of components that may be used in open distributed systems. We discuss CORBA in Chapter 4.

### Exercise

**2.6**    Discuss the relationship between evolvability and open systems.

## 2.2.10  Productivity

Productivity is a quality of the software production process, referring to its efficiency and performance. An efficient process results in faster delivery of the product.

Individual engineers produce software at a certain rate, although there are great variations among individuals of different ability. When individuals are part of a team, the productivity of the team is some function of the productivity of the individuals. Very often, the combined productivity is much less than the sum of the parts. Management tries to organize team members and adopt processes in such manner as to capitalize on the individual productivity of the members.

Productivity offers many tradeoffs in the choice of a process. For example, a process that requires specialization of individual team members may lead to high productivity in producing a certain product, but not in producing a variety of products. Software reuse is a technique that increases the overall productivity of an organization in producing a collection of products, but the cost of developing reusable modules can be amortized only over many products.

While software productivity is of great interest due to the increasing cost of software, it is difficult to measure. Clearly, we need a metric for measuring productivity— or any other quality, for that matter—if we are to have any hope of comparing different processes in terms of their productivity. Early metrics, such as the number of lines of code produced, have many shortcomings. In Chapter 8, we discuss metrics for measuring productivity and team organizations for improving productivity. As with other engineering disciplines, we shall see that efficiency of the process is affected strongly by automation. Modern software engineering tools and environments lead to increases in productivity. These tools will be discussed in Chapter 9.

### Exercise

**2.7**   Critically evaluate the number of lines of code as a productivity measure. (This issue will be analyzed in depth in Chapter 8.)

## 2.2.11  Timeliness

Timeliness is a process-related quality that refers to the ability to deliver a product on time. Historically, timeliness has been lacking in software production processes, leading to the "software crisis," which in turn led to the need for—and birth of— software engineering itself. Today, due to increased competitive market pressures, software projects face even more stringent time-to-market challenges.

The following example illustrates how one company handled its delivery difficulties in the late 1980s: The company had promised the first release of its Ada compiler for a certain date. When the date arrived, the customers who had ordered the product received, instead of the product, a letter stating that, since the product still contained many defects, the manufacturer had decided that it would be better to delay delivery rather than deliver a product containing defects. The product was promised for three months later.

After four months, the product arrived, along with a letter stating that many, but not all, of the defects had been corrected. But this time, the manufacturer had decided that it was better to let customers receive the Ada compiler, even though it contained several serious defects, so that the customers could start their own product development using Ada. The value of early delivery at this new time outweighed the risk of delivering a defective product, in the opinion of the manufacturer. So, in the end, what was delivered was late *and* defective.

Timeliness by itself is not a useful quality, although being late may sometimes preclude market opportunities. Delivering on time a product that is lacking in other qualities, such as reliability or performance, is pointless. But some argue that the early delivery of a preliminary and still unstable version of a product favors the later acceptance of the final product. The Internet has facilitated this approach. Vendors are able to place early versions of products on the Internet, enabling potential users to try the product and providing feedback to the vendor.

Timeliness requires careful scheduling, accurate estimation of work, and clearly specified and verifiable milestones. All other engineering disciplines use standard project management techniques to achieve timeliness. There are even many computer-supported project management tools.

Standard project management techniques are difficult to apply in software engineering because of the inherent difficulties of defining the requirements and the abstract nature of software. These difficulties in turn lead to problems in measuring the amount of work required for producing a given piece of software, problems in measuring the productivity of engineers—or even having a dependable metric for productivity—and problems in defining precise and verifiable milestones.

Another reason for the difficulty in achieving timeliness in the software process is continuously changing user requirements. Figure 2.2 plots user requirements against actual system capabilities and indicates why most current software developments fail. (The units of scale are not shown and can be assumed to be nonuniform.) At time $t_0$, the need for a software system is recognized, and development starts with rather incomplete knowledge of the requirements. As a result, the initial product delivered at time $t_1$ satisfies neither the initial requirements of time $t_0$ nor the user's requirements of time $t_1$. Between times $t_1$ and $t_3$, the product is "maintained," in order to get closer to the user's needs. Eventually, it matches the original user's requirements at time $t_2$. For

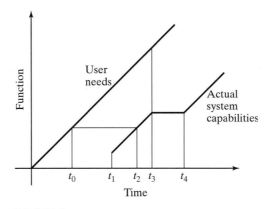

FIGURE 2.2

Software timeliness shortfall. (From Davis et al. [1988], ©1988 IEEE, reprinted by permission of IEEE.)

the reasons we have seen in Section 2.2.5, at time $t_3$ the cost of maintenance is so high that the software developer decides to do a major redesign. The new release becomes available at time $t_4$, but the gap with respect to the user's needs at that point is even greater than before.

Outside of software engineering, a classic example of the difficulty in dealing with the requirements of complex systems is offered by advanced defense systems. In several well-publicized cases, the systems became obsolete by the time they were delivered, or they did not meet the requirements, or, in many cases, both. But after 10 years of development, it is difficult to decide what to do with a product that does not meet a requirement stated 10 years before. The problem is exacerbated by the fact that requirements cannot be formulated precisely in these cases because the need is for the most advanced system possible at the time of delivery, not at the time the requirements are defined.

One technique for achieving timeliness is through the *incremental delivery* of the product. This technique is illustrated in the following—more successful—example of the delivery of an Ada compiler by a different company from the one we described before. This company delivered, very early on, a compiler that supported a very small subset of the Ada language—basically, a subset that was equivalent to Pascal with "packages." The compiler did not support any of the novel features of the language, such as tasking and exception handling. The result was the early delivery of a reliable product. As a consequence, the users started experimenting with the new language, and the company took more time to understand the subtleties of the new features of Ada. Over several releases, which took a period of two years, a full Ada compiler was delivered. Incremental delivery allows the product to become available earlier, and the use of the product helps in refining the requirements incrementally.

Obviously, incremental delivery depends on the ability to break down the set of required system functions into subsets that can be delivered in increments. If such subsets cannot be defined, no process can make the product available incrementally. But a nonincremental process prevents the production of product subsets even if such subsets can be identified. Thus, the combination of a product that can be broken down into subsets and an incremental process can achieve timeliness.

Incremental delivery of useless subsets, of course, is not of value. Timeliness must be combined with other software qualities. Chapter 4 discusses many techniques for achieving product subsets, and Chapter 7 discusses techniques for achieving incremental processes.

### 2.2.12  Visibility

A software development process is *visible* if all of its steps and its current status are documented clearly. Another term used to characterize this property is *transparency*. The idea is that the steps and the status of the project are available and easily accessible for external examination.

In many software projects, most engineers and even managers are unaware of the exact status of the project. Some may be designing, others coding, and still others testing, all at the same time. This, by itself, is not bad. Yet, if an engineer starts to redesign a major part of the code just before the software is supposed to be delivered for integration testing, the risk of serious problems and delays will be high.

Visibility allows engineers to weigh the impact of their actions and thus guides them in making decisions. It allows the members of the team to work in the same direction, rather than, as is often the case currently, in opposing directions. The most common example of the latter situation is, as mentioned earlier, when the integration group has been testing a version of the software assuming that the next version will involve fixing defects, while the engineering group decides to do a major redesign to add some functionality. This tension between one group trying to stabilize the software while another group is destabilizing it is common. The process must encourage a consistent view of the status and current goals among all participants.

Visibility is not only an internal quality; it is also external. During the course of a long project, many requests arise about the status of the project. Sometimes these requests require formal presentations on the status, and at other times the requests are informal. Sometimes the requests come from the organization's management for future planning, and at other times they come from the outside, perhaps from the customer. If the software development process has low visibility, either these status reports will not be accurate, or they will require a lot of effort to prepare each time.

One of the difficulties of managing large projects is dealing with the turnover of personnel. With many software projects, critical information about the software requirements and design has the form of folklore, known only to people who have been with the project either from the beginning or for a sufficiently long time. In such situations, recovering from the loss of a key engineer or adding new engineers to the project is very difficult. In fact, adding new engineers often reduces the productivity of the whole project as the folklore is being transferred slowly from the existing crew of engineers to the new engineers.

The preceding discussion points out that visibility of the process requires not only that all of its steps be documented, but also that the current status of the intermediate products, such as requirements specifications and design specifications, be maintained accurately; that is, visibility of the product is required as well. Intuitively, a product is visible if it is clearly structured as a collection of modules, with clearly understandable functions and available and accurate documentation.

## 2.3    QUALITY REQUIREMENTS IN DIFFERENT APPLICATION AREAS

The qualities described in the previous section are generic, in the sense that they apply to any software system. But software systems are built to automate a particular application, and therefore, we can characterize a software system on the basis of the requirements of the application area. In this section, we identify four major application areas of software systems and examine their additional requirements. We also show how these areas stress, in different ways, some of the general qualities that we have discussed.

### 2.3.1    Information Systems

One of the largest application areas for computers is the storage and retrieval of data. We call this class of systems "information-based systems" or simply "information systems," because the primary purpose of the system is managing information. Examples of information systems are banking systems, library-cataloguing systems, and personnel systems. At the heart of such systems is a *database* against which we apply *transactions* to create, retrieve, update, or delete items. Many such systems provide a Web interface to operate on the information.

Information systems have gained in importance because of the increasing value of information as a resource. The data that these systems manage is often the most valuable resource of an enterprise. Such data concern both the processes and the resources internal to the enterprise—plants, goods, people, etc.—as well as information on external sources—competitors, suppliers, clients, etc.

Information systems are data oriented and can be characterized on the basis of the way they treat data. Following are some of the qualities that characterize information systems:

- **Data integrity**. Under what circumstances will the data be corrupted when the system malfunctions?
- **Security**. To what extent does the system protect the data from unauthorized access?
- **Data availability**. Under what conditions will the data become unavailable and for how long?
- **Transaction performance**. Because the goal of information systems is to support transactions against information, the performance of such systems can be uniformly characterized in terms of the number of transactions carried out per unit of time.

Another important characteristic of information systems is the need for providing interaction with end users who have little or no technical background (e.g., sales clerks, administrative staff, and managers). Thus, human-computer interaction requirements, such as user-friendliness, are of prime relevance in this case. Such interaction should use menu-based graphic interfaces. Menus should be designed uniformly, and navigation among the different functions should be easy. Users should never get the feeling of being lost; they should always be in control of the interaction with the application, and the application should guard against possible misuse by the users.

Modern information systems go further in this direction. Not only do they support easy access by the user, but also, they encourage active user involvement in the creation of simple applications. In addition to providing a fixed set of functionality, many modern information systems offer simple customization facilities. With these customizations, the user may, for example, define specialized new reports or formats for reports. This feature is called *end-user computing*.

## 2.3.2   Real-Time Systems

Quite apart from information systems is another large class of software systems called real-time systems. The primary characteristic of these systems is that they must respond to events within a predefined and strict period of time. For example, in a factory-monitoring system, the software needs to respond to a sudden increase in temperature by immediately setting certain switches or sounding an alarm. Similarly, flight software that controls an airplane needs to monitor the environmental conditions and current position of the airplane and control the flight path accordingly.

While the real-time classification is usually used to refer to factory automation, surveillance systems, etc., real-time requirements can be found in many more traditional settings. An unusual, but interesting, example is the mouse-handling software in a computer system that needs to respond to mouse click interrupts within a certain period. For example, in many systems, a single mouse click is a command to select an object, while a double click, if the two clicks are sufficiently close in time, is a (different) command to "open" the object. This kind of interface establishes a real-time requirement on the software, because the software must process the first click quickly enough so that it can accept the second interrupt and determine whether the user initiated a double click or two successive single clicks.

There is a common misconception regarding real-time systems which says that such a system requires "fast response times." This is neither true nor sufficiently precise. "Fast" is a qualitative property of an application; what is required for a real-time system is a quantitatively specifiable and verifiable notion of response time. Also, in some real-time systems, a response that comes too early may be as incorrect as a response that comes too late. For instance, in the previous mouse-click example, if the first click is processed "too fast," the double click may not be detected correctly.

Real-time systems have been studied extensively in their own right. We can call information systems data oriented and real-time systems control oriented. At the heart of real-time systems is a *scheduler* that orders or *schedules* the actions of the system. There are two basic types of scheduling algorithms used: priority and deadline. In *priority scheduling*, each action has an associated priority. The action with the highest priority is the one executed next. In *deadline scheduling*, each action has a specified time by which it must be started or completed. It is the responsibility of the scheduler to ensure that actions are scheduled in such a way as to satisfy the scheduling requirements.

Another classification of real-time systems is event based versus time triggered. In event-based systems, each component of the system responds when it detects an event. In time-triggered systems, all components execute their actions at specified times. Time synchronization is expected to ensure that all components observe the same time.

In addition to the generic software qualities, real-time systems are characterized by how well they satisfy the response time requirements. Whereas in other systems response time is a matter of performance, in real-time systems response time is one of the correctness criteria. Furthermore, real-time systems are usually used for critical operations (such as monitoring patients and in defense systems and process control) and have very strict reliability requirements.[4]

In the case of highly critical systems, the term *safety* is often used to denote the absence of undesirable behaviors that can cause system hazards. Safety deals with requirements other than the primary mission of a system and requires that the system execute without causing unacceptable risk. Unlike functional requirements, which describe the intended correct behavior in terms of input-output relationships, safety requirements describe what should *never* happen while the system is executing. In some sense, they are negative requirements: They specify the states the system must never enter. For example, an X-Ray medical system must observe the safety property that the radiation it applies is always below a certain limit.

Finally, other software qualities also may be important in the case of real-time systems. We have shown that human-computer aspects are relevant in the case of information systems. They may be relevant in real-time systems as well. For example, the external interface with a control system monitoring a critical industrial plant must be designed in such a way that the operator perfectly understands the state of the system under control, so that he or she can always operate the plant safely.

---

[4] The term "mission critical" is used to characterize such systems.

### 2.3.3    Distributed Systems

Advances in processor and network technology have made it possible to build so-called distributed systems, which consist of independent or semi-independent computers connected by a communication network. The high-bandwidth, low-error-rate network makes it possible to write distributed software applications whose components run on different computers.

While the generic software qualities apply to distributed software, there are also some new requirements. For example, the software development environment must support the development of software on multiple computers, on which users are compiling, linking, and testing code.

The ability of components to be loaded and executed on different machines has driven the development of new languages such as Java and C#. For example, Java defines an intermediate language (the Java bytecode) that can be efficiently interpreted on any computer of the distributed system. This allows components to be loaded from the network dynamically as needed.

Among the characteristics of distributed systems are (1) the amount of distribution supported—for example, are the data distributed, or is the processing, or both? (2) whether the system can tolerate the partitioning of the network—for instance, when the network link makes it impossible for two subsets of the computers to communicate; and (3) whether the system tolerates the failure of individual computers.

One interesting aspect of distributed systems is that they offer new opportunities for achieving some of the qualities discussed. For example, by replicating the same data on more than one computer, we can increase a system's reliability, and by distributing the data on more than one computer, we can increase both the performance and the reliability of the system. Of course, replicating or distributing data is not so simple and requires significant design work. There are many established techniques for dealing with these issues. We will see some of them in Chapter 4.

Another interesting issue is whether we can take advantage of the technology that supports *code mobility*—that is, the ability of the code to migrate over the network at run time. Mobile code has advantages over the traditional client-server model when the network connections are not permanently enabled to support interactions between clients and servers. There may also be performance advantages if we can move the code to the node that stores the data on which the code needs to operate. Java applets are a simple example of mobile code.

### 2.3.4    Embedded Systems

Embedded systems are systems in which the software is one of many components and often has no interface to the end user; rather, the software has interfaces with the other system components and probably controls them. Embedded software is now used in airplanes, robots, microwave ovens, dishwashers, refrigerators, automobiles, cellular phones, and other appliances.

What distinguishes embedded software from other kinds of software is that the interface of embedded software is with other devices rather than humans; for example, the software sends speed control data to the motors of a robot instead of displaying such data as a curve on the screen. This removes some requirements from the interface design and allows trade-offs to be made in deciding what the system interface will be like. For example, it is often possible to modify the software interface—thereby complicating the software—in order to simplify the design of a hardware device.

Consider a coin-operated vending machine that accepts different-sized coins. We can either build a hardware device to determine the monetary value of each inserted coin—perhaps even having a different slot for each acceptable kind of coin—or let the hardware decide the weight and dimension of the coin and report them to the software. In the latter case, the software is responsible for determining the value of each coin and whether enough money has been inserted. Putting the decision-making capability in software allows a more flexible system: Changing the machine to accept newly released coins, to raise the price of items dispensed, or to work in a different country will not require the design of a new hardware device. With proper software design, such changes will require just the resetting of some internal switches and tables.

Although in our discussion so far, we have assumed that the four preceding application areas are distinct, in practice many systems exhibit characteristics that are common to several of these areas. For instance, it is easy to imagine an information system that may also have some real-time requirements. Such a system may, of course, be distributed. Furthermore, the system may be embedded in a larger monitoring system. As another example, embedded systems are often real time in nature.

A hospital patient-monitoring system is a good example of a system that may exhibit multiple characteristics. It must maintain a database of patient histories. It can be distributed to allow entry and retrieval of data from nurses' stations or various laboratories. It may have some real-time characteristics—for example, to monitor devices in the emergency room. Finally, it may have some requirements of embedded systems, because it may interact with laboratory devices in order to update patient records automatically on the basis of test results.

## 2.4    MEASUREMENT OF QUALITY

Once we have decided on the qualities that are the goals of software engineering, we need principles and techniques to help us achieve them. We also need to be able to *measure* a given quality. In software organizations, this activity is called quality assurance.

If we identify a quality as important, we must be ready to measure it to determine how well we are achieving it. This, in turn, requires that we define each quality precisely, so that it is clear what we should be measuring. Without measurements, any claims of improvement are without basis. But without defining a quality precisely, there is no hope that we can measure it precisely—let alone quantitatively.

The established engineering disciplines have standard techniques for measuring quality. For example, the reliability of an amplifier can be measured—among other ways—by determining the range within which it operates. The reliability of a bridge can be measured by—among other ways—the amount of pressure it can withstand. Indeed, these tolerance levels are released with the product as part of the product specification.

Although some software qualities, such as performance, are measured relatively easily, most qualities unfortunately have no universally accepted metrics. For example, whether a given system will evolve more easily than another is usually determined subjectively. Nevertheless, metrics are needed, and indeed, much research work is currently under way for defining objective metrics. In Chapter 6, we shall examine this issue in depth.

## 2.5    CONCLUDING REMARKS

Software engineering is concerned with applying engineering principles to the building of software products. To arrive at a set of engineering principles that apply uniformly to widely differing software products, the first step is to devise a set of qualities that characterize the products. That is what we have done in this chapter: We have presented a set of qualities that determine the merit of any software product. Our next task is to learn what principles to apply so that we can build software products that achieve these qualities. That is the topic of the next chapter.

## FURTHER EXERCISES

**2.8**    In this chapter, we have discussed the software qualities that we consider to be the most important. Some other qualities are testability, integrity, ease of use, ease of operation, and learnability. Define each of these—and possibly other—qualities, give examples, and discuss the relationships between the qualities you have defined and the qualities we have discussed in the chapter.

**2.9**    Classify each of the qualities discussed in this chapter as internal, external, product, or process, giving examples. The classes are not mutually exclusive.

**2.10**    Show graphically the interdependence of the qualities discussed in this chapter: Draw a graph in which each node represents a software quality and an arrow from node $A$ to node $B$ indicates that quality $A$ contributes toward achieving quality $B$. What does the graph show you about the relative importance of the software qualities? Are there any cycles in the graph? What does a cycle imply?

**2.11**    Sometimes, new managers use many of the techniques they employed on their most recent project. Using this as an example, discuss the concept of reusability applied to the software process.

**2.12**    If you are familiar with the TCP/IP protocols (for example ftp and telnet), discuss their role in interoperability.

**2.13**    We have discussed interoperability as a product-related quality. We can also talk about the interoperability of processes. For example, the process followed by a quality assurance organization must be compatible with that followed by a development organization in the same company. Another example is offered by a company that contracts with an independent organization to produce the documentation for a product. Use these examples and others of your own to analyze interoperability as applied to a process.

## HINTS AND SKETCHY SOLUTIONS

**2.1**  In some cases, human-interface decisions may affect the reliability of a system. For example, one should ensure that two switches which issue two commands with opposite effects are not placed close to each other, in order to prevent the inadvertent choice of one switch instead of the other.

**2.2**  As components are more and more reused, they are likely to become more and more reliable, since residual errors are progressively eliminated.

## BIBLIOGRAPHIC NOTES

For a discussion of software, its nature, and its characteristics, refer to Boehm [1976], Wegner [1984], Parnas [1985], Freeman [1987a], and Brooks [1987]. Weinberg [1971] and Weinberg and Schulman [1974] deal with human aspects of software development.

Different views of the software production process are provided by Boehm [1981], Agresti [1986], Curtis et al. [1988], Humphrey [1989], and Cugola and Ghezzi [1999].

A classification of software qualities is presented by Boehm [1976] and discussed in detail by Boehm et al. [1978]. For each quality, in turn, there is a specialized bibliography. The International Conference on Reliable Software by ACM [1975] had an important role in stimulating research in the area.

Musa et al. [1987] give an in-depth view of software reliability that follows a statistical approach. Program correctness is studied by Manna [1974] and Mandriol and Ghezzi [1987]. We shall return to these issues in Chapter 6. The concept of software safety has been investigated by Leveson [1986], security has been formalized by McLean [1990], and trusted computer systems are illustrated by Ames et al. [1983].

General texts on performance are Ferrari [1978] and Smith [1989]; a classic on computational complexity is Aho et al. [1974]. Practical approaches to writing efficient programs are illustrated by Bentley [2000, 1988].

For user-friendliness and the issue of human-computer interaction, refer to Rubinstein and Hersh [1984], Schneiderman [1998], and Norman and Draper [1986]. Norman [1998] is an entertaining and easy-to-read book on how to make the computer interface so natural that we don't even notice it.

Maintenance and software evolution are studied extensively by Lientz and Swanson [1980], Belady and Lehman [1979], and Lehman and Belady [1985]. The distinction between corrective, adaptive, and perfective maintenance is due to Lientz and Swanson, who also report the figures we gave in this chapter. Cusumano and Yoffie [1999b] discuss Netscape's approach to cross-platform design and portability and the company's initial disappointments and problems with Java in this regard.

Reusability is discussed by Freeman [1987b] and Biggerstaff and Perlis [1989].

Kernighan and Pike [1984] illustrate how the UNIX environment influences interoperability.

Productivity is discussed at length by Boehm [1981] and Capers Jones [1986]. Cusumano and Yoffie [1999a] discuss the impact of short time-to-market ("Internet-time") requirements on software development.

A characterization of real-time systems is given by Wirth [1977] and Stankovic [1988]. Kopetz [1997] covers the design of distributed real-time systems. Leveson [1995] discusses the safety risks in computers software and some ways to avoid them.

Early surveys of the state of the art in software quality metrics are given by Basili [1980] and Conte et al. [1986]. Some advances are illustrated in the special issue of *IEEE Software* [1990b]. Fenton and Pfleeger [1998] give a comprehensive study of software metrics for quality.

CHAPTER 3

# Software Engineering Principles

In this chapter, we discuss some important and general principles that are central to successful software development. These principles deal with both the *process* of software engineering and the final *product*. The right process will help produce the right product, but the desired product will also affect the choice of which process to use. A common problem in software engineering has been an emphasis on either the process or the product to the exclusion of the other. Both are important.

The principles we develop are general enough to be applicable throughout the process of software construction and management. Principles, however, are not sufficient to drive software development. In fact, they are general and abstract statements describing desirable properties of software processes and products. But, to apply principles, the software engineer should be equipped with appropriate *methods* and specific *techniques* that help incorporate the desired properties into processes and products.

Note that we distinguish between methods and techniques. Methods are general guidelines that govern the execution of some activity; they are rigorous, systematic, and disciplined approaches. Techniques are more technical and mechanical than methods; often, they also have more restricted applicability. In general, however, the difference between the two is not sharp. We will therefore use the two terms interchangeably.

Sometimes, methods and techniques are packaged together to form a *methodology*. The purpose of a methodology is to promote a certain approach to solving a problem by preselecting the methods and techniques to be used. *Tools*, in turn, are developed to support the application of techniques, methods, and methodologies.

Figure 3.1 shows the relationship between principles, methods and techniques, methodologies, and tools. Each layer in the figure is based on the layer(s) below it and is more susceptible to change, due to the passage of time. The figure shows clearly that principles are the basis of all methods, techniques, methodologies, and tools. The figure can also be used to explain the structure of this book. In this chapter, we present essential software engineering principles. In Chapters 4, 5, and 6, we examine methods and

FIGURE 3.1

Relationship between principles, methods and techniques, methodologies, and tools.

techniques based on the principles of the current chapter. Chapter 7 presents some methodologies, and Chapter 9 discusses tools and environments.

In our discussion of principles, we try to be general enough to cover every type of application. The same applies to the specific methods and techniques we develop in the chapters that follow. The emphasis we place on some principles and the particular methods and techniques we have selected, however, are deliberate choices. Among the qualities that were discussed in the previous chapter, we stress reliability and evolvability; and this choice, in turn, affects our emphasis in discussing principles, methods, and techniques.

As mentioned in Chapter 1, we consider the case where the software to be developed is not just an experiment to be run a few times, possibly only by its developer. Most likely, its expected users will have little or even no knowledge of computers and software. Or the software might be required to support a critical application—one in which the effects of errors are serious, perhaps even disastrous. For these and other reasons, the application must be reliable.

Also, we assume that the application is sufficiently large and complex that a special effort is required to decompose it into manageable parts. This is especially true in team projects, but it is also true in the case of a single software engineer doing the job. In both cases, there is a need for an approach to software development that helps to overcome its complexity.

In all the circumstances just described, which represent typical situations in software development, reliability and evolvability play a special role. Clearly, if the software does not have reliability and evolvability requirements, the need for software engineering principles and techniques diminishes greatly. In general, the choice of principles and techniques is determined by the software quality goals.

In this chapter, we discuss seven general and important principles that apply throughout the software development process: rigor and formality, separation of concerns, modularity, abstraction, anticipation of change, generality, and incrementality. The list, by its very nature, cannot be exhaustive, but it does cover the important areas of software engineering. Although the principles often appear to be strongly related, we prefer to describe each of them separately in quite general terms. We will revisit these principles at the end of the chapter with the help of two summarizing case studies. They will also be taken up in more concrete, detailed, and specific terms in the chapters that follow. In particular, the principle of modularity will be presented in Chapter 4 as the cornerstone of software design.

## 3.1 RIGOR AND FORMALITY

Software development is a creative activity. In any creative process, there is an inherent tendency to be neither precise nor accurate, but rather to follow the inspiration of the moment in an unstructured manner. *Rigor*—defined as precision and exactness—

on the other hand, is a necessary complement to creativity in every engineering activity: It is only through a rigorous approach that we can repeatedly produce reliable products, control their costs, and increase our confidence in their reliability. Rigor does not need to constrain creativity. Rather, it can be used as a tool to enhance creativity: The engineer can be more confident of the results of a creative process after performing a rigorous assessment of those results.

Paradoxically, rigor is an intuitive quality that cannot be defined in a rigorous way. Also, various degrees of rigor can be achieved. The highest degree is what we call *formality*. Thus, formality is a stronger requirement than rigor: It requires the software process to be driven and evaluated by mathematical laws. Of course, formality implies rigor, but the converse is not true: One can be rigorous and precise even in an informal setting.

In every engineering field, the design process proceeds as a sequence of well-defined, precisely stated, and supposedly sound steps. In each step, the engineer follows some method or applies some technique. The methods and techniques applied may be based on some combination of theoretical results derived by some formal modeling of reality, empirical adjustments that take care of phenomena not dealt with by the model, and rules of thumb that depend on past experience. The blend of these factors results in a rigorous and systematic approach—the methodology—that can be easily explained and applied time and again.

There is no need to be always formal during design, but the engineer must know how and when to be formal, should the need arise. For example, the engineer can rely on past experience and rules of thumb to design a small bridge, to be used temporarily to connect the two sides of a creek. If the bridge were a large and permanent one, on the other hand, she would instead use a mathematical model to verify whether the design was safe. She would use a more sophisticated mathematical model if the bridge were exceptionally long or if it were built in an area of much seismic activity. In that case, the mathematical model would take into account factors that could be ignored in the previous case.

Another—perhaps striking—example of the interplay between rigor and formality may be observed in mathematics. Textbooks on functional calculus are rigorous, but seldom formal: Proofs of theorems are done in a very careful way, as sequences of intermediate deductions that lead to the final statement; each deductive step relies on an intuitive justification that should convince the reader of its validity. Almost never, however, is the derivation of a proof stated in a formal way, in terms of mathematical logic. This means that very often the mathematician is satisfied with a rigorous description of the derivation of a proof, without formalizing it completely. In critical cases, however, where the validity of some intermediate deduction is unclear, the mathematician may try to formalize the informal reasoning to assess its validity.

These examples show that the engineer (and the mathematician) must be able to identify and understand the level of rigor and formality that should be achieved, depending on the conceptual difficulty and criticality of the task. The level may even vary for different parts of the same system. For example, critical parts—such as the scheduler of a real-time operating systems kernel or the security component of an electronic commerce system—may merit a formal description of their intended functions and a formal approach to their assessment. Well-understood and standard parts would require simpler approaches.

This situation applies in all areas of software engineering. Chapter 5 will go deeply into this issue in the context of software specifications. There, we shall show, for example, that the description of what a program does may be given in a rigorous way by using natural language; it can also be given formally by providing a formal description in a language of logical statements. The advantage of formality over rigor is that formality may be the basis of mechanization of the process. For instance, one may hope to use the formal description of the program to create the program (if the program does not exist yet) or to show that the program corresponds to the formal description (if the program and its formal specification exist).

Traditionally, there is only one phase of software development where a formal approach is used: programming. In fact, programs are formal objects: They are written in a language whose syntax and semantics are fully defined. Programs are formal descriptions that may be automatically manipulated by compilers: They are checked for formal correctness, transformed into an equivalent form in another language (assembly or machine language), "pretty-printed" so as to improve their appearance, etc. These mechanical operations, which are made possible by the use of formality in programming, can improve the reliability and verifiability of software products.

Rigor and formality are not restricted to programming: They should be applied throughout the software process. Chapter 4 shows these concepts in action in the case of software design. Chapter 5 describes rigorous and formal approaches to software specification. Chapter 6 does the same for software verification.

So far, our discussion has emphasized the influence of rigor and formality on the reliability and verifiability of software products. Rigor and formality also have beneficial effects on maintainability, reusability, portability, understandability, and interoperability. For example, rigorous, or even formal, software documentation can improve all of these qualities over informal documentation, which is often ambiguous, inconsistent, and incomplete.

Rigor and formality also apply to software processes. Rigorous documentation of a software process helps in reusing the process in other, similar projects. On the basis of such documentation, managers may foresee the steps through which a new project will evolve, assign appropriate resources as needed, etc. Similarly, rigorous documentation of the software process may help maintain an existing product. If the various steps through which a project evolved are documented, one can modify an existing product, starting from the appropriate intermediate level of its derivation, not the final code. More will be said on this crucial point in the chapters that follow. Finally, if the software process is specified rigorously, managers may monitor it accurately, in order to assess its timeliness and improve productivity.

## 3.2    SEPARATION OF CONCERNS

Separation of concerns allows us to deal with different aspects of a problem, so that we can concentrate on each individually. Separation of concerns is a commonsense practice that we try to follow in our everyday life to overcome the difficulties we encounter. The principle should be applied also in software development, to master its inherent complexity.

More specifically, there are many decisions that must be made in the development of a software product. Some of them concern features of the product: functions to offer, expected reliability, efficiency with respect to space and time, the product's relationship with the environment (i.e., the special hardware or software resources required), user interfaces, etc. Others concern the development process: the development environment, the organization and structure of teams, scheduling, control procedures, design strategies, error recovery mechanisms, etc. Still others concern economic and financial matters. These different decisions may be unrelated to one another. In such a case, it is obvious that they should be treated separately.

Very often, however, many decisions are strongly related and interdependent. For instance, a design decision (e.g., swapping some data from main memory to disk) may depend on the size of the memory of the selected target machine (and hence, the cost of the machine), and this, in turn, may affect the policy for error recovery. When different design decisions are strongly interconnected, it would be useful to take all the issues into account at the same time and by the same people, but this is not usually possible in practice.

The only way to master the complexity of a project is to separate the different concerns. First of all, we should try to isolate issues that are not so closely related to the others. Then, we consider issues separately, together with only the *relevant* details of related issues.

There are various ways in which concerns may be separated. First, one can separate them in *time*. As an everyday example, a university professor might apply separation of concerns by scheduling teaching-related activities such as holding classes, seminars, office hours, and department meetings from 9 A.M. to 2 P.M. Monday through Thursday; consulting on Friday; and engaging in research the rest of the time. Such temporal separation of concerns allows for the precise planning of activities and eliminates overhead that would arise through switching from one activity to another in an unconstrained way. As we saw in Chapter 1 and will see in more detail in Chapter 7, separation of concerns in terms of time is the underlying motivation of the software life cycle models, each of which defines a sequence of activities that should be followed in software production.

Another type of separation of concerns is in terms of *qualities* that should be treated separately. For example, in the case of software, we might wish to deal separately with the efficiency and the correctness of a given program. One might decide first to design software in such a careful and structured way that its correctness is expected to be guaranteed *a priori* and then to restructure the program partially to improve its efficiency. Similarly, in the verification phase, one might first check the functional correctness of the program and then its performance. Both activities can be done rigorously, applying some systematic procedures, or even formally (i.e., using formal correctness proofs and complexity analysis). Verification of program qualities is the subject of Chapter 6.

Another important type of separation of concerns allows different *views* of the software to be analyzed separately. For example, when we analyze the requirements of an application, it may be helpful to concentrate separately on the flow of data from one activity to another in the system and the flow of control that governs the way different activities are synchronized. Both views help us understand the system we are working on better, although neither one gives a complete view of it.

Still another type of separation of concerns allows us to deal with *parts* of the same system separately; here, separation is in terms of size. This is a fundamental concept that we need to master to dominate the complexity of software production. Indeed, it is so important that we prefer to detail it shortly as a separate point under modularity.

There is an inherent disadvantage in separation of concerns: By separating two or more issues, we might miss some global optimization that would be possible by tackling them together. While this is true in principle, our ability to make "optimized" decisions in the face of complexity is rather limited. If we consider too many concerns simultaneously, we are likely to be overwhelmed by the amount of detail and complexity we face. Some of the most important decisions in design concern which aspects to consider together and which separately. System designers and architects often face such trade-offs.

Note that if two issues associated with one problem are intrinsically intertwined (i.e., the problem is not immediately decomposable into separate issues), it is often possible to make some overall design decisions first and then effectively separate the different issues. For example, consider a system in which on-line transactions access a database concurrently. In a first implementation of the system, we could introduce a simple locking scheme that requires each transaction to lock the entire database at the start of the transaction and unlock it at the end. Suppose now that a preliminary performance analysis shows that some transaction, say, $t_i$ (which might print some complex report extracting many data from the database), takes so long than we cannot afford to have the database unavailable to other transactions. Thus, the problem is to revise the implementation to improve its performance yet maintain the overall correctness of the system. Clearly, the two issues—functional correctness and performance—are strongly related, so a first design decision must concern both of them: $t_i$ is no longer implemented as an atomic transaction, but is split into several subtransactions $t_{i1}$, $t_{i2}$, ..., $t_{in}$, each of which is atomic itself. The new implementation may affect the correctness of the system, because of the interleaving that may occur between the executions of any two subtransactions. Now, however, we have separated the two concerns of checking the functional correctness of the system and analyzing its performance; we may, then, do the analyses independently, possibly even by two different designers with different levels of expertise.

Perhaps the most important application of separation of concerns is to separate problem-domain concerns from implementation-domain concerns. Problem-domain properties hold in general, regardless of the implementation environment. For example, in designing a personnel-management system, we must separate issues that are true about employees in general from those which are a consequence of our implementation of the employee as a data structure or object. In the problem domain, we may speak of the *relationship* between employees, such as "employee *A* reports to employee *B*," and in the implementation domain we may speak of one object pointing to another. These concerns are often intermingled in many projects.

As a final remark, notice that separation of concerns may result in separation of responsibilities in dealing with separate issues. Thus, the principle is the basis for dividing the work on a complex problem into specific assignments, possibly for different people with different skills. For example, by separating managerial and technical issues in the software process, we allow two types of people to cooperate in a software project. Or, having separated requirements analysis and specification from other activities in a software life cycle, we may hire specialized analysts with expertise in the application domain, instead of relying on internal resources. The analyst, in turn, may concentrate separately on functional and nonfunctional system requirements.

## Exercises

**3.1**    Show in a simple program (or program fragment) of your choice how you can deal separately with correctness and efficiency.

**3.2**    Read about aspect-oriented programming, and examine it with respect to separation of concerns. How is separation of concerns supported in aspect-oriented programming?

**3.3    MODULARITY**

A complex system may be divided into simpler pieces called *modules*. A system that is composed of modules is called *modular*. The main benefit of modularity is that it allows the principle of separation of concerns to be applied in two phases: when dealing with the details of each module in isolation (and ignoring details of other modules) and when dealing with the overall characteristics of all modules and their relationships in order to integrate them into a coherent system. If the two phases are executed in sequence first by concentrating on modules and then on their composition, then we say that the system is designed *bottom up*; the converse—when we decompose modules first and then concentrate on individual module design—is *top-down* design.

Modularity is an important property of most engineering processes and products. For example, in the automobile industry, the construction of cars proceeds by assembling building blocks that are designed and built separately. Furthermore, parts are often reused from model to model, perhaps after minor changes. Most industrial processes are essentially modular, made out of work packages that are combined in simple ways (sequentially or overlapping) to achieve the desired result.

**Exercise**

---

**3.3**    Describe the work packages involved in building a house, and show how they are organized sequentially and in parallel.

---

The next chapter emphasizes modularity in the context of software design. Modularity, however, is not only a desirable design principle; it also permeates the whole of software production. In particular, modularity provides four main benefits in practice:

- the capability of decomposing a complex system into simpler pieces,
- the capability of composing a complex system from existing modules,
- the capability of understanding the system in terms of its pieces, and
- the capability of modifying a system by modifying only a small number of its pieces.

The *decomposability* of a system is based on dividing the original problem top down into subproblems and then applying the decomposition to each subproblem recursively. This procedure reflects the well-known Latin motto *divide et impera* (divide and conquer), which describes the philosophy followed by the ancient Romans to dominate other nations: Divide and isolate them first, and then conquer them individually.

The *composability* of a system is based on starting bottom up from elementary components and combining them in steps towards finally producing a finished system. As an example, a system for office automation may be designed by assembling together existing hardware components, such as personal workstations, a network, and peripherals; system software, such as the operating system; and productivity tools, such as document processors, databases, and spreadsheets. A car is another obvious example of a system that is built by assembling components. Consider first the main subsystems into which a car may be decomposed: the body, the electrical system, the power system, the transmission system, etc. Each of them, in turn, is made out of standard parts; for example, the battery, fuses, cables, etc., form the electrical system. When something goes wrong, defective components may be replaced by new ones.

Ideally, in software production we would like to be able to assemble new applications by taking modules from a library and combining them to form the required product. Such modules should be designed with the express goal of being reusable. By using reusable components, we may speed up both the initial system construction and its fine-tuning. For example, it would be possible to replace a component by another that performs the same function, but differs in computational resource requirements.

The *capability of understanding* and modifying a system are related to each other as understanding is often the first step to applying modifications. We have stressed evolvability as a quality goal because software engineers areoften required to go back to previous work to modify it. If the entire system can be understood only in its entirety, modifications are likely to be difficult to apply, and the result will probably be unreliable. When it is necessary to repair a defect or enhance a feature, proper modularity helps confine the search for the fault or enhancement to single components. Modularity thus forms the basis for software evolution.

To achieve modular composability, decomposability, understandability, and modifiability, the software engineer must design the modules with the goal of *high cohesion* and *low coupling*.

A module has high cohesion if all of its elements are related strongly. Elements of a module (e.g., statements, procedures, and declarations) are grouped together in the same module for a logical reason, not just by chance: They cooperate to achieve a common goal, which is the function of the module.

Whereas cohesion is an internal property of a module, coupling characterizes a module's relationship to other modules. Coupling measures the interdependence of two modules (e.g., module *A* calls a routine provided by module *B* or accesses a variable declared by module *B*). If two modules depend on each other heavily, they have high coupling. Ideally, we would like modules in a system to exhibit low coupling, because it will then be possible to analyze, understand, modify, test, or reuse them separately. Figure 3.2 provides a graphical view of cohesion and coupling.

A good example of a system that has high cohesion and low coupling is the electric subsystem of a house. Because it is made out of a set of appliances with clearly definable functions and interconnected by simple wires, the system has low coupling. Because each appliance's internal components are there exactly to provide the service the appliance is supposed to provide, the system has high cohesion.

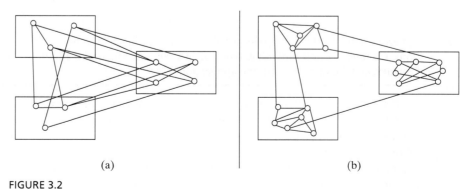

(a)             (b)

**FIGURE 3.2**

Graphical description of cohesion and coupling. **(a)** A highly coupled structure. **(b)** A structure with high cohesion and low coupling.

Modular structures with high cohesion and low coupling allow us to see modules as black boxes when the overall structure of a system is described and then deal with each module separately when the module's functionality is described or analyzed. In other words, modularity supports the application of the principle of separation of concerns.

### Exercises

**3.4** Suppose you decide to modularize the description of a car by considering the car as comprising small cubes 15 inches on a side. Discuss this modularization in terms of cohesion and coupling. Propose a better way of modularizing the description, if there is any. Draw some general conclusions about how one should modularize a complex system.

**3.5** Explain some of the causes of, and remedies for, low cohesion in a software module.

**3.6** Explain some of the causes of, and remedies for, high coupling between two software modules.

## 3.4 ABSTRACTION

Abstraction is a fundamental technique for understanding and analyzing complex problems. In applying abstraction, we identify the important aspects of a phenomenon and ignore its details. Thus, abstraction is a special case of separation of concerns wherein we separate the concern of the important aspects from the concern of the less important details.

What we abstract away and consider as a detail that may be ignored depends on the purpose of the abstraction. For example, consider a digital watch. A useful abstraction for the owner is a description of the effects of pushing its various buttons, which allow the watch to enter various modes of functioning and react differently to sequences of commands. A useful abstraction for the person in charge of maintaining the watch is a box that can be opened in order to replace the battery. Still other abstractions of the device are useful for understanding the watch and performing the activities that are needed to repair it (let alone design it). Thus, there may be many different abstractions of the same reality, each providing a *view* of the reality and serving some specific purpose.

### Exercise

**3.7** Different people interacting with a software application may require different abstractions. Comment briefly on what types of abstractions are useful for the end user, the designer, and the maintainer of the application.

Abstraction is a powerful technique practiced by engineers of all fields for mastering complexity. For example, the representation of an electrical circuit in terms of resistors, capacitors, etc., each characterized by a set of equations, is an idealized abstraction of a device. The equations are a simplified model that approximates the behavior of the real components. The equations often ignore details, such as the fact that there are no "pure" connectors between components and that connectors should also be modeled in terms of resistors, capacitors, etc. The designer ignores both of these facts, because the effects they describe are negligible in terms of the observed results.

This example illustrates an important general idea: The models we build of phenomena—such as the equations for describing devices—are an abstraction from reality, ignoring certain facts and concentrating on others that we believe are relevant. The same holds for the models built and analyzed by software engineers. For example, when the requirements for a new application are analyzed and specified, software engineers build a model of the proposed application. As we shall see in Chapter 5, this model may be expressed in various forms, depending on the required degree of rigor and formality. No matter what language we use for expressing requirements—be it natural language or the formal language of mathematical formulas—what we provide is a model that abstracts away from a number of details that we decide can be ignored safely.

Abstraction permeates the whole of programming. The programming languages that we use are abstractions built on top of the hardware: They provide us with useful and powerful constructs so that we can write (most) programs ignoring such details as the number of bits that are used to represent numbers or the specific computer's addressing mechanism. This helps us concentrate on the solution to the problem we are trying to solve, rather than on the way to instruct the machine on how to solve it. The programs we write are themselves abstractions. For example, a computerized payroll procedure is an abstraction of the manual procedure it replaces: It provides the *essence* of the manual procedure, not its exact details.

Abstraction is an important principle that applies to both software products and software processes. For example, the comments that we often use in the header of a procedure are an abstraction that describes the effect of the procedure. When the documentation of the program is analyzed, such comments are supposed to provide all the information that is needed to understand the use of the procedure by the other parts of the program.

As an example of the use of abstraction in software processes, consider the case of cost estimation for a new application. One possible way of doing cost estimation consists of identifying some key factors of the new system—for example, the number of engineers on the project and the expected size of the final system—and extrapolating from the cost profiles of previous similar systems. The key factors used to perform the analysis are an abstraction of the system for the purpose of cost estimation.

## Exercises

**3.8**   Variables provided in a programming language may be viewed as abstractions of memory locations. What details are abstracted away by programming-language variables? What are the advantages of using the abstraction? What are the disadvantages?

**3.9**   Variables in programs are also used as abstractions in the problem domain. Explain how a variable called employee is an abstraction of a problem-domain concept.

**3.10**   A software life cycle model, such as the waterfall model outlined in Chapter 1, is an abstraction of a software process. Why?

## 3.5   ANTICIPATION OF CHANGE

Software undergoes changes constantly. As we saw in Chapter 2, changes are due both to the need for repairing the software-eliminating errors that were not detected before releasing the application-and to the need for supporting evolution of the application as new requirements arise or old requirements change. This is why we identified maintainability as a major software quality.

The ability of software to evolve does not happen by accident or out of sheer luck-it requires a special effort to anticipate how and where changes are likely to occur. Designers can try to identify likely future changes and take special care to make these changes easy to apply. We shall see this important point in action in Chapter 4 in the case of design. In that chapter, we show how software can be designed such that likely changes that we anticipate in the requirements, or modifications that are planned as part of the design strategy, may be incorporated into the application smoothly and safely. Basically, likely changes should be isolated in specific portions of the software in such a way that changes will be restricted to such small portions. In other words, anticipation of change is the basis for our modularization strategy.

Anticipation of change is perhaps the one principle that distinguishes software the most from other types of industrial productions. In many cases, a software application is developed when its requirements are not entirely understood. Then, after being released, on the basis of feedback from the users, the application must evolve as new requirements are discovered or old requirements are updated. In addition, applications are often embedded in an environment, such as an organizational structure. The environment is affected by the introduction of the application, and this generates new requirements that were not known initially. Thus, anticipation of change is a principle that we can use to achieve evolvability.

Reusability is another software quality that is strongly affected by anticipation of change. As we saw, a component is reusable if it can be directly used to produce a new product. More realistically, the component might undergo some changes before it can be reused. Hence, reusability may be viewed as low-grain evolvability—that is, evolvability at the component level. If we can anticipate the changes of context in which a software component might be embedded, we may then design the component in a way that such changes may be accommodated easily.

Anticipation of change requires that appropriate tools be available to manage the various versions and revisions of the software in a controlled manner. It must be possible to store and retrieve documentation, source modules, object modules, etc., from a database that acts as the central repository of reusable components. Access to the database must be controlled. A consistent view of the software system must always be available, even as we apply changes to some of its components. As we mentioned in Section 2.1.2—and as we shall see again in Chapters 7, 8, and 9—the discipline that studies this class of problems is called *configuration management*.

In our discussion of anticipation of change, we focused attention more on software products than on software processes. Anticipation of change, however, also affects the management of the software process. For example, managers should anticipate the effects of personnel turnover. Also, when the life cycle of an application is designed, it is important to take maintenance into account. Depending on the anticipated changes, managers must estimate costs and design the organizational structure that will support the evolution of the software. Finally, managers should decide whether it is worthwhile investing time and effort in the production of reusable components, either as a by-product of a given software development project or as a parallel development effort.

**Exercise**

---

**3.11** Take a sorting program from any textbook. Discuss the program from the standpoint of reusability. Does the algorithm make assumptions about the type of the elements to be sorted? Would you be able to reuse the algorithm for different types of elements? What if the sequence of values to sort is so long that it should be stored on secondary storage? How would you modify the program to improve its reusability under these circumstances? Based on this experience, produce a list of general suggestions that would favor anticipation of change in a program.

---

## 3.6   GENERALITY

The principle of generality may be stated as follows:

> Every time you are asked to solve a problem, try to focus on the discovery of a more general problem that may be hidden behind the problem at hand. It may happen that the generalized problem is not more complex—indeed, it may even be simpler—than the original problem. Moreover, it is likely that the solution to the generalized problem has more potential for being reused. It may even happen that the solution is already provided by some off-the-shelf package. Also, it may happen that, by generalizing a problem, you end up designing a module that is invoked at more than one point of the application, rather than having several specialized solutions.

On the other hand, a generalized solution may be more costly, in terms of speed of execution, memory requirements, or development time, than the specialized solution that is tailored to the original problem. Thus, it is necessary to evaluate the tradeoffs of generality with respect to cost and efficiency, in order to decide whether it is worthwhile to solve the generalized problem instead of the original problem.

For example, suppose you are asked to merge two sorted sequential files into one. On the basis of the requirements, you know that the two source files do not contain any records with identical key values. Clearly, then, if you generalize your solution to accept source files that may contain different elements with the same key value, you provide a program that has a higher potential for reusability. Also, you may be able to use a merge program that is available in your system library.

As another example, suppose that you are asked to design an application to handle a small library of cooking recipes. Suppose also that the recipes have a header—containing information such as a name, a list of ingredients, and cooking information—and a textual part describing how to apply the recipes. Apart from storing recipes in the library, it must be possible to do a sophisticated search for recipes, based on their available ingredients, maximum calories, etc. Rather than designing a new set of facilities, these searches can be viewed as a special case of a more general set of text-processing facilities, such as those provided by the AWK language under UNIX or the language PERL. Before starting with the design of the specialized set of routines, the designer should consider whether the adoption of a generalized text-processing tool would be more useful. The generalized tool is undoubtedly more reliable than the specialized program to be designed, and it would probably accommodate changes in the requirements or even new requirements. On the negative side, however, there may be a cost of acquisition, and possibly overhead, in the use of the generalized tool.

Generality is a fundamental principle that allows us to develop general tools or packages for the market. The success of such tools as spreadsheets, databases, and word processors is that they are general enough to cover the practical needs of most people when they wish to handle their personal business with a computer. Instead of customizing specific solutions for each personal business, it is more economical to use aproduct that is already on the market.

Such general-purpose, off-the-shelf products represent a rather general trend in software. For every specific application area, general packages that provide standard solutions to common problems are increasingly available. If the problem at hand may be restated as an instance of a problem solved by a general package, it may be convenient to adopt the package instead of implementing a specialized solution. For example, we may use macros to specialize a spreadsheet application to be used as an expense-report application.

This general trend is identical to what happens in other branches of industry. For example, in the early days of automobile technology, it was possible to customize cars according to the specific requirements of the purchaser. As the field became more industrialized, customers could only choose from a catalogue of models—which correspond to prepackaged solutions—provided by each manufacturer. Nowadays, it is not possible for most people to acquire a personal car design.

The next step in this trend in the software industry is the development of *application servers* that provide the general functionality on remote server machines. In this way, the user does not even need to install the application on his or her own machine, but instead uses the functionality available remotely. For example, such common functions as mail and calendar management are now routinely offered and used remotely.

## 3.7    INCREMENTALITY

Incrementality characterizes a process that proceeds in a stepwise fashion, in *increments*. We try to achieve the desired goal by successively closer approximations to it. Each approximation is an increment over the previous one.

Incrementality applies to many engineering activities. When applied to software, it means that the desired application is produced as a result of an evolutionary process.

One way of applying the incrementality principle consists of identifying useful *early subsets* of an application that may be developed and delivered to customers, in order to get *early feedback*. This allows the application to evolve in a controlled manner in cases where the initial requirements are not stable or fully understood. The motivation for incrementality is that in most practical cases there is no way of getting all the requirements right before an application is developed. Rather, requirements emerge as the application—or parts of it—is available for practical experimentation. Consequently, the sooner we can receive feedback from the customer concerning the usefulness of the application, the easier it is to incorporate the required changes into the product. Thus, incrementality is intertwined with anticipation of change and is one of the cornerstones upon which evolvability may be based.

Incrementality applies to many of the software qualities discussed in Chapter 2 We may progressively add functions to the application being developed, starting from a kernel of functions that would still make the system useful, although incomplete. For example, in some business automation systems, some functions would still be done manually, while others would be done automatically by the application.

We can also add performance in an incremental fashion. That is, the initial version of the application might emphasize user interfaces and reliability more than performance, and successive releases would then improve space and time efficiency.

When an application is developed incrementally, intermediate stages may constitute *prototypes* of the end product; that is, they are just an approximation of it. The idea of rapid prototyping is often advocated as a way of progressively developing an application hand in hand with an understanding of its requirements. Obviously, a software life cycle based on prototyping is rather different from the typical waterfall model described earlier, wherein we first do a complete requirements analysis and specification and then start developing the application. Instead, prototyping is based on a more flexible and iterative development model. This difference affects not only the technical aspects of projects, but also the organizational and managerial issues. The unified process, presented in Chapter 7, is based on incremental development.

As we mentioned in connection with anticipation of change, evolutionary software development requires special care in the management of documents, programs, test data, etc., developed for the various versions of software. Each meaningful incremental step must be recorded, documentation must be easily retrieved, changes must be applied in a controlled way, and so on. If these are not done carefully, an intended evolutionary development may quickly turn into undisciplined software development, and all the potential advantages of evolvability will be lost.

### Exercise

---

**3.12**   Discuss the concept of the software prototype illustrated here, as opposed to the concept of a prototype used by engineers in other industrial branches (e.g., the prototype of a bridge or a car).

---

## 3.8   TWO CASE STUDIES ILLUSTRATING SOFTWARE ENGINEERING PRINCIPLES

In this section, we present two case studies that will help us understand more deeply the principles illustrated in this chapter. The first examines a fairly typical software product, namely, a compiler; the second examines a nonsoftware system, namely, an elevator system. Both case studies show how the principles illustrated in the chapter are general engineering principles. Both also serve to better illustrate commonalities and differences between traditional engineering and software engineering. This chapter—and indeed, the entire book—try to emphasize the relationships of software engineering to other engineering disciplines. The second case study will also help emphasize the notion that in most cases software is just a component of a more complex system that integrates artifacts of different types.

### 3.8.1   A Case Study in Compiler Construction

Let us examine how the principles illustrated in this chapter can be applied during the development of a compiler.

### 3.8.1.1 *Rigor and formality*

There are many reasons that compiler designers should be rigorous and, possibly, formal. First, a compiler is a critical product: A compiler that generates incorrect code is as serious a problem as a processor that executes an instruction incorrectly. An incorrect compiler can generate incorrect applications, regardless of the quality of the application itself. Second, when a compiler is used to generate code for mass-produced software such as databases or word processors, the effect of an error in the compiler is multiplied on a mass scale. Thus, in general, it is important to approach the development of a compiler rigorously, with the aim of producing a high-quality compiler.

Compiler construction is one of the fields in computer science where formality has been exploited well for a long time. In fact, formal languages and automata theory were largely motivated by the need for making compiler construction more effective and reliable. Nowadays, the syntax of programming languages is formally defined through Backus-Naur form (BNF) or an equivalent formalism. It is not by chance that, most often, problems associated with compiler correctness are related to the semantic aspects of the language, which are usually defined informally, rather than the syntactic aspects, which are well defined by BNF.

The formality achieved through BNF and the application of automata theory also produce major benefits in terms of generality, as we will see in Section 3.8.1.6.

### 3.8.1.2 *Separation of concerns*

As in most nontrivial engineering artifacts, the construction of a compiler involves several concerns. Correctness (i.e., producing an object code consistent with the source code and producing appropriate error messages in the case of erroneous source programs) is, as usual, a primary concern. Other important issues are efficiency and user friendliness. Efficiency could be related to compile time (in which case it amounts to performing source code analysis and translation quickly or using little memory) or to run time (in which case it involves producing an object code that is itself efficient). User-friendliness also has several aspects, ranging from the precision, thoroughness, and helpfulness of the diagnostics to the ease of interacting with the human-computer interface (e.g., through well-designed windows and other graphical aids).

These and other aspects of the compiler should be analyzed separately, as far as possible. For instance, there is no reason to worry about diagnostic messages while one is designing a sophisticated algorithm to optimize register allocation. This is not to say, as we already noticed in general, that different concerns do not affect each other. Typically, in an attempt to make object code as efficient as possible, we might incorrectly overload some register. Also, attempts to produce good run-time diagnostics (e.g., checking that array indexes are within their bounds) may produce run-time inefficiencies.

Run-time diagnostics and efficiency are a typical case where separation of concerns can and should be applied keeping in mind the mutual dependencies between the different aspects. In this case, in fact, the two concerns are often well separated by offering the user the option of enabling or disabling run-time checks. During the development and verification phases, when correctness is still being established and is a major concern, the user turns on run-time checks, making diagnostics the prevailing concern for the compiler. Once the program has been thoroughly checked, efficiency becomes the major concern for its user and, therefore, for the compiler, too; thus, the user could turn off the generation of run-time checks by the compiler.

### 3.8.1.3 *Modularity*

A compiler can be modularized in several ways. Here, we propose a fairly simplistic and traditional modularization based on the several "passes" performed by the compiler on the source code. Such a modular structure should be good enough for our initial purposes. In Chapter 4, we criticize the schema proposed here, and we show that alternative solutions may produce better results from the point of view of other principles, such as generality and design for change.

The well-established literature on compiler construction suggests that compilation proceeds in several phases or passes, each one performing a partial translation from an intermediate representation to another one, that the last pass eventually transforming its input intermediate code into the object code, which is then (almost) ready to run.

The following are the usual compiler phases:

- *Lexical analysis*, which analyzes program identifiers, replaces them with an internal representation, and builds a symbol table with their description. It also produces a first set of diagnostic messages if the source code contains lexical errors (e.g., ill-formed identifiers).

- *Syntax analysis* or *parsing*, which takes the output of the lexical analysis and builds a syntax tree, describing the syntactic structure of the original code. It also produces a second set of diagnostic messages related to the syntactic structure of the program (e.g., missing parentheses).

- Code generation, which produces the object code. This last phase is itself usually done in several steps. For example, a machine-independent intermediate

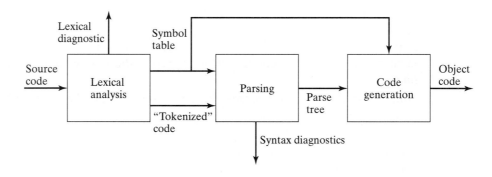

FIGURE 3.3a

The modular structure of a compiler.  Boxes represent modules and arrows represent inputs and outputs.

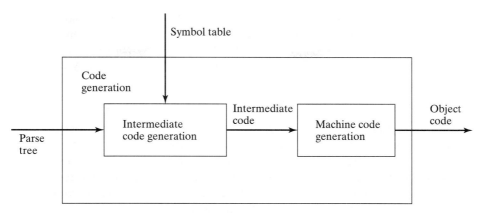

FIGURE 3.3b

A further modularization of the code-generation module.

code is produced as a first step, followed by a translation into machine-oriented object code. Each one of these partial translations may include an optimizing phase that rearranges the code to make it more efficient.

The foregoing description suggests a corresponding modular description of the structure of the compiler, depicted graphically in Figure 3.3a.

Despite the oversimplification present in the figure, we can already derive a few distinguishing features of modular design:

- System *modules* can be drawn naturally as boxes of any shape—here they are rectangular.
- Module *interfaces* are drawn as directed lines connecting the boxes representing the modules. An interface is an item that somehow connects different modules; it represents anything that is shared by them. Notice that the graphical metaphor suggests that everything that is inside a box is hidden from the outside; the rest of the system can communicate with a module exclusively through its interface. In the figure, it is convenient to represent interfaces with arrows to emphasize the fact that the item they describe is the output of some module and the input to another one. We shall see other cases in which the notion of an interface may be more symmetric (e.g., a shared data structure); in such cases, it is more convenient to represent the item with an *un*directed line.

  Notice also that the lines representing the source code, the diagnostic messages, and the object code are the input or output of the whole "system"; they are, therefore, drawn without source and target, respectively.

- The modular structure of Figure 3.3a lends itself to a natural iteration of the decomposition process. For instance, according to the description of the code-generation phase, the box representing this pass can be refined as suggested in Figure 3.3b.

Such diagrams as we have used here are referred to as box-and-line diagrams and are commonly used to informally show the overall structure or architecture of software systems. Many variants of box-and-line diagrams have been developed to make them more formal. We give examples of such graphical notations in Chapters 4 and 5.

### 3.8.1.4 Abstraction

Abstraction can be applied in compiler design along several directions. From a syntactic point of view, it is fairly typical to distinguish between concrete and abstract syntax. Abstract syntax aims at focusing on the essential features of language constructs, neglecting details that do not affect a program's structure. For instance, a conditional statement consists of a condition paired with a "positive" statement to be executed if the condition holds and, possibly, a negative one to be executed if the condition does not hold. This description remains valid both if we include the keyword `then` before the positive statement, as it happens in Pascal, and if we do not, as it happens in C. Similar remarks apply to the use of the C-like pair "{,}" and of the Algol-like pair "**begin-end**."

Another typical abstraction is often applied with respect to the target code: As we saw in the previous section, the first phase of code generation produces an intermediate code, which can be viewed as the code for an *abstract machine*. The second phase then translates the code of this abstract machine into code for the concrete target machine. In this way, a major part of the compiler construction abstracts away from the peculiarities of the particular processor that must run the object code. The Java language, indeed, defines a Java Virtual Machine, whose code (Java bytecodes) can be executed by interpreting it on different concrete machines.

In both examples of abstraction in this section, abstraction is naturally combined with the generality principle, as we shall emphasize further in Section 3.8.1.6. For instance, producing intermediate code for an abstract machine, rather than producing object code directly for a concrete one, allows us to build a general compiler that can be adapted, with minor modifications, to the production of code for different machines, thus enhancing the reusability quality.

### 3.8.1.5 Anticipation of change

Several changes may occur during the lifetime of a compiler:

- New releases of the target processors may become available with new, more powerful, instructions.
- New input-output (I/O) devices may be introduced, requiring new types of I/O statements.
- Standardization committees may define changes and extensions to the source language.

The design of the compiler should anticipate such changes. For instance, the Pascal language tried to "freeze" I/O statements within a rigid language definition. This decision conflicted with typical machine dependencies, and the result was often a number of dialects of the same language differing mainly in the I/O part. Later, it was recognized that attempts to freeze language I/O were not effective. Thus, languages such as C and Ada encapsulated I/O into standardized libraries, reducing the amount of work to be redone whenever I/O changes occurred.

Also, the more likely it is to want to adapt the compiler to different target machines, the higher are the benefits of separating the code-generation phase into two subphases as we showed above.

### 3.8.1.6  *Generality*

Like abstraction, generality can be pursued along several dimensions in compiler construction, depending on the overall goals of the project (e.g., producing a fairly wide family of products, as opposed to a highly specialized compiler).

Earlier, we mentioned the need to be parametric with respect to the target machine. The case of Java's bytecodes is a striking example of general design and its benefits. In fact, bytecodes are also independent of the source language, allowing them to be used as the target for compilers of languages other than Java.

Sometimes, a compiler can be parametric even with respect to the source language. A fairly extreme example of such a generality is provided by so called *compiler compilers*: They take as input the definition of the source—and possibly of the target—language and automatically produce a compiler translating the source language into the target one. Perhaps the most successful and widely known example of a compiler compiler is provided by the UNIX `lex` and `yacc` programs that are used to automatically produce the lexical and syntactic modules of a compiler.

Such generality can be achieved thanks to the formalization of the syntax of the language; thus, the generality principle is exploited in conjunction with formality. Another fairly obvious relation exists between the principles of generality and design for change: we usually want to be parametric—general—with respect to those features which are most likely to change.

### 3.8.1.7  *Incrementality*

Incrementality, too, can be pursued in several ways. For instance, we can first deliver a kernel version of a compiler that recognizes only a subset of the source language and then follow that by subsequent releases which recognize increasingly larger subsets of the language. Alternatively, the initial release could offer just the very essentials: translation into a correct object code and a minimum of diagnostics. Then we can add more diagnostics and better optimizations in further releases. The systematic use of libraries offers another natural way to exploit incrementality: It is quite common that the first release of a new compiler includes a very minimum of such libraries (e.g., for I/O and memory management) and later on new or more powerful libraries are released (e.g., graphical and mathematical libraries).

### 3.8.2    A Case Study in System Engineering

Suppose that we want to design an *elevator system*, to be included as a part of one or more buildings. Notice that we are talking about the *design*, not about a single physical instance of the elevator.

As a preliminary remark, let us address the question, "What does the design of an elevator system have to do with software engineering?" This is a typical example of the strong relationships software engineering has with system engineering: As we pointed out in Section 1.6.2, most software products are part of more complex systems, such as manufacturing plants, buildings, and cars. Thus, a software engineer must be able to act as a system engineer. Most of the initial analysis and design of any system will have to be done at the system level, possibly involving specialists from different engineering fields. Only in later phases will the designers be able to focus exclusively on software issues, such as coding the programs that control the computer devices, which in turn control the whole system. Not surprisingly, most of the qualities and principles examined in Chapters 2 and 3 apply to any engineering activity, not only to software construction.

Let us therefore verify how the principles examined in this chapter can be applied to the design of an elevator system. We shall use this same example in other parts of the book to illustrate several techniques.

### 3.8.2.1 *Rigor and formality*

There are several fairly obvious reasons for a designer to be rigorous in developing our hypothetical elevator system throughout its phases. First of all, the system is safety critical, because failures can cause serious damage and even the loss of human lives. Thus, we must first rigorously define applicable safety requirements, such as the following:

- Any elevator will be able to carry up to 400 kilograms without a failure occurring.
- In case of cable separation, emergency brakes will be able to stop the elevator within 1 meter and 2 seconds after separation under all circumstances.
- A safety warning will be sounded if the elevator is overloaded, and in such a case it will be impossible to operate the elevator.

Later, we will have to *verify* that such requirements are actually enforced by our design and fulfilled after installation of the elevator.

Second, being rigorous and precise is mandatory to avoid contractual disputes. For instance, if the initial specifications used as the basis of the contract between the customer and the supplier do not state the speed of the elevator, how can complaints that the elevator is slow be handled after installation?

Third, suppose that during a test of the system we verify the correct behavior and performance of any elevator by pushing all internal and external buttons. For example, we verify that pushing internal button number 4 once causes the elevator to reach the fourth floor within the specified time. Later, during the elevator's actual operation, it may happen that a strange combination of several internal and external buttons being pushed causes an overloading of part of the memory of a microprocessor that controls the system. In turn, this causes an undesired behavior, such as the elevator's missing a floor. Certainly, such behavior could and should be prevented by a more rigorous analysis of all possible sequences of events that could occur during system operation.

Finally, suppose that, under the pressure of our customer, we signed a contract that calls for the following requirements:

- Given some probabilistic conditions about user requests and the speed of the elevator, the elevator's service policy should minimize the average waiting time of the users.
- Every request must be eventually served.

It may happen that adopting a policy which optimizes performance from a statistical point of view does not guarantee fairness (i.e., eventually serving every request), or conversely. Thus, a rigorous analysis of requirements must uncover and avoid conflicting specifications.

As we stated in Section 3.1, applying some formal technique can help in being rigorous in specifying and verifying requirements such as those just discussed. We shall see some examples of appropriate techniques in Chapter 5.

### 3.8.2.2  Separation of concerns

An elevator system exposes the designer to several concerns that are fairly typical of most engineering artifacts. The following are some examples of such concerns:

- Safety
- Performance
- Usability (space, accessibility, illumination of buttons, and so on)
- Cost

Of course, most of these concerns are interrelated, so that a design decision about one of them may easily affect another. For instance, if we reduce costs by using cheap material, we may easily endanger safety. Nevertheless, separation of concerns remains a useful design principle. For example, we may perform cost analysis in a different time and with different techniques than safety verification, still keeping in mind that requirements referring to both concerns must be satisfied. Similarly, at a different time we may pay attention to usability, later verifying that the choices we adopted do not exceed cost limits.

### 3.8.2.3  Modularity

A rough modularization of an elevator system is shown in Figure 3.4a. Here, too, we can comment on a few distinguishing features of modular design from the diagram:

- As we did in describing the modular structure of a compiler in Figure 3.3a, in Figure 3.4a we use boxes to denote modules and lines to denote their interfaces. In this case, however, we use undirected, and not directed, arrows. This choice emphasizes that the lines represent items (say, electric signals) that flow in both directions. Perhaps, at a more refined stage of the design we could represent unidirectional items. For instance, we might represent a command given by the control apparatus to the elevator engine by an arrow going from the former to the latter. Conversely, we could represent the information about the current location of the elevator by an arrow going from the elevator box to the control box.
- This example also emphasizes the fact that it is often convenient to modularize a system by describing it as a collection of *objects*. This is the case, in fact,

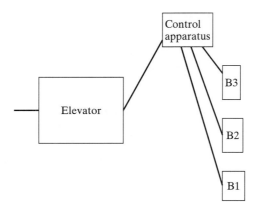

FIGURE 3.4a

A modular description of a simple elevator system.

for most systems that we have to design. For many such systems, we may identify and derive objects as natural units of modularization. The notion of an object, however, must be seen in a more general way than just physical objects: Typically, a piece of software such as a table of names or a queue of requests to be served can also be seen as an object. Consider the difference between the elevator, viewed as a set of cooperating objects, and the compiler, viewed as a collection of modules associated with different functions or passes of the compilation. We investigate object-oriented vs. function-oriented design thoroughly in Chapter 4.

- Here, too, the modular structure of Figure 3.4a can be further decomposed naturally. For instance, the box representing the elevator can be refined as suggested in Figure 3.4b.

Furthermore, the control apparatus can be described as the pairing of a microprocessor (the hardware part) and some software that implements the control policies (e.g., managing the queue of requests, sending commands to the engine or the brakes, or governing the illumination of the elevator buttons). Here we see clearly that the notion of *object* goes beyond purely *physical objects*.

Buttons, too—both the buttons on the floors and those inside the elevator—can be defined in more detail by showing the individual buttons on each floor and in the elevator.

### 3.8.2.4 *Abstraction*

The principle of abstraction can be applied to the design of our elevator system in many ways. First, notice that parts a and b of Figure 3.4 themselves are abstractions of the whole system, focusing on the modular structure while neglecting most other aspects, such as the mechanical and electrical behavior of the elevator and of its engine.

A different abstract view may concentrate just on those factors neglected in the figures, to help decide the required power of the engine and the brakes. Yet another abstraction should focus on the illumination of buttons, using a Boolean variable to

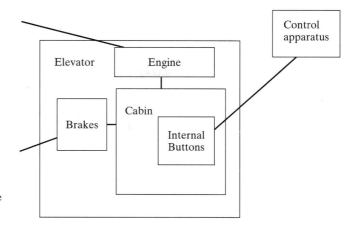

**FIGURE 3.4b**

A further decomposition of the elevator system.

represent the fact that a button is illuminated or is not, thus abstracting from, say, the power of the bulb in the physical button.

Finally, yet a different abstraction could describe the external layout of the buttons with respect to the concern of usability: how big they are, how strong their illumination is, and how far above the floor of the elevator they are.

### 3.8.2.5 *Anticipation of change, generality, and incrementality*

The principles of anticipation of change, generality, and incrementality enlighten the main difference between software engineering and more traditional system engineering, a difference due to software's malleability. For instance, whereas it is quite natural to build and deliver a subset of a compiler and then augment it, for example, by delivering new libraries, it is unlikely that we deliver, say, an elevator without doors and then deliver doors and other accessories later on. The principles, nevertheless, do have their relevance in system engineering, too, but, in general, their application is restricted to the design phase, which is more sharply separated from the delivery and maintenance of the product.

As an example, we may want a design of an elevator system that can be applied to several similar—but not identical—buildings. In this case, we may decide to make our design *parametric* with respect to a few distinguishing features that are likely to change from instance to instance, but whose range of variation can be easily stated *a priori*. We could design a system suitable for skyscrapers, with the number of floors ranging from 30 to 80, with the number of elevators ranging from 4 to 10, with variable speed and power, etc. Then, whenever we need to build a new skyscraper whose features satisfy these ranges, we merely have to instantiate those parameters in our elevator system design, obviating the need to redo the design from scratch.

Even the design notation could be adapted to emphasize such a parametric design. For instance, Figure 3.5 depicts the system of Figure 3.4a, but with the elevator and button boxes modified to denote a parametric number of instances of the same object type.

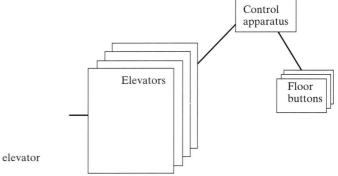

**FIGURE 3.5**

A parametric structure of an elevator system.

In this case, generality can go a little further than just the design phase. In fact, we could build several components, such as cabins, engines, and control apparatuses, that are usable in several buildings of the same category. Then, when we build the actual skyscraper, we only have to assemble those components according to the particular design, which in turn consists simply of fixing up a few parameters, as we stated earlier.

## 3.9    CONCLUDING REMARKS

In this chapter, we have discussed seven important software engineering principles that apply throughout the software development process and during software evolution. We emphasized that these principles are, first of all, engineering principles and that analyzing similarities and differences in the way they are applied in different engineering fields may help one understand them more deeply.

Because of their general applicability, we have presented the principles separately, as the cornerstones of software engineering, rather than in the context of any specific phase of the software life cycle. Another reason for presenting the principles separately is to establish a uniform terminology that we will use in the rest of the book.

The software engineering principles, as stated here, might seem too abstract. We shall make them concrete with more details in the rest of this book in the context of software design, specification, verification, and management. We shall do so partly explicitly, by pointing out the relevant principles (where appropriate), and partly implicitly, leaving it to the reader to recognize them as they come up.

We emphasized the role of general principles before presenting specific methods, techniques, and tools. The reason is that software engineering—like any other branch of engineering—must be based on a sound set of principles. In turn, principles are the basis for the set of methods used in the discipline and for the specific techniques and tools used in everyday life.

As technology evolves, software engineering tools will evolve. As our knowledge about software engineering increases, methods and techniques will evolve, too—although less rapidly than tools. Principles, on the other hand, will remain more stable; they constitute the foundation upon which all the rest may be built. They form the bases for the concepts discussed in the remainder of this book.

## FURTHER EXERCISES

**3.13** Suppose you are writing a program that manipulates files. Among the facilities you offer is a command to sort a file in both ascending and descending order. Among the files you manipulate, some are kept automatically sorted by the system. Thus, you might take advantage of the fact: If the file is already sorted, you do not take any action; or you apply a reverse function if the file is sorted in the opposite order. Discuss the pros and cons of using such specialized solutions instead of executing the sort algorithm every time the sort command is issued.

**3.14** Discuss briefly the relationships between generality and anticipation of change.

**3.15** Discuss briefly the relationships between generality and abstraction.

**3.16** Discuss briefly the relationship between incrementality and timeliness.

**3.17** Discuss briefly the relationship between formality and anticipation of change.

**3.18** Complete the case studies of Section 3.8 along various directions: You may consider more requirements; you may go deeper into the modular structure of the systems; you can better investigate interfaces with the environment of the systems; you may investigate other cases where incrementality could be applied.

**3.19** A *railroad crossing* (RC) consists of one or more rail tracks that intersect a street. The crossing is protected by a gate that must be operated automatically in such a way that cars cannot enter the crossing while a train is going through it.

- Describe the structure of the railroad-crossing control system by showing its components and their interfaces.
- State clearly and precisely the requirements that should be satisfied by the system in order for it to operate safely and usefully. For instance, deciding to keep the gate always closed would be safe, but useless, since no car could ever cross the track.
- Which features of the system are likely to change in different contexts?

## HINTS AND SKETCHY SOLUTIONS

**3.5** Dividing a long program into contiguous pieces does not necessarily generate a good structure with high cohesion. Grouping together statements that realize some conceptual function gives higher cohesion. (This approach corresponds to the conventional decomposition of programs into subroutines.) It is even better if we can group together the data and the routines that access the data, because doing so enhances the program's readability and modifiability.

**3.6** Modules that do not interact with each other have minimum coupling but this also means that they do not "cooperate" in any sense. If one module can access the local variables of another—that is, if it can directly modify the state of the other module—the coupling is higher than it is if a module calls a procedure defined in another module.

**3.7** The end user is interested only in an abstract description of how to operate the application; all details concerning how the application has been designed and implemented may (and should) be abstracted away. The designer should know what the requirements are and, when designing a part, should have an abstract view of the rest of the system that allows him or her to have a clear picture of how that part interacts with the rest, without having to take into account the details. When maintaining a system, one should also have an abstract view of the rationale of the design (why certain design decisions were made and why others were discarded). This would allow a system to be modified in a reliable way without impairing its structure.

**3.10**   We will see in Chapter 7 that the waterfall life cycle is an idealized view of software development. For example, the model of Figure 1.1 ignores the fact that some steps must be repeated as one phase reveals inconsistencies or mistakes in the previous phase.

**3.12**   The software prototype illustrated here is an evolutionary prototype, whereas in other fields we see more of throwaway prototypes. These terms will be discussed in Chapter 7.

**3.16**   By delivering an application incrementally, we might deliver a useful subset of the application earlier. That is, we can be early on the market with a product, although it is incomplete.

## BIBLIOGRAPHIC NOTES

Several textbooks emphasize formal approaches to programming; among these, we mention Alagic and Arbib [1978], Gries [1981], and Mills et al. [1987a]. Landmark contributions to the field are given by Wirth [1971], Dahl et al. [1972], and Dijkstra [1976]. Liskov and Guttag [1986] provide rigorous foundations for programming in the large; the approach they propose is deeply rooted in the concept of data abstraction. Liskov and Guttag [2001] apply these principles to Java.

Parnas's work on design methods and specification is the major source of insight into the concepts of separation of concerns, modularity, abstraction, and anticipation of change. All of Parnas's papers referenced in this bibliography help enlighten these fundamental issues. In particular, Parnas [1978] illustrates important software engineering principles. Thirty of Parnas's important papers have been collected in Hoffman and Weiss [2001], along with some updates and commentaries.

Aspect-oriented programming is a programming methodology that aims to support separation of concerns in system design and programming. It supports the programmer not only in concentrating on one aspect—concern—independently of another, but also in expressing the *cross-cutting* concerns in different program units. For example, the programmer might express memory management, synchronization, and functionality of a bounded buffer in syntactically different parts of the program. Of course, the designer still has to decide what is of concern to him or her. Kiczales et al. [1997] presents the idea. There have been many follow-on papers, as well as several prototype systems that have implemented the idea in Java and other languages.

The concepts of cohesion and coupling are discussed by Yourdon and Constantine [1979] and Myers [1978], who attempts to provide objective measures for the "goodness" of a design.

Anticipation of change, generality, and incrementality are justified in the work of Belady and Lehman [1979], Lehman and Belady [1985], and Lientz and Swanson [1980] on software evolution. Bennett and Rajlich [2000] goes so far as to say that, since maintenance consumes such a large portion of software costs, labeling the last phase of the development process as maintenance is no longer sufficient. The authors propose a software life cycle that takes evolution explicitly into account. The cycle involves development, servicing, and the phaseout of the software.

Configuration management is discussed by Babich [1986], Tichy [1989], Estublier [2000], and later in this book in Chapters 7 and 9. The language AWK is presented by Aho et al. [1988].

Rapid prototyping is discussed by Boehm et al. [1984]; the special issue of *IEEE Computer* edited by Tanik and Yeh (Computer [1989a]) contains several papers on the subject.

Both the elevator system described in Section 3.8 and the railroad-crossing system that is the subject of Exercise 3.19 have been proposed and widely explored in the literature as benchmarks for testing the suitability of software engineering techniques for the solution of realistic problems. The elevator system was initially proposed in IWSSD[1987]; the railroad-crossing system is presented and thoroughly investigated in Heitmeyer and Mandrioli [1996].

# Design and Software Architecture

Design is a fundamental human activity. In a general sense, design provides a structure to any complex artifact. It decomposes a system into parts, assigns responsibilities to each part, and ensures that the parts fit together to achieve the global goals of the system. This is true in any field, not only software: Architects design shopping malls (i.e., the layout, buildings, parking lots, air-conditioning and heating system, power supply, etc.), and novelists design novels—their characters, the overall plot, and the decomposition into chapters. Some design principles—how to decompose a system into parts, what properties the parts should have, and the like—are fairly general; others are domain specific.

In the case of software, the concepts of design apply in two different, but strictly related, contexts. On the one hand, design is the activity that acts as a bridge between requirements and the implementation of the software. Once we have determined the need for a software system and we have decided on its desirable qualities, including the interface it provides for interaction with the external world, we must proceed to design that system. The first result of our design activity is an architectural design that shows the major parts of the system and how they fit together and cooperate. The architecture shows the gross structure of the system. On the other hand, as we said, any complex artifact must be designed. According to this context, design is the activity that gives a structure to the artifact. So, for example, the requirements specification document itself must be "designed"; that is, it must be given a structure that makes it easy to understand and evolve. This chapter deals with both these contexts for design.

There is a mutual dependency between this chapter and the next, which talks about specification. On the one hand, according to the first context of design that we have mentioned, in a typical development life cycle, requirements specification occurs before architectural design. This argues for discussing specification before design. On the other hand, according to the second context, the principles of structuring large artifacts apply equally well to the structuring of requirements specifications. In addition, architectural designs must be specified. As a result, we have decided to talk about design prior to dealing with specification in the next chapter.

The current chapter starts by discussing the design activity and its fundamental goals. The chapter shows how we can achieve the desired qualities illustrated in Chapter 2; in particular, it emphasizes the need for designing systems that are reliable and evolvable. The principle of rigor and formality will inspire us to adopt appropriate notations for describing the resulting designs. Separation of concerns, modularity, and abstraction will be applied to tame the complexity of the design activity and produce designs that are characterized by high understandability, to enhance our confidence in the correctness of our solutions. Finally, anticipation of change and incrementality will allow us to design systems that can evolve easily as requirements change, or systems that can be enriched progressively in their functions, starting from an initial version with only limited functionality. *Design for change* is the motto we adopt from Parnas to stress the principles of anticipation of change and incrementality in the context of design.

We also tackle the problem of designing families of applications. Very often, the applications we design are not just individual products, but a family of products that may differ in some of the functions they offer, the hardware configuration on which they run, the set of services they provide, etc. Despite their differences, there is much in common that can be analyzed and designed once for the whole family. The principles of generality and anticipation of change support the design of product families. In fact, various members of the family may be designed on the basis of the same architecture. A carefully designed family architecture supports the development of different system designs for individual members of the family.

To achieve high quality of design, the software engineer must address two crucial and strictly related issues. First, the engineer must provide a careful definition of the modular structure of the system—a definition that specifies the modules and their interrelationships. These concepts are discussed in Section 4.2.1. Second, the engineer must choose appropriate criteria for decomposing a system into modules.

The main criterion we introduce in Section 4.2.2 and discuss throughout the book is *information hiding*: A module is characterized by the information it hides from other modules, which are called its clients. The hidden information remains a secret of the client modules. Section 4.2.3 introduces a design notation (TDN/GDN) that is used to document the results of the design activity. Information hiding is further analyzed and specialized to deal with the changeable nature of data, leading to the concept of abstract data types, presented in Section 4.2.4. Further techniques supporting design for change are discussed in Section 4.2.5. Section 4.2.6 introduces a popular design technique called stepwise refinement. This technique produces software designs in a top-down manner, whereas information hiding proceeds mainly from the bottom up. Design strategies (top down vs. bottom up) are contrasted in Section 4.2.7 from several viewpoints.

To achieve the goal of reliability, we deal with the problem of designing software that can respond to adverse events and behave in an acceptable manner even when it enters anomalous processing states. A careful design activity must address this robustness requirement, which is extremely important in safety-critical applications. These issues are treated in Section 4.3.

The principles of good design cannot be taught as a fixed set of rules to be applied according to a rigid recipe. If they are formulated in abstract terms, they do not provide designers with deep insights and convincing suggestions. Their effectiveness is best communicated through examples. Unfortunately, for reasons of space, it is impossible to illustrate the complete designs of real applications in a textbook. Thus, we illustrate the various design concepts through small practical examples. We do, however, provide a more comprehensive design case study in Section 4.4.

In Section 4.5, we discuss how concurrency, distribution, and real-time issues affect design. We do not go deeply into this subject here, for several reasons. First, a discussion of how concurrent components may interact and be synchronized is a specialized topic that deserves a separate treatment. Traditionally, this subject is studied in courses and textbooks on operating systems, distributed systems, real-time software, etc. Second, the issue is highly related to the specific constructs available in the operating system or the programming language used to implement concurrency. Thus, going deeply into details would require dealing with several different notations. Accordingly, we stick to general concepts and refer to selected concurrency schemes in our discussion, without aiming for completeness.

Our discussions in Sections 4.2–4.5 are mostly based on traditional design concepts. Section 4.6 shows how the concepts of information hiding and abstract data types eventually found a coherent unified application in object-oriented design. We discuss the specific additional concepts introduced by object-oriented design, and we show how that technique supports software evolution and reuse. Furthermore, we introduce the Unified Modeling Language (UML) standard design notation.

Designs are ultimately mapped onto programs; that is, the structures and components we identify during the design activity will be represented in terms of constructs of the programming language that we use to implement our software. This mapping of designs onto programs can be done more easily for some languages than for others; in particular, there are languages for which the design techniques we present can lead to programs almost directly. For example, information hiding and the design structures illustrated in this chapter may be easily mapped onto conventional modular languages such as Ada. Object-oriented languages, such as C++ or Java, would be the natural candidates for implementing object-oriented designs.

Increasingly, software is not built from scratch, but rather integrates components that may be bought off the shelf. The long-anticipated goal of reuse through "componentization" is becoming reality, both because new languages allow reusable components to be designed and because generalized support is becoming available for making different components that are capable of being integrated into a coherent architecture. Examples include the STL library of C++, Java and Java Beans, COM, and CORBA. The problem of specifying a software architecture at a higher level than TDN/GDN or even UML is also becoming increasingly important, and is a topic of active research. Other important problems are the identification of common design patterns that can be collected and classified for later reuse and the definition of adaptable architectures that define some generalized application framework. Such issues of component-based development are discussed in Section 4.7.

Design is a difficult and critical activity. It is also highly creative: In each new design, the engineer invents something that never existed before. There are many decisions and trade-offs to be made along the way. This chapter is about the methods we can use to overcome these difficulties and to guide and discipline the creative process. Systems, however, may be complex, requirements may be conflicting, and the general methods to apply are far from precise prescriptions. Unfortunately (or fortunately?), in software design there are no general and easy-to-use recipes that can be adopted once and for all and followed faithfully in all circumstances. Specific prescriptions are applicable only in restricted domains. The designer must be equipped with general principles and methods whose practical application will then depend on how and where they are to be applied and other constraints, such as the qualities desired of the product, the composition of the development team, and schedules. It is important for the designer to practice applying the principles and methods we present here, so that they become second nature to him or her, just like the laws of mathematics.

To ease the application of good principles and methods, some have been prepackaged into standardized methodologies. There is a high demand for such methodologies from industry, because they tend to standardize software development by making the application of methods more uniform within an organization. Standardization, in turn, makes it easier to cope with management issues such as personnel turnover in software development groups. Some of these methodologies have been widely adopted in practical software development, although quite often they are just based on common sense and lack truly convincing, general, and rigorous foundations. We briefly account for some of the important methodologies in Chapter 7, which deals with the organization of the software life cycle. In the current chapter, we concentrate on general, application-independent design principles that can be used to meet the software quality goals stated in Chapter 2.

## 4.1    THE SOFTWARE DESIGN ACTIVITY AND ITS OBJECTIVES

The design activity is a fundamental phase in the software development process that progressively transforms the system requirements through a number of intermediate stages into a final product. The output of the design activity is a *software design*.[1] We define a software design as a *system decomposition into modules*—a description of what each module is intended to do and of the relationship among the modules. Often, a *software architecture* is produced prior to a software design, and it guides the development of the design. The architecture shows the gross structure and organization of the system to be defined. A description of a software architecture includes a description of the main components of a system, the relationships among those components, the rationale used for the decomposition of the system into its components, and the constraints that must be respected by any design of the components. The goal of the architectural design activity is to define the software architecture; the goal of the software design activity is the definition of the software design according to the guidelines set forth in the software architecture. Because the principles used in developing an architecture and a design are similar, in this chapter we will often refer to design and architecture interchangeably.

We can view design as a process in which the views of the system are described through steps of increasing detail. First, the architecture is developed on the basis of the system requirements; next, a high-level design is produced on the basis of the architecture; then, a low-level design is derived on the basis of the high-level design; and so on. Each new step implements the requirements specified in the previous one, the final step being the implementation, which completes the transformation of the software architecture into programs.

---

[1]As we observed earlier, the term "design" is used to denote both the activity and its result. When an ambiguity may arise, we explicitly call the former "design activity" and the latter "software design" or "architecture."

The modularity principle is of paramount importance in the design of software; it is why the components of a system identified during the design activity are called, simply, modules. In the software literature, however, the concept of a module is rather elusive. Sometimes the term is used to name a boxlike iconic symbol in a blueprint that is intended to represent a design. In other cases, it is used to denote a well-identified piece of a program, such as a collection of routines. In still other cases, it is used to denote individual work assignments within a complex system. We will clarify our idea of a module in the sections that follow; for now, we rely upon an intuitive notion that may encompass all of the foregoing possibilities.

The decomposition of a system into modules can be accomplished in several ways and in several steps. For example, as we mentioned, one might first decompose the system into higher level components. Relations among the components are then defined, and their intended behavior is agreed upon by the designers. Next, each component is analyzed separately, and the procedure is iterated until we reach the point where the complexity of each component is sufficiently small that it can be implemented readily by a single person.

When a module M is decomposed into other modules, we say that these are used to *implement* M. Thus, in this approach, implementation is performed by recursively decomposing (sub)modules into modules, until we reach the point where implementation can be done in terms of a programming language in a straightforward way.

The reader will recognize here several of the principles and concepts that were presented in Chapter 3, in addition to modularity. Rigor and formality are useful in the description of the software architecture. The more precise the description, the easier it is to divide software development into separate tasks that can proceed in parallel with little risk of inconsistencies. Also, precision makes it easier to understand the system should the need arise to modify it. Finally, the effectiveness of the aforementioned design process depends on how well the techniques selected for modularization allow us to deal with each module separately, according to the principle of separation of concerns. Using two concepts already introduced in Chapter 3, we may state that modules should have high cohesion and low coupling.

According to the definition we gave in Chapter 3, the process of module decomposition just described can be called *top down*. It is also possible to proceed in a *bottom-up* manner. For example, a module may be designed to provide an easy, abstract way of accessing a peripheral device, masking the low-level hardware-oriented primitives provided by the device. The module acts like a layer that applies cosmetics (i.e., abstraction) to the device and lets it appear with a better and easier-to-deal-with look. Here, the process is intrinsically bottom up: We start from an existing, but intricate, object, and we build an abstraction around it.

According to a bottom-up strategy, the design process consists of defining modules that can be iteratively combined together to form higher level components. This is typical when we are reusing modules from a library to build a new system, instead of building such a system from scratch. The entire system is constructed by assembling lower level components in an iterative fashion.

The topic of bottom-up versus top-down design will be taken up later, in Section 4.2.7. We will see that it is possible—and often convenient—to combine the two, for different parts of the system or at different points in the design activity.

Before discussing the criteria that may be followed to modularize a system, we examine two important goals that drive the design of a software architecture: *design for change*, in Section 4.1.1, and *product families*, in Section 4.1.2. Design for change is a way to design software that can be modified easily as requirements change. Similarly, the concept of a product family allows us to view several end products as a family of products that share a single architecture that is reused—specialized and modified in varying degrees—in different contexts, giving rise to different designs. Thus, both concepts—design for change and product families—fall within the general framework of software reusability and support software evolvability.

## 4.1.1    Design for Change

In Chapter 3, we presented anticipation of change as a general software principle to cope with the evolutionary nature of software. To apply this principle in the context of software design means that during the design activity we anticipate the changes that the software may undergo during its lifetime and, as a result of this anticipation, produce a software design that will accommodate the changes easily. Following Parnas, we refer to the techniques used to accomplish this goal as *design for change*.

Design for change promotes a design that is flexible enough to accommodate changes easily. This, however, cannot be achieved in general, for *every* type of change. Special care in the initial phase is necessary to anticipate likely changes when the requirements for software are stated. At this initial stage, we should not concentrate exclusively on what is *presently* needed in terms of functions to offer or even, more generally, qualities to achieve. We must also consider the expected or possible evolution of the system. In fact, very often, the application we are designing is the first step of a known, preplanned sequence of steps that will lead to the final automated system. In such cases, we must make sure that the initial design will easily accommodate the anticipated evolution of the product.

Still more often, however, required changes are not precisely known *a priori*, although they will almost inevitably arise afterwards. Here, the previous experience of the software engineer and the deep understanding of the problem domain by the end user may play a major role in identifying potential areas of change and the future evolution of the system. After the requirements for changes are identified, the designer should ensure that the product's design will easily accommodate those changes in the future.

Software engineers must realize the importance of design for change. A common mistake is to design a system for today's requirements, paying little or no attention to likely changes. The consequence of this approach is that even a marvelous design may turn out to be extremely difficult and costly to adapt to requests for changes, and it will have to be redone almost completely in order to incorporate even seemingly "minor" changes. Another unfortunate consequence is that, in the process of trying to accommodate changes, the designer may have to clutter the initial elegant structure, resulting in an application that is more and more difficult to maintain and that inspires little confidence in its reliability.

### 4.1.1.1  *What changes? The nature of evolvability*

What types of changes should a design try to anticipate? To understand this issue, we must go back to the problems we discussed in Chapter 2 under the rubric of maintainability and, in particular, to the notion of evolvability (Section 2.2.5.2). As we saw, it has been reported in the literature that maintenance usually accounts for more than 60 percent of software costs. One reason these costs are so high is that software engineers tend to overlook the issue of maintainability during software development. In fact, they do not anticipate it at all.

Recall from Chapter 2 that maintenance may be classified into three categories: perfective, adaptive, and corrective. Adaptive and perfective maintenance are the real sources of change in software; they motivated the introduction of evolvability as a fundamental software quality and anticipation of change as a general principle that should guide the software engineer.

In this section, we mostly discuss changes that may fall under perfective or adaptive maintenance. These changes are not exhaustive of all such changes, but they are a sample of common ones. Other important cases of change, which are more under the software engineer's control, occur in the case of a development strategy based on iterative prototyping. In such a strategy, at a certain stage, certain parts are designed and implemented in a preliminary form; at a later stage, they are turned into a more finished version.

**Change of algorithms.**   This change is probably the best-understood type of change that we can apply to software: To improve the efficiency of some part, to deal with a more general case, etc.

Consider, for example, sorting algorithms. In order to choose among the many existing algorithms, we should know the size of the list to be sorted, the likely distribution of the data in the list, etc. Consequently, the choice of the most suitable algorithm to be used in an application may depend on experimental data acquired after the system is operational. We might start with a simple and straightforward algorithm as our initial choice and then replace it with a better solution as more experimental data are acquired. If the algorithm is confined to a well-identified module (e.g., a routine of the programming language), the change will be easy to apply because the portion of the program that requires changing is easily identified, being bound by its unique entry and exit points.

### Exercise

---

**4.1**   Give an example of two sorting algorithms whose execution profiles depend strongly on the distribution of data in the array to be sorted. Discuss how data distribution affects the execution profiles.

---

**Change of data representation.**   The efficiency of a program can change dramatically if one changes the structure used to represent some relevant data. As an example, changing the structure used to represent a table from a sequential array to a linked list or to a hash table can change the efficiency of the operations accessing the table. Typically, inserting an element into an array is costly if array entries are to be kept sorted according to, say, increasing index values. In fact, inserting an element at position i must be preceded by an operation that shifts all the elements at positions i through n, n being the number of stored entries, in order to provide room for the entry to be stored at position i. This shift operation, whose average cost in terms of processing time is proportional to n, is not needed if we choose a linked-list implementation of the table.

Another example is a tree data structure, implemented via pointers. Each node of the tree has two pointer fields, one pointing to its right sibling, if any, the other pointing to its first direct descendant, if any. (See Figure 4.1(a).) One more pointer may be added to make it easier (i.e., more efficient) to move along the data structure from the leaves towards the root of the tree. The pointer we add connects any node to its parent node, if there is any (See Figure 4.1(b).)

As another example of a change in data representation, not dictated by efficiency issues, one might wish to add fields to (or delete fields from) records as more (or less) information is needed to be saved in a file. One instance of this is when a new field is added to records representing students enrolled in a class in order to store the data on the other courses the student is currently taking.

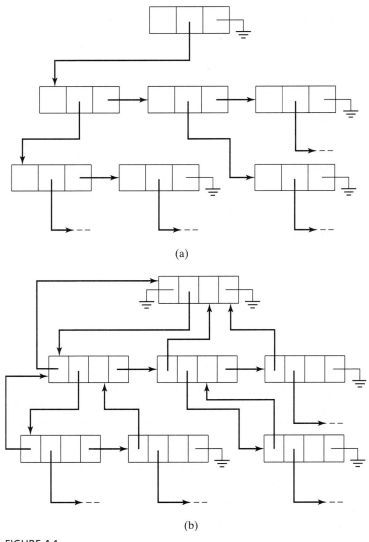

(a)

(b)

FIGURE 4.1

Two sample data structures representing a tree.

It has been reported that changes in data structures have a profound influence on the costs of maintenance (about 17 percent of total maintenance costs!).[2]

Although we have discussed change of algorithms and change of data structures separately, they are often related. For example, we may apply a change in a data structure in order to provide a better algorithm. Or, vice versa, a change in algorithms may require changes in a data structure.

### Exercise

**4.2**  Discuss some possible motivations for changing the tree data structure presented in Figure 4.1. Discuss whether (and why) the change of data structure requires a change of algorithms.

**Change of underlying abstract machine.**    The programs we write are run by some abstract (or virtual) machine. The machine coincides with the hardware in the (happily unlikely) case where no higher level languages are available for programming. More frequently, the abstract machine we use corresponds to the high-level language in which we write programs, the operating system to which we issue system calls, possibly the database management system we use to store and retrieve persistent data, etc. The abstract machine, by itself, hides details of the underlying physical machine.

Very often, however, we need to modify applications in order to be able to run them under a new release of the operating system and take full advantage of the new facilities offered. Similarly, new releases of the compiler we use may be available, and the new version might perform additional optimizations in order to generate faster and smaller object code. Or there might be a new version of the database management system (DBMS) that saves disk space and offers improved functions in terms of protection from undesired access and recovery from failures. Or again, a newer, more efficient, more reliable version of some library used by the application may become available. This means that the underlying abstract machine changes, and the changes may affect our application. Sadly, the benefits do not come for free. For example, if the new DBMS is able to store our data in half the original space, we have to reformat our existing databases. We may also have to change our data access programs to take advantage of the saving in space. Even if the functions offered by our software remain totally unchanged, the change in the underlying abstract machine affects the software.

### Exercise

**4.3**  Do you have any personal experience with software changes in the underlying abstract machine? Briefly present your experience and discuss what made your software difficult to change.

**Change of peripheral devices.**    A change of peripheral devices is strongly related to a change of the underlying abstract machine. We can view it as a specialization of that type of change in such cases as embedded computer applications, avionic systems, and process control systems, in all of which control software needs to interact with many different

---

[2]See Lientz and Swanson [1980].

and special-purpose peripheral devices. Such devices may be subject to change; in particular, they are progressively becoming "more intelligent"; that is, data-processing functions are being progressively decentralized to be performed locally, without disturbing the main application running on the main machine. Ideally, we would like to be able to accommodate such changes without affecting or redesigning the entire application.

**Change of social environment.** A change of social environment is similar to the previous two types of change. It is, however, not motivated by the need for modification arising in the software itself. Rather, the social environment in which the application is embedded requires our software to change.

For example, in a tax application, suppose that a change in legislation requires the rules for deductions to change slightly. Then the concept of a deductible item remains, but the list of deductible items changes. Software must change accordingly, in order to make the application valid for the new tax rules.

As another example, several countries of the European Union decided to unify their currencies by introducing the euro. This change in legislation affects existing software. Think of banking applications or any type of financial system that must now deal with euros instead of Italian lire or Austrian schillings. Eventually, all the software that deals with specific currencies and conversions among them will be retired.

### Exercise

---

**4.4** For some existing or hypothetical application, give an example of a software change that might be due to a change in the social environment.

---

**Change due to the development process.** Following the motivation we discussed in Chapter 3, software is often developed incrementally. Incrementality is another source of change that requires special care. For example, we may try to isolate useful portions of the application and release them so that the customer can start using the system and give us feedback based on experience. Later, when new parts are added to the system, it is important that we concentrate on the new developments and leave the early subsets unchanged. To make the approach feasible, the new and old parts must fit together cleanly, so that complex software changes will not be necessary as the new parts are released and integrated with the previously running, but incomplete, application.

### 4.1.2 Product Families

In many practical situations, changes consist of building new versions of the same software; every version constitutes an individual product, but the set of versions constitutes a *family*. Often, a new version is supposed to supersede the previous one; say, it eliminates some known errors or adds improved features to the product. In other cases, a new version is simply another product that coexists with the previous one; maybe it works on a different hardware, it has special requirements in terms of memory available, or it provides different functions for some parts of the system. The reason we regard the different versions of a software product as a family, rather than a set of different products, is that all members in the family have much in common and are only partially different. Frequently, they share the same architecture. By designing a common architecture for *all* members of the family jointly, rather than doing separate designs for each member of the family, we avoid the cost of designing the common parts separately.

A good example of a product family is the mobile (cellular) phone. Manufacturers want to sell their phones in different countries. While the basic functionality of the phones are the same in different countries (placing calls, receiving calls, maintaining a list of phone numbers, etc.), the phones may need to deal with different network standards, different natural languages for interaction with the user, different safety requirements, and so forth. The basic software that controls the phone is the same, but its interface to the environment depends on the geographic location.

Another example is a database management system that is required to run on different machines, possibly on different operating systems, and for various configurations.

In both cases, we should identify commonalities among the different versions of the software and delay the point at which any two versions start being different. The more we stress commonality, the less work is done for each new version. This decreases the chance of inconsistencies and reduces the combined maintenance effort expended on all the products.

Earlier approaches to software and product development did not pay special attention to designing product families, but rather proceeded from version to version in a sequential manner. A common mistake is illustrated by the very informal, but intuitive, trees shown in Figure 4.2. Starting from the requirements, version 1 of the application (corresponding to node 3 in Figure 4.2(a)) is developed through a sequence of design steps (represented by directed edges). Nodes represented by circles stand for intermediate

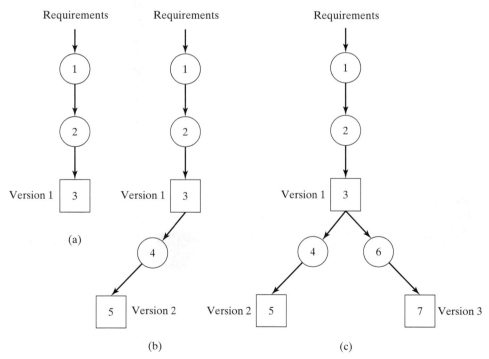

**FIGURE 4.2**

Sequential design of a product family.

design descriptions; nodes represented by squares represent a complete, executable version of the software. Thus, Figure 4.2(a) illustrates that the requirements are first transformed into the intermediate design stage 1, then 2, and, finally, version 1 of the product.

At this point, if the need for a new version—version 2—arises, we start modifying version 1. Initially, the application is put in the intermediate design stage represented by node 4 (Figure 4.2(b)) by deleting parts of the code of version 1; then it is transformed into a fully operational version, represented by node 5, which in turn may be the starting point of the derivation of further versions not illustrated in the figure. Also, a branch representing a different version may start from node 3, as illustrated in Figure 4.2(c).

This type of approach for deriving the members of a product family is not satisfactory. In fact, the family illustrated in Figure 4.2 must be biased by the design decisions made while version 1 was initially developed, since versions 2 and 3 are derived as modifications of version 1. No effort was made to isolate what is common to all versions and, iteratively, what is common to smaller and smaller subsets of the family. Thus, the derivation of a new member of the family becomes particularly difficult if the new member differs substantially from the previous member.

New versions of software are derived by modifying the code of the previous version because, often, intermediate design steps (represented in the figure by circles) are not documented. Programs are the only available trustable descriptions that can be used as a starting point for modifications. But programs (even well-written and well-documented ones) may be difficult to understand in sufficiently precise terms to allow modifications to be applied reliably. We can never be sure whether a modification done to a part of the system will adversely affect other parts. Also, we may inadvertently make design decisions that were discarded before, but never documented.

A systematic approach to the design of product families that solves these problems will be presented in Section 4.2. This approach is based on the general principle of designing for change, where changes are restricted to capturing the differences among the various members of the family. In the late 1990s, several techniques were developed to deal with the systematic development of product families. These techniques exploit better analysis techniques, software architectures, and modularization.

## 4.2   MODULARIZATION TECHNIQUES

In this section, we discuss techniques that can be used during design to achieve the objectives stated in Section 4.1. In particular, we distinguish between two complementary aspects of design—one (Section 4.2.1) that addresses the problem of defining the overall structure of the architecture in terms of relationships among modules and the other (Section 4.2.2) that deals with the design of each module, to which we apply the principle of information hiding.

As stated in Chapter 1, these two aspects are often called *architectural* (or *high-level*) *design* and *detailed design*. Even though several design methodologies suggest that the two be performed as two consecutive steps, we do not see them as separate steps, whereby the second necessarily follows the first. Rather, we view design as a continuum in which the interplay between these two activities takes place in a flexible way.

In order to document and analyze our designs, we need a *design notation*. We introduce a simple design notation in Section 4.2.3. The purpose of this notation, which comes in both a textual and a graphical form, is to serve our pedagogical needs in this book. It is not intended that the notation be used in industrial software development. Rather, the notation serves to show the features needed in a design notation and why they are needed. Later, in Section 4.6, we will refer to a standard notation (UML), when we discuss object-oriented design.

After introducing information hiding as a general principle, we illustrate a particular instance of it that leads to the important concepts of abstract objects and abstract data types, defined and illustrated in Section 4.2.4. Then we analyze design strategies and distinguish between top-down and bottom-up design. The two approaches are compared critically in Sections 4.2.6 and 4.2.7.

## 4.2.1    The Module Structure and its Representation

A module is a well-defined component of a software system. It is common to equate modules and routines, but this view of a module is too narrow. A module is a software fragment that corresponds to more than just a routine. It may be a collection of routines, a collection of data, a collection of type definitions, or a mixture of all of these. In general, we may view a module as a *provider of computational resources* or *services*.

When we decompose a system into modules, we must be able to describe the overall modular structure precisely and state the relationships among the individual modules.

We can define many relationships among modules. For example, we may define a relation which states that one module must be implemented before another or that it is more important than another. The first relation may be used by a manager to monitor the development of the system; the second may be used as a guideline for assigning work to programmers according to their skills and experience.

What we are interested in here, however, are the kinds of relations on modules that define the software architecture and that help us understand and control it—for example, whether a module uses the facilities provided by another module or is a part of the other module. As we shall see soon, these are two useful relationships among modules that may be used to define our system architecture.

In what follows, we address three particular issues: What is the structure of software in terms of its constituent modules? How can we define that structure precisely? And what are the desirable properties of such a structure?

First, from an abstract viewpoint, the modular structure of a system can be described in terms of various types of mathematical relations. Let $S$ be a software system composed of modules $M_1$, $M_2 \ldots$, $M_n$; that is,

$$S = \{M_1, M_2, \ldots, M_n\}.$$

A *relation* $r$ on $S$ is a subset of $S \times S$. If two modules $M_i$ and $M_j$ are in $S$, we represent the fact that the pair $<M_i, M_j>$ is in $r$ by using the infix notation $M_i \ r \ M_j$. Since we are interested in describing the mutual relationships among different modules, we will always implicitly assume the relations of interest in this text to be *irreflexive*. This means that $M_i \ r \ M_i$ cannot hold for any module $M_i$ in $S$.

The *transitive closure* of a relation $r$ on $S$ is again a relation on $S$, written $r^+$. Let $M_i$ and $M_j$ be any two elements of $S$. Then $r^+$ can be defined recursively as follows: $M_i r^+ M_j$ if and only if $M_i \ r \ M_j$ or there is an element $M_k$ in $S$ such that $M_i \ r \ M_k$ and $M_k \ r^+ M_j$. A relation is a *hierarchy* if and only if there are no two elements $M_i$, $M_j$ such that $M_i r^+ M_j$ and $M_j \ r^+ \ M_i$.

The transitive closure of a relation captures the intuitive notion of *direct* and *indirect* relationships. For example, for two modules A and B, A CALLS⁺ B implies that either A CALLS B directly or A CALLS B indirectly through a chain of CALLS.

Mathematical concepts can usually be grasped more effectively and intuitively if we can give them a graphical representation. Relations are a good example of this general principle. A relation can be represented in graphical form as a directed graph whose nodes are labeled by elements in S, and a directed arc exists from the node labeled $M_i$ to the node labeled $M_j$ if and only if $M_i$ r $M_j$.

A relation is a *hierarchy* if and only if there are no cycles in the graph of the relation; this type of graph is called a *directed acyclic graph* (DAG). Figure 4.3(a) illustrates a generic graph, and Figure 4.3(b) represents a hierarchy (a DAG).

The next two subsections discuss two types of relations among modules that are very useful for structuring software designs: USES and IS_COMPONENT_OF.

#### 4.2.1.1 *The* USES *relation*

A useful relation for describing the modular structure of a software system is the so-called USES relation. For any two distinct modules $M_i$ and $M_j$, we say that $M_i$ USES $M_j$ if $M_i$ requires the presence of $M_j$, because $M_j$ provides the resources that $M_i$ needs to accomplish its task. If $M_i$ USES $M_j$, we also say that $M_i$ is a *client* of $M_j$, since $M_i$ requires the services that $M_j$ provides. Conversely, $M_j$ is called the *server*. More concretely, a USES relation is established if module $M_i$ accesses a resource provided by module $M_j$. For example, $M_i$ USES $M_j$ if $M_i$ contains a call to a procedure contained in module $M_j$ or if $M_i$ uses a type defined in $M_j$.

A good restriction to impose on the USES relation is that it should be a hierarchy. Hierarchical systems are easier to understand than nonhierarchical ones: Once the abstractions provided by used components are understood, client components may be understood without looking at the internals of the used modules. In other words, separation of concerns can be applied by traversing the USES structure, starting with the nodes of the DAG that do not use any other nodes, up to the nodes that are not used by any other node. When we encounter a node, the corresponding module may be

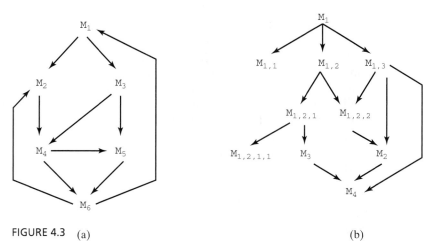

FIGURE 4.3 (a)  (b)

Graph representation of a relation among modules. **(a)** General graph. **(b)** Directed acyclic graph (DAG).

understood by referring to the abstractions provided by used modules (if any) that have been previously encountered and understood.

As a consequence of the hierarchical USES structure, we obtain another beneficial practical effect: Quoting Parnas, if the structure is not hierarchical, "we may end up with a system in which nothing works until everything works."[3] In fact, the presence of a cycle in the USES relation implies a strong coupling between all the modules in the cycle, meaning that no subsets of the modules in the cycle may be used or tested in isolation.

The restriction on a hierarchy has a methodological implication, too: The resulting structure defines a system through *levels of abstraction*. This often-used (and misused) term can be illustrated by reference to Figure 4.3(b). At the most abstract level, the entire system can be viewed as providing the services defined by module $M_1$. To implement such services, module $M_1$ uses modules $M_{1,1}$, $M_{1,2}$, and $M_{1,3}$. In turn, the abstract services offered by, say, $M_{1,2}$ are implemented by using the lower level modules $M_{1,2,1}$ and $M_{1,2,2}$.

We define the *level* of a module in a hierarchy r as follows:

1. The level of a module $M_i$ is 0 if there is no module $M_j$ such that $M_i$ r $M_j$, and
2. For each module $M_i$, let k be the maximum level of all nodes $M_j$ such that $M_i r M_j$. Then the level of $M_i$ is k + 1.

A system described by a hierarchical USES relation may be understood in terms of successive levels of abstraction: A module at level i USES only modules at any level j such that i>j. For example, in Figure 4.3(b), the levels of $M_{1,3}$, $M_2$, and $M_4$ are 3, 1, and 0, respectively; $M_{1,3}$ USES $M_2$ and $M_{1,3}$ USES $M_4$.

Given any two modules $M_i$ and $M_j$ whose levels are i and j, respectively, we say that $M_i$ is a *higher level* module than $M_j$ if and only if i>j.

Another common term used in connection with a hierarchical USES relation, especially in the case of the structure of operating systems, is *abstract (virtual) machine*. We already introduced this term in Section 4.1.1.1. Its meaning is that the modules at a certain level—say, i—provide a set of services that correspond to an abstract (or virtual) machine. Such services are used by higher level modules to implement the services they are expected to provide. In the implementation of such services, the services provided by modules at level i are used as if they were provided by some virtual machine. Virtual machines are progressively detailed by relying on other virtual machines, until no further levels are given.

As an example, consider the case of a module $M_R$ that provides input-output of record values. Let $M_R$ use another module $M_B$ that provides input-output of a single byte at a time. When $M_R$ is used to output record values, its job consists of transforming the record into a sequence of bytes and isolating a single byte at a time, to be output by means of the output operation provided by $M_B$. As viewed by its clients, module $M_R$ is a virtual machine that implements input and output operations for record values. But in order to perform its services, $M_R$ uses a lower level module $M_B$ that corresponds to a simpler virtual machine.

The USES relation among modules is defined statically; that is, the identification of all pairs <$M_i$, $M_j$> belonging to USES is independent of the execution of the software. In fact, it is exactly the purpose of design to define the relation once and for all.

---

[3]Parnas [1979].

To clarify this issue, consider a module M that uses modules $M_1$ and $M_2$ by calling one of their procedures. If the client module M contains the code structure

```
if cond then proc1 else proc2
```

where proc1 is a procedure of module $M_1$ and proc2 is a procedure of module $M_2$, then M USES $M_1$ and M USES $M_2$, although during any particular execution it may well happen that either $M_1$ or $M_2$, but not both, is invoked.

As another example, consider the dynamic reconfiguration of a distributed system: At run time, module $M_i$ may use module $M_j$ up to the point where dynamic reconfiguration causes $M_i$ to use module $M_k$. $M_j$ and $M_k$ provide exactly the same functionality, but reside on different nodes of the distributed system. Upon failure of the node where $M_j$ resides, any request for the services that were provided by $M_j$ is redirected to $M_k$. Thus, in terms of the USES relation, we have both $M_i$ USES $M_j$ and $M_i$ USES $M_k$, although only $M_j$ is actually used in the normal case.

The graphical view of the relation USES provides an intuitive, although partial, description of the coupling among modules. If each node of the graph is connected to every other node of the graph (i.e., the graph is complete: There is a pair $<M_i, M_j>$ in USES for each $M_i$, $M_j$ in S), then the modular structure is highly intricate and does not provide a manageable partitioning of the entire system into parts.

Actually, these comments also hold for most other relations among modules. If the graph of a relation $r$ is such that every module is related to every other module, then no part is independent of the whole. In such a case, the cardinality of $r$ is $n(n - 1)$, where n is the cardinality of S. On the opposite side, if $r$ is empty, then the relation describes a modular structure in which no two modules are related. Thus, the system is split into parts that can be designed and understood in complete isolation. While an empty $r$ is unrealistic in practice, this situation shows that we should try to achieve modular structures in which the cardinality of $r$ is much smaller than $n^2$.

The USES relation provides a way to reason about coupling in a precise manner. With reference to the USES graph, we can distinguish between the number of outgoing edges of a module (called the module's *fan-out*) and the number of incoming edges (called *fan-in*). It has been suggested that a good design structure should keep the fan-out low and the fan-in high. A high fan-in is an indication of good design because a module with high fan-in represents a general abstraction that is used heavily by other modules.

In order to evaluate the quality of a design, however, merely evaluating the structure of the USES relation is not sufficient. Also important is the nature of the interaction among modules. Here are examples of how modules may actually use one another:

1. An unstructured type of use occurs when a module modifies data—or even instructions—that are local to another module. This may happen in the case of assembly-language programs.
2. A module may use another module by communicating with it through a common data area, like a C static variable or a FORTRAN COMMON block.
3. The data exchanged between two modules may be "pure" data, or they can be control information, such as flags. Exchanging control information often results in a tricky kind of interaction that impairs the readability of programs.

4. A subprogram may communicate with another by invoking it with suitable parameters. This is a disciplined and traditional way of how two functional modules interact.

5. In a concurrent environment, a client module may communicate with a server through a remote procedure call (or a remote method invocation, as in Java). In a similar fashion, in the Ada programming language, a module M enclosing task $T_M$, may use a module M' enclosing task $T_{M'}$, by having a call to an entry of task $T_{M'}$. These are disciplined ways for two concurrent modules to communicate with each other.

## Exercises

**4.5**   Consider the case where the USES relation is defined by a tree. What does the fact that the structure is a tree, and not a DAG, represent? In general, would you prefer a design in which the USES relation is a tree or a design in which the relation is a DAG?

**4.6**   Consider procedure calls that may be taken to be instances of the USES relation. Mutually recursive modules do not form a hierarchy. Direct recursion within a module, however, is allowed in a hierarchy. Are these statements correct? If so, what is their justification?

**4.7**   Can you define the concept of *level* for a general graph rather than for a DAG? Why? Why not? What does this imply about a USES relation that is not a hierarchy?

**4.8**   Suppose that we use a language supporting procedure parameters. For example, module $M_i$ may call a procedure P of module $M_j$, passing to it procedure Q of module $M_k$ as a parameter. How could you define the USES relation for $M_j$, considering the modules it uses by calling its formal procedure parameter?

### *4.2.1.2 The* IS_COMPONENT_OF *relation*

IS_COMPONENT_OF is another relation among modules that is useful for describing designs. This relation allows designers to describe an architecture in terms of a module that is composed of other modules that may themselves be composed of other modules, and so on.

Let S be a set of modules. For any $M_i$ and $M_j$ in S, $M_i$ IS_COMPONENT_OF $M_j$ means that $M_j$ is realized by aggregating several modules, one of them being $M_i$. It is also possible to define COMPRISES as the inverse relation of IS_COMPONENT_OF; that is, for any two elements $M_i$ and $M_j$ in S, we say that $M_i$ COMPRISES $M_j$ if and only if $M_j$ IS_COMPONENT_OF $M_i$. Let $M_{S,i}$ be a subset of S defined as follows:

$$M_{S,i} = \{ \ M_k | M_k \text{ is in S and } M_k \text{ IS\_COMPONENT\_OF } M_i \ \}$$

Then we can say that $M_i$ IS_COMPOSED_OF $M_{S,i}$ and, conversely, $M_{S,i}$ IMPLEMENTS $M_i$.

If a module $M_i$ is composed of a set of other modules $M_{S,i}$, then the modules of set $M_{S,i}$ actually provide all of the services that $M_i$ should provide: They are the result of $M_i$'s decomposition into components, and therefore, they implement $M_i$.

In design, once $M_i$ is decomposed into the set $M_{s,i}$ of its constituents, it is replaced by them; that is, $M_i$ is an abstraction that is implemented in terms of simpler abstractions. The only reason to keep $M_i$ in the modular description of a system is to be able to refer to it, thus making the design structure more clear and understandable. At the end of the decomposition process, however, only the modules that are not composed of any other modules can be viewed as composing the software system. The others are kept just for descriptive purposes.

The relation IS_COMPONENT_OF can also be described by a directed graph, as shown in Figure 4.4(a). The relation is irreflexive and is also a hierarchy. Therefore, in this relation, we can define one module as being at a higher level than another module, as we did in the case of the USES relation. In practice, it is more useful to introduce the concept of level with reference to the relation COMPRISES. Figure 4.4(b) describes the system of Figure 4.4(a) in terms of this relation.

The concept of level defined by IS_COMPOSED_OF is such that if $M_i$ IS_COMPOSED_OF $\{M_{i,1}, M_{i,2}, \ldots, M_{i,n}\}$, then $M_i$ is a higher level module than any of $M_{i,1}, M_{i,2}, \ldots, M_{i,n}$. Note that the concept of a level of abstraction used in design descriptions is ambiguous, unless we explicitly specify whether it is intended as the level with respect to the USES relation or the COMPRISES relation. In the case of USES, all modules $M_{i,1}, M_{i,2}, \ldots, M_{i,n}$ used by a given module $M_i$ are lower level modules than $M_i$; thus, $M_i$ provides the services it exports to its clients by using the services provided by the lower level modules $M_{i,1}, M_{i,2}, \ldots, M_{i,n}$. In the case of COMPRISES, all modules implementing a given module $M_i$ are lower level modules than $M_i$: They actually stand for $M_i$ (i.e., $M_i$ is refined by substituting $M_{i,1}, M_{i,2}, \ldots, M_{i,n}$ for it).

The graphical representation of IS_COMPONENT_OF also describes IS_COMPOSED_OF, IMPLEMENTS, and COMPRISES. For example, in Figure 4.4, $M_2$, $M_3$, and $M_4$ are components of $M_1$; $M_1$ IS_COMPOSED_OF $\{M_2, M_3, M_4\}$; $\{M_2, M_3, M_4\}$ IMPLEMENTS $M_1$; and $M_1$ COMPRISES $M_i$, for $2 \leq i \leq 4$. The entire software system is ultimately composed of modules $M_4$, $M_5$, $M_6$, $M_7$, $M_8$, and $M_9$. The other modules that appear in the graph do not have a physical existence; their only purpose is to help describe the modular structure in a hierarchical way.

For example, suppose that Figure 4.4 describes the modular structure of an application in which $M_2$ is the module providing input facilities, $M_3$ is the heart of the system, providing all the processing, and $M_4$ provides output facilities. In turn, module $M_2$ is composed of various modules ($M_7$, $M_8$, and $M_9$), each providing certain input services, such as input through digitalization of input forms, input through I/O terminals, etc. Module $M_3$ is

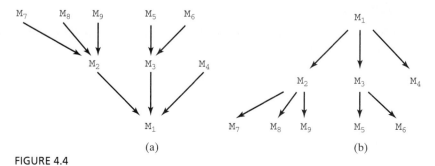

(a)  (b)

FIGURE 4.4

An example of the IS_COMPONENT_OF relation (a), and the corresponding COMPRISES relation (b).

decomposed into $M_5$ and $M_6$. The final system contains only physical modules that correspond to the elements of the IS_COMPOSED_OF relation that are not further decomposed into other modules—in the example, $M_4$, $M_5$, $M_6$, $M_7$, $M_8$, and $M_9$.

So far, in our discussion of IS_COMPONENT_OF, we have assumed that a module is a component of at most one module. Although this represents the typical case, we do not impose such a restriction in the definition of the IS_COMPOSED_OF relation. Therefore, it is possible to complete the graph of Figure 4.4 with a directed arc from node $M_6$ to, say, node $M_4$, to indicate that $M_6$ is a component of both $M_3$ and $M_4$. When a module $M_i$ is a component of both modules $M_j$ and $M_k$, one can give an obvious alternative description according to which $M_i$ is a component of just $M_j$ and use a copy of $M_i$ as a component of $M_k$. Another solution adopted by some languages consists of defining a macro or a *generic* (*template*) module and then generating instances to be used in the different contexts in which they become actual components. We will elaborate on this later.

The two relations USES and IS_COMPONENT_OF can be, and usually are, used together. For example, we may start a higher level description of a system's architecture by saying that SYSTEM is composed of modules $M_1$, $M_2$, and $M_3$, where $M_1$ uses both $M_2$ and $M_3$. Later, we specify $M_1$ as composed of $M_4$ and $M_5$, and so on.

Although we have discussed the USES and IS_COMPONENT_OF relations in the context of software architectural design, the concepts those relations embody apply equally to any other kind of design. In the context of requirements specification, for example, we should come up with specification modules and relations that describe their dependencies. A specification module may use another module if it refers to a concept that is specified in the other module. A specification module may also be a component of another module if it specifies a part of the system that is specified by the other module.

## Exercises

**4.9**    Are IS_COMPOSED_OF and IMPLEMENTS relations on S?

**4.10**    Suppose you decide to adopt the following policy: A module $M_1$ may be implemented before a module $M_2$ if $M_1$ has no components and does not use $M_2$ or any module comprising $M_2$. Describe this policy formally as a relation between modules.

### 4.2.1.3  *Product families revisited*

We can use the relations USES and IS_COMPONENT_OF to restate some points concerning product families.

Suppose you are designing a system S that you decompose into the set of modules $M_1$, $M_2$, ..., $M_i$, with some USES relation on it. Then, suppose you turn to the design of any of such modules, say, $M_k$, $1 \leq k \leq i$. At this point, you may realize that any design decision you take will separate one subset of family members from others; for example, $M_k$ is an output module, and its design may need to discriminate between textual output and graphical output, to be dealt with by two different family members. Suppose you make the decision to follow one of the design options (in the example, the graphical output), which leads you to decompose $M_k$ into $M_{k,1}, M_{k,2}, \ldots, M_{k,i_k}$, with some USES relation defined on this set.

You should record these design decisions carefully, so that future changes will be made reliably. Suppose that at some later time a different member of the family needs to be designed (for example, the system that provides support for textual output). You should never allow yourself to modify the final implementation by changing the code in order to meet the new requirements. Rather, the recorded documentation of the structure of the modules should force you to resume the design from the decomposition of module $M_k$, so that you may provide a different implementation in terms of lower level components. Note, however, that the rest of the system will remain untouched; that is, modules $M_1$, . . . , $M_{k-1}$ and $M_{k+1}$, . . . , $M_i$ will not be affected by the design of the new family member.

### 4.2.2    Interface, Implementation, and Information Hiding

The relations USES and IS_COMPONENT_OF provide only a partial description of the software architecture. For example, more remains to be said regarding the exact nature of the interaction between two modules participating in the USES relation and about the details of IS_COMPONENT_OF. That is, when a module $M_i$ that uses module $M_j$ is refined into its components $M_{i,1}, M_{i,2}, . . . , M_{i,n}$, it is necessary to state exactly what the USES relation between the modules in the set $\{M_{i,1}, M_{i,2}, . . . , M_{i,n}\}$ and $M_j$ means.

Intuitively, we would like to divide the software into components such that each component can be designed independently of the others. If each component becomes a work assignment to a different programmer on a team, then each programmer should be able to work on a component with as little knowledge as possible about how other members of the team are building their components. Once again, this is the essence of separation of concerns and modularity, as discussed in general terms in Chapter 3.

To be more precise, we must define how the interaction among modules actually takes place—that is, the exact nature of the USES relation between any two modules. The set of services that each module provides to its clients (i.e., the purpose of the module as it relates to other modules) is called its *interface*. The corresponding services are said to be *exported* by the module and *imported* by the clients. The way these services are accomplished by the module is the module's secret and is embedded in its *implementation*. A clear distinction between the interface of a module and its implementation is a key aspect of good design, because it supports the principle of separation of concerns.

The interface of a module M describes exactly what the client modules need to know in order to utilize the services provided by M. The interface is an abstraction of the module as viewed by its clients. The designer who is in charge of M, while working on the design, needs to know only the interfaces of the other modules used by M and may ignore their implementation. M's interface is viewed by the designer as his or her task description: The goal is to provide exactly these services through a suitable implementation. An implementation of a module is its decomposition in terms of components—described by the relation IS_COMPONENT_OF—or, if the module is sufficiently simple, its representation in terms of code in some programming language, which possibly uses the services provided by other, lower level modules.

The interface of a module M may be viewed as a *contract* between M and its clients; that is, the interface records all and only the facilities the designer in charge of M agrees to provide to other designers. Clients may depend only on what is listed in the interface. Thus, as long as the interface remains the same, M may change without affecting its clients.

In most practical cases, interfaces describe computational resources, such as (1) a variable that belongs to a module and is made accessible to other modules to provide a form of interaction or (2) procedures (functions) that must be called to have some operation performed. The examples we give here also make this assumption. Interfaces, however, are not limited to these types of resources. For example, information concerning the response time of an exported routine may be part of the nonfunctional description of the interface in the case of a real-time application. It is a kind of information that clients need to know in order to decide whether and how to use the module.

We can go deeper into the distinction between an interface and an implementation by introducing the concept of *information hiding*. The clients of a module know about its services only through its interface; the implementation is hidden from them. This means that the implementation may change without affecting the module's clients, provided that the interface remains unchanged. Thus, a crucial aspect of design consists of defining precisely what goes into a module's interface—and therefore is visible to its potential clients—and what remains hidden in the implementation and can be changed at any time without affecting the clients. The addition of facilities for the definition of module interfaces in the current generation of programming languages marks a significant development in programming-language technology in the direction of better support for software engineering.

### Exercises

**4.11**  For the Ada programmer; Consider the specification part of Ada packages as a module interface description. What is the difference between exporting a type and exporting a private type? Describe this difference in terms of the exported functionality.

**4.12**  For the Java programmer; The interface construct in Java allows a programmer to specify an interface of a module independently of its implementation. What entities are exportable in Java interfaces? How does the programmer provide an implementation for an interface? Is it possible to have two implementations for the same interface?

**4.13**  Compare and contrast the support for interface definition in Eiffel, Ada 95, C++, and Java.

#### 4.2.2.1  *How to design module interfaces*

A commonly used analogy to describe the concepts of an interface, an implementation, and information hiding is illustrated in Figure 4.5: A module is like an iceberg, the interface—the visible part—is like the tip of the iceberg, and the implementation is what is hidden by the surface of the sea. The tip is just a small part of the whole.

If we scratch the surface of this analogy, however, we observe that it is far from satisfactory: The tip does not provide a very satisfactory abstraction of the iceberg as viewed, for example, by a ship. That is, relying upon the shape of the tip does not prevent the ship from crashing into the iceberg! As opposed to the tip of the iceberg, the interface of a module describes all that must be known to operate the module correctly.

Still, the iceberg analogy sheds light on a very important point: What should go in the description of the interface and what should remain hidden in the implementation? Clearly, the interface of a module should reveal as little information as possible, but

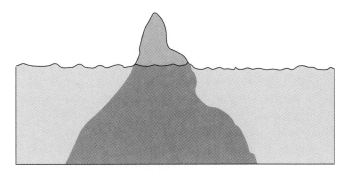

FIGURE 4.5

The interface as the tip of the iceberg.

sufficient information for other modules to use the services provided by the module. Revealing unnecessary information makes the interface unnecessarily complex and reduces the understandability of the design of the system. Also, by revealing knowledge of internal details that is not necessary, it is more likely that a change to a module will affect not only its implementation, but also its interface. Even worse, other modules might take advantage of the information we make public by operating on it in an undesirable manner. On the other hand, not exporting services that need to be imported by clients would make the module less usable.

### Exercise

**4.14**  Discuss a remote-control device as an interface for the user who wants to watch TV. Is the interface adequate if the user wants to connect the appliance to other devices (e.g., a stereo system, VCR, or video camera) through its input and output channels?

Exercise 4.14 illustrates an important concept: The interface we design depends on what services we wish to offer to clients and, conversely, on what we decide to hide within the module. We can hide certain things if we expect that the clients will not use them, but we cannot hide them if the clients are expected to use them. The art of designing module interfaces consists of balancing carefully what we want to hide and what we need to provide. If everything is hidden, then modules neither communicate nor cooperate with one another, they are autonomous subsystems. If everything is visible, then the module's structure is intricate and characterized by too high a coupling.

### Example 4.1

Suppose we are designing an interpreter for a very simple programming language, MINI, operating on integers and integer arrays. We provide a symbol-table module that is used to store information about the variables of a program. The symbol table exports a procedure GET that accepts as input the symbolic name of a variable and, possibly, the value of an index (in the case of an array) and returns the value of the variable. Similarly, a procedure PUT makes it possible to store a new value for a given variable. When a new variable declaration is encountered, a new entry is created in the symbol table by calling a procedure CREATE, passing it the name of the variable and its size (the number of integer entries it represents).

The purpose of the interface we are designing is to hide the physical structure of the table from the clients of the symbol-table module. To warn clients when they either try to read or write the value of a variable that does not exist or try to access an array with an invalid index value, the procedures GET and PUT return an additional parameter, POS. The value returned for POS is a pointer to the variable stored in the table if such variable exists, or it is the null pointer if the variable does not exist.

This design can be criticized because of the redundancy in the interface. If our purpose is just to provide operations to store and retrieve data (and signal the case where access to the data is incorrect), then we are providing additional information (i.e., the position in the table where the data are stored). Such redundancy has negative side effects on the ease of changing the design, as we shall show shortly. It also provides a loophole into information hiding. ∎

So how should we proceed in the design of modules through information hiding in order to improve cohesion and reduce coupling, in terms of both the number of interconnections in the graph of the USES relation and the type and amount of information exported through interfaces?

To answer this question, we should first define what the overall primary goal of our design actually is. As before, we assume here that ease of change is a primary goal: We want our design to be able to evolve easily and reliably according to some anticipated changes and possibly others. The next section gives some guidelines on how to design modules that can accommodate future changes.

### Exercise

---

**4.15**  Consider changing the interface of the module of Example 4.1 to have a separate call for asking whether a variable exists (and thus can be read or written safely). Discuss this change in terms of the quality of the modular structure, the efficiency of the system, etc.

---

### 4.2.2.2 *Module secrets and design for change*

To maximize the evolvability of a module implementation, its interface should export the minimum possible amount of detail. Another goal is to hide low-level details and provide an abstract interface in order to make the design more understandable. Doing this would be an application of the principles of abstraction and separation of concerns. Once the changes we wish to facilitate are identified, we can try to structure the system in such a way that changeable decisions are hidden in the implementation part of some modules, whereas module interfaces represent stable information (i.e., information that is not affected by the changes).

We say that the changeable, hidden information becomes the *secret* of the module; also, according to widely used jargon, we say that such information is *encapsulated* within the module implementation.

### Example 4.2

The secret of the symbol-table module of Example 4.1 is the data structure chosen for internal representation. We may choose to use a linear array, a hash table, a linked list, a binary tree, or even other, more sophisticated data structures. The important goal we wish to reach is the ability to change the data structure without affecting client modules. The reason is that we want to design and implement the system quickly, by first concentrating on the module's structure, without spending too much time designing and tuning the data structures in each module. We want to postpone the decision about the nature of the internals of each module, such as the "best" type of data structure, to a later point, after we have completed the entire design of the interpreter and, maybe, collected some execution profiles.

If we examine the interface closely, however, we see that it reveals more than is necessary; in particular, it reveals part of its (supposed) secret. By knowing the address of the storage area for a variable (revealed by both GET and PUT), we are allowed to access that variable directly, without being obliged to go through the interface procedures. For example, if a client accesses the same simple variable—say, X—repeatedly, the client might be tempted to obtain the value of POS and then use the pointer directly to access the variable X. This method would work correctly only if the position at which the value is stored does not change over time. That would be the case in a simple implementation of the symbol table module in which new declarations encountered are merely appended at the end of a sequential data structure.

Even if the software might work in this case, which may correspond to the initial release of the system, it would become incorrect in a future release of the symbol table that replaces the sequential data structure by one that keeps its entries sorted. In fact, as new declarations were encountered, they would have to be recorded in the appropriate position in the data structure, and this might imply shifting some existing entries, invalidating the values previously returned by POS. ■

As we anticipated in Section 4.1.1.1, details of the abstract machine underlying the software are examples of information that should be hidden. This includes details of some operating system calls, as well as intricacies of the required interactions with some special peripheral devices. The main reason for hiding these details is to protect the application against changes in the underlying abstract machine. Such changes may result from anticipated hardware evolution or to achieve portability of the application. Another strong reason for encapsulating abstract-machine-dependent aspects in *ad hoc* modules is separation of concerns: Mixing low-level machine-dependent details with higher level application-dependent features would hamper the understandability of the software.

## Example 4.3

Suppose that a computer is used to control a remote plant. The computer must provide an input acquisition capability to get measurements from some physical devices located at different points in the plant. For example, the computer would receive the value of the temperature at points $P_1$, $P_2$, and $P_5$, the value of the pressure at points $P_1$, $P_3$, and $P_4$, etc. As a function of input data, control signals must be sent back to the controlled plant, and a history log must be kept in a file to facilitate maintenance of the plant. Input data are presently received as sequences of bytes that must be decoded by the control application being designed. It is anticipated, however, that the system will evolve to a new distributed configuration in which physical inputs will be processed remotely by special devices and sent to the controlling computer as recordlike structured information.

An appropriate design here would define an input acquisition module whose secret would be the physical way input data are acquired. Such a module would provide client modules with a query operation to be invoked to get the next input datum (what kind of measure it was, where it was measured, etc.) and the value of the measure (an integer or real value, depending on the type of measure). ■

In conclusion, the purpose of information hiding is to design modules that protect some changeable design decision by making it a secret and to provide a meaningful abstraction through stable module interfaces. The identification of likely changes is crucial to this approach. A tentative set of likely changes should be found in the requirements document that sets the objectives for the application. As already mentioned, when the requirements of a new system are being determined, special attention should be paid to define not only what is needed now, but also what is likely to be needed in the future. Example 4.3 illustrates this point. Other points are illustrated by the next example.

## Example 4.4

Suppose that the requirements for the control application of Example 4.3 contain a description of how historical data must be processed. Suppose they also describe a predefined set of fixed-format queries that can be used to extract information in the maintenance phase of the software. Future enhancements of the system are anticipated that will allow natural-language-like queries.

A good modularization in this case will encapsulate in one module the physical structure of the files used to store the historical data; that is, the module will provide procedures to access the various items stored in the data structure. Another module will provide abstract queries; that is, it will encapsulate the way queries are actually provided by the user—in natural language or in a fixed format—and how they must be analyzed in order to extract the exact meaning of the user's request.                                  ◼

As we saw in Chapter 3, an important class of likely changes has to do with the strategy followed to produce the application. The strategy of incremental development tries to identify useful subsets of the application that might be developed and delivered earlier than others. Although some parts of the system are not dealt with at some point and are delayed to a later effort, special care is needed in the design stage to define exactly the interfaces with respect to the parts that are left for later development. This will allow those parts to be added to the system without disturbing the previously delivered functions. In other cases, in the initial stage, some parts of the system are deliberately implemented in a highly simplified manner. They are then redesigned and reimplemented at a later stage. The symbol table of Example 4.1 is one such example. Another example is illustrated next.

## Example 4.5

Suppose we are developing a completely new type of database management system that we hope will become a revolutionary product in the marketplace. The great new features of the system are in the language used for queries, which permits the sophisticated use of both natural language and pictorial interaction.

Before starting development of this new system, we would like to be able to assess the validity of the approach with respect to its innovative human-computer interaction aspects. Thus, we decide to implement the user interface, but delay the implementation of the "real" database management system (i.e., the definition of the physical file structures, the various algorithms for storage and retrieval, recovery procedures, concurrency control, etc.).

What we will implement is a *prototype* of the application that can only deal with a limited amount of information, because all data will be kept in main memory using arrays. Potential users will be asked to play with the system and give feedback to the designers regarding its usability. They will be warned that the performance, robustness, reliability, etc., of the prototype have nothing to do with the expected performance of the future system: They should pay attention only to the way queries may be submitted with a mixture of natural language and pictures.

If the interface between the module providing human-computer interaction and the module providing database access has been designed carefully, then the two modules may evolve independently. For example, we may concentrate first on implementing a robust version of the human-computer interaction module and later turn the prototype implementation of the database module into a realistic version without affecting the rest of the system. In other words, if we design stable interfaces among the various modules, then modules may evolve independently from the prototype implementation to their final version.    ◼

### 4.2.2.3 *More on likely changes*

The examples we gave in the previous sections are just a small sample of software change requests that may be encountered in practice. We can divide changes that we might anticipate into a few classes. Information-hiding modules should then be designed to accommodate these classes of changes reliably and efficiently. In Section 4.1.1, we discussed a list of likely changes: in algorithms, in data representation, in the underlying abstract machine, and in the social environment. Encapsulation via information-hiding modules supports such changes. For example, if we use a procedure to encapsulate an algorithm, changing the algorithm requires changing the body of the procedure, and this can be done without affecting the procedure's clients. Similarly, by hiding a data structure and providing abstract interface operations to access and modify it, we can protect users of the data structure from changes in the representation of data.

Policies are another kind of design decision that should be encapsulated within information-hiding modules. Often, they involve the order in which certain operations are performed. For example, suppose we are designing a module to provide clients with a sorted list of items. Suppose also that it must be possible to INSERT an item in the list, DELETE it from the list, and PRINT the list of item names in alphabetical order. Then INSERT, DELETE, and PRINT constitute the module's interface.

This module can hide various kinds of policies—for example, in an eager policy, the list is kept sorted as each item is inserted or deleted; in an incremental policy, the list is sorted just prior to printing it; in a lazy policy, the list is never kept sorted, but the PRINT operation simply prints the items in the right order. Note, however, that a change in the policy would leave the clients unaffected, as the policy is a secret of the module. The policy, however, would affect the execution time of each operation. That is, an eager policy makes it possible to support a fast PRINT at the expense of a slow INSERT and DELETE, since these must keep the list sorted.

As another example of this issue, consider the case of the concurrent application, where it is vital to distinguish between *mechanisms* and *policies*. In this type of application, we need mechanisms to suspend processes if they need to access some shared resource (e.g., a printer or a buffer). The underlying *scheduler* should then use some policy to resume suspended processes; for example, it might resume processes on a purely first-in, first-out basis, or it might use more complicated policies on the basis of, say, priorities or execution times. Either of these policies can be implemented by providing a module that exports the mechanisms to suspend and resume processes:

- suspend (P) would be invoked to suspend process P;

- resume (P) would be invoked to resume the next process; it also provides the identifier of the resumed process in the output parameter.

The module would hide the policy used to select the next process to be resumed. Future changes in the policies will then integrate smoothly with the rest of the system: Only performance will be affected, not correctness.

What can be hidden depends also on the type of application. For example, in many real-time applications, scheduling policies cannot be hidden from client modules. They are thus made part of the interface. They are not hidden in the implementation because they cannot be changed irrespective of the clients' wishes. Rather, the fact that, say, certain events are handled according to one policy or another (e.g., FIFO versus priority-based events) may affect the ability of a module to react to some incoming stimuli within specified time constraints, and a failure in this regard may cause serious, dangerous, or even catastrophic effects in the real-time system.[4]

### Exercise

---

**4.16**  Discuss the previous example of the sorted list of items in the case of real-time applications. Can a change in policy affect the clients? Why? Why not?

---

#### 4.2.2.4  *Summing up*

No matter what method we follow to modularize an application, module interfaces should represent all and only the information that client modules need to know in order to make use of the module's services. By examining just the interface, the designers of other modules must be able to decide whether they would benefit from using the module. This obviously requires a way to describe module interfaces precisely, so that no ambiguities arise in the interpretation of the exported services. We examine the issue in the next section (and partly in Chapter 5). Before tackling this problem, however, two summary comments are in order here.

First, a clear distinction between the interface and the implementation and a precise definition of the interface are necessary for module (re)usability. A module may be (re)used in any context, provided that the services listed in its interface match the clients' expectations, no matter what the implementation is.

Second, the interface must contain all the information that is needed to characterize the module's behavior as viewed by the clients. As we pointed out, in most cases interfaces provide descriptions of routines to be invoked by client modules. They can also provide a description of shared data. Furthermore, in real-time applications, the response time of an exported operation is part of the interface.

### 4.2.3   Design Notations

We have so far discussed software design issues informally: Architectures have been described in a colloquial style, using English prose. But English prose, or any other form of natural language description, is not an adequate medium for describing artifacts like software designs. More precision, rigor, and even formality are required for an unambiguous description. Thus, software engineers need special notations to specify their designs.

---

[4]Actually, note that often it is not necessary—or useful—to make the policy manifest in the interface. For example, one can provide a more abstract view of the policy by stating constraints on the response times of certain operations.

Actually, the preceding statement is true for every field of engineering. For example, electrical engineers produce blueprints in which complex appliances are described in terms of interconnected iconic symbols representing elementary devices such as resistors, capacitors, and transistors. These elementary devices may be viewed as standard components that may be assembled to produce a new system. Suitable annotations describe the types of elementary devices to be assembled—for example, the voltage to be supplied between two given points or the value, in ohms, of resistors. The layout of such blueprints is standardized, and no ambiguities arise when descriptions are interpreted in the construction phase, when the circuit is built. (The blueprint may be analyzed to uncover inconsistencies or errors before the implementation phase begins.) Similar considerations apply to the case of civil or mechanical engineering: In all such cases, designs are expressed in a standardized, graphical notation.

No standardized notation for expressing software designs has emerged yet, although various proposals have been entertained and some have been adopted in practice. The Unified Modeling Language (UML) is a combination of several earlier notations and is being promoted as a universal standard for object-oriented design. In the next two subsections, we illustrate two notations, one based on a programming-language-like textual syntax (called TDN) and the other based on a graphical interface (called GDN). These notations have many similarities to the notations used in practice. The reason we chose our own notation is that we do not want to be distracted by details of syntax that do not add much to the expressiveness of the notation. Later, when we address object-oriented design, we will instead refer to the standard UML notation.

The notations we introduce next describe the software architecture by specifying modules and their relationships. The notation is formal as far as the *syntax* of interfaces is concerned. For example, it says, in a syntactically correct form, how to formulate a request for a service exported by a module. But it does not formally specify the *semantics* of the exported services (i.e., what a service actually accomplishes for the clients, along with possible constraints or properties that clients need to know). The semantics is described only informally, by means of comments. The issue of formally specifying the semantics of modules is examined in Chapter 5.

### 4.2.3.1  TDN: A textual design notation

In this section, we illustrate TDN, our textual design notation. It is somewhat inspired by the syntax of traditional modular programming languages such as Ada or Modula-2, but its aim is to focus on issues of modularization. Thus, some features are added, and a large number of details typical of programming languages are deliberately ignored. Also, some aspects of the language are deliberately left informal and can be filled in by the designer, depending on his or her taste, in accordance with the type of application being designed, the programming language that will be ultimately used for implementation, etc. Above all, assuming that the reader knows a modular programming language such as C++, Modula-2, Ada, or Java, the notation should be self-explanatory.

We assume that a module may export any type of resource: a variable, a type, a procedure, a function, or any other entity defined by the language. As we mentioned, comments are used to provide semantic information about the exported services. In particular, comments are used to specify the *protocol* to be followed by the clients so that exported services are correctly provided. For example, the protocol might require that a certain operation which does the initialization of the module be called before any other operation. Or the protocol may require that the clients of a table-handling module not insert items into the table if it is full.

In general, if a module requires a special protocol to be followed to request one of the module's exported services, then this requirement should be stated as a comment associated with the syntactic description of the exported service in the module interface. Although written informally, the protocol is an essential part of the contract between the module's clients and the module's implementer, and it should be agreed upon by the designers and users of all such modules.

Comments are also used to describe the exact nature of the exported resource, once the required protocol is satisfied by the clients. Finally, comments are used to specify aspects of the interface that do not correspond to computational resources, such as routines or variables, but that deal with response times or other aspects. Time bounds and any other kind of additional constraints or properties of the exported entities may be stated as comments written in natural language when appropriate.

The parts of the module's description discussed so far define the interface—that is, what is visible to client modules. TDN, in addition, supports the description of other aspects of the architecture that may be necessary for its proper documentation. In particular, a **uses** part specifies the names of used modules (if any), and an **implementation** part gives a high-level description of the implementation, which may be useful for understanding the module's rationale. Typically, the **implementation** part gives the list of internal components, according to IS_COMPOSED_OF. Using informal comments, we may also describe which secrets are encapsulated within the module and why. This part may constitute a guideline for the implementation, or, after developing an implementation, it may document the important implementation choices. In any case, it does not concern the clients.

Figure 4.6 provides a sample TDN module description, and the reader is invited to read it carefully before proceeding. Note that the TDN description does not specify a module by itself, but rather a module that is part of an architecture.

```
module X
uses Y, Z
exports var A: integer;
    type B: array (1..10) of real;
    procedure C (D: in out B; E: in integer; F: in real);
    Here is an optional natural-language description of what
    A, B, and C actually are, along with possible constraints
    or properties that clients need to know; for example, we
    might specify that objects of type B sent to procedure C
    should be initialized by the client and should never
    contain all zeroes.
implementation
    If needed, here are general comments about the rationale
    of the modularization, hints on the implementation, etc.
    is composed of R, T
end X
```

FIGURE 4.6

A sample TDN module description.

```
module R
uses Y
exports var K: record ... end;
        type B: array (1..10) of real;
        procedure C (D: in out B; E: in integer; F: in real);
implementation
        .
        .
        .
end R

module T
uses Y, Z, R
exports var A: integer;
implementation
        .
        .
        .
end T
```

FIGURE 4.7

Sample components of module X in Figure 4.6.

What characterizes a module from its client's viewpoint (i.e., the module's interface) is exactly what appears in the **exports** section. The rest of the description does not deal with the interface, but serves to document the architecture in a precise manner. Thus, a change in the **exports** clause will affect the functional correctness of the clients, whereas changes to other sections will not.

The benefit of using a design notation like TDN instead of an unstructured and colloquial description lies not only in the rigor and precision of such a notation, but also in the fact that the design description can be checked for consistency and completeness. The check can be done manually, by carefully examining the textual description, or mechanically if we provide a specific tool to perform it. The way it can be done is explained next.

In the example of Figure 4.6, modules R and T eventually must be defined; if they aren't, we have a manifest case of incompleteness. Since R and T actually replace X, one or both must use one of Y or Z, or both. (Otherwise the **uses** clause of X would be wrong.) In addition to importing from Y and Z, R and T may import from one another. Also, what X exports should be a subset of the union of the sets of resources exported by R and T.[5] All of these constraints should be checked to assess the consistency and completeness of the description. One correct description of modules R and T is given in Figure 4.7.

The **uses** clause in a module specification describes exactly the USES relation introduced in Section 4.2.1.1. The clause simply states that a module may access any resource exported by another module. It may be useful to refine the **uses** clause by stating exactly which resources are imported by the module. Should this be required, we will use the notation

```
uses <module_name> imports (<resource_name_list>);
```

---

[5]For simplicity, we assume that the sets exported by R and T are disjoint.

```
module W
uses X imports (B, C),
           XX
exports ...
implementation
                .
                .
                .
end W
```

**FIGURE 4.8**

An example of a module with selective import.

If no **imports** clause is provided, all exported resources may be imported by the module. An example of a module W that uses modules X and XX is given in Figure 4.8. The example shows that W imports specific resources from X *(selective import),* whereas it imports all of the resources exported by XX.

When we refer to an entity E exported by a module M, we can use the dot notation M.E or, if no ambiguity arises, simply E. We might keep on adding new features to TDN and defining all the syntactic and semantic details. For example, if a module uses several modules and imports resources from them that have the same name in the exporting modules, the language might provide a way to resolve naming conflicts by renaming imported resources. We will not follow this path, however, in order to keep TDN as concise and general as possible. By adding features to TDN, we would make it closer to some programming language, and this would reduce its generality. We leave it up to the designer to add new features to the language if doing so turns out to be useful.

If TDN is to be used only with a specific programming language, it is possible to extend it with some language-specific features. But this must be done carefully, since a useful design notation should stay away from the low-level details of a programming language.

## Example 4.6

Example 4.1 and Example 4.2 introduced the problem of writing an interpreter for the MINI programming language. Here we address the problem of defining a compiler for MINI. One possible architecture is the following:

```
module COMPILER
exports procedure MINI (PROG: in file of char;
                        CODE: out file of char);
        MINI is called to compile the program stored in PROG and produce
        the object code in file CODE
implementation
        A conventional compiler implementation. ANALYZER performs both
        lexical and syntactic analysis and produces an abstract tree, as well
        as entries in the symbol table; CODE_GENERATOR generates code
        starting from the abstract tree and information stored in the symbol
        table. Module MAIN acts as a job coordinator.
        is composed of ANALYZER, SYMBOL_TABLE,
            ABSTRACT_TREE_HANDLER,
            CODE_GENERATOR, MAIN
end COMPILER
```

Modules MAIN, ANALYZER, and CODE_GENERATOR are specified as follows:

```
module MAIN
uses ANALYZER, CODE_GENERATOR
exports procedure MINI (PROG: in file of char;
                        CODE: out file of char);
    .
    .
    .
end MAIN

module ANALYZER
uses SYMBOL_TABLE, ABSTRACT_TREE_HANDLER
exports procedure ANALYZE (SOURCE: in file of char);
    SOURCE is analyzed; an abstract tree is produced by using the
    services provided by the tree handler, and recognized entities, with
    their attributes, are stored in the symbol table.
    .
    .
    .
end ANALYZER

module CODE_GENERATOR
uses SYMBOL_TABLE, ABSTRACT_TREE_HANDLER
exports procedure CODE (OBJECT: out file of char);
    The abstract tree is traversed by using the operations exported by the
    ABSTRACT_TREE_HANDLER and accessing the information stored
    in the symbol table in order to generate code in the output file.
    .
    .
    .
end CODE_GENERATOR
```

The reader is invited to complete the description of the remaining modules as an exercise. In particular, for the symbol-table module, we suggest going back to Example 4.1 and Example 4.2.    ■

### Exercise

**4.17**  Does the module structure described in Figure 4.6 represent a hierarchy? If not, how could you turn it into a hierarchy? If so, how could you turn it into a nonhierarchical structure?

#### 4.2.3.2  GDN: A graphical design notation

The reason engineers customarily adopt pictorial notations for their blueprints is that graphical descriptions can be more intuitive and easier to grasp than textual descriptions. A picture is worth a thousand words, according to folk wisdom. In this section, we provide a graphical design notation (GDN) that reflects the TDN textual description we defined in Section 4.2.3. land that is based on the graphical descriptions referred to earlier to describe relations among modules.

A module is represented by a box whose incoming arrows represent its interface (i.e., the exported resources). The reason exported resources are represented by incoming arrows is motivated by the fact that exported resources are accessible from the outside; that is, they represent an access path *into* the module.

Figure 4.9 gives a graphical description of the module X described textually in Figure 4.6. The fact that X uses modules Y and Z is shown by bold directed edges connecting X to Y and Z. Details of the exported resources—such as the number of procedure parameters, their type, and the type of variables—are omitted for simplicity, but may be added as annotations on the incoming arrows.

A box is empty if the module is elementary—that is, if it is not composed of any subcomponents. This is not the case with module X, which is composed of R and T. Since modules R and T are components of X, we can expand their definition, according to Figure 4.7, inside X; the resulting description is shown in Figure 4.10.

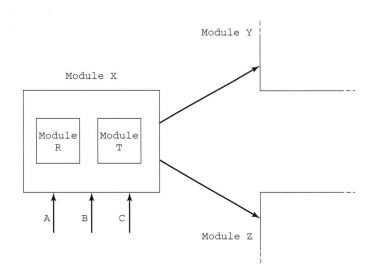

FIGURE 4.9

Graphical description of
module X of Figure 4.6.

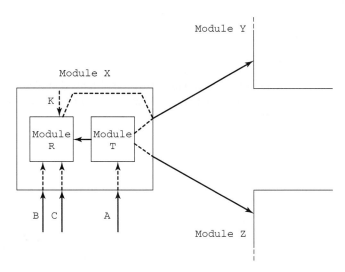

FIGURE 4.10

Module X is composed of modules
R and T.

Figure 4.10 shows explicitly which inner modules actually originate the resources exported by module X: B and C are provided by R, and A is provided by T. Graphically, this relationship is depicted by using shadow lines to connect export arrows of module X with the corresponding export arrows of modules R and T. Similarly, boldface shadow lines are used to specify which of R and T actually uses the modules used by X.

If a module M is a component of both modules L and N, we draw a box labeled M in both L and N. Should M be composed of other modules, the IS_COMPONENT_OF structure for M is described separately. This is sketched in Figure 4.11 in the case where M exports A and B and is composed of G and H.

## Exercises

**4.18**  Give a TDN description of module T of Figure 4.10.

**4.19**  Describe the module structure of Example 4.6, using GDN.

**4.20**  Describe the module structure of Figure 4.11, using TDN.

### 4.2.4    Categories of Modules

Modules can often be designed to export any combination of resources (variables, types, procedures and functions, events, exceptions, etc.). Of course, the nature of the exported resources also depends on what the programming language used to implement the modules actually supports. In general, however, modules can be classified into standard categories. Such a categorization is useful because it provides a uniform classification scheme for documentation and, possibly, for retrieval from a component library. Also, using a limited set of module categories makes a design more uniform and standard. As we discussed in Chapter 2, standard parts are the sign of the maturity

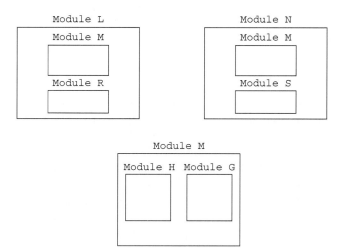

FIGURE 4.11

Module M is a member of both L and N.

of an engineering discipline. Categorization of modules is a step towards the development of standard software engineering components.

In this section, we illustrate three standard categories: procedural abstractions, libraries, and common pools of data. Two more general and abstract categories—abstract objects and abstract data types—are illustrated in the sections that follow.

A commonly used type of module provides just a procedure or a function that implements some abstract operation. In other words, such modules provide a *procedural abstraction* and are used to encapsulate an algorithm. Typical examples are sorting modules, fast Fourier transform modules, and modules performing translation from one language into another. The usefulness of procedural abstractions has been recognized since the early times of computing, and programming languages provided special support for them via routines.

A module may also contain a *group* of related procedural abstractions. A typical and successful example is represented by libraries of mathematical routines. Such libraries provide solutions to the most commonly encountered mathematical problems, such as those involving gradients and derivatives. Another example is a library of routines that provide algebraic operations on matrices. Still another is a library of routines for manipulating graphical objects. Modules of this type are used to package together a related set of routines. We use the term *library* to denote this class of modules.

Another common type of module provides a *common pool of data*. Once the need for sharing data among several modules is recognized, we can group such data together in a common pool that is imported by all client modules, which are then allowed to manipulate the data directly, according to the structure used to represent the data, which is visible to them.

An interesting use of a common data pool module is one that groups system configuration constants. For example, suppose that the supervisor of a control system is parameterized with respect to the number of input lines and the length of buffers in which inputs are temporarily stored. Each installation of the control system requires constant values to be assigned to these parameters, which are accessed by the modules that make up the supervisor. A typical solution consists of grouping all configuration constants in a common pool of data that may be easily accessed for configuration purposes.

In general, however, a common pool of data is a rather low-level type of module. Such a module does not provide any form of abstraction: All details of the data are visible and manipulable by all clients. The ability to group shared data in a common block only provides limited help in terms of readability and modifiability.

Establishing common pools of data is easily implemented in conventional programming languages. For example, it can be done in FORTRAN by means of the COMMON construct, or in C and Java with the use of static variables.

Most of the examples we gave in Sections 4.2.2 and 4.2.3, however, demand more abstract modules that can *hide* particular data structures as secrets of the module. For example, the symbol table module used in the interpreter (Example 4.1 and Example 4.2) and in the compiler (Example 4.6) of language MINI hides the specific data structure used to represent the table and exports the operations used to access it. This module is an example of the important class of modules that package together both data and routines, a class that is discussed in the next subsection.

#### 4.2.4.1 *Abstract objects*

We have already mentioned that nearly 17 percent of the costs involved in software maintenance are due to changes in the representation of data. Thus, a very important type of encapsulation is one that hides the details of data representations and shields clients from changes in them.

A symbol-table module illustrates a typical module that hides a data structure as a secret and exports routines that may be used as operations to access the hidden data structure and modify the values stored in it. Should the data structure change, all we need to change are the algorithms that implement the access routines, but client modules do not need to be changed, since they continue to use the same calls to perform the required accesses.

From their interface, these types of modules look like libraries. But they have a special property that mathematical libraries do not exhibit: They have a permanent, hidden, encapsulated data structure in their implementation part which is visible to routines that are internal to the module, but is hidden from client modules. In the symbol-table example, the data structure is used to store the entries as they are inserted into the table.

The hidden data structure provides these modules with a *state*. In fact, as a consequence of calls to the routines exported by the module, the values stored in the data structure may change from call to call; therefore, the results yielded by two calls with exactly the same parameters may be different. This behavior is unlike that of a pool of procedures or functions that constitute a library, because the library does not have a state: Two successive calls of the same function with the same parameters always yield the same result.

The difference between a module with state and library modules does not show through the syntax of the interface. In both cases, the module exports just a set of routines. We, however, distinguish between these two types of modules in our classification scheme. Modules that exhibit a state will be called *abstract objects*. We use a comment to indicate that a module is an abstract object.

**Example 4.7**

Arithmetic expressions may be written in parenthesis-free form by using so-called Polish postfix notation, wherein operators follow their operands. An example of an expression written in Polish postfix form is

```
a b c + *,
```

which corresponds to the infix expression

```
a*(b + c).
```

We restrict our attention to arithmetic expressions with only binary operators and integer operands. Also, we assume here that the input string is a syntactically correct postfix expression.

A way to evaluate arithmetic postfix expressions is to use a last-in, first-out data structure—a stack. The expression is scanned from left to right, and the values of the operands are pushed onto the stack as they are encountered. When the next symbol scanned is an operator, the two topmost values are taken off the stack, the operator is applied to the two operands, and the result is pushed on top of the stack. As an example, the reader is invited to simulate by hand the evaluation of the expression a b c + * when a = 2, b = 3, and c = 5.

Stacks can be implemented in several different ways, as any textbook on data structures illustrates. If their size is bounded, we may use an array; otherwise, we may use a linked list.

If we wish to encapsulate a stack in a module, we may define the following interface:

```
exports
    procedure PUSH (VAL: in integer);
    procedure POP_2 (VAL1, VAL2: out integer);
```

Procedure PUSH is used to insert a new operand on top of the stack; procedure POP_2 is used to extract the pair of topmost operands in the stack.

The hidden part of the module may then choose any data structure to represent the stack; the data structure is a secret of the module. ■

The design of the abstract object described in Example 4.7 may be criticized with respect to its generality and hence its reusability. First, it provides a specialized primitive to pop two elements at a time. This approach is useful when we have only binary operators; it fails when we extend the expression evaluator to the more general case where we can also have unary operators. To accommodate both binary and unary operators, one could provide a pop operation that pops one element at a time and let client modules call the operation twice when needed. The second shortcoming is that the design is based on the assumption that the expression to be evaluated is correct. If this is not the case, a run-time error will occur when we try to, say, pop an element from the stack when it is empty.

A more reliable design would define another interface routine, called EMPTY, that would deliver a Boolean result if the stack is empty. Of course, this design does not prevent the run-time error, but it provides a way for the client to avoid it. Notice, of course, that such a solution requires more from the client, but it is the price we pay to make our design more reusable and reliable.

## Exercises

**4.21**  Redesign the interface of the stack module so that it takes account of the previous comments. Also, discuss the use of a fixed-size data structure to implement the stack. Under what assumption is the interface correct? Is the module easily reusable? If not, how can you improve its reusability?

**4.22**  An output module is used to print single characters. As viewed by client modules, output is performed one character at a time. The output module, however, hides the exact way output is performed. This allows a family of programs to be designed in which the different members differ in the type of devices to which the output is directed. Some devices output data on a character-by-character basis, while others group characters in longer sequences and add special control characters.

Would you classify this output module as a procedural abstraction or as an abstract object? Sketch the TDN and GDN descriptions of the output module in the case where physical output is performed by a (hardware) module that buffers up to 16 characters.

### 4.2.4.2 *Abstract data types*

In this section, we introduce modules defining abstract data types as another category of modules that help in structuring our designs in a uniform and standard manner. We use Example 4.7 to motivate the introduction of this new category. The example utilized a stack abstract object. What if an application requires more than one stack? In this situation, we need the ability to define a type and then generate instances of that type. We also need a way to (a) associate a set of procedures with the type, in order to manipulate instances of that type, and (b) encapsulate the details of the type in the module, so that it can be changed without affecting the interface. Figure 4.12 illustrates this kind of module, using our textual design notation

A new notational device is introduced in the figure: the "?" symbol. It is used to export a type definition, leaving the details of the corresponding data structure hidden in the implementation part of the module. The fact that a type is exported allows client modules to declare variables of that type; the fact that the type definition is hidden, however, implies that variables of that type can be manipulated solely by procedures or functions exported by the module, since they are the only ones that "know" about the secret. Client modules must pass variables of the type in question as parameters to the exported routines for proper manipulation.

An *abstract data-type* module is a module that exports a type, along with the operations needed to access and manipulate objects of that type; it hides the representation of the type and the algorithms used in the operations. Such a module can be implemented directly in Ada by exporting a (limited) private type, in Modula-2 by exporting an opaque type, and in Java and C++ by a class.

Instances of an abstract data type are abstract objects that behave exactly like those discussed before. In particular, they can be manipulated only by the routines implemented and exported by the abstract data-type module.[6] Such routines may

```
module STACK_HANDLER
exports
        type STACK = ?;
        This is an abstract data-type module; the data structure
        is a secret hidden in the implementation part.
        procedure PUSH (S: in out STACK ; VAL: in integer);
        procedure POP (S: in out STACK ; VAL: out integer);
        function EMPTY (S: in STACK) : BOOLEAN;
          .
          .
          .
end STACK_HANDLER
```

FIGURE 4.12

An abstract data-type module in TDN.

_____

[6]The only syntactic difference in the case of an instance of an abstract data type is that the object to which an operation must be applied is a parameter of the operation.

include those needed to assign an abstract object to a variable and those needed to compare two abstract objects for equality. To simplify the notation, instead of listing these operators among exported routines, we use the conventional operators ":=" and "=" for them and list the operators after the "?" symbol in the type clause. Thus, writing

```
type A_TYPE: ? (:=, =);
```

in a module interface means that clients can assign an object of type A_TYPE to a variable of the same type and can compare two objects of type A_TYPE for equality. If ":=" or "=" is missing in the type declaration, the corresponding operation would not be available to clients.

### Example 4.8

Suppose we are designing a simulation system for a gasoline station. The purpose of the system is to find the "optimal size" (in terms of number of service lines, length of lines, etc.) of the station, given the expected arrival rates of cars, together with their requests for service. Each request for a service is characterized by a certain duration.

We represent each service line (gasoline, car wash, etc.) by an abstract object that represents the cars waiting for their turn to be served. There will be an operation to place a car in a service line, another to extract a car from the line, another to check whether the line is empty, and another to merge two lines associated with the same kind of resource, should the resource provided by one of them be exhausted. The policy is strictly first in, first out for all service lines.

We introduce an abstract data-type module FIFO_CARS that describes FIFO queues of cars. We also assume that cars are described by another abstract data-type module CARS, exporting type CAR, used by FIFO_CARS to perform operations on the cars extracted from the queues. The following is a sketch of module FIFO_CARS:

```
module FIFO_CARS
uses CARS
exports
    type QUEUE : ?;
    procedure ENQUEUE (Q: in out QUEUE; C: in CARS);
    procedure DEQUEUE (Q: in out QUEUE; C: out CARS);
    function IS_EMPTY (Q: in QUEUE): BOOLEAN;
    function LENGTH (Q: in QUEUE): NATURAL;
    procedure MERGE (Q1, Q2: in QUEUE; Q: out QUEUE);
    This is an abstract data-type module representing queues of cars,
    handled in a strict FIFO way; queues are not assignable or checkable
    for equality, since ":=" and "=" are not exported.
    .
    .
    .
end FIFO_CARS
```

This module allows other modules to declare instances of type QUEUE, such as

```
    gasoline_1, gasoline_2, gasoline_3: QUEUE;
    car_wash: QUEUE;
```

and operate on them using the exported operations. For example, we might write

```
ENQUEUE (car_wash, that_car);
MERGE (gasoline_1, gasoline_2, gasoline_3);
```                                                                            ■

There is an important reason for distinguishing between abstract object modules and abstract data-type modules, even though an abstract object can certainly be obtained by generating an instance of the abstract data type encapsulated in the abstract data-type module. The reason is that, intrinsically, an abstract data-type module can generate any number of instances, but we know *a priori* that abstract objects exist in only a single instance. Also, an abstract object module has a state, and an abstract data-type module does not. In an object-oriented framework, however, the two concepts are unified. Abstract data types are implemented by classes. Abstract objects exist only at run time, as instances of an abstract data type.

### Exercise

---

**4.23**  A key-manager module provides a different key every time a key is requested by a client. A key-manager can return keys to its clients, compare them for equality, and determine which of two keys is smaller. Design the key-manager module and describe the design, using TDN.

---

### 4.2.4.3 *Generic modules*

In this section, we present an extension of TDN that provides a powerful tool for writing reusable components. This extension, called generic modules, can be motivated by going back to Example 4.7. In that example, the physical way of storing the values and managing the LIFO structure was hidden from clients through an interface that listed the appropriate operations to be invoked. If we need to evaluate expressions of other types, such as real values or Booleans, we should provide new, specialized modules. All such modules, however, would behave similarly, differing only in the types of the values stored in their stacks.

It would be useful to be able to provide a single (abstract) description for all such modules implementing an abstract object, by factoring all the variations into a single module, instead of duplicating a number of almost identical modules. By providing just one description for all modules, we eliminate the chance (and danger) of having inconsistencies among different modules; moreover, we localize the effect of possible modifications to exactly one unit. What we obtain is a single, highly reusable component.

A solution to this problem is given by enriching TDN to support generic modules. A generic module is a module that is parameterized with respect to a type. In our case, we would write

```
generic module GENERIC_STACK_2 (T)
uses ...
exports
    procedure PUSH (VAL : in T);
    procedure POP_2 (VAL1, VAL2 : out T);
      .
      .
      .
end GENERIC_STACK_2
```

Here, module `GENERIC_STACK_2` is generic with respect to type `T`, and the routines `PUSH` and `POP_2` require parameters of that type. A generic module is not directly usable by clients. In fact, strictly speaking, it is not even a module; rather, it is a *module template*. In order to be used, it must first be instantiated by providing actual parameters. For example, to instantiate a stack module for integers, we write

    **module** `INTEGER_STACK_2` **is** `GENERIC_STACK_2 (INTEGER)`

If there are constraints on the possible types to be sent as parameters at instantiation time, these constraints should be specified via comments in the interface of the generic module.

If the generic module requires its parameter type to support a particular operation, this must be specified in the module header. For example,

```
generic module M(T) with OP(T)
uses ...
         .
         .
         .
end M
```

indicates that the operation `OP` must be supported by any type that is provided to module `M` when it is instantiated. At instantiation time, an actual procedure must be passed as a parameter along with the type, as in the declaration:

    **module** `M_A_TYPE` **is** `M(A_TYPE) PROC (M_A_TYPE)`

As the previous examples have shown, generic modules allow software designers to factor several algorithms into a single, abstract, generic representation that is instantiated before being used. A typical example would be a generic sorting module, which is left parametric with respect to the type of the elements to be sorted. Thus, intrinsically, a generic module is a reusable component, because it factors several modules into a unique algorithmic abstraction that is easily reused in different contexts by simple instantiation.

Similar situations arise in the case of abstract data types, which can often be written as generic modules and then instantiated in various specialized modules. For instance, in Example 4.8, we introduced a module to represent FIFO queues of cars. Suppose now that we wish to model the tellers in a bank, where customers queue up waiting to be served. In both cases we must describe what a queue is, the only difference being the types of items we end up queuing in our abstract objects. Thus, again, we might solve the problem by defining a generic abstract data-type module (call it `GENERIC_FIFO_QUEUE`) and then generating as many module instances as are necessary.

The use of generic modules can be viewed as an application of the principle of generality: Instead of solving a specific problem for, say, integers, we solve a more general problem for a class of types. Special-case solutions can then be derived from the general solution. Viewed in this way, generic modules can be useful for developing families of programs.

## Exercises

**4.24** Define precisely module GENERIC_FIFO_QUEUE, and instantiate a module that represents the abstract data type "queue of integer values." Show how you can then generate an abstract object instance.

**4.25** We have described a generic module as parameterized by types. Propose other possibilities for parameterizing modules.

**4.26** Give an example of a module that allows an array of elements of any type to be sorted. The constraint is that it must be possible to compare elements of such a type to see which is bigger.

### 4.2.5  Some Specific Techniques for Design for Change

So far in this chapter, we have presented a body of general methods that may be used for designing well-structured software—software that can be easily understood and, most important, easily modified. These methods are valuable also for achieving the two significant goals of producing families of programs and generating reusable components. Modularization via information hiding may be used to encapsulate the differences between family members, so that such differences are invisible outside the generic module. Similarly, the definition of simple, nonredundant, and clear interfaces can favor the reuse of modules: To understand whether a component is reusable, one should conform to its interface. As mentioned earlier, reusability is further enhanced by genericity.

As a complement to the general principle of information hiding and the methods we have been discussing so far, the sections that follow illustrate some specific techniques for implementing modules that accommodate change easily.

#### 4.2.5.1 *Configuration constants*

One difficulty with software modifications is that the specific information which is going to change may be hard coded into, and spread throughout, the program. As a simple example, consider the size of an integer table that is initially set to 10, but is required to become 50. The initial system might contain declarations such as

```
a: array (1..10) of integer;
```

if we want a to store a local copy of the table. If we want to check whether an integer k used as an index in the table does not exceed its bounds, the program might contain a statement like

```
if k ≥ 1 and k ≤ 10 then
            perform indexing;
else
            do other actions;
end if;
```

Clearly, changing the upper bound of the array to 50 requires changing both declarations and statements like those just shown. However, in cases where the required changes in software can be factored out into a set of constants (called *configuration constants*), the problem may be solved by changing the values of those constants and then recompiling the program.

Many languages, such as C, Ada, Java, and C++, provide symbolic constants as a simple solution to the problem of making programs easily adaptable to a change of configuration constants. Being constants, configuration data may not be changed inadvertently by the program; being symbolic, they may be given names that suggest their meaning, in order to improve readability and modifiability.

As we mentioned before, configuration constants may be grouped together in a module that provides a common pool of data. This module would then be used by all clients that need to access the configuration data.

Another example of the use of symbolic configuration constants is the case of a device handler in which the lengths of buffers may vary from configuration to configuration. Each configuration may be viewed as a different member of the same family, and different family members may be generated by recompiling the application with different values of configuration constants.

### Exercise

**4.27**  Changing the value of a configuration constant requires recompilation. Is it always necessary to perform a *complete* recompilation (i.e., a compilation of all the modules)? Discuss the issue by giving examples in C, Pascal, Modula-2, Java, C++, or Ada.

### 4.2.5.2  *Conditional compilation*

Configuration constants support only simple ways of representing multiple-version software. More flexible and general schemes may be provided by means of conditional compilation.

With this approach, all versions of a family are represented by one single source copy, and the differences between various versions are taken into account by conditional compilation. Source code that is relevant to only some versions is bracketed by macro commands recognized by the compiler. When the compiler is invoked, some parameters must be specified that describe which version of object code is to be produced; the compiler automatically ignores source statements that are not part of the proper version.

### Example 4.9

Suppose we are requested to write a program in which some parts (e.g., device drivers) must be tailored to a specific hardware configuration. During the design, we try to factor out all parts that do not depend on the specific hardware. If the final program is to be written in the C programming language, we may use the C preprocessor to specify what parts are to be tailored to the chosen hardware architecture. This is a sketchy example of what the C program would look like:

```
            ...source fragment common to all versions...
# ifdef hardware-1
            ...source fragment for hardware 1...
# endif
# ifdef hardware-2
            ...source fragment for hardware 2...
# endif
    .
    .
    .
```

If, at compilation time, we specify the switch `D = hardware-1`, only the code associated with `hardware-1` will be compiled.                                           ▮

### Exercises

**4.28**   Discuss the effectiveness of conditional compilation as the differences between the various versions become complex.

**4.29**   How can you use the generic facility in Ada to carry out the same task as in Example 4.9, without resorting to conditional compilation?

### 4.2.5.3 *Software generation*

Symbolic constants and conditional compilation achieve evolvability by allowing programs to be sufficiently general to cover some anticipated changes and to be able to be specialized at compilation time. Another appealing strategy is to generate automatically a new solution for each requested change.

*Generators* have been used successfully in restricted application domains. A typical example is a compiler generator, such as yacc in the UNIX environment, which can generate (part of) a compiler, given the formal definition of the language to be translated. If we decide to change the source language for which we have developed a compiler, we do not need to modify the compiler directly; rather, we rerun yacc on the newly defined language. This approach is particularly useful when the source language is not frozen yet and is subject to modifications.

Another example is a system for generating user interfaces that can be found in most database management systems on personal computers. In such systems, the layout of the panels used for human-machine interaction is directly "painted" on the computer screen. This declarative description is then automatically transformed into run-time actions that support the interaction of the user with the application. Changing the layout of the screen according to the user's taste can be accomplished quite easily and does not require any coding—just regeneration.

Other examples of software generators will be given in Chapter 5, where we show that certain specification languages may be executable. In some cases, the specification is translated into an implementation, thus generating the application directly from some abstract description. Although this approach is not in common practice today, it is used in restricted domains in many software production environments. We discuss this point further in Chapter 9.

### 4.2.6    Stepwise Refinement

Introductory programming courses often focus the attention of students on systematic approaches to program design and validation. The most popular approach followed is called *design by stepwise refinement*. Such a design strategy is easy to describe and understand.

As its name states clearly, stepwise refinement is an iterative process. At each step, the problem to be solved is decomposed into subproblems that are solved separately. The subsolutions that constitute the solution of the original problem are then linked together by means of simple control structures. They may be executed in a sequence, they may be selected alternatively, or they may be iterated in a loop. Thus, if P is the statement of the original problem, $P_1, P_2, \ldots P_n$ are the statements of the subproblems, and C is a Boolean expression that represents a condition, P may be decomposed and solved according to one of the following patterns:

```
(1)  P1; P2; ...; Pn
(2)  if C then
              P1;
     else
              P2;
     end if;
(3)  while C loop
              P1;
     end loop;
```

Often, we need to express multiple branch selection. Thus, instead of using deeply nested **if** statements, which may adversely affect a program's readability, we may employ a generalized **case** statement:

```
(2') case
              C1: P1;
              C2: P2;
              ...;
              Cn: Pn;
              otherwise P0;
     end case;
```

Each $C_i$ represents a Boolean expression, and all the $C_i$'s are required to be mutually disjoint.

Problem statements at each step of the decomposition are usually given as natural-language-like descriptions. Each refinement step is represented by rewriting the natural-language description in terms of subproblem statements glued together by means of the control structures represented by the foregoing patterns. Subproblem statements, in turn, are made more detailed at the next refinement step.

Thus, the design process starts with an overall description of the problem to be solved (the "top" function), recursively applies functional decomposition, and terminates as we reach the point where each subproblem is easy to express in terms of a few lines of code in the chosen programming language. (In turn, one may view programming-language statements as formal statements of very simple subproblems whose solutions are directly provided by the underlying abstract machine.)

## Example 4.10

As an example, we discuss the derivation of the selection sort algorithm by stepwise refinement. This is a small programming example, not a design exercise. However, the example clearly illustrates how stepwise refinement works. Shortly, we shall see another example in which stepwise refinement is applied at the design level. The selection sort algorithm proceeds as follows:

Step 1

```
let n be the length of the array a to be sorted;
i := 1 ;
while i < n loop
    find the smallest of a_i .. .a_n, and exchange it with the
    element at position i;
    i := i + 1;
end loop;
```

Step 2

```
let n be the length of the array a to be sorted;
i := 1 ;
while i < n loop
    j := n;
    while j > i loop
        if a(i) > a(j) then
            interchange the elements at positions j and i;
        end if;
        j := j - 1;
    end loop;
    i := i + 1;
end loop;
```

Step 3

```
let n be the length of the array a to be sorted;
i := 1 ;
while i < n loop
    j := n;
    while j > i loop
        if a(i) > a(j)then
            x :=a(i); a(i) :=a(j); a(j) := x;
        end if;
        j := j-1;
    end loop;
    i := i + 1;
end loop;
```

■

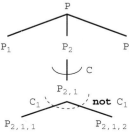

FIGURE 4.13

Graphical representation of stepwise refinement. (Legend: solid arc represents iteration; dotted arc represents selection.)

Design by stepwise refinement can be represented graphically by means of a *decomposition tree* (DT)—a tree in which the root is labeled by the name of the "top" problem, every other node is labeled by the name of a subproblem, and the child nodes of any given node are labeled by the names of the subproblems that detail it in a refinement. The left-to-right order of child nodes of a given node represents the order in which subproblems are to be solved during program execution. Nodes representing alternative subproblems are identified by a dotted line which groups the arcs that connect the nodes to their parent node; arcs are also labeled by the condition under which the connected subproblems must be chosen. Iteration is represented by a solid line, to which the condition governing the **while** structure is added as a label.

For example, Figure 4.13 represents the DT corresponding to the following stepwise refinement:

Step 1

```
P;                              P is the problem to solve.
```

Step 2

```
P₁; P₂; P₃;                     P is decomposed into the
                                   sequence of P₁, followed by P₂,
                                   followed by P₃.
```

Step 3

```
P₁;
while C loop
        P₂,₁;                   P₂ is decomposed into
end loop;                          an iteration.
P₃;
```

Step 4

```
P₁;
while C loop
        if C₁ then              P₂,₁ is decomposed into
            P₂,₁,₁;                a selection.
        else
            P₂,₁,₂;
        end if;
end loop;
P₃;
```

One might wonder about the relationships that obtain between a DT and the graph of the IS_COMPOSED_OF relation or, equivalently, between top-down design achieved through iterative decomposition of a module in terms of its components and stepwise refinement. Indeed, they are similar concepts; but there are differences, too.

For example, suppose you wish to describe the stepwise refinement illustrated in Figure 4.13 in terms of the IS_COMPONENT_OF relation or, more conveniently, in terms of IS_COMPOSED_OF. Let $M, M_1, M_2$, and $M_3$ be the modules that represent $P$, $P_1$, $P_2$, and $P_3$, respectively. Notice that we cannot simply state the relation

```
M IS_COMPOSED_OF {M₁,M₂,M₃}
```

because there would be no component in the system responsible for arranging the sequential flow of execution from $M_1$ to $M_2$ and then $M_3$, which is implicit in Figure 4.13. Thus, we need to introduce an additional control module $M_4$ that acts like a glue to impose the sequential flow from $M_1$ to $M_2$ to $M_3$. This would allow us to state the following relation:

```
M IS_COMPOSED_OF {M₁,M₂,M₃,M₄}
```

In turn, $M_2$ would be decomposed in terms of $M_{2,1}$ (associated with $P_{2,1}$) and $M_{2,2}$, which acts as a control module used to impose iterative use of $M_{2,1}$:

```
M₂ IS_COMPOSED_OF {M₂,₁, M₂,₂}
```

Finally, $M_{2,1}$ would be decomposed into $M_{2,1,1}$, $M_{2,1,2}$ (associated with $P_{2,1,1}$ and $P_{2,1,2}$, respectively), and $M_{2,1,3}$, which acts as a control module performing selection between $M_{2,1,1}$ and $M_{2,1,2}$ according to the value of $C_1$:

```
M₂,₁ IS_COMPOSED_OF {M₂,₁,₁,M₂,₁,₂, M₂,₁,₃}
```

This example shows that a design produced by stepwise refinement may also be described top down in terms of the `IS_COMPOSED_OF` relation. In fact, the method we used may be applied in general to transform one description into the other. The resulting description in terms of `IS_COMPONENT_OF`, however, does not correspond to a meaningful modularization. Actually, stepwise refinement should be considered more a method for describing the logical structure of a given algorithm, implemented by a single module, than a method for describing the decomposition of a system into modules. The description of the sorting program we just gave is an illustration of the virtue of the method when it is applied in the small. A complex and large system cannot be designed and described via stepwise refinement; rather, its design requires decomposition into modules, the separate development of each module, and the consistent application of information hiding.

### Exercises

**4.30**  Describe the USES relation among the modules we introduced to represent the stepwise refinement illustrated in Figure 4.13, and show the module structure, using GDN.

**4.31**  Describe the stepwise refinement of the sort-by-straight-selection example discussed in Example 4.10 in terms of the corresponding decomposition tree.

#### 4.2.6.1 An assessment of stepwise refinement

A common misconception about stepwise refinement is that it can provide a strategy for finding a solution to a problem by suggesting a smooth and almost mechanical way of recursively decomposing the problem into simpler subproblems. This misconception derives from examples of derivations found in some introductory textbooks, where the program seems to come out naturally by stepwise refinement. Contrary to appearances, however, the process of deriving a program often demands creativity and may require that various alternatives be explored before the appropriate solution is found. Take a well-known problem like sorting; it is certainly not by following stepwise refinement carefully that we can invent a good solution like, say, a quicksort, as opposed to, say, a bubblesort or a selection sort!

What is certainly true is that stepwise refinement is an effective way of describing a solution after it has been invented. It is a way of describing—*a posteriori*—the rationale behind an algorithm by positing an ideal and rational process whereby the algorithm is derived. Hence, stepwise refinement can be a good program documentation technique. Furthermore, if code is written by following stepwise refinement systematically, the resulting program is easy to read and understand.

Stepwise refinement is an effective technique for describing small programs. It fails, however, to scale up to systems of even moderate complexity. Thus, stepwise refinement is a method that works in the small, but fails in the large. In particular, it neither matches the goals that information hiding tries to solve nor helps designers reuse components from previous applications or design reusable components for larger programs. Here are a few reasons that explain these shortcomings:

**Subproblems tend to be analyzed in isolation.**   No emphasis is put by stepwise refinement on trying to generalize subproblems in a way that would make them reusable at different points within the derivation of the system, let alone across different designs.

When a problem is to be made more detailed, it is studied in the context of the decomposition subtree in which it appears. On the other hand, when a problem is being decomposed into subproblems, it may be useful to see whether a suitable generalization of the problem would make it similar to another problem being solved elsewhere, so that we can unify the two problems and design a single module for them.

**No attention is paid to information hiding.**   Stepwise refinement does not draw the designer's attention to the need for encapsulating changeable information within modules. In fact, the modules we derive when we apply stepwise refinement are pure procedural abstractions. A problem represented by some abstract function is recursively decomposed into subproblems, all of which are represented by abstract functions.

In stepwise refinement, the strategy never emphasizes the need for grouping together functions to define an abstract object or data type, nor is there a way to derive modules that provide selective export of a collection of resources. The only principle that guides functional decomposition by stepwise refinement is the striving for readability of the resulting solution.

**No attention is paid to data.**   This is a corollary of the previous point. Stepwise refinement does not stress the use of information-hiding modules. For example, the method does not stress the derivation of modules that hide a data structure and export abstract operations to access it.

**The top function may not exist.**   The method starts by stating the top problem, which is recursively detailed in terms of subproblems. A minor, but annoying, issue is that the top problem may be unnatural to state. Remember that the top problem should describe the problem as a very high-level function that transforms the input data into the expected results. Such a function, however, does not always exist.

For example, what is the function performed by a word processor? Clearly, a word processor is a system that reacts to input commands that create text, append or insert new characters into an existing file, and do complex text manipulation in response to commands supplied by the user. Of course, one can always write the top function as "respond to all user commands." but this is of little help in the subsequent decomposition steps.

**There is a premature commitment to the control structures that govern the flow of control among modules.**   The case study of translating the stepwise refinement of Figure 4.13 into a hierarchy of IS_COMPOSED_OF illustrates this point clearly. When $P_2$ is decomposed into the iteration of $P_{2,1}$, two modules are introduced conceptually: $M_{2,1}$ and $M_{2,2}$. $M_{2,1}$ corresponds to $P_{2,1}$; $M_{2,2}$ is just a control module that simply contains the statement

> **while** C **loop** $P_{2,1}$ **end loop**;

to force the repeated execution of $M_{2,1}$. A similar situation then arises in the decomposition of $M_{2,1}$. The concept is further emphasized by Example 4.11.

## Example 4.11

Suppose we are designing a program to check the syntactic correctness of programs written in a given computer language. In accordance with stepwise refinement, we may write the following:

Step 1
```
Recognize a program stored in a given file f;
```

Step 2
```
correct:= true;
analyze f according to the language definition;
if correct then
      print message "program correct";
else
      print message "program incorrect";
end if;
```

Step 3
```
correct:= true;
perform lexical analysis:
    store the program as a sequence of tokens in file f_t and the
    symbol table in file f_s, and set the Boolean variable
    error_in_lexical_phase according to the result of lexical
    analysis;
if error_in_lexical_phase then
    correct:= true;
else
    perform syntactic analysis on file f_t and set the
    Boolean variable error_in_syntactic_phase according to the
    result of the analysis;
    if error_in_syntactic_phase then
            correct:= false;
    end if;
end if;
if correct then
      print message "program correct";
else
      print message "program incorrect";
end if;
```

Without proceeding any further with the example, we can see that we have made strong commitments about the flow of control from the early stages of our development.

For example, we decided that lexical analysis should come first, that it should operate on the entire input program, and that it should produce the corresponding sequence of tokens in an intermediate file, to be used by the subsequent phase of syntactic analysis.

Suppose now that we decide to change strategy; for example, we decide that we do not want to perform recognition in two passes, but we wish to let the syntactic analyzer drive the process. In this case, the syntactic analyzer repeatedly activates the lexical analyzer, asking for the next token. This change has a profound impact on the structure of the program as described by stepwise refinement: Everything must be redone, starting from Step 3.

The impact of this change would not be so dramatic, however, if we followed an approach based on information hiding—for example, by defining the following sample modules:

- CHAR_HOLDER: hides the physical representation of the input file and exports an operation for accessing the source file on a character-by-character basis;
- SCANNER: hides the details of the lexical structure of the language from the rest of the system and exports an operation for providing the next token in the sequence;
- PARSER: hides the data structure used to perform syntactic analysis (the parse tree), which might be encapsulated in an internal abstract-object module (PARSER). ■

### Exercise

---

**4.32** Complete the design of the language recognizer. Use both TDN and GDN to describe your design. Describe what changes are needed to transform a two-pass solution into a one-pass solution.

---

## 4.2.7     Top-Down Versus Bottom-Up Design

What strategy should we follow when we design a system? Should we proceed from the top down, by recursively applying decomposition through IS_COMPOSED_OF, until we break down the system into manageable components? Or should we proceed from the bottom up, starting from what we wish to encapsulate within a module, recursively defining an abstract interface, and then grouping together several modules to form a new, higher level module that comprises them?

Stepwise refinement is an intrinsically top-down method. Some of the criticisms we raised about the method are attributable to its specific characteristics. In particular, the premature commitment to control structures and the orientation to design in the small are due to the programming-language-based style used to describe the refinements. Other major criticisms, however, apply to the top-down strategy in general. Among these are the facts that subproblems tend to be analyzed in isolation, that no emphasis is placed on the identification of commonalities or on reusability of components, and that little attention is paid to data and, more generally, to information hiding.

Information hiding proceeds mainly from the bottom up. It suggests that we should first recognize what we wish to encapsulate within a module and then provide an abstract interface to define the module's boundaries as seen from the clients. Note, however, that the decision of what to hide inside a module (such as the decision to hide certain policies) may depend on the result of some top-down design activity. Since information hiding has proven to be highly effective in supporting design for change, program families, and reusable components, its bottom-up philosophy should be followed in a consistent way.

Design, however, is a highly critical and creative human activity. Good designers do not proceed in either a strictly top-down or strictly bottom-up fashion. For example, should they decide to proceed from the top down, they also tend to pay attention to identifying commonalities and possible reusable components (i.e., they combine a predominantly top-down strategy with a bottom-up attitude).

A typical design strategy may proceed partly from the top down and partly from the bottom up, depending on the phase of the design or the nature of the application being designed, in a way that might be called *yo-yo design*. As an example, we might start decomposing a system from the top down in terms of subsystems and, at some later point, synthesize subsystems in terms of a hierarchy of information-hiding modules.

The top-down approach, however, is often useful as a way to document a design. Even though the design activity should not be constrained to proceed according to a fixed, rigid pattern, but should be a blend of top-down and bottom-up steps, we recommend that the *description* of the resulting design be given in a top-down fashion. Such descriptions make it easier to understand the system because they give the big picture first before showing the supporting details.

## 4.3 HANDLING ANOMALIES

A systematic design approach followed by a rigorous and disciplined implementation is the best way of dominating the complexity of software development and building reliable products. Unfortunately, software products can be quite complex, subjecting software production to human fallibility. No matter how careful we are during development, we cannot trust our software unconditionally. This lack of complete trust can be frustrating to the conscientio us programmer who must be aware of the criticality of many applications, for which the effect of a program failure may lead to disastrous consequences.

Any engineering product, from bridges to airplanes to software, is prone to failure. The designer must anticipate failures and plan to either avoid or tolerate them. That is, the designer must employ *defensive design*. He or she should try to shield the application from errors that may creep in during development or that may arise due to adverse circumstances during program execution. We must build *robust* systems: Our programs should continue to behave reasonably even in unexpected circumstances.

We define a module to be *anomalous* if it fails to provide a service as expected and as specified in its interface. So far, our design descriptions—whether textual or graphical—are mainly syntactic in nature and do not support a formal description of the semantics of the services exported by a module. A semantic enrichment of the notation may be given according to the concepts we shall discuss in Chapter 5. For simplicity, we assume here that semantics is specified by means of comments appearing in the interface, as explained in Section 4.2.3. We do, however, extend our design notations to associate a set of exceptions (defined next) with each service exported by a module. The *exceptions* associated with a service denote the anomalies that may occur while that service is being performed. For simplicity, we assume that the services exported by a module correspond to routines; what we say here, however, may be restated for other types of services.

Either a module executes correctly, in which case it performs the requested service and returns to the client in a normal way, or it enters an anomalous state. Defensive design requires that in the latter case the module should signal the anomaly by *raising an exception* to the client. In other words, we distinguish between the correct behavior and the anomalous behavior of the module. If something goes wrong and the module cannot complete the requested service correctly, it should return with an indication of the anomalous situation by raising an exception, which may be viewed as an event that is signaled to the client. The server module terminates execution, and the client, notified of the occurrence of the exception, responds by suitably handling the exception.

Why should a module M fail to provide its service as specified? Following what we said in Section 4.2.2, this may happen because M's client does not satisfy the required protocol for invoking one of M's services. For example, M's exported operation op requires a positive parameter, but the client may invoke op with a negative value for the parameter. Failure also may occur if M does not satisfy the required protocol when trying to use a service exported by another module—say, N. In the latter case, N's failure is signaled back to M, and M's *exception handler* is activated accordingly. The handler may try to recover from the anomaly, or it may simply do some cleanup of the module's state and then let the routine fail, signaling an exception to its caller.

If the recovery is successful, M does not fail; otherwise, some cleanup may be necessary to ensure that subsequent uses of M by other clients do not find the module in an inconsistent state. Note, however, that exception handlers are hidden in the module's body; that is, the exact way an exception is handled by a module is part of the module's secret. Therefore, we do not go deeply into the issue here. We do not examine how signaled exceptions are bound to handlers or what happens if a client module does not possess a handler for the signaled exception. These issues are very much dependent on the programming language we choose for the implementation. From a design point of view, the important point is that clients of a module can determine from its interface what exceptions they may expect from the module. In a robust system, clients anticipate and handle all possible exceptions that may be raised by server modules that they use.

Apart from these types of failures, a module may fail to provide its service because of an unforeseen condition, such as an overflow or an array index that is out of bounds, occurring during execution of the module. In the latter case, we assume that the underlying abstract machine is able to trap the abnormal condition and pass it on to the software for appropriate handling. Many programming languages are also capable of detecting and reporting the violation of logical-correctness assertions during execution. Once such violations are passed to the software, they may be treated as

```
module M
exports ...
        procedure P (X: INTEGER; ...)
            raises X_NON_NEGATIVE_EXPECTED,
                INTEGER_OVERFLOW;
                X is to be positive; if not, exception
                X_NON_NEGATIVE_EXPECTED is raised;
                INTEGER_OVERFLOW is raised if internal
                computation of P generates an overflow
        .
        .
        .

end M
```

FIGURE 4.14

A partial module interface, including exceptions.

```
module L
uses M imports P (X: INTEGER;..)
exports ...;
        procedure R (...)
                raises INTEGER_OVERFLOW;
        .
        .
        .

implementation
        If INTEGER_OVERFLOW is raised when P is invoked, the
        exception is propagated
        .
        .
        .

end L
```

FIGURE 4.15

A design fragment with a propagated exception.

were the previous types of exceptions. In addition, it is possible to specify that certain conditions should be treated as exceptions that deserve special treatment on the client's side after they are detected by the server module.

In the discussion that follows, we extend TDN interface descriptions so that a list of exception names may be associated with exported services. These are the names of exceptions that may be raised by the service to signal its anomalous completion.

Let us give some examples. Suppose that when interfaces are defined, designers agree on certain restrictions that apply to parameters of a procedure P enclosed in some module M. For example, they might agree that P should receive a nonnegative value for parameter X. This decision is recorded in M's interface as a comment. (See Figure 4.14.) Of course, in a perfect world, there is no reason to suspect that client modules do not satisfy this requirement. Defensive design, however, requires that we not trust clients to behave properly and that we therefore protect M by sending back an exception if P is called with a negative value for X.

As another example, consider Figure 4.15, in which module L uses module M of Figure 4.14. Should the exception INTEGER_OVERFLOW occur when procedure P is called by procedure R of L, we might decide that R's handler will do some cleanup and bookkeeping and then raise an appropriate exception (perhaps INTEGER_OVERFLOW again) to be handled by M's client. The same policy might also be followed by the client, and so on. Indeed, this can be a way of performing an organized shutdown of the system as a consequence of an unrecoverable error.

From the fragment of Figure 4.15, we observe that L does not raise an exception corresponding to the condition X_NON_NEGATIVE_EXPECTED, which may be raised by P. This means that either L guarantees that the exception never arises or L will recover from it.

### Exercises

**4.33** Define the interface of a module that implements the abstract data-type STACK, where operation pop raises an exception if called to operate on an empty stack.

**4.34** Suppose we are asked to build a cross-reference table for the variables appearing in a program. A cross-reference program is an aid to reconstructing documentation from other programs that are, by assumption, correct. Thus, according to the specification, it should never happen that a variable is used without or before being declared. For simplicity, we assume that the language does not provide rules specifying the scope of variables: All variable names are global.

We design a cross-reference table module CRT—an abstract object—that exports two operations: (1) Procedure NOTIFY is called to insert a variable's name in the table, along with the number of the line on which the declaration of the variable occurred. (2) Procedure OCCUR is called to record the occurrence of a variable in a statement, by specifying the variable's name and the number of the line on which the variable occurs.

As part of the contract with client modules, we specify in the interface that NOTIFY cannot be called if a variable with the same name is already in the cross-reference table. Also, OCCUR can be called only if the variable we are transmitting as a parameter has already been declared (i.e., it was in the cross-reference table). These protocols are consistent with the assumption that the source program is correct.

Design a robust CRT module and provide its TDN description. Implement your design in a programming language of your choice, assuming that suitable other modules drive CRT. Discuss the pros and cons of the language as far as exception handling is concerned.

**4.35** Compare and contrast the exception-handling facilities of C++ and Java. Is it possible in one of these languages for a client module to not have a handler for an exception that it may encounter? Which language enforces defensive design?

## 4.4    A CASE STUDY IN DESIGN

In this section, we illustrate the concepts presented in the previous sections in the context of a case study in design. Our goal is not to provide a general recipe of "what makes a good design." Design is a creative activity that cannot be done mechanically; it requires human insight and experience. Accordingly, we examine here a hypothetical design process in action, showing some of the problems that may arise in practice and discussing examples of what makes a good module.

Let us consider a small group of software engineers designing the compiler of yet another programming language: MIDI is considerably more complex than the MINI language of Example 4.1 and Example 4.6 and is an ALGOL-like, block-structured pro-

```
module   SYMBOL_TABLE
         Supports up to MAX_DEPTH block nesting levels
uses ...imports (IDENTIFIER, DESCRIPTOR)
exports procedure INSERT (ID: in IDENTIFIER;
                          DESCR: in DESCRIPTOR);
        procedure RETRIEVE (ID: in IDENTIFIER;
                          DESCR: out DESCRIPTOR);
        procedure LEVEL (ID: in IDENTIFIER; L: out INTEGER);
        procedure ENTER_SCOPE;
        procedure EXIT_SCOPE;
        procedure INIT (MAX_DEPTH: in INTEGER);
end SYMBOL_TABLE
```

FIGURE 4.16

TDN fragment representing the initial version of the symbol table interface.

gramming language. The overall design of Example 4.6 is supposed to be valid here, too, and is not discussed any more. In what follows, we concentrate our attention on the design of the module SYMBOL_TABLE. The designers agree on the following design decisions, which affect module interfaces: First, SYMBOL_TABLE's operations are invoked only as long as the program is syntactically and semantically correct. In particular, blocks are correctly bracketed by **begin, end** pairs, no two identifiers with the same name appear in the same block, and each variable is declared before being used. Second, for reasons of style, the maximum depth of block nesting is predefined, and programs with a nesting level higher than the predefined value are considered erroneous.

SYMBOL_TABLE is an abstract object that hides the physical data structure used to represent the table it creates. Its interface is tentatively represented by the TDN fragment in Figure 4.16. According to the figure, client modules may insert an identifier, along with its attributes, into the table via procedure INSERT. Clients are also allowed to retrieve the attributes of previously recorded identifiers via procedure RETRIEVE. Attributes are supposed to be stored in a descriptor. Operations are available to signal when a new lexical scope is entered (via procedure ENTER_SCOPE) and when a scope is exited (via procedure EXIT_SCOPE). An operation (LEVEL) is available to compute the lexical nesting level of an identifier. The level is zero if the identifier is declared locally—that is, in the most recently entered, and not yet exited, scope; the level is one if the identifier is nonlocal and declared in the previously entered scope; and so on.

The designers of the MIDI compiler soon realize that the current version of the SYMBOL_TABLE interface is not satisfactory. The assumption of syntactic and semantic program correctness and the assumption that the maximum depth of block nesting levels should not be exceeded might be violated by an incorrect behavior of client modules. Consequently, to improve the compiler's robustness, it is decided that illegal invocations should raise an exception. This improvement in the design of SYMBOL_TABLE's interface has the additional benefit of making the module reusable

```
module SYMBOL_TABLE
uses ...imports (IDENTIFIER, DESCRIPTOR)
exports
        Supports up to MAX_DEPTH block nesting levels; INIT
        must be called before any other operation is invoked
        procedure INSERT (ID: in IDENTIFIER;
                          DESCR: in DESCRIPTOR)
                          raises MULTIPLE_DEF,
        procedure RETRIEVE (ID: in IDENTIFIER;
                          DESCR: out DESCRIPTOR)
                          raises NOT_VISIBLE;
        procedure LEVEL (ID: in IDENTIFIER;
                          L: out INTEGER)
                          raises NOT_VISIBLE;
        procedure ENTER_SCOPE raises EXTRA_LEVELS;
        procedure EXIT_SCOPE raises EXTRA_END;
        procedure INIT (MAX_DEPTH: in INTEGER);
end SYMBOL_TABLE
```

FIGURE 4.17

TDN fragment representing a revised version of the symbol table interface.

in other contexts, in which the assumptions of syntactic and semantic correctness do not hold. In conclusion, the following design decisions are adopted:

1. Operation INSERT raises an exception if insertion cannot be accomplished because an identifier with the same name already exists in the current scope.
2. Operations RETRIEVE and LEVEL raise an exception if an identifier with the specified name is not currently visible.
3. Operation ENTER_SCOPE raises an exception if the maximum nesting depth is exceeded;
4. Operation EXIT_SCOPE raises an exception if no matching block entry exists.

Based on these three points, the designers produce a revised version of the SYMBOL_TABLE interface, shown by the fragment in Figure 4.17.

Let us now follow the job of the designer of SYMBOL_TABLE. The program's block structure requires that information concerning the various scopes be allocated and deallocated according to a LIFO policy. Thus, when a new scope is entered, a new block of descriptors is allocated, and the block is deallocated upon exit from the scope. We can, therefore, use a stack for storing descriptors. Thanks to the information on the maximum nesting level, the designer decides to implement the stack as an array (of size MAX_DEPTH) of lists, each list representing the declarations occurring in a block in terms of <identifier, descriptor> pairs.

Defining a list is not a new problem for our designer. She has faced the same problem over and over—redefining a new list from scratch every time it is needed—and this is quite frustrating! Thus, the designer decides to define a rather general list-handling module that will be reusable in future designs.

LIST is designed as a generic abstract data type. Being generic, it can be instantiated to a module that handles a list of elements of any specific type. Being an abstract data type, it allows several list objects to be instantiated. A tentative version of the module's interface is shown by the TDN fragment of Figure 4.18.

LIST exports a SEARCH procedure that searches the list to find an element that "matches" a given parameter. In the SYMBOL_TABLE example, since T is an

```
generic module LIST(T) with MATCH (EL_1, EL_2: in T)
exports
        type LINKED_LIST:?;
        procedure IS_EMPTY (L: in LINKED_LIST): BOOLEAN;
        Tells whether the list is empty.
        procedure SET_EMPTY (L: in out LINKED_LIST);
        Sets a list to empty.
        procedure INSERT (L: in out LINKED_LIST; EL: in T);
        Inserts the element into the list
        procedure SEARCH (L: in LINKED_LIST; EL_1: in T;
                     EL_2: out T; FOUND: out boolean);
                Searches L to find an element EL_2 that
                matches EL_1 and returns the result in FOUND.
        end LIST(T)
```

FIGURE 4.18

TDN fragment representing the initial version of the interface for a list-handling module.

<identifier, descriptor> pair, two elements of type T match if their identifiers are the same. In general, what "match" means should be specified by a procedure associated with the formal parameter T and sent as an actual parameter when the module is instantiated. Also, the module provides a procedure INSERT to store an element of type T. Where the element is actually stored is not specified in the interface: It may be at the beginning of the list, at the end, or at any intermediate point (e.g., in order to keep the list sorted). The choice is thus left to the implementation.

### Exercises

**4.36**  Consider the design of module SYMBOL_TABLE shown in Figure 4.16. Consider a MIDI program in which the number of **begin** symbols is greater than the number of **end** symbols. Clearly, the program is syntactically incorrect. How does the module of Figure 4.16 behave in this case? How can you improve the design to deal with such a situation?

**4.37**  The module SYMBOL_TABLE shown in Figure 4.16 requires client modules to follow a precise protocol in the invocation of the exported services. (INIT must be called before any other operation.) How can this policy be enforced through SYMBOL_TABLE's interface via exceptions?

## 4.5    CONCURRENT SOFTWARE

So far, we have implicitly assumed that the application we are designing has a single stream of execution (also called *thread of control*)—that is, that it is a purely sequential system. With the proliferation of networked computers and other computing devices such as personal digital assistants, many applications must deal with multiple threads of control, and the consequence is additional complexity of both design and analysis. Such classes of applications are increasingly important, and they deserve special treatment. Usually, they are studied as a separate topic in the courses and textbooks on operating systems, distributed systems, or real-time systems. Here, we examine the fundamental characteristics of these applications in relation to other types of software and show how the previously examined design techniques are affected by concurrency.

One of the key problems in designing concurrent software is to ensure the consistency of data that are shared among concurrently executing modules. We discuss this problem and solutions to it in Section 4.5.1. We then consider two particular classes of concurrent software: real-time software, in Section 4.5.2, and distributed software, in Section 4.5.3.

### 4.5.1    Shared Data

We can generalize the concepts of modularity we have studied thus far to the case where we have an abstract object that is accessed by more than one sequential activity (or *process*)[7] at a time. For example, suppose we have the abstract object BUFFER of

---

[7]In general, one should distinguish between threads and processes (i.e., sequential activities within a given name space or in different name spaces). For our purposes, we may ignore this distinction.

type QUEUE of characters. This object might be an instance of a type obtained by first instantiating the generic type of Figure 4.19, that is,

    **module** QUEUE_OF_CHAR **is** GENERIC_FIFO_QUEUE (CHAR)

and then instantiating a variable

    BUFFER: QUEUE_OF_CHAR.QUEUE;

assuming that QUEUE is the name of the type exported by GENERIC_QUEUE and using dot notation to specify the selection of a resource exported by a specific instance.

    We assume here that the following operations on objects of type QUEUE of characters are available:

- PUT: inserts a character in a QUEUE;
- GET: extracts a character from a QUEUE;
- NOT_FULL: returns **true** if its QUEUE parameter is not full;[8]
- NOT_EMPTY: returns **true** if its QUEUE parameter is not empty.

    Object BUFFER is accessed concurrently by client processes that produce characters (say, PRODUCER_1, PRODUCER_2, etc.) and call operation PUT to insert a new character into the buffer. BUFFER is also accessed concurrently by client processes that remove characters (say, CONSUMER_1, CONSUMER_2, etc.), and call procedure GET to extract one character from the buffer. Assume that operation PUT may be called only if the buffer is not full and that operation GET may be called only if the buffer is not empty.

    To use the module BUFFER correctly, we might try to embed calls to GET and PUT issued from the clients into the following structures:

(i)  **if** QUEUE_OF_CHAR.NOT_FULL (BUFFER) **then**
        QUEUE_OF_CHAR.PUT (X,BUFFER);
   **end if**;

(ii) **if** QUEUE_OF_CHAR.NOT_EMPTY (BUFFER) **then**
        QUEUE_OF_CHAR.GET (X,BUFFER);
   **end if**;

    Unfortunately, this approach does not suffice to access the buffer correctly, for it may happen that CONSUMER_1 checks the buffer and does not find it empty. Thus, it chooses to enter the **then** branch and gets ready to perform a GET. Before it actually executes GET, however, CONSUMER_2 also checks the buffer and finds it nonempty; it, too, enters the **then** branch and gets ready to perform a GET. If BUFFER initially contained only one character, we reach an invalid state in which two authorizations to GET a character have been issued. This will certainly lead to an error during execution.

---

[8]We assume that queues have a finite capacity. Unbounded queues are similar (and simpler) to deal with. They do not require this operation.

**Exercise**

---

**4.38** Suppose that the code implementing operation PUT contains the statement TOT := TOT + 1, TOT being the total number of buffered characters, while operation GET contains the statement TOT := TOT - 1. Suppose also that PRODUCER_1 and CON-SUMER_2 are concurrently performing PUT and GET on the buffer. Show that the system may enter an invalid state.

---

The BUFFER example illustrates the need for *synchronization* of concurrent activities. Two concurrent activities proceed in parallel as long as their actions do not interfere with one another. But if they need to cooperate or compete for access to a shared resource, such as BUFFER in the example, then they cannot simply proceed independently and must synchronize their actions.

There are several ways to effect synchronization of processes. One is to ensure that any shared resource the processes access is used in *mutual exclusion*. This means that when a process is executing a PUT (or a GET), no other process should be allowed to access BUFFER; otherwise an error, as in Exercise 4.38, might arise. Also, the structure containing operations (i) and (ii) shows that when a consumer executes operation (ii), it should access the object in mutual exclusion; that is, no other process should be allowed to execute any other operation on the shared buffer. The same holds if a producer executes operation (i).

More generally, operations that affect the internal state of a shared object should always be executed in mutual exclusion, so that they leave the object in a consistent state. The same holds for sequences of operations that test the value of an object and possibly modify the value, depending on the result of the test.

The problem of accessing shared data in a concurrent environment is actually a generalization of the same problem in the sequential environment. Variables that are shared among modules in a sequential environment also require special care, because two successive calls to a module M may observe different values of a variable due to an intervening call to M issued by some other module. This arrangement may be intentional (in the case of an abstract object), or it may be an error. In the sequential environment, such interactions of modules are explicit in the design of the application.

In a concurrent environment, however, the interactions are dependent not only on the design of the application, but also on the particular implementation of concurrency in the execution system. This additional difficulty is due to the fact that the order of execution of operations (e.g., accesses to the shared data) cannot in general be determined at the time the program is written, but rather depends on the speed of execution of the various tasks. Indeed, different tasks may be executed on different processors and exhibit different speeds during different executions of the application.

The potential problems we observed in the case of producers and consumers concurrently accessing the same buffer are due to the unfortunate occurrences of particular sequences of actions. It may happen that the system works correctly in the majority of executions, but when the actions occur in some particular sequence, the system fails. Different sequences of actions in the access to the buffer may correspond to different speeds of execution of processes.

There are several ways of influencing the speed of execution of processes. First, processes may share the same processor, and the scheduler may assign them a fixed slice of processing time periodically. Or, alternatively, some processes may have a higher priority than others. Or each process may run on a separate, dedicated physical processor. In these three cases, the speed of execution of the processes is subject to variation.

We would like to be able to design our software in a way that its correct behavior is ensured, independently of the speed of execution of processes. The system should have the same correct behavior whether it is executed on a uniprocessor or a multiprocessor, whether the time-shared uniprocessor uses fixed time slices or priorities, and so on. This would make our solution more general, allowing it to work for a family of implementations of the underlying abstract machines. Thus, changing the underlying abstract machine would affect only the *performance* of the software, not its correctness. Also, reasoning about the correctness of the design would be easier, since the design could be assessed without taking execution speeds of processes into consideration.

To do this, we extend the concepts and the notation of abstract objects and abstract data types to the case of concurrent software. In particular, we follow two common paradigms of concurrent software design. These paradigms, in turn, are reflected in the constructs provided by some existing concurrent programming languages.

The first approach, inspired by the Concurrent Pascal programming language and now popularized by Java, leads to the notions of *monitors*, which represent concurrently accessed objects as protected passive entities. We shall call this approach *monitor based*. The second approach, inspired by the Ada programming language, leads to the concept of a *resource guardian*, which is used to represent a concurrent active object. The mechanism used for synchronization is called rendezvous, and thus we call this approach *rendezvous based*.

Although the approach chosen for describing a software design is independent of the implementation language, the mapping of a design onto a program is more direct if the two are based on the same philosophy. Certain design structures (e.g., a rendezvous-based design) are easier to map onto a certain language (e.g., Ada). Also, considerably more effort goes into the implementation if the language we use is sequential, and concurrency must then be achieved via calls to the underlying operating system.

### 4.5.1.1 Monitors

A *monitor* is an abstract object that may be accessed in a concurrent environment. The monitor guarantees to its clients that the operations it exports are executed in mutual exclusion. If a process P requests the execution of an operation in a monitor while another process is already executing an operation in the same monitor, the monitor suspends the execution of P. Execution is resumed only when P can gain exclusive access to the operations of the monitor.

From the clients' viewpoint, mutual exclusion is guaranteed by the monitor through its interface; the way it is actually provided by the monitor depends on the monitor's implementation. If we implement our system in a language like Concurrent

Pascal or Java, mutual exclusion can be guaranteed directly by the language. If the language does not provide any automatic way of enforcing mutual exclusion, then we must guarantee it in implementing our application.

Of course, mutual exclusion in the execution of individual operations is not sufficient to guarantee correctness in the access to shared objects. As we saw earlier, two consumers may invoke operation NOT_EMPTY to check whether the buffer is not empty, and both may be authorized to perform the removal of a character. If the buffer originally contained a single character, the second attempt to remove a character would generate an erroneous state.

To solve problems of this kind, we extend our textual design notation by permitting exported operations to be coupled with an optional **requires** clause. As viewed by clients, this clause is automatically checked when the operation is called. If its result is **true**, then the operation is executed normally, but in mutual exclusion. If the result is **false**, the process issuing the call is suspended and waits for the condition to become **true**. Suspension of the process releases the mutual exclusion that was previously acquired, so that other processes may be allowed to enter the monitor. At some point, a process executing some monitor operation might cause the condition on which other processes were suspended to become **true**. Such processes would then become eligible for resumption; when resumed, a process executes the operation in mutual exclusion, as if it had requested the operation just then. In this way, testing the **requires** clause and executing the associated operation result in an atomic action.

If we choose—say—Java as a programming language, all the suspensions and resumptions needed to handle the **requires** clause properly are automatically provided by the monitor implementation. If we use a sequential programming language, mutual exclusion and the **requires** clause may be implemented by appropriate calls to the operating system.

Figure 4.20 is an example of a monitor representing a buffer of characters. We simply add the keyword **concurrent** to specify the monitor's semantics for the module.

Monitor types can be defined accordingly and can be generic. An example of a generic monitor type representing FIFO queues of any component type is illustrated in Figure 4.19.

Operations exported by a monitor may raise exceptions, and the syntax for specifying the exception associated with an operation is the same as before. For example, in the case of the CHAR_BUFFER monitor, suppose that the interface specifies that the character sent to PUT should satisfy some constraint. The specification of PUT would then be modified to read

```
procedure PUT (C: in CHAR) requires NOT_FULL
        raises PAR_ERROR;
```

where PAR_ERROR is the exception raised by PUT if the parameter does not satisfy the constraints specified in the interface.

We conclude our brief discussion of monitors and monitor types at this point, without trying to add details to our design notation. Going into details would raise several critical issues that would make our notation more intricate and more programming-language oriented.

```
concurrent module CHAR_BUFFER
    This is a monitor (i.e., an abstract object module in a
    concurrent environment.)
uses ...
exports
    procedure PUT (C: in CHAR) requires NOT_FULL;
    procedure GET (C: out CHAR) requires NOT_EMPTY;
    NOT_EMPTY and NOT_FULL are hidden Boolean
    functions yielding TRUE if the buffer is not empty and not
    full, respectively. They are not exported as operations,
    because their purpose is only to delay the calls to PUT and
    GET if they are issued when the buffer is in a state where it
    cannot accept them.
        .
        .
        .
end CHAR_BUFFER
```

FIGURE 4.19

Example of a monitor in TDN.

```
generic concurrent module   GENERIC_FIFO_QUEUE (EL)
    This is a generic monitor type (i.e., an abstract data type
    accessed in a concurrent environment.)
uses ...
exports
    type QUEUE: ?;
    procedure PUT (Q1:in out QUEUE; E1: in EL)
        requires NOT_FULL (Q1: QUEUE);
    procedure GET (Q2:in out QUEUE; E2: out EL)
        requires NOT_EMPTY(Q2: QUEUE);
        .
        .
        .
end GENERIC FIFO_QUEUE (EL)
```

FIGURE 4.20

Example of a monitor type in TDN.

## Exercise

**4.39** Extend GDN by providing a graphical notation for monitors and monitor types.

### 4.5.1.2 *Guardians and the rendezvous*

The monitor-based approach to the design of concurrent software views a software system as composed of two kinds of entities: active entities (i.e., processes), which have independent threads of control, and passive objects. Passive objects may be either instances of an abstract type or single-instance abstract objects. Passive objects may be shared among processes or may be used as private resources by a process. A shared object must be either a monitor or an instance of a monitor type; otherwise, there would be no guarantee that access to the object would preserve a consistent state.

As we anticipated, there are other paradigms for the design of a concurrent system. One such paradigm is exemplified by the approach taken by the Ada programming language. In this approach, private objects are the only passive entities of a system. Active objects come in two "flavors": processes, as before (called *tasks* in Ada), and *guardians* of shared resources.

Guardians are themselves tasks whose sole purpose is to guarantee orderly access to a hidden secret representing an encapsulated resource, possibly a data structure. Guardians are never-ending tasks that await requests to perform some operation. A guardian may or may not accept a request, depending on some condition based on the internal state of the resource controlled by the guardian. A guardian accepts requests one at a time.

A task issuing a request to a guardian becomes suspended until the guardian accepts the request and completes execution of the associated action Following Ada terminology, this form of interaction between a task and a guardian is called a *rendezvous*.

The same syntactic notation we gave before in the case of the monitor-based approach may be used to describe a rendezvous-based design approach. What changes, of course, is the semantics. As an example, take the concurrent module CHAR_BUFFER of Figure 4.20. If we interpret the design notation in the context of the rendezvous-based approach, CHAR_BUFFER is a task that accepts requests to operate on its guarded state by performing either a GET or a PUT. A GET request is accepted only if the buffer is not empty; a PUT request is accepted only if the BUFFER is not full. A task issuing one of these requests (via a suitable call) is suspended until the request is fulfilled by the guardian—that is, until the guardian finds the **when** clause true, decides to respond to the request, and executes the body of the request. The guardian repeatedly accepts valid requests in a never-ending loop.

To clarify these issues, one may assume that, in a rendezvous-based language, the internals of module CHAR_BUFFER might look like the sketchy program of Figure 4.21. The program, written in a self-explaining Ada-like style, describes the structure of a guardian implementing the CHAR_BUFFER concurrent module of Figure 4.20. The example shows that the guardian repeatedly checks for requests from clients.

Both the monitor-based approach and the rendezvous-based approach provide *nondeterministic* solutions to concurrency problems. The CHAR_BUFFER guardian is specified as a server accepting requests to access the buffer, either to add new characters to it or to remove characters from it. Requests to add new characters are accepted if the buffer is not full; similarly, requests to extract symbols from the buffer are honored if the buffer is not empty. From the client's viewpoint, when the buffer is neither full nor empty, pending requests (if any) are handled nondeterministically, as is suggested by the **select ... or ... end select** construct of Figure 4.21. Note that we do not specify what happens when several requests of the same kind (e.g., GET) are issued to the same guardian. Here, too, we may assume that the choice of which request to fulfill is made nondeterministically.[9] Similarly, in the monitor-based approach, several processes may be waiting for the mutual exclusion condition to be released. Which of them is actually resumed when the monitor is freed? Finally,

---

[9]Actually, Ada says that these requests must be handled in a first-in, first-out fashion.

```
loop
    select
        when NOT_FULL
            accept PUT (C: in CHAR);
            This is the body of PUT; the client calls it as if it
            were a normal procedure
            end;
        or
        when NOT_EMPTY
            accept GET (C: out CHAR);
            This is the body of GET; the client calls it as if it
            were a normal procedure
            end;
    end select;
end loop;
```

FIGURE 4.21

Typical internal structure of a guardian task.

if some processes are suspended on a **requires** clause and the condition becomes true, which of them is chosen?

In all these cases, the module's behavior, as viewed by its clients, is nondeterministic. That is, the interface does not reveal how the module actually makes its choices. Nondeterminism is an important property at the specification level, because it is independent of particular implementations of concurrency. Thus, our design is not sensitive to the ways the nondeterminism is resolved later. The programming language we use to implement the system may make specific choices where we have left things nondeterministic, and other choices may be made by the abstract machine that supports the execution of the programming language. Whatever choices are made by the implementation, the system will be correct, and only its performance will be affected. Avoiding nondeterminism at the specification level forces the designer to overspecify the behavior of the system, constraining implementations unnecessarily.

In designing a concurrent system, special care is needed to prevent certain undesirable anomalous situations from occurring during execution, which would cause the entire system (or a subsystem) to become blocked indefinitely. This anomalous situation is called a *deadlock*. For example, consider the case where a process A is suspended on a **requires** X clause of a monitor. Suppose that the only way for X to become true is to have another process B execute another fragment of code. But process B is also blocked on a **requires** clause Y of some monitor, and the only way for Y to become true is to have process A terminate its call to the monitor and execute a certain fragment of code that follows the call to the monitor. Processes A and B are thus blocked indefinitely. They wait for each other to proceed further in their respective computations. Chapters 5 and 6 discuss how anomalous situations of this kind may be detected. Detection may be performed by first providing a formal model for the software architecture and then applying suitable analysis methods to the formal model. For example, we shall illustrate Petri nets as a formal notation in which a concurrent architecture of this kind may be modeled, and we shall show how potential deadlocks can be detected by analyzing the Petri net model.

**Exercise**

---

**4.40** Consider a programming environment composed of a sequential programming language (e.g., C) and an operating system (e.g., UNIX). Provide implementation guidelines for both monitor-based and rendezvous-based designs.

---

### 4.5.2 Real-Time Software

In the previous section, we solved the problem of concurrent access to shared data by assuming that we can resolve contention for resources by suspending the execution of competing processes for a period of time. For example, in monitor-based design, producers could be suspended if the buffer they were accessing was full.

Unfortunately, suspending processes is not always feasible. For example, an operation invoked on an abstract object may belong to the thread of control of a process that cannot be suspended, perhaps because the process is a physical activity existing in an environment whose temporal evolution is not under the control of the computer system. Suppose, for example, that in a controlled chemical plant a producer is a sensor that samples data sent to the controller (a computer). In this case, there is no way to, say, slow down or suspend the plant! If a datum sent by the plant is not accepted in time by the controller, it will simply be lost. It is the controller's job to comply with the speed requirements of the plant in such a way that the data sent on the line are accepted, with no losses. Problems of this kind characterize real-time systems, which may be defined as systems for which reasoning about their correct behavior requires dealing with the speed of execution of the processes that make up the system. When we design such systems, we must comply with requirements that specify time limits within which certain operations must be executed. If some operations are not executed within the limit (i.e., if they occur either too early or too late), the system is incorrect.

This time constraint shows the fundamental difference between a pure concurrent system and a real-time concurrent system. A concurrent system is designed by ignoring the speed of processes. By applying suitable design principles, we may ensure that the system is correct independently of the speeds of the processes that constitute the system. Processes may be explicitly suspended (i.e., they may be slowed down as much as we wish) in order to ensure the validity of certain logical properties. For example, in the case of the monitor-based solutions discussed in the previous section, we are able to say, "At the future point where the producer will be allowed to perform a PUT operation, the buffer will have some free space to store the value delivered by the client." This was stated by means of the **requires** clause. Such statements do not make any sense in the case of a real-time system. If incoming signals arrive at a frequency of, say, one every 5 milliseconds, and, for security reasons, no incoming signal must be lost, knowing that "eventually the incoming signal will be buffered" does not solve our problems: The signal *must* be buffered within 5 milliseconds (i.e., before the next signal arrives); otherwise the signal is lost.

To deal with real-time issues in our design notations, we do not propose any specialized constructs, but rather suggest using comments to attach the needed requirements. For example, a comment may be used to say that the execution time of a certain exported routine is bounded by given lower and upper bounds.

Real-time systems often interact with an external environment that produces stimuli autonomously, at unpredictable times. Therefore, such systems may be viewed

```
concurrent module REACTIVE_CHAR_BUFFER
This is a monitorlike object working in a real-time environment.
uses ...
exports
        reactive procedure PUT (C: in CHAR);
        PUT is used by external processes, and two consecutive
        PUT requests must arrive more than 5 msec apart;
        otherwise, some characters may be lost
        procedure GET (C:out CHAR);
            .

            .

            .

end REACTIVE_CHAR_BUFFER
```

(a)

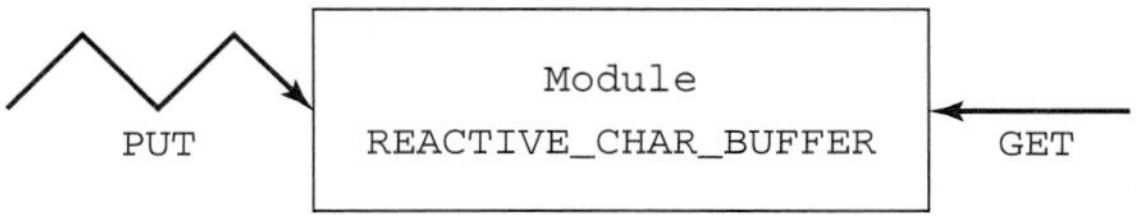

**FIGURE 4.22**

**(a)** Textual and **(b)** graphical design notation describing events.

(b)

as reactive systems that respond to incoming stimuli provided by the external world.[10] It is thus useful to have a way to specify that a given routine represents the response to an unpredictable request coming from the external environment. In TDN, we specify that by using the keyword **reactive**; in GDN, we indicate it by means of a zigzag arrow. (See Figure 4.22.)

If an operation is classified as **reactive**, it means that its execution cannot be delayed—for example, by suspending the caller and resuming it at a later, more convenient time. In practice, reactive operations are specified by stating constraints on their execution times (e.g., "The operation can occur every x milliseconds, with $5 \leq x \leq 15$"). Thus, it is the designer's responsibility to make sure that when an incoming request for such an operation arrives, no other operation of the module is being executed. Otherwise, the result would be unpredictable.

Practical experience has shown that timing issues are extremely critical, and this is what makes real-time systems difficult to design and verify. The complexity of design and verification scales up as we move from purely sequential systems to concurrent systems and from purely concurrent systems to real-time systems, and what makes the difference is time. In the case of sequential systems, time has to do only with the performance of a program. In the case of a concurrent system, we can suitably organize the system so that proper synchronization ensures correctness in a time-independent manner. Thus, again, time affects only the performance of the resulting program. In the case of real-time systems, however, time affects correctness. Accordingly, it introduces one more dimension that must be taken into account when we design, implement, and verify our systems.

Besides being intrinsically complex, real-time systems often provide critical functions, so that the effect of errors may be disastrous, possibly causing heavy financial losses or even loss of human lives. Thus, one of the qualities required of many real-time

---

[10]The fact that the environment activates some operation at unforeseen instants of time is typical of, though not exclusive to, real-time systems.

software systems is *dependability*. The design and verification of dependable real-time systems are subjects of active current research.

### 4.5.3    Distributed Software

One important class of concurrent software consists of concurrent activities that run on different computers connected by a communication network. For example, computers in an organization or in a home are often connected by a local area network (LAN). Such a network allows the users of the different computers to communicate (e.g., via electronic mail), share resources (e.g., printers and files), and otherwise cooperate. A set of LANs that are geographically distributed may be connected over a wide area network (WAN). Such an interconnection of networks is called an *internet*. An internet that belongs to, and is under the control of, a single organization is called an *intranet*. An intranet may support several distributed applications, including an internal mailing service or an internal web-based service to disseminate relevant information to employees.

In this section, we provide an initial overview of the issues involved in dealing with distributed software. Additional comments will be provided after we introduce object-oriented design in the next section. We start by observing that distribution imposes further requirements on the concepts of modules and relationships among modules studied so far. The resource guardian modules developed in Section 4.5.1 are directly applicable to a distributed software application and can serve as a unit of distribution. We must, however, impose certain restrictions on the USES relation between two modules that reside on different machines. In particular, because the modules on different machines have independent address spaces, we cannot allow one module directly to access variables defined in other modules. We will however, allow indirect access of such variables, through access procedures exported by the module, described in Section 4.6.3.3.

With distributed software, we must consider these new design issues:

- **Module-machine binding.** Sometimes a module is required to run on a particular machine. For example, if the module's purpose is to provide a printing service, the module may have to run on a computer that is attached to a printer. Other times, the module may be able to run on any number of a class of machines—for example, those that have a gateway connection to enable them to reach networks outside the organization.

- **Intermodule communication.** If two modules reside on different machines, how should they communicate? We have seen that modules which reside on the same machine can communicate by using a shared global area: One module records some information in the global area, and the other reads the information. This approach, which works for both sequential programs and concurrent programs, does not extend directly to the distributed environment, because the two modules are on different machines. Another approach to intermodule communication in the sequential environment is through parameter passing at procedure call and return times. The procedure call mechanism has been extended to a *remote procedure call* (RPC) in which the caller and the callee are not required to be on the same machine. The Java language introduced the notion of *remote method invocation* (RMI), which allows an object to call a procedure in an object that resides on another machine.[11] Another approach to intermodule communication in a distributed environment is sending *messages*. A number of libraries and operating system facilities support the development of applications using remote procedure calls or message passing.

- **Efficient access to abstract objects.** We have identified abstract objects as important types of modules that are derived naturally during the design of a system. In a centralized system, we do not incur a large cost by encapsulating a piece of data needed by module $M_1$ as part of an abstract object $M_2$. In a distributed system, however, if the two modules are located on different machines, it takes $M_1$ a much longer time to access data in $M_2$ through, say, a remote procedure call than the data that are local in $M_1$. Nonlocal access times may be orders of magnitude higher for remote data. Two approaches to making abstract objects more efficient in a distributed environment are *replication* and *distribution*.

We examine the preceding issues more closely in Sections 4.5.3.2 through 4.5.3.4. But first, in Section 4.5.3.1, we discuss briefly a particular model for structuring a distributed system: the *client-server* model.

### 4.5.3.1 *The client-server model*

We have said that the role of modules is to provide services to other modules called client modules. This model is directly applicable to distributed architectures. The most popular architecture for a distributed application is in terms of clients and servers residing on different machines. For example, consider a printing service facility on a network of computers. In this network, some computers have printers attached to them and others do not. We can design the printing service to consist of client and server modules. The server receives a file and prints it on a printer. The client accepts a file name from the user and sends the contents of the file to a server module, along with information about the user who requested the print operation.

Some of the modules that we have encountered already can be viewed naturally as server modules in a client-server architecture. For example, a module similar to the BUFFER example of Section 4.5.1 can be used by client modules of the printing service application to deposit the files to be printed. The client modules are the producers, and the server module is then the consumer, of the application. Similarly, the resource guardian modules of Section 4.5.1.2 can model servers in a distributed application.

### Exercise

**4.41** The same module may be a client in one context and a server in another. For example, consider a printing service facility that consists of a number of client modules running on machines without printers, a number of BUFFER modules running on any machine, and a

---

[11]The terms *object* and *method* are defined in Section 4.6, which deals with object-oriented design.

number of server modules running on machines that have printers. Discuss whether the BUFFER is a client or a server.

### 4.5.3.2 Binding a module to a machine

As we have said, an issue that we face in a distributed software architecture is that of binding modules to machines. Sometimes, as in the print server example, the binding is imposed by the physical environment or underlying infrastructure. Other times, there is a choice, and this choice may be guided by several considerations. For example, in order to reduce the cost of communication, we may want to place server modules on machines that are close to their clients, perhaps even on the same machine if possible.

Another issue is whether the binding is static or dynamic. A static binding is simpler, but the ability to choose the location of execution of a module dynamically allows us, for example, to choose a lightly loaded system in order to improve the application's performance. This ability is also essential for supporting highly reliable systems, because the failure of one machine can be tolerated by moving the modules that were running on it to another machine. Such dynamic movement of processes is called *migration*. We will not deal with the many details of this problem, which may be found in the specialized literature.

A special issue pertaining to the static or dynamic binding of modules to machines is whether a module can be instantiated (i.e., created) dynamically in the first place. Some systems support the creation of processes at run time, and others do not. If processes may be created dynamically, then the application can determine at run time how many instances of the process it needs to run. The ability to create a process on a specific machine is an additional feature. Different languages and libraries that support distributed software offer a large variety of options for the designer.

### Exercises

**4.42**  Explain why the dynamic creation of processes may not be desirable in real-time systems.

**4.43**  Consider an application that is required to be accessible from any machine on a particular network. There are thousands of machines on the network, but we expect that the application will not be run by more than 10 users at any one time. Design a solution to this problem. Is the dynamic binding of modules to machines useful in this example? How can you use process migration in this application? What is your solution if you are required to have a static binding of modules to machines?

### 4.5.3.3 Intermodule communication

Two models of communication are used in distributed applications: remote procedure call and message passing.

The remote procedure call mechanism is an extension of the traditional procedure call that allows the calling and the called modules to reside on different machines. Commercial packages are available that support this type of interaction under different operating systems. These packages offer an *Interface Definition Language* (IDL) and a compiler. Using IDL, the designer defines an interface for any procedure that may be called by remote clients. The compiler processes the definitions and generates header (or include) files that are included by clients and servers at compile time and that provide access to stub procedures which support the inter-module communication. Because of the similarity of remote procedure calls to traditional procedure calls, it is possible to design applications without making any distinction between service requests for local and remote modules: Any module interface that is written in terms of procedure calls can be supported in a distributed application. In practice, however, there are many details that hamper this approach.

The first difference between local and remote procedure calls is in performance. Since the call parameters have to be transmitted over the network, the overhead of an RPC is an order of magnitude higher than that of a local call. Switching a call from local to remote can have a significant impact on the performance of an application. Whereas a compiler may sometimes generate in-line code for local calls in order to improve efficiency, this is not possible for remote calls.

Another major difference between local and remote procedure calls is in the forms of parameter passing. Even if the ideas of a procedure call and a return are implemented rather naturally, not all forms of parameter passing can be supported remotely. For example, because the calling and called modules reside in two different address spaces, the two modules cannot communicate in terms of pointers. This means that parameter passing by reference, or passing linked data structures, is problematical, if possible at all. Thus, commercial remote procedure call systems generally do not support the passing of pointer structures.

The message-passing paradigm for intermodule interaction may be thought of in terms of mailboxes. Each module may be considered to have a mailbox in which it can receive messages from other modules. Client modules can send requests to the mailbox of a server module. A server picks up a request from its mailbox, acts upon it, and, if necessary, sends a reply to the mailbox of the appropriate client. The chief considerations in the use of message passing involve the size of mailboxes (how many messages can be buffered), whether message sending is synchronous or asynchronous, and whether a module can choose a target mailbox dynamically or the choice is static.

Although the two paradigms of remote procedure call and message passing are equal in power, in that each can be simulated with the other, they are appropriate for different software architectures. The most significant difference between the two is that remote procedure call is inherently a synchronous form of interaction and message passing is asynchronous. This means that a module making a procedure call must wait until the callee returns, but a client sending a message may continue with its thread of control. The existence of different threads of control means that the designer must deal with concurrent threads explicitly.

## Exercises

**4.44** Consider an application in which a sensor module reads a series of values on an incoming line and sends these values to a recorder module for further processing. If these two modules are distributed on two different machines, which form of inter-module communication would you choose to use? Why?

**4.45** For the previous exercise, sketch each module in a suitable extension of TDN, once using remote procedure call and once using message passing.

#### 4.5.3.4 Replication and distribution

The final consideration in software design for a distributed environment is to make access to data efficient. In particular, we have emphasized that one useful type of module is an abstract object, which provides client modules with access to an encapsulated data structure. This means that the client module makes a request—usually through a procedure call—for any data that it must access. The cost of accessing a piece of data through a procedure call rather than through memory directly—which is done for local data—is considered excessive even in some centralized applications. The cost is considerably higher if the abstract object is on a remote machine. The cost of a remote access on the fastest networks is around four times the cost of a local access and can be as much as an order of magnitude higher. We therefore need a way to make access to abstract objects efficient if we are going to use them in a distributed application. Two general methods exist for doing this.

The first approach is to replicate the distributed object on several machines—indeed, on every machine if necessary. In the latter case, each client has access to the abstract object locally. The problem now is that if a client modifies a copy of the object, all copies of the object must be kept consistent so that the different clients continue to observe the same abstract object rather than many different objects. Numerous techniques have been developed, in both the operating system and database areas, for solving this data consistency problem.

Another solution to speed up access to remote data is to distribute the abstract object on different machines. That is, even though logically the object is a single object, we can partition it physically and store the partitions on different machines, with each partition close to the clients that are likely to access it.

For each particular abstract object to be used in a distributed application, we must consider whether it makes sense to replicate it, partition it, do both, or do neither.

#### Exercises

**4.46** Extend both TDN and GDN to cope with the problems of dynamic allocation, intermodule communication, replication, and distribution.

**4.47** Consider a printing service application. A BUFFER module stores the job requests. Should we partition or replicate BUFFER? Why or why not?

**4.48** Consider an application for managing bank accounts in a bank. An abstract object represents all the customer accounts in the bank, which has many branches all over the country. Each branch has a computer that is used to access the customer-account object. Would you replicate or partition the object? Why or why not?

**4.49** Sketch the design of a conference room reservation application. Hundreds of rooms may be reserved for any particular time. The application may be accessed from thousands of machines on the network.

**4.50** Consider an application that is expected to receive stock market data that arrive on an incoming wire service and make it available to all the computers on a network for different types of queries. We decide to use an abstract object to represent the stock market data. Would you partition or replicate the data? Why or why not?

### 4.5.3.5 Middleware

The proliferation of networks, internets, and intranets has resulted in the development of many distributed software applications that rely on many of the same underlying facilities to perform their tasks. For example, they all need to locate services such as a print service on the network, and they need to locate various processes and communicate with them. The recognition of such common services has given rise to a new layer of software called middleware. The middleware layer resides between the network operating system layer and the application layer. Just as operating systems provide, for example, file and directory services to application programs, middleware provides distribution services to distributed applications. Typically, middleware provides the following two services:

- Name services: to find processes or resources on the network.
- Communication services: various forms of communication between processes, such as message passing or remote procedure call.

The facilities that make these services available are used by almost all distributed applications. The communication facilities provide the important service of packaging the parameters and transporting them across heterogeneous machines. Without such facilities, the application developer would have to take care of data-type conversions when processes on different computers communicate.

Today's middleware systems provide services for building applications that are distributed across local area networks. Research systems attempt to extend these facilities to operate across Internet-scale systems. The challenges in these middleware systems are to deal with scalability and reliability issues. Internet-scale applications must be able to handle millions of clients and cope with partial network failures.

Thanks to middleware, a software architect designing a distributed system does not start from scratch. The architect can depend on, and indeed use, preexisting components. Middleware systems provide many such components besides those associated with naming and communication. Common services are logging, transactions, event notification, security, and so on. We illustrate CORBA, a typical, standard middleware specification, in Section 4.7.

## 4.6    OBJECT-ORIENTED DESIGN

Object-oriented (OO) design is a technique that pushes to the extreme a design approach based on abstract data types. OO design became increasingly popular as OO languages—Smalltalk, C++, Java, and others—became more and more widely used in practice. In OO design, there is only one kind of module: the abstract data-type module. Using OO design terminology, we call such modules classes. A *class* exports the operations that may be used to manipulate its instances. Such operations are defined by procedures, usually called methods in OO terminology. Classes can also disclose part of their internal secrets, through exported attributes.[12] Objects are instances of classes and variables are *references* to objects.[13]

We modify TDN to express the fact that all modules implement just abstract data types. Instead of using the notation "`type X = ?`" in the interface of some module X to introduce the type's name, we let client modules use the class name directly. Hence, instead of declaring, say, a reference to an object of the abstract data type XX exported by module X as "`a: XX.X`", we would write "`a: X`". Since classes implement abstract data types, we use the abbreviation "object a is of class X" to mean—more precisely—"a is a reference to an instance object of the abstract data type implemented by class X."

Another substantial change occurs in the syntax of operations that are invoked on instance objects. In the case of the abstract data-type module X exporting XX, the invocation of operation `op` that manipulates the object referenced by a is written as

```
op(a,other_parameters)
```

In the case of OO design, we write

```
a.op(other_parameters)
```

indicating the invocation of operation `op` provided by instance a of class X. Thus, all operations exported by an OO module operate on a current instance object.

OO design insists on identifying classes and relations among classes. Relations are used by OO in a very broad and abstract way. We discuss the various kinds of OO relations in Sections 4.6.1 through 4.6.3. Along with this discussion, we introduce a graphical notation that specializes and replaces our GDN in the case of OO design. This notation, called Unified Modeling Language (UML), is commonly used for describing OO designs. UML is discussed further in Section 4.6.4.

## 4.6.1   Generalization and Specialization

OO design allows abstract data types to be organized in a hierarchy through generalization-specialization relations. Such a hierarchy defines a classification scheme for abstract data types. If class B specializes class A (conversely, A generalizes B), then the abstract data type implemented by B defines objects that behave like A's instances, but may provide more methods and attributes. Thus, all methods and attributes defined for A can be used to manipulate B's objects (which also may be manipulated by the methods and attributes defined specifically for B). B is said to be a *subclass* of A, with A being B's *superclass*.

Generalization-specialization can be implemented in a straightforward way through the inheritance mechanism provided by OO programming languages. This is why we often say "B inherits from A" as a synonym of "B specializes A" Accordingly, we can also say that B is A's heir class and A is B's parent class.

As an example, consider class EMPLOYEE defined in TDN in Figure 4.23. Class EMPLOYEE defines what is common to any kind of employee. All instances of EMPLOYEE (representing individuals) are characterized by the operations provided by the class for manipulation of the instances. For example, an employee instance may be hired with an

---

[12]A read-only attribute is like an exported function that yields the value of the attribute.
[13]We implicitly refer to the data model supported by Java.

```
class EMPLOYEE
exports
  function FIRST_NAME(): string_of_char;
  function LAST_NAME(): string_of_char;
  function AGE(): natural;
  function WHERE(): SITE;
  function SALARY: MONEY;
  procedure HIRE (FIRST_N: string_of_char;
                  LAST_N: string_of_char;
                  INIT_SALARY: MONEY);
```
*This operation initializes a new EMPLOYEE, assigning a
new unique identifier.*
```
  procedure FIRE();
  procedure ASSIGN (S: SITE);
```
*It is not possible to assign an employee to a SITE if he or she is
already assigned to it (i.e., WHERE must be different from S). It is the
client's responsibility to ensure the truth of this property. The effect is
to delete the employee from those in WHERE, add the employee to
those in S, generate a new id card for the employee with security code
to access the site overnight, and update WHERE.*
```
end EMPLOYEE
```

**FIGURE 4.23**

Class EMPLOYEE defined in TDN.

initial salary, by which it receives a unique identifier; it may be fired, by which the unique identifier is released; it may be assigned to a work site of the company, it may be promoted, and it may be queried for its name, age, salary, unique identifier, etc.

Some employees are members of the technical staff, others are members of the administrative staff, and still others are a member of neither staff. For this purpose, we define in Figure 4.24 two subclasses: TECHNICAL_STAFF and ADMINISTRA-TIVE_STAFF. A member of the administrative staff enjoys all properties of employ-

```
class ADMINISTRATIVE_STAFF inherits EMPLOYEE
exports
        procedure DO_THIS (F: FOLDER);
        This is an additional operation that is specific to
        administrators; other operations may also be added.
end ADMINISTRATIVE_STAFF

class TECHNICAL_STAFF inherits EMPLOYEE
exports
        function GET_SKILL(): SKILL;
        procedure DEF_SKILL (SK: SKILL);
        These are additional operations that are specific to
        technicians; other operations may also be added.
end TECHNICAL_STAFF
```

**FIGURE 4.24**

Defining subclasses in TDN.

ees: indeed, he or she *is* an employee! From an abstract data-type viewpoint, this means that the corresponding objects may be manipulated by all operations defined by the parent class EMPLOYEE, as well as others that characterize the heir module itself. In OO terminology, we say that ADMINISTRATIVE_STAFF inherits automatically all methods and attributes defined from EMPLOYEE That is, members of the administrative staff may be hired, fired, etc. In addition, they may be assigned some work to do by passing them a folder. The latter operation is specific to the heir class; it is not inherited from the parent class. Similarly, members of the technical staff, apart from the methods and attributes inherited from EMPLOYEE, are characterized by additional methods that make it possible to define and query their main skill. Finally, those individuals who are neither members of the technical staff nor members of the administrative staff are represented as instances of class EMPLOYEE and do not belong to any of its subclasses.

From a software design perspective, generalization-specialization may be used to factor out in a parent class what is common to different components, and then single out the variations in heir classes. This approach has the potential to improve reusability. In fact, we may try to factor out in a module all features that are likely to be sufficiently general to be reusable. The additional features needed in specific applications may be added afterwards by means of heir modules.

We can also look at inheritance as *a way of building software incrementally*. Thus, inheritance facilitates system evolution as new requirements arise. More generally, it can make maintenance easier to perform. The idea is that whenever the need arises to modify an existing module $M_1$ in order to obtain a new behavior as described in a module $M_2$, instead of modifying $M_1$, we inherit from $M_1$ and apply the changes that would transform $M_1$ into $M_2$. The types of changes we have examined so far consist exclusively of adding new operations to the abstract data types. We will examine other types of changes shortly.

In essence, we used incrementality to define the two heirs of EMPLOYEE. The two heir modules were defined by just listing the differences with respect to the parent module. To be more precise, the heir module is obtained from its parent module as a copy of its implementation with some new resources added.

Another way of looking at the generalization-specialization hierarchy is to see an heir class as implementing a subtype of the type defined by its superclass. An element of a subtype should be allowed to appear wherever a member of its parent type may appear. This is often called the *substitutability* principle. Since all instances of a subclass inherit the attributes and methods of its parent class, the substitutability principle is trivially satisfied. OO design, however, adds more features to the generalization-specialization relation. A subclass cannot only add new attributes and methods: It can redefine the methods defined in its parent class.

For example, suppose that EMPLOYEE provides a method for promotion, which increases the salary of an employee by a given fixed amount. Classes TECHNICAL_STAFF and ADMINISTRATIVE_STAFF might each redefine the method by increasing the salary by different amounts. Suppose now that some code manipulates an object X of type EMPLOYEE. According to the substitutability principle, such code should work fine if an instance of any of EMPLOYEE's subtypes is actually provided (e.g., TECHNICAL_STAFF). If the method for promotion is invoked on X, then, since X is bound to an instance of class TECHNICAL_STAFF, the method for promotion redefined in class TECHNICAL_STAFF is actually called. The important concepts behind this approach are *polymorphism* and

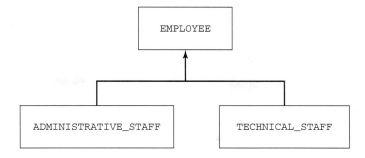

FIGURE 4.25

UML representation of generalization.

*dynamic binding*. Since X is an object of type EMPLOYEE, we can bind it to objects of any of its subtypes (polymorphism), and the methods that get invoked depend on the type of the object that is bound to X at run time (dynamic binding).

Let us conclude our discussion of generalization-specialization by providing a graphical notation that can describe it. As we mentioned, in this section we will gradually introduce elements of the UML notation, where classes are represented by boxes divided into three parts—corresponding to the class name, attributes, and methods—and the generalization-specialization relation is represented by a triangular connector between classes.

Figure 4.25 shows a UML description of the textual representation shown in Figure 4.23 and Figure 4.24. Observe that the uses relation between classes is not shown explicitly. Rather, it is implicit in the fact that the types of certain attributes or method parameters are not elementary, but are defined by other classes (which are therefore used).

### 4.6.2 Associations

Associations represent relations that the implementation is required to support between instances of classes. For example, members of the technical staff may be asso-

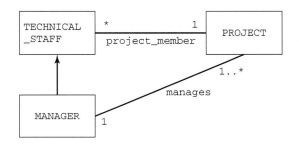

FIGURE 4.26

Representation of associations in UML.

ciated with the project they are working on. (Each technician works on exactly one project, but several technicians may work on the same project)

Figure 4.26 shows how associations can be represented by a UML fragment of a class diagram. The fragment introduces another subclass of TECHNICAL_STAFF, called MANAGER, and a further association between managers and projects. The diagram shows that managers are particular kinds of technical staff members (that is, in the particular world we are dealing with, a member of the administrative staff cannot be a manager), and a manager is associated with one or more projects that he or she manages. For simplicity, Figure 4.26 does not provide the details of the interface of the classes. (For classes EMPLOYEE and TECHNICAL_STAFF, the reader may refer to Figure 4.24.)

Associations in UML are represented by links—labeled by the name of the association—connecting the boxes that represent classes. Associations can involve several classes. In most cases, however, they are binary relations (i.e., they involve two classes). In what follows, we implicitly assume associations to be binary. Furthermore, associations may be described by specifying the multiplicity constraints on them, indicating how many objects can participate in the relation. For example, Figure 4.26 shows that any number of technicians can be involved in a project (indicated by the multiplicity constraint "*" on the end of the association at the TECHNICAL_STAFF side), while a technician may be associated with only one project (indicated by the multiplicity constraint "1" on the association at the PROJECT side). In general, multiplicity constraints are given by specifying "lower_bound..upper_bound". The abbreviation "*" actually stands for "0..infinity", and "1" stands for "1..1". For example, should we require that at least one technician be in a project, the multiplicity constraint "*" would be replaced by "1..*". The multiplicity constraints given on the association between MANAGER and PROJECT show that a manager can manage several projects (but at least one!). If we require that managers may not manage more than three projects, the multiplicity constraint "1..*" should be replaced by "1..3".

The specification of associations in a class diagram like the one shown in Figure 4.26 does not provide enough information to derive an implementation. For example, it specifies that managers are associated with the projects they manage and projects are associated with the technicians who manage them. But is the implementation required to support navigation both from the projects to their managers and from the managers to the projects they manage? By navigation from managers to projects, we mean that, given a manager, we are able to determine all the projects he or she manages. Similar questions may be asked for the association between TECHNICAL_STAFF and PROJECT. To answer such questions, UML allows one to *decorate* associations with a navigability arrow. For example, the design fragment shown in Figure 4.26 indicates that the association between MANAGER and PROJECT is such that we only need to navigate from a manager to the projects he or she is responsible for. However, if no navigability arrows are provided to guide the implementation, we should assume that navigation can occur in both directions. So, for example, one should support navigation from a technician to the project he or she is assigned to and from a project to the technicians assigned to it.

The preceding discussion shows that the associations we introduce at the design level constrain implementation to support a way to navigate among classes. For example, a possible implementation of the association between MANAGER and PROJECT may consist of having a variable in each instance of MANAGER that is an array of references to objects of class PROJECT. Furthermore, the discussion illustrates that an association between classes implicitly defines a USES relation—for example, in the case of Figure 4.26, MANAGER USES PROJECT.

As a final remark, we wish to point out that, during design, the distinction between attributes (or methods) and associations is not always obvious. For example, in Figure 4.26, we decided that method DO_THIS is used to assign a folder to a member of the administrative staff. Alternatively, we could have defined a class FOLDER and an association between ADMINISTRATIVE_STAFF and FOLDER to describe the binding between a member of the administration and the folder he or she is working on. Of course, the difference would be that the explicit association would imply support for navigation from folders to members of the administration.

### 4.6.3  Aggregation

In describing a class, it may be useful to define the objects of that class as composed of simpler components that constitute the parts of those objects. This is often called the PART_OF relation. For example, we may define a class TRIANGLE and its relation to class POINT as an aggregation (Figure 4.27). For simplicity, the figure does not provide the details (methods and attributes) of class interfaces, but shows the cardinality constraints for the aggregation relation: Three points constitute one triangle.

Notice that the PART_OF relation differs from the IS_COMPOSED_OF relation we introduced in Section 4.2.1.2. In fact, the component that comprises the parts has its own properties which are not directly provided by the parts. Rather, the component uses its parts to provide its own behaviors (i.e., attributes and methods).

A—say—Java implementation of the design fragment shown in Figure 4.27 requires that class TRIANGLE provide the methods and attributes needed to manipulate triangles, represented as three references to objects of class POINT. Thus, implicitly, this says that TRIANGLE USES POINT.

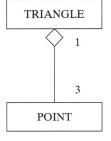

FIGURE 4.27

Example of aggregation.

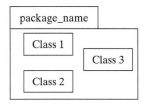

FIGURE 4.28

Package construct of UML for the IS_COMPONENT_OF relation.

### 4.6.4    More on UML Class Diagrams

UML class diagrams can be seen as an evolution of the simple GDN we introduced earlier for documenting designs. The USES relationship we introduced for GDN is replaced by a variety of relations: generalization-specialization, associations of various kinds, and aggregation. Generalization-specialization is implemented through inheritance by using OO languages. The other kinds of relations can be implemented straightforwardly by embedding in an object references to the objects it is related to. In all cases, USES relations are implied. If a class B inherits from class A, B USES A. If an association exists between classes A and B, with a navigability constraint indicated from B to A, then B USES A.[14] If B is described as an aggregation of A, then again, B USES A. In a sense, we may conclude that UML introduces a number of more abstract relations than the USES relation we used for TDN and GDN. These relations are more abstract because they describe semantically richer relational concepts that may eventually be implemented in terms of the USES relation.

UML also provides a notation to describe the IS_COMPONENT_OF relation: the package construct. The package groups several classes or packages (see Figure 4.28). It is also possible to draw dependency links between packages to show that the entities enclosed in a package depend in some loose sense on the entities defined in another package.

Besides providing notations to describe the static structure of an architecture, UML provides notations that can be used to complement class diagrams by describing dynamic aspects of an architecture: state diagrams and activity diagrams. State diagrams describe all possible states the objects of a given class may enter and how an object's state changes as results of operations performed on the object. Activity diagrams describe work flows that traverse the executions of methods of different objects. The key concept of activity diagrams is that they define work flows that can proceed in parallel. State diagrams and activity diagrams are illustrated in Section 5.7.

## 4.7    ARCHITECTURE AND COMPONENTS

An architecture of a system describes the overall organization and structure of the system in terms of its major constituents and their interactions. For example, for a modern hospital administration system, the architectural description might show that the system consists of many subsystems, such as patient-monitoring devices, nurses' stations, portable data entry devices to be used by doctors, a patient database, and so on. The architecture is the first high-level design of the system. In coming up with an architecture, the designer considers many options, constraints, and trade-offs. The trade-offs determine many of the overall properties of the system, such as its performance, reliability, and security. The architecture, therefore, provides the medium for reasoning about and analyzing the global properties of the system, since global properties are determined not by individual components, but by the interaction of the whole set of components.

In designing the architecture, the designer must consider many functional requirements as well as many nonfunctional requirements, such as cost and reliability.

---

[14]Notice that if navigability is in both directions, then the resulting USES relation is not a hierarchy.

While the architecture of a system is, of course, influenced by these requirements, there are also some structuring principles that govern the design of the architecture. In particular, depending on the system requirements, some specific decomposition of the system into components and modes of interaction among those components is most appropriate. We have already seen an example of such structure for distributed systems in the client-server architecture, which provides guidance to the architect of any distributed system that may be organized as a set of providers of services and clients that seek those services.

There are many benefits to developing and studying such architectures. First, knowing about architectures that have already been tried and tested in previous systems allows the architect to start on a design quickly and with confidence. Such an architecture embodies the experiences of previous designers, and its use builds on those experiences. Associated with each architecture are the design decisions that must be addressed. Second, because an architecture establishes the modes of communication among the components of the system, it defines a kind of generic interface at which those components meet. The existence of such interface specifications supports the development of standard components which may be used in systems that use the architecture. Third, an architecture serves as an integration platform for interconnecting the different subsystems of the system. Some of these subsystems may be developed for the particular system to be designed, or they may be existing software systems, such as databases. In the subsections that follow, we will study these issues in detail.

### 4.7.1    Standard Architectures

By studying existing systems, designers and researchers have found that certain architectures occur frequently. Here we list some of the prominent ones. We examine architectures for distributed systems in Section 4.7.4.

**Pipeline architectures.**    Sometimes, subsystems may be organized to form a pipeline of processing elements. Each subsystem accepts input from the previous subsystem, processes the input, and delivers output to the next subsystem. The first subsystem reads the system input, and the last subsystem produces the system output. Such an architecture may be useful, for example, for the part of a plant-monitoring system in

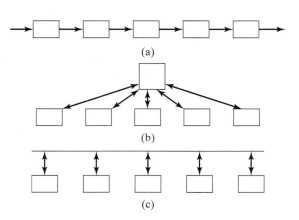

(a)

(b)

FIGURE 4.29

The relationship of components in various architectures: (a) pipeline; (b) blackboard; (c) event based.

(c)

which sensors read environmental data and pass them on to other subsystems for further processing. A pipeline architecture is also called a *pipe-and-filter* architecture, because each subsystem is viewed as filtering the data it receives and the data are considered to flow along pipes between the filters. By starting with a pipeline architecture, the designer can immediately concentrate on issues such as the performance requirements for data flow on the pipes, the synchronization requirements among neighboring filters, potential bottlenecks in the pipeline, and so on. A graphic view of this architecture is shown in Figure 4.29a.

**Blackboard architecture.**    In a pipeline architecture, the communication between two filters is local. Sometimes, it is necessary for subsystems to be able to communicate with more than just their neighbor subsystem. If many subsystems need to communicate with each other, then a blackboard architecture may be appropriate. In this architecture, one subsystem is designated as the "blackboard" and serves as the communication medium among the other subsystems. Essentially, the blackboard is an interfaces for writing information and receiving queries. A stock market brokerage system or an auction system may be structured as a blackboard system, with requests and offers posted to the blackboard and clients querying the blackboard for information. A graphic view of this architecture is shown in Figure 4.29b.

**Event-based architecture.**    In traditional architectures, components communicate and invoke operations by way of procedure calls. In an event-based architecture, components respond to the occurrence of events. An event might be the detection of a signal by a sensor or the arrival of a message. Components are designed to create events or start their operations when they receive an event. Event-based architectures are appropriate when components wait for input from the environment or when clear client-server relationships are not definable. User interfaces are often structured to utilize mouse clicks or mouse drags as events. Conceptually, we may imagine a bus on which events are announced and propagated. Different models of event-based systems support component operations such as advertising of events and subscribing to events. Types of events are dependent on the application.

Event-based architectures satisfy a *publish-subscribe* paradigm or pattern. Components publish events that are delivered to those components which have previously subscribed to those events. Key to this architecture is an event dispatcher, which is responsible for the run-time distribution of events from publishers to subscribers. The event dispatcher may be provided as part of middleware. A graphic view of this architecture is shown in Figure 4.29c.

**Domain-specific architectures.**    Pipeline, blackboard, and event-based architectures codify a certain set of components, along with their relations and communication patterns. Many such standard architectures are emerging in practice. These architectures are aimed at abstracting the common structural properties of classes of systems without paying particular attention to the domain of use of those systems. Another class of standard architectures tries to exploit the common properties of a given application domain. These architectures are called domain-specific architectures. For example, domain-specific architectures have been developed for the domains of real-time systems and user-interface systems. Domain-specific architectures embody many assumptions about the domain—for example, the way that components communicate, the speed with which they must communicate, and the existence of time-out mechanisms in connection with communicating messages. Domain-specific architectures speed up the development of systems in particular domains. Further, they encourage and support the development of components that may be reused in many systems in the domain. Finally, they enable tools such as editors, generators, and analyzers to be developed in support of the domain. For example, user-interface generators can be easily based on a standard user-interface architecture.

**Example 4.12**

One well-known domain-specific architecture is the model-view-controller for software that has a significant amount of user interaction. The architecture is composed of three separate components: the model, which purports to be a model of the "real world," the view, which displays the model to the user, and the controller, which communicates with the user and controls the other two components. As an example of the use of the model-view-controller architecture, consider a file editor that stores the user's data for subsequent display in different formats, such as textual or graphic. The model would manage the storage of the data, the view would request the data from the model and then display the data, and the controller would interact with the user to decode the user commands and would update the data in the model. By providing different view components, the system can support different viewing options in a modular way. For example, one view component can display an outline and another a page. Each component specializes in its own semantics or hides its formatting information. Figure 4.30 shows the structure of the model-view-controller architecture. The arrows in the figure represent requests for services.

Many actual libraries for user-interface development, such as the Java Swing library, implement the model-view-controller architecture.    ■

**4.7.2    Software Components**

In engineering disciplines, products are almost always constructed from parts, or components. Component-based software engineering has been a goal of software engineering from the beginning of its history. Much research and development have gone into efforts to make it possible to use standard components in building software prod-

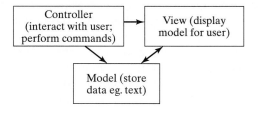

FIGURE 4.30

The model-view-controller architecture.

ucts. Software technology has finally developed to a level where languages and methodologies support the development and use of components.

The most fundamental question about software components is what form they should take. That is, what is the unit of packaging for a software component as an independent entity? Until the early 1990s, the only successful units of packaging in software engineering were routines and libraries of routines. For example, scientific libraries of routines for matrix manipulation are widely and commercially available. There are several reasons for the success of these libraries as components, among which the most important are the following:

- *Clear interfaces.* The specification of the component is precisely defined by its mathematical properties. Further, those properties are purely functional, which makes the component easier to describe, understand, and integrate with other components.

- *Useful and separable service.* The service provided by a component is clearly identifiable as useful to many clients and is separable from the functions of the client itself.

- *Clear domain of applicability.* Programmers and engineers writing scientific programs are deeply knowledgeable about the domain of mathematics involved and the boundaries of applicability of the components in that domain.

Given these properties, it is easy for engineers to know when they might need a component, to examine and understand the interface of a component, and to make use of the component in their applications.

In the 1990s, with advances in programming-language technology, component-packaging mechanisms other than routines became possible. Among these mechanisms are (1) generic constructs in languages such as Ada and C++ and (2) objects and frameworks in object-oriented languages. We examine one example of each of these mechanisms next.

**STL.** The standard template library is a collection of software components designed for C++ and eventually merged into the C++ standard library. The library consists of common data structures, such as lists and stacks, and frequently used algorithms, such as those for searching and sorting. By defining a uniform interface for both algorithms and data structures, STL achieves an orthogonal design that allows most algorithms to be applied to most data structures. For example, a single `find` algorithm for searching for an element in a collection may be applied to arrays, singly linked lists, and doubly linked lists. Algorithms and data structures in STL are packaged as C++ templates. This means that the source code in the STL library must be available to the programmer so that it can be compiled with the C++ program.

STL uses a uniform principle for structuring the interfaces of components. Most algorithms that operate on collections of items take references to the first and last elements of the collection as input. For example, the interface for the `find` algorithm, a function that searches a sequence of elements for a particular element, is

```
template < class InputIterator, class T >
InputIterator find(InputIterator first, InputIterator last,
const T& value);
```

The generic algorithm is defined for any sequence of elements of type $T$. Data structures—collections—are able to return references to their first and last elements. This uniform structure for interfaces establishes guidelines for designers of new algorithms and data structures to follow. If an algorithm adheres to these guidelines, then it may be combined with any of the data structure components of STL. Likewise, if a data structure follows the guidelines, it may be combined with any of the algorithms of STL. This means that with $m$ data structures and $n$ algorithms, we have $m \times n$ possible component combinations.

A unique feature of STL is its use of C++ templates. Templates allow the expression of generic algorithms and data structures, while preserving the type-checking ability of the compiler. STL includes over 100 components. A typical component is quite small in terms of number of lines. The components achieve their power by their generality and their being able to be composed with other components.

**JavaBeans.**   The object-oriented languages promote components constructed as classes and objects. The Java programming language also offers packages and archive files (Jar, for "Java archive" files) to augment facilities for component-based development. The JavaBean component framework promotes the visual approach to software development in an environment where components are represented by icons that may be dragged and positioned on the screen and connected to other icons. A *framework* is a collection of related classes that are designed to be used together in developing applications in a certain domain. The JavaBean framework defines a set of methods that must be supported by each component. These methods ensure that components may be composed visually. The framework defines the semantics that each prescribed method must provide to ensure that the connections between components work properly.

**Swing.**   Java has a number of libraries to support software development for different applications. For example, there are libraries for networking and security. The Swing library supports the development of graphical user interfaces. Swing is representative of a number of domain-specific component libraries designed for graphical user interfaces. Because the representation of these interfaces has become rather standard, consisting of windows, buttons, menus, and so on, libraries like Swing provide facilities for constructing user interfaces by combining such so-called *widgets*. The object-oriented paradigm is ideally suited for this domain. Each widget is represented as an object that supports methods which specify what the widget does if the mouse points to it, if it is dragged, if it is clicked, and so on. As we mentioned before, Swing follows the model-view-controller architecture.

One of the issues researched in the development of software components is the granularity of the components. STL components are fine-grained code-level components, while Swing and JavaBeans are medium-grained components. It is also possible to use large-grained components such as database management systems. Indeed, since many applications utilize databases, it is quite beneficial to be able to use database management systems as components in applications. To be able to use existing database management systems as components, the Open Data Base Connectivity (ODBC) standard defines a set of interfaces to a relational database.

These interfaces have been mapped to most existing relational database management systems. The availability of the mappings means that a designer may assume the existence of a relational database as a component in the architecture of the system. At the design and implementation levels, a particular database management system may be selected on the basis of cost, performance, compatibility with other products, and so on.

### 4.7.3    Architecture As the Framework for Component Integration

The component-based development of software assumes a two-step process. First, a high-level architecture or design of the system is developed, identifying components that should be combined to make the system. Second, an attempt is made to find the needed components off the shelf, already available on the market. Obviously, these two steps are mutually reinforcing. On the one hand, knowing what components are available on the market motivates architects to select architectures that can take advantage of those components. On the other hand, knowing about architectures that architects design motivates component developers to develop components that fit within popular architectures.

As particular domains mature, more and more components become available for those domains. In these cases, designing an architecture for an application becomes more an attempt to compose an existing set of components in order to achieve the goals of the application. In this way, we can view an architecture as a framework for integrating a set of components. The architecture specifies the way that the components should be arranged and connected in order to meet the application's requirements.

The *Common Object Request Broker Architecture* (CORBA) is an example of a standard architecture that may be viewed as such an integration platform. CORBA assumes a client-server paradigm in a distributed environment. It assumes that clients and servers reside on a network and establish connections with each other through an Object Request Broker (ORB). Servers inform the ORB of their availability, and clients query the ORB for the availability of servers. Once a client finds out about a server through the ORB, it can communicate directly with the server. The ORBs on different networks may communicate with each other (through an Inter-ORB protocol) in order to provide

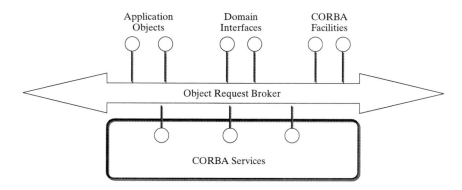

FIGURE 4.31

The CORBA architecture.

access to servers across multiple networks. Thus, ORB serves as the name server in the CORBA architecture. In Section 4.5.3, we mentioned that one of the tasks pursued in distributed software design is to bind a module to a machine. The ORB makes it possible to query for this binding at run time. Once the CORBA standard was defined, a number of commercial ORBs became available, and they are now widely used.

The CORBA standard essentially defines the architecture of a generic distributed system based on clients and servers. Figure 4.31 shows the CORBA architecture. The job of a designer of a particular system is to provide clients and servers that fit within this framework—that is, they are able to communicate with ORBs.

One of the most influential contributions of the CORBA standard is its *Interface Definition Language* (IDL). The designer of a server uses this language to define the interfaces provided by the server. Clients use the interfaces to compile and link programs. The language provides a set of data types that may be used in procedure signature definitions. Interfaces may inherit from other interfaces. From a software engineering point of view, the existence of IDL is quite significant. The IDL specifications clearly separate the responsibilities between designers and programmers of clients and servers. The IDL specification serves as a module specification for servers.

CORBA provides a framework for building distributed applications. It is especially suitable for building new distributed systems. We can build new components and integrate them into the CORBA framework. In many cases, however, we may want to integrate already existing components into the framework. For example, we may have a personnel system or other legacy software that we want to make available to the distributed network. One way to integrate such systems into a CORBA framework is to write IDL specifications for their services and then write programs that map the interface into interactions with the legacy software. Such mapping software is called *wrapper* software, because it wraps the legacy software into a package that may be used in a new environment. Wrapping is not always possible, however. For example, an interactive legacy software cannot be easily wrapped to operate in a client-server environment.

In the Microsoft world, the *Distributed Component Object Model* (DCOM) was designed specifically to be able to integrate legacy software. One of the design goals for the model was to allow integration of binary code. DCOM is in many respects similar to CORBA, but it is proprietary and continuosly evolving.

### 4.7.4  Architectures for Distributed Systems

One of the main advantages of modeling a system at the architecture level is that it is then possible to understand the overall structure of the system and analyze its global properties. We can even discover structural patterns that are more generally useful than the system we are currently designing. For example, we have seen that the client-server paradigm has been codified in the CORBA standard as a standard architecture for distributed systems.

With the proliferation of networks and the increasing availability of distributed environments, the importance of standard architectures for distributed systems and applications has grown. In this section, we review two related architectural approaches for distributed systems: the three-tiered architecture and application servers.

The *three-tiered architecture* is an outgrowth of the client-server architecture, which may be viewed as *two tiered*. In a client-server architecture, there are two levels

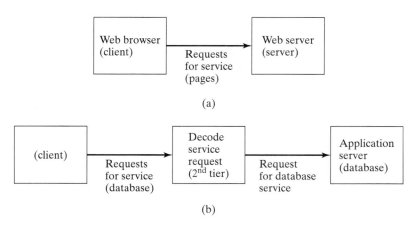

FIGURE 4.32

(a) Two- and (b) three-tiered architectures.

of components: the client level and the server level. The client level relies on the services of the server level. For example, the World Wide Web (WWW) architecture exhibits this structure. The Web browser resides on the client's computer and communicates with the Web server that resides on the server's computer. The browser sends requests for pages to the server and displays them on the screen when it receives them. There are only two kinds of components: clients and servers. This architecture is shown in Figure 4.32a.

In many distributed applications, however, we may distinguish a third layer of functionality. Suppose that the request from the browser is not for a simple page, but for a service such as a database access. In this case, the Web server must send the request to the machine that hosts the database (which may, of course, be the same physical machine on which the browser resides), retrieve the results, and forward them to the client. We can characterize such applications as three tiered, consisting of the client tier, which runs the user interface; the business logic layer, which interprets the user's requests and determines what is to be done; and the application tier, which actually performs the requested service. The application is often, but not always, a database server. A three-tiered architecture is shown in Figure 4.32b.

With the spread of three-tiered architectures, it becomes possible to identify specific applications that are commonly requested from the application tier. In this regard, it is possible to construct *application servers* that provide a single application. For example, an entire application such as a mail service may be provided by a mail application server. The application server approach promotes the creation of highly specialized and optimized servers aimed at carrying out specific tasks. Such servers may be viewed as large-grained components to be integrated in distributed architectures. The architect merely has to select, from among available application servers, the one that best fits into the system being built.

## 4.8    CONCLUDING REMARKS

In this chapter, we have examined the various facets of software design and architecture. Most of the general software principles we presented in Chapter 3 have been examined in more depth here, in the context of software design. In particular, we emphasized modularity, which is the very essence and the common theme underlying the whole chapter. Separation of concerns, abstraction, generality, and incrementality have also been discussed extensively. In particular, they have been viewed as benefits derived from appropriate modularization techniques. Finally, rigor and formality have been shown to be essential goals of our design documentation, inspiring the definition of a design notation that was presented in two forms: textual (TDN) and graphical (GDN). Such notation provides a clear way of documenting a software design, to facilitate communication among software designers and future maintainors of the system.

Design is a critical and creative activity. It can be inspired by general principles and guidelines, but it cannot be mechanized by fixed, absolute rules or theorems. We have shown that design consists of (1) defining an architecture in terms of a set of relations on modules and (2) defining the interfaces between the modules. These activities may be driven by the general principles that the architecture should have low coupling and high cohesion and that interfaces should enforce information hiding. Putting such principles into practice, however, requires insight, maturity, and experience on the part of the designer. The principles are *not* recipes!

Information hiding was assumed as a cornerstone upon which a solid design is based. Thus, we paid much attention to the question of how to design interfaces through information hiding. In particular, we identified several categories of modules that may be used as guidelines during design. Most notable were abstract objects and abstract data types.

Among the qualities of software design, we stressed evolvability and reliability. Evolvability is achieved through design for change. Reliability is also a by-product of a disciplined approach to design. Good methods help overcome the complexity of design and hence promote the likelihood that flaws are absent from a particular design. But we also addressed the issue of defensive design, by showing that possible anomalies should be considered during the design phase and described in the documentation.

We addressed the issue of design for concurrent, real-time, and distributed systems, by extending the design principles and the proposed design notation to these cases. Our goal here was to show that the principles and the approaches that we presented for designing sequential software may be extended to deal with concurrency, real time, and distribution.

Information hiding, abstract objects, and abstract data types led to the concept of object-oriented design, an approach to software design that has become dominant in the past decade because of the advent of programming languages, such as C++ and Java, that support the approach by providing linguistic features missing in traditional languages. Object-oriented design, together with its related languages, takes the idea of information hiding to its logical conclusion, with the aim of helping software designers get closer to such goals as design for change, the design of program families, incremental development, the production of reusable components, and ease of maintenance. The UML design notation has been introduced for object-oriented design. UML is increasingly adopted as a standard notation to document the architecture of object-oriented applications.

Finally, we examined a number of issues related to the component-based development of software. These issues revolve around standard architectures and interfaces that allow the development of standard components and their integration into applications. We concluded the chapter with a discussion of the evolution of two-tiered and three-tiered architectures for distributed systems.

## FURTHER EXERCISES

**4.51** Define some useful relations among modules other than the relations discussed in this chapter.

**4.52** Classify the changes discussed in Section 4.1.1.1 as either perfective, adaptive, or corrective maintenance.

**4.53** Consider a program you have written in the past in a programming language like Ada, Modula-2, C, or Pascal. (Here we employ Ada, but the exercise can be adapted quite easily to any of these languages.) Consider Ada library units as corresponding to the concept of a module that we are using in this chapter. Also, define a relation CALLS between any two modules such that $M_i$ CALLS $M_j$ if and only if a call to a procedure or function in $M_j$ is issued within $M_i$.

   **a.** Unlike the assumption we made in Section 4.2.1, would it make any sense to define CALLS as a reflexive relation?

   **b.** What follows from requiring CALLS to be a hierarchy?

   **c.** Draw the CALLS graph for your sample program, and check whether the graph is a DAG or not.

**4.54** Prove that the inverse of a hierarchy is also a hierarchy.

**4.55** With reference to Figure 4.4, we may say that

   {$M_1$} ENCAPSULATES {$M_4$, $M_5$, $M_6$, $M_7$, $M_8$, $M_9$}
   {$M_2$} ENCAPSULATES {$M_7$, $M_8$, $M_9$}
   {$M_3$} ENCAPSULATES {$M_5$, $M_6$}

   Thus, the relation ENCAPSULATES relates each module to the set of elementary modules that it comprises. Define ENCAPSULATES formally.

**4.56** Explain why a design with low coupling helps maintainability.

**4.57** Study the COMMON construct of FORTRAN, and discuss the difference between labeled and unlabeled COMMONs, as well as their possible use. Also, discuss the mechanisms provided by FORTRAN to initialize COMMON areas.

**4.58** Describe how to use C to define a common area for storing data. Do the same for Pascal.

**4.59** We have criticized the POP_2 interface to the stack of Example 4.7 on the grounds of being too *specialized*. We said that if we *generalize* the interface to POP, clients have more flexibility in its use. Specialization, however, is sometimes necessary for reasons of efficiency. For example, consider a stack that is implemented on one node of a distributed system. Compare POP and POP_2 in terms of efficiency of the interface for clients.

**4.60** According to the definition of the Ada programming language, what is the difference between **private** and **limited private** types exported by a package, as far as client modules are concerned?

**4.61** Example 4.8 used objects of type FIFO_CARS to represent any queue at the gas station. We would like, however, to treat a queue of cars waiting for gas differently from a queue of cars waiting for, say, a tune-up. In particular, if there is no gas left, we do not want to merge the two queues. In Example 4.8, the proper handling of queues was left to the client modules. Clients would choose appropriate names for objects (such as gasoline_1 or car_wash) in order to avoid merging inhomogeneous queues inadvertently. Suggest a better solution using generic modules.

**4.62** In Section 4.2.4.3, we described generic modules parameterized by types. Study the Java language specification. Does it support parameterized modules? Does C++?

**4.63** We did not provide an enrichment of GDN to describe exceptions and exception handling. Propose a notation to describe the fact that an exception may be raised by a module when a request for a service is being served. Your notation should also provide a way to show that an exception is propagated after being signaled to a client.

**4.64** Suppose you wish to model the elevator system of a multifloor building. The system is composed of m floors and n elevators. Each elevator has a set of buttons, one for each floor. The buttons light up when pressed and cause the elevator to visit the corresponding floor. The light goes out upon the elevator's reaching the floor. Each floor (except for the ground and top floors) has two buttons, one to request an up elevator and one to request a down elevator. The illumination goes out when the elevator visits the floor and either is moving in the desired direction or has no outstanding requests. Each elevator has an emergency button that, when pressed, causes a warning signal to be sent to the site manager. The elevator is then deemed "out of service." Each elevator has a mechanism to cancel its out-of-service status.

**a.** Model this system in an object-oriented style.

**b.** Suppose that the elevators are divided into two sets, the first comprising the elevators that serve floors zero through $m_1$, the second comprising those which serve floors $m_1$ through m. What would change in your design to accommodate this feature?

**4.65** After the first step of design described at the beginning of Section 4.4, the designer of the SYMBOL_TABLE module anticipates that he will store the information contained in the various blocks in contiguous locations. Therefore, the algorithms for RETRIEVE and LEVEL will be almost identical: To search for the value of a variable, first the most recently entered block is searched, and then, if the variable is not found, the previously entered block is searched, and so on. The designer proposes to his colleagues that they should take advantage of this near identity of algorithms and change the interface. Toward that end, instead of having procedures RETRIEVE and LEVEL, he will provide a procedure (RETRIEVE_LEVEL) that merges the two. Its proposed interface is as follows:

```
procedure RETRIEVE_LEVEL (ID: in IDENTIFIER;
    DESCR: out DESCRIPTOR; L: out integer);
```

After some discussion, the designer's colleagues convince him that merging the two operations into one is not such a good idea. Do you agree with this decision? Why? Why not?

**4.66** Referring to the module QUEUE_OF_CHAR discussed in Section 4.5, do you expect two concurrent executions of NOT_EMPTY and NOT_FULL to require execution in mutual exclusion? Why? Why not? How about two concurrent executions of NOT_EMPTY and GET?

**4.67** Is it completely correct to say that the **requires** clause defined in Section 4.5.1.1 is part of the interface of a concurrent module? Why? Why not?

**4.68** Consider the module of Figure 4.19 and assume that the operations NOT_FULL and NOT_EMPTY are exported by the module. Would the exported operations in Figure 4.19 provide any useful abstraction when they are called by the module's clients? Why? Why not?

**4.69** What difficulties may be encountered if a monitor operation is allowed to use another monitor operation (perhaps even exported by the same monitor)?

**4.70** Study concurrency features in Ada, and provide a detailed description of the case where any number of consumers (defined by a task type) and one producer may access a given buffer to append characters to it and remove characters.

**4.71** At the turn of the century, much attention was drawn to the so-called Y2K ("year 2000") problem. Most existing software was designed to handle dates by using two digits to denote the year. This would have generated errors because, for example, "00" could have been interpreted as the year 1900. Discuss the Y2K problem as a problem of software evolution. In particular, address the following issues: What was the source of the problem? Could the problem have been anticipated? Why was it not? How would you detect such errors in a program and how could you solve them?

**4.72** Examine case study A in the Appendix. Show how the company would have been able to deal with the different needs of different customers by exploiting some of the techniques illustrated in this chapter.

**4.73** Modify the class diagrams in Figure 4.25 and Figure 4.26 by specifying an association that describes the team working in a project. The team is composed of a manager, an administrator, and a group of technicians.

## HINTS AND SKETCHY SOLUTIONS

**4.9** IS_COMPOSED_OF and IMPLEMENTS cannot be defined as mathematical relations on S because they relate an element of S with a subset of elements of S.

**4.38** Observe that the two statements are actually performed as a sequence of more elementary actions. It may happen, then, that both processes read TOT, then PRODUCER_1 increases the read value and stores it back into TOT, and finally CONSUMER_2 decreases the read value and stores it back into TOT!

**4.51** A semantic equivalence relation between modules is useful for deciding whether one module can replace another during software evolution. As far as compilation is concerned, there can be order relations between modules, of the type "$M_1$ must be compiled before $M_2$." In distributed systems, there could be a relation stating that two modules must be allocated to the same machine.

**4.65** A different implementation might cache the descriptors of all visible identifiers at block entry, without caching the level. This would invalidate the proposed interface.

**4.67** Strictly speaking, a concurrent module can be used properly even without "knowing" the **requires** clause. The clause, however, provides useful information for a better understanding of the effect of the associated operations. It also has an impact on performance analysis, since it helps find delays due to the mutual exclusion it enforces.

**4.68** Clients cannot rely on the result they get back, because other processes may change them in the meantime.

**4.69** Such a feature may increase the risk of deadlock.

**4.72** By using, say, object-oriented design, the company could first have factored out from a few modules all information and operations that are needed by all legal offices. Later, legal offices could have been specialized by applying inheritance to cope with different classes of needs. This approach would also have supported an incremental construction and delivery of the system.

Also, by following the approach suggested by Example 4.5, the company could have concentrated both design and promotion efforts on the innovative features of the system.

## BIBLIOGRAPHIC NOTES

The work of D.L. Parnas is the major source of inspiration of the view of design presented in this book.

Dijkstra [1968a, 1968b, and 1971] was the first to teach how to use the powerful principles of separation of concerns and levels of abstraction to deal with complexity of design.

Parnas pioneered all subsequent work on software design: Parnas [1972b] introduced the concept of information hiding—the cornerstone of good software design structures—while Parnas [1972a] introduced the notion of module specification, which we address in the next chapter. Parnas's subsequent work gave additional insights into the issues of program families (Parnas [1976]) and program modification for extension and contraction (Parnas [1979]). Parnas [1974] discusses the need for precision when we talk about hierarchical systems. Britton et al. [1981] discusses abstract interfaces for device interface modules. Hester et al. [1981] illustrates the use of good design documentation. Parnas's original papers are collected in Hoffman and Weiss [2001].

Hoffman [1989] discusses the issue of interface design and specification in a practical—yet rigorous—fashion. Hoffman [1990] discusses criteria for designing good module interfaces.

Work on module interconnection languages addresses the issue of providing linguistic mechanisms to describe the interconnection of software modules; examples are surveyed by Prieto-Diaz and Neighbors [1986].

The notion of an abstract data type is rooted in the work of Dahl et al. [1972] and Liskov and Zilles [1974]. Liskov and Guttag [1986] illustrates a methodical approach to software construction based on the recognition of abstractions.

Lientz and Swanson [1980] discusses the causes of change in software and reports figures showing the influence of various factors (such as a change in the data).

The TDN notation we used to illustrate designs is based on the programming languages Ada (see AJPO [1983]) and Modula-2 (see Wirth [1983]). The graphical representation we use resembles the HOOD notation, defined by the European Space Agency (see HOOD [1989]). Wasserman et al. [1990] describes another proposal; Buhr [1984] provides a graphical notation to describe Ada designs.

The issue of application generators is discussed in Software [1990c]. For conditional compilation, see Babich [1986], which places it in the context of configuration management.

Object-oriented design is illustrated by Booch [1986, 1987a, and 1987b] in the context of the Ada programming language and by Meyer [2000] in the context of the Eiffel programming language. Wegner [1987] presents a clear explanation and classification of the issues surrounding object-oriented language designs. Szyperski [1998] gives a comprehensive discussion of various object-oriented technologies and the solutions offered by *component* orientation.

Concurrent software design was addressed by Brinch Hansen [1977], who defined the programming language Concurrent Pascal. Rendezvous-based mechanisms were inspired by Communicating Sequential Processes (CSP), defined by Hoare [1974] and found their systematic application in the Ada programming language. Weihl [1989] discusses the use of abstract data types in a concurrent environment.

The issues of real-time systems are described by Wirth [1977] and Stankovic [1988]. Kopetz [1997] is a complete treatment of real-time systems with specific attention to time-triggered systems. The design of distributed systems is discussed by Shatz and Wang [1989].

The guardian concept in the context of distributed systems is due to Liskov and is the basis of the design of the ARGUS system (Liskov [1988]).

A design issue not specifically addressed in this book concerns user interfaces. The interested reader may refer to Schneiderman [1998] and the special issue of *IEEE Software* [1989a].

For a view of programming languages and their support of software design, refer to Ghezzi and Jazayeri [1998].

Other approaches to design are described in various books on "structured design," such as Yourdon and Constantine [1979] and Myers [1978]. These approaches are based on the notion of decomposition of a system into functional modules. The methods are part of a larger methodology, called structured analysis/structured design (SA/SD); we will address this methodology in Chapter 7. For a detailed discussion of the concepts of cohesion and coupling, refer to Yourdon and Constantine [1979] and Myers [1978].

Surveys of early software design techniques are presented by Bergland [1981] and Yau and Tsai [1986]. There are many books and papers on object-oriented design. Two ideas that have received a lot of attention in the OO work are design patterns and frameworks. Design patterns are recurring structures consisting of several components that appear in the design of many systems. Gamma et al. [1994] is the original source for this idea and contains 23 such patterns. Frameworks are a set of related classes that are almost like a skeleton for a particular application area or domain. We have used the word "framework" in this chapter in the generic sense. In the OO world, it has a strict definition. For examples of frameworks, see the special issue of the *Communications of the ACM* edited by Fayad and Schmidt [1997].

Although the term "architecture" was used even in the early 1980s by Parnas and Brinch Hansen, the systematic investigation of software architecture as an independent subject of study attracted attention only in the 1990s. Perry and Wolf [1992] argued for the systematic study of the subject. Shaw and Garlan [1996] is an initial systematic study of the field and explores the notion of components and connectors as the basic structuring abstractions for software architectures. Rechtin [1991] is an excellent source of commonsense ideas for system structuring. It emphasizes the importance of simplicity as an architectural principle.

A number of books report different experiences with software architecture. Among these are Bass et al. [1999], Hofmeister et al. [1999], and Jazayeri et al. [2000], which concentrates on architecture for product families. Buschmann et al. [1996] reports patterns to be used with software architecture. Kruchten [1995] is an influential paper that introduces the importance of different views of a software architecture. Garlan [2000] reviews the major issues in software architecture and predicts future developments.

Novel architectural paradigms are explored in many publications. Wolf and Rosenblum [1997] discusses event-based architectures, and Hauswirth and Jazayeri [1999] surveys push-based systems and compares them with event-based systems.

STL is described in detail by Musser and Saini [1996] and is analyzed from a software engineering viewpoint in Jazayeri [1995].

Fowler and Scott [1998] is a brief introduction to UML. Booch et al. [1999] is the original source.

There are many books on CORBA, DCOM, and other middleware. For example, see Emmerich [2000] and Orfali et al. [1997].

# C H A P T E R 5

# Specification

Every nontrivial engineering system must be *specified*. For instance, one can state that a bridge must support at least 1,000 tons, must be 30 meters wide, etc. In this sense, the specification is a precise statement of the requirements that the system—in this case, the bridge—must satisfy. Of course, we may specify not only the requirements of the final system, but also those of the subsystems and components that will be used to make up the system. So the bridge designer will specify, in addition, the requirements for the columns, the cables, the bolts, etc. Not only requirements, but also designs and architectures must be specified.

In traditional engineering disciplines, the word *specification* has a precise meaning. In software engineering, the term is used in several contexts with different meanings. We ourselves have used it informally several times in the previous chapters.

In general, we can view a specification as the statement of an agreement between a producer of a service and a consumer of the service or between an implementer and a user. Depending on the context, the implementer and the user are different, and the nature of the specification is different. A *requirements specification* is an agreement between the end user and the system developer. A *design specification*—for example, in terms of the USES hierarchy, a UML class diagram, or an IDL interface—is an agreement between the system architect (or designer) and the implementers. A *module specification* is an agreement between the programmers using the module and the programmer implementing the module. For instance, the exports clause of the modules in a TDN description can be viewed as a (syntactic) specification of those modules. Similarly, class diagrams can be enriched by listing the signature of all the exported operations.

As these examples show, the term "specification" is used at different stages of system development. Furthermore, a *specification* at some level states the requirements for the *implementation* at a lower level. Since the specification is an agreement between the user and the implementer, we can view it as a *definition* of what the implementation must achieve.

This relationship between the specification and the implementation is often explained in terms of the *what versus how* dichotomy described in Chapter 1. The specification states *what* a system should do; the implementer decides *how* to do it. In practice, however, the distinction between the two is often not so sharp. For instance, in some cases, the decision as to whether to distribute a banking system throughout the bank's branches or to keep it centralized in the main branch and use remote terminals at the other branches can be considered a design matter (i.e., a *how* matter). So one can claim that the physical distribution of the system is not a requirement, but an implementation issue. In other cases, the user can explicitly require a distributed architecture, which then automatically becomes part of the system specification. So an implementation that realizes all required functions, but uses a single mainframe, would be rejected as incorrect.

Furthermore, sometimes a simple way to describe *what* one wants is just to give an example of *how* it can be done. This implies not that it must be done in exactly that way, but that it must behave *as if* it were done that way. For instance, one can state that the execution of several concurrent transactions in an information system must be performed as if each transaction were executed in a noninterruptible way. This does not necessarily require the implementer to let each transaction run to completion before starting another one—which would be highly inefficient in the case of long transactions. Rather, the implementer is free to interleave the execution of different transactions, as long as each is perceived by the user to have run without interruption.

In principle, all desirable qualities should be specified, and the implementation should ensure that all desirable qualities are achieved by the product (e.g., in terms of functionality, usability, performance, portability, etc.). In this chapter, however, we concentrate mostly on the specification of software functionality (i.e., on *functional specifications*). We briefly address the specification of nonfunctional properties in Section 5.2.

The specification activity is a critical part of the whole design process. Specifications themselves are the result of a complex and creative design activity; they are subject to errors just as are the products of other activities, such as coding. As a consequence, all the design principles discussed in Chapter 3 should be applied as well to the specification process.

In this chapter, we first analyze the *uses* of specifications. Next, we point out the main specification *qualities* that should be kept in mind in writing specifications. Then we analyze some of the most relevant techniques of writing specifications, by classifying them according to different *specification styles*. We discuss the *applicability* of each class to various application areas. The role of specification throughout the development process will then be taken up in Chapter 6. Finally, we discuss the problems in, and the techniques for, *managing* the specifications of real systems, which inevitably tend to be complex and tedious.

## 5.1     THE USES OF SPECIFICATIONS

Specifications can be created and used for different purposes. Let us examine their major uses.

**A statement of user requirements.**     The primary purpose of a product is to meet its user's requirements. User requirements are often not clearly understood by the developer. If this is the case, a careful analysis, involving frequent interaction with the user, should be devoted to clarifying, and documenting a clear statement of requirements, in order to uncover and avoid possible misunderstandings. Sometimes, at the beginning of a project, even the user has no clear idea of exactly what the desired product is. For instance, a user with little previous experience with computer products may not appreciate the degree to which his or her problems may be automated. It is likely that an initial description produced by an inexperienced user will lack even a precise formulation of system functions and performance requirements.

Other times, however, the requirements can be very clear, and their specification may be straightforward. In traditional engineering, in fact, standard specifications exist for such things as nails, screws, and tiles. Such standards enable different producers to produce the "same" product. In software engineering, a programming language (and a target architecture) can be viewed as a standard specification for a compiler. This also enables different producers to build a product based on the same specification.

Many times, major failures occur because of misunderstandings between the producer and the user. Such misunderstandings are more likely to occur when the culture and the "language" of the two are widely different—for instance, when the user is a lawyer or works in the humanities. Case study A in the Appendix is an example of this problem.

When misunderstandings occur, unfortunately, going back to the document that specifies the requirements usually reveals an ambiguity that supports both the user's and the producer's interpretation. This situation shows a need for the ability to *verify* the specifications—for example, to check whether they adequately define what the product has to be—before implementing the product. For instance, submitting a specification document to the end user may help uncover previous misunderstandings of actual user needs. This way, improper definitions may be avoided by discovering them early. We shall analyze the issue of verification of specifications in more depth in Section 5.4. The issue of involving the user in the verification will be discussed in Section 5.7.3. We shall have more to say about the specification of user needs in Chapters 6 and 7.

**A statement of the interface between the machine and the controlled environment.** Computers interact with the external environment by receiving inputs (e.g., signals from the sensors of a controlled plant or commands from a user) and providing outputs (e.g., control data to actuators or responses to user commands). A flawed specification or a misunderstanding between software engineers and the experts in the given domain who know all about the phenomena affecting the control function to be implemented by software can have serious undesirable effects. Both may cause a later redesign and reimplementation of a large part of the application, thus increasing development costs. But—more seriously, in the case of a critical system—if these problems are not caught and propagate to the implementation, they may cause disasters from which it is impossible to recover. It is therefore necessary to specify the interface between the machine and the controlled environment by describing precisely inputs, outputs, and expected relationships, including perhaps a specification of time constraints that the controller should satisfy.

This example and the previous one share a common essence. What the specification aims at is a precise description of the borderline between the machine and the external world with which the machine interacts. In the case of human-centered systems, the external environment can be described and understood in terms of what the end user expects in order to accomplish his or her tasks. In the case of embedded systems, the external environment is the set of devices controlled by the machine.

**A statement of the requirements for the implementation.**    Specifications are used as a reference point while the product is being implemented. In fact, the ultimate goal of the implementation is to build a product that meets the specifications. Thus, the implementer uses the specifications during the design phase to make design decisions and during the verification activity to check that the implementation complies with the specifications.

We have already remarked that the whole design process is a chain of definition-implementation-verification steps. Thus, it is likely that several different specification documents will exist. As already mentioned, a specification that defines the external behavior of the system is called a *requirements specification*, and a specification of the software architecture, possibly at several levels of abstraction, is called a *design specification*.

In general, different uses of the specifications stress the required qualities in different—perhaps even contrasting—ways. For instance, if specifications must be used as part of a contract, then all parties to the contract must be able to understand the specifications. This may restrict the *language* used for writing them, since technical terminology and notation may not be acceptable to many users. In contrast, the specification of, say, a module interface, is more useful for guiding its implementation if it is written in a formal notation of the type introduced in Chapter 4.

**A reference point during product maintenance.**    In Chapters 2 and 4, we saw that several kinds of maintenance may occur during a product's life cycle. All involve specifications.

In the case of corrective maintenance, usually only the implementation is changed. Thus, specifications are needed to check whether the new implementation corrects the errors contained in the previous version of the product. An exception could be when the error is in the specification itself, but is not discovered until the product is used. In this case, one must first correct the specification and then modify the implementation accordingly.

Adaptive maintenance occurs because of changes in the requirements. Among such changes are modifications of the functionality of the product—say, coping with a new tax law in a payroll system—and modifications in the operating environment—say, a change in the automatic teller mechanisms in a banking system. In such cases, the original specifications must be adapted to the new requirements. Then the new implementation must be checked against the specifications again for correctness. Sometimes engineers try to reduce development time by changing the implementation, without first updating the specifications. This practice, however, creates inconsistencies between specification and implementation and leads to bigger problems in the future. One of the worst examples of such an approach is when "patches" are applied to the object code, as in Case Study A. The patches produce inconsistencies even between the source code and the object code.

In perfective maintenance, sometimes the functional requirements do not change. For example, one may wish to restructure the design of a product in an attempt to gain an improvement in performance. In other cases, such as the inclusion of new functions or the modification of an existing function, the functional requirements also change. Again, what is important is the use of specifications to understand the impact of the change clearly and to accomplish the change reliably. Similar considerations apply to changes that must be made to product modules. If a precise specification of a module is available, it is possible to understand whether the change affects the module implementation only, in which case the client modules are unaffected, or whether it affects the interface, too. In the former case, the burden of dealing with the change rests only on the module's developer; in the latter, all the developers of the client modules also are involved.

## 5.2    SPECIFICATION QUALITIES

Of course, one can write good specifications or bad ones. Most of the qualities listed in Chapter 2 as general software qualities contribute to the production of good specifications. For instance, usability is a relevant feature for specifications as well as for the whole software product. As with software, usability applied to specifications implies different requirements, depending on who the user of the specification actually is (e.g., the end user or the implementer). Maintainability is also desirable for specifications, because, as we saw in the previous section, specifications are likely to change during a product's life as the product itself changes.

In this section, we discuss three qualities that are especially relevant to specifications. The first set of qualities required of specifications is that they should be *clear, unambiguous*, and *understandable*. This claim sounds obvious, but it cannot be overemphasized. In particular, informal specifications, written in a natural language, are likely to contain subtle ambiguities.

For instance, consider the common example of a word processor providing a **select** command, specified in the following way:[1]

> Selecting is the process of designating areas of the document that you want to work on. Most editing and formatting actions require two steps: first you select what you want to work on, such as text or graphics; then you initiate the appropriate action.

Such a definition does not specify exactly what the term "area" means. It turns out that in most tools the definition implicitly assumes an area to be a "*contiguous* sequence of characters." A user unaware of this assumption might, however, interpret the term "area" as the collection of *scattered* sequences of characters, so that one could go through a text, selecting different, not necessarily contiguous, words and then, say, italicizing all of them with a single command. This is not possible in traditional word processors. The main point, however, is that the original specification does not make clear whether it is possible or not.

Another example is the following fragment of a specification taken from the documentation of a real project for a mission-critical system:

> The message must be triplicated. The three copies must be forwarded through three different physical channels. The receiver accepts the message on the basis of a two-out-of-three voting policy.

Intuitively, this specification states that, for reasons of reliability, messages are triplicated. Upon receiving three copies of a message, the receiver determines the content by comparing the copies: If two of them match, their content is assumed correct. It is not clear, however, whether the message may, or should, be considered received *as soon as* two identical copies have been received, without waiting for the third one, or whether the receiver should wait for all three copies before comparing their contents. Since we are

---

[1] From the manual of *Microsoft Word 4.0.*

talking about a real-time system, this point can make a significant difference when it comes to acting on the message.[2]

The application of rigor and formality can help significantly in achieving these and many other qualities of specifications. For instance, the ambiguity in the voting policy just mentioned was discovered because it was decided to formalize the informal specification. Later in the chapter, we shall see how to formalize the voting policy to remove *all* ambiguities.

The second major quality requirement for specifications is *consistency*. For instance, as regards a word processor, one could state that

- The whole text should be kept in lines of equal length, with the length specified by the user.
- Unless the user gives an explicit hyphenation command, a carriage return should occur only at the end of a word.

This definition, however, does not cover the case where a particular word is longer than the length specified for lines. In such a case, the specification is self-contradictory, or *inconsistent*. Therefore, no implementation can satisfy it. The probability of inadvertently including some inconsistency in a specification increases as the specification documents become longer and more complex, which is often the case in real-life projects.

The third quality requirement for specifications is that they should be *complete*. There are two aspects of completeness. First, the specification must be *internally complete*. This means that the specification must define any new concept or terminology that it uses. A glossary is often helpful for this purpose. For example, if the specification of an elevator system states that "in the absence of any outstanding requests, the elevator enters a *wait-for-request* state," the specification must also define the meaning of "wait-for-request state."

The second aspect (*external completeness*) refers to completeness with respect to requirements: The specification must document all the needed requirements. In the elevator example, if it is required that an elevator with no outstanding requests go to the first floor and open its doors, this requirement must be stated explicitly and not left to the designer's discretion. External completeness implicitly refers to functional requirements. Although normally functional requirements are the most crucial kinds of requirements, they are not the only ones that matter. Nonfunctional, or quality, requirements (usability, reliability, performance, etc.) are also quite important. For example, response-time performance often is not specified for non-real-time systems (e.g., word processors). Upon using the product, however, the customer may complain that the system is too slow. Exceptional cases also are rarely specified, yet they are quite relevant; for instance, one would not be very happy if a power failure caused all open files to be lost.

---

[2]By looking at the design documentation, we found that, actually, neither of the two suggested interpretations was chosen by the implementer. In fact, the receiver polled the three channels periodically, so that an implicit time-out was defined: If the three copies were received within a given period of time, all of them were compared; if, however, after the given period of time, only two copies of the message were available and they matched, then the message was accepted without waiting for the third transmission.

It is often unrealistic to ask for complete specifications in a strict sense. This is because many requirements can be identified clearly only after one gains some experience with the system. Moreover, too many details would need to be specified. More realistically, some requirements are considered to be common to every system and are assumed to be implicit in all specifications. This assumption, in turn, may lead us to accept some amount of imprecision and ambiguity. For instance, one will often be satisfied with sentences of the type "response times should be about two seconds" or "the system should be robust with respect to power failures." The aim, however, is to keep such imprecision within limits that avoid the risk of dangerous ambiguities of the type mentioned earlier. It is the responsibility of both the user and the producer to decide when some imprecision can be accepted on a commonsense basis and when it must be avoided as dangerous.

One might even argue that in many practical cases, including the examples we have discussed in this section, specifications are stated informally on purpose, because the choice of which interpretation should be given to remove ambiguities is viewed as an implementation decision: One or another way of removing these ambiguities is equally acceptable from the user's standpoint. According to this view, providing a precise specification would overspecify the system and unduly constrain the implementer. The weakness in this position is that one does not ordinarily know whether the lack of precision in the specification is deliberate or due to oversight. Moreover, the use of an informal language does not help in highlighting the places where ambiguities are hidden. Only when one tries to describe the requirements formally do the questions arise. At that point, one can make a conscious and explicit decision: Either the specification should precisely state what is to be done, or the resolution of the ambiguity should be deferred to the implementation.

Because of the difficulties in achieving complete, precise, and unambiguous specifications, the use of the *incrementality* principle is especially important in deriving specifications. That is, one may start off with a fairly sketchy specification document and expand it through several steps, perhaps after some experience with early prototypes. We shall see examples of this strategy later in the chapter. For similar reasons, the modularity principle is also important for specifications.

### Exercises

**5.1**   Go through all the software qualities listed in Chapter 2, and state clearly which are relevant for specifications and which are not.

**5.2**   Give a precise specification for the *justify* function in a word processor.

## 5.3    CLASSIFICATION OF SPECIFICATION STYLES

We may classify the many different styles of specifications according to two different, independent criteria.

Specifications can be stated *formally* or *informally*. Informal specifications are written in a natural language; they can, however, also make use of figures, tables, and other notations to provide more structure and help the understanding. They can also be structured in a standardized way. A notation that has a precise syntax and meaning is called a *formalism*. We use formalisms to create *formal specifications*. It is also useful to talk of *semiformal* specifications, since, in practice, we sometimes use a notation without insisting on a completely precise semantics for it. The TDN and GDN notations introduced in Section 4.2.3.1 are an example of semiformal notations, since they put together a formal syntactic description of module interfaces and an informal statement of their meaning. We shall see later how the informal comments in our TDN module specifications can be made precise by formalizing the semantics of the operations. Similarly, UML class diagrams can be used as a semiformal notation to describe a design. A formal language called OCL is also available to provide precise semantics of classes.

The second major distinction between different specification styles is between operational and descriptive specifications. *Operational specifications* describe the intended system by describing its *desired behavior*, usually by providing a model implementation of the system (i.e., an abstract device that in some way can simulate its behavior). By contrast, *descriptive specifications* try to state the *desired properties* of the system in a purely declarative fashion.

For example, suppose you give the following specification of a geometric figure E: E is a geometric figure that can be drawn as follows:

1. Select two points $P_1$ and $P_2$ on a plane.
2. Select a string of a certain length and fix its ends to $P_1$ and $P_2$ respectively.
3. Position a pencil as shown in Figure 5.1.
4. Move the pen clockwise, keeping the string tightly stretched, until you reach the point where you started drawing.

What we have just given is an operational definition of the curve known in geometry as an ellipse with foci $P_1$ and $P_2$. An alternative definition of the same curve could be given by providing its equation, $ax^2 + by^2 + c = 0$, where $a$, $b$, and $c$ are suitable constants.

The example shows that an operational definition readily allows us to check whether the specification describes the kind of curve that we had in mind when we gave the specification. It is in fact easy to draw a curve with paper and pencil following the specification and then examine whether the curve satisfies, say, the aesthetic requirements we had in mind. Of course, the implementation of the curve might turn out to be entirely different from what is given in the specification; for example, it might be a curve to be displayed on a graphics terminal. Nevertheless, experimentation helps us understand whether the specification we gave is correct. By contrast, if we want to check whether, say, a given point P at position $(x_1, y_1)$ lies on the curve, we can do that more easily by referring to the equation, which might also help in assessing the adequacy of the requirements: The curve might be the trajectory of a robot, point P

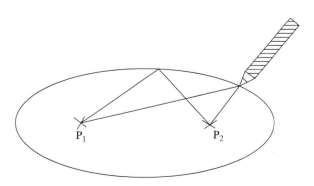

FIGURE 5.1

Construction of an ellipse.

might represent the site where a human should work, and safety reasons might require that the robot never cross point P.

For a software example, consider the following informal operational specification of the sorting of an array:

> Let a be an array of n elements. The result of sorting a is an array b of n elements that may be built as follows:
>
> 1. Find the smallest element in a, and assign it as the first element in b.
> 2. Remove the element you found in step 1 from a, and find the smallest of the remaining elements. Assign this element as the second element in b.
> 3. Repeat steps 1 and 2 until all elements have been removed from a.

This specification suggests a natural and simple (although not very efficient) way of implementing the sorting of an array. The suggestion, however, does not imply that a sorting algorithm *must* sort a in that way: It must only produce the same result. Thus, quicksort, for example, is a perfectly adequate implementation of the specification. The problem with this kind of specification, however, is that it is difficult for the reader to determine what it actually prescribes, what must be implemented, and what is not.

A possible descriptive specification of the sorting of a is the following:

> The result of sorting a is an array b that is a permutation of a and is sorted.

If the concepts of *permutation* and being *sorted* are not considered to be clear enough, they can be further specified. If, on the other hand, they are deemed to be primitive concepts, specification may be considered to be complete at this stage.

There are several trade-offs between descriptive and operational specification styles. It is sometimes claimed that descriptive specifications are *more abstract* than operational specifications, because they do not bias the reader towards any particular implementation. Rather, they help focus on essential properties of the system without modeling the behavior of any implementation. Although this is basically true, we must recognize that some hidden implementation schema is present in *any* specification. For instance, the foregoing descriptive specification of sorting an array suggests the following trivial implementation: "Enumerate all permutations of the original array. The first permutation that is sorted is an acceptable output for a sorting algorithm."

One could also write specifications that are in some sense halfway between operational and descriptive. For instance, one could define a new operation to be applied to an array a in the following way:

- First, a must be sorted, where the definition of "sorted" is given in the previous descriptive way.
- Then, any duplicate elements of the sorted array must be deleted from the array.

This specification is operational in the sense that it specifies a sequence of two operations to be performed to obtain the desired result. But part of it—the meaning of the term "sorted"—is given in a descriptive way.

In sum, the distinction between operational and descriptive specifications is not always sharp and is sometimes subjective. It is, however, an adequate distinction for categorizing different specification styles.

In this chapter, we develop a deeper understanding of specification styles, techniques, and goals by describing and critically evaluating some sample specification techniques. While we have selected these techniques because they are important representatives of specification styles, it is not the particular choices that are our main subject. Since there is no style that is right for all circumstances, our purpose is to help the reader develop the ability to analyze a specification technique or style critically and then select or reject it, depending on the situation. The appropriate style or notation can help a designer express a design or problem clearly. An inappropriate notation makes it difficult to do so. Some notations, however, are gaining wide acceptance and are increasingly being adopted in practice. As a consequence, they have become subject to standardization. The UML notation, which we introduced in Chapter 4 and which will be further illustrated in this chapter, is a notable example of a standardized notation.

No style or notation, however, formal or informal, can guarantee that the designer will come up with a good design or an insightful formulation of a problem. Good specification and design require adequate skills, experience, taste, judgement, and even creativity. Since so much in the design activity depends on subjective criteria, it is important to develop a critical intuition that enables one to adapt the right specification style, technique, and notation to the problem at hand.

### Exercises

**5.3**   Give a completely descriptive specification of the previous example that used a mix of descriptive and operational styles to describe the construction of a sorted array with no duplicates.

**5.4**   Consider the operational and descriptive specifications of the sort operation given in this section. Are there ambiguities in these specifications? How are duplicate elements to be treated?

## 5.4    VERIFICATION OF SPECIFICATIONS

We have stated that one important use of specifications is to serve as a reference against which we can verify an implementation. But we also observed that the specification itself must be verified. In Chapter 2, we saw that the correctness of an application does not automatically imply that the functions performed by the application are exactly the ones that were meant by the customer. The same observation holds for all software qualities. Even if the implementation eventually satisfies the specification, we may still end up with a product that does not match the user's expectations. It is thus important that specifications be verified prior to starting an implementation, in order to assess their correctness.

There are two general ways of verifying a specification. One consists of observing the dynamic behavior of the specified system in order to check whether it conforms to the intuitive understanding we had of the behavior of the ideal system. The other consists of analyzing the properties of the specified system that can be deduced from the specification. The properties that are deduced are then checked against the expected properties of the system.

The effectiveness of both techniques increases as a function of the degree of formality of the specification. In fact, in a completely formal setting, a way of observing the dynamic behavior of the specified system may consist of providing an interpreter of the formal language in which the specifications are written and then executing formal specifications on sample input data. Similarly, deducing new properties from the ones stated as part of the (descriptive) specification can be made mechanical in some formal logic setting, as we shall see.

In the example of an ellipse shown in Figure 5.1, the observation of the dynamic system behavior can also be called *simulation*. Simulation is obtained by executing the formal specification, and this, following the concepts we introduced in Chapter 2, yields a *prototype* of the specified system, before any implementation has been started. In a less formal setting, execution may be simulated in the human mind, rather than mechanically, and this more easily accommodates informality. Similarly, *property analysis* can be done by human inspection, especially if the specifications are not fully formal.

It is perhaps useful to compare software engineering with more traditional engineering fields. There, descriptive specifications are often given in terms of (or on the basis of) mathematical equations that model the system. Think of a bridge of a given shape connecting two banks of a river: The mathematical model provided by the engineer supports a property analysis, in terms of whether the bridge can or cannot sustain a given distribution of static or dynamic forces. An operational model of the system is often built as a mock-up (a prototype, in our terminology), which is usually viewed not as a specification, but rather as an aid in verifying the specifications. In both bridge building and software building, an inadequate specification can lead to system failure. Bridges have been known to collapse in storms because the specifications did not take into account unusual wind formations.

So far, we have discussed only the verification of functional specifications. It is also important to verify the completeness and consistency of specifications. Again, with formal specifications, some of this verification may be done mechanically (e.g., verifying that all terms used in the specification document are defined); some verification, however, may require the use of more sophisticated proofs. Informal specifications are harder to verify automatically, but even for them, some mechanical checks are possible and should be used.

We will take up the issues of the verification of requirements later in the chapter and also in Chapters 6, 7, and 9.

## 5.5 OPERATIONAL SPECIFICATIONS

In this section, we describe a few widely known and applied notations for giving specifications in an operational style. We start from semiformal notations that are widely adopted in practice for the description of information systems. Then we illustrate formal notations that are suitable for describing control aspects in system modeling.

### 5.5.1 Data Flow Diagrams: Specifying Functions of Information Systems

*Data flow diagrams* (DFDs) are a well-known and widely used notation for specifying the functions of an information system and how data flow from functions to functions. They describe systems as *collections of functions* that manipulate *data*. Data can be organized in several ways: They can be stored in *data repositories*, they can flow in *data flows*, and they can be transferred to or from the external environment.

One of the reasons for the success of DFDs is that they can be expressed by means of an attractive graphical notation that makes them easy to use.

The following are the basic elements of a DFD:[3]

- Functions, represented by *bubbles*.
- Data flows, represented by *arrows*. Arrows going to bubbles represent input values that belong to the domain of the function represented by the bubble. Outgoing arrows represent the results of the function—that is, values that belong to the range of the function.
- Data stores, represented by *open boxes*. Arrows entering (exiting) open boxes represent data that are inserted into (extracted from) the data store.
- Input-output, represented by special kinds of *I/O boxes* that describe data acquisition and generation during human-computer interaction.

Figure 5.2 gives examples of these graphical symbols. Figure 5.3 shows how the symbols can be composed to form a DFD. The DFD describes the evaluation of the arithmetic expression

```
(a + b) * (c + a * d),
```

assuming that the data a, b, c, and d are read from a terminal and the result is printed. The figure shows that arrows can be "forked" to represent the fact that the same datum is used in different places.

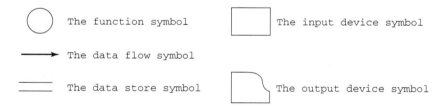

**FIGURE 5.2**

The basic graphical symbols used to build data flow diagrams.

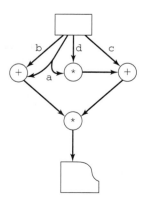

**FIGURE 5.3**

A data flow diagram for specifying the evaluation of an arithmetic expression.

---

[3] The DFD notation is not standardized. The literature contains several slightly different definitions.

**Example 5.1**

Figure 5.4 describes a simplified information system for a public library. The data and functions shown are not necessarily computer data or computer functions. The DFD describes physical objects, such as books and shelves, together with data stores that are likely to be, but are not necessarily, realized as computer files. Getting a book from the shelf can be done either automatically—by a robot—or manually. In both cases, the action of getting a book is represented by a function depicted by a bubble. The figure could even represent the organization of a library with no computerized procedures.

The figure also describes the fact that, in order to obtain a book, the following are necessary: an explicit user request consisting of the title, the name of the author of the book, and the user's name; access to the shelves that contain the book; a list of authors; and a list of titles. These provide the information necessary to find the book.

The way the book is actually obtained, however, is not at all mentioned in the figure. If we did not use our previous experience about the way one borrows a book from a library, there would be no way to deduce this information from the figure. Thus, we should consider this DFD as a *first approximation* of the description of a library information system. A finer description of how a book can be selected from the library shelves is given in Figure 5.5, which can be seen as a *refinement* of (a part of) Figure 5.4. Figure 5.5 is still somewhat imprecise, in that it does not specify whether both the title of the book and the name of the author are necessary to identify a book or whether only one of them is enough. We do know that, in general, one

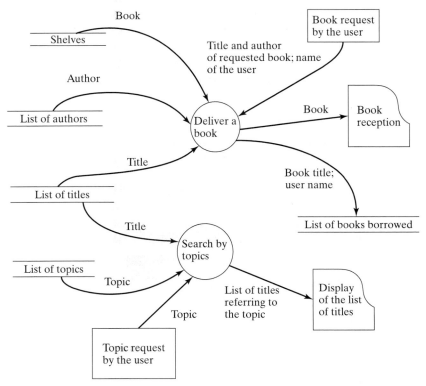

FIGURE 5.4

A DFD describing a simplified library information system.

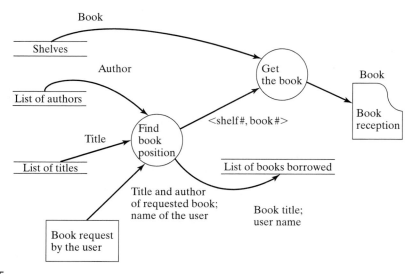

**FIGURE 5.5**

Partial refinement of the function "Deliver a book" of Figure 5.4.

is sufficient, but occasionally, both are necessary. This distinction, however, is not explained by the figure.                                                                ∎

In Example 5.1, Figures 5.4 and 5.5 provide an intuitive description of the system, but they lack precision. This is true in general for DFDs, which lack a precise meaning, chiefly for the following reasons:

1. The *semantics* of the symbols used is specified only by the identifiers chosen by the user. Sometimes this is sufficiently precise; for example, the symbol '+' clearly denotes the function "add," and no further explanation is needed. Other times, however, more explanation is necessary. For instance, the function "Find book position" of Figure 5.5 has some intuitive meaning, but does not fully specify what happens if some information is missing. A realistic (but still informal) definition could be the following:

   ```
   If the user supplies both author name(s) and book title then
           determine book position (if the book does not
           exist, give an appropriate message)
   elsif only the author is given then
           supply a list of all existing books by that
           author and ask the user for a selection;
   elsif only the title is given then...
       .
       .
       .
   end if
   ```

2. *Control* aspects are not defined by the model. For example, Figure 5.6 shows a simple DFD in which the outputs of three bubbles, A, B, and C, are inputs to D and D's two outputs are inputs to the bubbles E and F. By itself, this diagram does not specify clearly the way in which inputs are used and outputs are pro-

duced by the function D. In particular, there are many different, equally plausible alternatives for both input and output. For the inputs,

- D may need all of A, B, and C; that is, D may be unable to execute unless A, B, and C are all present together.
- D may need only one of A, B, and C to execute; that is, the associated data transformation could take place when only one of A, B, and C is present.

For the outputs,

- D may output a result just to one of the two output bubbles E and F, again in a nondeterministic, but exclusive, way.
- D may output the same data to both E and F.
- D may output distinct data to E and F.

Other interpretations of D's inputs and outputs are also compatible with Figure 5.6.

Another case where DFDs leave synchronization between components of a system completely unspecified is shown in Figure 5.7, where two bubbles A and B are connected by a single data flow, with A's output being B's input. There are at least two possible interpretations of this DFD:

- A produces a datum and then waits until B has consumed it. (This is often the case when A and B denote arithmetic operations on simple data.)
- A and B are autonomous activities that have different speeds, but there is a buffering mechanism between them (some sort of bounded queue or unbounded pipe) which ensures that no data are lost or duplicated (for instance, if A denotes computing the time spent by employees in their work and B denotes computing a payroll).

In sum, DFDs are an attractive graphical notation that is suitable for capturing, in a fairly immediate and intuitive way, the flow of data and the operations involved in an information system. However, DFDs lack a precise semantics. Although the notation can be seen as operational, the behavior of the abstract machine corresponding to

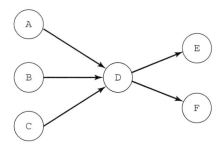

FIGURE 5.6

A DFD that is ambiguous in its use of inputs and outputs.

FIGURE 5.7

A DFD that does not specify synchronization between modules.

a DFD is not fully specified. Rather, different interpretations are generally possible for the control regime associated with a DFD.

These drawbacks have some negative consequences. First, if a rough description of the system modeled is not sufficient, and we need a precise and detailed definition, DFDs simply cannot do the job. Second, imagine that you want to build a machine to simulate the system modeled, in order to test whether the specifications reflect the user's expectations. Such a machine cannot be derived *directly* from the DFD, because no machine execution is possible without a precise semantics for the notation. A human reader is able to fill the semantic gap thanks to the intuitive meaning of the identifiers. But the machine, lacking intuition, will not be able to interpret a notation of the type given in Figure 5.7.

For these reasons, we say that traditional DFDs are a *semiformal notation*. Their syntax—the way they compose bubbles, arrows, and boxes—is sometimes defined precisely, but their semantics is not.

Several methods have been designed to overcome these difficulties. They can be classified roughly as follows:

- *Using a complementary notation to describe those aspects of the system that are not captured adequately by DFDs.* Thus, the complete system specification will consist of the integration of different descriptions provided in different notations. We shall see examples of this technique later in the chapter.

- *Augmenting the DFD model in order to cope with aspects that are not captured by its traditional version.* For instance, we can handle control aspects by introducing *control flow arrows*. A control flow arrow going to a bubble means that the computation of the function associated with the bubble may occur only when a signal is present in the arrow. Figure 5.8 shows the notation and an example of the use of control flow arrows.

- *Revising the traditional definition of a DFD to make it fully formal.* For example, one could define a formal DFD model that would make it possible to express all desirable interpretations of original DFDs in an unambiguous fashion. Thus, one might use different notations to distinguish the case where the arrow between two bubbles specifies the flow of a single datum from that where the arrow represents a pipe. Or one could annotate the diagram to specify whether all input data flows are needed, or whether only one is required, to compute the function performed by a given bubble. Finally, one could provide a notation that would formally specify the function performed by a bubble.

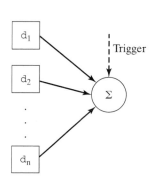

**FIGURE 5.8**

A partial DFD augmented with control flow arrows. The trigger is a control flow arrow that is dashed rather than continuous. The function "sum" associated with the bubble is applied to all data existing in the boxes as soon as a trigger occurs.

## Exercises

**5.5** Give a more complete description of a library information system, including several other operations, such as returning or reserving a book or doing a bibliographic search. Then, refine the operations up to a level where all of them are explained in sufficient detail.

**5.6** Give a completely detailed specification of a reasonably powerful and realistic function, "finding book position." You are invited to reflect on how many details are involved in the full specification of such a small and seemingly simple part of a seemingly simple information system.

**5.7** Provide a DFD description of how one can apply for admission to, and then become enrolled in, your university.

### 5.5.2    UML Diagrams for Specifying Behaviors

As we mentioned in Chapter 4, UML is a collection of languages that provide specific notations to specify, analyze, visualize, construct, and document the artifacts of a software system. The notations are used by software engineers to produce standardized blueprints that contain a number of different diagrams, each enlightening a certain aspect of the software system. In this section, we illustrate use case diagrams, sequence diagrams, and collaboration diagrams, all of which can be used to model the dynamic aspects of a system.

*Use case diagrams* provide a global view of the actors involved in a system and the actions that the system performs, which in turn provide an observable result that is of value to the actors. Use case diagrams describe the overall context of a system by partitioning the system's functionality into transactions that are useful to actors and showing how actors interact with them. Actors are an abstraction of an external person, process, or entity interacting with the system being described. Actors are linked to use cases by associations, which represent the communication path between the actor and the use case it participates in.

For example, consider the description of a library in Figure 5.9. The system allows customers to borrow and return books. These actions involve both customers and librarians. Librarians can update the library by inserting copies of new books and eliminating copies of old ones.

*Sequence diagrams* and *collaboration diagrams* are two equivalent notations that can be used to describe how objects interact by exchanging messages. They provide a dynamic view of a system by graphically displaying *scenarios* that may occur at run time when objects interact to accomplish certain tasks.

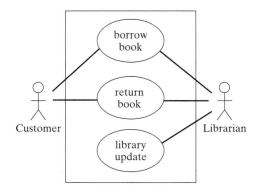

FIGURE 5.9

A use case diagram.

As an example, the sequence diagram of Figure 5.10 illustrates a fragment of the specification of a library system by describing one of the scenarios that may occur when the customer of a library borrows a book. In the scenario, first the customer provides his or her membership card to the librarian, and then the librarian checks whether the membership card is expired. If the card is valid, the catalogue is checked to see whether the book is available. If it is, then finally the customer can borrow the book. The sequence diagram visually indicates the progression of time in the vertical direction and the temporal sequence of messages exchanged between objects (the customer, the librarian, and the catalogue).

Figure 5.11 describes the same scenario by means of a collaboration diagram. The diagram indicates the objects involved in the interaction and describes the temporal sequence of events by numbering the relevant labels on the arcs connecting collaborating objects. As we mentioned, sequence diagrams and collaboration diagrams are semantically equivalent, but syntactically different. The choice of which of the two to use is a matter of personal taste. Collaboration diagrams make the structural properties of a collaboration more evident, whereas sequence diagrams highlight the temporal evolution of the scenario.

The specifications of use cases and possible scenarios of the behavior of the system are quite useful in the requirements phase, when the software engineer interacts with the expected user to elicit his or her expectations. The diagrams describe in a very intuitive way a number of representative cases of the system behavior. By reading these diagrams, the expected user can confirm whether the specifications capture the expected behaviors faithfully.

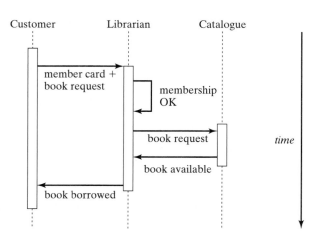

FIGURE 5.10

A sequence diagram.

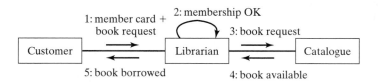

FIGURE 5.11

A collaboration diagram.

### 5.5.3    Finite State Machines: Describing Control Flow

In the description of information systems, the emphasis is on the organization of functions and data flows. We saw, however, that to make specifications more precise, some attention must be paid to *control* aspects as well. For instance, sooner or later, one may wish to specify in a DFD whether the execution of a function must wait for all inputs or whether it can start as soon as some of them are available. In a similar way, programming languages have constructs both to describe data organization and to describe the flow of control.

In the specification of different systems, the balance between data and control flow may be different. For instance, in a communication system, one might first like to state requirements such as the following:

- One must not write into a full buffer or read from an empty one.
- One should not access a buffer while another process is writing into it.
- Reading from a buffer must have a higher priority than writing into it.
- Every message must be forwarded through some channel within 2 milliseconds from its arrival.

Then, one could also attend to functional aspects such as the following:

- For each message received, the parity must be checked.
- For every 10 messages received, a new message is synthesized that is the concatenation of the 10 messages, preceded by a header that specifies the address of the receiving station.

Thus, both information systems and control systems—and, indeed, all other kinds of systems—have functional and data aspects as well as control aspects. The models used, however, could put different emphases on the two, according to the nature of the systems.

*Finite state machines* (FSMs) are a simple, widely known, and important formal notation for describing control aspects. An FSM consists of[4]

1. a finite set of states, $Q$;
2. a finite set of inputs, $I$;
3. a transition function $\delta: Q \times I \rightarrow Q$. $\delta$ can be a partial function; that is, it can be undefined for some values of its domain.

An FSM may be shown by a graph whose nodes represent states; an arc labeled $i$ goes from $q_1$ to $q_2$ if and only if $\delta(q_1, i) = q_2$. Figure 5.12 shows a simple FSM.

As the term itself suggests, FSMs are suitable for describing systems that can be in a finite set of states and that can go from one state into another as a consequence of some event, modeled by an input symbol. For instance, a lamp can be either on or off and can go from on to off as the consequence of an external action consisting of pushing a button on the attached switch. Pushing the button again causes the opposite transition. This simple system is described by the FSM of Figure 5.13. Another simple example of the use of FSMs is given next.

---

[4] More precisely, this is the definition of a *deterministic* finite-state machine.

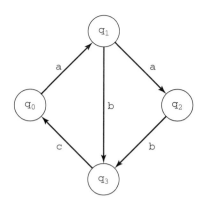

FIGURE 5.12

A finite state machine.

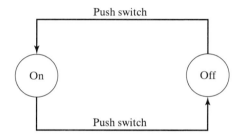

FIGURE 5.13

A finite state machine description of a lamp switch.

## Example 5.2

Consider the control of a (small part of a) chemical plant. Temperature and pressure levels must be monitored for safety reasons. Sensors are installed to detect and generate appropriate signals when either of these levels exceeds some predefined values. A trivial policy for managing the plant is the following: When either one of the signals is raised by the corresponding sensor, the control system shuts the plant off and raises an alarm signal; the system is restarted manually when the cause of the failure has been rectified. All this is described by the FSM of Figure 5.14.

This simple policy is obviously inadequate. A better way of managing the plant is as follows: When one of the two signals is raised, the system enters a recovery state in which it tries to apply a recovery action. If, after a while, the recovery action succeeds, the system is automatically reset to the "normal" state, and a message, "everything OK," is issued to the external environment. Otherwise, the alarm signal must be raised and the plant must be shut off. The system must also be switched off if it is trying to recover from one kind of anomaly—temperature or pressure—and the other signal is raised. It is assumed that the two signals cannot occur simultaneously. This new policy is described by the FSM of Figure 5.15. ∎

FSMs are often used to specify sets of acceptable strings of input symbols (i.e., formal languages). In such a case, they are augmented by defining an *initial state* $q_0 \in Q$ and a subset $F$ of $Q$, called the set of *final* or *accepting* states, graphically denoted by doubly circled nodes. The set $I$ is the set of characters used to form the input strings.

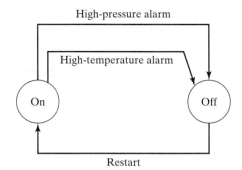

**FIGURE 5.14**

An FSM describing the control of a chemical plant.

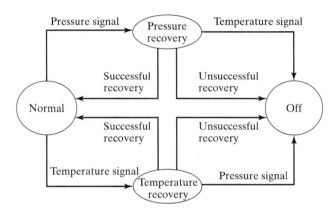

**FIGURE 5.15**

A refined policy for the control of a chemical plant described by an FSM.

An input string is *accepted* by the FSM if and only if there is a path in its graphical representation leading from $q_0$ to any final state such that the concatenation of the labels of the edges of the path is the input string. For instance, the machine of Figure 5.16 accepts the words **begin** and **end**. The machine of Figure 5.17 accepts the valid identifiers of a programming language.

Sometimes, FSMs are augmented with the possibility of producing *output signals*. In this case, the transition function $\delta$ is augmented as

$$\delta : Q \times I \rightarrow Q \times O,$$

where $O$ is the finite set of output symbols. Graphically, the label <i/o> labels an arc going from $q_1$ to $q_2$ if and only if $\delta(q_1, i) = <q_2, o>$.

FSMs are a simple and widely used model. Their applications range from the specification of control systems to compilation, pattern matching, protocol and hardware design, and even applications outside of computer science. The simplicity of the model, however, may become a weakness in some more intricate cases. We shall discuss the most relevant ones from the point of view of system specification, with primary reference to the specification of control systems, which is one of the major fields of application of FSMs.

First, FSMs are finite-memory devices, as their name suggests. This implies that in many cases their expressive power is limited. For instance, in Example 5.2, suppose that, in response to abnormal temperature, a cooling effort is attempted that is proportional to DiffTemp, the difference between the present temperature and a reference

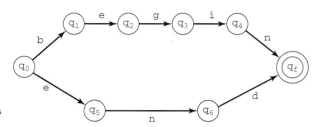

**FIGURE 5.16**

An FSM accepting the keywords **begin** and **end**.

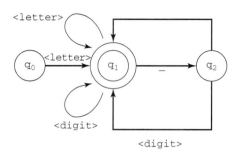

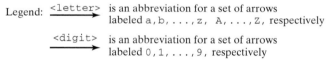

**FIGURE 5.17**

An FSM accepting the identifiers of a programming language.

Legend:    `<letter>` →    is an abbreviation for a set of arrows labeled `a, b, ..., z, A, ..., Z`, respectively

`<digit>` →    is an abbreviation for a set of arrows labeled `0, 1, ..., 9`, respectively

value. This effort cannot be modeled by a finite state device, because the possible cooling states are infinite (one for each possible value of `DiffTemp`).

Even when the range of possible values is finite—which is the case for many physical quantities of practical interest—the description of the responses may become extremely cumbersome. The previous natural-language description is a much better specification than an FSM that uses a different arc for each distinct integer temperature value within, say, a 50-degree range. Similarly, even though the physical memory of any computer is always finite, it consists of an unmanageably large number of states: Describing an eight-bit register by means of an FSM requires $2^8$ different states!

When such situations occur, we can cope with them in different ways:

- We may give up on describing all details of the system and be satisfied with an approximation that ignores requirements of the type just discussed. After all, Figure 5.14 provides some meaningful information, even without specifying the "amount of cooling effort."
- We may complement the diagram with informal natural-language comments.
- We may change models. Actually, a large variety of other models has been proposed to overcome this and other problems of FSMs. Some appear as modifications of the original FSM; others are totally different models.
- We may *enrich* the model by adding new features to the description to cope with the new requirement.

For instance, in the system of Example 5.2, we can state, formally or informally, that the transition from the "normal" state to the "temperature-recovery" state must be accompanied by an action described as

```
Cooling_effort:= k*(present_temperature-standard_value)
```

Also, one could add *predicates (guards)* to transitions. This means that the predicate must be true in order for the state transitions to occur. For example, one could add to the finite state machine of Figure 5.15 a transition from the state "normal" to the state "off" and attach the following guard to it:

```
temp ≥ very_dangerous_value
```

In addition, the following guard could be attached to the transition from the "normal" state to the "temperature-recovery" state:

```
temp < very_dangerous_value
```

Actually, if we carry such a way of enriching the original model to its logical extreme, we end up with a full definition of a new FSM-like model. This was done several times in the past, both for FSMs and for many other models, in order to provide new *ad hoc* formal specification languages.[5]

FSMs have another drawback that is somewhat typical of control system descriptions. This shortcoming is illustrated in the next example.

### Example 5.3

A producer process produces messages and puts them into a two-slot buffer. A consumer process reads the messages and removes them from the same buffer. If the buffer is full, the producer must wait until the consumer process has emptied a slot. Similarly, if the buffer is empty, the consumer process must wait until the producer has inserted a message. The two processes and the buffer may be described separately by the FSMs of Figure 5.18.

Although it can be useful to examine the three components separately, it is clear that the two processes, together with the buffer, are a single, synchronized system that must also be described as a whole.

A natural way of attacking this problem is to compose the different FSMs to obtain a new FSM that describes the whole system. Intuitively, the resulting state set should be the Cartesian product of the component state sets; furthermore, arcs denot-

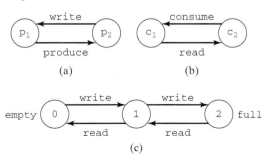

**FIGURE 5.18**

Three separate FSMs describing a producer-consumer system. **(a)** Producer. **(b)** Consumer. **(c)** Buffer.

---

[5]We shall see later that the Statecharts language supports the definition of guards and actions associated with transitions of a finite state machine.

ing the same action in different components should become single arcs in the resulting graph. Applying this composition to Figure 5.18, we would obtain the result shown in Figure 5.19. In this FSM, a state such as $<0, p_2, c_2>$ corresponds to the buffer being empty, the producer being in state $p_2$, and the consumer being in state $c_2$.

The approach, however, is not without drawbacks. First, we see that, even in the fairly simple case under consideration, the cardinality of the state space grows dramatically: If we compose n subsystems, each with $k_i$ states, the resulting system has a cardinality of $k_1 \cdot k_2 \cdot \ldots k_n$.

This objection, however, is mitigated somewhat by the consideration that what we need is actually a *complete description of the system*, not a complete FSM describing the system. Thus, we can argue that full information about the system is given by the three components of Figure 5.18, augmented with precise—even algorithmic—rules for composing FSM "modules" into "full FSMs," with no need for the explicit description of Figure 5.19. In some sense, we have built a modular specification of the system, leaving its integration to a straightforward "FSM linker."

Still, there is a more serious objection to the use of FSMs for the description of systems that consist of several concurrent units. If we look at Figure 5.19, we realize that it is an adequate description of the system under certain somewhat restrictive assumptions. Basically, the system described is always in a unique state and performs exactly one action at any instant of time. There is, however, no reason to impose a serialization between production by the producer and consumption by the consumer, two actions that are absolutely independent.

A possible rebuttal to this objection is that the figure is still an adequate specification of the concurrent system because the effect of two concurrent—and compatible—actions, say a write and a consume, is the same as the effect of *any serialization* of the two actions, either write followed by consume or consume followed by write. This answer is partially true. It works fairly well if we can assume that the time for any transition is short enough that, for example, at any instant $t$ we can say "the present

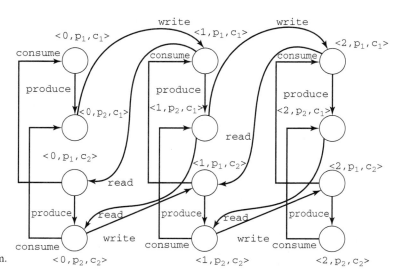

**FIGURE 5.19**

An integrated FSM description of a producer-consumer system.

state of the system is $<1, p_1, c_2>$." In such a case, we could even define new transitions that are the "parallel execution" of elementary transitions in order to cope with truly simultaneous events.

Instead, suppose that the various operations take fairly different execution times; for example, consuming is longer than producing, which in turn is far longer than reading from and writing into the buffer. In this case, it may happen that the producer and consumer start together (producing and consuming, respectively). After a while, the producer is finished with producing and may start writing. This, again, may be finished before the consumer is finished with its original operation, and a new instance of production may start. Thus, we see that the transitions of the various components occur in an *asynchronous way* that is no longer described well by the FSM of Figure 5.19.  ■

Example 5.3 shows that FSMs are essentially a *synchronous model*. (At any time, a global state of the system must be defined and a single transition must occur.) Other models are more appropriate for describing systems consisting of concurrent and asynchronous components, more so if timing aspects (i.e., stating time constraints for the completion of several transitions) are important. In the next section, we present and evaluate an operational model that is explicitly aimed at describing concurrent systems.

### Exercises

**5.8**  Using FSMs, describe a lighting system consisting of one lamp and two buttons. If the lamp is off, pushing either button causes the lamp to switch on, and conversely.

**5.9**  Describe a system with two lamps and one button. When the lights are off, pushing the button causes the first lamp to go on. Pushing the button again causes the second lamp to go on and the first to go off. Pushing the button yet again causes both lamps to go on, and pushing it once more switches both lamps off.

**5.10**  Modify the specification given by the FSM of Figure 5.15 in order to cope also with simultaneous signals.

**5.11**  Modify the specification given by the FSM of Figure 5.15 by considering the case where temperature and pressure each have two different associated signals, one indicating a slight deviation from the acceptable value and the other a dangerous deviation from the acceptable value. In the latter case, the system must be shut off immediately.

### 5.5.4  Petri Nets: Specifying Asynchronous Systems

Petri nets are a formalism for specifying systems that contain parallel or concurrent activities. They are defined by a quadruple $(P, T, F, W)$, where

1. $P$ is a finite set of *places*;
2. $T$ is a finite set of *transitions*;
3. $P \cup T \neq \emptyset$;
4. $F \subseteq \{P \times T\} \cup \{T \times P\}$ is the *flow relation*; and
5. $W: F \to N-\{0\}$ is the *weight function*, which associates a nonzero natural value to each element of $F$. If no weight value is explicitly associated with a flow element, the default value 1 is assumed for the function.

A Petri net (PN) can be given an appealing graphical representation, which makes specifications intuitively understandable. Places are represented by circles, transitions by bars, and flow elements by arrows. Whenever useful, a bi-directional arrow connecting a place P and a transition t will be considered as an abbreviation for a pair of arrows, one going from P to t, the other going from t to P. Figure 5.20 shows a sample Petri net.

A PN is given a *state* by marking its places. Formally, a *marking* is a function M from places to natural numbers:

$$M:P \rightarrow N$$

A marking is represented graphically by inserting a number x of *tokens* in every place of the net, such that x = M(p). Figure 5.21(a) shows one marking of the PN of Figure 5.20. The evolution of a PN—that is, its progression through state changes, is regulated by the rules explained next.

A transition may have one or more input and output places. If an arrow goes from a place to a transition, the place is said to be one of the transition's *input places*; if an arrow goes from a transition to a place, the place is said to be one of the transition's *output places*. A place can be both an input and an output for a transition. A transition is said to be *enabled* if each of its input places contains a number of tokens that is greater than or equal to the weight of the flow element connecting the input place to the transition. In the default case, where the weight of the flow element is one, each input place must contain at least one token. A transition with no input places is always enabled.

An enabled transition may *fire*. The firing of transition t removes from each input place $p_i$ a number of tokens that equals the weight of the flow element from $p_i$ to t and then inserts into each output place $q_i$ a number of tokens equal to the weight of the flow element from t to $q_i$. In Figure 5.21(a), both $t_1$ and $t_2$ are enabled; no other transition is enabled. In such a case, the marking of the net may evolve in at least two different ways: either by firing $t_1$ or by firing $t_2$. Thus, the model is *nondeterministic*, in the sense that, given an initial marking, different evolutions of the PN are possible. In the case of Figure 5.21(a), the firing of $t_1$ produces the marking of Figure 5.21(b), whereas the firing of $t_2$ produces the marking of Figure 5.21(c). Notice that, after $t_1$ fires, $t_2$ is still enabled and could fire. Correspondingly, $t_1$ would still be enabled if $t_2$ fires first. Transitions $t_1$ and $t_2$ can also fire in parallel. In any case, one would eventually reach the marking of Figure 5.21(d). At this point, $t_3$ and $t_4$ are both enabled, and either can fire in a nondeterministic way. This time, however, the firing of one prevents the other from firing. For example, if $t_3$ fires, $t_4$ will no longer be enabled.

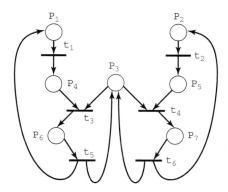

FIGURE 5.20

A sample Petri net.

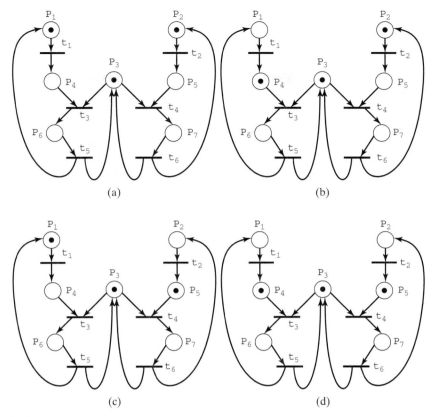

FIGURE 5.21

Evolution of a Petri net.
**(a)** Initial marking. **(b)** $t_1$ fires from initial marking.
**(c)** $t_2$ fires from initial marking. **(d)** $t_1$ and $t_2$ both fire from initial marking.

A *firing sequence* of a given PN with a given initial marking is a sequence of transition firings, denoted as a string of transition labels $<t_1, t_2, \ldots, t_n>$, such that $t_1$ is enabled in the initial marking, $t_2$ is enabled in the marking obtained by firing $t_1$, and so on.

Before going further into the analysis of the behavior of PNs, let us interpret them as a model for the description of concurrent systems. In a PN, a transition usually models an event or an action, and its firing represents the occurrence of the event or the execution of the action. Thus, a transition is enabled if the *conditions* are satisfied that allow the occurrence of the modeled event or action. The presence of a token in a place denotes the existence of some condition or state. For instance, a place may model a resource, and the existence of one or more tokens in that place signifies the availability of one or more instances of that resource.

Let us look at the net of Figure 5.21(a). We can interpret its two parts, consisting of transitions $t_1$, $t_3$, $t_5$, and $t_2$, $t_4$, $t_6$, respectively, as two independent activities flowing through the events modeled by the transitions. The two activities share a common resource, modeled by place $P_3$. They could be two different programs using the same CPU, two students sharing a book, etc.

Initially, the two activities can proceed in an independent and asynchronous way. In fact, $t_1$ and $t_2$ are both enabled, and the firing of one does not prevent the other from firing. In such a case, we say that the two transitions are *concurrent*. This arrangement could model, say, the independent editing of two programs at different terminals or the reading of personal lecture notes by two students. After both transitions have fired,[6] however, both activities are again enabled to proceed, but in mutual exclusion. This is shown in Figure 5.21(d). The resource modeled by $P_3$ is actually available, but only for one of the two activities, the choice being nondeterministic. In this case, we say that the two transitions are in *conflict*.

Suppose that the resource is given to the activity on the left-hand side of the figure. Then the net can proceed through $t_3$ and $t_5$, leaving the other activity temporarily blocked. The firing of $t_5$ frees the resource, which is now available again for further use. At this point, $t_4$ could fire. But it is also possible that, on the contrary, $t_1$ fires again, and then the choice between $t_3$ and $t_4$ is resolved once more in favor of $t_3$. This sequence of events can be repeated forever.

The model does not impose any policy to resolve conflicts. In the concurrent system terminology, the scheduling policy is not *fair*, and a process that never receives access to a needed resource is said to suffer *starvation*. Thus, a firing sequence where only transitions $t_1$, $t_3$, $t_5$ occur leads to starvation of the activity on the right-hand side of the figure.

Now, assume that the initial marking of the PN has two tokens in $P_3$ instead of one. This means that two indistinguishable resources are available. As a consequence, $t_3$ and $t_4$ are no longer in conflict, but are concurrent. If the two activities represent computer processes, and two CPUs are available for them in a multiprocessor machine, the two processes may be executed in parallel.

Figure 5.22 is a modification of Figure 5.21(a) that models the case where the two activities need two identical copies of a resource to proceed. These copies are modeled by two tokens in place R. After an activity—say, the leftmost—starts by firing $t_1$, it may obtain any one of the available resources (firing $t'_3$) Then, it attempts also to obtain the other resource (firing $t''_3$). Once the activity has obtained both resources, execution can proceed, eventually releasing both (firing $t_5$).

Consider, however, the firing sequence $<t_1,\ t'_3,\ t_2,\ t'_4>$, which leads to a marking wherein no transition is enabled. Thus, the net is prevented from any further progress. Each of the activities has obtained one of the two resources and needs the other one to go further. But this cannot happen, because the needed resource is owned by the other activity, which is also waiting for one more resource.

This is a typical *deadlock*, which is modeled quite well by a PN. Formally, a PN with a given marking is said to be in deadlock if and only if no transition is enabled in that marking. A PN in which no deadlock can ever occur starting from a given marking is said to be *live*.

Deadlocks lead to system "freezes." Designers obviously try to avoid deadlocks, but detecting them is difficult. Modeling formalisms such as Petri nets make it possible to analyze properties of the system. In this example, we were able to derive the deadlock property of a system by manually analyzing the PN that models the system.

---

[6]Notice that this does not necessarily happen. For example, after $t_1$ has fired, $t_3$ could fire. This would disable $t_2$ until $t_5$ fires.

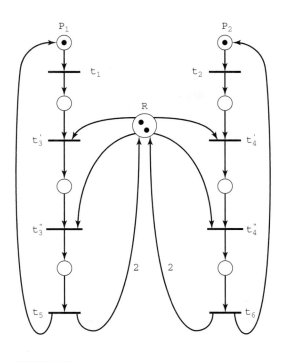

FIGURE 5.22

A Petri net that can enter a deadlock state.

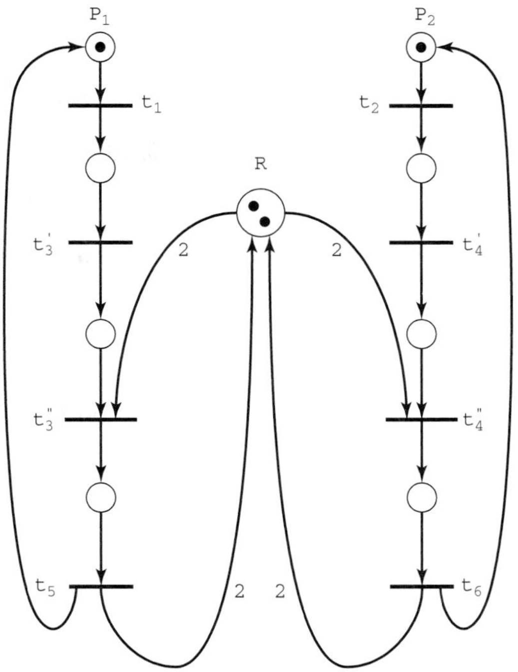

FIGURE 5.23

A modification of the Petri net of Figure 5.22 that is live.

FIGURE 5.24

A Petri net with partial starvation.

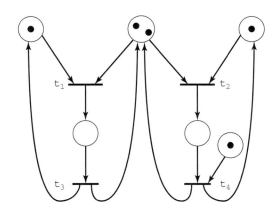

## Exercises

**5.12** Show that the modification of the PN of Figure 5.22 given in Figure 5.23 is live. How do you interpret the modification introduced?

**5.13** Consider the PN of Figure 5.24. Clearly, this PN is live. The activity modeled by transitions $t_2$ and $t_4$, however, can go into starvation. In fact, the net could reach a marking from which the two transitions can never be enabled. Comment briefly on the difference between this type of starvation and the one illustrated before.

## Example 5.4

Let us go back to the producer-consumer system modeled as an FSM in Example 5.3. We can use the PNs of Figure 5.25 to describe the three separate components of the system.

Graphically, the composition of the three subsystems into a PN is shown in Figure 5.26. The figure shows that the major drawbacks of the corresponding FSM representation (given in Figure 5.19) are now resolved satisfactorily. First, the graphical complexity of the figure is not based on multiplying the state space of the components, but is only additive. In fact, in Figure 5.19 the number of nodes coincided with the number of states. In Figure 5.26, the number of states is given by the number of possible markings. The reader is invited to compare a PN describing a system of two producers and three consumers using a four-position buffer with the corresponding FSM representation.

Second—and more important—in Figure 5.26, the concurrency of independent activities is described properly. In fact, if the system is in the state $<1, p_1, c_2>$ (i.e., a token is in each one of those places), both of the transitions produce and consume

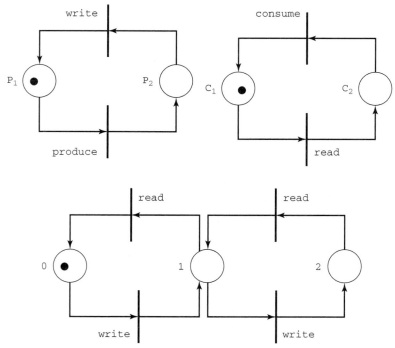

FIGURE 5.25

Three separate Petri nets describing a producer-consumer system.

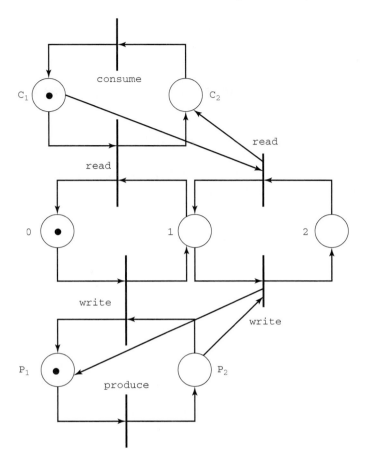

FIGURE 5.26

An integrated Petri net describing a producer-consumer system.

are enabled. That is, the two transitions are concurrent. They can be executed in parallel without preventing each other from firing. Also, looking at the firing sequence

`<produce, write, produce, read, consume, write, read, consume>`

shows immediately which actions could happen concurrently and which ones have to be serialized because the termination of one is necessary for the start of the other. ■

## Exercises

**5.14**  Give examples of firing sequences for the net of Figure 5.21(a).

**5.15**  Describe some of the systems previously described by FSMs by means of PNs, and compare the different specifications.

### 5.5.4.1  *Limitations and extensions of Petri nets*

Even though PNs model certain aspects of systems quite well, their use in applications has revealed some weaknesses when they are used for software specification. First, they are—like FSMs—a control-oriented model. Tokens typically represent the flow of control in the execution of several actions. The tokens, however, are anonymous. For example, the presence of a token in a place may denote only the presence of a message in a buffer, not what the message says.

This simplicity may be useful. Often—for example, when we are interested in analyzing the flow of messages within a communication network—the important issue is whether a message that has been produced somewhere will be delivered somewhere else. In such cases, the actual content of the message may be an irrelevant detail.

But this is not always the case. For example, suppose you wish to specify a system in which a message is to be forwarded through one of two different channels: channel$_1$ is selected if the message is well formed; channel$_2$—the "error" channel—is selected if the message is incorrect. The message is well formed if it contains an even number of 1's (i.e., if it has correct parity).

Figure 5.27 shows a tentative PN specification of such a system. This net, however, suggests that the choice between the two channels is nondeterministic when a message is ready to be forwarded (represented by a token in place P). The figure is not an adequate description of the system we have described with words, since the choice between the channels is dictated by the contents of the message.

In our example, however, the firing of a transition *should* depend on what the message says. But since the message is represented by the token, this is clearly impossible. The token can denote only the presence of a message. We should be able to associate what messages say (their *values*) with tokens, and we should be able to *compute* the value of the tokens. Then, on receipt of a message, a station could modify the message before forwarding it (e.g., by adding another address field). These problems are common to all control-oriented models.

Another drawback of PNs is the fact that, in the general case, it is not possible to specify a *selection policy* between different transitions that are enabled. For instance, going back to the net of Figure 5.21(a), we already noticed the possibility of the firing sequence <$t_1$, $t_3$, $t_5$> repeating indefinitely, starving the activity consisting of <$t_2$, $t_4$, $t_6$>. To avoid starvation in this case, we could enforce an alternation policy by modifying the net slightly as shown in Figure 5.28. This modified net prevents $t_3$ from firing a second time before $t_4$ has fired once.

It can be mathematically proven, however, that, in the general case, PNs do not have the ability to describe a selection policy such as the following:

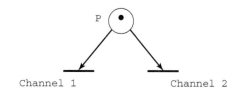

FIGURE 5.27

A portion of a Petri net describing the forwarding of messages through different channels.

Channel 1                    Channel 2

```
if transition t is enabled then
   fire t;
else
   fire the first enabled transition
   according to some ordering criterion
end if;
```

*Timing issues* are another critical aspect of some systems. As we have seen in Chapters 2 and 4, in some real-time systems, the failure to compute an answer within a given time has the same severe effect as not computing it at all or computing it incorrectly. Also, the result of a computation may depend on the speed of execution of some actions.

For instance, suppose that an external line sends messages to a computer at some given speed. Every message that is received is put into a buffer and then processed. If a message is not taken from the buffer before the next message arrives, it is overwritten. Thus, the results of the processing may vary, depending on the arrival times of the messages.

Unfortunately, most models of computer systems, including PNs, do not take time into account explicitly. The consequence is a lack of depth in modeling and analysis.

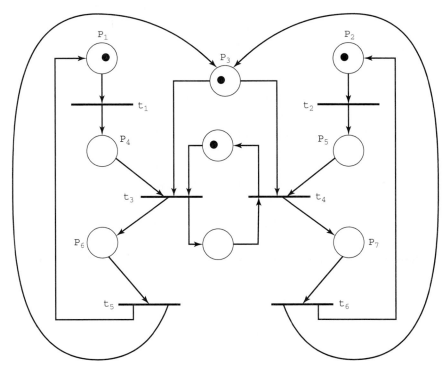

FIGURE 5.28

A modification of the Petri net of Figure 5.21(a), enforcing an alternation policy.

For instance, consider again the PN of Figure 5.21(a). Let us assume that the actions occur as soon as they are enabled. Let us also assume that the firing of a transition occurs when the corresponding actions modeled by the transition ends. If the actions modeled by $t_1$, $t_3$, and $t_5$ take 1 second each to be completed, and the action modeled by $t_2$ takes 5 seconds, then, clearly, the firing sequence $<t_1, t_2, t_3, t_5, t_4>$ is not feasible, contrary to what is suggested by the net. In fact, suppose that at time 0 both $t_1$ and $t_2$ start. At time 1, $t_3$ can start, but $t_2$ is not completed. Thus, the firing of $t_2$ cannot occur before the firing of $t_3$.

Luckily, the flexibility of the Petri net model has allowed it to be extended in several directions while maintaining its original features. Let us review some fairly standard modifications of PNs that have proved useful in several circumstances. For simplicity, we will assume the default case, where the weight is 1 for all elements of the flow relation.

**Assigning values to tokens.**    Tokens can be modified to carry a value of an appropriate type: an integer, an array of bytes, or even a full *environment* consisting of several variables and associated values. Transitions are also modified to have associated *predicates* and *functions*. The firing rule for transitions is now based on the values, as well as the presence, of tokens. A transition with $k$ input places and $h$ output places is enabled if there exists a $k$-tuple of tokens—one for each input place—such that the predicate associated with the transition is satisfied by the values of the tokens of the tuple. These tokens are together called a *ready* tuple.

Notice that the predicate is evaluated on exactly one token for each input place. Thus, there could be more than one ready tuple for some transition; that is, the same token could belong to different ready tuples. When an enabled transition fires, this implies all of the following:

- the cancellation of all tokens that belong to a ready tuple from the input places (if there is more than one ready tuple, its choice is nondeterministic);
- the evaluation of $h$ new token values on the basis of the values of the ready tuple by applying the function associated with the transition (thus, such a function has a domain of $k$-tuples and a range of $h$-tuples);
- the production of one token for each output place—the value of the token is computed by the function associated with the transition.

For instance, consider the PN of Figure 5.29, where tokens are assumed to carry integer values. The notation is self-explanatory: The name of a place in a predicate or function stands for a token in that place. Both transitions $t_1$ and $t_2$ are enabled. Transition $t_1$ has two ready tuples, namely, $<3, 7>$ and $<3, 4>$, since both tuples satisfy the predicate $P_2 > P_1$. Transition $t_2$ has one ready tuple, namely, $<4, 4>$, which satisfies the predicate $P_3 = P_2$. The token with value 1 in $P_2$ does not belong to any ready tuple. Thus, the firing of $t_1$ by using the tuple $<3, 4>$ would produce a token with value 7 in $P_4$ and would therefore disable $t_2$, since the tokens 3 and 4 would disappear from $P_1$ and $P_2$, respectively. Instead, the firing of $t_1$ by using $<3, 7>$ would produce the value 10 in $P_4$. After that, $t_2$ could still fire, producing the values 0 in $P_4$ and 8 in $P_5$.

This first enrichment to the PN model allows a natural and simple solution to the problem of Figure 5.27. In fact, it is sufficient to consider tokens as carrying a value of the type of messages, say, sequences of bits. Then the predicate "P has an even number

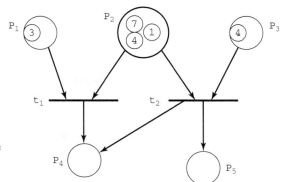

**FIGURE 5.29**

A Petri net whose tokens carry values. The predicate $P_2 > P_1$ and the function $P_4 := P_2 + P_1$ are associated with $t_1$; the predicate $P_3 = P_2$ and the functions $P_4 := P_3 - P_2$ and $P_5 := P_2 + P_3$ are associated with $t_2$.

of 1's" can be attached to transition $\text{channel}_1$, and similarly for transition $\text{channel}_2$. Also, if the forwarding of the messages through the channels implies some modification of the message, this can be done in a natural way by adding appropriate functions to the transitions.

### Exercise

**5.16**  Use the foregoing PN extension to describe a message dispatcher that works along the following lines: The dispatcher receives messages from two different channels and then checks the parity of each message. If the parity is wrong, it sends a "nack" (negative acknowledgment) through a reply channel (there is one such channel for each input channel); if the parity is right, it places the received message into a buffer. The buffer may store 10 messages. When the buffer is full, the dispatcher sends the whole contents of the buffer to a processing unit through another channel. No message can be placed into a full buffer.

**Specifying scheduling policies.**   When the pure nondeterminism of the Petri net model is not adequate, we face the problem of specifying a policy for selecting a transition to fire among all the enabled transitions. A fairly simple way of doing this is to attach priorities to transitions. Formally, they can be defined by a priority function $\text{pri}$ from transitions to natural numbers:

$$\text{pri}:\text{T} \rightarrow \text{N}.$$

Then we modify the firing rule in the following way: If, in some state, several transitions are enabled, only the ones with maximum priority are actually allowed to fire.

According to our definition, priorities are static. If tokens carry a value, however, we could also define dynamic priorities whose values depend on the values of the tokens of the input places of the transitions.

### Exercise

**5.17**  Add suitable priorities to the PN you built to solve Exercise 5.16. If the dispatcher is in a condition where it can receive a message from an input channel, send a "nack" reply, or forward the contents of the buffer to the processor, then it must order its priorities as follows: First get the message, then send the "nack", and then forward the contents of the buffer.

**Timed Petri nets.** Subtle theoretical problems arise when one introduces time within formal computation models. Such theoretical issues are beyond the scope of this text; accordingly, we just mention that the notion of time has been added to Petri nets in several ways. We describe one of the most simple and natural ways of introducing time into PNs by scratching only the surface of this hard problem.

*Timed PNs* are PNs in which a pair of constants $<t_{min}, t_{max}>$ is associated with each transition. In more sophisticated models, it is also possible to define the temporal bounds so that they are computed as functions of the values of tokens at the input places. An initial marking is given at some value of time t, say t = 0. The idea is that once a transition is enabled, it must wait for at least $t_{min}$ to elapse before it can fire. Also, if enabled, it *must* fire before $t_{max}$ has elapsed, unless it is disabled by the firing of another transition before $t_{max}$. A timed PN is equivalent to an original PN if, for every transition, $t_{min} = 0$ and $t_{max} = \infty$.

Temporal and other modifications can obviously be combined. So if we attach both times and priorities to transitions, care is needed in determining which transition can or must fire at which time. A natural rule is that if several transitions can fire according to the token-presence rule and the time-bound $[t_{min}, t_{max}]$ interval rule, then only transitions with maximum priorities can actually fire, within a time that is less than or equal to their own $t_{max}$.

For instance, consider the net of Figure 5.30, with its initial marking at time zero. It may happen that $t_1$ fires within a time less than 2. If it does not fire within that time, however, then it cannot fire anymore, because, at time t = 2, $t_2$ can fire, too, and it has a higher priority than $t_1$. Now, if at time t = 1 a token is produced into $P_4$, then, during the interval $1 \le t < 2$, both $t_3$ and $t_1$ can fire, but $t_1$ cannot fire before $t_3$, because it has lower priority.

Now, let us go back to the problem of giving a precise meaning to the informal specification

> The message must be triplicated. The three copies must be forwarded through three different physical channels. The receiver accepts the message on the basis of a two-out-of-three voting policy.

which was discussed in Section 5.2. Timed PNs, augmented with tokens carrying the values of messages, can easily provide a precise description of the possible interpretations of this informal specification.

The first interpretation suggested in Section 5.2 was that the message should be considered received as soon as two identical copies have been received. This interpretation is formalized by the PN of Figure 5.31. With this formulation, as soon as two tokens

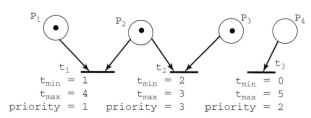

FIGURE 5.30

A timed Petri net.

with identical values are present in $P_1$, $P_2$, or $P_3$, the corresponding transition fires. A different interpretation of the informal requirements, based on the decision to wait until all three copies have been received before performing the comparison, is formalized by the net of Figure 5.32.

This example of receiving triplicate messages shows that the use of a formal model allows us to attach a precise meaning to a system specification. Furthermore, the formal model may be the basis of a rigorous *analysis*. For instance, if we are interested in determining the maximum time that may be spent to deliver an incoming message, we can easily see that it is $k_1 + k_2$ in both cases. If, however, we assume that transmission of the copies through the three channels takes a time that is randomly distributed within $c_2$ and $k_2$, we find that the probability of receiving the message in place Forwarded Message within time t (with $c_1 + c_2 \leq t \leq k_1 + k_2$) is higher in the case of Figure 5.31 than in the case of Figure 5.32.

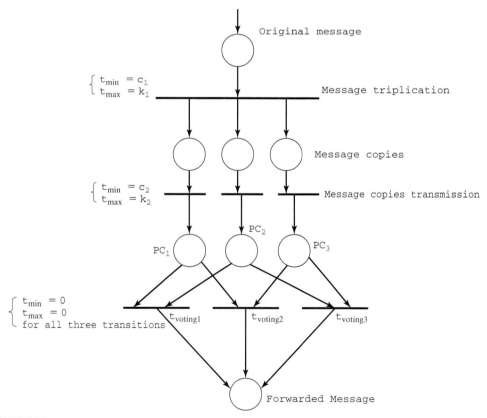

FIGURE 5.31

A possible formalization of message replication and selection through augmented Petri nets. The predicate $PC_1 = PC_2$ is associated with $t_{voting1}$. The predicate $PC_1 = PC_3$ is associated with $t_{voting2}$. The predicate $PC_2 = PC_3$ is associated with $t_{voting3}$. The predicate true is associated with all other transitions. The identity function is associated with all transitions. $c_1$ and $k_1$ ($c_2$ and $k_2$) are the lower (upper) bounds of the duration of operation Message triplication (Message copies transmission).

Now, assume that each channel has some probability of failure during transmission. (This state of affairs could be modeled by adding three more transitions, each connected to the input places "message copies" places, whose firing would destroy the tokens that represent the messages.) Then the model of Figure 5.31 would have a lower probability of global failure (i.e., not forwarding the message to place `Forwarded Message`) than the model of Figure 5.32. Since message triplication is apparently done just to enhance the PN's performance or fault tolerance, it is clear that such a difference between the two interpretations of the informal specification is quite useful.

The preceding analysis could have been made even more precise by further enriching the PN model with stochastic features, such as probabilistic distributions of firing times and probabilistic distributions of the firing of enabled transitions. The interested reader can find models of this type in the literature suggested in the bibliographic notes.

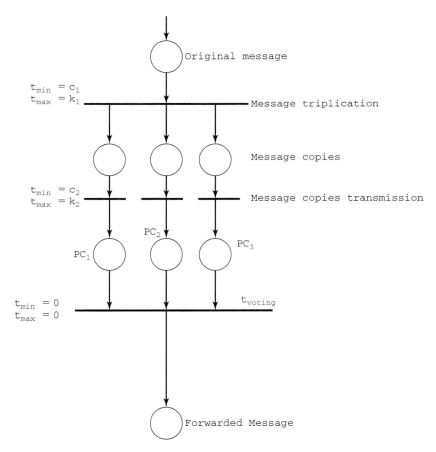

**FIGURE 5.32**

An alternative formalization of message replication and selection. The predicate $PC_1 = PC_2$ **or** $PC_2 = PC_3$ **or** $PC_1 = PC_3$ is associated with $t_{voting}$. The function "**if** $PC_1 = PC_2$ **then** $PC_1$ **elsif** $PC_2 = PC_3$ **then** $PC_2$ **elsif** $PC_1 = PC_3$ **then** $PC_1$ **else** "ERROR" **end if**" is associated with $t_{voting}$. The predicate **true** is associated with all other transitions. The identity function also is associated with all other transitions.

### Exercises

**5.18**  Give a formalization, in terms of augmented PNs, of the third interpretation mentioned in Section 5.2, in which the receiver polls the three channels periodically. If three copies are received within a given time period, all of them are compared. If only two are received within the given time period, and they are identical, then the message is accepted.

**5.19**  The formalization of Figure 5.31 has a minor flaw that may become relevant if the PN is part of a cyclic system. Find and fix the error (i.e., modify the PN in such a way that it behaves properly even if repeated cyclically).

### 5.5.4.2  *A case study using Petri nets*

Let us now apply the Petri net model—and some of its variations—to describe a more complex and realistic system, namely, an elevator system. Consider the following informal specification, which has been proposed and used in the literature as a benchmark for evaluating the applicability of specification techniques:

> An n-elevator system is to be installed in a building with m floors. The manufacturer supplies the elevators and the control mechanisms. The internal mechanisms of each are assumed given. The problem concerns the logic to move elevators between floors according to the following constraints:
>
> 1. Each elevator has a set of buttons, one for each floor. The buttons light up when pressed and cause the elevator to visit the corresponding floor. The lights switch off when the elevator visits that floor.
> 2. Each floor other than the ground floor and the top floor has two buttons, one to request an up elevator and one to request a down elevator. These buttons light up when pressed. The lights switch off when the elevator visits the floor and either is moving in the desired direction or has no outstanding requests. In the latter case, if both floor-request buttons are pressed, only one is canceled. The algorithm to decide which to service first should minimize the waiting time for both requests.
> 3. When an elevator has no requests to service, it should remain at its final destination with its doors closed and await further requests.
> 4. All requests for elevators from floors must be serviced eventually, with all floors given equal priority.
> 5. All requests for floors within elevators must be serviced eventually, with floors being serviced sequentially in the direction of the elevator's travel.
> 6. Each elevator has an emergency button that, when pressed, causes a warning signal to be sent to the site manager. The elevator is then deemed "out of service." Each elevator has a mechanism to cancel its "out of service" status.

Before translating these statements into a formal model, let us substantiate the value of doing so. Although people are generally familiar with this type of system, the specifications should be examined with some attention. It would be interesting for the reader to postpone reading the comments that follow and first try to analyze and perhaps formalize the specifications on his or her own.

Let us focus our attention on point 2. First, we read that every floor, except the first and the last, has two buttons. Note that there is no implication here—or elsewhere in the specifications—that rules out as incorrect an implementation in which the first floor has nine buttons and the last one four. This remark, however, could appear to be overly critical: There is an "obviously correct" interpretation—that is, that the first floor has only the button to go up and the last floor has only the button to go down. We make this interpretation because it is part of our ordinary knowledge about elevators and we can easily integrate that knowledge into our design for the system with explicitly stated requirements. Indeed, we could even use the remark as an argument in favor of informality in specifications: A formal definition would have forced us to specify in full detail even things that are perfectly understood, resulting in wasted effort.

In general, formality is a tool for achieving precision *whenever it is needed*. Full precision may be useless and even boring if the intended reader of the specifications is a human being. Thus, it is the responsibility of the specifier to choose an appropriate *level of formality*. Sometimes, the simplicity, immediateness, and generality of natural language may be preferable to the semantic rigor of mathematical formalisms. Other times, a—perhaps graphical—semiformal notation can give a quick and sufficiently clear idea of the desired system. In still other cases, especially if the system is complex or critical, the effort of going through a full formalization may be worthwhile. In general, formality is required when we cannot afford the risk of being misinterpreted.

Now, let us go further into the analysis of point 2. The rule states that

> The light associated with a button switches off when the elevator visits the requested floor and is either moving in the desired direction or ....

This sentence can be interpreted in at least two different ways. Consider an elevator going up. (The case when the elevator is going down is symmetric.) Then the rule could mean either of the following:

- Switch off the up button as soon as the elevator reaches the floor, coming from below. (This interpretation has an exception for the first floor).
- Switch off the up button after an elevator reaches the floor and starts moving in the up direction. (This interpretation has an exception for the last floor).

By examining different elevators, we can see that both interpretations have been used in practice. As we observed earlier, one might argue that the ambiguity was left in the specification on purpose to allow the implementer to choose the best solution without unnecessary constraints. This might be an acceptable explanation in this case, where one solution or the other does not make any difference. In general, however, one does not realize the ambiguity in a sentence until one builds a formal model of it.

Finally, notice the imprecision in the requirement

> The algorithm to decide which floor to service first should minimize the waiting time for both requests.

What does "minimize the waiting time for both requests" mean? Here are two possible interpretations:

- In no other way should it be possible to serve either request in a shorter time. This interpretation could be infeasible: Minimizing the waiting time of one request could require a longer waiting time for the other request;
- The sum of the two waiting times should be minimized. But why the sum?

Even worse, the waiting time that is forecast at the moment of making the decision could be changed by the initiation of other requests during the service. For example, imagine that an elevator moves from floor 2 to serve a request issued at floor 60. While going up, the elevator stops to serve a new call issued at floor 40. This call could not have been considered to "minimize" the waiting time when that specific elevator was chosen to serve the original request.

### Exercise

**5.20**  Continue with the analysis of the preceding specifications, trying to discover ambiguous or questionable points.

Let us try to specify the elevator system by means of a Petri net. Figure 5.33 gives a sketchy initial view of the system. This description has some intuitive attraction: It provides a pictorial display of the elevators' position and of the events that determine the movement of the elevators. It stresses the fact that, in order to move from one floor to an adjacent floor, some button must be illuminated, and that the movement, in turn, is the result of pressing the said button.

The description in Figure 5.33, however, is far from satisfactory. Here are a few of its shortcomings:

1. The description is terribly incomplete: Many other facts must be taken into account. There are not only internal, but also external, buttons. The movement of the elevator can be caused by any of the buttons: Even an elevator at floor 1 can move up when the down button of floor 40 is pushed. Nor does the net explain how a button is reset. What about the case of an elevator that is going from, say, floor 4 to floor 27, and the external up button of floor 20 is pressed just when the elevator is crossing that floor? What is the latest acceptable calling time in such a case?

2. The description shows immediately that the full formalization of the system is likely to be enormous and totally unmanageable. Think of a system with 100 floors and seven elevators!

3. The description is clearly wrong in many of its details. For instance, the figure suggests that a button lights up when it is pushed; this is modeled by the presence of a token in place "button illumination." If the button is pressed twice before it is reset, however, we have two tokens in that place, so that when the request is eventually serviced and one token is consumed, the other token remains, incorrectly indicating that the button is still lit up.

### Exercise

**5.21**  Find other inadequacies and trouble spots in the foregoing initial formalization.

Despite its shortcomings, Figure 5.33 can be taken as a starting point to obtain a correct and full specification of the system by means of Petri nets.

First, let us face the problem of managing the complexity of the system. Here, we must recall that specification is a *design* activity and that a complete specification document is, in general, the result of many trials and corrections. It is not a document that is to be built from scratch and never modified. Thus, we must apply all of the design principles illustrated in Chapters 3 and 4 to the design of the specifications as well.

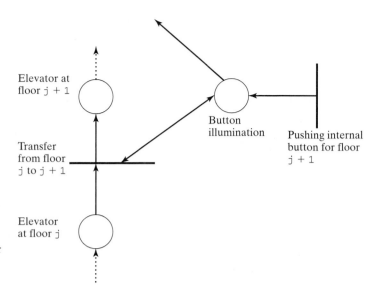

**FIGURE 5.33**

A first sketch of the elevator button switching through a Petri net.

In particular, it is quite useful in this case to define suitable *specification modules*, intended as portions of a final PN. Each module describes a component of the system. A complete description is the result of integrating all the modules together. In this case, it seems natural to use different portions of the net to represent the elevators' positions, on the one hand, and the setting and resetting of internal and external buttons, on the other.

Also, we can observe that, with the exception of the first and last floors, the description of what happens at floor j will be identical to that of what happens at floor k. And since the same will hold for elevators and buttons, this suggests a *parameterized* specification that refers to generic floor j, elevator m, button of floor h, etc., as was to some extent already suggested in Figure 5.33. Thus, we obtain the following natural structure for the specification.

**System description.**    The overall specification is decomposed into modules. There are n specification modules of type ELEVATOR and m specification modules of type FLOOR. Each module is described by a suitably extended PN, with suitable interconnections.

Each module of type ELEVATOR is decomposed into two submodules, one of type ELEVATOR_POSITION, which represents the position of the elevator, and the other of type ELEVATOR_BUTTONS, which represents the state of buttons internal to the elevator. More precisely, the latter can be decomposed into m modules of type BUTTON, each of which represents one of the m buttons internal to each elevator.

Each module of type FLOOR, in turn, is decomposed into two modules of type BUTTON, which represent the calls to elevators to go up or down. The modules representing the first and last floor are an exception, since they are described by only one module of type BUTTON, representing calls to go up and down, respectively.

Now let us face individual problems of description, going problem by problem. We start with the rules for lighting up buttons, which seem fairly simple, but contain an apparent mistake in the first attempt. We will make use of timed PNs with priorities.

**Button description.**    Modules of type BUTTON may be described as in Figure 5.34. Pushing a button is represented by the firing of transition Push, which is always enabled, to represent the fact that the button may be pushed at any time. If the button is off (a token is in Off) and Push fires, then Set immediately fires (thus, $t_{min}$(Set) = $t_{max}$(Set) = 0) and sets the button to on (a token is in On). To prevent the meaningless accumulation of tokens in P, one can set $t_{min}$(Push) = 0.1 and $t_{min}$(C) = $t_{max}$(C) = 0.005 (transition C acts as a token consumer).[7] In such a way, an on button can be pushed many times (with a minimum idle time of 0.1) without any undesirable consequences.

The firing of transition Reset represents the resetting of the button. The way other modules can reset a module of type BUTTON will be described later. (This means that other arrows not shown here will be connected to Reset for other specification modules.)

## Exercise

**5.22**  Give an alternative specification for lighting up a button by using PNs augmented with priorities, instead of timed PNs. Discuss the differences between the two representations.

**Description of elevator position and movement.**    As a first rough approximation, each module of type ELEVATOR_POSITION can be represented as in Figure 5.35. Intuitively, the figure describes how an elevator can move from one floor to the next in each direction. A token in place $F_i$, $1 \le i \le m$, represents an elevator standing at floor $i$. A token in place $DF_i$ ($UF_i$), $2 \le i \le m-1$, represents an elevator passing through floor $i$, moving downwards (upwards). Appropriate times should be associated with the transitions in order to account for the elevator's speed.

We insist on the importance of describing complex facts in an incremental way. Thus, Figure 5.35 first gives an idea of elevator movement, by distinguishing between the case of standing and moving elevators. In a more detailed view, the

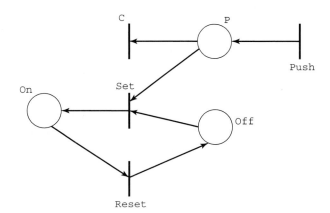

FIGURE 5.34

Switching the buttons on.

---

[7]By default, time is given in seconds. Note that any arbitrary value less than 0.1 can replace 0.005.

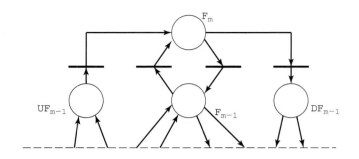

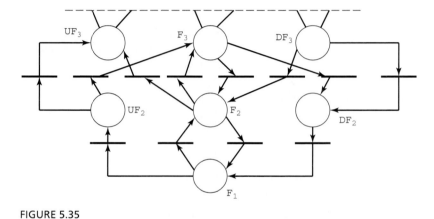

**FIGURE 5.35**

A first description of elevator movement.

conditions that cause an elevator to move upwards are expressed by the fragment of net shown in Figure 5.36, with reference to an elevator initially standing at floor $F_i$. (The conditions that cause the elevator to move downwards can be modeled in much the same way.)

Now, let h be any integer greater than $j+1$ and less than or equal to m. An elevator standing at floor j can move up if there is either an internal request to stop at floor $j+1$ or at some floor h or an external request at floor $j+1$ or any floor h. Such requests are modeled by the presence of a token in the place On of the nets of type BUTTON that represent internal and external buttons. In the figure, $ILB_{j+1}$ and $ILB_h$ are nets of type BUTTON that represent the internal buttons for stops at floors $j+1$ and h, respectively. Similarly, $UP_{j+1}$, $DOWN_{j+1}$, $UP_h$, and $DOWN_h$ represent the buttons for external calls from floors $j+1$ and h, to go up or down, as indicated.[8]

The specification of Figure 5.36 uses two intermediate places, $F'_j$ and $F''_j$, between $F_j$ and both $F_{j+1}$ and $UF_{j+1}$. The firing of transitions $t_1$ through $t_6$ represents the response of the elevator to a request to move up; as a consequence, a token enters

---

[8]Floors 1 and m are an exception, because they only have buttons $UP_1$ and $DOWN_m$, respectively.

place $F\,'_j$. The firing of transition $t$ between $F\,'_j$ and $F\,''_j$ represents the time needed to move from floor $j$ to floor $j+1$; in fact, we define $t_{min}(t) = t_{max}(t) = \Delta t$, the time needed to move from one floor to an adjacent floor. (For simplicity, we ignore the fact that such time is not constant because it may include a noninfinite acceleration.) For every other transition shown in Figure 5.36, we set $t_{min} = t_{max} = 0$. (This, again, corresponds to the assumption that times taken to make a decision whether to stop at some floor can be ignored. That assumption is an abstraction of the supposed real situation, wherein the mechanism that governs the system (e.g., a microprocessor) has negligible reaction times compared with the times that are required by the mechanical system.)

Transitions $t_7$ through $t_{12}$ represent the (nondeterministic) choice among requests for service. In this way, we model the fact that the elevator may also service incoming requests concerning floor $j+1$, provided that they occur during the transfer time from floor $j$ to floor $j+1$.

The description of an elevator in transit through floor $j+1$ (represented by a token in place $UF_{j+1}$) can be given similarly (but not identically) to that just given. Note that a token appears in place $UF_{j+1}$ only if there are pending (internal or external) requests for service to some higher floor $h$.

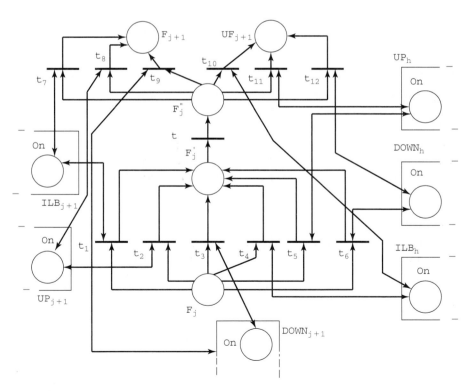

FIGURE 5.36

A more precise description of elevator movement.

In our description, so far we have not made any assumptions about a decision policy for selecting a request to be served if more than one request is pending. Thus, at the stage we are now, the model is still highly nondeterministic. For example, the model does not require the elevator to stop at floor $j+1$ if an internal request to stop there is issued before passing floor $j+1$ in the upward direction. Our choice is to concentrate all policy decisions within a SCHEDULER module, which is discussed shortly.

Let us now browse through the specification of the remaining aspects of the elevator system.

**Switching the buttons off.**   Figure 5.37 models how an internal button $ILB_j$ is switched off when the elevator reaches floor $j$. (We have drawn a dashed box around the components of $ILB_j$ to clarify the module's boundaries.) Transition Reset has $t_{min} = t_{max} = 0$ and the highest priority, so we are guaranteed that the light is switched off as soon as the elevator reaches the corresponding floor. Again, notice how the specification is built up in parts (i.e., incrementally and in a modular way). In the figure, we are referring to place $F_j$ without repeating all the previous connections to it.

Figure 5.38 sketches how floor buttons $UP_j$ $(1 \leq j \leq m-1)$ are switched off. Transition $t'_i$ is the duplication of any transition $t_i$ $(1 \leq i \leq 6)$ of Figure 5.36. (They are all treated identically.) Transitions $t'_i$ also have $t_{min} = t_{max} = 0$, but have higher priority than transitions $t_i$; in this way, a transition $t'_i$ is chosen to fire instead of the corresponding $t_i$ if the floor button is to be switched. In other words, both transitions $t_i$ and $t'_i$ model the "decision" of the elevator to go up. In addition, the latter transition models the resetting of the floor button. Transition Reset fires to reset the button when there are no pending requests. We define $t_{min}$ (Reset) = $t_{max}$ (Reset) = dp, where dp is the delay time needed to model a person entering the elevator and pushing a button. Floor buttons $DOWN_i$ $(2 \leq i \leq m)$ are modeled in the same way. As a consequence, both floor buttons are switched off if no internal service request occurs in due time. Note that here we are changing the informal requirements slightly. Note also that the formalization of Figure 5.38 disambiguates the informal statement about switching the button off by choosing the second of the two interpretations we suggested in analyzing the deficiencies of the informal requirements.

### Exercises

**5.23**  Formalize the first of the two interpretations of the rule on switching the button off that were discussed in our assessment of the informal specification.

**5.24**  Formalize the original rule of the informal specifications—that is, "in the latter case, if both floor-request buttons are pressed, only one should be canceled,"—instead of the present choice that switches both buttons off.

**Decision policies.**   The model described so far is highly nondeterministic. In many cases, nondeterminism is a desirable property of a specification, since it allows one to specify a set of acceptable behaviors without restricting the model to one specific behavior, which can be chosen later at implementation time—for example, for performance reasons. Sometimes, however, nondeterminism would allow undesirable behav-

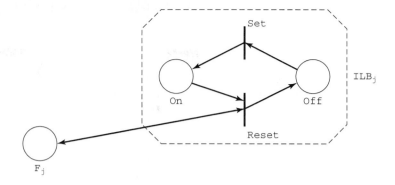

FIGURE 5.37

Switching the internal buttons off. The dashed box shows the boundaries of module ILB$_j$.

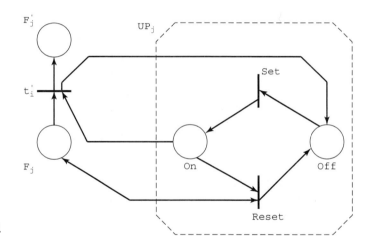

FIGURE 5.38

Switching the floor buttons off.

iors that we wish to exclude at specification time. In our example, up to now we specified only the mechanisms that govern the elevator's movements; we did not specify the policies involved. These policies, however, need to be specified if we wish to prove that all requests are eventually serviced by the elevators. (See informal requirement 4.) We decided to encapsulate all decision policies in a module called SCHEDULER. This is an application of information hiding to specifications: Encapsulation of the decision policies will allow us to change such policies without affecting the mechanisms described by the rest of the net; for example, we will be able to fine-tune the system's performance at the requirements specification level by simulating different policies in the model.

Here, we simply sketch a simplest instance of SCHEDULER. The chosen policy differs from the fuzzy requirement of the informal specifications: It guarantees *fairness* among the service requests; that is, it guarantees that every request will be served eventually (but does not try to "minimize waiting times," whatever that means). Thus, no request will ever suffer starvation.

We assign each elevator a "direction state," which is either U (up) or D (down). (See Figure 5.39.) A token in U (D) means that the elevator direction is up (down). Our policy consists of keeping the direction state unchanged as long as there are calls that would force the elevator to go in that direction. Otherwise, transitions U_D and D_U fire when the direction of movement changes from up to down and down to up, respectively. $U_K$ denotes any transition of the overall net (e.g., $t_1$, ..., $t_{12}$) representing an upwards movement; and $D_K$ denotes any transition of the overall net representing a downwards movement. (Remember that these transitions have $t_{min} = t_{max} = 0$; that is, they fire immediately as they are enabled.) Transitions U_D and D_U, conversely, represent actions that have a non null duration (i.e., they have $t_{min} = t_{max} = x$ msec), where $x$ is non null). Such a duration represents the decision time taken by the scheduler to check whether there are requests to go up or down. Furthermore, in the portion of the net of Figure 5.36, and in similar ones, we give higher priority to transitions $t_7$, $t_8$, and $t_9$ than to transitions $t_{10}$, $t_{11}$, and $t_{12}$. This way, an elevator is forced to stop at any floor if there are internal or external requests to serve that floor. As one may easily observe, the elevator continues to move in a certain direction—say, up—as long as there are pending requests to go up. If there are no more requests to serve in that direction, after a certain time the elevator switches to the down mode of movement if there are pending requests to go down. If there are no such pending requests, the elevator keeps checking for them to become available.

A more general way of modeling scheduling policies consists of introducing a place, SCHEDULER, which contains a distinguished token that carries information about the overall state of the system. Suitable predicates can then be associated with transitions in such a way that those transitions which are enabled are exactly those which are allowed to fire according to the scheduling policy. This general model is sketched in Figure 5.40.

Once we have completed the formalization of the elevator system in terms of PNs, we can analyze it to verify whether it defines the intended behavior properly. As we anticipated in Section 5.4, one way to verify the adequacy of a specification is by *simulating* it. In this case, simulation through PNs is quite natural: We just need to apply the firing rules to the model, starting with an initial state, and then observe the resulting behavior.

For instance, we could consider an initial marking wherein an elevator is at floor 1 (i.e., a token is in place $F_1$) and all of the internal and external buttons are off. Now assume that somebody enters the elevator and pushes the internal button 2. This corresponds to the firing of transition Push in the portion of the net describing the button. (See Figure 5.34.) Then Set fires immediately, which corresponds to switching the button on. Thus, transition $t_4$ in the net of the type of Figure 5.36 is enabled and fires immediately. After a time $\Delta t$, a token will be in $F''_2$, enabling transition $t_7$. This transition will fire immediately. Just after that, transition Reset for the internal button of the elevator corresponding to floor 2 fires. (See Figure 5.37.) This simulation allows us to conclude that, if an elevator is at floor 1 and no button is On when the elevator's internal button 2 is pushed, then after $\Delta t$ seconds, the elevator will reach floor 2 and the button will be reset. Similarly, one could simulate external calls by using the rules formalized in Figures 5.34 and 5.38. This would make apparent the chosen interpretation for the informal requirement

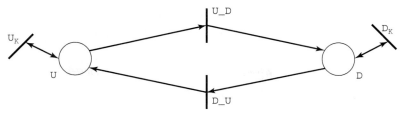

**FIGURE 5.39**

A simple scheduling policy.

**FIGURE 5.40**

A more general way of representing scheduling policies. Each transition has a predicate of the type OK(Scheduler) (in conjunction with other possible conditions). The token in SCHEDULER stores all information about the state of the system that is useful for the selection of which transition to fire. The token is "permanent," since it is always reproduced after the firing of any transition and, possibly, after being updated.

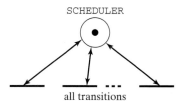

The light associated with a button is switched off when the elevator visits the floor and is either moving in the desired direction, or ...

If it turns out that this is not the interpretation meant by the customer, the specification must be modified accordingly. (See Exercise 5.23.)

The ability to create a simulation is a strong reason in favor of using a formal model for specifications: Formal specifications can be simulated automatically with the help of an interpreter for the model. The benefits of this approach should be quite obvious. The usefulness of simulation, however, depends on the model. Interpreting an FSM—even a fairly complex one—is easy and efficient. Interpreting a PN is conceptually simple, but its efficiency is affected by the intrinsic nondeterminism of the model, which may require the use of time-consuming backtracking techniques. In fact, suppose you are executing a PN to check whether, from a given marking m, a different marking m' can be reached. During the interpretation, nondeterministic choices are made whenever several transitions are enabled. If it turns out that these choices do not produce the marking m', you must undo some of them to try different ones. We will comment further on the use of models to verify specifications in Sections 5.6.2.4 and 5.7.3.

## Exercise

**5.25** Give reasonable interpretations of the phrase "minimize the waiting times" in the informally stated requirements of the elevator system. Formalize the chosen interpretations as selection functions to be attached to a PN schema of the type of Figure 5.40. Check whether your policy still guarantees that all requests will eventually be served.

## 5.6    DESCRIPTIVE SPECIFICATIONS

As we stated in Section 5.3, descriptive specifications try to describe the desired *properties* of a system rather than its desired *behavior*. In this section, we start a short review of descriptive specification notations with a semiformal and widely used model. Then we move to completely formal notations. We illustrate different notations that can be used to specify systems at different stages of the development process. Some notations are suitable for use at the requirements level. Others are suitable for specifying the semantics of module interfaces. Still others are suitable for specifying individual program fragments. All of the notations, however, share the same flavor of the descriptive style.

A natural way of providing precise descriptive specifications is through the use of *mathematical formulas*. Unlike natural language, mathematical formulas have a precise syntax and semantics. Furthermore, they can be managed by automated tools as well as formal operational models.

Many mathematical formalisms have been proposed for the description of system properties. In this section, we will review two major approaches, one based on the use of mathematical logic and the other based on the use of algebra.

### 5.6.1    Entity-Relationship Diagrams

We have seen that DFDs are a useful notation for describing the operations used to access and manipulate the data of a system—typically, an information system. However, this is often not enough to specify all the interesting features of the system: A conceptual description of the structure of the data and of their relations is also necessary.

Actually, it is unclear which of the two descriptions, of operations or of data structures, should come first. On the one hand, understanding the operations to be provided by the system helps in understanding the logical structure of the data. On the other hand, the logical structure holds irrespective of the operations performed on the data. One may even argue that it represents our knowledge of the application area, which is more stable than the operations provided by the application.

The two views are clearly complementary, and both are useful for understanding and specifying an application. Therefore, we start our review of descriptive specifications with the *entity-relationship* (*ER*) model, a widely known and adopted notation for describing the relations among the data of an information system.

The ER model was motivated by the need for a conceptual model of data suitable for specifying user views and logical requirements in information systems and, more generally, in applications that are centered around large collections of interrelated data. The model is based on three primitive concepts: *entities, relations*, and *attributes*. The model has an associated graphical language, which is particularly easy to understand; the descriptions given in the graphical language are called *ER diagrams*.

Figure 5.41 shows a simple example of an ER diagram that describes the entities STUDENT and CLASS, with the relationship ENROLLED_IN, which may hold between a STUDENT and a CLASS. An entity—represented by a box—stands for a collection of items that share common properties; the concept is thus similar to that of a type in programming languages. The properties of an entity are its attributes and the relations in which it participates. Attributes are listed next to the entity, and relations are represented as diamond-shaped boxes. In our example, STUDENT is a collection of individuals; NAME, AGE, and SEX are attributes of STUDENT; and every student is characterized by a triple of values representing the student's name, age, and sex. A relation on two entities such as STUDENT and CLASS is a set of pairs <a, b>, where a is an element of STUDENT and b is an element of CLASS. The relation shown in Figure 5.41 could represent the fact that student a is enrolled in class b.

ER diagrams have not been standardized. This means that there is no official, universally recognized version of the notation, and many variations exist in practice. Some ER languages allow relations to be n-ary (i.e., they may relate any number of entities); others support binary relations only. Also, some permit relations to have attributes, while others do not. If attributes of relations were permitted, we could define the attribute PROFICIENCY to be associated with ENROLLED_IN. Then the attribute associated with any given pair <a, b> in ENROLLED_IN would represent the proficiency of student a in class b. Finally, some ER languages support a kind of inheritance among entities, often called the IS_A relation in ER jargon. For example, one could define UNDERGRADUATE and GRADUATE as two subentities of STUDENT, inheriting the properties of STUDENT and adding new ones in terms of attributes and participation in relations (UNDERGRADUATE IS_A STUDENT).

Most ER languages allow relations to be partial; that is, not every element in the related entities has to participate in the relation. In addition, they often allow the relation to be annotated as one to one, one to many, many to one, or many to many. If a relation R between A and B is one to one, then, for any <a, b> in R, there exists no a' in A such that <a', b> is in R and a' ≠ a; and, in addition, there exists no b' in B such that <a, b'> is in R and b' ≠ b. If R is many to one, it is required only that, for any <a, b> in R, there exist no b' in B such that <a, b'> is also in R and b' ≠ b, etc. Graphically, this is represented as shown in Figure 5.42. We can see that the relation ENROLLED_IN in Figure 5.41 is many to many.

The annotations in Figure 5.42 describe simple constraints on the relationship. In practice, however, when we specify requirements, we would like to be able to state more general and complex kinds of constraints on our data that might characterize

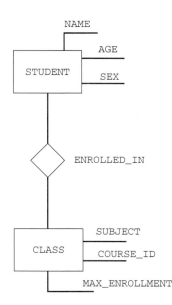

**FIGURE 5.41**

An ER diagram describing a relationship between students and classes.

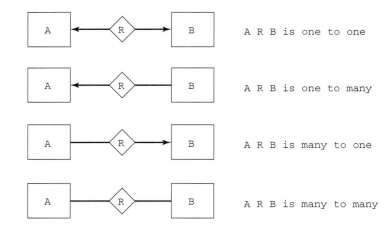

**FIGURE 5.42**

Annotations describing constraints on the relationship R.

A R B is one to one

A R B is one to many

A R B is many to one

A R B is many to many

some important properties of the world we are modeling. Unfortunately, the power of the ER language is rather limited, and more complex concepts must be expressed separately by using a different notation. For example, there is no way to specify graphically that a class can exist only if the number of enrolled students is greater than five and that the number cannot exceed the value MAX_ENROLLMENT that is an attribute of each class. If we want, this constraint can be stated as a comment in natural language, associated with the diagram as further documentation.

According to the classification discussed in Section 5.3, ER diagrams are a semiformal notation, because their syntax and semantics are not stated precisely and because their lack of expressive power forces us to add properties as informal comments. Also, they are a descriptive notation, because they state what the entities and their properties are in terms of attributes and participation in relations. In Section 5.6.2, we will comment on the relation between ER diagrams and the formal descriptive notation provided by logic.

The reader may have noticed that ER diagrams are similar to a simplified form of class diagrams. In fact, class diagrams have been defined as an evolution of ER diagrams wherein data entities are modeled along with their operations in an object-oriented style. In a conventional style, in which functions and data are defined separately, ER diagrams are used to complement DFDs. In an object-oriented style, the two aspects are clustered together in classes.

ER diagrams are still widely used in practice especially in data-oriented applications. Since they are graphical, they are rather understandable even by nonspecialists. It is also claimed that they are effective for the assessment of requirements, since end users may be trained to understand them and thus may verify whether the description provided by the software engineer models the application's domain adequately in terms of the relevant entities and their relationships.

### Exercises

**5.26** Suppose that your ER language does not support attributes associated with relations, but does support n-ary relations. Following the discussion in Section 5.6.1, how would you represent the students' proficiency levels in a given class?

**5.27** Augment the ER diagram of Figure 5.41 by introducing the entity PROFESSOR and suitable relations TEACHES (with entity CLASS) and ADVISES (with entity STUDENT). How can you specify a (funny) constraint like "a student cannot take a class that is taught by his or her advisor"?

## 5.6.2 Logic Specifications

A formula of a *first-order theory* (FOT) is an expression involving variables, numeric constants, functions, predicates, and parentheses, as in traditional arithmetic. The usual logical connectives—**and, or, not, implies,** and ≡ (which denotes logical equivalence) —are also used. The type of the result of a first-order-theory formula must be Boolean. As opposed to the Boolean-valued formulas of many programming languages, however, FOT formulas may also use *quantifiers*—that is, the symbols **exists** and **for all** that can be applied to variables.

The following are a few examples of FOT formulas:

1.     x > y **and** y > z **implies** x > z;
2.     x = y ≡ y = x;
3.     **for all** x, y, z (x > y **and** y > z **implies** x > z);
4.     x + 1 < x - 1;
5.     **for all** x (**exists** y(y = x + z));
6.     x > 3 **or** x < -6.

The semantics of such formulas should be sufficiently clear from the intuitive meanings of the symbols used.

Notice that some of the preceding formulas are true, others are false, and still others are true or false, depending on the values of the unquantified variables. So formulas 1 and 2 are true regardless of the values of x, y, and z, formula 4 is false regardless of the value of x, and formula 6 is true for some values of x and false for others.

A variable that occurs in a formula is said to be *free* in that formula if it is not quantified; a variable that is not free is said to be *bound*. So x is free in formula 1 and is bound in formula 3. If all variables in a formula are quantified, the formula is said to be *closed*. Thus, formula 3 is closed. A closed formula is always either true or false. The *closure* of a formula is obtained by quantifying all of its free variables with the **for all** quantifier. So the closure of formula 4 is **for all** x(x + 1 < x - 1). If a formula is true for all values of its free variables, so is its closure. Thus, the closure of formula 1 is true, but the closure of formula 4 is false.

In some cases, the truth of a formula depends on the domain chosen for its variables. For instance, the formula

7.     **for all** x (x ≥ 1) **or** (x ≤ - 1) **or** (x = 0)

is true if x is an integer; it is false if x is a real number. In this book, however, we will deal with variables whose domains should be understood without ambiguity. In particular, numeric variables will be assumed to be integers, unless stated otherwise.

Earlier, we observed that ER diagrams can be classified as a semiformal descriptive notation. We can illustrate this property by showing that ER diagrams may be easily restated in terms of logic; moreover, logic provides a formal notation to express the constraints that are not expressible in terms of ER diagrams. For example, in the discussion relating to Figure 5.41, the constraint that "a class can exist only if the number of enrolled students is greater than five, and the number cannot exceed the value MAX_ENROLLMENT" can be stated as

```
for all a in CLASS
        5 ≤ cardinality {b|< a, b > in ENROLLED_IN}≤
        a.MAX_ENROLLMENT
```

where we use the dot notation to denote the value of an entity's attribute. Also, the function **cardinality** has been introduced to indicate the number of elements in a set.

We shall demonstrate the use of logical formulas in the style of the so-called Floyd-Hoare program specification. First, we show how complete programs can be specified by stating logical formulas that relate the program's input and output. These formulas are called input-output assertions. Next, we show the use of intermediate assertions logical formulas that are used to specify fragments of a program by making statements about the state of the program's execution at particular points in the program. We then briefly discuss how this specification style can be extended to object-oriented design to specify classes. Finally, we use both types of specification to present the case study of the elevator system in terms of logical specifications.

### Exercises

**5.28** Build the closures of the preceding formulas 1 through 7.

**5.29** Is the closure of formula 6 true?

### 5.6.2.1 Specifying complete programs: input–output assertions

We start with the simplest use of mathematical formulas to express software properties. Let P be a sequential program. Let $<i_1, i_2, \ldots, i_n>$ denote the sequence of P's input values and $<o_1, o_2, \ldots, o_m>$ the sequence of P's output values. More precisely, assume that P reads all input values from, and writes all output values to, sequential files; $<i_1, i_2, \ldots, i_n>$ is the sequence of values stored in the input file in the order in which P reads them, and $<o_1, o_2, \ldots, o_m>$ is the sequence in which P writes its output.

A *property*, or *requirement*, for P is specified as a formula of the type

```
{Pre(i₁, i₂, ..., iₙ)}
P
{Post(o₁, o₂, ..., oₘ, i₁, i₂, ..., iₙ)}
```

where $\mathrm{Pre}(i_1, i_2, \ldots, i_n)$ denotes a FOT formula having $i_1, i_2, \ldots, i_n$ as free variables and $\mathrm{Post}(o_1, o_2, \ldots, o_m, i_1, i_2, \ldots, i_n)$ denotes a FOT formula having $o_1, o_2, \ldots, o_m$, and, possibly, $i_1, i_2, \ldots, i_n$, as free variables. Pre is called the *precondition* of P, and Post is the *postcondition* of P. The preceding formula is intended to mean that if Pre holds for the given input values before P's execution, then, after P finishes executing, Post must hold for the output and input values.

Let us give some simple examples of program specifications in terms of pre- and postconditions:

**1.**
```
{exists z(i₁ = z*i₂)}
P
{o₁ = i₁/i₂}
```

This states that, if the input value $i_1$ is a multiple of the input value $i_2$, then the output must be the result of the division $i_1/i_2$. A stronger requirement for a division program is the following:

**2.**      $\{i_1 > i_2\}$

P

$\{i_1 = i_2{}^{\ast}o_1 + o_2 \text{ and } o_2 \geq 0 \text{ and } o_2 < i_2\}$

This requirement is stronger in the sense that it imposes fewer constraints on the input values and more constraints on the output values. A precondition of $\{\texttt{true}\}$ does not place any constraint on input values; it always holds, regardless of the input values, implying that the program will achieve its result for all input values. The specification

**3.**      $\{\texttt{true}\}$

P

$\{o = i_1 \text{ or } o = i_2) \text{ and } o \leq i_1 \text{ and } o \leq i_2\}$

requires that P produce the greater of $i_1$ and $i_2$. The specification

**4.**      $\{i_1 > 0 \text{ and } i_2 > 0\}$

P

$\{(\textbf{exists } z_1, z_2 \ (i_1 = o \ast z_1 \text{ and } i_2 = o \ast z_2)$
**and not**
$(\textbf{exists } h \ (\textbf{exists } z_1, z_2 \ (i_1 = h \ast z_1 \text{ and } i_2 = h \ast z_2) \text{ and } h > o)))\}$

requires that P compute the greatest common divisor of $i_1$ and $i_2$.

Assuming that n is a positive value denoting the length of the input sequence, the specification

**5.**      $\{n > 0\}$

P

$$\left\{o = \sum_{k=1}^{n} i_k\right\}$$

requires that P compute the sum of the sequence. Finally, the specification

**6.**      $\{n > 0\}$

P

$\{\textbf{for all } i \ (1 \leq i \leq n) \ \textbf{implies} \ (o_i = i_{n-i+1})\}$

requires that P produce the reverse of its input sequence, assuming that the input sequence is not empty.

## Exercises

**5.30**  Give a logic specification for a program that reads a sequence of $n + 1$ values and checks whether the first value also appears in the next n input values.

**5.31**  Give a logic specification for a program that, first, reads two words (i.e., two sequences of alphabetic characters, separated by a blank and terminated by the special character '#'). The second word may be null; the first must not. Then, the program reads a sequence of other words, separated by blanks and terminated by '#', and rewrites the sequence, substituting all occurrences of the first word by the second.

You should just sketch the solution without going into all the details. Then you should go back to the exercise after reading the rest of this section.

The previous examples and exercises have shown that the formulas which are needed to specify even simple problems may require many details and may be hard to understand. We have already faced this inconvenience in our previous examples of operational specifications. In Section 5.7, we shall consider the problem of managing complex specifications in its full generality. We anticipate, however, some suggestions for improving the readability of logic specifications, just as we did when we built non-trivial specifications with PNs and FSMs.

Consider, for instance, the problem given in Exercise 5.31. The major source of trouble is that even simple and intuitive concepts, such as "word," have no predefined meaning in the FOT syntax. Thus, if we want to formalize a sentence such as "two words are equal" or "one word is substituted by another one," we have to go through many details. This, however, can be done once and for all by the use of suitable *definitions*.

For example, we could introduce the predicate input_word (m, n) to state that the sequence of characters in the input stream, from the mth through the nth positions, is a word. This notion is formalized by the formula

input_word (m, n) $\equiv$ (**for all** i (m $\leq$ i $\leq$ n) **implies** alphabetic($c_i$))

where $c_i$ represents the ith input character and alphabetic (c) means that c is an alphabetic character. (The formalization of this predicate is a trivial exercise.)

Now we can use the predicate input_word as a compact and understandable abbreviation whenever it is needed. In particular, we can define the predicate input_text (m, n) to state that the sequence of elements of the input file from the mth through the nth positions is a piece of text that is, a sequence of words separated by a blank and bracketed by a pair of symbols, '#'. Precisely,

input_text(m,n) $\equiv$
        ($i_m$='#' **and** $i_n$='#' **and**
           (**exists** k ( **for all** j (1 $\leq$ j $\leq$ k) **implies**
               (**exists** $h_j$, $m_j$ (input_word ($m_j$, $m_j$ + $h_j$) **and**
                    $m_1$ = m + 1 **and** $m_k$ + $h_k$ + 1 = n **and**
                    (1 $\leq$ j < k)**implies** ($m_{j+1}$ = $m_j$ + $h_j$ + 2 **and**
                    $i_{mj}$ + $h_j$ + 1=' '))))))

Once this definition is stated, one can go on to define suitable predicates for the output file and, eventually, an overall relation between input and output files based on the previous definitions. We leave this task to the reader.

### Exercise

**5.32** Find some detail of the informal specification of Exercise 5.31 that was not defined precisely, and check it against the formal definition.

### 5.6.2.2 *Specifying program fragments: intermediate assertions*

In the previous section, we used pre- and postconditions on I/O values to specify complete programs. Often, however, it is useful to specify just portions of programs. For instance, if we are building a library of general-purpose modules, we do not even know the context in which some procedures will be executed.

Such a generalization is quite straightforward. All we need to do is to allow expressions in pre- and postconditions to refer to program variables as well as to I/O values. For instance, suppose you want to specify a procedure `search` with input parameters `element`, `table` (an array of integers), and `n`, the number of elements stored in `table`. The procedure is to check whether `element` exists in `table`. This can be done as follows:[9]

**7.**  `{n > 0} -- n is a constant value`
       **procedure** `search (table: in integer_array; n: in integer;`
                          `element: in integer; found: out Boolean);`
       `{found ≡ (exists i(1 ≤ i ≤ n and table(i) = element))}`

Similarly, one could write the following specification for a subprogram that reverses the contents of an array of integers:

**8.**  `{n > 0}`
       **procedure** `reverse (a: in out integer_array; n: in integer);`
       `{for all i (1 ≤ i ≤ n) implies (a(i) = old_a(n - i + 1))}`

In this specification, we needed to state a relation between the values of the program variables before and after the execution of the procedure. Thus, we used the auxiliary variable $old\_a$ to denote a's value prior to the execution of the procedure.

The following is a specification for a sort procedure:

**9.**  `{n > 0}`
       **procedure** `sort (a: in out integer_array; n: in integer);`
       `{sorted(a,n)},`

As we did before, we define the new predicate

       `sorted(a,n) ≡ (for all i(1 ≤ i < n) implies a(i) ≤ a(i+1))`

### Exercise

**5.33**  Is specification 9 an appropriate specification for a sorting procedure? Why? If not, give such an appropriate specification.

### 5.6.2.3 *Specifying classes*

Specifying properties of the state of program execution, rather than just I/O relations, becomes even more important in the case of object-oriented languages when we wish to specify a class. More precisely, specifying such properties becomes important whenever we wish to specify the behavior of objects of the class during their lifetime, from their creation, as operations are applied to them to change their state and to inquire about their state. In this case, in fact, there is no notion of a computation that we wish to specify with well-defined starting and ending points. Rather, to understand the effect of an operation applied to an object, we need to be able to characterize the current state of the object, which is the result of any previous sequence of operations applied to it.

---

[9]We implicitly assume here that the lower bound of arrays is 1.

One way to characterize object states is through an *invariant* predicate. The invariant defines a property that characterizes the object from its creation, throughout its lifetime. The invariant must be preserved by the operations. For example, if an array `IMPL` of size `length` is used in a class to implement the abstract data type `SET`, the invariant might state that no two elements of `IMPL` are equal:

> **for all** i, j (1 ≤ i ≤ length **and** 1 ≤ j ≤ length **and** i≠j) **implies**
> IMPL[i]≠IMPL[j]

In addition, each operation can be specified by stating a precondition and a postcondition. The precondition is a predicate on the initial state of the object (input parameters and object instance variables) which specifies a constraint that client modules are expected to satisfy when they invoke the operation. The postcondition is a predicate on the object's state after the invocation that the implementation of the operation must establish. For example, suppose that operation `DELETE` is defined to eliminate an element x from a set. Then a precondition for `DELETE` could be

> **exists** i (1 ≤ i ≤ length **and** IMPL[i]= x)

The postcondition would be

> **for all** i (1 ≤ i ≤ length **implies** IMPL[i] ≠ x) **and**
>   **forall** i ((1 ≤ i ≤ *old*_length **and** *old*_IMPL[i] ≠ x) **implies**
>   **exists** j (1 ≤ i ≤ length
>   **and** IMPL[i]= *old*_IMPL[i]))

According to this specification, if the client module ensures that the precondition is true when the operation is invoked, the implementation of the operation provided by the class must ensure that the postcondition is true after its execution.

In general, let us assume that `INV` is an invariant predicate for a class. For each operation $op_i$ defined in the class, let $pre_i$ be its precondition and let $post_i$ be its postcondition. The complete specification for the code implementing operation $op_i$ defined by the class, may then be given as

> {INV **and** $pre_i$} *program fragment for* $op_i${INV **and** $post_i$}

This formula formalizes the property that `INV` is an invariant (it holds after the operation is executed, assuming that it holds before the operation is executed) and $pre_i$ and $post_i$ are the pre- and postcondition, respectively. To complete the specification, we must also depend on the fact that in its initial state the object satisfies the invariant. Assuming that a constructor operation `cstr` is provided by the class to create objects, we require that

> {true} *program fragment for cstr* {INV}

In fact, by induction, since initially the object satisfies the invariant and since every operation preserves it, we can conclude that the invariant is always true during the object's lifetime, before and after the execution of any operations on the object.

### 5.6.2.4 *Specifying nonterminating behaviors*

Very often, we need to specify systems whose behaviors are described by nonterminating programs. One such system is a reactive system, which waits continuously for signals from the external environment and provides responses to those signals. An operating system is a typical example of a reactive system, responding to user requests, interrupts coming from peripheral devices, etc. Computer control systems, such as the elevator we discussed in Section 5.5.4.2, are another typical example. As a case study, let us consider here the classical producer-consumer system introduced in Section 4.5.1.1. Informally, a major requirement for such a system is that, at any time, the sequence of items produced by the producer (i.e., passed to operation PUT as parameters) coincide with the sequence of items consumed (i.e., obtained through GET), except for the most recently produced elements, which are kept in the buffer. This property must always hold; that is, it must be invariant during system execution. If the producer and the consumer processes are in **repeat-forever** loops, however, the two sequences are not even defined. (A sequence has to be finite). Accordingly, what we are actually interested in is that, at any given critical point, the two sequences coincide. This property must hold infinitely many times, independently of how many items are produced and consumed. Again, it must be invariant during system execution. Let us examine a producer-consumer system in more detail.

## Example 5.5

Consider the producer-consumer system of Section 4.5.1.1. To specify the desired system behavior, we need to state a predicate based on the sequences of characters that are read and written. These are neither I/O nor program variables in the strict sense: There is neither a declaration nor any use of such variables. We may refer to them, however, as if they were program variables in the same way we did when referring to the values of the same variable at different points in the execution of a sequential program.

Thus, we define the variables INPUT_SEQUENCE and OUTPUT_SEQUENCE, and we assume that each PUT operation of a producer (into CHAR_BUFFER) appends the written character at the end of INPUT_SEQUENCE and that each GET operation of a consumer appends the character read at the end of OUTPUT_SEQUENCE.

Now, we realize that it is not exactly true that we want the two sequences to be always the same. In fact, they may differ up to the present contents of the buffer. Thus, the invariant property that can be assumed as a specification is

```
INPUT_SEQUENCE = append (OUTPUT_SEQUENCE,
                    contents(CHAR_BUFFER))
```

where the meanings of the append and contents operations should be obvious.

Analyzing this property more deeply, however, we realize that even its new formulation cannot be claimed to be an invariant property in a strict sense. In fact, when, say, the consumer is executing the monitor procedure GET, the buffer contents and OUTPUT_SEQUENCE are not even well defined. We do not, however, need such a strong requirement on the invariance of the desired property. For our purposes, it is perfectly satisfactory that the invariant property hold whenever the system is not executing a monitor procedure.

Thus, the *critical execution points* at which we need to guarantee that the invariant property holds are the entry and the exit of monitor procedures. (In fact, the variables of interest are affected *only* by monitor procedures.)

In the foregoing example, we have seen that the specification describes properties of the state of execution of the system. In Chapter 6, we give more examples of such specifications. ∎

### Exercises

**5.34** Specify a procedure that is intended to merge two sorted arrays into a single one. You should distinguish two different cases:

   **a.** Duplicate elements in input arrays should appear as duplicates in the output array.
   **b.** Input and output arrays should contain no duplicate elements.

**5.35** Consider the system outlined in Figure 5.43. It consists of three processes: `Line`, `Producer`, and `Consumer`. `Line` represents the external environment of the system. It writes single characters into `Port`, from which `Producer` gets them. The two are synchronized through a monitor. `Producer` puts the character into `Buffer` through another monitor, from which `Consumer` gets packets of n ≤ `size(Buffer)` characters. `Consumer` does not have to wait until the buffer is full. Formalize a correct behavior of this system by means of an appropriate invariant assertion.

### 5.6.2.5  *A case study using logic specifications*

To tackle a larger problem, let us now apply logical formalism to the elevator case study analyzed in Section 5.5.4.2. This will allow us to compare and contrast such formalism with the PN analysis used there. The first step of our specification effort is to define a set of elementary predicates that describe relevant properties about the state or operation of the system. For instance, `at(E, F, T)` could be used to state that elevator `E` is at floor `F` at time `T`. Similarly, `start(E, F, T, up)` could state that elevator `E` left floor `F` at time `T` in the up direction, and so on.

Then, one could write a set of formulas that describe the behavioral rules of the system. For instance,

$$(\text{at}(E, F, T) \textbf{ and } \text{on}(EB, F_1, T) \textbf{ and } F_1 > F) \textbf{ implies } \text{start}(E, F, T, up)$$

specifies that, if at time `T` elevator `E` is at floor `F`, and its internal button referring to floor $F_1$, with $F_1 > F$, is on, then, at the same time, the elevator starts moving in the up direction.

Notice that here we are predicating properties of system objects such as elevators, floors, etc., in the same way that in previous examples we stated properties of program variables. We introduce new predicates (e.g., `at` and `on`) and specify their semantics through FOT formulas in the same way that we could state the property

$$x > y \textbf{ and } y > z \textbf{ implies } x > z$$

for the predicate '>' in arithmetic.

**FIGURE 5.43**

A simple producer-consumer system.

This is a good example of the different uses of specifications. If we specify properties of system objects such as elevators and buttons, we are specifying system requirements; if we specify properties of program variables, we are specifying program *design* and *implementation*.

For syntactic convenience, we denote variable identifiers by strings beginning with uppercase letters and predicates by strings beginning with lowercase letters. Notice that we explicitly take time into account as a system variable. This will allow us to state time constraints between the occurrence of different events (e.g., the request for an elevator and its arrival at the floor in question).

To continue formalizing the elevator system further requires a systematic approach, such as the one we adopted in Section 5.5.4.2 based on PNs. First, we partition the set of elementary predicates with which we intend to describe the system's evolution into *elementary states* and *events*. States describe a condition of the system that has a non null duration. The global notion of a system state at a given time is the conjunction of all elementary states that hold during that time. For the sake of brevity, in the following we will call *elementary states* just *states*. The term *global state* will identify the state of the whole system. Events describe conditions that can hold only at a particular instant of time. For example, the event

```
arrived(E, F, T)
```

means that elevator E arrived at floor F at time T, while the state

```
standing(E, F, T₁, T₂)
```

means that elevator E has been parked at floor F from time $T_1$ to time $T_2$.

In this description, then, time is represented explicitly, by a single value for events, which are by definition instantaneous, and a pair of time values for states, where the pair denotes the interval during which the state holds.

We describe the behavior of the system by implicative formulas, or *rules*—that is, by a set of premises, followed by the keyword **implies**, followed by a conclusion, which is supposed to follow logically from the premises. The rules are implicitly universally quantified for symbols occurring on the LHS and existentially quantified for symbols that occur *only* on the RHS. They allow one to deduce the occurrence of an event or the change of a state at a particular moment as the consequence of a set of events or states holding at that moment or before, possibly under certain conditions. Since a state changes due to the occurrence of an event, another group of rules extends the period of time during which a state holds, until a modifying event occurs.

For the sake of simplicity, we make a few assumptions. First, we assume *zero decision times*, as we assumed in Section 5.5.4.2. Furthermore, we exclude *simultaneous events* generated from the external environment. This does not affect our specification substantially, but allows a simplification of certain rules. If they turn out to be unrealistic, the assumptions may be removed easily—at the price of a slight increase in the number of formulas used.

Next, we give a sample of events, states, and rules that constitute the system specification. Exercises will then guide the reader through the completion of the specification and some variations of it. Remember that there are m floors and n elevators. The system is turned on at time $t_0$.

**Events**

- arrival(E, F, T)
  E in [1..n], F in [1..m], $T \geq t_0$
  ($t_0$ is the initial time)

represents the arrival of elevator E at floor F at time T. This event does not indicate whether, once it has arrived, the elevator would stop at that floor or leave immediately for another floor; nor does it imply anything about the direction of motion of the elevator or about the floor from which the elevator has left.

- departure(E, F, D, T)
  E in [1..n], F in [1..m], D in {up, down}, $T \geq t_0$

describes the departure of elevator E from floor F in direction D at time T. We shall see in the rules that this event puts elevator E in the state of motion from floor F in direction D.

- stop(E, F, T)
  E in [1..n], F in [1..m], $T \geq t_0$

represents the arrival and stopping of elevator E at floor F at time T. The stop is for servicing an internal or external request. We shall see in the rules that this event puts elevator E in the state of standing at floor F.

- new_list(E, L, T)
  E in [1..n], L in [1..m]*, $T \geq t_0$

At every instant T, each elevator has an associated list L of integers[10] between 1 and m. The list represents the set of floors at which the elevator will eventually stop, according to the scheduling decisions performed, up to that time, by the control component of the system. A list is associated with each elevator because, that way, the scheduling strategy for internal and external requests can be easily and naturally expressed by rules—to be given later—managing the lists of the different elevators. At any instant, each elevator "decides" what to do according to the contents of its list. new_list (E, L, T) means that the list associated with elevator E becomes L at time T; thus, this predicate represents the event that transforms the control state of elevator E by setting its reservation list to L.

- call(F, D, T)
- request(E, F, T)
  E in [1..n], F in [1..m], D in {up, down}, $T \geq t_0$

These two predicates denote events generated from outside the system: external calls from floor F in direction D at time T and the reservation of floor F from inside elevator E at time T, respectively. Both events are associated with the pushing of the corresponding buttons by someone who wants to make a reservation. If F = 1 or F = m, there is a further condition on the parameter values: D must be equal to up and down, respectively.

**States**

Since states are properties of objects that have a duration, all predicates which refer to states have two time parameters that represent the boundaries of the time interval

---

[10]The * indicates the transitive closure operation; a* stands for a sequence of zero or more a's.

during which the property holds. We use the convention that time intervals associated with state predicates are closed at the left and open at the right; that is, the lower extreme of the time interval is included in the interval, and the upper extreme is excluded from the interval. (The notation adopted to indicate such time intervals is $[T_1, T_2[$.) The motivation for this convention is the fact that any effects of events are assumed to be instantaneous, so that a new state holds from the instant (included) when the event that generates it occurs up to the instant (excluded) when the event that determines the next, instantaneous, state change occurs.

From the definition of a state, it is clear that if a property that characterizes a state holds during a given interval, it will hold during any interval contained in the given one. Also, given an interval during which a state holds, the state may also hold during a larger interval. For example, if we state that

```
moving(E, F, D, T₁, T₂)
```

(i.e., the state of movement of elevator E from floor F in direction D) holds in the interval $[T_1, T_2[$, it must be possible to deduce

**for all** $T_3, T_4 (T_1 \leq T_3 < T_4 \leq T_2)$ moving($E, F, D, T_3, T_4$)

Nothing, however, prevents

```
moving(E, F, D, T₃, T₄)
```

with $T_3 < T_1 < T_2 < T_4$ from holding as well. We will later give appropriate rules to enforce these assumptions about the semantics of states.

Next, we provide a list of elevator states:

- standing($E, F, T_1, T_2$)
  $E$ in $[1..n[$, $F$ in $[1..m[$, $t_0 \leq T_1 < T_2$

specifies that in the interval $[T_1, T_2[$, elevator E is standing at floor F. As just pointed out, this does not necessarily imply that elevator E arrived at floor F at time $T_1$ or that it will leave floor F at time $T_2$.

- moving($E, F, D, T_1, T_2$)
  $E$ in $[1..n]$, $F$ in $[1..m]$, $D$ in {up, down},
  $t_0 \leq T_1 < T_2$

specifies that in the interval $[T_1, T_2]$, elevator E is moving in direction D and the last floor it visited was F.

- list ($E, L, T_1, T_2$)
  $E$ in $[1..n[$, $L$ in $[1..m[$*, $t_0 \leq T_1 < T_2$

specifies that in the interval $[T_1, T_2[$, the list associated with elevator E is L. Unlike the predicates standing and moving, which denote a physical property of the elevators, the predicate list denotes a control property.

We now illustrate the rules that describe the behavior of the system. We give the rules that describe the movement of elevators, followed by those which express the control strategies. In each group, we partition the rules into those leading to the deduction of events and those leading to the deduction of states.

**Elevator rules that relate events and states**

We first give the rules that govern the relationships between states and events in the system in English and then formalize the rules with logical expressions.

$R_1$ Elevator E, upon arrival at floor F, leaves immediately if that floor does not require service and the list is not empty. If the next floor to be serviced is higher than the one being passed, the departure is in the upward direction; otherwise, it is in the downward direction. We adopt the convention that the floor to be serviced is the one in the first position on the list. (This is denoted by the function `first` applied to the variable L.)

```
arrival(E, F, T_a) and
list(E, L, T, T_a) and
first(L) > F
implies
        departure(E, F, up, T_a).
```

A similar rule applies to the departure of an elevator in the opposite direction.

$R_2$ Elevator E, upon arrival at floor F, stops there if that floor must be serviced—that is, if the floor number appears as the first element of the list associated with the elevator.

```
arrival(E, F, T_a) and
list(E, L, T, T_a) and
first(L) = F
implies
        stop(E, F, T_a).
```

$R_3$ If elevator E arrives at a floor F with an empty list, it will stop there. Assuming that all elevators are moving to service the floors that appear on their respective lists, they should leave from, and arrive at, floors with nonempty lists. This rule then becomes significant if the scheduling policy allows for *canceling* elements from the list of a moving elevator. (See control rules described shortly.)

```
arrival(E, F, T_a) and
list(E, empty, T, T_a)
implies
        stop(E, F, T_a).
```

$R_4$ We assume that elevators have a fixed and known service stop time $\Delta t_s$. If the elevator list is not empty at the end of such an interval, the elevator leaves the floor immediately.

```
stop(E, F, T_a) and
list(E, L, T, T_a + Δt_s) and
first(L) > F
implies
        departure(E, F, up, T_a + Δt_s).
```

A similar rule applies for departures in the opposite direction.

**R$_5$** At the end of the period of service, if there are no floors to be serviced (i.e., if the elevator list is empty) the elevator will leave only when the list becomes nonempty.

```
stop(E, F, Ta) and
list(E, empty, Ta + Δts,Tp) and
Tp > Ta + Δts and
list(E, L, Tp, T) and
first(L) > F
implies
        departure(E, F, up, Tp).
```

As usual, a similar rule describes the departure in the opposite direction.

**R$_6$** As we did with PNs, we assume that the time $\Delta t$ taken by an elevator to move from one floor to the next, in either direction, is known and fixed. The arrival at a floor then takes place at a time $\Delta t$ after the departure time from the previous floor.

```
departure (E, F, up, T)
implies
        arrival (E, F + 1, T + Δt).
```

A similar rule applies to departure in the opposite direction.

**R$_7$** The event of stopping at floor F at time T initiates a state of standing at the floor that lasts at least for the interval $[T, T + \Delta t_s[$.

```
stop(E, F, T)
implies
        standing(E, F, T, T + Δts).
```

**R$_8$** At the end of a service stop of length $\Delta t_s$, if there are no floors to be serviced, the elevator will remain standing at the floor as long as the list remains empty.

```
stop(E, F, Ts) and
list(E, empty, Ts + Δts, T)
implies
        standing(E, F, Ts, T).
```

**R$_9$** The event of the departure of elevator E from floor F in direction D at time T initiates a state of movement that lasts for the interval $[T,T + \Delta t]$.

```
departure(E, F, D, T)
implies
        moving(E, F, D, T, T + Δt).
```

**R$_{10}$**. If a state is proven to hold for the interval $[T_1,T_2[$, then it also holds for all intervals $[T_3,T_4[$ included in $[T_1,T_2[$.

```
standing(E, F, T1,T2) and
T1 < = T3 and T3 < T4 and T4 ≤ T2
implies
        standing(E, F, T3,T4).
```

There are similar rules for all other states.

**Control Rules**

Control rules are rules that allow one to deduce events of the type new_list and states of the type list; in other words, they express the scheduling strategy. As an example, we give the rules that express the simple strategy according to which requests that come from inside elevators are immediately inserted in the elevator's list in such a way that the list is sorted either in the order from the current floor to the top if the elevator is moving up or in the reverse order if the elevator is moving down. An element is removed from an elevator's list as soon as the elevator stops at the floor corresponding to the element. External calls can be managed similarly (e.g., by inserting the requested floor in the list of the closest elevator that is moving in the right direction or in an elevator that is standing).

$R_{11}$. The event of reserving a floor F from inside an elevator E that is not standing at that floor causes an instantaneous update to the list L associated with E, according to the policy just mentioned. This event can be described by

```
request(E, F, T_R) and
not (standing(E, F, T_a,T_R)) and
list(E, L, T_a,T_R) and
LF = insert_in_order(L, F, E)
implies
        new_list(E, LF, T_R).
```

The relation insert_in_order is a function that produces the new list by inserting F on the basis of the position and direction of elevator E, according to the defined policy. The detailed formalization of the function is left to the reader as an exercise. As we did in the case of the Petri net specification, we hide the service policy in one function so that a change in policy would require only the replacement of the insert_in_order function. This is an example of the principle of design for change, applied to writing specifications.

$R_{12}$. The effect of the arrival at floor F of an elevator E that stops there is to remove the first element F from the list.

```
arrival(E, F, T_a) and
list(E, L, T, T_a) and
F = first(L) and
L_t = tail(L)
implies
        new_list(E, L_t,T_a).
```

The predicate tail(L) denotes the remaining part of L, after its first element has been deleted.

$R_{13}$. The control state of an elevator E is represented by the list that specifies all reservations scheduled for E. The list remains unchanged as long as no new_list events occur.

```
new_list(E, L, T_1) and
not (new_list(E, L, T_2) and T_1 < T_2 < T_3)
implies
        list(E, L, T_1, T_3).
```

## Exercises

**5.36** Complete the preceding set of events, states, and rules. In particular, describe the events that switch internal and external buttons on and off. Define the policy for canceling external reservations in both interpretations described in Section 5.5.4.2.

**Warning**: You should pay attention to the consistency between the contents of lists and the lighting up of buttons. That is, if an internal button is switched on, the corresponding floor must appear in the elevator's list. Also, some inconsistency could arise between rule $R_{12}$ and the policy of switching external buttons off only when the elevator leaves the floor in the desired direction. Why? How can you avoid the risk of inconsistency?

**5.37** Is the policy described here to serve internal and external requests the same as that in Section 5.5.4.2?

**5.38** Define and formalize other service policies.

### 5.6.2.6 *Verifying specifications: a comparison of descriptive and operational style*

In the previous section, we used logic to specify an elevator system. We gave rules that described the system's behavior in the sense of defining how the system reacts to some stimuli when it is in a certain state. Now let us analyze the elevator's specification as we did in the case of Petri nets. We can "simulate" the system by assuming a given state at a given time and checking the effect of the occurrence of some events. This approach is formalized by formulas that are assumed to be true a priori (and therefore denote facts). Then, the rules given in the previous section can be used to deduce the consequences of these facts.

For instance, we can define the elevator state

```
standing (2, 3, 5, 7);
```

That is, elevator 2 has been at floor 3 at least from time 5 to time 7; the elevator enters this state as a consequence of `stop(2, 3, 5)`. Also, we can state

```
list(2, empty, 5, 7);
request(2, 8, 7);
```

Then, by applying the rules of the specification, we can deduce the fact

```
new_list(2, {8}, 7),
```

and, if we exclude the occurrence of other events, we can also deduce the facts

```
departure (2, 3, up, 7 + Δt_s);
arrival (2, 8, 7 + Δt_s + Δt_a · (8-3))
```

by means of a few simple logical deductions.

Thus, the logical formalism describes the system's operation by means of *deductions*. Now, the set of formulas is a specification of the system in the sense that every implementation must guarantee that all of the given rules are true. But if this is so, then all of the consequences of the rules will be guaranteed.

Logical deduction can be applied not only to simulate system behavior, but also to *analyze* system properties. In fact, in a descriptive specification such as the foregoing logical description of the elevator system, a system property is just another formula on system variables. For instance, the property that all requests will eventually be served can be formalized as (Notice that in this formula, the symbols $l_1$ and $t_1$ occur only on the right-hand side of the formula and are therefore, according to our quantification rules, assumed to be existentially quantified.)

```
new_list (E, L, T) and F ∈ L implies
        new_list (E, L₁,T₁) and F ∉ L₁ and T₁ > T₂.
```

If we succeed in deducing this formula from the previous system specification, we will be able to rely on its truth in any valid implementation of the system. Thus, proving properties of a logic specification is just the same logical deduction activity as deducing system dynamics.

Here we see a major difference between operational and descriptive specification styles. In operational specifications, the description of the *state* of the system is quite different from the description of the *properties* of the system. This fact has a major impact on the way we can use a—possibly automatic—specification interpreter to verify specifications. For instance, we could use a PN interpreter to verify that, after initializing an elevator system with 30 floors, four elevators, a given speed, and a given sequence of calls, all requests will be serviced with a maximum delay of 30 seconds. The interpreter, however, cannot provide a *proof* that for any system with n floors, m elevators, and speed z, for any sequence of no more than y calls per minute, the maximum delay between a call and its service is w, a suitable function of n, m, z, and y. In other words, a PN interpreter could be used to simulate specifications, but not to prove their properties—at least not directly.

These remarks apply in general to all operational and descriptive styles and to all properties. For instance, consider FSMs. If we want to know what the state of the system will be, starting from a given state and applying a given sequence of transitions, we just have to "execute the automaton." If, instead, we want to know whether the system can behave periodically, we must check the graph that represents the FSM for the presence of cyclic paths.

As a further example, consider the property of a system's being *deadlock free*. PNs are provided with a clear formal definition of this property, as we saw in Section 5.5.4. A PN interpreter, however, cannot be used to *decide* whether a given net is deadlock free; we can, at most, *test* the model in several different cases to check whether in those cases a deadlock occurs. Thus, if we want to decide whether a system modeled by a PN has the risk of running into a deadlock, we must analyze the model in some manner different from executing it.[11]

Instead, suppose you have given a formal definition of the same system using FOT formulas. Then the desired property is, again, an FOT formula, such as

```
for all S₁, S₂ ((state (S₁) and state (S₂)
and reachable (S₂, S₁)) implies
        exists S₃ (state (S₃) and S₃ ≠ S₂ and reachable (S₃, S₂))
```

---

[11]It turns out that freedom from deadlock is decidable for "pure PNs" (i.e., PNs given according to the original definition), but that the problem is of intractable complexity in the general case.

That is, for any state $S_1$, and for any state $S_2$ that is reachable from $S_1$, the system can evolve into a new state $S_3$ that is reachable from $S_2$. As a consequence, we can use the same interpreter of FOT formulas to simulate a system or to decide system properties. Of course, an undecidable property will not become decidable just because we used a descriptive style to express it: We have only a homogeneous language to describe both the system and its properties.

On the other hand, executing logical specifications (i.e., building interpreters for them) may not be as simple as it is for operational specifications. For instance, "interpreting" a set of FOT formulas requires applying rules of deduction that, in general, involve much nondeterminism: Often, from a set of premises, several partial conclusions may be derived, and many of them do not necessarily lead to the desired final conclusion.

It is worth recalling that the problem of *proving theorems* within FOTs is undecidable; in other words, we cannot automatically decide whether a given property (a FOT formula) is implied by a given specification (another FOT formula). Executable logic languages such as PROLOG, however, succeed fairly well in *approximating* the deductive power of FOTs through effective interpretation techniques. For this reason, they can be used as *prototyping languages*.

In conclusion, operational formalisms seem more naturally oriented towards the simulation of systems, whereas descriptive formalisms are more naturally applied to analysis of properties.

### Exercise

**5.39**   Define (not prove!) a property of the elevator system stating that the waiting time for each request is bounded. Formalize this property as a FOT formula.

## 5.6.3   Algebraic Specifications

Another popular descriptive specification style is based on the use of *algebra* rather than logic as the underlying mathematical formalism. Essentially, algebraic specifications define a system as a *heterogeneous algebra*—that is, a collection of different sets on which several operations are defined.

Traditional algebras are *homogeneous*. A homogeneous algebra consists of a single set and several operations. For instance, the integers, together with the operations addition, subtraction, multiplication, and division, are a homogeneous algebra. By contrast, alphabetic strings (i.e., sequences of characters), together with the operations of concatenation and length, are not a homogeneous algebra, since the range of the length operation is the set of integers, not the set of strings. Thus, strictly speaking, we say that this algebra consists of two sets—strings and integers—on which the operations length and concatenation are defined.

It turns out that many software systems can be naturally defined as heterogeneous algebras; after all, the definition "collection of sets together with operations" is quite close to the notion of an abstract data type introduced in Section 4.2.4.2. We shall state some important connections between heterogeneous algebras and abstract data types in Section 5.7.2.1.

Let us explore the essential features of algebraic specifications through a few examples. As a starting point, consider the simple case of strings.

## Example 5.6

Suppose that we want to specify a system to manage strings. The first relevant facts that one should record are the operations needed and the sets involved in such operations. In this case, assume we want to manage strings by

- creating new, empty strings (operation new);
- concatenating strings (operation append);
- adding a new character at the end of a string (operation add);
- checking the length of a given string (operation length);
- checking whether a string is empty (operation isEmpty); and
- checking whether two strings are equal (operation equal).

A short inspection of this list shows that the sets involved, besides the set of strings itself, here called String, are

- Char: the set of alphabetic characters;
- Nat: the set of natural numbers; and
- Bool: the set of logical values, {true, false}.

The collection of sets that form the heterogeneous algebra is called its *signature*. Each set, in turn, is called a *sort* of the algebra. Thus, to define a heterogeneous algebra, we first need to specify its signature, the involved operations, and their domains and ranges. This definition is called the algebra's *syntax* and can be expressed in any of several notations. We shall adopt a notation based on the Larch specification language. The notation is quite intuitive and is fairly close to that of other algebraic languages. Here is the syntax of the algebra for strings in a "Larch-like" notation:

```
algebra StringSpec;
introduces
        sorts String, Char, Nat, Bool;
        operations
            new: () → String;
            append: String, String → String;
            add: String, Char → String;
            length: String → Nat;
            is Empty: String → Bool;
            equal: String, String → Bool.
```

Sort String is just one of the sets involved. The fact that we are actually interested in its definition and that natural numbers and Booleans are in some sense "auxiliary sorts" has only intuitive relevance and is noted by the name given to the algebra in the first line. Notice that the new operation has no arguments (i.e., no domain). This is a conventional way to denote constant values. In fact, a function with no argument must have just one value. In this case, it is the "empty string."

The meaning intended for the preceding operations is quite clear in this instance. Nevertheless, such a meaning must be defined precisely. This is done in the algebra's *semantics*, using *equations* that are intended to define essential *properties* that must always hold when the operations are applied. For this reason, such equations are also called the *axioms* of the algebra.

The following are some obvious properties of the operations of the `String` algebra: (1)The string created by the `new` operation is the `empty` string. (This is actually more a definition than a property.) (2)The result of concatenating the `empty` string to any other string is that same string (i.e., the empty string is a *unit* with respect to concatenation). (3)The result of adding a character to any string is not `empty`.

The formalization of these and other properties in our Larch-like notation yields the following construct:

```
constrains new, append, add, length, isEmpty, equal so that
for all [s,s₁,s₂:String;c:Char]
        isEmpty(new()) = true;
        isEmpty(add(s,c)) = false;
        length(new()) = 0;
        length(add(s,c)) = length(s)+1;
        append(s,new()) = s;
        append(s₁,add(s₂,c)) = add(append(s₁,s₂),c);
        equal(new(),new()) = true;
        equal(new(),add(s,c)) = false;
        equal(add(s,c),new()) = false;
        equal(add(s₁,c),add(s₂,c) = equal(s₁,s₂);
end StringSpec.
```

Let us examine the foregoing equations. To start with, observe that we used five undeclared and undefined symbols, namely, $0$, $1$, $+$, `true`, and `false`. The other symbols, including parentheses and '=' (not to be confused with the operation "is equal to"), either are symbols of the notation or have been declared in the syntax. If we wanted to be absolutely rigorous, we should have declared '+' as an operation of the `Nat` algebra and $0$, $1$, `true`, and `false` as constants (i.e., functions with zero arguments) of their respective sorts. Furthermore, we should have given axioms to specify properties of those algebras; in particular, according to Peano's classical axiomatization of arithmetic, we should have stated that, actually, '1' is the result of applying the elementary operation "successor" to the constant '0'. To avoid an excessive number of fairly obvious equations, however, we left them as implicit—and as an exercise for the reader.

Next, let us proceed to analyze the specification. There is no doubt that the equations of this specification describe "truths" about strings. What we are interested in, however, is the ability to derive other properties from them, as we did with logic specifications. It is for this reason that the equations are called *axioms*.

For instance, the following property should hold for every character c:

```
append(new(),add(new(),c)) = add(new(),c)
```

This property can be derived from the axioms in the following way: If we let $s_1, s_2$ = new () in the axiom

```
append(s₁,add(s₂,c)) = add(append(s₁,s₂),c)
```

we obtain

```
append(new(),add(new(),c)) = add(append(new(),new()),c) (i)
```

Then, by substituting s = new () in the axiom append (s, new()) = s, we obtain append (new(),new()) = new (). Substituting this into **(i)**, we obtain the desired property.

Similarly, let $< c_1, \ldots, c_n >$ be an abbreviation for

```
add(add...(add(new(), c_1),...), c_n).
```

Then it is an easy exercise to prove that

```
append (<c_1,c_2>,<c_3,c_4>) = <c_1,c_2,c_3,c_4>
```

for every $c_1, c_2, c_3, c_4$.

Now, consider properties such as

```
append(new(), s) = s
```
                                                                    **(ii)**

and

```
append (s_1, append(s_2,s_3)) = append(append(s_1,s_2),s_3)
```
                                                              **(iii)**

These two properties can be proved by induction. We do so for **(ii)**. Now, **(ii)** holds for s = new () by applying the axiom append (s, new())= s with s = new (). Assume that **(ii)** holds for a given string $s_1$, and let s be add($s_1$, c). Then append (new(),s)= append(new(),add($s_1$, c))= add(append(new(),$s_1$), c)= add($s_1$, c)= s. Thus, **(ii)** holds for s, too.

The preceding intuitive reasoning, however, assumes that every string s, other than new(), is of the type add($s_1$, c), for some $s_1$, c. The operations new and add are thus called the *generators* of the algebra StringSpec. Although this sounds obviously intuitively, it is not explicitly stated in the formalization of StringSpec. To specify this fact, we modify the header of the earlier semantic definition to read as follows:

```
constrains new, append, add, length, isEmpty, equal so that
       StringSpec generated by [new, add]
       for all [s,s_1,s_2: String; c: Char]
```

This construct states explicitly that all elements of sort String can be obtained as a suitable combination of the operations new and add. Similarly, all natural numbers can be generated by the constant '0' and the "successor" operation.

Now, let us assume that the previous algebra has been enriched by introducing constant characters, such as 'a', 'b', .... (The constants are enclosed within quotes.) Formally, these constants are introduced by defining them as functions with no arguments, as we did for the new operation; for example, a: () → Char. 'a' will be used as an abbreviation for a (). Then, consider the property given by the formula

```
equal(add(s,'a'),add(s,'b')) = false
```

Intuitively, this formula appears to be true. There is, however, no way to prove that it is true[12] within the framework of the system.

---

[12]The reader should pay some attention to the intricacies of mathematical formulas. Here, we want to prove (i.e., to derive the truth of) a formula that states the falsity of another formula. We should keep in mind that, in general, the fact that there is no proof of a formula does not mean that the formula is false. There is no proof of equal (add(s,'a'),add(s, 'b'))= true. There is also no proof of equal (add(s,'a'),add(s,'b'))= false, but we "feel" that this formula should be true, and we would like to be able to prove it. Again, our exposition of these theoretical issues relies much on the reader's intuition and leaves a deep mathematical treatment of the topic to the appropriate literature.

The inability to prove the formula in question shows that the axioms given for the system are *incomplete*—that is, they do not allow us to deduce all the desired "truths" of our algebra. Happily, in this case, the specifications formalized by previous equations can easily be *completed* (it is not, however, always so simple to achieve completeness!) by enhancing the syntax of the language as follows:

- adding the new operation equalC, defining *equality between characters*. This operation should be *constrained* by equations of the type

```
equalC('a','a') = true;
equalC('a','b') = false;
  .
  .
  .
```

- replacing the last equation of the previous semantics by

$$\text{equal(add}(s_1,c_1),\text{add}(s_2,c_2)) = \text{equal}(s_1,s_2) \textbf{ and } \text{equalC}(c_1,c_2) \qquad \textbf{(j)}$$

Clearly, in writing algebraic specifications, as with other styles, incompleteness is not the only risk. We could *overspecify* (i.e., unduly constrain) a system, as would happen, for instance, if we included the axiom

$$\begin{aligned}\text{equal(add}(s_1,c_1),\text{add}(s_2,c_2)) = \text{equal}(s_1,s_2) \textbf{ and } \\ \text{equalC}(c_1,c_2) \textbf{ and not } \text{equalC}(c_1,\text{'a'}) \qquad \textbf{(jj)}\end{aligned}$$

instead of the previous (j). In fact, (jj) improperly states that two strings can be equal only if they do not contain the character 'a'!

We could also write contradictory or inconsistent specifications, as would happen if we added

```
equal(add(s,c),s) = true
```

to the axioms. In general, a set of algebraic equations is *contradictory*, or *inconsistent*, if it allows us to prove true = false.

We could write *redundant* specifications if we added, say,

```
append(new(),s) = s
```

to the set of axioms, since this formula can already be proved as a consequence of the other axioms. In practice, redundancy in algebraic specifications is a much lesser problem than inconsistency and incompleteness and can usually be ignored.

In conclusion, an algebraic specification defines a system as the collection of all sets and related operations stated in the signature of the specification, whose elements satisfy all equations of the semantic part of the specification and, therefore, even all equations derivable from them.    ■

We now gain a better insight into algebraic specifications through a more elaborate example.

## Example 5.7

Suppose you want to specify a text editor. The specification must indicate the data types on which the editor must operate (i.e., the sorts, the available operations, and their meanings). Initially, let us consider an oversimplified text editor, suitable for handling simple text files, with the following set of operations:

- newF: creates a new, empty file (the suffix F is used to indicate that the operation is related to files; in some cases, there are similar operations for other sets);
- isEmptyF: states whether a file is empty;
- addF: adds a string of characters to the end of a file;
- insertF: inserts a string at a given position of a file. The rest of the file will be moved to just after the inserted string (word);
- appendF: concatenates two files;
- other operations that will be discussed later or that can be imagined by the reader as an exercise.

Thanks to the similarity with the previous example, the following algebraic specification for the text editor should be sufficiently clear:

```
algebra TextEditor;
introduces
        sorts Text, String, Char, Bool, Nat;
        operations
            newF: () ⟶ Text;
            isEmptyF: Text ⟶ Bool;
            addF: Text, String ⟶ Text;
            insertF: Text, Nat, String ⟶ Text;
            appendF: Text, Text ⟶ Text;
            deleteF: Text ⟶ Text;
            lengthF: Text ⟶ Nat;
            equalF: Text, Text ⟶ Bool;
            addFC: Text, Char ⟶ Text;
            {This is an auxiliary operation that will be needed to
            define addF and other operations on files. Also, we
            assume that all operations previously introduced in
            StringSpec are still available. To make clear the
            distinction between the two kinds of operations, the
            latter are suffixed by 'S'. We assume that the syntax
            and the semantics of these belong to TextEditor also,
            without explicitly copying them}
constrains newF, isEmptyF, addF, appendF, insertF, deleteF so that
TextEditor generated by [newF, addFC]
for all [f, f₁,f₂: Text; s: String; c: Char; cursor: Nat]
    isEmptyF(newF())= true;
    isEmptyF(addFC(f, c))= false;
    addF(f, newS())= f;
    addF(f, addS(s, c))= addFC(addF(f, s), c);
    lengthF(newF())= 0;
    lengthF(addFC(f, c))= lengthF(f) + 1;
    appendF(f, newF())= f;
    appendF(f1, addFC(f₂,c))= addFC(appendF(f₁,f₂), c);
    equalF(newF(),newF())= true;
    equalF(newF(),addFC(f, c))= false;
    equalF(addFC(f, c),new())= false;
```

```
equalF(addFC(f₁,c₁),addFC(f₂,c₂)=
                equalF(f₁,f₂) and equalC (c₁,c₂);
insertF(f,cursor, newS())= f;
((equalF(f,appendF(f₁,f₂)) and (lengthF(f₁)= cursor - 1))
implies
equalF(insertF (f,cursor,s), appendF(addF(f₁,s),f₂)))= true;
end TextEditor.
```

The last equation looks rather complicated. To make such equations more understandable, we may write them as

```
if (equalF(f,appendF(f₁,f₂)) and (lengthF(f₁)=cursor - 1)) then
        (insertF(f,cursor,s) = appendF(addF(f₁,s),f₂))
```

These kinds of equations are called *conditional equations*.

Let us examine the real meaning of the operations defined by the preceding equations. Algebraic equations state relations among the elements of the sets involved, not relations on *variables that store values*. Thus, it would be plausible, but not necessary, to deduce from the previous equations that the result of applying insertF (f, cursor, s) is the *modification of the state of file* f consisting of inserting the string s between portions $f_1$ and $f_2$ on the file. This formula just states a property of the value of type file that is the result of the operation. To stress the difference with the concepts of conventional programming languages, our syntax for algebraic specifications uses the keyword **operations** rather than the traditional keywords **procedure** and **function**.

Thus, both of the following two *implementations* of the insert operation would be adequate with respect to the foregoing specification:

- Implementation 1: The operation modifies f in the specified way;
- Implementation 2: The operation creates a new file whose value is computed in the specified way.

In general, of course, direct-access file systems tend to work according to implementation 1 (if no explicit command states the opposite), whereas sequential, batch-processing file systems necessarily work according to implementation 2.

Even though the specification contains a considerable number of equations (the reader should not forget that some of them have been left implicit), it is still far from specifying a realistic text editor. The way to achieve such a goal, however, should now be clear.    ■

Algebraic specifications are a useful notation for specifying the semantics of modules such as abstract data types. Hence, they can complement design notations like TDN/GDN or UML class diagrams to add semantic information on modules. Algebraic specifications differ from preconditions, postconditions, and invariants in that they provide more abstract specifications of abstract data type semantics. Preconditions, postconditions, and invariants are expressed in terms of the *implementation* of the abstract data type (i.e., in terms of class variables and parameters).

## Exercises

**5.40**  Prove that the following properties hold for the StringSpec algebra introduced in this section:

```
equal(<'a','c','a','d'> , <'a','c','a','d'>)= true
equal(<'a','c','a','d'> , <'a','c','d','a'>)= false
```

**5.41**    If we imagine that the operations of Example 5.7 are interactive user commands to manipulate text files, we readily see that they are definitely too limited. The main shortcoming is the fact that the user has no way to *name* files. It is possible only to build new files and then operate on them. Augment the previous specification to include a naming facility. The user must be able to give identifiers to files when creating them and use an identifier to specify the file to which an operation must be applied.

You may consider the name, or identifier, of a file as different from the previous variables $f$, $f_1$, and $f_2$ of sort Text. In other words, the name should be an attribute of a file, uniquely identifying it.

**5.42**    Augment the specification given in Example 5.7 with operations such as the following:

- change ($f, s_1, s_2$) : substitutes all occurrences of $s_1$ in $f$ with $s_2$;
- find($f, s$) : returns a Boolean value that states whether s is in $f$ and, if it is, returns the position of the first character of s in $f$. (There are a couple of trouble spots in this informal definition; can you spot them?)

## 5.7    BUILDING AND USING SPECIFICATIONS IN PRACTICE

In the previous section, we saw a sample of models and notations that can be used for giving specifications of different systems. Although most of the examples we used were inspired by real software problems, the systems involved were very simple. In this section, we look at the problem of applying specification techniques to real-life systems. After examining what more is needed for writing and using specifications in practice, we look at a few ways that help tackle the practical problems of dealing with large and complex systems.

### 5.7.1    Requirements for Specification Notations

Let us examine critically the benefits obtained and the problems raised by the use of the formalisms introduced in Sections 5.5 and 5.6. Certainly, by exploiting the principles of rigor and formality, we were able to make clear and precise many specifications that otherwise might have been left vague or ambiguous until later design or implementation phases.

It turned out, however, that even in specifying relatively simple systems, many details had to be taken into consideration. For instance, a full description of an elevator system for a skyscraper in terms of PNs would be a huge, unmanageable, unintelligible network; and the algebraic specification of even a toy text editor would require many equations, both explicit and implicit.

Thus, building requirements specifications for real-life systems is likely to be as complex an activity as designing the implementation of these systems: The resulting specification document—whether we use a formal notation or English—would be as complex as the design documentation and code itself! Consequently, all principles stated in Chapter 3 should be applied to the construction of complex specifications.[13] Even many "design techniques" examined in Chapter 4 are highly useful for managing the "design" of complex specifications.

---

[13]In fact, our presentation of the derivation of the elevator system specification was carried out in a *modular* way, even if we did not give a formal definition of "PN module" or "FOT module."

Having emphasized the importance of rigor and formality in previous sections, let us briefly examine a few other principles separately. All "specification languages" we have presented so far—finite state machines, DFDs, PNs, logic, and algebraic equations—are related to real specification languages in the same way that so-called toy programming languages, such as those of the "Mini-Pascal style" used in many introductory computer science courses, are related to real programming languages. They grasp the essentials of the real languages, but they are suitable only for expressing simple systems, such as how to code sorting algorithms and trigonometric functions, and not, say, real-life payroll systems or compilers. What they lack most with respect to (good) real programming languages are abstraction and modularization mechanisms. The next section shows that specification formalisms may be provided with such mechanisms in much the same way as in the case of programming languages.

The principle of *separation of concerns* also has some natural implications for specifications. For instance, whenever possible, *functional specifications* (i.e., the definition of what the system should do as a consequence of the given input) should be kept separate from *performance specifications* (the definition of efficiency requirements), from *user interface specifications*, and so on.

Sometimes, separation of concerns may even result in using different notations for specifying different aspects of a system. For instance, suppose that you wanted to describe the production of a document in an office automation system. The DFD of Figure 5.44(a) describes which sources of information and what kind of data are necessary to produce the document: a library of `Predefined Templates` (say, contracts of several types in which specific data, such as names, dates, and amounts, are missing); a database of `Customers` who already have been in touch with the office; the customers themselves; and a set of `Predefined Formats` to be selected to print the document.

The figure, however, does not specify the order of execution of the actions that lead to the composition and printing of the document. This is specified by the FSM of Figure 5.44(b), which shows that, after having gotten the customer's name, we may get further data—the customer's address, date of birth, etc.—either from the `Customer` database or through more interaction with the customer. There is intuitive evidence that if the customer's record is already in the database, then the edge "get other data from the database" is followed. The alternative edge is followed if the customer's record is not in the database. This, however, is not stated explicitly in the figure. If we wanted to be more precise, we could augment the model by adding suitable labels to the edge to specify the conditions under which it would be followed. As an alternative to an FSM to show the control requirements, we can use UML sequence or collaboration diagrams.

Similarly, we already noticed in Section 5.6.1 that DFDs and ER diagrams can complement each other by supplying different "views" of system descriptions, the former being oriented to the specification of system functions, the latter to the description of relations among data.

Incrementality is perhaps even more important for specifications than for implementation. It is seldom the case that all requirements are well understood at the very beginning of a software project. More often, their final formulation is the result of a long process involving much trial and error. Furthermore, it is in any case wise initially to focus attention on the most relevant and critical requirements of a system. Later on, minor requirements will be taken into consideration and stated clearly in the appropriate documents.

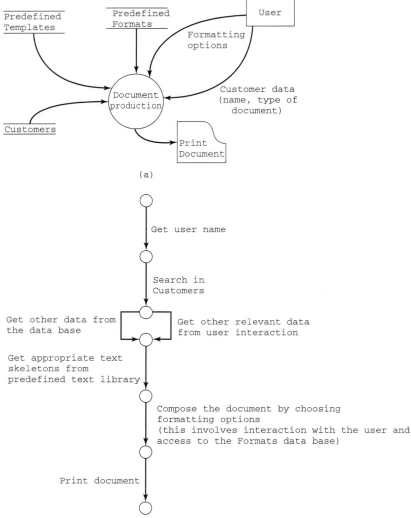

(a)

**FIGURE 5.44**

Two views of document production.
**(a)** Data view through a DFD.
**(b)** Control view through an FSM.

Incrementality should be applied in the construction of specifications, even to the level of rigor and formality, in the sense that, initially, things can hardly be formulated in a fully precise way. In many cases, things are not very precise even in the mind of the person stating the requirements. Thus, initial formulations are likely to be informal and rather fuzzy notes, whether written in a natural language or sketched in some graphical notation. Later, the specifications will likely change, and even the "language" in which they are expressed will move from informal to semiformal or formal.

Several examples of specifications given in Sections 5.5 and 5.6 were derived in an incremental way, both by moving from an informal statement to a formal one (recall the elevator system, particularly with reference to switching the button lights on and off) and by modifying earlier formulations given in the same formalism (again, the case of switching the button lights of the elevator system on and off is illustrative).

In writing specifications, a full and complete formalization of the document is not usually necessary. We already remarked in Chapter 3 that even mathematicians, when formulating and proving theorems, proceed by incrementally adding details and formality in the critical steps of definitions and proofs. In the same way, a specification document could be a mixture of informal natural-language sentences, semiformal figures, and fully formalized models, when needed, under the complete responsibility of the designer.

Another reason to adopt combinations of "languages" for specifications is that specifications are often used by different people with different purposes, as we pointed out in Section 5.1. For example, it is quite unlikely that a contract for a software product will be signed on the basis of a document written in mathematical logic. Thus, further requirements may be imposed on specification documents if they must be managed by the end users. We shall briefly examine a few techniques for tackling this problem in Section 5.7.3.

In sum, talking about *specification languages* is at least as difficult as talking about programming languages. A specification document is not likely to be just a huge, yet well-structured and well-modularized, PN. Nor is it likely to be a single FOT formula. In many cases, a specification document uses different formalisms to achieve different purposes. Thus, the specifier may naturally wish to integrate several formal, informal, and semiformal specifications into a unique document whose major goals are clarity, precision, and immediate understandability. Quite often, a full description in a single formal language looks more like implementation code than a system definition. Therefore, the "ideal specification language" is even less realistic than the "ideal programming language." This, however, is certainly not a good reason for using no specification language at all!

Finally, the process of writing, analyzing, modifying, and using specifications to check an implementation can benefit highly from the use of appropriate tools. In the most trivial case, one can use just a word processor to edit and modify documents written in a natural language. It is clear, however, that much more is desirable, much more is already available, and still much more is likely to be offered in the future to help the whole process. For instance, graphical editors to aid in writing, say, DFDs or PNs are already widely available, as are many tools that assist in examining specifications for the presence of various properties. In the next section, we shall see how the Unified Modeling Language combines several notations into a specification language intended for use in practice.

### Exercises

**5.43**  Can performance specifications be separated from functional specifications in real-time systems? Justify your answer.

**5.44**  Give a PN control view of the production of a document.

**5.45**  Discuss the application of the principles of generality and anticipation of change to the construction of specifications.

### 5.7.1.1  The UML notations

We introduced the Unified Modeling Language (UML) in Chapter 4. In particular, we presented class diagrams as a way to describe the static architecture of an object-oriented system. Class diagrams, however, are just one of several notations provided by UML. The motivation for offering several notations is that they can enlighten different aspects of a system, and thus they can provide different and complementary viewpoints under which the system may be understood. Furthermore, they can be used at different stages during the software development process.

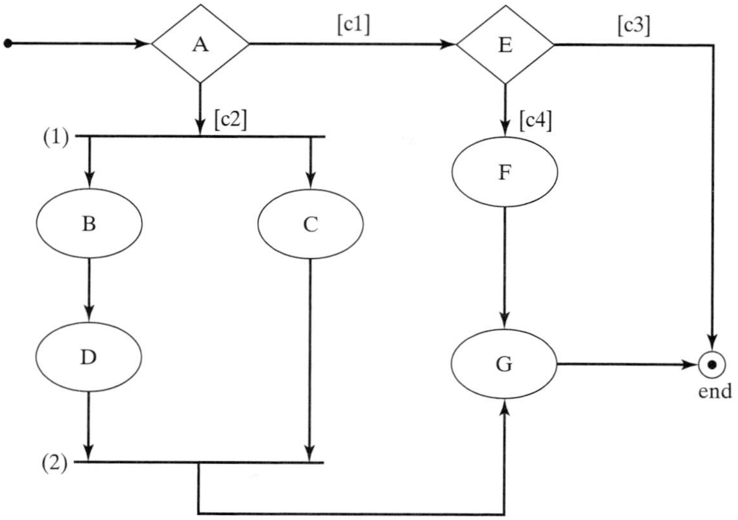

**FIGURE 5.45**

Activity diagram.

For example, class diagrams provide a static description of the software architecture in terms of classes and associations. As we shall see later in this chapter, state diagrams (using Statecharts) can specify the state evolution of the objects of a given class, as operations are applied to them. Yet another notation (Activity Diagrams) can be used to describe how methods executions may be combined, both sequentially and in parallel, and how they may synchronize. An example is shown in Figure 5.45. Activity diagrams are reminiscent of Petri nets, as can be seen in the figure.

The figure shows the flow of a set of activities (in our context, executions of methods) A through G. All of the activities have an entry and an exit point, except decision activities (like A and E), which have two possible exit points, corresponding to different conditions ($c_1$ and $c_2$ for A; $c_3$ and $c_4$ for E). Synchronization bars (similar to Petri net transitions) are used to generate parallel sequences of activities (as in the case of (1)) and to synchronize the termination of parallel flows (as in the case of (2)).

The different notions provided by UML make the language rich and expressive. They can also cause some confusion, however, because the distinct viewpoints they describe may overlap, and the effect of their combination can be unclear or, worse, inconsistent.

## 5.7.2 Building Modular Specifications

This section is devoted mainly to showing how appropriate constructs, suitably embedded in the specification language, can help in applying the principles of modularity, abstraction, and incrementality to specifications. First, we present a language based on algebraic equations. Then we show how appropriate constructs can be added, in principle, to any language, to make it more suitable for writing specifications in practice.

### 5.7.2.1 A sample algebraic specification language

Let us go back to the TextEditor algebra of Example 5.7. We have already noticed that many equations are missing: equations to define strings, equations to define natural numbers, those to define characters, and those to define Booleans. In some sense, writing in full detail all of the equations to specify a text editor would entail as much effort as implementing the system in Pascal by using only the Boolean data type and the array constructor.

Whether we use `Naturals`, `Booleans`, etc., as algebras or as programming language data types, they always denote sets and operations that are widely known and widely used, so that one should not need to redefine them every time they are required. In programming languages, these features are built in; that is, they are defined and implemented once and are accessible to all programmers. Languages also often provide *libraries* of other widely useful data types and operations. So, we have trigonometric routines, I/O packages, and even packages to handle tables and the like. Furthermore, and most important, we have mechanisms to build our own abstractions and modules and to build complex systems by integrating them together.[14]

Several specification languages also provide this kind of support. Let us briefly see how this happens by taking inspiration from Larch. As we said in Section 5.6.3, Larch is a well-developed specification language based on the algebraic style. Basically, Larch's modules are algebras. In Larch, one can define *hierarchies* of algebras by means of suitable relations that are based on the same principles described in Chapter 4. Let us begin illustrating them with a simple example.

We saw that the `StringSpec` algebra used some elementary sets and operations, such as `Nat`, `Bool`, `Char`, and '`+`'. Assume that these have been previously defined as independent algebras as follows:

```
algebra BoolAlg;
introduces
        sorts Bool;
        operations
            true () → Bool;
            false () → Bool;
            not: Bool → Bool;
            and: Bool, Bool → Bool;
            or: Bool, Bool → Bool;
            implies: Bool, Bool → Bool;
             ≡ : Bool, Bool → Bool;
constrains true, false, not, and, or, implies,  ≡ so that
Bool generated by [true, false]
for all [a, b: Bool]
        not (true)= false;
        not (false)= true;
        a and b = not (not (a) or not (b));
        a implies b = not (a) or b;
        .
        .
        .

end BoolAlg.
```

---

[14]This is especially true in the case of object-oriented programming languages.

```
algebra NatNumb;
introduces
        sorts Nat, Bool;
        operations
                0: () → Nat;
                Succ¹⁵: Nat → Nat;
                +: Nat, Nat → Nat;
                -: Nat, Nat → Nat;
                =: Nat, Nat → Bool;¹⁶
                  .
                  .
                  .

constrains 0, Succ, +, -, =, ..., so that
NatNumb generated by [0, Succ]
                  .
                  .
                  .

end NatNumb.
algebra CharAlg;
introduces
        sorts Char, Bool;
        operations
                'a': () → Char;
                'b': () → Char;
                  .
                  .
                  .

end CharAlg.
```

StringSpec may now be defined completely by *using* these specifications. This is done in Larch through the **imports** clause, which simply states that the imported algebra is enclosed in the new one, in the sense that all its sorts and operations may be used, with their given meanings, in the new algebra. The clause specifies, in addition, that the semantics of the imported algebras *cannot be modified* by additional constraints in the new theory; it can only be *used*. In other words, we should not expect that the properties of, say, '+' are further specified in StringSpec. In our case, we just need the following declaration:

```
algebra StringSpec;
imports BoolAlg, NatNumb, CharAlg;
introduces
        sorts String, Char, Nat, Bool;
        operations
                new: () → String;
                  .
                  .
                  .

end StringSpec.
```

---

[15] This is the "successor" operator, which increments a natural number by one unit.

[16] Strictly speaking, we should use a different operation symbol, such as "equalN", to denote equality between naturals, since '=' is a reserved symbol of the algebra's syntax. However, to avoid the heavy notation equalN (5,5), we have decided to overload the two operation symbols.

After that, everything may proceed as before.

Notice that **imports** defines a relation between *algebras*. Semantically, it implies the USES relation between modules, but it says something more than this. In fact, the USES relation simply states that if $M_1$ USES $M_2$, then $M_1$'s correctness depends on $M_2$'s correctness. The **imports** clause states also that $M_1$ can use $M_2$, through its operations. The **imports** clause is required to be a hierarchy, whereas USES is not, although we saw in Chapter 4 that hierarchical relations are desirable. Also, in both cases, the semantics of operations exported by $M_2$ cannot be affected by $M_1$.

## Exercise

**5.46**  Build the TextEditor algebra of Example 5.7 by importing suitable other algebras. In so doing, you should notice that a problem of identifying the scope of identifiers arises in the same way as it does in programming languages. For instance, different "new" operations are needed for different sorts. The problem is not taken into consideration here, since it can be handled by applying traditional techniques—hiding rules, overloading, etc. You are invited, however, to define your own scope rules for the Larch-like language that will be defined.

## Example 5.8

We often deal with several types of data structures: stacks, queues, sets, etc. These different data structures have some properties in common and others that distinguish them from each other. The properties, however, are rarely stated precisely, and, in general, we find different definitions for them. Here, we seek to find out common and different aspects of many classical (dynamic) data structures and arrange them in a well-structured algebraic hierarchy that resembles the inheritance hierarchy of object-oriented design.

First, observe that any data structure is a place for storing data; that is, it is a *data container*. Thus, assuming that all items to be stored are of sort, say, DataType, we start by defining a Container algebra, with the idea that all other data structures should be seen as particular cases of this structure. (Thus, we see an application of the principle of generality.) Elements of type Container can be created via the usual new operation, items may be stored in them through an insert operation, Containers may be either empty or nonempty, and they have a specific size. Since all possible configurations of any data structure may be reached by appropriately inserting some elements into the data structure, new and insert are generators of the Container algebra, just as new and add are generators of the StringSpec algebra. Thus, we have the following simple algebra:

```
algebra Container;
imports DataType, BoolAlg, NatNumb;
introduces
      sorts Cont;
      operations
            new: () → Cont;
            insert: Cont, Data → Cont;
             {Data is the sort of algebra DataType, to which elements
             to be stored in Cont belong}
            isEmpty: Cont → Bool;
            size: Cont → Nat;
```

```
constrains new, insert, isEmpty, size so that
Cont generated by [new, insert]
for all [d: Data; c: Cont]
        isEmpty(new())= true;
        isEmpty(insert(c,d))= false;
        size(new())= 0;
end Container.
```

Our next step is to define a TableAlg algebra as a specialization of Container. That is, we consider a table as a particular case of a data container with more operations, perhaps with slightly different semantics than the operations of a container. We assume that a table insert is done in an ordered way, by inserting the new item as the *last* element of the table. Thus, last and rest are two other simple operations belonging to the algebra. Furthermore, we want to check tables for equality, and we want to delete elements from a table. (Since the same element could be inserted several times into the table, we want to delete all of its occurrences, if any.) The following new definition makes use of the new relation **assumes** between algebras:

```
algebra TableAlg;
assumes Container;
introduces
    sorts Table;
    operations
        last: Table → Data;
        rest: Table → Table;
        equalT: Table, Table → Bool;
        delete: Table, Data → Table;
constrains last, rest, equalT, delete, isEmpty, new, insert so that
for all [d, d₁,d₂: Data; t, t₁,t₂: Table]
        last(insert(t, d)) = d;
        rest(new()) = new ();
        rest(insert(t, d)) = t;
        equalT(new(),new()) = true;
        equalT(insert(t, d), new()) = false;
        equalT(new(), insert(t,d)) = false;
        equalT (t₁,t₂) = equalD¹⁷(last (t₁), last (t₂)) and
                            equalT(rest (t₁)), rest (t₂));
        delete(new(),d)= new();
        delete(insert(t,d),d)= delete (t, d);
        if not equalD (d₁,d₂) then
            delete(insert(insert(t,d₁),d₂) = insert(delete(t,d₂),d₁);
end TableAlg.
```

As with **imports**, the **assumes** clause gives access from the "assuming algebra" to the signature and semantics of the "assumed" one. Also, both **imports** and

---

[17]We assume that algebra DataType is provided with an equality operation.

**assumes** are transitive in the sense that they allow access to operations of other algebras that are further imported or assumed by the assumed—or imported—algebra. Again, we do not deal here with any newly generated problems of scope; we simply add appropriate suffixes to common operations, such as new and equal.[18]

The difference between **imports** and **assumes** is that **assumes** allows the semantics of the assumed operations to be modified, whereas imports does not. In our example, TableAlg equations impose new constraints on the new and insert operations. This is not the same as, say, using the '+' operation anywhere, without altering its meaning. Thus, the **assumes** clause states a typical *inheritance* relation between algebras, in the same sense that this relation has in the object-oriented terminology.

Another type of data container is a *FIFO queue*, which has operations last and equal, as do tables. The FIFO delete operation, however, is both syntactically and semantically different from the table delete. Furthermore, FIFO queues have a first operation, which returns the first element that has been inserted into the queue and has not yet been removed. Next, we provide the definition of QueueAlg:

```
algebra QueueAlg;
assumes Container;
introduces
      sort Queue;
      operations
            last: Queue → Data;
            first: Queue → Data;
            equalQ: Queue , Queue → Bool;
            delete: Queue → Queue;
constrains last, first, equalQ, delete, isEmpty, new, insert so that
for all [d: Data; q, q1,q2: Queue]
            last(insert(q, d)) = d;
            first(insert(new(), d)= d
            first(insert(q, d)) = if not isEmpty (q) then first (q);
            equalQ(new(), new()) = true;
            equalQ(insert(q, d), new()) = false;
            equalQ(new(), insert(q, d)) = false;
            equalQ(insert(q1,d1),insert(q2,d2)) = equalD(d1,d2) and
                                                  equalQ(q1,q2);

            delete(new()) = new();
            delete(insert(new(), d))= new();
      if not equalQ(q, new()) then
            delete(insert(q,d)) = insert(delete(q), d);
end QueueAlg.
```

Figure 5.46 (a) summarizes the algebras defined so far and the relations among them.

---

[18]Another important issue we do not deal with here is *error conditions*. For instance, suppose that the delete operation is applicable only if the element to be deleted exists in the table. Then we must specify that delete(t,d) results in an error in such a case. Also, last(new()) should result in an error. The reader is invited to augment these and other sets of equations with appropriate error conditions by introducing the keyword **error**.

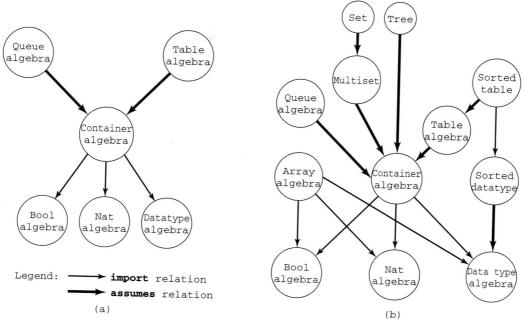

Legend: ⟶ **import** relation

➤ **assumes** relation

(a)

(b)

FIGURE 5.46

Hierarchies of algebras. **(a)** A simple hierarchy. **(b)** A richer hierarchy: `SortedDataType` assumes `DataType` and adds a total ordering to it (operation '<'). `SortedTable` contains sorted tables, with no duplicate elements.

## Exercise

**5.47** Build the algebras shown in Figure 5.46(b), which completes Figure 5.46(a). Notice that equality has different meanings in different algebras. For instance, multisets are sets with possible repetitions of elements, but in which the order is not relevant. Thus, {a, b, a, c} = {b, a, c, a} ≠ {a, b, b, c}. Sets are considered a specialization of multisets, because they can be obtained by adding more equations to the equations for equality between multisets.

The mechanisms introduced to build hierarchies of algebras exploit the principle of incrementality, since they allow the construction of complex new algebras as modifications of existing ones. Incrementality is favored by algebraic specification languages in other ways also: In general, it might be difficult to obtain a complete and consistent set of equations stating the properties of an algebra at the first writing, even applying suitable modularization mechanisms; such a set of equations, however, can be obtained incrementally, allowing early versions of specifications to be partially incomplete.

For instance, consider the queue equality operation of Example 5.8. One could first write the equation

$$\mathtt{equalQ(insert(q_1,d_1),\ insert(q_2,d_2))= equalD(d_1,d_2)}\ \textbf{and}\ \mathtt{equalQ(q_1,q_2)}$$

which seems to contain the essential aspects of the desired operation. Then, further equations may be added to cope with "extreme conditions." It is also possible to do the opposite: First clarify special cases, and then cope with the general one. With both techniques, the set of equations is built incrementally, focusing attention on different aspects at different moments.

In some sense, we could call the aforementioned two ways of exploiting incrementality *incrementality in the large* and *incrementality in the small*. The former deals with the construction of families of algebras, the latter with the construction of a single algebra.

## Exercises

**5.48** Why did we not add the equation `size(insert(c, d))= size(c) + 1` in the specification of the `Container` algebra?

**5.49** Discuss the technical differences between **assumes** and the object-oriented INHERITS_FROM, in one or more of its forms discussed in Chapter 4.

**5.50** `QueueAlg` and `TableAlg`, each given in Example 5.8, actually have more in common than just `Container`. Define an "intermediate algebra" that contains all that is common to the two.

**Going from specification to implementation.**    The whole design process can be seen as a chain of definition-implementation steps, often resulting in a hierarchy of modules. The IS_COMPOSED_OF relation is an example of such a hierarchy. During the process of design, several "languages" can be used, according to different needs. For instance, one could write initial specifications in an algebraic language, then design a software architecture using the UML notations, and finally code the system in Java.

The transition between different levels of the definition-implementation hierarchy may proceed more or less naturally, depending also on the languages used. For instance, implementing the hierarchy of modules of Figure 5.46(b) in terms of TDN/GDN is a smooth transition.

In the case of Larch, several *interface languages* have been defined, with the purpose of helping to effect a natural transition from specifications written in the basic language outlined previously (called the Larch *shared language*, since it is common to any design, independently of the programming language used) to the implementation, which may be coded in different languages. Thus, there is a Larch/C++ language and a Larch/Pascal language, and others can be defined.

Let us briefly examine the essential features of the Larch/Pascal language. As a first step, it is quite natural to see an algebra as an abstract data type. The most obvious way of implementing an abstract data type in Pascal is as type declarations coupled with function or procedure declarations.

Here, we must take into account the most relevant difference between shared Larch and Pascal. The former is *purely functional*; that is, its operations do not modify any execution state. The latter is operational; that is, in it, procedures and even functions can have side effects. Thus, translating a specification written in shared Larch into a Pascal-like notation essentially consists of defining which operations become functions, which operations become procedures, and which variables the procedures can modify. We explain this through an example.

Consider the `StringSpec` algebra described in Example 5.6. Its signature is transformed, in Larch/Pascal, into the following declaration:

**type** String **exports** is Empty, add, append, ...
　　　　{Notice that new has been dropped; in fact, we could either use
　　　　the Pascal **new** statement, which would force us to implement
　　　　strings through pointers, or accept the limitation of not being
　　　　able to create string variables at run time}
**based on** Boolean, integer, character
**function** isEmpty (s: String): Boolean
　　　　**modifies at most** []{i.e., it has no side effects};
　　　　**procedure** add (**var** s : String; c : char)
　　　　**modifies at most** [s]
　　　　{it has no effects on execution state other than modifying the
　　　　string parameter s};
　　　　**function** length (s: String) : integer
　　　　**modifies at most** [];
　　　　**procedure** append (**var** $s_1, s_2, s_3$: string)
　　　　**modifies at most** [$s_3$]
　　　　{although we decided, for convenience in the implementation,
　　　　that all procedure parameters are passed by reference, actually
　　　　only $s_3$, which is meant as the result of the operation, is
　　　　modified};
　　　　　.
　　　　　.
　　　　　.
**end** StringSpec.

This translation from Larch signature into a notation closer to Pascal can be obtained, in principle, as the result of an interactive, syntax-directed translation. A translator could, in fact, automatically generate portions of the code, interacting with the designer, who decides whether an operation is to be implemented as a procedure or as a function and which elements—not necessarily parameters—can be modified.

The Larch/Pascal interface language is an example of a transition technique that helps along the complex process leading from specifications to implementation. In principle, it can also be applied to other specification and implementation languages.

### 5.7.2.2 *Modularizing finite state machines: the case of Statecharts*

As we have said, appropriate modularization mechanisms are needed, and should be provided, for any formalism. In this section, we discuss the issue in the context of finite state machines.

The language of Statecharts is the best known graphical notation that supports specifications based on modular descriptions of finite state machines. Here we refer to two of the notions provided by Statecharts: *superstates* and *state decomposition*. A superstate is a complex state that is further refined by a decomposition into a finite state machine.

Figure 5.47 shows a statechart restating the control policy of the chemical plant of Figure 5.15. The superstate Recovery is entered from the Normal state whenever an anomaly is detected. In this superstate, a recovery policy is attempted. It is possible to

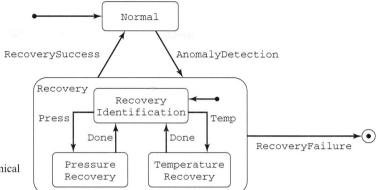

**FIGURE 5.47**

Statechart describing the control policy of the chemical plant of Figure 5.15.

define transitions from and to superstates. Any transition—like `AnomalyDetection`—that leads to a superstate implicitly enters the default initial state of the superstate. Similarly, a transition exiting a superstate stands for a transition that can exit from any of its internal states. In the example, transition `AnomalyDetection` leads to state `RecoveryIdentification`. (An initial state is denoted by an arrow with a black filled circle.) Further, a transition labeled `RecoverySuccess` can exit any of that state's substates and lead to state `Normal`. Similarly, a transition `RecoveryFailure` can exit any of that state's substates and lead to the final state. (A final state is denoted by a filled black circle surrounded by an unfilled circle.)

Statechart transitions may be labeled. Labels, in general, can be triples: `<event, guard, action>`, where event is what makes the transition eligible to occur if the event is received by the object in a certain state, guard is a predicate that must be true in order for the transition to occur, and action is an executable atomic action executed by the object while it is performing the transition. In our example, transitions are labeled only by events.

Figure 5.47 illustrates the sequential decomposition of a superstate. In Statecharts, it is also possible to decompose a superstate into concurrent substates. Figure 5.48 depicts a superstate decomposed into three concurrent substates, defining a producer, a consumer, and a buffer, as discussed earlier in Example 5.3. The figure describes a superstate, `ConcurrentWork`, which is a collection of three concurrent substates (`Producer`, `Consumer`, and `Buffer`). This is an AND decomposition, since at any time the three components are in one of their own states and evolve concurrently. The state space of the superstate is the Cartesian product of the states of its components, but such state space is not shown explicitly. To make things clearer, we added a state with respect to the original description of Figure 5.18, representing the initial state from which the concurrent behavior is generated.

Statecharts have been incorporated into UML to describe the dynamic evolution of the objects of a given class by describing how the state of the objects changes as operations are applied to them. For example, the state transition diagram shown in Figure 5.49 describes the behavior of objects of class `STACK`. Transition labels describe the invoked operation as an event and the condition under which the transition fires, if any, as a guard. (There is no explicit action part.) Objects of class `STACK` can be manipulated by pushing an item on top of them, by popping off the latest introduced item, and by inquiring about the top item stored in them.

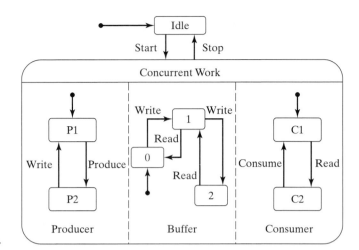

**FIGURE 5.48**

Statechart describing a producer-buffer-consumer system in terms of concurrent substates.

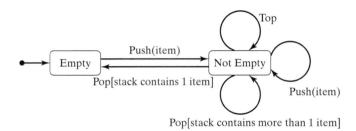

**FIGURE 5.49**

Transition diagram for a stack object.

The decomposition facilities of Statecharts can specify the dynamic behavior of objects characterized by a large and complex state space. Usually, this is done by decomposing higher level superstates in terms of sequential substates. Sometimes, however, objects may be specified by introducing concurrent substates.

Going back to our discussion in Section 5.7.1.1, UML is a specification language composed of several sublanguages, each devoted to describing specific aspects of the system. So far, we have seen several such sublanguages: class diagrams, through which the static properties of an object-oriented architecture can be specified; Statecharts, through which aspects of the dynamic evolution of objects may be added; and activity diagrams, which provide a specification of concurrent sets of activities and of their synchronization. The sublanguages aim at providing complementary views of the system. In Chapter 6, we shall see that UML provides an even richer set of sublanguages, and we discuss how these different notations may be used throughout the development process.

## Exercises

**5.51**  Describe the dynamic behavior of objects of class QUEUE. The operations available on such objects are ENQUEUE, to insert an item in the queue; DEQUEUE, to extract an item from a nonempty queue; IS_EMPTY, to query whether the queue is empty; and MERGE, to merge a queue with the current queue.

**5.52** Statecharts introduce the useful notion of a *history state*. Normally, when a transition enters a composite sequential state, it enters that state's initial substate (unless the transition targets a substate explicitly). However, in some cases, it can be useful to model the fact that the composite state "remembers" the substate that was active prior to leaving the state, so that entering the composite state could resume from such a state. For example, in modeling the interrupts in a computer system, we would like to specify that the action being executed when the interrupt was received will be taken up after the response is taken care of. A history state is represented by a circle containing the symbol H. If we want a transition to activate the most recent substate, we show a transition from outside the composite state pointing directly to the history state. There is also a transition from the history state to a sequential substate, to indicate the substate that becomes active the first time we enter the composite state (i.e., before the composite state has a history). Describe a generalization of the lamp switch example of Figure 5.13 using composite states and history states. The generalization consists of this: A general switch provides power to the building in which the lamp is located. The switch must be in the on position to allow the lamp to operate, and whenever the general switch is turned on, the lamp will be on or off, depending on the state in which it was the last time the general switch was turned off.

### 5.7.2.3 *Modularizing logic specifications: the case of Z*

Z is a formal specification language based on the mathematical concepts of sets, functions, and first-order predicate logic. The language is typed; that is, types are introduced to define the entities that model the system of interest. A system is specified by describing its state space (i.e., the collection of typed variables that characterize the system). The properties of the state space are described in terms of *invariant* predicates that are required to be maintained as the system moves from state to state. State transitions are described by providing the relationships between inputs and outputs of the operations and predicates specifying the resulting state changes. Z *schemas* are the modularization constructs used to define states and how they are affected by the operations. A horizontal line separates state variable declarations from predicates in the graphical representation of a schema. Predicates are expressed as FOT formulas. The $\mathbb{Z}$ language also defines the effect of the combinations of the various schemas that specify different parts of the system.

We introduce Z through an example that illustrates the specification style enforced by the language and the most relevant features of the notation. We will refer to the elevator case study, assuming for simplicity that only one elevator exists in the system. Also, for simplicity and unlike our previous treatments of the elevator example, we ignore timing issues in this section.

We start by introducing the types that are used in the specification. Z has a built-in type $\mathbb{Z}$, which represents the set of integer numbers. Other types, such as $\mathbb{N}$ (representing natural numbers), are also available: They are predefined, using $Z$. It is then possible to introduce new types through various linguistic constructs. As an example, a *free type* definition allows one to define a new type by enumerating the values it comprises. The first two lines of Figure 5.50 show two new enumerated types (SWITCH and MOVE) that can be defined to describe the status of illumination of buttons and the movement of the elevator, respectively.

Z allows objects to be introduced by a construct (called *axiomatic definition*) which defines the constraint that is assumed to hold anytime the object name is used

$$SWITCH ::= on \mid off$$

$$MOVE ::= up \mid down$$

$$
\begin{array}{|l}
\hline
FLOORS : \mathbb{N} \\
\hline
FLOORS > 0 \\
\hline
\end{array}
$$

$$
\begin{array}{l}
\text{--- IntButtons} \text{---------------------} \\
IntReq : 1 .. FLOORS \rightarrow SWITCH \\
\hline
\end{array}
$$

$$
\begin{array}{l}
\text{--- FloorButtons} \text{-------------------} \\
ExtReq : 1 .. FLOORS \rightarrow \mathbb{P} MOVE \\
\hline
down \notin ExtReq(1) \\
up \notin ExtReq(FLOORS) \\
\hline
\end{array}
$$

$$
\begin{array}{l}
\text{--- Scheduler} \text{----------------------} \\
NextFloorToServe : 0 .. FLOORS \\
\hline
\end{array}
$$

**FIGURE 5.50**

A Z specification fragment for the elevator example.

$$
\begin{array}{l}
\text{--- Elevator} \text{-----------------------} \\
CurFloor : 1 .. FLOORS \\
CurDirection : MOVE \\
\hline
\end{array}
$$

in the specification. The third line of Figure 5.50 shows an example of a global constant (FLOORS) that is introduced to denote the number of floors served by the elevator. An alternative way of providing the same definition would be to write

FLOORS : $\mathbb{N}_1$

which uses another predefined Z type, $\mathbb{N}_1$ (the set of positive natural numbers).

The fourth line of Figure 5.50 defines schema IntButtons, which specifies the buttons internal to the elevator. These are represented as a function IntReq from floors to the illumination of a button. More precisely, the function is specified by providing the type of the domain and the type of the range; the symbol → denotes a total function, the symbol ↠ a partial function. In the example, the domain of the function is defined by the type 1 . . . FLOORS. This is yet another way to define a new type in Z, as a finite subrange of integer values. The range of the function is defined by type SWITCH.

FloorButtons is another example of a Z schema. Here, function ExtReq's range type is defined to be the powerset($\mathbb{P}$) of type MOVE. This means that an external request maps a floor into a set of moves. The set ($\mathbb{P}$) is empty if no outstanding request exists for the elevator at a given floor. If it is not empty, the reservation can be for an up ride, a down ride, or both. In contrast to the IntButtons schema, FloorButtons also has a section, separated by a horizontal line, in which two predicates are listed. These predicates are required to hold at any time: Their conjunction represents an *invariant* property for the variables of the schema. In the example, the invariant simply states that a down ride is not possible from the first floor and an up ride is not possible from the top floor.

The next two schemas specify two other components of the system state. The Scheduler component is responsible for yielding, at any time, the next floor to be served by the elevator. (We shall use the fictitious floor 0 to represent the fact that no floor is to be visited next—that is, there are no pending requests.) The Elevator schema models the elevator state by a pair: the current floor it is at and the current direction of its movement. (We shall see that even a standing elevator has a current direction: the direction in which it was moving when it arrived at the floor.)

Figure 5.51 shows how the schemas defining the various components of the system are combined to define the complete system state. By including the declarations Elevator, IntButtons, ExtButtons, and Scheduler, schema System implicitly includes above the line all the declarations from those schemas and implicitly includes below the line all their invariants. Furthermore, an additional invariant is provided as a first attempt to constrain the various state variables of the components to achieve the expected properties of the global system state. In the example, we define a very simple invariant which constrains the scheduler by requiring that if a floor is the next one to be served, then a request should be pending for the floor (either an internal request issued to stop at the floor or an external request issued to go up or down). It is easy to see that this invariant is very weak. It does not even guarantee that whenever a pending request to serve a floor exists, the scheduler yields a (nonzero) next floor to serve. In fact, the invariant is satisfied even if NextFloorToServe is 0 and there is a pending request for the elevator. To remove this drawback, a new version of schema System is provided in Figure 5.52. The new invariant of that figure is a conjunction of the previous invariant and a new one, which ensures that if NextFloorToServe is 0 then all floors f satisfy the condition that both IntReq(f) is off and the set ExtReq(f) is empty.

A revised version of the invariant is shown in Figure 5.52. The invariant here is a list of two predicates that deal with the two cases where there is a next floor to serve and there are no floors to serve. In Z, the predicates in a list are implicitly combined in a conjunction. The second predicate says that if NextFloorToServe is 0 (i.e., the elevator does not recognize the existence of a floor to serve), then there are no pending internal and external requests. (The spot • is just a delimiter in universal and existential quantifiers.)

FIGURE 5.51

Z specification of the complete state space: first attempt.

$$
\begin{array}{|l}
\hline
\text{System} \\
\hline
\textit{Elevator} \\
\textit{IntButtons} \\
\textit{FloorButtons} \\
\textit{Scheduler} \\
\hline
\textit{NextFloorToServe} \neq 0 \\
\quad \Rightarrow \textit{IntReq}(\textit{NextFloorToServe}) = \textit{on} \lor \textit{ExtReq}(\textit{NextFloorToServe}) \neq \emptyset \\
\hline
\end{array}
$$

FIGURE 5.52

Z specification of the complete state space: second attempt.

$$
\begin{array}{|l}
\hline
\text{System} \\
\hline
\textit{Elevator} \\
\textit{IntButtons} \\
\textit{FloorButtons} \\
\textit{Scheduler} \\
\hline
\textit{NextFloorToServe} \neq 0 \Rightarrow \\
\quad \textit{IntReq}(\textit{NextFloorToServe}) = \textit{on} \lor \textit{ExtReq}(\textit{NextFloorToServe}) \neq \emptyset \\
\textit{NextFloorToServe} = 0 \Rightarrow \\
\quad (\forall f : 1 \mathinner{..} \textit{FLOORS} \bullet (\textit{IntReq}(f) = \textit{off} \land \textit{ExtReq}(f) = \emptyset)) \\
\hline
\end{array}
$$

The invariant provided in Figure 5.52, however, is still too weak. According to this specification, any floor for which a request is pending can be chosen as the next floor to serve. Thus, the specification does not guarantee that eventually all requests issued by the users of the elevator will be satisfied. Surely, though, this is a requirement that any elevator should guarantee. To meet this requirement, we provide a new specification for the scheduling policy in Figure 5.53. The complex invariant described here is an existential predicate that deals separately with the case where the elevator is moving up and that where the elevator is moving down. The two cases, however, are handled in a similar way. The rationale of this new specification is that, in selecting the next floor to serve, the elevator proceeds in its current direction of motion, as long as there are pending requests it can satisfy in that direction. Consider, for example the case of an elevator moving up. The set `Pri1` denotes those floors higher than the current floor for which there are internal requests to stop or external requests for up rides. If such a set is not empty, the next floor the elevator visits will be the lowest among all such floors. Otherwise, if the set is empty, then the elevator selects from among the requests to stop at floors for down rides and the internal requests to stop at floors that are lower than the current floor. These floors constitute the set `Pri2`. Among the floors of `Pri2`, the next floor to serve is the highest floor. If `Pri2` also is empty, then the scheduler will consider the set `Pri3` of floors that are lower than the current floor and for which there is an external pending request for an up ride. Among all elements of `Pri3`, the scheduler selects the lowest floor as the next floor to visit. If, however, `Pri3` is also empty, then there is no next floor to visit (i.e., the elevator stays at the current floor).

This example illustrates an important point: If we wish to change the policy adopted by the elevator to choose how to serve pending requests, all we need to change is the invariant predicate encapsulated in the SYSTEM schema. Other schemas do not change. This is a beneficial effect of the modularity of Z specifications.

$$
\begin{array}{|l}
\hline
\textit{System} \\
\hline
\textit{Elevator} \\
\textit{IntButtons} \\
\textit{Floor Buttons} \\
\textit{Scheduler} \\
\hline
\exists \; Pri1, Pri2, Pri3 : \mathbb{PN}_1 \bullet \\
\quad CurDirection = up \; \Rightarrow \\
\quad (Pri1 = \{f:1..FLOORS \mid f \geq CurFloor \wedge (IntReq(f) = on \vee up \in (ExtReq(f))\} \wedge \\
\quad Pri2 = \{f:1..FLOORS \mid down \in ExtReq(f) \vee (f < CurFloor \wedge IntReq(f) = on)\} \wedge \\
\quad Pri3 = \{f:1..FLOORS \mid f < CurFloor \wedge up \in ExtReq(f)\} \wedge \\
\quad ((Pri1 \neq \emptyset \wedge NextFloorToServe = min(Pri1)) \vee \\
\quad (Pri1 = \emptyset \wedge Pri2 \neq \emptyset \wedge NextFloorToServe = max(Pri2)) \vee \\
\quad (Pri1 = \emptyset \wedge Pri2 = \emptyset \wedge Pri3 \neq \emptyset \wedge NextFloorToServe = min(Pri3)) \\
\quad \vee (Pri1 = \emptyset \wedge Pri2 = \emptyset \wedge Pri3 = \emptyset \wedge NextFloorToServe = 0))) \wedge \\
\quad CurDirection = down \; \Rightarrow \\
\quad (Pri1 = \{f:1..FLOORS \mid f \leq CurFloor \wedge \\
\quad (IntReq(f) = on \vee down \in ExtReq(f))\} \wedge \\
\quad Pri2 = \{f:1..FLOORS \mid up \in ExtReq(f) \vee \\
\quad (f > Curfloor \wedge IntReq(f) = on)\} \wedge \\
\quad Pri3 = \{f:1..FLOORS \mid f > CurFloor \wedge down \in ExtReq(f)\} \wedge \\
\quad ((Pri1 \neq \emptyset \wedge NextFloorToServe = max(Pri1)) \vee \\
\quad (Pri1 = \emptyset \wedge Pri2 \neq \emptyset \wedge NextFloorToServe = min(Pri2)) \vee \\
\quad (Pri1 = \emptyset \wedge Pri2 = \emptyset \wedge Pri3 \neq \emptyset \wedge NextFloorToServe = max(Pri3)) \\
\quad \vee (Pri1 = \emptyset \wedge Pri2 = \emptyset \wedge Pri3 = \emptyset \wedge NextFloorToServe = 0))) \\
\hline
\end{array}
$$

**FIGURE 5.53**

Z specification of the complete state space: final version.

To proceed with our specification exercise, we need to describe the effect of the operations on the system state. We introduce the following operations, formally specified in Figure 5.54 (parts 1 and 2),

MoveToNextFloor, describing the effect of moving from one floor to the next;

InternalPush, describing the effect of pushing an internal button;

ExternalPush, describing the effect of pushing an external button at a floor;

ServeIntReq, describing the effect of servicing a request to stop at a floor, issued by pushing an internal button;

ServeExtReqSameDir, describing the effect of servicing a request to stop at a floor, issued by pushing a external button, and requesting the elevator to continue to move in the same direction;

ServeExtReqOtherDir, describing the effect of servicing a request to stop at a floor, issued by pushing an external button, and requesting the elevator to change its direction of motion.

All these operations may affect the system's state, a fact that is indicated by writing "$\Delta$ schema_name" in the declaration part of the specification. For example, operation MoveToNextFloor may modify System. The predicate part of the operation contains a list of predicates that (as we have done so far) are implicitly combined through a logical

---

**MoveToNextFloor**
$\Delta System$
───────────────
$NextFloorToServe \neq 0$
$CurFloor \neq NextFloorToServe$
$CurFloor > NextFloorToServe \Rightarrow$
$CurFloor' = CurFloor - 1 \wedge CurDirection' = down$
$CurFloor < NextFloorToServe \Rightarrow$
$CurFloor' = CurFloor + 1 \wedge CurDirection' = up$
$\theta IntButtons' = \theta IntButtons$
$\theta FloorButtons' = \theta FloorButtons$

---

**InternalPush**
$\Delta System$
$f? : 1 .. FLOORS$
───────────────
$IntReq' = IntReq \oplus \{f? \mapsto on\}$
$\theta Elevator' = \theta Elevator$
$\theta FloorButtons' = \theta FloorButtons$

---

**ExternalPush**
$\Delta System$
$f? : 1 .. FLOORS$
$dir? : MOVE$
───────────────
$ExtReq' = ExtReq \oplus \{(f? \mapsto (ExtReq\ (f?) \cup \{dir?\}))\}$
$\theta Elevator' = \theta Elevator$
$\theta IntButtons' = \theta IntButtons$

---

**ServeIntRequest**
$\Delta System$
───────────────
$NextFloorToServe = CurFloor$
$IntReq(CurFloor) = on$
$IntReq' = IntReq \oplus \{(CurFloor \mapsto off\ )\}$
$ExtReq' = ExtReq$
$CurFloor' = CurFloor$
$CurDirection' = CurDirection$

**FIGURE 5.54**

(a) Z specification of the elevator operations

$$\begin{array}{|l}
\hline
\quad\textit{ServeExtRequestSameDir} \\
\quad\Delta\textit{System} \\
\hline
\quad \textit{NextFloorToServe} = \textit{CurFloor} \\
\quad \textit{IntReq}(\textit{CurFloor}) = \textit{off} \\
\quad \textit{CurDirection} \in \textit{ExtReq}(\textit{CurFloor}) \\
\quad \textit{IntReq}' = \textit{IntReq} \\
\quad \textit{ExtReq}' = \textit{ExtReq} \oplus \{(\textit{CurFloor} \mapsto (\textit{ExtReq}(\textit{CurFloor}) \setminus \{\textit{CurDirection}\}))\} \\
\quad \textit{CurFloor}' = \textit{CurFloor} \\
\quad \textit{CurDirection}' = \textit{CurDirection} \\
\hline
\end{array}$$

$$\begin{array}{|l}
\hline
\quad\textit{ServeExtRequestOtherDir} \\
\quad\Delta\textit{System} \\
\hline
\quad \textit{NextFloorToServe} = \textit{CurFloor} \\
\quad \textit{IntReq}(\textit{CurFloor}) = \textit{off} \\
\quad \textit{CurDirection} \notin \textit{ExtReq}(\textit{CurFloor}) \\
\quad \textit{IntReq}' = \textit{IntReq} \\
\quad \textit{ExtReq}' = \textit{ExtReq} \oplus \{(\textit{CurFloor} \mapsto \emptyset)\} \\
\quad \textit{CurFloor}' = \textit{CurFloor} \\
\quad \textit{CurDirection}' = \textit{CurDirection} \\
\hline
\end{array}$$

$$\begin{array}{|l}
\hline
\quad\textit{SystemInit} \\
\quad\textit{System}' \\
\hline
\quad \forall\, i : 1 \,..\, \textit{FLOORS} \bullet \textit{IntReq}'(i) = \textit{off} \wedge \textit{ExtReq}'(i) = \emptyset \\
\quad \textit{NextFloorToServe}' = 0 \\
\quad \textit{CurFloor}' = 1 \\
\quad \textit{CurDirection}' = \textit{up} \\
\hline
\end{array}$$

**FIGURE 5.54**

(b) Z specification of the elevator operations.

*and*. Some of these predicates use variable names with a prime (e.g., see CurFloor in schema MoveToNextFloor). By convention, the prime denotes the value of the variable *after* the operation is executed. Another convention used by Z is a "?" that may be added as a postfix to a variable name, such as f in the case of schema InternalPush. This indicates the input parameter of the operation. Similarly (although no example is shown here), a "!" used as a postfix identifies an output parameter.

A predicate that does not involve either a primed variable or a variable with a "?" postfix is called a *precondition*, since it denotes a property of the state prior to executing the operation in question. Similarly, a predicate containing primed variables or variables with a "!" postfix is called a *postcondition*, since it denotes a constraint on the values that are required to hold after the operation in question is executed. Observe that the operations are either events or external operations. An *event* is an operation that occurs spontaneously as its precondition becomes true (in the example, MoveToNextFloor, ServeIntReq, ServeExtReqSameDir, and ServeExtReqOtherDir). An *external operation* is an operation that must be explicitly activated by the external environment (in the example, InternalPush and ExternalPush).

The notation $\theta X' = \theta X$ indicates that no component of schema $X$ changes in the operation. The symbol $\oplus$ used by operations InternalPush and ExternalPush is the override operator, which applies to functions. A function is viewed as a set of pairs of elements, the first from the domain and the second from the range. The operator $\oplus$ yields a function that contains the same pairs as the left operand, except that the pairs in the right argument replace any pairs in the left argument that have the same first component. For example, after execution of an internal push for floor f, the new value of *IntReq* is equal to the value before the action was executed, except that the button light for floor $f$ is on. The notation $\{f? \mapsto on\}$ stands for a set containing a simple pair. The set denotes a function that maps the input value $f?$ onto the value "on". Another Z symbol that requires a little explanation is the operator "\\" appearing in the first of the schemas of Figure 5.54 (part 2). This operator stands for the set difference. Observe that the schemas ServeIntRequest, ServeExtRequestSameDir, and ServeExtRequestOtherDir describe the actions that switch off the button lights when the requests they issued are satisfied. For example, the last schema describes the satisfaction of a request from a floor that would require a change in the elevator's direction of motion. According to the system's invariant, this action may occur only if no other pending requests exist that would allow the elevator to continue moving in the same direction. Also, note that the actual change in the elevator's direction of motion occurs only as a consequence of operation `MoveToNextFloor`.

With the state of the system and the operations that modify it defined, the final step is to specify the initialization of the system. Initialization is described by schema `SystemInit`, which can be viewed as the result of an operation that does not refer to the state of the system before its application. Rather, `SystemInit` simply provides a new state.

We have now completed the specification of the elevator, which consists of the schemas appearing in Figure 5.50, Figure 5.53, and Figure 5.54. Once a specification is given, as we discussed, it is necessary to verify it. In the case of a Z specification, the analysis process may consist of verifying that the specification is syntactically correct and does not contain any type errors. Other checks are of a semantic nature. For example, one should also check that the initial state is not vacuous—that is, that there exist values for the state variables that satisfy both the predicate in the `Init` schema and the invariant. All these kinds of analyses can be performed manually, or they can be supported by tools that assist the specifier in writing and checking formal specifications.

### Exercises

**5.53**  Modify the specification discussed in this section by introducing the elevator's door and the operations that open and close the door, respectively.

**5.54**  Modify the specification of the elevator, assuming that the elevator moves continuously from the first to the last floor and back, instead of responding to the internal and external requests of users.

## 5.7.3   Specifications for the End User

Specifications can be used as a common reference for both the producer and the user of an application. For such a purpose, a specification written in a mathematical formalism is not very useful because most users would not be able to understand such formalisms. Often, the only common language between producer and user is their natural language.

The previous statement is not an argument against the use of formal models. Rather, formal system descriptions could be used to help the producer-user interaction in two different ways. First, once one has used formal models to spot and disambiguate informal and imprecise specifications, it is easy to translate the formalization back into a prose description. The advantage of this approach is that the resulting description does not suffer from the problems of ambiguity or incompleteness that most likely affects the initial informal description.

For instance, we realized in Section 5.5.4.2 that the informal specifications of the elevator system did not state in a clear way when buttons had to be switched off. Once a precise definition was achieved through formalization, however, it was not difficult to reformulate it as an English sentence that states precisely what we want from the system.

Second, one may go further and build a prototype of the system by providing an interpreter of the specification language. This could be supplied to the user in order to check whether the producer has properly understood the requirements. Clearly, in some cases the prototype can be operated directly by the user, and in others it cannot. An appropriate *user interface*, however, can make the prototype always manageable directly by the end user.

Another conclusion that may be drawn from the elevator example is that the PN specification cannot be understood by the end user. We could, however, use the PN description as an *internal form* and provide the user with an abstract view in terms of intuitive iconic symbols. The end user would see an elevator icon moving up and down the screen. (This is the result of translating a token flow in terms of icon movement.) The user could also see some buttons to click with the mouse; this would correspond to the pushing of a button in the real system, etc. Such an activity is often called *system animation*. Formal, executable models make it possible to produce and ensure the accuracy of animations relatively easily.

## 5.8   CONCLUDING REMARKS

This chapter has been devoted to the subject of specification. A specification is a precise statement. Specifications can help document many things in a software engineering project, such as the following:

- what the users need from a system (requirements specification);
- the design of a software system (design and architecture specification);
- the features offered by a system (functional specification);
- the performance characteristics of a system (performance specification);
- the external behavior of a module (module interface specification);
- the internal structure of a module (internal structural specification).

Depending on its nature, the specification is intended for a particular user: the system designer, the system implementer, the end user, the system manager, etc. Principles that are similar, though not identical, in content can be used to develop good specifications for these different users.

After having discussed the major desirable qualities for specifications, we classified specification techniques as formal or informal and operational or descriptive. We presented the major operational techniques of data flow diagrams, finite state machines, statecharts, and Petri nets and the major descriptive techniques of entity-relationship diagrams, class diagrams, logic, and algebraic specifications. Data flow and entity-relationship diagrams are examples of the semiformal approach; logic specifications are an example of the formal approach. We contrasted the operational and descriptive approaches, using an elevator system as a case study.

Like software systems, specifications can be large, complex objects that undergo many changes during their lifetime. We therefore need appropriate principles and techniques for managing the development of specifications. Accordingly, we showed that the principles of Chapters 3 and 4 apply to building and managing specifications as well as to software. We developed requirements for managing the writing of complex specifications and examined the impact of these requirements on the different styles of specifications. We argued that modularity is the key to managing complex specifications, and we showed how the different specification styles may be used to develop modular specifications. We presented the specification languages UML, Larch, and Z that support such features, and, in particular, we discussed how the Z specification language provides a way to modularize large specifications.

We have stressed that there is no ideal specification style or language. Considering the variety of details that need to be specified for a complex system, the best approach is to use several styles and languages, either for the different objectives that are specific to different stages of the development process, for different parts of the same system, for different views, or even for different users of the specifications. Such an eclectic approach can encompass a mixture of formal and informal specifications, as well as descriptive and operational ones. UML is an example of this attitude. Obviously, the benefits one may gain in terms of expressiveness are often counterbalanced by the difficulty of providing seamless integration of the different notations. Again, this explains why it is so difficult to formulate a rigorous, unified semantics for the various diagrams that specify a system in UML.

Finally, we discussed the use of specifications in enhancing the interaction between the end user and the developer, with an eye toward producing more accurate specifications. In particular, we discussed system animation and rapid prototyping. The software specification literature contains a dichotomy between specifying and prototyping. The idea is that either you go from (nonexecutable) specifications to code, or you build a prototype that is a first version of the system and develop it into the final system. We saw, however, that there is no contradiction between the two approaches: We can start with a—possibly executable—specification that is our first prototype. The organizational issues related to this topic will be discussed in Chapter 7. In Chapter 6, we shall examine one of the most important uses of specifications: that of verification.

## FURTHER EXERCISES

**5.55** Consider the following specification of a `change` command for a word processor:

```
change (p,q) is defined by:
for any sequence of characters s in the text
        if p = s then
                replace p by q;
        end if;
end change;
```

Is this specification formal or informal? Is it operational or descriptive? Is it ambiguous?

**5.56** Build an FSM that accepts the set of strings that contain an even number of 0's and an odd number of 1's and that begin with 1 and end with 0.

**5.57** Give an FSM description of a system consisting of several independent programs that share the same CPU, the same memory device, and the same I/O devices in such manner that access to them occurs in mutual exclusion.

**5.58** Modify the preceding exercise by considering a system with different instances of physical resources (CPUs, disks, etc.), but in which programs may share some files. Is the model used in the previous case still adequate? Why?

**5.59** Show that any FSM can be "translated" into an equivalent PN—that is, a PN whose set of acceptable firing sequences is the same as the transition sequences of the FSM. Also, show that the converse operation is not always possible.

How can you analyze the deadlock-freedom property by means of FSMs?

**5.60** The time required to process some data often depends on some property of the data. For example, sorting a sequence of items depends on the size of the sequence. Imagine that some transition of a PN models a process of this type. Provide a modification of the timed PN model presented here that is able to cope with this case.

**5.61** Consider the portion of a PN given in Figure 5.55. Suppose you want to model a requirement of the type "Once a token is produced in place $P_3$, it can be consumed, either through transition $t_1$ or through transition $t_2$, within a time $t_{max}$. If neither of these alternatives happens, the token cannot be consumed any more." Show that timed PNs, as defined in this chapter, cannot describe such a requirement. Outline an alternative way of defining timed PNs that could cope with the problem.

**5.62** Complete the specification of the elevator system given in Section 5.5.4.2 with a description of the emergency button and its effects.

**5.63** Complete the specification of the elevator system given in Section 5.5.4.2 by describing the opening and closing of the doors.

**5.64** Modify the specification of the elevator system given in Section 5.5.4.2 by taking into account the fact that $\Delta t$, the transfer time between two adjacent floors, depends on whether an elevator does or does not stop at a floor. Consider also the case in which the elevator moves from a floor where it is standing.

**5.65** Sketch how the elevator system described in Section 5.5.4.2 could be specified in terms of FSMs. You don't need to go into all the details. Rather, you should point out what FSMs are able to describe and where they fail to capture the desired requirements.

**5.66** Use PNs to model office organization and automation. You should describe all relevant activities that occur in an office (producing documents, computing invoices and salaries, etc.), the data such activities involve, the way the activities operate on the data, and the precedence relations among different activities (e.g., one cannot mail a letter if it has not

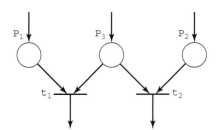

**FIGURE 5.55**

A portion of a Petri net.

been written). You do not need to produce a long list of activities and data stores. Rather, you should focus attention on a few of them and analyze them in some depth. You may refer to Section 5.7.1 for hints on this project.

**5.67**  Augment the ER diagram of Figure 5.41 so that you can specify the prerequisites for each class (i.e., which classes must be taken before taking the given class).

**5.68**  Give an ER diagram complementing the DFD of Figure 5.5, in order to describe the entities involved in the application and their relationships.

**5.69**  Give a logic specification for a program that computes the integer square root of nonnegative integers.

**5.70**  Augment the specification of Exercise 5.69 by imposing the requirement that, if the input value is negative, an appropriate error message is printed.

**5.71**  Go back to the specification of the `search` procedure (number 7) given in Section 5.6.2.2. Would the procedure still be adequate if the variable `table` were a global variable instead of an input parameter?

**5.72**  Modify the logic specification of the elevator system by taking the elevator's acceleration into consideration.

**5.73**  Go back to the PN of Figure 5.33. Is it incomplete? Is it inconsistent? Why?

**5.74**  Describe, in both an operational style and a descriptive style, the following problem (not its solution!):

A farmer has to carry a goat, a cabbage, and a wolf from one side of a river to the other side. She has a boat to do so, but the boat cannot carry more than three items, whether farmer, goat, cabbage, or wolf. If she leaves both the goat and the cabbage on the same side of the river or in the boat without being present, the goat will eat the cabbage. Similarly, the wolf will eat the goat if left unattended.
Compare the two specifications from several points of view.

**5.75**  Describe, in both an operational style and a descriptive style, the fact that a fixed number of processes can access any of a fixed number of common resources in mutual exclusion. Compare the two specifications.

**5.76**  Write a paper comparing the specification of Section 5.5.4.2 with the specification of Section 5.6.2.5 from several points of view.

**5.77**  Here is an example of a real-time specification that does not involve mission-critical systems (it has been mentioned in Section 2.3.2): With many computer windowing systems, the user may click or double-click the mouse. If two clicks occur within a given time $\Delta t$, their meaning is different from the case in which they are separated by a longer interval. Describe the Macintosh click and double-click semantics both in an operational (e.g., by means of timed PNs) and in a logic style. Compare the two specifications.

**5.78**  Build a PN interpreter that will work both interactively and in batch. In the former case, the nondeterminism of the model can be resolved by the user through a dialog. In the latter case, nondeterministic choices should be taken randomly, but the user should be able to give appropriate scheduling options, possibly on the basis of previous experiences, before the relevant command is executed. For instance, one could ask for "complete execution." In this case, the interpreter should provide all firing sequences, up to a predefined point.

Alternatively, one could start from an existing firing sequence and ask for a change in some firing choices to obtain a new firing sequence as a modification of the previous one.

**5.79** How could you analyze the property of equivalence between two different systems described in terms of FSMs? Could you make use of an FSM interpreter?

**5.80** Give a complete description of the library system described in Figure 5.4 and Figure 5.5, possibly integrating the use of DFDs with other notations.

**5.81** Give an algebraic specification of the module FIFO_CARS introduced in Example 4.9.

**5.82** Discuss an enrichment of the Larch specification language described in Section 5.7.2.1 by allowing genericity.

**5.83** Discuss the differences between specifying the behavior of objects of a certain class by using (1) Statecharts, (2) an algebraic language like Larch, and (3) preconditions, postconditions, and invariants.

**5.84** Define a specification-design language for algebraic equations based on Larch and on the design notation of Section 4.2.3.1. Give examples of the use of this language, and sketch its translation into a programming language. The main idea is to move from the definition of an algebra to the definition of an abstract data type by specifying which operations become procedures and which become functions.

**5.85** Give examples of translations from DFD descriptions into skeletons of code in some programming language (e.g., the declarative part of an Ada package). You do not need to define algorithms for the translation.

**5.86** Discuss how to define and build modular PNs.

**5.87** Give rules for building complex DFDs by stepwise refinement of higher level ones.

**5.88** Modify the policy of the elevator in the Z specification in Section 5.7.2.3 by supposing that the highest floor is the VIP floor. Any external request from the VIP floor must be handled with higher priority than any other request.

## HINTS AND SKETCHY SOLUTIONS

**5.19** You need to add transitions that remove the tokens, corresponding to copies of messages, that are not removed by the firing of a "voting" transition.

**5.20** a. In point 4, what does "with all floors given equal priority" mean?
- That all floors must be served in a nondeterministic way, provided that eventually they will be served?
- That all floors must be served in a FIFO way?
- Consider the case in which there are two elevators at floor 2, with one request for floor 60 and one request for floor 3. Then both elevators go to floor 60 first, and then both go to floor 3. Is this case compatible with the specification?

b. Why do points 4 and 5 state different requirements for external and internal requests? (Point 5 is more precise than point 4.)

c. From the point of view of the *organization* of the specifications, it should be noticed that there is a mixture of specifications defining the behavior of the system (e.g., switching buttons), specifications stating requirements on system properties (e.g., "all requests must be serviced"), and specifications on scheduling decisions ("the algorithm...should minimize... ").

**5.25** In the general case, the token in place SCHEDULER should contain information about the whole state of the system (i.e., elevator positions and button illuminations), because the waiting times depend on this information. Once the information is stored in SCHEDULER, a *decision* function could be attached to a transition connected only to SCHEDULER. Such a function embeds the algorithm chosen to minimize waiting times and must be computed in a time that is negligible with respect to the dynamics of the system. In other words, the maximum time associated with the transition must be very small compared with the time $\Delta t$ that is required for an elevator's moving from one floor to an adjacent one.

**5.26** Introduce a third entity, PROFICIENCY, and define a ternary relation.

**5.32** The informal specification did not state how many blanks could exist between two consecutive words. Also, it was not stated whether the terminator '#' should immediately follow the last character of the last word or whether a blank was needed before it. The formal specification makes this clear. It is quite easy to change options if desired.

**5.33** No. The procedure

```
procedure sort (a: in out integer_array) is
begin
        for i in a'first. . a'last loop
                a (i):= i;
        end loop;
end sort;
```

would satisfy the given requirement.

An appropriate specification for a sorting procedure is

```
{n > 0}
P
{perm(a,old_a) and sorted(a,n)}
```

where perm (x, y) states that x is a permutation of y. (However, when giving a full definition of perm, you should pay attention to the case in which some element occurs more than once in the array.)

**5.41** The new operation name: Text → Identifier is defined; the other operations are modified accordingly—for instance,

```
newF: Identifier → Text.
```

The following is a sample of the modified semantics:

```
name newF(id))=id;
if name(f1)=name(f2) then f1=f2;
if (equalF(f, appendF(f1, f2)) and (lengthF(f1)=cursor) and
name(f)=id)then
(insertF(id, cursor, s)=appendF(addF(f1, s), f2) and
name(insertF (id,
    cursor, s)=id)
```

**5.42**  Here is the solution for operation find.

First, the range of the operation is the Cartesian product `Bool` $\times$ `Nat`, with obvious restrictions.

Second, if `s` is the empty string, it always occurs in `f` in any position.

Third, what if `s` occurs several times in `f`? What if some occurrences are intersecting? Some of these remarks apply even to the `change` command.

**5.49**  We saw in Chapter 4 that the `INHERITS_FROM` relation is still quite controversial, and different definitions are given for it in different languages. Whenever unconstrained redefinition of inherited operations is allowed, it makes inheritance different from **assumes**, since **assumes** can only add new properties to the inherited operations, without canceling previous equations. Some object-oriented languages, however, at least aim at a semantics of the inheritance relation that coincides with **assumes**.

**5.52**  Figure 5.56 provides a solution.

**5.59**  PNs can have an infinite number of states because, in some cases, the marking of places can grow unboundedly.

**5.61**  A simple solution consists of attaching pairs $<t_{min}, t_{max}>$ to places instead of transitions. Thus, if a token is produced into a place P, it cannot be consumed before $t_{min}$ has elapsed. Furthermore, if, at time $t_{max}$, an output transition of P is enabled, it must fire at $t_{max}$; if several are enabled, the choice is, as usual, nondeterministic. If $t_{max}$ elapses and the token has not been consumed, it can never be consumed by any transition (i.e., the token is "lost").

A more general solution that could handle many different timing situations is outlined as follows:

Each token carries a *time stamp*, which is a value representing the time at which the token has been produced. Predicates associated with transitions are defined on the time stamps of the tokens in the input places. A definition of the semantics of these nets is given by Ghezzi et al. [1989a].

**5.71**  No, because the procedure could modify `table` during execution. In this case, the output assertion would require the variable `found` to be true if and only if the value `element` exists in `table` after execution, not before. Thus, the postcondition should be changed by using `old_table` instead of `table`.

**5.76**  Simulating PNs is simpler and more natural than simulating logical specifications by deductions, whether this is done by hand or automatically. By contrast, analyzing properties is perhaps easier in logic.

Dealing with—and changing—implementation policies is easier in a logic style. In fact, for PNs, we might need strong changes in the model.

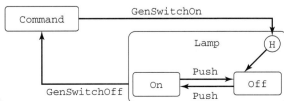

FIGURE 5.56

A sequential composition of a superstate.

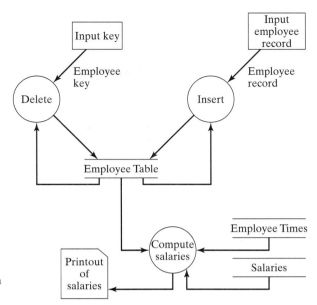

FIGURE 5.57

A DFD describing part the computation
of employees' salaries.

"Putting together" several components of the specifications is perhaps more complex with PNs. In fact, the graphical representation becomes unmanageable. The difficulty lies in checking possible inconsistencies among several components. In a set of logical rules, we have the same problem, but following the flow of logical deductions to check possible inconsistencies is perhaps more systematic.

**5.82** Apply the examples and techniques used in Chapter 4.

**5.85** The DFD of Figure 5.57 can be translated into the Ada package interface outlined as follows:

```
package Employees is
        Empl_Table: ...
        Empl_Record: ... —contains an Empl_Key declaration—
        Empl_Time: ...
        Salaries: ...
        procedure Insert (Empl_Record: in...; Empl_Table: in out...);
        procedure Delete (Empl_Key: in...; Empl_Table: in out...);
        procedure Comp_Sal (Empl_Times: in...;
                            Empl_Table: in...; Salaries: out...);
end Employees;
```

**5.86** PNs can be described in several structured ways. In particular, one could see a transition as describing a fairly complex activity that could be further detailed by suitable subnets. Figure 5.58 gives a hint on how to produce this kind of *refinement*. Alternatively, one could define several components of a PN as independent subnets that are to be aggregated by following suitable *composition rules*. Figure 5.25 and 5.26 can be used as a source of inspiration for defining such rules.

**5.87** Apply *functional decomposition* to operations denoted by bubbles. For instance, a "compute salary" function may be decomposed into "compute number of hours at work," "compute gross salary," "compute taxes," and "compute net salary."

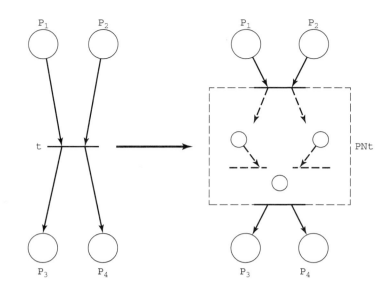

**FIGURE 5.58**

Refinement of a Petri net transition.

## BIBLIOGRAPHIC NOTES

For the basic terminology on specification, refer to the standards document IEEE [1999]. Davis [1990] and Davis [1993] are two books on software requirements and specification. Jackson [1995] is an enlightening glossary on requirements and specification. In particular, it proposes a systematic framework for dealing with the acquisition and specification of the requirements that an application must satisfy in order to interact properly with its surrounding environment. Van Lamsweerde [2000a] provides a research perspective of requirements engineering. Nuseibeh and Easterbrook [2000] gives an overview of issues in requirements engineering.

Boehm [1984b] distinguishes between verification (compliance with the specified requirements) and validation (the system serves its intended purpose). Parnas [1972a] is a seminal paper advocating a clear distinction between specification and implementation. Parnas [1977] provides a lucid introduction to, and requirements for, specifications.

Data flow diagrams are one of the most popular notations for software specification. They are presented, in many slightly different versions, in numerous papers and books, such as DeMarco [1978]. Ward and Mellor [1985] have extended DFDs with control flow arrows and other features in order to make them suitable for real-time systems analysis and specification. Real-time specifications are also described by Hatley and Pirbhai [1987]. A complete formalization of DFDs is proposed in Fuggetta et al. [1993].

FSMs are probably the most widely known, most simple, and most used model in computer science. They are described in much detail in many different textbooks, such as Mandrioli and Ghezzi [1987].

Petri nets are due to Petri [1962], who defined them originally to describe interacting finite state machines. They are described by Peterson [1981] and Reisig [1985]. Among the many variations and extensions that have been proposed for the basic model, we mention predicate-transition networks by Genrich [1987], in which tokens are allowed to carry values and the firing of transitions may depend on those values through predicates that are associated with the transitions. Time has been added to Petri nets in several ways; the one presented here is due to Merlin and Farber [1976]. Ghezzi et al. [1989a] presents a general way to introduce time into Petri nets. AjmoneMarsan et al. [1984] proposes a stochastic extension by making the firing of transitions probabilistic.

The case study of the elevator system has been used extensively in the literature as a benchmark for specification methods and languages. The informal definition presented here is taken from the call for papers of the 4th IEEE International Workshop on Software Specification and Design [IWSSD, 1987], where it was explicitly proposed as a challenging exercise. The formalization of the definition in terms of Petri nets is from Ghezzi and Mandrioli [1987].

The entity-relationship model was introduced by Chen [1976].

The application of mathematical logic to computer science was pioneered by McCarthy [1962], Floyd [1967], and Hoare [1969]. The text by Manna and Waldinger [1985] is an excellent introduction to mathematical logic, with particular emphasis on computer science applications. A shorter introduction is provided in the theoretical computer science text by Mandrioli and Ghezzi [1987]. The application of logic to the specification of concurrent and real-time systems has been undertaken on the basis of the initial work of Hoare [1972].

Much interest is presently devoted to the use of temporal logic. A good tutorial on this extension to classical logic and its applications to computer science is provided by Kroeger [1987]. Ostroff [1989] discusses the application of temporal logic to real-time systems. The elevator formalization in terms of logic is taken from Garzotto et al. [1987].

The use of algebraic formalisms for software specification has been advocated by several researchers. Initial efforts were due to Guttag [1977] and Goguen et al. [1978]. The language Larch discussed in this chapter is due to Guttag and Horning [1983, 1986a, and 1986b] and Guttag et al. [1985a and 1985b]. Jalote [1989] discusses how to test the completeness of specifications given in an algebraic style.

CCS (calculus of communicating systems), due to Milner [1980], is a well-known and extensively studied algebraic approach to the specification of concurrent systems.

The Z specification language is defined by Spivey [1989]. Woodcock and Davies [1996] is a textbook on formal specifications in Z. Spivey [1990] and Wordsworth [1990] describe practical case studies using Z.

Statecharts have been defined in Harel [1987], Harel et al. [1990], and Harel and Naamad [1996].

For UML, the reader can refer to Booch et al. [1999] and Fowler and Scott [1998].

In this chapter, we presented only a sample of specification languages. Others have been developed on the basis of the models presented in the chapter. Several have found practical application. Most are associated with appropriate tools to support their use. The following is a partial list of these languages:

- RSL (Requirement Statement Language) is based on the so-called R-Nets, a semiformal extension of FSMs. Part of the Software Requirements Engineering Methodology (SREM) developed by TRW for the U.S. Strategic Defense Command, RSL is presented by Alford [1977].
- PSL (Problem Statement Language) is an operational language developed by Teichrow and Hershey [1977]. PSL is a computer-aided technique for structured documentation and analysis of information-processing systems.
- SADT was developed by Ross [1977] as part of a complete methodology.
- VDM (Vienna definition method) is a formal language based on the *denotational approach* to formal semantics, a descriptive method that consists of defining the meaning of a notation as the solution (minimal fixed point) of a suitable set of

equations in suitable domains. The language has been presented by Bjorner and Jones [1982], Bjorner and Prehn [1983], and Jones [1986a and b].

- ASLAN, developed by Auernheimer and Kemmerer [1985], is also based on first-order predicate calculus. The language has been extended by Auernheimer and Kemmerer [1986] to deal with real-time systems. ASTRAL (Coen-Porisini et al. [1997]) is another language that inherits from ASLAN and TRIO (see *shortly*).

- OBJ2 is a specification language that derives from Goguen's early work on algebraic specifications. The language is described by Futatsugi et al. [1985]; Nakagawa et al. [1988] describes a practical application of the language, which evolved into the CafeOBJ specification language (Nakajima and Futatsugi [1997]).

- LOTOS is a specification language for communications applications, based on Milner's CCS. It is described by Bolognesi and Brinksma [1987].

- TRIO is a specification language for real-time critical systems (Ghezzi et al. [1990]). Based on temporal logic, TRIO is supported by an extensive set of tools and has been validated in several large-scale case studies, as reported in Ciapessoni et al. [1999].

- The SCR (Software Cost Reduction) requirements method was introduced in the late 1970s at the Naval Research Laboratories (Heninger [1980], Bharadwaj and Heitmeyer [1999]) to specify the software requirements of embedded real-time systems. It has been used extensively, and more recent work has strengthened its formal underpinnings (Heitmeyer et al. [1996]).

Heitmeyer and Mandrioli [1996] is a collection of papers on the formal specification of real-time systems that provides a broad view of the state of the art in the area.

Writing specifications is difficult and prone to error. This is why we need to verify (validate) them, according to Boehm [1984b]. The issue of executing specifications has been advocated by Kemmerer [1985]. Prototyping is discussed by Luqi and Ketabchi [1988] and Luqi et al. [1988]. The special issue of *IEEE Computer* edited by Tanik and Yeh (Computer [1989a]) may be consulted for a sample of rapid prototyping techniques and applications. Boehm et al. [1984] compares software design based on specification with an approach based on prototyping.

Moriconi and Hare [1986] and Harel [1988] advocate the use of *visual languages* to make specifications more understandable. Roman and Cox [1989] illustrates the use of animation for visualizing concurrent computations.

An eclectic approach to writing specifications has been advocated by Ghezzi and Mandrioli [1987] and Sanden [1989b].

The issue of viewpoints in specifications and the need for establishing some form of correlation among the different viewpoints has been analyzed by Nuseibeh et al. [1994].

Van Lamsweerde [2000b] provides a road map for the field of formal specifications. Engels and Groenwegen [2000] offers a road map of object-oriented modeling, and Jackson and Rinard [2000] presents a road map of the analysis of specifications.

# CHAPTER 6

# Verification

In Chapters 3, 4, and 5, we saw how to develop software methodically so that a product meets its intended uses. In a perfect world, we could stop here. Human beings, however, are fallible, and they make mistakes: Even if they adopt the most sophisticated and thoughtful design techniques, erroneous results can never be avoided *a priori*. Consequently, the product of any engineering activity—a bridge, an automobile, a television set, or a word processor—must be *verified* against its requirements throughout its development.

During the design and construction of, say, a bridge, one must repeatedly verify the product in all its intermediate development stages. For instance, the first blueprints of the bridge are verified by using suitable equations to forecast whether the bridge will sustain the required loading. Possibly, a physical model is also built, to further enhance the reliability of the forecast. The raw materials used in the construction are inspected, and their quality is verified. The construction process is also verified for its adherence to certain required standards. Finally, in some cases, the real bridge is checked by loading it with a number of trucks of a given weight before opening it to the public.

As we said, not only the *products* of bridge design and construction are verified, but even the *process* must be checked. For instance, before starting the actual construction of the bridge, one should verify that the building site has been prepared appropriately—perhaps including schools for the children of the workers if the bridge has to be built in an undeveloped area. There are even government agencies that must approve the design before any work can begin. The site, likewise, must be prepared by the contractor and approved by an appropriate agency.

Software must be verified in much the same spirit. In this chapter, however, we shall learn that verifying software is perhaps more difficult than verifying other engineering products. We shall try to clarify why this is so.

The chapter is devoted to software verification. We first discuss the goals and requirements of the verification activity and then present, compare, and evaluate major verification techniques.

Before proceeding with the technical details, we should discuss some issues regarding terminology. The field of software verification is progressing rapidly, and the terminology is evolving. The terms *verification* and *validation*, in particular, are used with many, often inconsistent, meanings. We shall avoid the term *validation* and only use *verification* in this chapter. By verification, we mean all activities that are undertaken to ascertain that the software meets its objectives. As we shall see, these activities encompass a wide spectrum of efforts, including testing, mathematical proofs, and informal reasoning.

At the beginning of the chapter, we shall use the terms *error* and *defect* interchangeably in place of the more common and affectionate (but sloppy) term, "bug." We shall define these and other terms more precisely later in the chapter.

This chapter is organized as follows: Section 6.1 discusses the goals and requirements of verification. Section 6.2 presents the two prominent approaches to verification: testing and analysis. Section 6.3 addresses testing, and Section 6.4 deals with analysis. Section 6.5 introduces symbolic execution, a less standard, but promising, technique that can be seen as a middle way between analysis and testing. Section 6.6 introduces model checking, a new verification technique that allows us to obtain the certainty of correctness in some simple cases. Section 6.7 aims at building a global view of the verification activity by summarizing and integrating the various techniques examined separately in previous sections. Section 6.8 examines the role of debugging in software verification. Finally, the verification of other software qualities is discussed in Section 6.9.

## 6.1    GOALS AND REQUIREMENTS OF VERIFICATION

Just as a bridge or any other engineering work must be verified, so must both the process of software development and all of its products. With small programs, with programs we write for our own use, and with programs that do not have critical requirements to meet, program verification often consists of trying a few sample cases to see whether the results of running the code match our expectations. Although this practice is unprofessional and is inadequate even for such simple programs, the consequences of errors in these cases can usually be tolerated. Unfortunately, people are often tempted to carry over the approach to the verification of software *products*.

Trying a few sample cases, however, is too limited to provide us with any confidence in the software, for at least two reasons. First, we shall see later that we can *never* gain such absolute confidence in the correctness of software. Second, even if we could, we would still be quite far from software that we could trust: The software might perform poorly, or its documentation might be inadequate, preventing its effective use or its evolution. Furthermore, performing verification only after the running code is available would make it very difficult to repair any defects that were discovered. Experimental data from industrial projects have shown that the cost of removing an error after the software has been developed completely is much higher than if errors are eliminated earlier.

In sum, the verification activity—like other software design activity—must follow rigorous principles and suitable techniques; it cannot be left exclusively to human insight, experience, or luck.

Let us now go through the requirements for verification in a more systematic way.

### 6.1.1    Everything Must Be Verified

In principle, all design processes and all of the products of these processes must be verified. We already have discussed the issue of verifying specifications in Chapter 5, where we showed that simulation and property analysis are two means of achieving it.

In some sense, even *verification must be verified*. In fact, once we have tested a system for proper behavior, we should check whether our tests were executed properly themselves. Verifying the validity of experiments is standard practice in established scientific disciplines. Going back to the bridge example, after having tested the strength of the bridge in several cases, we should check whether all the experiments have been carried out in the right way and whether more experiments are needed. Similarly, if we have been able to prove some desirable property of a system we are working on, we must critically analyze whether the proof we made is "correct." Of course, such a "recursive" application of the verification activity must eventually stop.

Also, *every software quality must be verified*. Not only must we check, through verification of correctness, whether the software we have implemented behaves according to the specification document(s), but also, we must certify the software's portability, performance, modifiability, etc.

The foregoing remarks suggest that verification may be performed at different points of time by different people with different goals and by applying different techniques. For instance, in some cases it may be useful for a product to be verified by a person other than the one who implements it; in other cases, verification could be performed by applying precise algorithms, etc. These organizational issues will be treated in part in Chapters 7 and 8. Here, we are concerned mainly with principles and related techniques to be applied during the verification activity.

### 6.1.2    The Results of Verification May Not Be Binary

We tend to think of verification as a "yes or no" activity: After having performed as many tests as needed and as much analysis as required, eventually the result of the verification is either acceptance or rejection of the final product. Even though it is true that, ultimately, the producer either decides to deliver the product or decides not to, and the user either decides to accept it or decides not to, there are many verification activities whose results cannot be reduced to a binary answer.

As we observed in Chapter 2, even correctness itself (i.e., compliance with functional specifications) is a matter of degree. In other words, it cannot be stated that a piece of software is absolutely error free, but an approximation of ideal correctness is often considered satisfactory and may in some way be certified. It is common to hear or read sentences such as "The new release of this product corrects several errors." (That is, the new release is more correct than the previous release.) This claim implies that

- The presence of defects in large and complex software cannot be avoided completely in practice.
- Sometimes, some defects can be tolerated. (Recall from Chapter 2 that correctness is related to, but is not the same as, reliability or robustness.)
- In practice, correctness is relative. Unfortunately, this does not imply that it is easy to measure.

Efficiency is a typical example of a software quality that can be exhibited at different levels. Efficiency is often explicitly mentioned in requirements documents and can be measured in several ways. For instance, efficiency could be expressed in terms of complexity by a formula such as "The time required to perform computations is given by the function f(n) of the length n of the input stream"; or one could experimentally build tables that state the number and kind of resources needed to run a system in several representative cases.

Furthermore, we shall see at the end of the chapter that one can apply statistical criteria to define, measure, and thus verify reliability.

### 6.1.3    Verification May Be Objective or Subjective

Some instances of verification may be the result of an objective activity, such as performing a test by supplying some input data to the system and checking the output, or measuring the response time of an interactive system to given stimuli.

Not all qualities, however, can be quantified in such an objective way. For instance, portability and maintainability can be made precise only by specifying an environment—porting a software system from a given architecture to another specific one, or modifying existing software in order to meet a precisely stated new requirement. In many cases, one would like to state a generic level of portability, even though one is unable to specify exactly the technical features of possible new architectures. Similarly, one would like to estimate reusability even when one cannot specify exactly in which new context the software will have to be reused.

In such cases, objective measures must be replaced by, or integrated with, subjective estimates. For instance, we stated in Chapter 4 that the use of object-oriented techniques may be expected to enhance reusability. We substantiated this claim by providing examples showing that "essential parts" of existing code could be naturally adapted to operating conditions different from their original ones. Such a claim, however, could not be related to any objective measure of the reuse of code—say, the number of lines of unaffected code. Even this rough quantification of reusability could be misleading: It would imply that complexity of software reuse is measured by the number of lines of code—an often assumed, but questionable, hypothesis.

Still, we need to estimate a level of modifiability even in the absence of an objective criterion to measure it.

### Example 6.1

Consider the following real situation showing how, in practice, reusability may be empirically evaluated. Manufacturer *A* wants to buy a graphical text editor to market with its new line of computers. Software vendor *B* claims to have developed an editor that could easily be adapted to various environments. The editor already runs on the processors that the manufacturer is using. What manufacturer *A* is really interested in is whether the editor can be adapted to support different kinds of display terminals. *B* claims that this can be done easily and that the editor already supports many different types of display terminals. In the absence of any objective measure of evolvability of the code, *A* and *B* agree on an experiment: *A* will try to add the support for a new terminal. If this can be done in less than a week, then *A* will buy the software. Thus, while the goal of "modifiability" was a subjective one for *B* during the development of the editor, it became the deciding factor for making the sale, based on a precise, although subjective, experiment.    ■

Other aspects of software products are even more intrinsically subjective—after all, bridges and other artifacts may also be more or less beautiful. Certainly, understandability and usability are, by definition, subject to human judgment, and such judgment varies from person to person.

All this suggests is that subjective evaluation must be a part of the whole verification process, even though the results of a subjective evaluation are less dependable than those of an objective evaluation. In much the same way, despite its greater fallibility, subjective evaluation is used in other engineering fields. Instead of avoiding subjective evaluation, precautions are taken to reduce the associated risks. For instance, committees—and supercommittees—are set up to contrast several opinions against each other.

### 6.1.4    Even Implicit Qualities Must Be Verified

The desired software qualities should be stated explicitly in the requirements specification document. Some requirements, however, may have been left out, either because they are implicit or because they were forgotten. In Chapter 2, we used the term *robust* to characterize software whose functional behavior remains acceptable, even in unspecified circumstances.

Let us consider the case of implicit requirements. For example, requirements for conventional data-processing systems often are only functional requirements and, worse, are frequently incomplete. This does not mean that such systems have no performance requirements. It is just that these requirements are omitted because they are not considered to be critical and they can be left to professional judgment and common sense. For instance, people are expected to know that a transaction at an automatic teller machine *normally* should not exceed one minute; and furthermore, the term "normally" should be quantified as—say—about 95% of the time.

Maintainability is a typical example of a software quality that is seldom explicitly asked for, yet is often highly desirable. We also saw that it is hardly quantifiable. This notwithstanding, a good software engineer should strive not only to design maintainable software, but also to verify the maintainability of the product during each step of the design process. For instance, once the requirements for a user interface are specified, one should ask how, when, and why they are likely to change. Similarly, suppose you have decided to buy some piece of software that is to be integrated into a system you are building. If you are not completely sure that such a piece of software will meet all your present and future needs, you should analyze the implications of changing your decision in the future, perhaps by redeveloping the same piece of software. Example 6.1 illustrates this point: The software of company *B* was adequate for the needs of company *A*, but company *A* needed to perform an experiment to ensure that the decision to buy from company *B* would not preclude them from supporting different display terminals later.

**Exercise**

---

**6.1** Go back to the software qualities discussed in Chapter 2. Classify all of them with respect to the following verifiability issues:

a. Are they objective or subjective?
b. Are they binary or not?
c. Are they more or less relevant in different applications and environments?

---

## 6.2 APPROACHES TO VERIFICATION

There are two fundamental approaches to verification: experimentation and analysis. The first consists of *experimenting with the behavior* of a product to see whether the product performs as expected (i.e., *testing* the product). The other consists of *analyzing* the product—and any design documentation related to it—to deduce its correct operation as a logical consequence of the design decisions. The two categories of verification techniques are also classified as *dynamic* and *static*, respectively, since, by definition, the former requires executing the system to be verified, while the latter is based on examining static models of the product. Not surprisingly, the two techniques turn out to be nicely complementary.

We already saw an instance of the difference between dynamic and static verification in Chapter 5, when we discussed the issue of the verification of specifications. There, we distinguished between simulating the specifications and analyzing the properties that can be deduced from them. In the current chapter, we shall focus our attention mainly on the verification of software correctness. As suggested in the previous section, however, much of the proposed techniques can, and should be, applied also to the verification of other qualities. We provide some hints on this topic later in the chapter. In particular, we discuss the problem of assessing the more subjective qualities, such as understandability and modifiability, and we present some techniques for doing so, along with some difficulties associated with them.

## 6.3 TESTING

The most natural and customary way of verifying any piece of work is just to operate it in some representative situations and verify whether it behaves as expected. In general, it is impossible to test it under all possible operating conditions. Thus, it is necessary to find suitable *test cases* that provide enough evidence to give us confidence that the desired behavior will be exhibited even in cases that have not been tested. This is often a difficult, and sometimes even impossible, job. Furthermore, in the case of software testing, the usual analogies between traditional engineering fields and software engineering fail to provide useful suggestions.

Consider our familiar example of constructing a bridge. Suppose you wish to test the bridge's ability to sustain weight. If you have verified that the bridge can sustain 1,000 tons, then it will sustain any weight less than or equal to 1,000 tons under the same circumstances.

This criterion cannot be applied to software, as is shown by the following example.

**Example 6.2**

Consider the following binary search procedure:

```
procedure binary-search (key: in element;
      table: in element Table; found: out Boolean) is
begin
      bottom := table'first; top := table'last;
      while bottom < top loop
            if (bottom + top) rem 2 ≠ 0 then
                  middle := (bottom + top - 1)/2;
            else
                  middle := (bottom + top)/2;
            end if;
            if key ≤ table (middle) then
                  top := middle;
            else
                  bottom := middle + 1;
            end if;
      end loop;
      found := key = table (top);
end binary-search;
```

What happens if we omit the **else** clause of the first **if** statement? The procedure will still work properly for all tables whose size is such that the first **if** condition will always be true (i.e., the size of the table is a power of 2), but this does not guarantee that it works properly for all tables of smaller size. ∎

This example shows that small changes in the input to a program may result in significantly different behavior of the program. In contrast, the features of most engineering constructions exhibit a *continuity* property, so that we can rely on the fact that small differences in operating conditions—for example, between the system's operation under testing and its normal operation—will not result in dramatically different behaviors. Such a continuity property is totally lacking in software, as Example 6.2 illustrates.

Testing is a critical activity in software engineering and should be performed as systematically as possible by stating clearly what result one expects and how one expects to obtain that result. On the contrary, in practice, testing often is performed in an unstructured way, without applying planned criteria. In the sections that follow, we first state testing goals and then give some precise terminology and explicitly point out the theoretical limitations of the testing activity. Finally, we explain testing strategies and how testing can be organized.

## 6.3.1   Goals for Testing

Program testing can be used to show the *presence* of bugs, but never to show their absence.

This famous statement by Dijkstra (in Dahl et al. [1972]) is a perfect synthesis of the goals of testing: If the results delivered by the system are different from the expected ones in just one case, this unequivocally shows that the system is incorrect; by contrast, a correct behavior of the system on a finite number of cases does not guarantee correctness in the general case. For instance, we could have built a program that behaves properly for even integer numbers, but not odd numbers. Clearly, any number of tests with even input values will fail to show the error.

This, of course, does not imply that testing is useless in verifying software. We should simply keep in mind that no absolute certainty can be gained from a pure testing activity. Then again, absolute certainty can hardly be obtained on the basis of *any* human activity. Even mathematical proofs, which are a more reliable means of guaranteeing any property than is informal reasoning, are error prone; many proofs have even been found to contain errors after *years* of usage. Thus, testing should be considered only one of the means of analyzing the behavior of a system and should be integrated with other verification techniques in order to enhance our confidence in system qualities as much as possible. We shall expand further on this point in Section 6.7.

Testing should be based on *sound and systematic techniques*, so that, after testing, we have a better understanding of the product's reliability. For instance, a natural approach, such as using randomly generated test cases, turns out to be inappropriate in many situations. In fact, consider the following program fragment:

```
read(x); read(y);
if x = y then
     z := 2;
else
     z := 0;
end if;
write(z);
```

Suppose that the programmer incorrectly wrote z := 2 instead of z := 22. If we supply the program with equal values for the variables x and y, we immediately discover the error. If x and y are, say, integers, however, and we use a random-number generator for supplying their values to the program, it is very unlikely that the condition x = y will be tested.

Testing should help *locate* errors, not just detect their presence. The result of testing should not be viewed as simply providing a Boolean answer to the question of whether the software works properly: Tests should be organized in a way that *helps isolate errors*. This information can then be used in *debugging*.

Testing should be *repeatable*; that is, tests should be arranged in such a way that repeating the same experiment—supplying the same input data to the same piece of code—produces the same results. This remark sounds fairly obvious—even more so if we compare it with some classical experimental law such as "At sea level, pure water will boil at 100 degrees centigrade, or 212 degrees Fahrenheit." Hard-to-repeat experiments, however, are not infrequent, and they are responsible for the major difficulties surrounding the debugging activity.

A major reason for the lack of repeatability in software testing is the influence of the execution environment on the semantics of erroneous programs. A typical source is the case of uninitialized variables. For instance, suppose that a piece of program contains the statement

```
if x = 0 then
    write("abnormal");
else
    write("normal");
end if;
```

and that the variable x is not initialized before this statement in the program code. Then if the language implementation does not provide any check against this type of error—which is often the case, for reasons of efficiency of execution—when the statement is executed, the contents of the physical memory cell corresponding to x will be read. In all likelihood, the cell will have an unpredictable value. Thus, in many executions of the program, the output normal will be read, but, in an absolutely unpredictable way, some execution of the same program, with the same input data, will yield the opposite result. The issue of repeatability becomes even more critical with concurrent software, as we shall see in Section 6.3.7.

Finally, testing should be *accurate*, a quality that will increase its reliability. Here, we should observe that the *accuracy* of the testing activity depends on the level of precision—and maybe even formality—of the software specifications. For instance, suppose that in a real-time system specification it has been stated that, as a consequence of input stimulus x, the system should produce output y within $\Delta t$ milliseconds. This suggests using input x as a test to check whether the appropriate output y is produced within $\Delta t$ milliseconds. But if the requirement reads "As a consequence of input stimulus x, the system should produce output y within $\Delta t$ milliseconds, no matter what other events occur in the system during this time," we must then test the system by supplying x in several different contexts, in order to check whether the response time is still acceptable in a busy system.

Furthermore, if a formula expresses a property of software outputs in a mathematical way, it will be easier to check, possibly automatically, whether the output produced exhibits that property. For instance, consider the formula

$$\{\textbf{for all } i(1 \leq i < n) \textbf{ implies } (a(i) \leq a(i+1))\}$$

which specifies that the variable array a is sorted. By checking whether a satisfies this formula after the program executes, we obtain an effective way to verify whether the program has produced a valid a.

Since it may be unclear whether the result of an execution is indeed correct (we explore this issue further in Section 6.3.4.4), verifying it against a formal specification can enhance the reliability of the testing activity.

## 6.3.2  Theoretical Foundations of Testing

In this section, we introduce some testing terminology in a precise manner and show the limitations of testing from a mathematical point of view. The terminology, however, is not standardized, so that the same terms may be used in other texts with a different meaning.

Let P be a program, and let D and R denote its input domain and its output range, respectively. That is, D is the set of all data that can correctly be supplied to P, and the results of P's executions, if any, are elements of R. Obviously, both D and R may contain (possibly unbounded) sequences of data if P contains several I/O statements, perhaps embedded within loops.

For simplicity, we assume that P behaves as a *function*—possibly partial[1]—with domain D and range R. This is quite often the case, at least for sequential programs. It is not difficult, however, to extend the basic definitions and properties to the more general case where P defines a *relation*[2] between D and R. Thus, we will denote the result of executing P on input datum d as P(d).

Let OR denote the requirement on output values of P as stated in P's specification, whether in a formal notation or not. Then, for a given d ∈ D, P is said to be *correct for* d if P(d) satisfies OR. Thus, P is correct if and only if it is correct for every d in D.

The presence of an *error* or *defect* is demonstrated by showing that P(d) is incorrect for some d—that is, that P(d) does not satisfy the output requirements. We call such a situation a *failure*—a manifest symptom of the presence of an error. We know well, however, that the presence of an error does not necessarily cause a failure. Thus, testing tries to increase the likelihood that program errors cause program failures, by selecting appropriate test cases.

A *fault* is an incorrect intermediate state that may be entered during program execution—say, a variable being assigned a value that is different from what it should be. Obviously, a failure occurs only if a fault happens during execution, and a fault occurs only if the program contains an error, but the two converse statements do not hold, in general.

A *test case* is an element d of D. A *test set* T is a finite set of test cases—that is, a finite subset of D. P is correct for T if it is correct for all elements in T. In such a case, we also say that T is *successful*[3] for P.

A test set T is said to be *ideal* if, whenever P is incorrect, there exists a d ∈ T such that P is incorrect for d. In other words, an ideal test set always shows the existence of an error in a program if an error exists. Obviously, for a correct program, any test set is ideal. Also, if T is an ideal test set and T is successful for P, then P is correct.

A *test selection criterion* C is a subset of $2^D_F$, where $2^D_F$ denotes the set of all finite subsets of D. In other words, C specifies a condition that must be satisfied by a test set. For instance, for a program whose domain D is the set of integers, C could require that test sets contain at least three elements: one negative, one positive, and one zero. A test set T *satisfies* C if it belongs to C. In general, C may be described by a suitable formula which must be satisfied by all elements of any of the subsets of D that belong to C. For example, the aforementioned requirement of C is described by the formula

$$C = \{<x_1, x_2, ..., x_n> \mid n \geq 3 \textbf{ and exists } i, j, k(x_i<0, x_j = 0, x_k > 0)\}$$

A selection criterion C is *consistent* if, for any pair of test sets $T_1$ and $T_2$, both satisfying C, $T_1$ is successful if and only if $T_2$ is. Thus, if one is provided with a consistent

---

[1] The function may be partial because, for some input data, the result is undefined (i.e., a run-time error occurs).

[2] This may happen when P is coded in a language that deals with concurrency or nondeterminism.

[3] Some authors define a test case's being successful in exactly the opposite way: A test succeeds if it causes the program to fail. (See the bibliographic notes for more explanation regarding this definition.)

criterion, there is no theoretical reason to make a specific choice of a test set among those satisfying C. Later we shall see, though, that there are practical reasons for preferring one test set over another.

A criterion C is *complete* if, whenever P is incorrect, there is an unsuccessful test set that satisfies C. Thus, were we provided with a consistent and complete criterion C, any test set T satisfying C could be used to decide P's correctness.

For instance, suppose that P is a program to sort sequences of integers and that P works properly only if the length of the sequence to be sorted is a power of two. Then a complete and consistent criterion for P would stipulate that any test contain at least one sequence whose length is not a power of two. By contrast, a criterion which requires that either all sequences in T have a length which is a power of two or that none of them have this property is complete, but not consistent.

Finally, we say that a *testing criterion* $C_1$ is *finer* than $C_2$ if, for any program P, for every test set $T_1$ satisfying $C_1$, there exists a subset of $T_1$, say, $T_2$, that satisfies $C_2$. For instance, suppose that

$C_2 = \{<x_1, x_2, x_3> | (x_1<0, x_2=0, x_3>0)\}$

and that

$C_1 = \{<x_1, x_2, ..., x_n> | n \geq 3$ **and**
$\qquad$ **exists** i, j, k, m, p$(x_i<0, x_j=0, x_k>0, x_m$ even **and** $x_p$ odd$)\}$

A test set satisfying $C_1$ is $\{-3, 0, 6\}$ which also satisfies $C_2$. Another test set satisfying $C_1$ is $\{-3, 0, 5, 8\}$, from which we can extract $\{-3, 0, 5\}$ which satisfies $C_2$.

Unfortunately, none of the preceding definitions is *effective*: We cannot derive an algorithm that states whether an object—a program, a test set, or a criterion—has the desired property.

First, consider the correctness of a program P. Suppose you may formally specify the functional requirements as a first-order formula FR (d, u), having d and u as free variables, and let P(d) be the function associated with the program. Then the correctness of P may be formally stated as

**for all** d **in** D, u **in** R (u = P(d) **implies** FR (d, u))

This statement, however, cannot be decided, since doing so would mean that we would have to decide the truth of any first-order formula—an undecidable problem. Second, in some cases, it might even be impossible to decide whether a value d is in a test set T, depending on how T is defined—another well-known undecidable problem. Thus, it is impossible to decide whether a test is ideal, whether a criterion is consistent or complete, etc. These are in the long list of major program properties such as correctness, termination, and equivalence that are undecidable.

Furthermore, we shall see next that many criteria used in practice are themselves undecidable; that is, it is not decidable whether a given test set satisfies them or even whether there exists a test set that satisfies them. As always with undecidable problems, this means that full mechanization is not possible, and our approach to verification must be based on common sense and ingenuity. In practice, mechanical support tools can provide clerical help, but they require human interaction at some critical points.

The next section proposes and evaluates some possible criteria for the selection of test sets.

### Exercise

---

**6.2**    We say that $C_1$ is *more reliable* than $C_2$ if, whenever a program P is incorrect, it cannot happen that a test set $T_2$ satisfying $C_2$ causes P's failure whereas $T_1$ satisfying $C_1$ does not. Show that it is not the case that if $C_1$ is *finer* than $C_2$, then $C_1$ is *more reliable* than $C_2$. Give a condition that does guarantee such an implication.

---

## 6.3.3    Empirical Testing Principles

We observed that, in general, the only testing of any system that can provide absolute certainty about the correctness of system behavior is *exhaustive testing*—that is, testing the system under all possible circumstances. Unfortunately, such testing can never be performed in practice. Thus, we need testing *strategies*—some criteria for selecting significant test cases. The notion of the *significance* of a test set, however, cannot be formalized, but it is an important intuitive notion, being an empirical approximation of the concept of an ideal test set.

A *significant* test case is a test case that has a high potential for uncovering the presence of an error. Thus, the successful execution of a significant test case increases our confidence in the correctness of a program. Intuitively, rather than running a large number of test cases, our goal in testing should be to run a sufficient number of significant test cases. If a significant test set $T_1$ is a superset of another significant test set $T_2$, we can certainly rely more on $T_1$ than on $T_2$. On the other hand, since testing is costly, we must limit the number of possible experiments.

## Example 6.3

This simple example shows that the number of test cases in a test set does not necessarily contribute to the significance of the set. Suppose you have written the following wrong program fragment to compute the greater of two numbers:

```
if x > y then
    max := x;
else
    max := x;
end if;
```

In this case, the test set {x = 3, y = 2; x = 2, y = 3} is able to detect the error, whereas {x = 3, y = 2; x = 4, y = 3; x = 5, y = 1} is not, although it contains more test cases.    ■

In spite of the theoretical limitations emphasized in the previous section, testing criteria are needed in practice to define significant test sets. A testing criterion attempts to group elements of the input domain into classes such that the elements of a given class are expected to behave in exactly the same way. That way, we can choose a single test case as representative of each class. If the classes $D_i$ are such that $\cup D_i = D$, we say that the testing criterion satisfies the *complete coverage principle*. We will see that many well-known practical testing criteria satisfy this principle.

## Example 6.4

Suppose you have to build a program to compute the factorial of any number. The specification of the program reads as follows:

> If the input value n is < 0, then an appropriate error message must be printed. If 0 ≤ n < 20, then the exact value of n! must be printed. If 20 ≤ n ≤ 200, then an approximate value of n! must be printed in floating-point format (e.g., using some approximate method of numerical calculus). The admissible error is 0.1% of the exact value. Finally, if n > 200, the input *can* be rejected by printing an appropriate error message.

In this case, it is quite natural to divide the input domain into the classes {n < 0}, {0 ≤ n < 20}, {20 ≤ n ≤ 200}, and {n > 200} and to use test sets containing one element from each class. Suppose that the results are correct for the data belonging to one test set (e.g., {-10, 5, 175}). Then the assertion that the program will behave correctly for any other value is just a reasonable expectation, not the truth!    ■

If we divide the input domain into disjoint classes $D_i$ such that $D_i \cap D_j = \emptyset$ for $i \neq j$ (i.e., if the classes constitute a *partition* of D), then there is no particular reason to choose one element over another as representative of a class. The classes of Example 6.4 are an example of a partition. If the classes are not disjoint, however, we have the possibility of choosing representatives to minimize the number of test cases. For example, if $D_i \cap D_j \neq \emptyset$, a test case in $D_i \cap D_j$ exercises both $D_i$ and $D_j$.

For instance, consider the following testing criterion: The program must be tested with classes $D_1$, $D_2$, and $D_3$ of values for x, where

```
D₁ = {dᵢ|dᵢ mod 2 = 0}
D₂ = {dᵢ|dᵢ <= 0}
D₃ = {dᵢ|dᵢ mod 2 ≠ 0}
```

Here, since $D_1 \cap D_2 \neq \emptyset$ and $D_2 \cap D_3 \neq \emptyset$, we can choose just two test cases to exercise the program and still satisfy the complete-coverage principle. For instance, the test set {x = 48; x = -37} would be acceptable.

The complete-coverage principle is subject to many interpretations, including several trivial ones. At one extreme, we could insist that each class consist of a single element; this would lead to exhaustive testing, which we have already ruled out as infeasible. At the other extreme, we could group all input data into just one class, which would lead to trying the system in just one case. Thus, we may evaluate the goodness of a testing criterion on the basis of how significant the representatives of the classes obtained by its decomposition are. The application of the principle to produce significant tests is quite a challenging task.

Ideally, the complete-coverage principle should help approximate consistent and complete criteria in the following way: If the input domain D is decomposed into several subsets $D_i$, then a test set may be chosen that contains at least one representative from each $D_i$, with the goal that if a test set $T_1$ differs from $T_2$ only with respect to which representative is chosen from each set $D_i$, then the results of test sets $T_1$ and $T_2$ are equivalent (in terms of failure or success). In such a case, the partition would provide a consistent criterion. On the other hand, completeness would be achieved if, in case the program contains an error, there is at least one $D_i$ such that any representative of $D_i$ exposes the error. Although we know from the previous section that, in general, it is impossible to find such a decomposition in an automatic way, common sense and insight can help in finding subsets that exhibit some degree of consistency and completeness.

In Example 6.3, any test set that causes the execution of both branches of the **if-then-else** statement would most likely show the error in the program fragment, no matter which data are selected from the classes $\{x > y\}$ and $\{x \le y\}$. As an exercise, the reader is invited to find the exceptions.

Thus, a careful selection of test cases, with the goal of satisfying the complete-coverage principle, can in some sense approximate consistent and complete criteria. We can increase the reliability of such criteria by choosing more than one element from each class. For example, if we feel that a particular partition is "rather" consistent and complete, but that there could be some exceptions, we could improve the method by generating several cases—perhaps randomly—from the same class.

It turns out that this general principle can be applied in many different—and sometimes complementary—ways. Next, we review how the testing activity can be organized in practice and how we can describe various empirical approaches to the determination of significant test sets in light of the complete-coverage principle. We do so by first distinguishing between *testing in the small* and *testing in the large*. Testing in the small addresses the issue of testing individual software components. Testing in the large, by contrast, addresses the issue of decomposing and organizing the testing activity according to the modular structure of complex programs. We discuss testing in the small in Section 6.3.4 and testing in the large in Section 6.3.5.

## 6.3.4   Testing in the Small

Testing in the small addresses the testing of individual modules. There are two main approaches: *white-box testing* and *black-box testing*. Testing a piece of software as a black box means operating the software without relying on any knowledge of the way it has been designed and coded. Test sets are developed and their results evaluated solely on the basis of the specification. By contrast, testing software as a white box means using information about the internal structure of the software and perhaps even ignoring its specification. The choice of partitioning possible test cases for the program of Example 6.3 into the classes $\{x > y\}$ and $\{x \le y\}$ is an example of white-box testing, and Example 6.4 is an instance of black-box testing.

Intuitively, both strategies are useful and somewhat complementary. White-box testing tests what the program *does*, while black-box testing tests what it is *supposed to do*. For this reason, we may refer to black-box testing as specification-based testing and to white-box testing as implementation-based testing. Thus, they can both increase our level of confidence in the reliability of the component. The next two subsections describe the two approaches in some detail.

### 6.3.4.1 *White-Box Testing*

White-box testing is also called structural testing, because it uses the internal structure of the program to derive the test data. Example 6.5 illustrates the concept. The first and simplest white-box testing strategy suggests that we should try to ensure that our test cases exercise all program statements at least once. This is called the statement-coverage criterion and is discussed next.

## Example 6.5

Consider the following well-known algorithm of Euclid:

```
begin
    read(x); read(y);
    while x ≠ y loop
        if x > y then
            x := x - y;
        else
            y := y - x;
        end if;
    end loop;
    gcd := x;
end;
```

This program contains a sequence of statements. We want to ensure that all of the statements are executed. First, we need to ensure that the **while** loop is executed at least once. Then, inside the loop, we need to ensure that both the statement x := x - y; and the statement y := y - x; are executed. A possible test set that exercises all the statements in the program is {<x = 3, y = 3> , <x = 4, y = 3> , <x = 3, y = 4>}.    ∎

**Statement Coverage**    Intuitively, the statement-coverage criterion is based on the observation that an error cannot be discovered if the parts of the program containing the error and generating the failure are not executed; thus, we should strive for complete coverage of statements.

In block-structured languages, where statements may be part of more complex statements, we must be precise about what we mean by a *statement*. A natural assumption is to refer to the BNF syntactic definition of programming languages and to assume as an *elementary statement* any statement that is derived from the <statement> nonterminal without producing any recursive occurrence of the same nonterminal. Thus, in a conventional block-structured language, assignment statements, I/O statements, and procedure calls are elementary statements. With this assumption, the criterion can be stated as follows:

> **STATEMENT-COVERAGE CRITERION**. Select a test set T such that, by executing P for each d in T, each elementary statement of P is executed at least once.

In general, the same input datum causes the execution of many statements. Thus, we are left with the problem of trying to minimize the number of test cases while still ensuring the execution of all statements. For instance, consider the following program fragment:

```
read(x); read(y);
if x > 0 then
      write("1");
else
      write("2");
end if;
if y > 0 then
      write("3");
else
      write("4");
end if;
```

Let us denote by $I_1, I_2, W_1, W_2, W_3$, and $W_4$, the first and second **if** statements and the write("1"), write("2"), write("3"), and write("4"), statements, respectively. Also, let $D_i$ denote the class of input values that cause execution of $W_i$, for $i = 1, ..., 4$. Clearly, $D_1 = \{x > 0\}$, $D_2 = \{x \leq 0\}$, $D_3 = \{y > 0\}$, and $D_4 = \{y \leq 0\}$. Thus, if a representative is chosen from each of the classes, we are guaranteed that all of $W_1, W_2, W_3$, and $W_4$ are executed at least once.

Therefore, we might choose the following test set:

```
{<x = 2, y = 3>, <x = - 13, y = 51>, <x = 97, y = 17>, <x = - 1, y = - 1>}
```

This test set, however, is not minimal with respect to the criterion, since every input datum belongs to two classes. Thus, we may reduce the number of test cases to two, for example, by selecting the following representatives:

```
{<x = - 13, y = 51>, <x = 2, y = - 3>}
```

A weakness of the statement-coverage criterion is illustrated by the following fragment:

```
if x < 0 then
      x := -x;
end if;
z := x;
```

Choosing a test set such that, at the beginning of execution of the fragment, x is negative, would result in the execution of all statements of the fragment. Not exercising the case $x \geq 0$, however, is in some sense a lack of completeness. In fact, we could see the fragment as a short notation for

```
if x < 0 then
      x := -x;
else
      null;
end if;
z := x;
```

In this formulation, the statement-coverage criterion would require executing even the **null** statement, and the experiment could show an error. Thus, different syntactic conventions could lead to different instantiations of the same criterion. We shall deal with this problem later.

**Edge Coverage**   The complete-coverage principle may also be applied to criteria on the basis of the program structure, described by a graphical representation of the program control flow. Assume again the case of a simple block-structured language.

For any program fragment P, its *control flow graph* $G_p$ is built inductively in the following way:

1. For each I/O, assignment, or procedure call statement, a graph of the type of Figure 6.1(a) is built. The graph has an edge, representing the statement.[4] The edge connects two nodes that represent entry into, and exit from, the statement. If needed, a unique label, labeling both the statement and the edge of the graph, may be used to make the correspondence between edges and statements explicit.

2. Let $S_1$ and $S_2$ denote two statements and $G_1$ and $G_2$ denote their corresponding graphs. Then

   - The graph of Figure 6.1(b) is associated with the statement

     ```
     if cond then
             S₁;
     else
             S₂;
     end if;
     ```

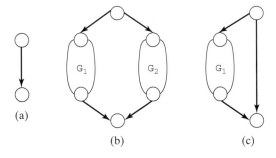

(a)

(b)

(c)

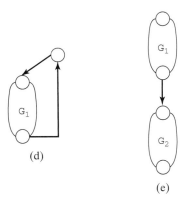

(d)

(e)

**FIGURE 6.1**

Construction of the control-flow graph of a program.
**(a)** Graph of an I/O, assignment, or procedure call statement.
**(b)** Graph of **if-then-else** statement.
**(c)** Graph of **if-then** statement.
**(d)** Graph of **while** loop.
**(e)** Graph of two sequential statements.

---

[4] More often, the control flow graph is defined in the literature by representing statements with nodes.

- The graph of Figure 6.1(c) is associated with the statement

```
if cond then
        S₁;
end if;
```

- The graph of Figure 6.1(d) is associated with the statement

```
while cond loop
        S₁;
end loop;
```

- The graph of Figure 6.1(e) is associated with the statement

```
S₁;

S₂;
```

Since we are interested in the flow of control in a program, we may consider a sequence of edges of the type of Figure 6.2, with no other edges leading to any node $n_2, \ldots, n_{k-1}$, or leaving any of them, as equivalent to a single edge going from $n_1$ to $n_k$. This construction may thus be used to simplify a control flow graph. Figure 6.3 shows the control flow graph of Euclid's algorithm given in Example 6.5.

Once we have associated a control flow graph with a program fragment, we can state the following criterion:

**EDGE-COVERAGE CRITERION.** Select a test set T such that, by executing P for each d in T, each edge of P's control flow graph is traversed at least once.

We can see that the test sets derived by the edge-coverage criterion exercise all conditions that govern the control flow of the program, in the sense that the criterion requires test cases which make each condition generate both true and false values (at different times, of course). The reader might prove that, in general, the edge-coverage criterion produces different results from, and is finer than, the statement-coverage criterion. As an exercise, the reader should also verify that the test we derived for Euclid's algorithm in Example 6.5 actually provides edge coverage.

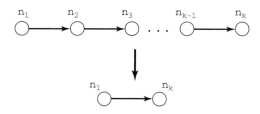

FIGURE 6.2

Equivalent portions of control flow graphs.

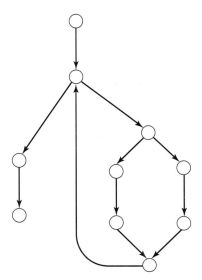

FIGURE 6.3

Control flow graph of Euclid's
algorithm coded in Example 6.5.

**Condition Coverage**   The edge-coverage criterion can be further strengthened to make it more likely to expose errors. Consider the following fragment, which searches for an element within a table (implemented as an array of items):

```
found := false; counter := 1;
while (not found) and counter < number_of_items loop
    if table(counter) = desired_element then
        found := true;
    end if;
    counter := counter + 1;
end loop;
if found then
    write("the desired element exists in the table");
else
    write("the desired element does not exist in the table");
end if;
```

This code contains a trivial and common error: "<" appears instead of "≤" in the loop condition. Let us choose the following test sets:

1. A table with no items (i.e., number_of_items = 0); this causes execution of the fragment without any iteration of the body of the loop.
2. A table with three items, the second being the desired one; this causes execution of the body of the loop twice, the first time without executing the **then** branch, the second time executing it. Notice that both branches of the final **if-then-else** statement are executed, so that the edge-coverage criterion is fulfilled.

The error is not discovered by the test set. Closer inspection of the program shows that the loop condition has two parts: "**not** found" and "counter < number_of_items". The two test cases we provided exercised the two possible values of the first part (one for each iteration), but only one of the possible outcomes of the second. A stricter criterion, requiring that both possible values of the second constituent of the condition be exercised, would have revealed the error.

In general, a compound Boolean expression may be true or false, depending on the values of its constituent expressions. For example, if C is a compound Boolean expression written as the conjunction or disjunction of several elementary clauses (i.e., C is of the type $c_1$ **and** $c_2$ **or** $c_3$..., with $c_i$ being either an atomic formula[5] or its negation), then these atomic formulas are called *constituents*, and their values affect the value of C. Often, as in the example, the different values taken by each individual constituent expression characterize significant test cases.

We can thus derive a new testing criterion that is finer than the edge-coverage criterion:

> **CONDITION-COVERAGE CRITERION**. Select a test set T such that, by executing P for each element in T, each edge of P's control flow graph is traversed, and all possible values of the constituents of compound conditions are exercised at least once.

Another way of looking at this situation is to observe that a statement such as

```
if c₁ and c₂ then
      Sₜ;
else
      S_f;
end if;
```

is equivalent to

```
if c₁ then
      if c₂ then
         Sₜ;
      else
         S_f;
      end if;
else
      S_f;
end if;
```

If one applies the edge-coverage criterion to the second form, one actually generates test sets that exercise all edges of the control flow graph and all possible values of atomic conditions. Thus, the condition-coverage criterion enhances the edge-coverage criterion by making explicit the edges that might be "hidden" in the control flow graph of the program.

The idea of exercising the various values of the constituents of the conditions has given rise to other criteria; the reader can find some interesting ones in Exercises 6.5 and 6.6.

---

[5] An atomic formula consists of a relational expression (i.e., a relational operator, such as = , ≠, or ≤ , applied to arithmetic expressions) or a Boolean variable.

**Path Coverage**    The next example shows that the edge-coverage criterion may fail to identify significant test cases.

## Example 6.6

In the program fragment

```
if x ≠ 0 then
     y := 5;
else
     z := z − x;
end if;
if z > 1 then
     z := z/x;
else
     z := 0;
end if;
```

the test set $\{<x = 0, z = 1>, <x = 1, z = 3>\}$ causes the execution of all edges, but fails to expose the risk of a division by zero. Such a risk would be uncovered by the test set $\{<x = 0, z = 3>, <x = 1, z = 1>\}$, which would exercise other possible flows of control through the fragment.    ■

Example 6.6 suggests that traversing single edges may not be enough to ensure the traversal of all important flows of execution. A natural extension would therefore lead to the following new testing criterion:

> **PATH-COVERAGE CRITERION**. Select a test set T such that, by executing P for each d in T, all paths leading from the initial to the final node of P's control flow graph are traversed.

Clearly, this new criterion is finer than the edge-coverage criterion. In the Example 6.6, the path consisting of the **else-then** branches of the two **if** statements would have shown the error. Unfortunately, in the general case, the number of possible execution paths, even in simple programs, is very large—too large, in practice, if not infinite. Traversing all control paths is almost as infeasible as exercising all possible input data. Thus, the path-coverage criterion turns out to be impractical in almost all cases.

The criterion, however, can be kept as a "reference guide" in order to determine a few critical paths, among the many possible ones, to be exercised. For instance, going back to the earlier program fragment that searches for an element within a table, we see that there is some intuitive evidence that an important sample of execution paths could be the following:

- Skipping the loop (the table is empty);
- Executing the loop once or twice and then finding the desired element;
- Searching the entire table without finding the desired element.

More generally, we could suggest the following empirical guideline for testing loops: Look for conditions that execute loops

1. zero times (or a minimum number of times in special cases, such as repeat-until loops);
2. a maximum number of times;
3. an average number of times (according to some statistical criterion).

Furthermore, when dealing with complex combinations of alternatives (several **if** or **case** statements), one should try to combine paths as much as possible. The major source of complexity is nested loops.

Before closing this section, we wish to discuss an important point. After we have chosen a coverage criterion (say, statement coverage or edge coverage), we get to the point of determining actual input values that would fulfill the criterion. For instance, consider the following fragment, and suppose we are trying to follow the statement-coverage criterion:[6]

```
read(x);
z := 2 * x;
if z = 4 then
      statement …
```

Here, it is obvious that if we want to execute the `statement`, we need to supply the value 2 to the `read` statement. In the following fragment, however, there is no input value that will cause the execution of `statement`.

```
if x > 0 then
      if x < 0 then
          statement …
```

This example shows that coverage of *all* statements in a program may be impossible if the program contains unreachable statements. Of course, one may still reformulate the criterion by requiring that *all reachable statements* be covered at least once by test data. In the general case, however, it is not decidable whether suitable input data exist that guarantee the execution of some given statement in a given program (i.e., whether some given statement is reachable). Consequently, the criterion is not effective.

Consequently, if we try to enforce the testing policy that "100% of statement coverage must be achieved," not only may the goal be unachievable, but also, we cannot decide algorithmically whether the 100% coverage was not reached because we were unable (or too lazy) to find test cases or because of the presence of unreachable statements.

This is yet another case where the theory of testing reveals unsolvable problems: Whatever coverage criterion we try to fulfill, we face problems that cannot be solved in a purely mechanical fashion, but rather require human intervention at some point. More will be said on this topic in Section 6.5.3 and in Chapter 9, where we will also discuss tools that help evaluate the thoroughness of testing by computing the percentage

---

[6] A similar reasoning applies to any other criterion.

of coverage reached, on the basis of some coverage criterion. Such percentages can be used to "verify" the testing activity.

Finally, we mention that structural or white-box testing can catch only errors of "commission" but not errors of "omission." That is, if the code omits the implementation of some part of the specification, the test cases derived from the code will also ignore that part of the specification. Test cases derived from specifications, on the other hand, can handle such errors of omission. In the next section, we discuss this class of testing strategies.

## Exercises

**6.3**    Consider the following two program fragments:

a.
```
found := false; counter := 1;
while (not found) and counter < number_of_items loop
    if table(counter) = desired_element then
        found := true;
    end if;
    counter := counter + 1;
end loop;
if found then
    write("the desired element exists in the table");
else
    write("the desired element does not exist in the table");
end if;
```

b.
```
found := false; counter := 1;
while (not found) and counter < number_of_items loop
    found := table(counter) = desired_element;
    counter := counter + 1;
end loop;
if found then
    write("the desired element exists in the table");
else
    write("the desired element does not exist in the table");
end if;
```

State whether the edge-coverage criterion may lead to different test sets in the two cases.

**6.4**    Let $\{c_i\}$ denote the set of all Boolean conditions used in a program P to govern the flow of execution. (For simplicity, we assume that control is driven only by Boolean conditions; for instance, **case** statements of Pascal are ruled out.) The edge-coverage criterion requires that a test set $\{d_j\}$ must be such that each $c_i$ is made true and false by some $d_j$ at least once.

For each $c_i$, let $D_i$ and $\overline{D}_i$ denote, respectively, the sets of input data that cause $c_i$ to be true and false during P's execution. Then the edge-coverage criterion is satisfied by test sets T that must contain at least one element of $D_i$ and one element of $\overline{D}_i$ for each $c_i$. This does not define a partitioning of D, however, Why?

As a consequence, there may be different test sets, with different cardinalities, satisfying the edge-coverage criterion. Thus, the problem arises of finding minimal test sets that satisfy the criterion. For the following fragments, find minimal test sets compatible with the edge-coverage criterion:

*a.*    **if** x > z **then**
        y := 3;
     **else**
        y := 2;
     **end if**;
     **if** x > z + 1 **then**
        w := 3;
     **else**
        w := 2;
     **end if**;

*b.*    **if** x > z **then**
        y := 3;
     **else**
        y := 2;
     **end if**;
     **if** a > b **then**
        w := 3;
     **else**
        w := 2;
     **end if**;

*c.*    **if** x > z **then**
        y := 3;
     **else**
        x := z + 2;
     **end if**;
     **if** x > z + 1 **then**
        w := 3;
     **else**
        w := 2;
     **end if**;

**6.5**    Let $\{c_i\}$ be defined as in Exercise 6.4. Consider the following *truth-assignment criterion*: Let $<tr_1, ..., tr_n>$ denote any truth assignment to conditions $\{c_i\}$; that is, $<tr_1, ..., tr_n>$ is an n-tuple of Boolean values to be assigned to each condition of P. For any such assignment, let $D_r$ denote the set of values of D that make all $c_i$'s true or false according to the assignment.

Show that $\{D_r\}$ is a partitioning of D. Show that the truth-assignment criterion is finer than the edge-coverage criterion.

**6.6**    Let $\{c_i\}$ be defined as in Exercise 6.4. The *multiple-condition-coverage criterion* can be defined as follows: Each test set must make all conditions $c_i$ true and false in all possible ways, based on the values of their constituents. For instance, if $c_i$ is $c_{i1}$ **and** $c_{i2}$, then we must generate four cases that would make $c_{i1}$ true and $c_{i2}$ true, $c_{i1}$ false and $c_{i2}$ true, etc.

Give (possibly minimal) test sets satisfying the multiple-condition-coverage criterion for the following program fragment:

```
if x > z and x > 3 then
     a := 1;
else
     a := 2;
end if;
if a > b or z < x then
     w := 1;
else
     z := x;
end if;
```

Clearly, the multiple-condition-coverage criterion is finer than the edge-coverage criterion. Which is finer, the multiple-condition-coverage criterion or the truth-assignment criterion? Which is finer, the multiple-condition-coverage criterion or the condition-coverage criterion?

**6.7**    Would the truth assignment criterion guarantee the discovery of the error in Example 6.6?

**6.8**    Compute the maximum number of possible execution paths for the two programs of Exercise 6.3 as a function of the size of the table.

### 6.3.4.2 Black-Box Testing

Black-box testing, also called functional testing, is based on the definition of what a (piece of) program is intended to do (i.e., it is based on the program's specification, rather than on its structure). We can apply the complete-coverage principle to black-box testing. Suppose that the specification of a program reads as follows:

> The program receives as input a record describing an invoice. (A detailed description of the format of the record is given.) The invoice must be inserted into a file of invoices that is sorted by date. The invoice must be inserted in the appropriate position: If other invoices exist in the file with the same date, then the invoice should be inserted after the last one. Also, some consistency checks must be performed: The program should verify whether the customer is already in a corresponding file of customers, whether the customer's data in the two files match, etc.

The following is an intuitive way to test this program:

1. Provide an invoice whose date is the current date.
2. Provide an invoice whose date is before the current date. (In some systems, this provision could be forbidden by law, depending on the country in which the system is operated.) This case, in turn, can be split into the two following subcases:

   Provide an invoice whose date is the same as that of some existing invoice.
   Provide an invoice whose date does not exist in any previously recorded invoice.

3. Provide several incorrect invoices, checking different types of inconsistencies.

This informal procedure is the result of decomposing the specifications into a set of relevant classes and analyzing the behavior of the program in at least one case for each class.

Here, again, we see a major motivation for being rigorous, and possibly even formal, in writing specifications: The more precisely the operating conditions of the system and the expected results are defined, the more precisely can one categorize input data and compare the observed results against the expected ones. Furthermore, when specifications are given in a formal notation, test sets could even be derived (semi) automatically by tools that apply the very same philosophy and technique as in the case of white-box testing.

Next, we present a few examples of black-box testing derived from formal specifications. First, we show how to use logic specifications as illustrated in Chapter 5 to produce test cases in a functional style. Next, we present a few more cases of black-box testing, perhaps more used in practice, that are suitable for more specialized application domains: *syntax-driven testing*, which is applicable to programs whose input is formally described by a grammar; *decision table-based testing*, which is applicable whenever a specification is described by a decision table; and the *cause-effect graphs* technique.

**Testing Driven by Logic Specifications**    Let us go back to the just-discussed specifications stating requirements on the insertion of an invoice record into a file. As a first step, we need to restate the informal specification in a formal way. We do this by adopting the logical notation introduced in Section 5.6.2:

- Let x, z be variables of type `invoice`, (i.e., tuples `<x.customer, x.amount, x.date, …>`, `<z.customer, z.amount, z.date, …>`, where the types of fields `customer`, `amount`, etc., are given.

- Let `current_date` denote a variable of type `date` storing the value of the day when the operation is executed.
- Let `f` be a variable of type `invoice_file` (i.e., a sequence of elements of type `invoice`). As usual, `f(i)` will denote the *i*th element of `f`.
- We also assume the existence of other files of types `customer_file`, ....
- Given a generic record `x` and a file `f` of such records (with no repeated elements), let `pos` be a function that returns the position `i` of `x` in `f`. Formally, `pos` satisfies the axiom

  `pos(x,f) = i ≡ f(i) = x`

- We also define the predicate `sorted_by_date`, which takes as argument a variable of type `invoice_file` and satisfies the axiom

  ```
  sorted_by_date(y)  ≡
        forall i, j in Integers (i < j implies f(i).date ≤ f(j).date
  ```

- Finally, let `result` and `warning` denote two Boolean variables used to signal the success of the insertion operation and the occurrence of some anomaly (not necessarily implying an error), respectively.

Once these definitions are given, the requirements of the insertion operation can be expressed through a pair of pre- and postconditions such as the following:

```
for all x in Invoices, f in Invoice_Files
{sorted_by_date(f) and not exist j, k (j ≠ k and f(j) =f(k)}
insert(x, f)
{sorted_by_date(f) and
for all k,z (old_f(k) = z implies exists j (f(j)=z)) and
for all k,z (f(k) = z and z ≠ x) implies exists j (old_f(j) = z) and
exists j (f(j).date = x. date and f(j) ≠ x) implies
        j < pos(x, f) and
result ≡
        x.customer belongs_to customer_file
        /*i.e., exists j (x.customer = customer_file(j))*/ and
        ...
and
warning ≡
        (x belongs_to old_f or
        x.date < current_date or
        ....)
```

Once we have formalized requirements such as those just set forth, we can use the specification "code" in much the same way as we did for white-box testing. For instance, we can see the preceding postcondition as the conjunction of several clauses, each characterized by some condition. A formulation that makes these conditions more explicit is as follows:

```
TRUE implies
        sorted_by_date(f) and
        for all k,z old_f(k)=z implies exists j (f(j) = z) and
        for all k,z (f(k)=z and z ≠ x) implies exists j (old_f(j) = z)
and
```

```
(x.customer belongs_to customer_file
      /*i.e., exists j (x.customer = customer_file(j))*/ and
      …)
implies result
and
not (x.customer belongs_to customer_file and
      …)
implies not result
and
x belongs_to old_y implies warning
and
x.date < current_date implies warning
and
…
```

Thus, we can apply the condition-coverage criterion to the foregoing conjunction, producing at least one test case for each condition. Doing so yields the following indications for a set of possible test cases:

- Any test case can be used to verify that the file which is produced contains all and only previous invoices plus the new one and is sorted.
- We need at least one test case with an invoice whose field customer exists in the customer_file, and one test case with an invoice whose field customer does not exist in such file.
- We need at least one test case with an invoice whose field date is the same as that of an already existing invoice, and one test case with an invoice whose field date is not that of an already existing invoice.

It is easy to verify that the test set so derived is a reformulation—yet more complete and obtained in a more systematic way—of the suggestions we derived from the informal specifications given originally.

**Syntax-Driven Testing**   A classical example of the application of formal specifications to drive testing can be seen in compiler verification. In this case, we have a complete formal specification of the syntax of the language, namely, its BNF or some equivalent definition. The specification can be used to generate test sets (i.e., sample programs to be compiled) in several ways. For instance, a simple criterion is to supply a set of test programs to the compiler such that each syntactic production of the BNF is applied at least once in some program. This criterion is called syntax-driven testing.

## Example 6.7

Suppose your program is an interpreter of simple arithmetic expressions defined by the following BNF grammar:

```
<expression> ::= <expression> + <term>|<expression> - <term> | <term>
<term> ::= <term> * <factor> | <term> / <factor> | <factor>
<factor> ::= ident | (<expression>)
```

A way to do syntax-driven testing is to take any rule of the grammar, say, `<term> ::= <term> * <factor>`, and generate a string, starting from the grammar's axiom `<expression>` so that the rule is applied. This means that the complete-coverage principle is applied here in such a way that all of the rules of grammar are covered by at least one test case. For example, we might choose the following derivation:

`<expression>` ⇒ `<expression> + <term>` ⇒ `<expression> + <term> * <factor>`

We may then complete the generation in any way (e.g., by generating the shortest possible derivation):

`<expression> + <term> * <factor>` ⇒ `<term> + <term> * <factor>` ⇒ …
⇒ `<factor> + <factor> * <factor>` ⇒ … ⇒ `ident + ident * ident`

This procedure generates a test case for each rule of the grammar. Some rules, however, are exercised as a consequence of trying to exercise another rule. For example, in the previous derivation, we exercised the following additional rules:

```
<expression> ::= <expression> + <term>
<term> ::= <factor>
<factor> ::= <ident>
```

We can therefore reduce the number of test cases by keeping track of the rules that have already been exercised by previous test cases. ■

Example 6.7 shows that there are many ways of generating tests based on a grammar. For example, we chose to generate the shortest possible derivation that exercises each rule, but other strategies are also possible. In general, the syntax of most classical ALGOL-like languages is such that we can even generate a single program that will exercise all statements of the language. That is, the whole test set could consist of one rather long, single test case.

Thus, the question arises as to what criteria should be followed to generate the test set. The notion of a *minimal test set* should be considered with some care in the case of syntax-driven testing. In fact, we usually refer to it by comparing the cardinalities of two test sets $T_1$ and $T_2$. But should we consider a test set $T_1$ consisting of one program of 1,000 characters preferable to a test set $T_2$ consisting of two programs of 100 characters each? Perhaps the *sum* of the lengths of the programs contained in the test set would be a better measure.

### Exercises

**6.9** Define a simple Pascal-like language by means of a BNF grammar. Then find one or more test sets that satisfy the syntax-driven testing criterion. Is it possible to have a test set consisting of just one program?

**6.10** Explain how syntax-directed techniques can be applied to programs that are not language processors.

**Decision Table-Based Testing** Decision tables are a simple formalism to describe how different combinations of inputs may generate different outputs. Decision tables find practical use particularly in data-processing applications. Their tabular form makes them easy to understand and supports a systematic derivation of tests. We introduce decision tables here through an example.

## Example 6.8

Consider the following informal specification for a word processor:

> The word processor may present portions of text in three different formats: plain text (p), boldface (b), and italics (i). The following commands may be applied to each portion of text: make text plain (P), make text boldface (B), make text italic (I), emphasize (E), and superemphasize (SE). Commands are available to dynamically set E to mean either B or I. (We denote such commands as E = B and E = I, respectively.) Similarly, SE can be dynamically set to mean B (command SE = B), I (command SE = I), or B and I (command SE = B + I).

The decision table corresponding to the specification is given in Table 6.1. The rows of the table describe conditions (here, the commands given to the word processor); columns represent rules (i.e., the actions that are the result of exercising the conditions). For example, the rule represented by the leftmost column of the table shows that condition P generates output p. (To avoid cluttering the table with too many entries, we show only true conditions, marked with the letter X.)

One can generate test cases naturally on the basis of the decision table, trying to apply the complete-coverage criterion so that each column of the table is exercised by at least one test. This "blind" application of the principle, however, may be too expensive in terms of the number of experiments to be carried out, because of the exponen-

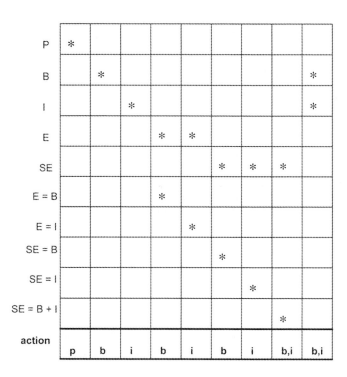

|          |   |   |   |   |   |   |   |     |     |
|----------|---|---|---|---|---|---|---|-----|-----|
| P        | * |   |   |   |   |   |   |     |     |
| B        |   | * |   |   |   |   |   |     | *   |
| I        |   |   | * |   |   |   |   |     | *   |
| E        |   |   |   | * | * |   |   |     |     |
| SE       |   |   |   |   |   | * | * | *   |     |
| E = B    |   |   |   | * |   |   |   |     |     |
| E = I    |   |   |   |   | * |   |   |     |     |
| SE = B   |   |   |   |   |   | * |   |     |     |
| SE = I   |   |   |   |   |   |   | * |     |     |
| SE = B + I |  |   |   |   |   |   |   | *   |     |
| **action** | p | b | i | b | i | b | i | b,i | b,i |

**TABLE 6.1**

Decision table specifying the word processor of Example 6.8.

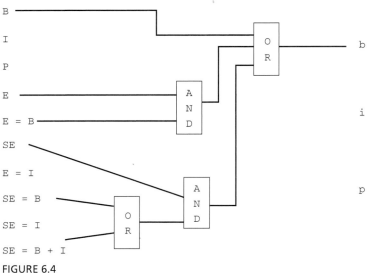

**FIGURE 6.4**

Partial and-or graph for a word processor.

tial growth in the number of test cases with respect to the number of conditions. In fact, in general, the number of columns can go up to $2^n$, where n is the number of conditions. Thus, we may need some technique to select a *significant subset* of all possible input classes. A way to tackle this problem is discussed in the next section.  ∎

**The Cause-Effect Graph Technique**    The cause-effect graph technique is based on a formal way of structuring complex input-output specifications called cause-effect graphing. To apply cause-effect graphing, one must first transform the specification of inputs and outputs into Boolean values and the transformation performed by the program into a Boolean function. We describe the technique in the next example.

## Example 6.9

Consider the informal specification for a word processor given in Example 6.8. An input command in {B, I, P, E, SE, E = B, E = I, SE = B, SE = 1, SE=B+I} can be represented by a 10-tuple of Booleans (called *causes*). For example, <true, false, false, false, false, false, false, false, false, false> represents command B, and <false, false, false, true, false, true, false, false, false, false> represents E = B and E. The same technique obviously applies to outputs, called *effects*. In our example, an output is an element in {b, i, p, }; for instance, <false, false, true> denotes a plain text output.

Once both the input and the output domains are restated in terms of Booleans representing causes and effects, the function is also restated as a Boolean function. In particular, it is synthesized as a combination of the logical operators **not, and,** and **or** and is graphically represented by using any one of the well-known techniques such as the and-or-graph. Figure 6.4 gives a pictorial representation of how a boldface output may be obtained; the reader should complete the graph as an exercise.

Suppose now that the informal requirements also specify the following constraints:

Both B and I exclude P (e. g., one cannot ask for both plain text and italics for the same portion of text). E and SE are mutually exclusive.

Since B and P are mutually exclusive, the tuple `<true, false, true, ... >` would not describe valid input commands, because it would request both bold and plain text. The following notation may be used to specify *constraints*:

- A dotted connection labeled *e* of the type of Figure 6.5 joining the logical variables a, b, and c states that *at most one* among a, b, and c may be true.
- A dotted connection labeled *i* states that at least one of the arguments a, b, and c must be true.
- A dotted connection labeled *o* states that one and only one of a, b, and c must be true.
- A dotted directed connection from a to b labeled *r* states that a *requires* b— that is, a **implies** b.
- A dotted directed connection from a to b labeled *m* states that a *masks* b— that is, a **implies not** b.

Similar constraints can be imposed on output variables as well. When such constraints are specified on both inputs and outputs, their *compatibility* must be verified. Figure 6.6 is an enrichment of Figure 6.4 that displays all constraints on input and output variables. ∎

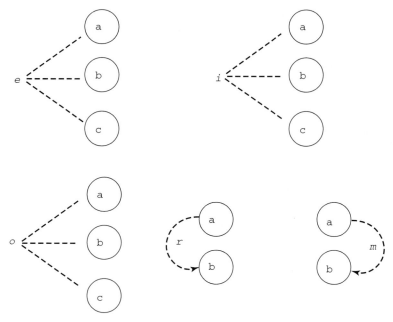

FIGURE 6.5

Graphical representation of constraints among logical variables.

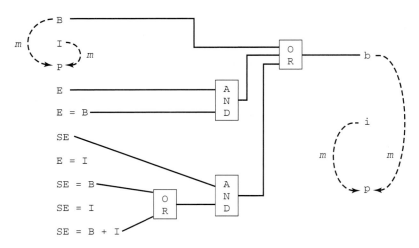

**FIGURE 6.6**

The fragment of Figure 6.4, augmented with a diagram showing the constraints among the variables.

The graph that is obtained by following the procedure set out in Example 6.9 is called the *cause-effect graph* of a program specification. The cause-effect graph can be used to drive program verification by applying the complete-coverage principle in a fairly obvious way, namely, by generating all possible combinations of inputs and checking whether the outputs correspond to the specification. Actually, the graph can also be used to assess the specification itself. In fact, it can show an inconsistency if, say, the output corresponding to an admissible input violates the graph's compatibility constraints. Also, the graph can show incompleteness if, say, no input value is found that supplies an admissible output.

If the size of the test set is considered excessive, the following procedure can be applied to reduce the size: For each admissible combination of output values, find *some* combinations of input values which cause that combination of output values, by tracing back through the graph.[7] The combinations of input values are selected among all possible ones by means of the following heuristic rules:[8]

1. In tracing back through an **or** node whose output is true, we use only input combinations that have exactly one true value. This way, each cause is tried independently, assuming that combining two causes does not alter the separate effects of each. For instance, if the output of an **or** node must be true, and $I_1, I_2$ are the inputs, we consider only $\{<I_1 = \text{true}, I_2 = \text{false}>, <I_1 = \text{false}, I_2 = \text{true}>\}$.

2. Similarly, in tracing back through an **and** node whose output is false, we use only input combinations that have exactly one false value.

---

[7] For simplicity, let us ignore any actions that are to be performed if some inconsistency or incompleteness is discovered during this procedure.

[8] These rules are a simplified version of those given by Myers [1979].

## Exercises

---

**6.11**  Consider a cause-effect graph in which you also represent constraints (e.g., take the graph shown in Figure 6.6.). How can you represent constraints by means of a decision table?

**6.12**  Give a mathematical definition of how the input-output specification of a program may be transformed into a Boolean function, as required by the cause-effect graph technique. State when this approach is ineffective and when it is not applicable at all.

---

### 6.3.4.3 *Testing Boundary Conditions*

We have based our testing criteria—both white box and black box—mostly on partitioning the input domain of the program into suitable classes, on the assumption that the behavior of the program is "similar" for all elements of each class. Some typical programming errors, however, just happen to be at the boundary between different classes.

For instance, quite often programmers use '<' instead of '≤', or conversely. This error is unlikely to be detected by applying any of the previous techniques. It is also one of the main reasons that pure random testing works poorly.

More precisely, suppose that a program fragment is of the type

```
if x > y then
      S₁;
else
      S₂;
end if
```

Many of the white-box testing criteria would lead to selecting at least one pair of values for x and y such that $x > y$ and at least one pair such that $x \leq y$. This could easily miss a test case with $x = y$, which would be the most natural way to detect the error of writing '>' instead of '≥'.

The preceding remark leads to a natural suggestion: After having partitioned the input domain D into several classes, test the program using input values not only "inside" the classes, but also at their boundaries. Notice that the suggestion applies to white-box techniques as well as to black-box techniques. This natural way of complementing many of the previous testing criteria is usually called *testing boundary conditions*.

In practice, the different testing criteria should always be applied in combination, because none is completely effective by itself. We ask you to ponder this point in Exercise 6.61.

### Exercise

---

**6.13**  Give an example of testing boundary conditions in black-box testing.

---

### 6.3.4.4 *Test Oracles*

So far, we have focused our attention mostly on building test cases—that is, input data to be supplied to the implemented software to verify whether it behaves properly or not. To achieve such a goal, however, selecting a meaningful test set is not enough: We must also guarantee that the test is accurate; that is, we must verify, by running our software on the selected test set, that the results obtained do indeed comply with the software goals, as stated in the specification. This raises the so-called oracle problem: How do we relate selected input data—the test cases—with corresponding outputs? How do we verify the correctness of the outputs we obtain? Such a problem is not always trivial: For instance, in an extreme scenario, once we have selected a suitable test set for an air traffic control system, we should actually run the system by applying it to real flights to verify whether it does in fact prevent accidents, an obviously dangerous approach. On the other hand, understanding whether the risk of aircraft collision is excluded by the routes designed by the control system is often hard; for this reason, we say that we need an "oracle" for such a job.

In some cases, test selection criteria provide little or no help at all in solving the oracle problem. Typically, this occurs with most white-box criteria. For instance, given a program fragment such as

```
if x > 0 then S₁ else S₂ end if;
```

it is quite natural to produce a test set that includes a case where $x > 0$ and a case where is $x \leq 0$. There is no indication, however, as to which outputs should be observed in response to the two input cases.

By contrast, black-box criteria are, at least in principle, much better suited to build not only test cases, but also the corresponding oracles. To illustrate, let us go back to the specification of the insertion of an invoice record into a file given in Section 6.3.4.2, or even better, its formalization in a logic notation. It is quite natural that such a specification can be used not only to derive "at least one test case with an invoice whose field `customer` exists in the `customer_file` and one with an invoice whose field `customer` does not exist in such file," but even to state that in the first case the resulting output variable should be `true`, whereas in the second case it should be `false`.

Notice that, even when the specification does not explicitly state the expected value of the program's output, it states the *properties* that such a value must satisfy, as we suggested in Section 6.3.1; these are what really matter and are, in general, easy to verify.

Once again, we emphasize the usefulness of formalization, which allows at least partial automation of the construction of both test cases and their corresponding oracles.

### 6.3.5  Testing in the Large

So far, we have been concerned with testing single pieces of software—that is, individual modules that will be combined with other modules to form a complete system. Actually, they could also be complete programs considered as a whole—programs whose testing was considered with respect to an overall definition of their expected behavior.

The combinatorial explosion of many of the techniques we illustrated in the previous sections might make them applicable only to small programs. Of course, when we are dealing with complex systems, we need techniques to master the complexity of their verification—and of their testing, in particular—just as we do for their design and specification. The current section deals with this problem.

#### 6.3.5.1  Testing and Modularity

The organization of the testing activity should in some way reflect the organization of the design activity. This implies that the modular architecture of the system is a natural candidate to drive the verification of the system. Just as we build a complex system by first designing it as a collection of related modules, we should be able to test modules separately, one by one, and eventually test the whole system on the basis of the relationships among the modules. There are several obvious benefits to be derived from testing a system modularly: It is easier to localize errors; it is easier to discover errors at early stages of their development; and it is easier to classify errors according to their scope (i.e., whether they are design errors, coding errors, etc.).

Thus, good design techniques result in better software, not only in the sense that the software is likely to contain fewer errors, but also in the sense that it is easier to catch and fix the errors that do occur. In other words, good design techniques enhance verifiability also.

We shall discuss module testing, integration testing, and system testing. *Module testing* is intended to verify whether a given module has been implemented correctly with respect to its expected external behavior: The module works correctly, no matter which modules are interacting with it, provided that these modules are using its interfaces correctly. *System testing* is intended to check whether a whole collection of modules behaves properly—possibly on the basis of the assumption that all of its constituent modules behave properly by themselves.

Systems are often integrated gradually: Collections of modules are put together to form a subsystem, and this may be progressively integrated with other modules or subsystems. Partial systems may thus be created and tested. We call the testing that is performed while a system is being integrated *integration testing*. At the final stage of integration that results in the whole system, integration testing coincides with system testing. In general, however, system testing is executed in the actual delivery environment (or as close as possible to it), as opposed to the development environment, in which module testing and integration testing take place. Related to system testing is *acceptance testing*, which is performed by the customer, possibly together with the developer, before taking delivery of the product. Depending on the application also, some levels of integration and system testing (e.g., testing an embedded application consisting of the hardware and the software running on it) are not pure software testing. We shall say a little more about testing systems that do not consist exclusively of software modules in Section 6.3.5.5.

### 6.3.5.2 *Module Testing in Context*

A single module should be tested on the basis of the techniques described as testing in the small. A module, however, often cannot be executed by itself. Using the terminology of Chapter 4, if $M_i$ USES $M_h$ and $M_i$ USES $M_k$, then the correct execution of $M_i$ requires the availability of correct versions of $M_h$ and $M_k$. If we wish to execute $M_i$ in isolation (e.g., because $M_h$ and $M_k$ are not yet available), then we need to provide a temporary context for $M_i$'s execution that simulates the real context that will be provided by $M_h$ and $M_k$.

Modules are ultimately mapped into different programming constructs—say, a procedure, a package, a task, or even a full program that is part of a system of programs that interact together through an operating system to form a complete application. To support the testing of a single module, we need a complete environment which provides all that is necessary for the execution of the module and is not included within the module itself. In particular, it may happen that

- the module uses an operation—say, it calls a procedure—that is not part of the module;
- the module accesses nonlocal data structures; or
- the module is itself used (called) by another module.

All these situations must be simulated in order to make the testing of the module possible.

Consider the case of an external procedure call occurring during the execution of a module. If the procedure that is called is not yet available (because it is still being developed), the simplest way to manage the call is to build a *stub*, that is, a procedure that has the same I/O parameters as the missing procedure, but a highly simplified behavior. For example, the stub might produce its expected results by reading them from a file or requesting them from a human tester interactively; or it might even do nothing and simply print some diagnostic message, should this be acceptable to the caller. The stub will then be linked with the module, just as if it were the real procedure.

The following declaration shows the development of a stub to replace a sorting procedure that is intended to sort sequences of n integers:

```
type sequence(max_size: NATURAL) is
    record
        size : INTEGER range 0. . max_size := 0;
        contents = array(1 .. max_size) of INTEGER;
    end record;
```

The stub looks like this:

```
procedure sort(seq : in out sequence) is
begin
        write("the sequence to be sorted is the following:");
        for i in 1 .. seq.size loop
            write(seq.contents(i));
        end loop;
        write("enter the result of sorting the sequence");
        for i in 1 .. seq.size loop
            read(seq.contents(i));
        end loop;
        -- a safer version of the stub could verify the
           consistency of
        -- the user-supplied data with respect to
           procedure
        -- specification
end sort;
```

Similarly, one can build *drivers*. A driver is a program that simulates the use of the module being tested. The driver sets the values of the shared data as they would be set in the real application by other modules that are yet to be designed. Figure 6.7 gives an intuitive picture of a module being tested. The module consists of a procedure, together with a stub and a driver.

As an example of a driver, suppose that you have built a procedure (called insert_table) that inserts an item (of type element_type) in a table in an appropriate order. Suppose that procedures to initialize (init_table) and print

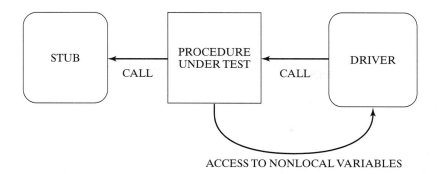

FIGURE 6.7

A procedure undergoing testing, with (1) a stub providing a functional abstraction and
(2) a driver.

(print_table) a table are already available; a procedure (input) is also available
to read values of type element_type via suitable interaction with the user. Then a
driver to help test procedure insert_table could be built along the following lines
(the details are left to the reader as an exercise):

```
init_table;
input(el1);
insert_table(el1);
--check whether insertion was done properly
print_table;
input(el2);
insert_table(el2);
--check whether insertion was done properly
print_table;
        .
        .
        .
```

All the support software developed for module and integration testing, including
the stubs, is sometimes called test *harness* or *scaffolding*. The term "scaffolding" is used
by analogy to the scaffolding that is used to hold buildings up during their construction: Scaffolds are not part of the final building, but they certainly are necessary.

Here, we see another opportunity for the use of formal, executable specifications
when the appropriate technology is available. In fact, suppose that a module M has
been formally specified by means of, say, a logic language that is executable. Then the
formal specification of M can be easily turned into a stub that is more reliable and
effective than, say, a stub that is completely simulated by user interaction.

## Example 6.10

Imagine a module compute_monthly_incomes. To do its job, this module accesses
a database that stores all invoices issued by the company. Access to the database is performed through appropriate procedures, which belong to a module DBM encapsulating

all of the "secrets" of the database. These procedures include a **select** operation that, given a predicate, returns an array of invoices that satisfy the predicate.

The DBM module is not available yet, so `compute_monthly_incomes` requires a stub in order to be executed. Because the **select** operation allows queries to specify sophisticated and complex logical selection policies that cannot be handled by a conventional database system, we cannot resort to conventional databases as temporary stubs.

A possible solution to the problem of testing `compute_monthly_incomes`, with present-day technology, without the DBM module might be to use the logical power of a language like PROLOG, provided that a suitable run-time connection is established between PROLOG and our programming language. In such a case, PROLOG may be viewed as an approximation to an executable specification language.   ■

### Exercises

**6.14** Sometimes, your stub can use existing facilities available, for example, from the operating system. Explain how to use the sort package available on most systems in the stub just discussed. If you can use the sort package in your stub, why not use it in the final product?

**6.15** Suppose you have built a module that implements a complete abstract data type `fifo_queue`, provided with operations `is_empty`, `enqueue`, `dequeue`, etc., with their natural meaning. Build a facility to drive the execution of such a module, consisting of a small program that allows the user to test the module.

### 6.3.5.3 *Bottom-Up and Top-Down Integration*

Integration testing can be performed by following different strategies. At one extreme, one could first test all of a system's modules separately and then the whole system at once. This is called big-bang testing. With big-bang testing, integration testing disappears, and we proceed abruptly from module testing to system testing. The problem with big-bang testing is that all intermodule dependencies are tested during the system test phase. Hence, if the system consists of many modules, many interactions wind up being tested at once. A more disciplined approach is needed to test the intermodule dependencies incrementally.

An alternative to big-bang testing is *incremental testing*. There are several reasons to apply the incrementality principle to integration testing. First, since modules are developed independently of each other, there is no reason to delay integration testing until all the modules of a system have been implemented; rather, we can start integration testing as soon as a reasonable subset of the modules has been developed.

Second, it is easier to localize errors incrementally. For instance, if a subset of n modules has been successfully and carefully tested, and a fault occurs when a new module that has itself been successfully tested is added, it is likely that the error is in the interface between the new module and the previous ones. If, by contrast, we integrate a whole set of modules at once, localization of errors is more difficult.

Third, partial aggregations of modules often constitute important subsystems that can have some autonomy. For instance, a complex office information system can integrate modules that perform financial computations, processing of documents, etc. Each of these modules, in turn, may consist of several modules such as `invoiceDB`, `lettersDB`, and `personnelFiles`. Clearly, it is worthwhile to test the integration of all the modules related to document processing independently of those having to do with financial processing, and conversely. This kind of testing will also help focus attention on critical relationships between the modules when one moves to higher level integration. Furthermore, if the subset provides a meaningful subsystem, it may be delivered to users according to an incremental delivery strategy.

Fourth, incremental testing can reduce or obviate the need for stubs or drivers. For instance, suppose you have a module `file_manager` that exports a set of traditional operations on files. After having tested this module separately, you may turn to testing a module `table_manager` that manages several kinds of tables, stored in memory or in secondary storage. Thus, `table_manager` uses the `file_manager` module. You could decide to link `table_manager` to `file_manager` immediately and test the two of them together. This will allow you to avoid constructing stubs that simulate the operations of `file_manager`, and you will be able to test `table_manager` independently, with a good chance to localize possible errors.

Once the incrementality principle is accepted, the question arises, "In what order should modules be aggregated?" Two natural approaches to answering this question are *bottom-up* and *top-down* aggregation. The former means starting aggregation and testing from the leaves of the USES hierarchy. It requires the implementation of drivers to substitute for higher level modules. The latter means starting from top-level modules and using stubs to simulate lower level ones. The complementary benefits of the two approaches should be fairly obvious and are left to the reader to ponder. Also, mixed solutions could easily be designed to cope with peculiar cases.

The top-down and bottom-up approaches may be used—and combined—in several ways by following a software architecture described in terms of both the USES and the IS_COMPOSED_OF relations. For example, consider the GDN structure of Figure 6.8. We can test $M_1$ by providing a stub for $M_2$ and a driver for $M_1$. Later, we can provide an implementation for $M_{2,1}$ and a stub for $M_{2,2}$. Alternatively, we can first implement $M_{2,2}$ and test it by using a driver, then we can design $M_{2,1}$ and test the combination of $M_{2,1}$ and $M_{2,2}$—which constitutes $M_2$—by using a driver. Finally, we can implement $M_1$ and test it along with $M_2$, using a driver for $M_1$.

## Exercises

**6.16**  Design an incremental testing strategy for the software architecture given in Example 4.6.

**6.17**  Discuss the advantages and disadvantages of top-down integration with respect to bottom-up integration.

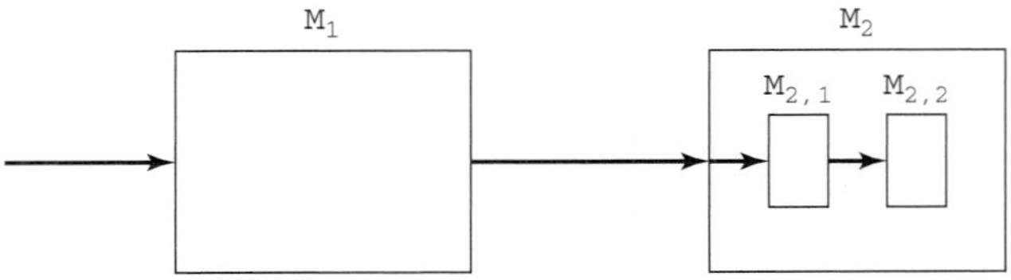

FIGURE 6.8

A GDN structure showing that $M_1$ USES $M_2$ and $M_2$ IS_COM-POSED_OF $\{M_{2,1}, M_{2,2}\}$.

#### 6.3.5.4 *Testing Object-Oriented Programs*

In Chapter 4, we saw that object-oriented (OO) design techniques push concepts such as modularization, information hiding, abstract data types, and designing for change to new boundaries by exploiting features such as inheritance, genericity, polymorphism, and late binding. It should be no surprise, therefore, that, when testing a program built as a collection of OO components, we face problems and we apply techniques that come from general modularization features, such as those examined in previous sections, as well as new ones that are typical of the OO realm. Let us examine some of the most distinguishing problems arising from the use of OO design techniques.

**Testing and Inheritance**    Inheritance is a major tool for reusing code, by specializing it towards more and more specific goals. Of course, as we wish to reuse code, we would also like to reuse testing—that is, reduce the amount of testing for an heir class by exploiting testing already done for an ancestor class. For instance, consider the class hierarchy of Figure 6.9, which is an extension of the one we saw in Chapter 4, defining Administrative_Staff and Technical_Staff as heirs of Employee. The figure defines an ancestor class, Personnel, and two heirs, Consultant and Employee. In turn, Employee has two heirs: Administrative_Staff and Technical_Staff.

In this hierarchy, some heirs add new elements (attributes or methods) to the ones they inherit from their ancestors. For instance, Technical_Staff adds method Assign to those inherited from Employee. In other cases, inherited items can even be redefined, as might happen with the class Manager if, say, payment procedures for managers are different from those adopted for other staff. Yet in other cases, defining methods may be delayed to heir classes, though introduced in ancestor classes: In our example, Payment is introduced in Personnel, but is deferred to the definition of Consultant and Employee, by exploiting the mechanism of late binding.

Thus, the question is, How do we test all those classes? A trivial answer could consist of "flattening" the whole hierarchy and considering every class as a totally independent component. The obvious drawback of such an approach is that, during testing, we lose all the incrementality and reusability we achieved during design through the inheritance mechanism: Clearly, we want to save in testing as well as in design and implementation. In principle, we should avoid repeating the testing of elements that are inherited with no change, we should test new items, and we should retest items that have been redefined. In practice, things are not always that easy. To illustrate, consider the following cases:

- Under normal circumstances, hiring a new person entails inserting a record with his or her attributes (age, name, ...) into some file. There is no reason to suspect that if such a procedure works correctly for a technical employee, it does not work for an administrator.

- On the other hand, it is clear that testing an `Assign` procedure that assigns a technical employee to some project makes sense only for class `Technical_Staff` and therefore must be done solely for instances of that class (and of its possible heirs).

- If, instead, some method is inherited, but is redefined, it will be necessary to test the method again in the heir class, even though it already was tested in the ancestor. For instance, `Payment` of `Managers` may require us to introduce some new attributes in the interface of the method, though part of the method could remain unaltered.

- In some even more subtle cases, we could leave the semantics of an inherited method unaffected, but we could decide to change its implementation, say, to increase efficiency. This could happen, for example, in the definition of a class `Square` as an heir of a class `Polygon`. If `Square` inherits the method `Perimeter` from its ancestor, clearly the interface of the method is the same, but we could decide to apply a more efficient code in its implementation by exploiting the geometric properties of squares. In such a case, a superficial verifier might ignore the change and avoid retesting the method, which could result in failing to catch errors in the implementation of the heir class.

The preceding remarks show that organizing the testing of an inheritance hierarchy in a safe, but "economical," way (i.e., exercising everything that is necessary to verify without wasting effort testing what has already been tested is not a trivial task. In the present state of the art, testing object-oriented software is more of a problem and a research issue than testing a collection of established techniques.

A major difficulty arises from the fact that a precise and standardized semantics of the notion of inheritance is still lacking. Indeed, different languages offer rather different implementations of this concept. Thus, systematic approaches to testing inheritance hierarchies must depend on both the particular definition of the inheritance mechanism in the programming language and the design methodology being followed. The designers can develop only *ad hoc* techniques to avoid repeating tests in a given project by examining the hierarchy structure of the design and deciding at any time which tests should be repeated or modified and how. For instance, a systematic way to structure such testing activity could consist of "labeling test cases" as follows:

- a test that does not have to be repeated for any heir;
- a test that must be performed for heir class `X` and all of its further heirs;

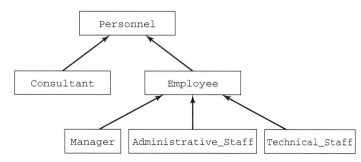

**FIGURE 6.9**

An inheritance hierarchy for
`Personnel`.

- a test that must be redone by applying the same input data, but verifying that the output is not (or *is*) changed;
- a test that must be modified by adding other input parameters and verifying that the output changes accordingly.

Even with systematic rules, the design of such a structured testing approach depends, in general, on the designer's knowledge of the design and of the language features.

**Testing Genericity and Polymorphism**    Genericity and polymorphism are powerful tools for achieving generality and reusability, but are yet another source of complexity for testing and for verification in general.

Consider, for instance, a generic class `Table(Element_Type)`, which is parametric with respect to the type of its elements. (We can instantiate it as a `Table` of `Invoices`, a `Table` of `Names`, etc.). Such a class contains several polymorphic operations, such as `Search`, `Insert`, and `Sort`. Now, suppose you have thoroughly tested the behavior of such a class by instantiating it as a `Table(Integer)`. How much of the results obtained through such a testing activity are still valid for, say, a `Table(Invoices)`? Should we redo from scratch all tests for all possible instantiations? In the extreme, testing all possible instantiations would degenerate to exhaustive and practically impossible kind of testing.

Here, too, the questions fall more in the province of open research problems than in the framework of well-developed techniques. A few guidelines based on common sense and sound design principles, however, may help in designing an effective test plan when faced with such generic classes:

- First, remember that the more abstract the design, the easier is the verification—testing in particular. For instance, if the implementation of the aforementioned `Table` uses the built-in operation '<', denoting the usual ordering relation, to implement searching or sorting operations, the operations may work for tables of numbers and, possibly, of alphabetically ordered items such as strings. The operations will not work, however, for *all* classes with *all* ordering relations, such as an `Invoices` class wherein ordering is based on dates and names (unless an explicit overloading of the '<' operator is allowed and defined). Instead, if we explicitly define a `Precedes` relation between items of the parameter class, and we require it in the interface of any class used as an actual parameter of the generic class, we know *a priori* that such a precedence relation will be *used* (not implemented!) correctly for all possible instantiations of the generic class.
- If we know *a priori* the context in which the generic class will be used, we can probably foresee which types of instances will be created, and we can direct the testing of the class towards those instances—perhaps even in an exhaustive approach if the instances are not too many. If, on the contrary, the generic class has to be stored in a library and used in contexts that cannot be foreseen *a priori*, then a more thorough and systematic testing may be needed. In such a case, we could, for instance, partition the set of all possible actual parameter classes according to some criterion (e.g., simple data type vs. structured type, numeric elements vs. nonnumeric elements, data with built-in ordering relation vs. data

whose ordering relation has to be defined *ad hoc*, or even data with no ordering relation if the definition of the generic class may exploit, but not mandate the existence of, such a relation, etc.); then we could apply the complete-coverage principle by testing the class with at least one actual parameter for each of these categories.

### 6.3.5.5 *System Testing*

We have been emphasizing that the term "system" is a relative concept: A software application is often a collection of integrated and interacting programs that in turn may each be organized as a collection of modules written in some programming language. The software application itself, however, is frequently part of a more complex system that may include computer hardware, plants, or even human organizations and rules.

The overall goal of verification—and of testing in particular—is therefore related to the whole system, with an appropriate definition of *system* on the basis of the context. Testing the control software of a car in isolation would be as unsafe as testing the wheels, the engine, and the suspension separately without testing the whole car. System testing, therefore, may require that the software engineer collaborate with other engineers.

Consider, for instance, how the principle of separation of concerns can be applied in several contexts. First, let us consider a traditional information system operated within a bank according to some well-established procedures. The system evolves as, periodically, the hardware is replaced by new machines, the software is updated with new releases with new features and more efficient implementation, and the operating personnel are affected by normal turnover, training, and changes in organizational procedures. In such a case, most likely, when we replace, say, a workstation with a new and more powerful one, we do not have to repeat the whole system testing process: It probably suffices that we verify that some critical software runs as well on the new hardware as it used to run on the old one.

Suppose, however, that we are instead building a new office automation system whereby previous operations such as shipping, paying invoices, purchasing, and controlling the budget, which used to be done either through regular mail and fax or through stand-alone applications running on personal computers, are now integrated into a single Internet-based distributed system. In such a case, proper *system testing* must involve not only verifying that the new applications run properly on the network, but even that their users exploit them appropriately (e.g., in managing purchasing through the Web).

As another example of the application of general principles to system testing, consider the case of scaffolding: In the context of testing of software alone, the term means setting up a suitable collection of stubs and drivers that allow testing of separate modules to evolve smoothly and gradually towards testing the whole system. The basic ideas of stubs and drivers, however, can be naturally extended to the case where some system modules are pieces of hardware or external devices to be controlled by the software. Thus, in testing the control software for an antilock braking system (ABS), we may use a simulator that supplies to our software input data that represent possible inputs coming from physical sensors in the real device. Later on, we will test the software *in the field*—that is, in an integrated fashion, with sensors attached to the wheel and running on the real microprocessor installed in the car.

### 6.3.6   Separate Concerns in the Testing Activity

Testing a whole system is a complex activity that involves, in general, several phases, with different goals, performed by different people. For instance, some testing could be done by the developers of the software themselves, some could be done by other people belonging to the same company that produces the system, and some could be done by the customer. Also, some tests could be done to ensure functional correctness, others to ensure robustness, etc. Applying the principle of separation of concerns is a key to a successful testing strategy.

Recall from Section 6.1.1 that all software qualities should be verified and, therefore, possibly tested. This suggests that testing should address not only compliance with precisely stated functional requirements, but also performance, robustness, usability, and all other requested qualities. We can use the principle of separation of concerns to design test cases for different qualities: One test set is designed to check functional behavior, another is designed to check performance, and so on.

One should not, however, forget that even qualities which are not explicitly specified in the requirements document are worth verifying. As we saw in Chapter 2, in practice it is often impossible to point out exhaustively and exactly all the requirements of a system; the requirements document should therefore be viewed as a *minimal* set of requirements for testing.

The following discussion gives a sampling of the different concerns that we can address with specific kinds of tests.

**Overload Testing.**   Suppose that a transaction system is required to execute at least 20 transactions per second with an average response time not to exceed 30 seconds. Then we should test how the system behaves during peak conditions, when, say, 30 transactions are requested in a second. Such testing is called overload testing. It is likely that many ideas and suggestions for overload testing arise after the system is implemented, rather than during its specification. Of course, many of the results derived during such overload testing will be a source of inspiration for future enhancements of the system and also for the future development of similar systems.

**Testing for Robustness.**   For much the same reason as in overload testing, we must test the system under unexpected conditions, such as erroneous user commands and power failures. Strictly speaking, it could seem a waste of time to schedule the testing of the system under unexpected conditions; instead, why not specify the expected response explicitly in the requirements document? The relevance of many unexpected conditions, however, may become clear only after some experience with early versions of the system.

**Regression Testing.**   Another concern that should be kept in mind during testing is that software will be modified during its lifetime, as we already have emphasized several times. For instance, suppose you are going to add new functionality to your software, or you are going to modify a module to improve its response time. The changes, of course, may introduce errors into software that was previously correct. For example, suppose the program fragment

```
x := c + 1;
proc(z);
c := x + 2;
x := 3;
```

works properly. Now suppose that in a subsequent redesign it is transformed into

```
proc(z);
c := c + 3;
x := 3;
```

in an attempt at program optimization. This may result in an error if procedure `proc` accesses variable x.

Thus, we need to organize testing also with the purpose of verifying possible *regressions* of software during its life—that is, degradations of correctness or other qualities due to later modifications. Properly designing and documenting test cases with the purpose of making tests repeatable, as well as using test generators, will help regression testing. By contrast, the use of interactive human input reduces repeatability and thus hampers regression testing. In practice, regression testing is done by keeping an archive of previous test runs and their results and then rerunning all the archived tests for each new release of the product.

Finally, we must treat test cases in much the same way as software. It is clear that such factors as evolvability, reusability, and verifiability are just as important in test cases as they are in software. We must apply formality and rigor and all of our other principles in the development and management of test cases. We will examine some organizational issues related to software evolution and testing in Chapter 7.

## 6.3.7    Testing Concurrent and Real-Time Systems

We have seen in Chapters 4 and 5 that concurrent systems are, in general, more difficult to design and specify than sequential systems. Not surprisingly, they are also more difficult to verify. In this section, we will discuss the additional problems that may arise in testing concurrent programs.

In principle, all of the testing techniques we have discussed so far should be applicable to sequential as well concurrent programs. Making tests repeatable, however, becomes a critical issue in concurrent programming. In fact, in traditional programming languages such as C, COBOL, FORTRAN, etc., the semantics of a program is a function from the set of possible input data to the set of output data. That is, if we provide the same input to a program twice, the program must produce the same results both times. This property does not hold in general in the case of concurrent and real-time systems, as we discussed in Chapter 4. We examine the issue here in the context of the Ada programming language. Similar comments apply to Java and any other language that supports concurrency.

## Example 6.11

Consider the following fragment of an Ada program that is a slight modification of the guardian task given in Figure 4.21:

```
task Char_Buffer_Handler is
    .
    .
    .
```

```
    loop
        .
        .
        .
    select
            when NOT_full accept PUT
                --code of PUT
        .
        .
        .
    or
            when NOT_empty accept GET
                --code of GET
        .
        .
        .
    end select;
        .
        .
        .
end loop;
    .
    .
    .
    end Char_Buffer_Handler;
```

This code defines a task whose job is to manage the use of a buffer of characters by other tasks, namely, producers, which may write (PUT) characters into the buffer, and consumers, which may read (GET) characters from it.

The critical issue here is the *nondeterminism* of the behavior of the task. The task Char_Buffer_Handler can serve requests for writing or reading, provided that their respective conditions hold. If requests of both types are pending, however, and the buffer is neither full nor empty, both requests can be accepted: The task may choose which request to serve in a way that is not specified by the programmer.

Let us examine the impact of nondeterminism on guaranteeing the repeatability of testing. If we apply the complete-coverage principle to a system composed of the Char_Buffer_Handler task and a set of producers and consumers, it seems natural to test the system in such a way that the loop shown in the code is entered at least once with a full buffer, at least once with an empty buffer, and perhaps once with a buffer that is neither full nor empty.

Now, imagine the programming error of leaving out the **when** NOT_Full clause. Intuitively, in testing the system with the buffer full, a failure should occur, in much the same way as if we had forgotten an **if** $x \neq 0$ clause before executing a division by $x$. When we are testing the effect of a PUT operation on a full buffer, however, a GET request may be issued by some consumer. Since we have neither control over nor knowledge of the policy used by the Char_Buffer_Handler to serve pending requests, it may happen that the GET request is served first. After that, at the next loop iteration, the PUT operation will be performed without exposing the fault.

This experiment, however, does not guarantee at all that by running the same system of tasks with the same input data on a different machine, the program will behave correctly. In fact, under the same condition, a different implementation could select the option to serve the PUT request, thus generating a fault. Even running the same system on the same machine with the same input data could provide different results if, for example, the operating system worked under a time-sharing policy that led sometimes to slowing down the consumer tasks and other times to slowing down the producer tasks. ■

The difficulties of testing concurrent systems become even more apparent when we move from testing in the small to testing in the large. In fact, it is intuitively clear that repeatability of testing is much more difficult to achieve with modules running concurrently than when they run sequentially. The producer-consumer program is an example that demonstrates this issue.

Real-time systems are even more difficult to verify, for similar reasons. In fact, their correctness, by definition, depends on execution speeds. Clearly, verifying such systems requires taking into consideration many more details than in traditional systems; typically, many aspects which are "implementation details" that can be abstracted away in traditional systems—such as scheduling policies, machine architecture, and speed—must be taken into account here.

In principle, a test case for a real-time system consists not only of input data, but also of the times when such data are supplied. For instance, a typical test case could look like a sequence of the type

$$<E_1, \ t_1>, \ <E_2, \ t_2>, ..., \ <E_n, \ t_n>$$

where $E_i$ denotes the occurrence of an input event such as an alarm and $t_i$ denotes the time when $E_i$ occurs. Clearly, including time as a critical part of the test case adds a new dimension of complexity to the whole testing activity.

In conclusion, the general testing principles we have discussed so far are certainly applicable to concurrent and real-time systems. Much more care and technical details, however, must be taken into account, and, in general, many more test cases need to be considered. In fact, the number of possible execution paths is further increased by the possible execution interleavings of several concurrent units, and in the case of real-time systems, completeness should be pursued even from the point of view of relative processing speeds. For example, with a producer-consumer system, one should test the case when production is fast relative to consumption, and conversely.

The topic of testing concurrent and real-time systems is an active research area. Thus, we do not go further into the topic here, but instead refer the interested reader to the appropriate literature in the bibliographic notes.

## Exercises

**6.18** Consider a system consisting of three tasks: a producer, a consumer, and a Char_Buffer_Handler, of the type outlined in Example 6.11. Consider also a fixed sequence of external stimuli and a fixed size of the buffer. (Say, the buffer has length 3, and the producer gets four items from the external environment, to be put into the buffer.)

Assume that concurrency is simulated on a uniprocessor with the following different scheduling policies:

- Policy 1: Every task runs until it is blocked by asking for an unavailable resource.
- Policy 2: Every task runs until it reaches a synchronization point. At that point, the `producer` has higher priority than the `consumer`. (The `Char_Buffer_Handler` has the lowest priority, since it depends on the task it has to serve.)
- Policy 3: Every task runs until it reaches a synchronization point. At that point, the `producer` has lower priority than the `consumer`.

Discuss execution flows and the possibility that a failure with respect to the error discussed in Example 6.11 will be detected.

**6.19** Consider the following real-time version of the producer-consumer system of Exercise 6.18: The `Char_Buffer_Handler` has no guard to block writing operations. Furthermore, when both PUT and GET requests are pending, the policy used to manage the **select** statement gives precedence to the PUT request. On the other hand, producers may be suspended only for a limited time on the PUT request, after which they skip the statement. Try to design a significant test set for such a system by taking into account possible (minimum and maximum) process execution speeds, the specified scheduling policy, etc.

## 6.4 ANALYSIS

In Section 6.3, we discussed verification by experimentation (i.e., testing). In the current section, we shall discuss verification by means of analysis. Analyzing any piece of work means inspecting it to understand its properties and capabilities. We observed that in the case of engineering products, analysis complements and integrates with experimental verification. For instance, one can check the minimum distance necessary to stop a car at a given speed by driving the car at that speed and braking, perhaps repeating the experiment several times. Or, alternatively, one can try to derive the braking distance by applying appropriate mathematical formulas that take into account such properties of the car as its speed, weight, and center of gravity, as well as the friction between the wheels and the road.

Cast in terms of software, testing characterizes a *single* execution, whereas analysis characterizes a *class* of executions. While this observation seems to show the advantage of analysis over testing, both approaches have complementary advantages and disadvantages. Analysis is subject to the fallibility of our reasoning. Also, it is generally based on a *model* of the product rather than on the product itself. Thus, it abstracts away from elements that could be crucial. Experiments, on the other hand, are bound to the context in which they are performed, and their generality is not always clear. For instance, what can we conclude about the braking distance of a car on a wet road after we perform an experiment on a dry road?

In the case of software, we have already noticed that testing is better suited to show the existence of errors rather than their absence. The goal of analysis is to prove that the system is free from error, but that cannot be done absolutely.

Verification of a piece of software in order to check a desired property is similar to the activity a mathematician undertakes in proving—or disproving—a theorem. Initially, a statement is formulated that is supposed to be true. At this point, it is a conjecture. Then, we start the process of trying to prove the truth of the conjecture—that is, to show that it is a theorem. Probably, some intuitive reasoning that supports the conjecture will be available, but more evidence (i.e., a more convincing proof) is needed. If the initial attempt to build a proof fails, we might start to doubt the truth of the statement. We can try to show its falsehood unequivocally by a counterexample, the search for which might be driven by the failure of our previous attempt at proof. Conversely, verifying that the conjecture is actually true in some critical case may provide useful suggestions for deriving a full proof. Eventually, the mathematician may come to either a proof or a counterexample of the conjecture. (In the former case, the conjecture becomes a theorem.) It could also happen that neither a proof nor a counterexample is found. In fact, the truth of a statement in a nontrivial theory—as well as the correctness of a particular program—may be undecidable.

Unfortunately, when decisions or proofs cannot be concluded mechanically, we are subject to human fallibility, and, in general, there is no guarantee that the right decision will be taken. Even in pure mathematics, erroneous theorems and proofs are sometimes accepted as valid, although this happens less frequently than the acceptance of defective software as error free. Once more, formality, when applicable, can help reduce—but not avoid—the risks of fallibility.

Software design analysis can apply many different techniques with different purposes. It can address the verification of highly different qualities (correctness, performance, etc.). It can be done by humans, be they the authors of the design, colleagues, or customers, or it can be done with the aid of machine instruments. It can apply formal techniques or be based on intuition and experience. It can be applied to any step of the development process and to the related products, etc.

For instance, in the case of programming-language code, much analysis is performed automatically by the compiler during program translation. This kind of analysis helps us catch many trivial errors, such as violating the type constraints of a variable. Unfortunately, less trivial errors are less easy to detect and require a deeper analysis. We examine this type of analysis next.

### 6.4.1 Informal Analysis Techniques

The most natural and simple analysis technique consists of just looking at the software—the requirements specification, the design specification, or the code—and trying to imagine its behavior by manual simulation, maybe with some help from pencil and paper to focus attention on the most relevant facts.

In this case, the cooperation of people other than the designers is helpful. In fact, in examining one's own work, it is easy to be biased by the same reasoning that was used in the design and thus fail to spot errors. Another person, with no previous misconceptions, is more likely to detect the errors.

The success of informal reasoning in software verification has led to attempts to organize this activity. Two particularly successful organized approaches are *code walkthroughs*, presented in Section 6.4.1.1, and *code inspections*, discussed in Section 6.4.1.2.

It is possible, also, to apply informal analysis techniques to something other than code. Consider, for example, the case of specifications. Completeness and consistency can be checked manually, even for informal specifications. One should check that every concept used is uniquely defined and that no undefined concepts are left in the specification document. If cross-references, glossaries, or decision tables are available, they can be helpful in this phase. If they are not available, or if they are incomplete, they can be created.

### 6.4.1.1 Code Walk-Throughs

A code walk-through is an informal analysis of code performed in a cooperative, organized manner by several participants. The analysis is based mainly on the game of "playing the computer." That is, participants select some test cases (the selection could have been done previously by a single participant) and simulate execution of the code by hand. This is the reason for the name walk-through: Participants "walk through the code" or through any design notation. States of execution may be recorded either on "private storage" (a piece of paper) or on "shared memory" (a blackboard).

Several guidelines have been developed over the years for organizing this naive, but useful, verification technique to make it more systematic and reliable. Of course, these guidelines are based on personal experience, common sense, and many subjective factors. Thus, they should be considered more as examples than as rules to be applied dogmatically.

In general, the following prescriptions are recommended:

- The number of people involved in the review should be small (three to five).
- The participants should receive written documentation from the designer a few days before the meeting.
- The meeting should last a predefined amount of time (a few hours).
- Discussion should be focused on the *discovery* of errors, not on fixing them, nor on proposing alternative design decisions.
- Key people in the meeting should be the designer, who presents and explains the rationale of the work,[9] a moderator for the discussion, and a secretary, who is responsible for writing a report to be given to the designer at the end of the meeting.
- In order to foster cooperation and avoid the feeling that the designers are being evaluated, managers should not participate in the meeting.

The success of code walk-throughs hinges on running them in a cooperative manner as a team effort: They must avoid making the designer feel threatened. They are run to examine the *code*, not the coder.

### 6.4.1.2 Code Inspections

Another organized activity devoted to analyzing code is called code inspection. The organizational aspects of code inspection are similar to those of code walk-throughs (i.e., the number of participants, duration of the meeting, psychological attitudes of the participants, etc., should be about the same), but there is a difference in goals.

In code inspection, the analysis is aimed explicitly at the discovery of common errors. In other words, the code—or, in general, the design—is examined by checking it for the presence of errors, rather than by simulating its execution. In such a case, it is useful to state *beforehand* the type of error for which we are searching. For instance, consider the classical error of writing a procedure that modifies a formal parameter

---

[9] Experience shows that most errors are discovered by the designer during the presentation, while trying to explain the design to other people.

and calling the procedure with a constant value as the actual parameter.[10] It is more likely that such an error will be discovered by looking for it in the code than by simply hand-simulating the execution of the procedure.

Since many errors in programs can be classified according to well-known categories, we can hope to discover most of them just by looking for them. The following is a list of some classical programming errors:

- use of uninitialized variables;
- jumps into loops;
- incompatible assignments;[11]
- nonterminating loops;
- array indexes out of bounds;
- off-by-one errors;
- improper storage allocation or deallocation;
- mismatches between actual and formal parameters in procedure calls;
- comparisons of equality for floating-point values.

Many of these errors (as well as others not listed here) have different symptoms and impacts, depending on the programming language. For instance, improper storage allocation or deallocation is not even possible for static languages such as FORTRAN. Or, in C++ and Java, many mismatches between actual and formal parameters can be caught at compile time, but there might be an exception for pointer parameters, etc. We might also use a language-specific list based on the error-prone features of the language.

Furthermore, despite the undecidability of most of the errors listed, many analytical tools exist to help in detecting such errors. In general, the human inspectors should concentrate on what cannot be inspected automatically. The reviewers should receive the reports produced by the analysis tools.

Software inspections are a major means of verification whose usefulness both has intuitive appeal and has been confirmed by a large amount of practical experience. Tailoring a software inspection to the peculiarities of a single project or organization, however, to minimize its cost-benefit ratio is far from a trivial task and is often based on naive and fairly superficial evaluations. To organize a software inspection, we must address practical issues such as the following:

- How many people should be involved in the inspections?
- How frequent should the meetings be (if they should be held at all)?
- Should every reviewer be responsible for detecting any type of defect, or should responsibilities be clearly separated among reviewers?

---

[10] In some cases, the compiler provides automatic protection against this type of error.

[11] Even though most modern programming languages have a strong typing system (i.e., they allow all type checks to be done at compile time), some incompatibilities in assignments will necessarily be detectable only at run time. For instance, suppose you have a type week_day that includes the seven days of the week as possible values and a *subtype* work_day that is restricted to values from Monday to Friday. Then, if x and y are two variables declared to be of types week_day and work_day, respectively, the language might allow the assignment y := x, but this may result in a run-time error if x's value is Sunday at execution time.

Some systematic experiments have tried to assess the effectiveness of the various inspection techniques and to help answer these questions. Some findings have been rather surprising. For instance, the effectiveness of meetings was found to be often overestimated. Also, well-defined inspection scenarios in which responsibilities of inspectors are clearly specified were found to be more effective than unstructured inspections. The results of these experiments, however, must be evaluated in their appropriate context. It is not clear how to relate such results among different types of projects. For example, projects in a specialized field such as building optimizing compilers, conducted by skilled personnel, may produce significantly different findings than projects performed in general industrial environments with high staff turnover.

## Exercises

**6.20**  Discuss the sample list of errors we presented in this section from the point of view of the programming language being used.

**6.21**  Complete the sample list of programming errors we presented in this section by including a discussion of their impact, depending on the programming language adopted.

## 6.4.2    Correctness Proofs

Informal analysis techniques are useful, but more rigorous and even formal approaches are needed to make verification more reliable. The next example illustrates how informal reasoning can fail to detect an erroneous fragment in a program.

## Example 6.12

The following incorrect program fragment is intended to merge two sorted arrays of n elements each:

```
i := 1; j := 1; k := 1;
while k ≤ 2 * n loop
    if a(i) < b(j) then
        c(k) := a(i);
        i := i + 1;
    else
        c(k) := b(j);
        j := j + 1;
    end if;
    k := k + 1;
end loop;
```

An informal analysis of this code may read as follows:

Three counters are defined: i for a, j for b, and k for c. They are all initialized to 1. At each step, the ith element of a and the jth element of b are compared. The smaller one is stored into c as the kth element. Then k and the counter of the array containing the selected element are incremented. The step is repeated until c is all built.

Superficially, this reasoning seems to confirm the correctness of the program, but actually it hides the subtle error that when the end of, say, a is reached (i.e., $i = n$), the loop may be executed again, and if $a(n) < b(j)$, i becomes $n + 1$, which is an error. Even testing may fail to show the error, since the program could access some physical location that does not correspond to any program variable, perhaps producing a result corresponding to the result of the test $a(i) < b(j)$.  ■

Formal program analysis is a verification aid that may enhance program reliability. Indeed, a program is a formal object, since the syntax and the semantics of programming languages can be defined formally. Once the program's specification has been given in a formal way, proving program correctness amounts to the (nontrivial) task of mathematically proving that the program's semantics implies its specification. Such a proof, of course, would enhance our confidence in the program, as is the case whenever we apply mathematical reasoning in an analysis.

In this section, we briefly describe the fundamentals of correctness proofs, trying to avoid excessive mathematical detail, but also trying not to hide their intricacies. This will enable us to assess the practical application of the approach. We organize our presentation in the following way: Section 6.4.2.1 introduces the basic notions of program correctness; Section 6.4.2.2 extends the concepts to a richer set of statements, including the ability to deal with arrays; and finally, Sections 6.4.2.3 and 6.4.2.4 address the issue of how to deal with formal verification in practice.

### 6.4.2.1 Basic Concepts of Correctness Proofs

To introduce the basic concepts of correctness proofs, let us consider the following simple example, which consists of a program and its specification, which uses the assertion notation introduced in Section 5.6.2.1:

```
{true}
begin
    read(a); read(b);
    x := a + b;
    write(x);
end
{output = input₁ + input₂}
```

Due to the semantics of the write statement, the postcondition {output = $input_1 + input_2$} holds after its execution if and only if, just before its execution, the predicate {x = $input_1 + input_2$} holds. Since the assignment statement stores the value of $a + b$ into x, the previous predicate is guaranteed to hold after execution of x := a + b if and only if the predicate {a + b = $input_1 + input_2$} holds just before its execution. Finally, since read (a) and read (b) will give a and b, respectively, the values of the first two input values $input_1$ and $input_2$, we realize that {a + b = $input_1 + input_2$} will certainly hold before execution of "x := a + b". As a consequence, we can conclude that the whole program guarantees the truth of {output = $input_1 + input_2$} at the end of its execution; that is, the program is correct.

The preceding reasoning is a formal derivation of the correctness of a program with respect to a specification given in input-output assertions. Essentially, it is based on the fact that for any postcondition Post on program variables, and for any assignment statement x := exp, where exp is an expression containing program variables, a necessary and sufficient condition for Post to hold *after* execution of the statement is that Post itself holds *before* its execution with exp substituted for any occurrence of x. Such substitution[12] is called *backward substitution*, and the resulting predicate is called a *precondition*.

The reader can reinforce his or her understanding of backward substitution by considering the following tautologies[13]:

```
{x = 5} x := x + 1 {x = 6}
{z - 43 > y + 7} x := z - 43 {x > y + 7}
```

Input and output statements can be treated as if they were assignment statements from the input file and to the output file, respectively. In the previous example, since we knew that the input file contained two values (to be read into a and b), we could treat the two read statements as if they were written as

```
a := input₁; b := input₂;
```

Similarly, we could treat the only output statement as if it were

```
output := x
```

The general way to deal with input and output, though, is more complicated and will be discussed in Section 6.4.2.2.

Backward substitution can be applied easily to *sequences* of assignment statements. In fact, if {z - 43 < y + 7} is a necessary and sufficient condition for {x > y + 7} to hold after x := z - 43—that is, if

```
{z - 43 > y + 7}
x := z - 43
{x > y + 7}
```

and if {a + b - 43 > y + 7} is a necessary and sufficient condition for {z - 43 > y + 7} to hold after z := a + b—that is, if

```
{a + b - 43 > y + 7}
z := a + b
{z - 43 > y + 7}
```

then {a + b - 43 > y + 7} is a necessary and sufficient condition for {x > y + 7} to hold after z := a + b; x := z - 43—that is,

```
{a + b - 43 > y + 7}
z := a + b; x := z - 43
{z - 43 > y + 7}
```

---

[12] For simplicity, we assume here that the evaluation of the expression on the right-hand side does not generate any side effects, which could happen if the expression involved a function call. As an exercise, the reader may verify why this hypothesis is needed and should consider how to modify the backward substitution rule to cope with side effects.
[13] A tautology is a statement that is always true, such as "7 is greater than 5."

More generally, suppose that, for any two statements $S_1$ and $S_2$, you have separately proven that

$\{F_1\}S_1\{F_2\}$,

and

$\{F_2\}S_2\{F_3\}$,

(i.e., the truth of $F_1$ guarantees that $F_2$ holds after the execution of statement $S_1$, and the truth of $F_2$ guarantees that $F_3$ holds after the execution of statement $S_2$). Then you can deduce

$\{F_1\}S_1; \ S_2\{F_3\}$

(i.e., if $F_1$ holds, then $F_3$ will hold after the execution of $S_1$ followed by $S_2$).

We can state this reasoning in the form of a *proof rule* for sequencing statements, as expressed in *Hoare's notation*:

$$\frac{\{F_1\}S_1\{F_2\}, \ \ \{F_2\}S_2\{F_3\}}{\{F_1\}S_1; \ S_2\{F_3\}}$$

This notation is used in the following way: If $\texttt{Claim}_1$ and $\texttt{Claim}_2$ have been proven, one can deduce $\texttt{Claim}_3$ from the rule

$$\frac{\texttt{Claim}_1, \ \texttt{Claim}_2}{\texttt{Claim}_3}$$

The proof rule for sequencing statements can even be stated more strongly. Suppose that $F_0$ implies $F_1$, $F_2$ implies $F_2'$, and $F_3$ implies $F_4$. Then, from $\{F_1\}S_1\{F_2\}$ and $\{F_2'\}S_2\{F_3\}$, you can deduce $\{F_0\}S_1; \ S_2\{F_4\}$. That is,

$$\frac{F_0 \ \textbf{implies} \ F_1, \ F_2 \ \textbf{implies} \ F_2', \ F_3 \ \textbf{implies} \ F_4, \ \{F_1\}S_1\{F_2'\}, \ \{F_2'\}S_2\{F_3\}}{\{F_0\}S_1; \ S_2 \ \{F_4\}}$$

All this should sound quite natural, and the reader is invited to check his or her understanding through the following exercise.

## Exercise

---

**6.22** Prove the following two properties:

**1.**    $\{$x > 0 **and** y > 0$\}$      **2.**    $\{$x > 0$\}$
       z := x * y                   y := x ** 2;
       $\{$z > - 1$\}$;             z := sqrt(y);
                           $\{$z > 0$\}$

---

Of course, programs do not consist exclusively of sequences of assignment and I/O statements. Thus, we need *proof rules* for all the different constructs of a given programming language in order to prove correctness with respect to a particular set of specifications. In what follows, we summarize the essential proof rules for a restricted set of conventional language constructs; for simplicity, we confine ourselves to programs that manipulate integers. The reader is referred to the more specialized literature for a more complete treatment of the topic.

First, let us examine conditional statements. As an introductory example, consider the following formula:

```
{true}
if x ≥ y then
    max := x;
else
    max := y;
end if
{(max = x or max = y) and (max ≥ x and max ≥ y)}
```

This formula states that, whatever the values of x and y are before execution of the code, the value of variable max must equal the larger of the two after execution of the code.

Now, assume at the outset that x ≥ y. Then the **then** branch of the statement is executed. Backward substitution of the desired postcondition yields {(x = x **or** x = y) **and** (x ≥ x **and** x ≥ y)}, and the predicate is implied by the condition x ≥ y, which guarantees execution of this branch. The same happens if x < y. Thus, we may deduce that in all cases indeed, this is the meaning of the true precondition the desired postcondition will hold after the conditional statement is executed.

More generally, let

```
if cond then S₁; else S₂; end if;
```

be any conditional statement, where S₁ and S₂ are any two statements. Then we can state the following proof rule for conditional statements:

$$\frac{\{\text{Pre and cond}\}S_1\{\text{Post}\},\ \{\text{Pre and not cond}\}S_2\{\text{Post}\}}{\{\text{Pre}\}\text{if cond then } S_1;\ \text{else } S_2;\ \text{end if};\{\text{Post}\}}$$

The proof rules that we are building for simple language constructs can be arbitrarily composed and nested. For example, **if-then-else** statements may contain other **if-then-else** statements in their **then** or **else** branches. (See Exercise 6.23 at the end of this section.)

Let us now consider **while** loops; other kinds of iterative statements may be modeled in a similar way. Let I be any assertion. The proof rule for **while** loops is

$$\frac{\{\text{I and cond}\}S\{\text{I}\}}{\{\text{I}\}\text{while cond loop } S;\ \text{end loop};\ \{\text{I and not cond}\}}$$

Intuitively, the meaning of this rule is as follows: Suppose we have been able to prove that, if assertion I holds, then executing the loop body S under condition cond preserves I's truth. Then I is a loop invariant; that is, I is a predicate which holds at loop entry and exit, no matter how many times we execute the loop. As a consequence, we may infer that, whenever I holds at loop entry, I will still be true at loop exit, along with **not** cond.

A trivial application of the foregoing rule is the following:

```
{x ≥ 0}
while x > 0 loop
    x := x - 1;
end loop;
{x = 0}
```

The formula $\{x \geq 0\}$ is a loop invariant for the loop. This can be seen in the fact that backward substitution through $x := x - 1$ yields $\{x - 1 \geq 0\}$, which is implied by $\{x \geq 0$ **and** $x > 0\}$, since $x$ is an integer. Thus, application of the rule gives the postcondition $\{x \geq 0$ **and not** $(x > 0)\}$; that is, $\{x = 0\}$.

We emphasize that this proof rule allows the derivation of a postcondition of a **while** loop that is guaranteed to hold at loop exit *if the loop is ever exited*. In other words, having proved the invariance of a loop assertion does not prove that the loop will eventually terminate, as is shown by the predicate

```
{x > y}
while x ≠ 0 loop
    x := x - 2;
    y := y - 2;
end loop;
{x > y and x = 0}
```

which can easily be proven to hold on the basis of the loop proof rule. The loop, however, will never terminate if $x$ is odd upon entry to it.

As a consequence, the proofs that we are able to provide with this technique are called *partial correctness proofs*; that is, the validity of the formula

```
{Pre} Program {Post}
```

guarantees only that if the precondition `Pre` holds before the execution of `Program`, *and if the program ever terminates*, then the postcondition `Post` will be achieved.

A *total correctness proof*, on the other hand, is a mathematical proof that `Pre` guarantees `Program`'s termination *and* the truth of `Post`. Total correctness proofs require a *termination proof* in addition to a partial correctness proof. For termination proofs, we refer the reader to the more specialized literature in the bibliographic notes. In what follows, we focus on partial correctness proofs, assuming that termination is verified separately.

We are now able to build correctness proofs of complete programs by applying the foregoing proof rules. Let us start with the following, simplest, case.

## Example 6.13

Consider the following program and its assertions:

```
{input₁ > 0 and input₂ > 0}
begin
    read(x); read(y);
    div := 0;
    while x ≥ y loop
        div := div + 1;
        x := x - y;
    end loop;
    write(div); write(x);
end;
{input₁ = output₁ * input₂ + output₂ and 0 ≤ output₂ < input₂}
```

The predicates of this program provide a specification of an integer division algorithm. Our goal is to prove that the implementation is correct with respect to the given specification.

Backward substitutions through the output statements leave us with the job of proving

```
{input₁ > 0 and input₂ > 0}
begin
        read(x); read(y);
        div := 0;
        while x ≥ y loop
                div := div + 1;
                x := x - y;
        end loop;
{input₁ = div * input₂ + x and 0 ≤ x < input₂}
```

At this point, we need to be able to invent a suitable loop invariant. Actually, many assertions are invariant—in a more or less trivial way—for the preceding loop. For instance, $z + w = 2$, $div \geq 0$, and $div > 10,000$, are all invariant for the loop. (Prove the invariance of these assertions as an exercise.) These invariants, however, are useless for us: We need an invariant that, conjoined with the negation of the loop condition, implies the truth of the assertion

```
{input₁ = div * input₂ + x and x < input₂}
```

The choice of a loop invariant is a key point in the correctness proof. The discovery of such an invariant, in general, requires insight into the algorithm of the program. In this example, the job of the loop is to increment $div$ by one unit at every iteration and to decrement x by the value of y. This action can be formalized as the following candidate invariant: $I_1$: input₁ = div * y + x.

Backward substitution through the loop body immediately shows that this formula actually is an invariant. The invariant is not sufficiently strong, however, to prove that the required postcondition holds at loop exit; that is, we cannot prove that $I_1$ **and** x < y **implies** {input₁ = div * input₂ + x **and** x < input₂}. To prove this, we need to strengthen $I_1$ so that y = input₂ **and** x ≥ 0 also hold. Since these additional conditions are also invariant, we deduce the following stronger loop invariant:

$I_2$: input₁ = div * y + x **and** x ≥ 0 **and** y = input₂

It is easy to verify that the conjunction of this invariant with x < y (the negation of the loop condition) implies the desired postcondition. Finally, we easily verify the fragment

```
{input₁ > 0 and input₂ > 0}
begin
    read(x); read(y); div := 0;
    {I₂: input₁ = div * y + x and x ≥ 0 and y = input₂}
```

and this completes the proof.    ■

Proof rules allow us to derive formulas that are assertions about properties that hold at intermediate points in a program. In Section 5.6.2.2, we called these assertions *intermediate assertions.* An intermediate assertion is associated with a particular point in the program and states a property that must hold at that point in any execution of the program. Loop invariants are a kind of intermediate assertion that characterize the semantics of a loop. The assertion {$input_1$ = div * $input_2$ + x **and** $0 \leq x < input_2$} holding before the output statements of the program discussed in Example 6.13 is another example of an intermediate assertion. In Section 6.8, we shall see that intermediate assertions may be useful in the error removal phase of software development.

## Exercises

**6.23** Prove formally that the following program fragments each store the maximum among x, y, z, and w into variable max:

**a.**
```
if x ≥ y and x ≥ z and x ≥ w then
   max := x;
elsif y ≥ x and y ≥ z and y ≥ w then
   max := y;
elsif z ≥ x and z ≥ y and z ≥ w then
   max := z;
else
   max := w;
end if;
```

**c.**
```
if x ≥ y and x ≥ z and x ≥ w then
   max := x;
end if;
if y ≥ x and y ≥ z and y ≥ w then
   max := y;
end if;
if z ≥ x and z ≥ y and z ≥ w then
   max := z;
end if;
if w ≥ x and w ≥ y and w ≥ z then
   max := w;
end if;
```

**b.**
```
if x ≥ y and z ≥ w then
   if x ≥ z then
      max := x;
   else
      max := z;
   end if;
elsif x ≥ y then
   if x ≥ w then
      max := x;
   else
      max := w;
   end if;
elsif z ≥ w then
   if z ≥ y then
      max := z;
   else
      max := y;
   end if;
else
   if w ≥ y then
      max := w;
   else
      max := y;
   end if;
end if;
```

**6.24** Does the proof of Example 6.13 also hold with the weaker precondition $input_1 \geq 0$ **and** $input_2 \geq 0$? Can the assumed precondition be weakened? How?

**6.25** Build correctness proofs for the following fragments:

**a.**
```
{input₁ > 0 and input₂ > 0}
read(z); read(y)
x := 1;
j := 1;
while y ≥ j loop
   j := j + 1;
   x := x * z;
end loop;
write(x);
{output = input₁^input₂}
```

**b.**
```
{input₁ > 0 and input₂ > 0}
read(x); read(y);
while x ≠ y loop
   if x > y then
      x := x - y;
   else
      y := y - x;
   end if;
end loop;
write(x);
{GCD(input₁, input₂, output)}
```

In the second fragment, the predicate GCD $(x, y, w)$, read "$w$ is the greatest common divisor of $x$ and $y$," stands for

```
exists z₁, z₂ (x = w*z₁ and y = w*z₂)
and not exists h (exists z₁, z₂ (x = h*z₁ and y = h*z₂) and h > w)
```

### 6.4.2.2 Programs with Arrays

The proof rules used so far help in proving the correctness of programs made up of very simple programming language statements, but real programming languages offer a richer set of statements which require more complicated proof rules. We do not give a detailed treatment of all programming language constructs here. Such a treatment may be found in the specialized literature. There is, however, one major issue of conceptual relevance that we must address.

Consider the following assignment statement involving the use of an indexed variable:

```
a(i) := 4;
```

If we apply the previous proof rule for assignment statements, we would obtain an assertion of the type

```
{a(3) = 2}
a(i) := 4;
{a(3) = 2 and a(i) = 4}
```

which is false if $i = 3$ when the statement is executed. Clearly, the problem arises because the effect of the statement depends on the value of the index variable. To cope with this problem, when the left-hand side of an assignment statement is an indexed variable, the backward substitution rule must be generalized. We show how to effect such a generalization next.

For any assertion Post, and for any statement of the type $a(i) :=$ expression, let Pre denote the assertion obtained from Post by substituting every occurrence of an indexed variable $a(j)$ by the term

```
if j = i then expression else a(j);
```

Then we can use the rule

```
{Pre} a(i) := expression; {Post}
```

for our correctness analysis.[14]

Applying the new rule to the previous example, we obtain

```
{(if 3 = i then 4 else a(3)) = 2 and (if i = i then 4 else a(i)) = 4}
a(i) := 4;
{a(3) = 2 and a(i) = 4}
```

which is simplified to

---

[14] A few mathematical intricacies have been omitted to simplify the notation. However, the simplified rule can be used safely in most practical situations.

```
{i ≠ 3 and a(3) = 2}
a(i) := 4;
{a(3) = 2 and a(i) = 4}
```

As a first application of the new rule, let us consider a program fragment that is intended to insert an integer $x$ into a table of $n$ elements. The table is implemented as an array with $nmax$ elements of type integer. If, before execution of the code, $n$ is less than $nmax$, then the program must guarantee that $x$ will be inserted into the table. A formal proof of this requirement calls for the verification of the following formula:

```
{n < nmax}
if n < nmax then
    n := n + 1;
    table(n) := x;
end if;
{n ≤ nmax and (exists i(1 ≤ i ≤ n and table(i) = x))}
```

By applying the augmented backward substitution rule, we obtain the following predicate:

```
{n + 1 ≤ nmax and
    (exists i (1 ≤ i ≤ n +1 and
            (if i = n + 1 then x else table(i)) = x))
    )
}
```

Now, $n < nmax$ implies $n + 1 \leq nmax$. On the other hand,

```
(exists i (1 ≤ i ≤ n + 1 and (if i = n + 1 then x else table(i)) = x))
```

is obviously satisfied by $i = n + 1$. Thus, the stated precondition guarantees the desired postcondition.

As another example, let us prove the following formula:

```
{n ≥ 1}
i := 1; j := 1;
found := false,
while i ≤ n loop
    if table(i) = x then
        found := true;
        i := i + 1
    else
        table(j) := table(i);
        i := i + 1; j := j + 1;
    end if;
end loop;
n := j - 1;
{not exists m (1 ≤ m ≤ n and table(m) = x) and
found ≡ exists m (1 ≤ m ≤ old_n and old_table(m) = x)}
```

In this formula, *old_table* and *old_n* are constants that denote the values of table and of $n$, respectively, before execution of the program fragment. (Recall from Section 5.6.2 that, sometimes, in formal specifications, we need to refer to values held by variables at previous points in the execution flow.)

Intuitively, the specification states that the program should delete from the table all occurrences of the value x, if any, and should store, in the variable found, a Boolean value indicating whether x occurred in table before execution. It is not explicitly requested, however, that all other elements of table be preserved.

Let us prove the correctness of the foregoing program fragment by means of the following loop invariant:

```
I: {(j ≤ i) and (i ≤ old_n + 1)
          and (not exists m (1 ≤ m < j and table(m) = x))
          and (n = old_n)
          and found ≡ exists m (1 ≤ m < i and old_table(m) = x)}
```

First, it is easy to prove that I **and** i > n implies the result of backward substitution of the postcondition through n := j − 1.

Second, let us prove I's invariance through the loop. Backward substitution through the **then** branch yields

```
{(j ≤ i + 1) and (i + 1 ≤ old_n + 1)
          and (not exists m (1 ≤ m < j and table(m) = x))
          and (n = old_n) and exists m (1 ≤ m < i + 1
            and old_table(m) = x )}
```

which is implied by I **and** i ≤ n **and** table(i) = x.

The **else** branch produces

```
{(j + 1 ≤ i + 1) and (i + 1 ≤ old_n + 1)
          and (not exists m (1 ≤ m < j + 1
                and (if m = j then table(i) else
                    table(m)) = x))
          and (n= old_n)
          and found ≡ exists m (1 ≤ m < i + 1 and
            old_table(m) = x)}
```

The fact that I **and** i ≤ n **and** table(i) ≠ x imply the first two clauses is obvious. Let us show that they also imply

```
(not exists m (1 ≤ m < j + 1 and (if m = j then table(i) else table(m)) = x))
```

To see that they do, note that, for all m, with 1 ≤ m < j, the statement is implied by the invariant; when m = j, it is implied by the condition of the **if** statement. In quite the same way, we may also prove

```
found ≡ exists m (1 ≤ m < i + 1 and old_table(m) = x)
```

Finally, it is clear that the precondition n ≥ 1 implies the result of backward substituting I through i := 1; j := 1; found := false. This completes the correctness proof.

The technique we have presented here to deal with arrays also allows us to deal with input-output statements in a formal way. In fact, we can view the files input and output as unbounded arrays having associated indexes $c_i$ and $c_o$, respectively, that are initialized to 1 and automatically incremented after any input-output operation. Specifically, the statement read(x) may be viewed as an abbreviation of

```
x := input(c_i);
c_i := c_i + 1;
```

Similarly, `write(x)` may be considered an abbreviation of

```
output(c_o) := x;
c_o := c_o + 1;
```

## Exercise

**6.26** Augment the preceding specification of the delete operation by requiring that no elements of *old_table* other than x be deleted and no other elements be added. Also, specify that the number of elements should never exceed `nmax`. Prove the correctness of the program with respect to the new assertions.

### 6.4.2.3  *Correctness Proofs in the Large*

The distinction between techniques "in the small" and "in the large" can be applied to correctness proofs as well as to testing, specification, and design: In no case can we manage large and complex artifacts by simply scaling up techniques that work fine for small ones. As usual, modularization is the major approach for progressing from the small to the large. Thus, it is no surprise that we can build and manage large correctness proofs by modularizing them as we do in all other contexts. In this section, we briefly hint at how we can build modular correctness proofs. Furthermore, as we did with testing, we show that often we cannot stop at pure software analysis, but must proceed to a complete system correctness proof.

## Example 6.14

Suppose we have defined and implemented an abstract data type `TABLE` along the following lines:

```
module TABLE;
exports
        type Table_Type (max_size: NATURAL): ?;
        no more than max_size entries may be stored in a table:
        user modules must guarantee this
        procedure Insert(Table: in out Table_Type; ELEMENT: in
            ElementType);
        procedure Delete(Table: in out Table_Type; ELEMENT: in
            ElementType);
        function Size(Table: in Table_Type) return NATURAL;
        provides the current size of a table
            .
            .
            .
end TABLE
```

Each abstract operation can be specified formally be means of suitable pre- and post-conditions, exemplified as follows:

```
{true}
Delete(Table, Element);
{Element ∉ Table};

{Size(Table) < max_size}
Insert(Table, Element)
{Element ∈ Table};
```

At this point, we can easily—and formally—prove properties about the abstract data type `TABLE` by using its abstract specification. For instance, we can prove that applying a `Delete` operation after an `Insert` operation guarantees that the deleted element is not present in the table if the `Insert` operation is applied when the table is not full. In fact, the proof follows easily from the two formulas about `Insert` and `Delete`.

To prove the correctness of module `TABLE`'s implementation, we must know what data structure is used to represent tables. Suppose that type `TableType` is implemented as

```
type TableType (max_size: NATURAL) is
    record
        size : INTEGER range 0.. max_size := 0;
        contents = array (1.. max_size) of INTEGER;
    end record;
```

Then it is explicitly stated that predicate `Element ∈ Table` is true if and only if there exists a value `i` such that $1 \leq i \leq size \leq max\_size$ **and** `Table.con-tents(i) = Element`. It is a simple exercise to prove the correctness of the procedures that implement the operations on `Table`.

The previous specifications, however, are too weak to prove a natural and desirable property such as

```
{Table.size < max_size}
Insert(Table, Element);
Delete(Table, Element);
{Table = Old_Table - {Element}}[15]
```

which states that after the foregoing two operations are executed, the table is the same as it was, except that `Element` is missing. (See Exercises 6.27 and 6.28.)   ■

Modular correctness proofs extend naturally towards system correctness proofs as well as system testing and other verification techniques. To illustrate, let us go back to the elevator system introduced in Chapter 3 and resumed in Chapter 5 in the context of formal specifications. A typical requirement we might state for such a system is that, if, in any elevator, we push the *i*th internal button, the request will be served within $\Delta$ seconds, which means that there is a time `t` belonging to the interval $[t_b, t_b + \Delta]$,

---

[15] The symbol ' – ' denotes set difference here.

where $t_b$ denotes the time the button is pushed, such that the elevator reaches the $i$th floor at time $t$; furthermore the $i$th button must remain illuminated during the interval $[t_b, t)$ (with the usual convention that $t_b$ is included in, and $t$ is excluded from, the interval). Let us examine how we can formally prove that our system implementation guarantees such a property.

Clearly, to produce such a proof, we must analyze a number of components in the system, such as

- the buttons and their illumination devices;
- the control apparatus, which receives information about the state of the elevators and about requests raised by the user through pushing a button. The control apparatus, in turn, consists of an electronic device, which receives signals from the context and sets registers to suitable values, and of a program that implements suitable service policies (e.g., FIFO); and
- the engine, which moves the elevator at some speed according to the commands received by the control apparatus.

All of these components influence the global correctness of the system with respect to the property under consideration. Thus, it seems natural to modularize the system correctness proof into the following pieces (we simplify the whole process that leads to a complete correctness proof and omit many details in order to focus attention on the essentials of modularization of the proof):

- One lemma must state that if we push internal button $i$ and the elevator is not at the $i$th floor, then the button lights up, and a signal is sent to the control apparatus notifying it of the request for floor $i$.
- A second lemma must state that whenever the control apparatus receives a request signal, it inserts the request into a list of pending requests and removes it from the list only when it sends a command to the engine to move towards the $i$th floor.
- A third lemma must state that the apparatus's scheduling algorithm is such that every request is eventually removed from the list and that no more than $n-1$ requests are served before this removal; in other words, it cannot be the case that a second request for floor $i$ is reinserted into the list before any requests that were pending at the time when the first request for floor $i$ was served. (For simplicity, we assume that the execution of the scheduling algorithm takes a time that is negligible in relation to the time taken by the elevator's movement.)
- A fourth lemma states that whenever the engine receives the command to go to floor $i$, the elevator reaches floor $i$ within $\Delta_1$ seconds.
- A fifth lemma states that whenever the elevator reaches the $i$th floor and the corresponding button is illuminated, the button is switched off.

Finally, on the basis of all these lemmas, one can deduce the desired property as a concluding theorem if, say, $\Delta < n * \Delta_1$. Notice that a better and more realistic policy (than, say, just a FIFO one) could allow us to prove a stronger requirement than the third lemma and, therefore, a better time bound $\Delta'$.

Of course, each of the preceding lemmas must be proven separately on the basis of the specifications of the corresponding module. In this case, the availability of a unifying formalism that allows us to describe the behavior and the properties of heterogeneous system components is highly valuable, because it provides a unique framework for global system analysis. Certainly, the analysis of engine behavior is quite different from the analysis of the scheduling algorithm and requires different types of knowledge—mechanics and electromagnetism, as opposed to algorithms and data structures—but it is important to have a unifying formalism to describe and analyze the whole system in a modular way, leaving to the specialists the proof of particular lemmas such as the fourth one.

### 6.4.2.4 Using Correctness Proofs in Practice

The examples and the exercises in the previous section demonstrate that formal correctness proofs are intricate even for fairly simple programs. Thus, the question naturally arises, "What about proving the correctness of a software system that is 10,000 lines or more?" In other words, we must assess the applicability of the proof techniques to practical situations. In fact, theoreticians proposed formal verification techniques over 30 years ago, but their application in practical projects is still an exception, and their practical usefulness is often questioned.

The following are some of the major objections raised against the use of formal verification techniques:

1. Formal proofs are often even longer and more complex than the programs they are intended to prove. Thus, they are at least as prone to error as those programs themselves. Hence, a correctness proof does not increase our confidence in the program's correctness.
2. Formal proofs require too much mathematical background to be used by the average software designer.
3. Formal proofs overwhelm designers with details that could easily be dispensed with if they used an informal analysis.
4. Even if we can achieve mathematical certainty of the correctness of a program, we cannot rely on it in an absolute way because there could be a failure in the implementation of the language (the compiler) or even in the hardware.
5. Formal proofs do not deal with the physical limitations of the computing device. For instance, a limited number of bits is used to approximate real numbers. Thus, assertions that are true in the idealized mathematical world may turn out to be false when actual computations are performed.

Some of these objections are serious. In evaluating the applicability of formal verification techniques, however, we must also consider counterobjections. Let us start by refuting the last two of the foregoing claims.

Of course, even when we have proven the formal correctness of a program for, say, air traffic control, we cannot rely 100 percent on the air traffic control *system*. An earthquake could destroy the hardware on which the program is running, the hardware itself could have a failure, or an error could be present in the compiler that translated the application program.

But this is not a new situation. Even if the design of a car is perfect, there could be an error in the assembly procedure or a defect in the material used to build the brakes, and the resulting product would not be reliable anymore. Still, we feel safer if the design has been in some manner certified. In a complex system, all of the components must be verified, and the application program is just one component of the whole system. Also, mathematical properties can be proven on mathematical models that are an abstraction of the real world. Thus, having verified that a mathematical model of a bridge tolerates certain circumstances does not guarantee that the real bridge will not collapse under those same circumstances. However, we justifiably accept conclusions drawn on the basis of the analysis of the model, as long as we keep in mind that the model does leave out the consideration of some risks.

On the other hand, the literature on formal correctness analysis does not deal, in general, with the problem of using finite computer memory to approximate infinite sets. This problem, however, is well understood, and powerful solutions are available in the literature on numerical computation.

Let us now focus attention on the remaining objections. It is true that a formal analysis takes longer and is more difficult, and even more tedious, than an informal analysis. And, of course, errors do exist in formal reasoning. Nonetheless, formal reasoning is universally considered to be a fundamental tool for deriving reliable conclusions. In the history of science, the introduction of formal objects has always been motivated by failures of previous, less rigorous, attempts. And pure mathematics, as we have observed, has used much informal reasoning to build sound and important theorems. Even the discovery of paradoxes has led to more formal approaches to certain branches of mathematics (e.g., set theory and mathematical logic). In general, when we have good reasons not to rely too much on informal reasoning, we must try to gain more confidence by using formulas. Such attempts often lead to the discovery of subtle errors.

To be useful in practice, formal verification techniques should be applied in conjunction with the modularity and incrementality principles, just as they are applied together in the design and specification activities. We have seen in Section 6.4.2.3 how modular formal proofs can and should be built: Modularization is a major principle used to master complexity and must be applied in any phase of development and to any technique.

Also, formality and modularity could be exploited jointly with incrementality. A critical module should be specified formally and its implementation checked carefully against the formal specification, perhaps by applying formal proof techniques, whereas other components of the system could be left to a more informal verification.

For example, a good candidate for formal specification and analysis is a library package that is used by many users or that is used in critical applications. Certainly, the reusability of a component can be enhanced if its potential users understand its functionality fully and can rely on its correctness.

As an example of how formal program proofs can be reserved for critical portions of a program, let us go back to the merge program of Example 6.12, which is repeated as follows for convenience:

```
i := 1; j := 1; k :=1;
while k ≤ 2 * n loop
    if a(i) < b(j) then
        c(k) := a(i);
        i :i + 1;
    else
        c(k) := b(j);
        j := j + 1;
    end if;
    k := k + 1;
end loop;
```

Initially, a simple informal analysis could raise the question of whether the indexes i, j, and k are guaranteed to remain within the ranges 1..n, 1..n, and 1..2 * n, respectively. The question may be easily rephrased as whether the assertion

I:{1 ≤ i ≤ n **and** 1 ≤ j ≤ n **and** 1 ≤ k ≤ 2 * n}

is a loop invariant.

An attempt to prove this assertion invariant—with the aid of the further relation k = i + j – 1—would fail much more clearly in a formal than in an informal analysis. In fact,

I **and** k = i + j– 1

does not imply

{1 ≤ i + 1 ≤ n **and** 1 ≤ j + 1 ≤ n **and** 1 ≤ k + 1 ≤ 2 * n}

(i.e., it does not imply the result of the latter's backward substitution through the loop body).

Actually, as we know, the program fragment is incorrect; after correcting it, we would be able to prove the assertion. The assertion, however, is not a complete specification of the fragment, but contains only facts that we consider critical. In reality, going through a complete specification and its related correctness proof would be quite complicated. (See Exercise 6.71.) But the example shows that we do not need to go through a complete specification and its correctness proof to assess the program. If there are critical facts that we want to verify (in the example, indexing in the arrays), then we may still specify and prove them in a formal way. This is an instance of the principles of separation of concerns and abstraction, namely, deal with the critical issues only, and is particularly valuable when the program is large and complex.

We should also emphasize that program assertions—pre- and postconditions and intermediate assertions—can be used as a formal way of expressing program comments. Accordingly, they can be used both to drive correctness proofs and to debug programs. In other words, the activity of formally specifying properties of the execution states at some critical points can be used both to help localize and repair errors (debugging) and to prove their absence (proving correctness). We will return to the topic of debugging, using assertions, in Section 6.8.

The usefulness of formal analysis techniques can be enhanced further by the use of (semi-) automatic tools. In fact, in a formal correctness proof, there are a few critical points where ingenuity must be applied (typically, to invent loop invariants and to prove logical implications), and there are many "clerical" steps that can easily be automated (typically, backward substitutions and some algebraic simplifications). It is natural to leave the carrying out of the latter to the computer and allow the user to concentrate on the critical aspects. The recent availability of well-engineered tools for proving program correctness has encouraged the adoption of this technique in some important industrial projects.

Finally, we believe that a good knowledge of formal analysis techniques will eventually enhance the reliability of even informal analysis. In fact, rigor and formality always enhance the reliability of informal, everyday types of reasoning. In sum, it is true that formal correctness proofs are still of limited practical application, but, if properly understood and used, they do offer a high potential for enhancing software and system qualities. In fact, recently, significant examples of successful applications in real-life projects have been reported, though they are still few in number. These facts will be considered further in the more general context of the industrial adoption of so-called *formal methods*. (See case study D in the appendix.)

## Exercises

**6.27**  Is the following provable with respect to the specification given for module TABLE in this section? Why? Why not?

```
{max_size > 1}
Delete(Table, Element);
Insert(Table, Element);

{Element ∈ Table}
```

**6.28**  Modify the specifications given in Section 6.4.2.3 for operations Insert and Delete in such a way that both

```
{Size(Table) < max_size}
Insert(Table, Element);
Delete(Table, Element);
{Table = Old_Table - Element}
and
{Size(Table) > 1}
Delete(Table, Element);
Insert(Table, Element);

{Element ∈ Table}
```

become provable. Then give an implementation, and either prove it correct with respect to the augmented specifications, or, if it is not correct, modify the implementation accordingly.

## 6.5    SYMBOLIC EXECUTION

Symbolic execution is a verification technique that can be classified as somewhere in between testing and analysis: It is a synthesis of experimental and analytical approaches to software verification.

Consider the following simple program:

```
read(a); read(b);
x := a + b;
write(x);
```

A computer needs to read some specific input values in order to perform its computation and produce the appropriate output. By contrast, a human analysis (for instance, during a walk-through) can proceed along the following lines:

> Let A and B be the first two values of the input file. They are assigned to variables a and b, respectively. Thus, the result of the assignment x := a + b is that x gets the value A + B. Finally, A + B is printed.

The advantage of this kind of reasoning over actual numeric computation is more generality: A and B represent *any actual values* for the input variables. Thus, they allow us to conclude that the program's output is their sum, no matter what their actual values are. By contrast, if we just test the program by supplying, say, 3 and 4 as input values, the fact that the output is the value 7 provides little evidence that the program's function is a sum.

The main difference between computer execution and hand simulation of the previous program is that in computer execution variables receive actual numeric[16] values, whereas in hand simulation we give them *symbolic values*. Thus, we said that a's value was A and that, after execution, x got the value A + B.

Without going into a formal theory of symbolic execution, for which we refer the reader to the specialized literature referenced in the bibliographic notes, we can say that the technique is based on the fact that the domain of possible values for program variables is the set of expressions made up of symbolic values and operation symbols. Even without many mathematical definitions, the reader can see that the results of symbolically evaluating the following programs are the expressions within brackets:

```
read(a); read(b);
x := a + 1; y := x * b;
write(y);
[(A + 1) * B]
```

```
read(a); read(b);
x := a + 1; x := x + b + 2;
write(x);
[A + B + 3]
```

We see from the second example that some simplification of formulas can be applied naturally to the symbolic results.

Symbolic evaluation is a candidate technique for general and reliable program analysis. For instance, consider the following program fragment with associated assertions:

---

[16] In this section, we talk about *numeric computation* and *numeric* values, as opposed to symbolic computation and symbolic values, respectively. Thus, the attribute "numeric" applies not only to genuine numeric values, but also to values that, strictly speaking, are nonnumeric, such as characters and Booleans.

```
{true}
read(a);
x := a * a;
x := x + 1;
write(x);
{output > 0}
```

Symbolic evaluation of this fragment easily produces the result output = $A^2$ + 1. Thus, a simple arithmetic deduction allows us to conclude that the specification is met. The method we follow is similar to what we did in correctness proofs. Also, much of the symbolic transformation involved in such an analysis can be performed automatically, just as backward substitution is done in correctness proofs.

The situation, however, becomes more intricate as soon as we deal with nontrivial programs. For instance, in the program fragment

```
read(a);
if a > 0 then
    DO_CASE_1;
else
    DO_CASE_2;
end if;
```

symbolic execution cannot proceed when it reaches the conditional, because a's symbolic value does not carry enough information to support the choice of either DO_CASE_1 or DO_CASE_2. One approach to dealing with such branches is to select a particular branch and continue along it.

We shall describe how this kind of problem can be treated in Section 6.5.1, which provides the basic concepts behind the symbolic execution of a simple conventional language. Section 6.5.2 discusses more intricate details that are needed to symbolically execute programs with arrays and concurrent programs (Section 6.5.2.1). Finally, Section 6.5.3 discusses the use of symbolic execution in testing.

### 6.5.1    Basic Concepts of Symbolic Execution

Consider the following program fragment, and assume that at the beginning of its execution the symbolic values of the variables are x = X, a = A, and y = Y:

```
x := y + 2;
if x > a then
    a := a + 2;
else
    y := x + 3;
end if;
x := x + a + y;
```

After execution of the first statement, we have x = Y + 2, with all other variables remaining unchanged. At the branching point, since the comparison Y + 2 > A may yield either true or false, we make an arbitrary choice, say, the **else** branch. This leads to the final state {a = A, y = Y + 5, x =2 * Y + A + 7}. We must, however, record the fact that such a result is obtained by selecting the **else** branch of the **if** statement. This can be done by keeping track of the path executed—for example, by referring to the control flow graph of the program and by recording the condition the symbolic values must satisfy in order to guarantee the traversal of the selected path. In this case, the condition is $Y + 2 \leq A$. As a result, we may claim that the symbolic execution we have described produces the triple

```
<{a = A, y = Y + 5, x = 2 * Y + A + 7}, <1, 3, 4> , Y + 2 ≤ A>
```

where `<1, 3, 4>` denotes the execution path with reference to the control flow graph shown in Figure 6.10.

The condition that guarantees the execution of a given path is called the *path condition*. Once a path condition is given, the corresponding execution path can be derived immediately from the program, and conversely. Thus, only one of the two is necessary to fully describe the symbolic execution. For the moment, however, we shall keep both. Indeed, we shall see later that the execution path is actually needed for concurrent programs.

In general, let P denote a program fragment, and let $G_P$ denote P's control flow graph. Then the result of symbolically evaluating P on a path of $G_P$ is the *symbolic state* of P, defined as the triple `< symbolic_variable_values, execution_path, path_condition>`. The set `symbolic_variable_values` describes the bindings of variables with their symbolic values by equations of the type

```
variable_identifier = symbolic_expression
```

where `symbolic_expression` is composed in the usual way from identifiers that denote symbolic variable values. (For simplicity, we use lowercase letters for variable identifiers and uppercase letters for symbolic values.) The execution path is a sequence of contiguous edges in $G_P$. The path condition is a logical expression involving symbolic values and denotes the condition that the symbolic values must meet to guarantee traversal of the execution path.

Before symbolic execution is started, the symbolic state of the interpreter is initialized to show the symbolic values of variables as undefined, the execution path as

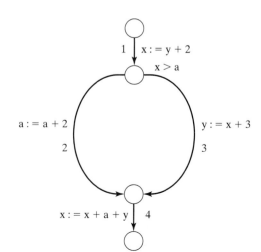

FIGURE 6.10

An annotated control flow graph. The branching node is marked by the corresponding condition in the program fragment, and edges are marked by the corresponding statements.

null, and the condition path as true. As new statements are encountered, the symbolic interpreter updates the symbolic state in the following way:

1. The execution of an input statement `read(x)` removes any binding for `x` that may exist in the state and adds the binding `x = X`, where `X` is a *newly introduced* symbolic value that does not occur in any previous state.

2. The execution of an assignment statement `x := expression` causes the construction of the symbolic value of the expression, `SV`, from the symbolic values of the variables involved in the expression. (The details of such construction should be obvious from the previous examples.) Subsequently, the binding `x = SV` is stored into the state, replacing the previous binding for `x`, if there is any.

3. The execution of an output statement `write(expression)` causes the symbolic evaluation of the expression as before and the binding `output(n) = computed_symbolic_value`, where `n` denotes a counter associated with the output file. The counter `n` is initialized to `1` and is automatically incremented after each output statement.

4. After execution of the last statement of a sequence that corresponds to an edge of $G_P$, the edge is appended to the execution path.

5. The execution of a conditional statement of the type **if** cond **then** $S_1$; **else** $S_2$; **end if** or of a **while** cond **loop...end loop** statement causes the following sequence of steps to be executed:

   **a.** The condition is evaluated by substituting the current symbolic values for variables into it. Let `eval(cond)` denote the symbolic result.

   **b.** If it can be deduced that `eval(cond)` is `true` or `false` independently of the values of the symbolic identifiers,[17] then execution proceeds by following the appropriate branch. Otherwise,

   **c.** A nondeterministic choice of `true` or `false` is made for the condition. In the former case, `eval(cond)` is conjoined to the current path condition. In the latter case, **not**`(eval(cond))` is conjoined to the path condition. Then, execution proceeds along the corresponding edge of $G_P$.

By applying this symbolic execution procedure to the fragment appearing at the beginning of this subsection, we obtain two different triples as results. Besides the one already mentioned, we have the following triple that is obtained by selecting the **then** branch of the conditional statement:

```
<{a = A + 2, y = Y, x = 2 * Y + A + 4}, <1, 2, 4> , Y + 2 > A>
```

Clearly, in many cases, the set of possible triples that are the result of symbolically executing a program fragment may be infinite, as may be the number of paths in the control flow graph.

---

[17] Remember that evaluating logical implications of symbolic expressions is, in general, undecidable. Thus, it cannot be done completely mechanically and may require human interaction.

Symbolic execution of traditional programming constructs such as **if-then-else** and **while** loops establishes a one-to-one correspondence between the execution path and the path condition; that is, a given path condition unequivocally determines an execution path, and conversely. This is due to the deterministic nature of these constructs (i.e., for any actual execution state, when variables have numeric values, the next statement to be executed is determined uniquely). In such a case, we can drop the execution path component from the symbolic state; this is not possible, however, if the language provides nondeterministic control structures or, as we shall see in Section 6.5.2.1, in the case of concurrent programs.

### Exercises

**6.29** Give symbolic evaluation rules for classical programming constructs such as **case**, **repeat-until**, and other constructs.

**6.30** Compute some symbolic evaluation triples by increasing the length of the execution paths for the programs of Exercise 6.25.

### 6.5.2   Programs with Arrays

Symbolic execution becomes more intricate when we are dealing with arrays for much the same reasons as it does in proving the correctness of programs with arrays. We shall briefly sketch two possible ways of tackling the problem.

In the first approach, any access to a given array whose index value is not numerically known is considered as if it were a branch, with an edge for each possible index value. In other words, let a be an array with 10 elements. Then the statement a(i) := exp is considered a shorthand notation for

```
case i of
        when 1 => a(1) := exp;
        when 2 => a(2) := exp;
          .
          .
          .
```

This approach is simple, but produces a proliferation of execution paths. It could be used in practice only in interactive execution or with small-sized arrays.

A more general approach is to let any assignment to an array value produce a new symbolic value for the whole array and to record suitable relationships between the old value and the new value. For instance, let $A_1$ be the symbolic value of array a at a given point where the statement a(i) = exp is executed. Then, after execution of the statement, a receives the new symbolic value $A_2$, which we shall denote as $A_2 = A_1 <i, exp>$, a shorthand notation for

```
for all k if k = i then A₂(k) = exp else A₂(k) = A₁(k)
```

We can see a similarity between this formula and the backward substitution rule given for correctness proofs.

We explain the second method with the help of the next example.

**Example 6.15**

Consider the following program fragment, where x denotes an integer array variable of length 5:

```
1.    read(i);
2.    y := x(i);
3.    x(3) := 9;
4.    read(i);
5.    x(i) := 3 + y;
6.    y := x(2);
7.    read(i);
8.    x(i) := x(i) - 1;
9.    y := y + x(i);
```

Let execution start in an initial state in which the symbolic value $X_1$ is bound to x. Then executing statements 1 through 9 produces the following bindings:

```
1.    read(i);            i = I_1
2.    y := x(i);          y = X_1(I_1)
3.    x(3) := 9;          x = X_2 where X_2 = X_1 <3, 9>
4.    read(i);            i = I_2
5.    x(i) := 3 + y;      x = X_3 where X_3 = X_2 <I_2, 3 + X_1(I_1)>
                                  that is, X_3(I_2) = 3 + X_1(I_1) [18]
6.    y := x(2);          y = X_3(2)
7.    read(i);            i = I_3
8.    x(i) := x(i) - 1;   x = X_4 where X_4 = X_3 <I_3, X_3(I_3) - 1>
9.    y := y + x(i);      y = X_3(2) + X_4(I_3)
```

Notice that the symbolic state can be expressed as a function of the symbolic values read and x's initial value $X_1$, using substitutions that "unfold" the additional relations stored into the state. By performing such operations, we obtain, at the end of the execution of the fragment,

$$y = X_1<3, 9><I_2, 3 + X_1(I_1)>(2) +$$
$$X_1<3, 9><I_2, 3 + X_1(I_1)><I_3, X_1<3, 9><I_2, 3 +$$
$$X_1(I_1)>(I_3) - 1>(I_3)$$  ∎

## Exercise

**6.31** Compute several execution paths for the program of Example 6.12. (Try the case where you execute the loop just once, and observe how the treatment of arrays becomes simpler when indexes have a numeric value even during symbolic evaluation.)

---

[18]Here, some optimization could be performed. In fact, since x has not been referenced since its last assignment, we could simply update its current value by means of the modification $x = X_2$ **where** $X_2 = X_1 <3, 9>< I_2, 3 + X_1(I_1) >$.

#### 6.5.2.1 *Symbolic Execution of Concurrent Programs*

In this section, we examine the use of symbolic execution in the analysis of concurrent software. Specifically, we base our analysis on Petri nets; the remarks we give, however, are general and do not depend on the particular formalism we use for describing a concurrent system.

Let us consider augmented Petri nets in which tokens have values and each transition has an associated action and a predicate that determines whether the transition can fire, based on the values of incoming tokens. Symbolic execution allows us to use symbolic values for tokens and evaluate the transition predicates symbolically.

In a sequential and deterministic program, the state of the symbolic interpreter at any particular point is given by a triple < `symbolic_variable_values`, `execution_path`, `path_condition` >, where `path_condition` fully determines the execution path. In a concurrent system, the execution path is a sequence of atomic execution steps. In the specific case of a Petri net, an atomic step is modeled by the firing of a transition, which consumes a tuple of tokens from its input places. If we make the simplifying assumption that no more than one token will ever be present in each place, a sequence of atomic steps can be modeled by a firing sequence, which resolves the nondeterminism that is due to several transitions being enabled. Thus, the triple < `symbolic_variable_values`, `execution_path`, `path_condition` > can be used to model the symbolic state of the interpreter, provided that we interpret `execution_path` as the firing sequence.

Consider the specification of a concurrent system given in Figure 6.11. The Petri net represents messages that may be received and dispatched on one of three channels. The action that generates a message in the mailbox is modeled by the statement `m := f()`. Function f with no argument states that messages are sent to the system by the external environment, without any relationship to the internal state of the system. Thus, f is actually used as a random-number generator.

When we execute a Petri net symbolically, we start with an initial value of `true` for the path condition. A transition can fire only if its associated predicate is implied by the path condition. If we decide to fire the transition, then the execution path (i.e., the firing sequence) is updated. A transition can also fire if the path condition implies neither the truth nor the falsity of its associated predicate. In this case, if we decide to fire the transition, then not only is the execution path updated as before, but the path condition is also updated by the conjunction of the evaluated predicate.

Now consider the path condition

$M_1$.`ok_parity` **and not** $M_2$.`ok_parity` **and** $M_3$.`ok_parity`

where $M_1$, $M_2$, and $M_3$ are the symbolic values of messages received (i.e., the tokens generated by the transition `message_reception`) and $M_i$.`ok_parity` (i = 1, 2, 3) indicates whether the parity bit of $M_i$ is correct. We can see that the path condition makes the following firing sequence possible:

```
<message_reception, send_ack₂, message_reception, send_nack,
 message_reception, send_ack₃>
```

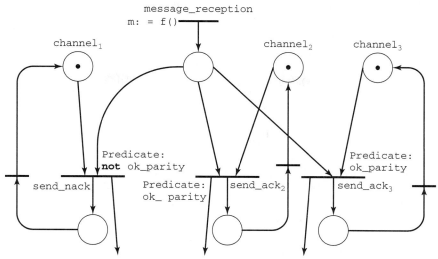

**FIGURE 6.11**

A Petri net describing a transmission channel.

In this example, when the path condition contains $M_i$.ok_parity, two transitions may fire, because the associated predicate is true. The firing sequence resolves the choice between the two.

Thus, both the path condition and the firing sequence are needed to characterize an execution path uniquely. We can then use the pair <firing sequence, path condition> to drive the testing activity. For example, if the net of Figure 6.11 is the specification of a communication system, we could use the path condition to derive constraints on the input messages submitted to the system when it is being tested and then check whether the system executes its actions in the same sequence as specified in the pair. Unfortunately, because of the system's nondeterminism, other sequences of actions would also be considered valid, and we should check whether the observed sequence is actually valid according to the description of the net in the figure.

On the other hand, if we want to reproduce exactly the same sequence of actions as specified in the pair, we may run into problems, because we must be able to resolve nondeterminism exactly as it is stated in the firing sequence member of the pair. This may be difficult to achieve if some actions are performed by the external environment in an unpredictable manner, as may be the case here for messages received in the mailbox. On this very specific topic, we refer the interested reader to the specialized literature mentioned in the bibliographic notes.

### 6.5.3  The Use of Symbolic Execution in Testing

Symbolic execution is a powerful tool that can be seen as an interesting middle ground between the generality and rigor—but also tedium and complexity—of correctness proofs and the conceptual simplicity—but also unreliability—of testing. In fact, the results of symbolic execution are *formulas* that in one way or another help in deducing program properties. The technique, however, is still evolving, and its practical applicability is questionable in the case of large and complex programs.

Symbolic execution, however, can be used indirectly as a testing aid. More precisely, it can help in the selection of test data for a particular execution path. In fact, once a given path in the control flow graph of a program has been selected (e.g., to reach a statement in the case of the statement-coverage criterion), a suitable path condition that guarantees the traversal of that path can be built algorithmically. Thus, the problem of guaranteeing path traversal is reduced to proving the satisfiability of a mathematical formula.

For instance, consider the following program fragment (which was discussed in Section 6.3.4.1), whose control flow graph is given in Figure 6.12:

```
found := false; counter := 1;
while (not found) and counter < number_of_items loop
    if table(counter) = desired_element then
        found := true;
    end if;
    counter := counter + 1;
end loop;
if found then
    write("the desired element exists in the table");
else
    write("the desired element does not exist in the table");
end if;
```

If we symbolically execute the path <1,2,3,5,6,7,9>, we obtain the path condition

```
table(1) = desired_element
```

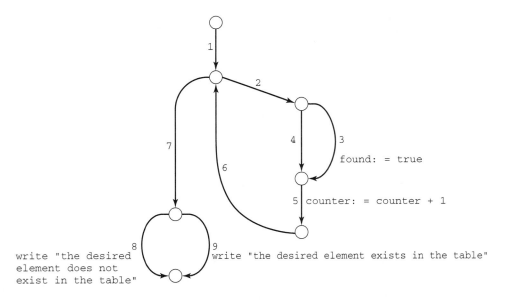

FIGURE 6.12

Control flow graph of the program fragment of Section 6.5.3. Edges are labeled by the relevant assignment statements.

On the other hand, if we try to execute the path `<1,2,3,5,6,2,3,5,6...>`, we obtain, as a partial path condition,

```
1 < number_of_items
and table(1) = desired_element
and not (true)
and 2 < number_of_items
```

which clearly is a contradiction, showing that the path in question is infeasible. In fact, the loop can be executed only once if the **then** branch of its inner **if** statement is executed.

Of course, in general, deciding the satisfiability of path conditions is still an undecidable problem, but finding values that make a formula true is often easier than directly looking for values that guarantee path traversal. In other words, symbolic execution can help make test data selection more systematic. Indeed, in special cases, such as linear path conditions, the process can be made algorithmic.

## 6.6    MODEL CHECKING

Software verification suffers from the fact that correctness, as well as most other relevant properties, is an undecidable problem. In other words, long-standing theoretical results imply that in no way can we algorithmically decide whether a given program computes the function we intend it to. For this reason, testing can only show the presence, not the absence, of errors, and correctness proofs require human ingenuity.

Even though such an unfortunate circumstance holds in general, there are, fortunately, some important particular cases which are not subject to that limitation. *Model checking* is a rather recent verification technique which exploits the fact that most interesting system properties become decidable (i.e., algorithmically verifiable) when the system is modeled as a finite state machine.

Essentially, model checking consists of describing a given system—software or otherwise—as an FSM, expressing a given property of interest as a suitable formula, and verifying whether the system's behavior does indeed satisfy the desired property. The major strength of the approach derives from the fact that this last step is performed automatically. Thus, model checking in some sense joins the features of testing with those of mathematical correctness proofs. It is a kind of dual-language approach combining system modeling for operations and an assertion language to specify the system's properties. In fact, the *model checker* (i.e., the algorithm that verifies the property) either provides a *proof* that the property holds or gives a *counterexample* in the form of a test case that exposes the system's failure to behave according to the property.

Let us now illustrate the essential features of model checking through a simple example. As we said, the first step is to build an FSM modeling the system to be analyzed. For instance, consider the PN of Figure 5.20 and its possible evolutions as described in Figure 5.21. Each state of the FSM represents a marking of the PN. For example, a state labeled $<P_1, P_2, P_3>$ represents the marking where only $P_1, P_2$, and $P_3$ contain one token each. Of course, it is possible to model a PN with an FSM only in the particular case where the number of markings is finite. Figure 6.13 illustrates our example.

The second step consists of describing the property to be verified through a suitable formula. Usually such a formula—or *proposition*—is built according to a syntax and a semantics inspired by temporal logic, such as the following inductive rules:

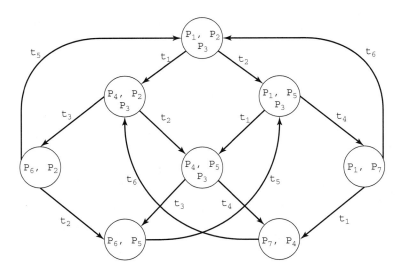

**FIGURE 6.13**

An FSM describing the behavior of the PN of Figure 5.20.

- First, a finite set AP of *atomic propositions* is defined. For instance, with reference to the PN of Figure 5.20 and to the corresponding FSM of Figure 6.13, we could define the following AP:

  - $C_1, C_r$, meaning that the processes described by the left and right portions of the net, respectively, are in the critical region (i.e., they "own" the resource modeled by place $P_3$).
  - $N_1, N_r$, meaning that the respective processes are in the noncritical region (tokens are in $P_1$ and $P_2$, respectively).
  - $R_1, R_r$, meaning that the respective processes requested the shared resource (tokens are in $P_4$ and $P_5$, respectively).

- Next, a subset of AP is associated with each state of the FSM. Such an association defines all elementary properties that hold in a given state. In our case, we associate $\{N_1, N_r\}$ with state $<P_1, P_2, P_3>$; $\{R_1, N_r\}$ with $<P_4, P_2, P_3>$; $\{N_1, R_r\}$ with $<P_1, P_5, P_3>$; $\{C_1, N_r\}$ with $<P_6, P_2>$; $\{R_1, R_r\}$ with $<P_4, P_5, P_3>$; $\{N_1, C_r\}$ with $<P_1, P_7>$; $\{C_1, R_r\}$ with $<P_6, P_5>$; and $\{R_1, C_r\}$ with $<P_7, P_4>$.

- Finally, let $F_1, F_2$ denote two generic formulas. Then the following are also formulas:

  - $F_1$ **and** $F_2$, **not** $F_1$, and $F_1$ **or** $F_2$, with the usual meaning of the propositional operators **not, or**, and **and**.
  - $AX(F_1)$, whose meaning is that it holds when the FSM is in a given state S (called the *current state*) if and only if $F_1$ holds in every state that can be reached from S in a single step. (Thus, AX is analogous to a *universal quantifier*.)
  - $EX(F_1)$, whose meaning is that it holds when the FSM is in state S if and only if $F_1$ holds in some state that can be reached from S in a single step. (Thus, EX is analogous to an *existential quantifier*.)
  - $A(F_1 \; \textbf{U} \; F_2)$, whose meaning is that it holds when the FSM is in state S if and only if, for every sequence $\sigma$ of transitions starting from S, $\sigma$ has a pre-

fix $\sigma_1$ such that $F_2$ holds in state s' reached by $\sigma_1$ and $F_1$ holds in all states preceding s' in $s_1$. (For this reason, **U** is called the *Until* operator.)

- $E(F_1 \ \textbf{U} \ F_2)$ whose meaning is that it holds when the FSM is in state S if and only if there is some sequence $\sigma$ of transitions starting from S such that $\sigma$ has a prefix $\sigma_1$ such that $F_2$ holds in state s' reached by $\sigma_1$ and $F_1$ holds in all states preceding s' during the application of $\sigma_1$.

- $AF(F_2)$ is an abbreviation for $A(\texttt{TRUE} \ \textbf{U} \ F_2)$, and $EF(F_2)$ is an abbreviation for $E(\texttt{TRUE} \ \textbf{U} \ F_2)$; they are read "$F_2$ is *inevitable*" and "$F_2$ *potentially* holds," respectively.

For instance, with reference to the FSM of Figure 6.13 $EF(C_1)$ holds in every state, but $AF(C_1)$ does not hold in any state that does not include $P_6$; this means that there is always a computation that allows the left process to enter the critical region, but there is no guarantee that the left process accesses the shared resource unless it already owns it.

At this point, the major strength of model checking comes into play: After we define the FSM describing the system's behavior and the property to be analyzed, well-known results of the theory of computation guarantee the decidability of the validity of the given property; thus, we only have to supply the FSM and the property to a model checker, which, by applying a natural inductive algorithm, can tell us whether the formula holds (and, if it doesn't, can "explain" why by providing a counterexample that falsifies the formula).

This sharp difference with respect to other major verification techniques, which all require ingenuity or do not provide guaranteed results, has made model checking a highly successful technique. Not surprisingly, however, it has its weaknesses.

First, its scope is restricted to finite-state systems, a feature that represents a fairly severe lack of generality. Second, even when FSMs are an adequate model for system description, the model-checking algorithm suffers from extremely high complexity due to the typical combinatorial explosion of the number of states of FSMs when the size of the system that is modeled increases. (A $k$-bit register is modeled by an FSM with $2^k$ states!)

For this reason, model checking has been successful mostly in the verification of hardware design and of communication protocols, wherein, reasonably small-sized FSMs are often a useful model. The potential benefits of the technique, however, are so encouraging that active research in the field is ongoing, especially to apply model checking to more general software engineering fields. For instance, using techniques inspired by symbolic execution, we can partition a large or even infinite state space into a reasonably small set of equivalence classes, each of which embodies the essential features of many states. For example, in some cases, an integer variable x can be "projected" into three states $\{x > 0, \ x = 0, \ x < 0\}$.

The literature reports some successful applications of these techniques to real-life problems.

## 6.7     PUTTING IT ALL TOGETHER

In this chapter, we have examined several major verification techniques. In principle, they lend themselves to a fairly natural contrast; in fact, we can categorize them as follows:

- Testing versus (correctness) analysis techniques.
- Formal versus informal techniques.
- White-box versus black-box techniques.
- Techniques in the small versus techniques in the large.
- Fully automatic techniques, such as model checking, versus interactive techniques, such as semiautomatic test case generation. Automatic techniques are rooted in the decidable properties of restricted models, whereas semiautomatic ones are rooted in the undecidable and more general properties of models.
- Techniques that exploit human ingenuity and leave much freedom to the verifier versus techniques that stress disciplined and rigid approaches.

These contrasts do not show the superiority of one approach or technique over another. Rather, they can lead us to exploit natural *complementarities* of the approaches. We already noticed that some skill in formal analysis techniques can help make informal analysis more reliable; also, testing and correctness proofs—perhaps limited to the verification of critical properties—may easily be integrated. (Symbolic execution is by itself already a kind of integration of testing and correctness proofs.) This means that a successful verifier must master several complementary techniques and apply them in an integrated way.

For instance, the construction of a complex system is likely to involve the inclusion of externally developed pieces of software, such as commercial off-the-shelf (COTS) software components. For such components, white-box testing is often out of the question, because source code is not available; however, in critical situations, these components may need an extra certification besides the one that may be supplied by the vendor (e.g., to guarantee safety or security properties). In such cases, black-box techniques, perhaps based on a formalization of the behavior of external components, may be mandatory. Also, verification in the large—at the system level—may require different strategies when the whole system is developed within a single industrial environment.

As a further example, suppose you wish to verify a highly critical module. Initially, you may build an approximation of it by using a finite state model: In this way, you may be able to verify the module fully automatically by applying, say, model checking. The result of model checking can then be used for more refined interactive analysis based on a more sophisticated model. For instance, an error signaled by model checking may be used as a suggestion to check whether such an error exists in the more general model of the system. Also, in real-time systems, it is quite likely that all properties of interest will show up within a time bound that can be predicted *a priori*. In such a case, testing within a finite time bound may make a property decidable that would be undecidable in the theoretically unbounded time domain.

The great variety of verification techniques and of the contexts in which they can be applied, however, introduces an extra complexity factor: Besides the intrinsic complexity of the system to be verified, we now have to manage also the choice of verification technique and the policies to apply to the various techniques. This is a significant challenge to the verifier.

Once again, appropriate tool support may offer the required solutions: Not only do we need tools supporting single techniques such as model checkers, test case generators, etc., but also we should be supported when applying our choices and putting them together. Unfortunately, the state of the art of verification tools is still at a fairly preliminary stage: Only prototype tools are available for the most advanced techniques, and their integration is done mostly manually.

## 6.8   DEBUGGING

In our discussion of testing, we said several times that the goal of testing is the discovery of errors ("bugs") in programs. According to the terminology introduced in Section 6.3.2, we can say that a program's failure is a clear symptom of the presence of an error, but the presence of an error does not necessarily cause a failure. The goal of testing is to discover program executions in which errors lead to failures. As we said before, however, the choice of an appropriate testing criterion enables us to view successful testing as more than an uninteresting experiment: It should, indeed, increase our confidence in the correctness of the program.

*Debugging* is the activity of locating and correcting errors. It can start once a failure has been detected. Unfortunately, going from the detection of a failure to correcting the error that is responsible is far from trivial. Although debugging is not a verification activity and thus—strictly speaking—should not be treated in this chapter, it is so intimately related to verification that we have decided to discuss it here briefly.

Debugging is one of the least understood activities in software development and is practiced with the least amount of discipline. It is often approached with much hope and little planning. While there is still a lot to be learned about debugging and, in particular, about what leads to successful debugging, our previous discussion of the testing and analysis of programs enables us to analyze debugging carefully, leading to a disciplined approach.

First, a failure is actually a behavior that does not match the program specifications. Thus, one should first consult the specifications themselves to determine whether they are clear enough and to consider the possibility that the error is located there, rather than in the implementation. Second, the location of the error, assuming that the error is in the implementation, is not always apparent. The failure could even be caused by a combination of several errors.

Accordingly, rigor and care must be used in locating errors during debugging. Certainly, a clear separation between testing in the small and testing in the large (i.e., modularizing the testing activity) helps in debugging. For instance, if two modules behave properly when operated separately, and a failure occurs when they are integrated, their interface should be checked for consistency.

Even when an error has been clearly localized to a given module, however, the module could still be too large and complex to enable the immediate detection of the error. Thus, in some sense, we need to practice some "testing in the smaller" *a posteriori*—for example, by breaking the module into small fragments whose intended behavior we understand clearly.

A simple and powerful principle to aid in localizing errors is *closing up the gap between faults and failures*. To understand this notion, recall from our terminology from Section 6.3 that we consider a fault to be an incorrect state during program execution—say, an incorrect value of a variable. The problem is that faults do not always lead to failures and therefore may go undetected.

We can, however, expose faults by means of suitable techniques. For instance, consider the old-fashioned technique of producing a *memory dump*: printing out the contents of memory at some given point of a program's execution. In principle, this technique tries to make any fault result in a failure. By dumping the memory, we are making the state of the program (i.e., the contents of the memory) an output of the program, so that any discrepancy in any part of the memory shows up as a failure in the output produced by the program. Of course, this requires that we state precise requirements for the results of memory dumps just as we do for other program outputs. If we are able to state the requirements precisely—and to check them—then we have turned a fault into a failure at the point of the dump, and we have closed the gap between the two.

The obvious drawback of this approach is that too many details are needed, in general, to analyze the result of a dump (even if it is represented symbolically). That is, the specification of the whole memory state is too complex to define and check. But the principle of pushing faults closer to failures by adding the specification of the program state can be applied in other, more flexible, ways.

A natural middle ground between examining dumps and examining only the program's output is to restrict our attention to some particular variables at some particular points of the program's execution. This can be done by using software monitors. A monitor used to inspect the value of a variable is called a *watch point* (or a *spy point*).

We can implement a watch point by inserting an output statement in the appropriate place in the program, or we can use a debugger's watch points without modifying the program manually. The latter eliminates many practical problems involved with adding ad hoc debugging statements to the program manually. For example, in the manual modes, we have to be sure that, after finding and fixing the error, we remove any debugging statements we have inserted.

In this section, however, we are interested only in the *concept* of a watch point, and we will use output statements. So if, for instance, we wish to check the value of array index variable i at a given point where the array is accessed, we just modify the code, changing, say,

```
a: array (1..10) of INTEGER;
   .
   .
   .
a(i) := …
```

to

```
a: array (1..10) of INTEGER;
   .
   .
   .
write(i);
a(i) := …
```

Suppose, however, that we are really interested not in the particular value of the variable, but rather in the fact that it satisfies a particular condition. For example, suppose the watch point on variable i is intended to check whether the array index is in the first half of the array; that is, we are interested in the truth or falsity of the assertion $\{1 \leq i \leq 5\}$ at the point where we have inserted write(i).

In Section 6.4.2, we saw the use of intermediate assertions for exactly this purpose. There, we tried to produce a proof that such an assertion holds in any execution of the program when execution reaches the point at which the assertion occurs. In debugging, we attempt to verify that the assertion holds for a particular execution. Thus, whether we realize it or not, whether we do it formally or informally, in debugging we are testing the validity of assertions. These assertions may have been embedded in the program by the programmer or may have been manufactured as hypotheses about the location and nature of the error by the person doing the debugging.

An effective way to add executable debugging assertions to a program is to use a procedure called `assert` that accepts a Boolean input. This procedure will evaluate its input and will do nothing if its input is true; it will produce a message or terminate the program if its input is false. Using the `assert` procedure in place of `write(i)` in the preceding code, we could use `assert (i > 0 and i < 6)`. One advantage of this approach is that calls to `assert` can be removed from the program relatively easily (through conditional compilation, the use of comments, etc.) after debugging is completed.

## Example 6.16

Consider the following procedure, intended to merge two sorted sequences with no duplicate elements into a single sorted sequence with no duplicate elements. The procedure is given together with appropriate type declarations and a formal specification written as a pair of logical formulas (pre- and postconditions).

```
type sequence (max_size: NATURAL) is
   record
        size : INTEGER range 0.. max_size:= 0;
        contents = array (1.. max_size) of INTEGER
   end record;

{(1 ≤ l < m ≤ a.size) implies a.contents(l) < a.contents(m)) and
(1 ≤ l < m ≤ b.size) implies b.contents(l) < b.contents(m))}

procedure strict_merge(a, b : in sequence; c : out sequence) is
        i, j, k : integer;
begin i := 1; j := 1; k:= 1;
while i ≤ a.size and j ≤ b.size loop
        if a.contents(i) < b.contents(j) then
           c.contents(k) := a.contents(i);
           i := i + 1;
        else
           c.contents(k) := b.contents(j);
           j := j + 1;
        end if;
        k := k + 1;
end loop;
while i ≤ a.size loop
     c.contents(k) := a.contents(i);
     i := i + 1; k := k + 1;
end loop;
```

```
while j ≤ b.size loop
    c.contents(k) := b.contents(j);
    j := j + 1; k := k + 1;
end loop;
c.size := k - 1;
end;
```

```
{(1 ≤ l < m ≤ c.size} implies c.contents (l) < c.contents (m)) and
(for all x
   ((exists l (x = a.contents(l)) or exists m (x = b.contents(m)))
   implies exists p (x = c.contents(p)) ) and
   (exists p (x = c.contents(p)) implies
   (exists l (x = a.contents(l)) or exists m (x = b.contents(m))
   ))
))
}
```

Executing the procedure with input data

```
a = {1,3,5,7}, b = {2,3,8}
```

produces the erroneous result c = {1,2,3,3,5,7,8}, which violates the output requirement

```
{(1 ≤ l < m ≤ c.size) implies c.contents(l) < c.contents(m))}
```

We can help localize the error by noting that, at each iteration of the first loop (as well as at each iteration of other loops), c should exhibit the property stated in the assertion up to the portion so far constructed. This stipulation can be formalized by the loop invariant

```
{(1 ≤ l < m < k} implies c.contents (l) < c.contents(m))}
```

Now, if we test the validity of the loop invariant during program execution by inserting the statement

```
if k > 2 and then c.contents(k - 2) ≥ c.contents(k - 1) then
        write("iteration #:"); write(k - 1);
        write("monotonicity error in c");
end if
```

as the last statement of the first loop, the fault will occur at the fourth loop iteration, and pinpointing this fact helps identify its source. ∎

In Section 6.4.2, we saw the central role of intermediate assertions, such as loop invariants, in program correctness proofs; here we have seen their application in the very practical debugging activity.

As another example, consider the following fragment of code appearing in a client of the table manipulation module sketched in Section 6.4.2.3;

```
read(Element);
Insert(Table, Element);
    .

    .

    .
Delete(Table, Element);
write(element);
```

To verify whether the table is used correctly, we could insert the following intermediate assertions within the code:

```
read(Element);
{Size(Table) < max_size}
Insert(Table, Element);
{Element ∈ Table};
    .
    .
    .

{Size(Table) > 0}
Delete(Table, Element);
{Element ∉ Table};
write(Element);
```

These assertions may be checked at run time in order to help detect and localize errors.

In conclusion, inserting and checking intermediate assertions within the code can be seen as a "specification *a posteriori*" of small program fragments. In fact, we have used the same notation as that employed for the logic specification of whole programs. In other words, the program is overspecified by adding details about its states of execution. The result is that whenever such more detailed specifications are violated, a program failure will occur (i.e., further failures are generated from program faults). The insertion of intermediate assertions can also be viewed as an attempt during debugging to check a proof of correctness for a particular execution of the program.

Yet another function of intermediate assertions is as formal comments used for program documentation. The benefit of formality is that debugging can be performed systematically by checking the truth of such assertions.

### Exercise

---

**6.32**  Modify the procedure of Example 6.16 by eliminating the second loop. Describe how you can use intermediate assertions to detect the errors in the program.

---

## 6.9    VERIFYING OTHER SOFTWARE PROPERTIES

At the beginning of this chapter, we stated that all software properties, or qualities, should be verified, although we deliberately restricted our attention to the verification of functional correctness (apart from a few remarks on testing for robustness and regression testing in Section 6.3.6). In the current section, we address the topic of verification of other relevant qualities. As usual, we do not try to be exhaustive. Rather, we want to help develop the reader's intuition in the complex verification process. First, we address the issue of a classical "objective" quality, namely, performance. Then, we go into the more elusive topic of measuring qualities such as reliability, understandability, and modifiability.

### 6.9.1    Verifying Performance

Performance has always been a major concern in software systems, whether one is dealing with strictly real-time systems, more traditional electronic data-processing systems, or end-user productivity tools. Since performance is a measurable software property, several methods have been developed to verify it.

Performance evaluation is a subject in its own right. It is treated in specialized books and courses outside of software engineering. Rather than summarizing these texts here, we wish to provide just a framework to put the different specialized techniques for evaluating software performance into a unified perspective.

Performance can be verified from several standpoints and with several techniques. In general, they all complement each other. One can be interested in *worst case analysis*, in which the focus is on proving that the system response time is bounded by some function of the external requests to the system, say, the number of incoming interrupts per second and the size of a file to be processed. Or we might be interested in the *average behavior* of the system, wanting to know the *average* response time rather than its maximum value.

Another relevant factor in performance is the standard deviation. Clearly, both worst case and statistical factors are pertinent here. Sometimes, though, these may conflict with each other. For instance, one of the best sorting algorithms, Quicksort, has a worst case performance that is $O(n^2)$, n being the number of elements to be sorted, whereas other algorithms that are worse on the average have a worst case performance that is only $O(nlogn)$.

Both worst case analysis and statistical analysis are supported by established models, techniques, and tools. In the former, computational complexity theory, and in the latter, statistics, probability and queuing theory, provide many analytical models.[19]

As with functional correctness, performance can be verified either by *analyzing* suitable models of the software or by *experimenting* directly with the system's behavior. Also, we can talk about static versus dynamic verification techniques, each with advantages and disadvantages. An important technique is that of *simulation*, which yields knowledge about system performance by running a mathematical model of the system. It is therefore considered a dynamic verification technique, even though it does not require running the real system. In general, simulation applies statistical models of the system. We can view simulation as a rapid prototyping technique devoted to the analysis of performance.

### 6.9.2    Verifying Reliability

Statistical and probabilistic methods work quite well for measuring system properties that we cannot measure with absolute certainty. In the case of software, we saw in the previous section that performance may naturally be modeled and evaluated in a statistical manner. In general, many properties of engineering artifacts, such as *reliability*, are measured and verified in this way. For instance, the reliability of an electrical appli-

---

[19] In some specialized literature, the term *performance evaluation* is reserved only for statistical analysis.

ance may be measured in terms of its probability of failure within a given time. Such reliability measures are helpful whenever we cannot guarantee the absence of failures.

In the case of software, we already saw in Chapter 2 that reliability is used intuitively to denote a broader and often more useful property than correctness. In fact, we saw that in many cases one may even accept an incorrect system, assuming that its defects are not serious or that failures do not occur too frequently. For instance, a word processor whose spell checker sometimes fails to catch some unusual misspelling may still be considered reliable if this type of error does not occur too frequently and if other more critical functions, such as saving files, are guaranteed to work.

Thus, it sounds rather natural to try to measure the reliability of software on a probabilistic basis, as has been done in other engineering fields. Unfortunately, however, there are some difficulties with this approach. First, as we remarked at the beginning of the chapter, the notion of continuity is generally lacking in software. This prevents us from quantifying concepts such as "small defect" and "acceptable failure" in any rigorous and measurable way. Furthermore, traditional probabilistic models are based on hypotheses that do not hold in the case of software.

For instance, we can assume that, *normally*, the separate events of two different customers entering a bank to ask for some service are *independent* in the same way that the results of flipping the same coin two times are independent. This independence allows us to estimate quantities such as the mean service time spent with some teller and the average length of the waiting queues. Similarly, the events of two different chip failures in the same processor can generally be considered independent. This allows us to state the probability of system failure both in the case where the whole system depends on the functioning of both chips and in the case where the functioning of one chip is enough to guarantee operation of the system.

This is not so in the case of software: Independence of *failures* cannot be assumed. For instance, consider the following program fragment:

```
if x > 0 then
    write(y);
else
    write(z);
    write(x);
end if;
```

Suppose that the programmer has made two independent errors. One generates the fault of making x's value incorrect, and the other makes z's value incorrect. But if the value of x is 6 instead of 7, evaluation of the condition still produces a correct result, and thus, neither error will cause a failure during execution. By contrast, if x is 0 instead of 1, both failures will occur; and if x is 2 instead of 0, we can infer the error in x (because y is printed instead of z and x), but not the error in z.

Nevertheless, measuring statistical reliability properties, such as the mean time between two software failures, is an attractive goal and has been pursued by researchers.

First of all, let us point out that reliability is concerned with measuring the *probability of the occurrence of failure*—that is, the probability of the observable effects of errors. Second, several quantities are taken into consideration as meaningful parameters for estimating software reliability, including, typically, the following:

- The *average total number of failures*, AF(t), observed at a given time. The average is obtained with respect to different observations on different installations of the same system. Ideally, experiments should be performed in such manner that n identical instantiations of the same system are initialized identically. Then, these n instantiations start operating independently (say, with different, unrelated, users). Next, for each of the n instantiations, the total number of failures at time t is computed. Finally, the average of such numbers with respect to the n instantiations is AF(t).
- The *failure intensity*, FI(t) (i.e., the number of failures per unit time). FI(t) is the derivative of AF(t) with respect to time t, using the terminology of continuous mathematics.
- The *average time interval between two failures*, also called the *mean time to failure (MTTF)*. Clearly, MTTF(t) = 1/FI(t).

In the preceding quantities, the time variable may be intended in different ways. It may denote either the actual *execution time* of the software under consideration, the *calendar time*, which includes also the time when the system is off, or even the machine *clock time*—that is, all the time that the hardware is running, including time spent on other programs. Clearly, these three times are related: In a system that is in a state of equilibrium, the ratio of any one to any of the other two can be thought of as constant. In more dynamic cases (e.g., when the number of applications running on the same processor varies over time), a more complex and deeper analysis is needed. We shall talk here about execution time only, without going into the subtleties of the differences among the various measures.

Thus, it is assumed that the occurrence of software failures follows some law of randomness. Here, we could discuss philosophical issues pertaining to determinism, nondeterminism, and randomness. In fact, some claim that even the result of throwing a coin is regulated by deterministic laws, so that, by knowing the force applied when flipping the coin, the density of air, the weight and the shape of the coin, etc., one could, in principle, forecast the result of a coin toss. However, since all of these elements are combined in a far too complex way for us to know what they are, a random model is much more practical for analyzing such a phenomenon. Of course, we cannot forecast the exact result of a single coin toss, but we can state that, for a large enough number of tosses, about 50% will be heads and 50% will be tails.

Similarly, it is claimed that software construction is often so complex that human programming errors which cause failures are distributed randomly,[20] and their effects occur randomly. In other words, failures, as well as the environment (external stimuli, input values, etc.) within which software must operate, are arranged randomly. Therefore, several classical models of random processes have been used to describe the variables involved. We discuss two such models next.

The *basic model* assumes that the decrement per failure experienced (i.e., the derivative with respect to the number of detected failures) of the failure intensity function is constant. In other words, the FI variable is a function of AF according to the law

---

[20] *Randomly* does not mean *uniformly*.

```
FI(AF) = FI₀ (1 - AF/AF∞)
```

where $FI_0$ is the initial failure intensity and $AF_\infty$ is the total number of failures.

Obviously, this law is based on the assumption that a decrease in failures is due to the fixing of the errors that were the sources of the failures. We know that detecting a failure is one thing and finding its cause and removing it is quite another, even without considering the risk of introducing a new error. The basic model is based on the optimistic hypothesis that the total number of failures is finite. Also optimistic is the hope that the ability to remove errors does not vary with time. In practice, however, the errors detected first are usually easier to remove than subtle errors that occur in intricate situations.

By contrast, the *logarithmic model* assumes, more conservatively, that the decrement per failure of FI decreases exponentially—that is, that

```
FI(AF) = FI₀ exp(-θ· AF)
```

where $\theta$ is called the *failure intensity decay* parameter. A comparison of the two models is given in Figure 6.14.

If failures actually occur according to either of these models, that model can be used to predict system reliability. In fact, it is sufficient to measure $FI_0$ and other constant parameters in the two formulas presented by performing a sufficient amount of testing so that average values are reasonably stable. Then, the application of the chosen formula allows the estimation of, say, the expected MTTF after 100 hours of execution time.

We must evaluate a given model on the basis of how it matches the actual failure phenomenon. Unfortunately, it is not clear whether and which statistical hypotheses can be assumed in regard to error and failure distribution. For instance, the basic model assumes that the total number of failures is finite, and the logarithmic model assumes the opposite. In other cases, we see claims of the type "After a reasonable amount of system experimentation, the number of remaining errors is likely to be proportional to the number detected so far," which clearly contradicts both models' assumptions.

Experimental evidence has been used to show that any of these models—basic, logarithmic, and others—does indeed work well for some class of applications. The fact that there exist arguments in favor of different models, however, shows at least that the applicability of these models must be restricted to carefully selected fields. For instance, the claim about the proportional relationship of detected to undetected errors is based on the observation of an old, highly complex system—the OS 360 operating system—that was not built with a rigorous approach. The main reason for this pessimistic assumption was the observation that trying to fix a detected error caused the introduction of new errors as a side effect.

We do not go deeper into the subject here, since it would require developing much d hoc theory. The topic is debated in the scientific community, and its industrial application is only beginning. We refer the reader to the relevant literature in the bibliographic notes. Here, we simply stress the point that by building a suitable formal model of the phenomenon at hand—in this instance, reliability—we can use the results of mathematics to gain some control over the phenomenon, such as the ability to predict. The critical issue, however, is whether and how well the formal models of reliability capture the peculiarities of software.

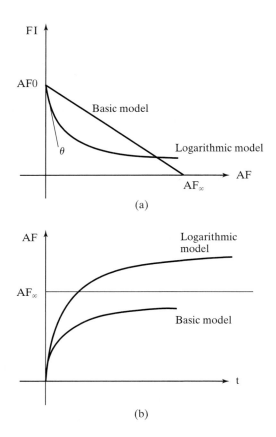

**FIGURE 6.14**

Comparison of the (a) basic model
and (b) the logarithmic model.

## Exercise

**6.33** Consider an application that contains errors causing an improper alarm. The consequence
of these failures is that the operator must restart the system. An independent error, however, is also present in the initialization routines executed by the operator. This error does
not cause a fault every time the system is restarted. Rather, both the fault and the failure
occur as a function of some external parameters set by the operator during the restart procedure. Discuss the correlation between the two types of failures.

## 6.9.3 Verifying Subjective Qualities

We often assess software qualities such as understandability, modifiability, and portability on the basis of common sense and experience. For instance, in Chapter 4, we
insisted that good modularization is important in achieving many of the desired qualities. But we did not give any objective measure to determine whether one program is
modularized "better" than another. There have been attempts, however, to make this
measurement more precise. In some books and manuals, for example, one can even
read suggestions of the type "a module length should not exceed 50 lines of code, or
one page." Such recommendations, however, are too simplistic: They measure the size
of a module independently of the module's logical organization. What if we are not

able to build a procedure or an abstract data type in fewer than 51 lines? Should we split it anyway just to satisfy the requirement? Even the notion of a *line of code* is rather elusive: Does a module become more acceptable (shorter) just because we write several statements on the same line?

Another example is interesting from a historical point of view. In the 1960s, Dijkstra observed that programs with many **goto** statements tended to contain more errors than programs with fewer or no **goto** statements at all. This remark started many years of debate about how to control the quality of programs by limiting the number of **goto** statements in them. In the end, even though counting **goto** statements did not prove to be useful, progress in programming has replaced **goto** statements with structured control statements.

In short, there is no doubt that we need to be able to evaluate software qualities in more systematic ways in order to increase the objectivity of our assessments. But unfortunately, the easy attempts to translate our common sense into mathematical formulas intended to measure software qualities may often be readily criticized by finding obvious counterexamples. Using the number of lines as a metric to evaluate a module is a good example of a simplistic attempt. Even the more elaborate models proposed so far have proven to be controversial.

In this section, we give a brief account of three important approaches to verifying such subjective qualities as simplicity, reusability, and understandability. First, we introduce two models that, despite several controversial aspects, contributed significantly to measuring a program's complexity.[21] Since the metrics of these models are based on quantities that are measured from the source program, they are called *source-code metrics*. Next, we summarize a more general approach that, on the basis of previous experiences, aims at building a more complete theory of measuring software qualities.

### 6.9.3.1 *Halstead's Theory*

Software science is an approach to measuring software qualities on the basis of objective code measures. The theory, due to Halstead and based on information theory, relies on the following measurable quantities, defined for a given program coded in any programming language:

- $\eta_1$, the number of unique, distinct operators appearing in the program;
- $\eta_2$, the number of unique, distinct operands appearing in the program;
- $N_1$, the total number of occurrences of operators in the program;
- $N_2$, the total number of occurrences of operands in the program.

Although the terms "operator" and "operand" have an intuitive meaning, a precise definition of them is needed to avoid ambiguities that may arise between different programming languages. For instance, a pair of parentheses, as well as a **begin-end** pair, is considered a single operator. A label is considered an operator if it is used as the target of a **goto** statement, since its purpose is to effect control; otherwise, it is con-

---

[21] Do not confuse this with computational complexity!

sidered a comment. A **goto** statement applied to a label is considered an operator. An **if-then-else-end if** 4-tuple is considered a single operator. A semicolon is considered a single operator. Many other such conventions are necessary. The exercises that follow are intended to convince the reader that much care is needed to define terms precisely. (In some cases, several answers are possible.)

### Exercises

**6.34**  How should a reference to an array element of the type a(i, 4) be considered? Should it be viewed as a single operand? As an operator a applied to the operands i and 4? What about the comma?

**6.35**  How should a procedure identifier be considered, both when declared and when called? What about the identifier of a procedure that is passed as a parameter to another procedure?

---

Once we have defined $\eta_1$ and $\eta_2$ precisely, we can define the program vocabulary as

$$\eta = \eta_1 + \eta_2$$

and the program length as

$$N = N_1 + N_2$$

At this point, we can already consider some relations between the preceding quantities. A first obvious relation is

$$\eta \leq N$$

Also, we can derive an upper limit on N as a function of $\eta$, based on the observation that it is quite unlikely that a program has several identical parts—in the terminology of formal languages, substrings—of length greater than $\eta$. In fact, once a piece of code occurs identically in several places, it is usually made into a procedure, a function, or a common subexpression to be stored in a temporary variable. Since repeated pieces of code are quite unlikely to contain all of a program's operands and operators, we can safely assume that any program of length N consists of $N/\eta$ substrings of length $\eta$ such that none of them occurs more than once in the program. Now, for any given alphabet of size k, there are exactly $k^r$ different strings of length $r$. Thus, $N/\eta \leq \eta^\eta$, and $N \leq \eta^{\eta+1}$. Also, since operands and operators in a program tend to alternate, we can further refine the upper bound into $N \leq \eta \cdot \eta_1^{\eta_1} \cdot \eta_2^{\eta_2}$. (See Exercise 6.79.)

Now, let us quote Halstead [1977], who derives an estimate $\hat{N}$ for the length of a program with $\eta_1$ operators and $\eta_2$ operands in the following way:

Now the upper limit $N \leq \eta \cdot \eta_1^{\eta_1} \cdot \eta_2^{\eta_2}$ must include not only the single ordered set of N elements that is the program we seek, but it must also contain all possible subsets of that ordered set. Fortunately, the family of all possible subsets of a set of N elements is so well known that it has a name, "the Power Set", and this family itself has $2^N$ elements. Consequently we may equate the number of possible combinations of operators and operands with the number of elements in the power set, and solve for the length of an implementation of an algorithm in terms of its vocabulary. From

$$2^N = \eta \cdot \eta_1^{\eta_1} \cdot \eta_2^{\eta_2}$$

we have

$$N = \log_2(\eta_1^{\eta_1} \cdot \eta_2^{\eta_2}) \text{ or } N = \log_2 \eta_1^{\eta_1} + \log_2 \eta_1^{\eta_1}$$

yielding the equation

$$\hat{N} = \eta_1 \log_2 \eta_1 + \eta_1 \log_2 \eta_2$$

where the "hat" has been placed on N to distinguish the quantity obtained, the calculated length, with this equation from the value of the length N obtained by direct observation.

We decided to quote Halstead's reasoning directly, since, in spite of its intuitive attractiveness, it suffers from flaws that make it questionable. The major flaw is that a program is not a "single ordered set of N [distinct!] elements," but a string, with possible repetitions. Consider, for instance, the string aba, for which the set of all possible strings obtained by "picking up" any subset of its elements, in any order, is

```
{ε(the empty string), a, b, ab, aa, ba, aba, baa, aab}
```

which contains more than $2^3$ elements. (It could contain even less. When?)

Disregarding the questionable reasoning that leads to its formulation, $\hat{N}$ is an *estimate* of the length of a program, not the measured value of the length. Thus, it is interesting and necessary to compare $\hat{N}$ and N on some relevant samples. Statistics performed on published algorithms seem to indicate an average value of the relative error $(N - \hat{N})/N$ to be less than 10%.

As defined by Halstead, program length is a reasonable formalization of conceptual length, but does not coincide with more traditional notions of the term (the number of characters in the source code, the number of lines of code, the number of statements, etc.). Clearly, the physical length of the program (which we assume here to be the number of characters in the code) depends on factors such as the choice of identifiers for operators and operands. To avoid this type of dependency, which would produce highly different measures for "essentially the same program," the notion of program volume is introduced:

$$V = N \log_2 \eta$$

Intuitively, the program volume V is the minimum number of bits needed to code the program. In fact, in order to represent $\eta$ different identifiers, we need at least $\log_2 \eta$ bits.

Then, the notion of potential volume V* is defined as the volume of the most succinct program in which an algorithm can be coded. Reasonably enough, it is claimed that such a form is given by assuming that the available programming language has just a single operator, say, op to perform the computation of the given algorithm. Thus, if the algorithm operates on input and output data $d_1, d_2, ..., d_n$, the most succinct program is

```
op(d₁, d₂, ..., dₙ)
```

which implies that $\eta_1 = 2$ (commas are not considered operators here!), $\eta_2 = n$, and, therefore, $V* = (2 + \eta_2 \cdot \log_2(2 + \eta_2))$.

The notion of potential volume is then used to introduce the concept of the program level

```
L = V*/V
```

L is an attempt to measure the *level of abstraction* of the formulation of an algorithm, assuming that the most abstract possible formulation is that having volume V*. Again, there is some intuitive evidence in favor of such a definition, although it can be criticized more or less in the same way as we have the previous definitions.

Another important quantity introduced by Halstead's theory is the *effort* E, defined as V/L. Halstead argues that E may be interpreted as the number of mental discriminations required to implement a program (the implementation effort) and also as the effort required to read and understand the program. Experience has shown that, for small programs, E is well correlated with the effort needed for maintenance.

Halstead's software science goes further, giving formal definitions to such concepts as language level, intelligence contents, program purity, and so on. As a result, the theory defines a set of parameters that may be measured in programs (or estimated before they are developed). Such parameters may be used for the quantitative assessment of properties in order to evaluate whether one program is better than another—for example, which of two programs solving the same problem has a higher complexity and hence requires more maintenance, or which has a higher abstraction level.

In conclusion, Halstead's theory tries to provide a formal definition for such qualitative, empirical, and subjective software qualities as program complexity, ease of understanding, and level of abstraction, based on the count of some low-level quantities, such as the number of operators and operands appearing in a program. The goal is to be able to predict the level of these qualities a program will have before the start of a project and then measure the level mechanically to assess the quality of the resulting product. In the next section, we review another theory that has the same goals as Halstead's software science, but is based on other quantities that can be measured in the source code.

## Exercise

---

**6.36**  It is interesting to examine how the ratio $(N - \hat{N})/N$ varies when a program is divided into parts. (Actually, some experiments show that the partitioning of vocabularies due to program modularization maintains the stability of the ratio. Two extreme situations may occur:

a.  $\eta_1$ and $\eta_2$ are the same for all parts;
b.  $\eta_1$ and $\eta_2$ are partitioned into disjoint subsets by modularization.

Compute the variations of $\hat{N}$ for a program with $N = \hat{N} = 72$, $\eta_1 = 4$, and $\eta_2 = 16$ when the program is divided into two parts, under the two extreme assumptions.

**Warning**: It may be difficult to "divide" a program in such a way as to satisfy the second assumption. (At least one procedure definition and call must share an identifier.) For large values of the quantities involved, however, we can at least assume that $\eta_1$ and $\eta_2$ have small intersections with respect to their size.

---

### 6.9.3.2 McCabe's Theory

Another source-code metric was developed by McCabe, who observed that the quality of a program depends on the complexity of its control flow, rather than on operators and operands, as in Halstead's theory. McCabe's complexity metric C is based on the control flow graph and is defined as

```
C = e - n + 2p
```

where e is the number of edges, n is the number of nodes, and p is the number of connected components of the graph (usually, 1).

In graph-theoretic terms, C is called the *cyclomatic* number of the graph, and thus McCabe's metric is called *cyclomatic complexity*. C defines the number of linearly independent paths in a program. It is possible to prove that, for structured programs with single-entry, single-exit constructs (i.e., with no **goto** statements), the cyclomatic number is equal to the number of conditions plus one. Also, for planar graphs, it is equal to the number of regions into which the graph divides the plane. For example, in the case of Euclid's algorithm, whose control flow graph is shown in Figure 6.3, the cyclomatic complexity is 5.

According to McCabe, the number of conditions that govern the control flow is an indication of how difficult the component is to understand, test, and maintain. McCabe also contends that well-structured modules have a cyclomatic complexity in the range from 3 to 7, and C = 10 is a reasonable upper limit for the complexity of a single module, as is confirmed by empirical evidence.

### Exercise

**6.37**  Evaluate McCabe's cyclomatic number for the merge program of Example 6.16.

### 6.9.3.3 The Goal/Question/Metric Approach to Measuring Software Qualities

Much research and experimental activity has been reported in regard to validating Halstead's and McCabe's theories, as well as other, similar ones. Some experiments seem to support the theories, while others are inconclusive.

Despite all controversial issues related to associating objective numbers with such subjective evaluations as understandability, complexity, and even size, designers and managers do need to express such measures. Not by chance, in fact, two most widely used measures for program size and design effort are still the number of lines of code and the person-year, no matter how rough, ambiguous, and imprecise they are.

Under the pressure of such an overwhelming need, software metrics continue to evolve, regardless of the evident difficulties. In this section, we briefly report on the goal/question/metric (GQM) approach, which aims at broadening and deepening previous experiences.

GQM is based on the following main principles:

- Any kind of software metrics must be used to analyze software qualities, but *not to evaluate people*. It is clear, in fact, that, whichever quantity we adopt to evaluate whichever quality, if a designer feels that he or she is being evaluated through that quantity, that designer will try to maximize (or minimize) the measured quantity rather than the real quality. For instance, if the manager states that in a good object-oriented design, all classes should have fewer than 10 public methods, programmers will most likely try to comply with such a requirement, even at the expense of a real design need that could exceptionally result in a class with 11 methods. Similar experiences occurred when managers attempted to measure programmer productivity through the number of lines of code delivered. (Programmers delivered lengthy and sloppy code, avoiding reuse, since that would have decreased their apparent productivity.) In some sense, the *means* of achieving or measuring the goal becomes itself the *goal* for the designer.

  Despite its compelling appeal, this principle is quite difficult to apply. It is difficult to set up a production process by indicating quantitative parameters that will be used to measure software qualities without giving designers the message that the measured quality of the product will also be interpreted as the quality of the designer.

- Quality evaluation must be applied not only to the product, but to the process as well. This principle is consistent with the general assessment of software qualities we stated in Chapter 2.

- Quality measures should be defined not only for the end product of the software process—the code—but for all intermediate steps of the whole process and for the product that is delivered. Thus, we must apply suitable metrics to requirement specifications, as well as to architectural design and to code; this principle extends previous approaches that were concerned exclusively with source code metrics.

- Any metrics must be defined in the context of a complete and well-designed quality improvement paradigm (QIP). In other words, quantities to be measured must be defined on the basis of a well-thought-out goal to be achieved; then the measure that is obtained must be validated and used to drive decisions aimed at improving that goal. For instance, a company could decide to move towards object-oriented design, and, when setting up the design methodology, managers could follow the aforementioned guideline recommending that no class have more than 10 public methods. After the first experiments, the guideline should be validated and perhaps modified on the basis of the experience gained.

  The more general issue of quality improvement, however, deals more with organizing the whole software development process than with verifying software qualities. In this chapter, we focus on the software quality. A few remarks on the impact of software metrics on process organization will be given in Chapter 8.

On the basis of the foregoing principles, the most distinguishing feature of GQM is its generality. In fact, unlike previous approaches, GQM does not consist of measuring a single quantity or group of quantities, such as program volume, or cyclomatic complexity. Rather, it is a true method that is intended to lead from a precise definition of the objectives of measuring qualities (the *goals*) to the quantities (the *metrics*) whose measures are used to verify the achievement of such qualities.

As the name itself suggests, the GQM approach to the verification of software qualities consists essentially of three phases:

1. First, the *goal* of the measurement is precisely defined. To help achieve precision and some level of standardization, the goal should be defined by filling out a *template* through a suitable instantiation of its parameters. The general template can be given as:

   *Analyze* <object of study>
   *with the purpose of* <objective>
   *the* <features>
   *from the point of view of* <stakeholders>
   *in the context of* <operating context>.

   Examples of <object of study> are: process, product, or process phase such as design or testing. Examples of <objective> could be: characterize, evaluate, foresee, or improve. Examples of <features> could be: cost, correctness, reliability, or user acceptance. Examples of <stakeholders> are: user, manager, programmer, or corporation. Examples of <operating context> are: a particular company or group within a company.

   Examples of goals defined in such a way are the following:

   - *Analyze* the information system
     *with the purpose of* estimating
     *the* costs
     *from the point of view of* the manager
     *in the context of* a major software house.

   - *Analyze* the testing phase
     *with the purpose of* increasing
     *the* reliability
     *from the point of view of* the end user
     *in the context of* the manufacturing firm.

   - *Analyze* the requirements specification
     *with the purpose of* evaluating
     *the* understandability
     *from the point of view of* the designer
     *in the context of* the manufacturing firm.

2. Second, a suitable set of *questions* aimed at achieving the stated goal is defined. For instance,

   - "Do there exist failures that are critical from the user's point of view?" or "What is the mean time to failure [MTTF]?" may be used to assess product reliability.
   - "How much effort has been devoted to the testing phase [or to test a given module]?" and "What percentage of source code has been covered during the testing phase?" are relevant to evaluate both costs and system reliability.

Examples such as these show that several questions can be useful in achieving a given goal, but also that the same question can be used for different goals. In a complete GQM methodology, we arrive at a collection of goals and related questions as suggested by Figure 6.15, thus saving time and effort through exploiting the same activity for several goals.

Notice also that some questions imply a human answer (e.g., "How much time has been devoted to debugging?"), whereas others can be answered—at least in principle—automatically (e.g., "What percentage of branches have been covered?").

3. Finally, a precise *metric* is associated with every question. For instance, the answer to the question "What percentage of branches have been covered?" will certainly be a number between 0 and 100; the user's evaluation of the criticality of a failure can be assigned a number conventionally ranging between 1 and 10, with 10 denoting maximum criticality; we could define, however, a more sophisticated measure in response to such a question by "weighing" the answer with an "expertise level" that is associated *a priori* with different users, so that the answer of an experienced user would then be more important than the answer of a novice. Here is where the difficulties associated with traditional approaches to software metrics come into play: We must assign a quantitative measure to what are often subjective evaluations. Even when the question has a fairly obvious and well-defined answer, such as the percentage of covered branches in a piece of code, the real impact of the measure on the goal that is being pursued may not be definitive. For example, we must carefully consider whether 95% coverage implies more reliability than 90% and whether the cost of achieving the added 5% is justified.

### Exercise

**6.38**   Give other examples of goal definitions using the GQM templates.

Of course, no silver bullet exists to overcome such a difficulty. Thus, much common sense, care, and experience must be applied in such critical definitions as the goals, the questions, and their relations and measures. GQM, however, provides a comprehensive methodology for structuring a measurement process and systematically deriving and interpreting relevant metrics. GQM has some distinguishing features that help the designer in the difficult task of measuring subjective qualities with objective measures.

FIGURE 6.15

The relations between goal and questions.

In the first place, although GQM is necessarily based on informal definitions and evaluations, rigor is strongly pursued, with precision always encouraged and enhanced, for example, through goal templates and other standardized techniques.

Second, as we mentioned before, GQM is part of an iterative process aimed at quality improvement. Thus, all decisions must be validated *a posteriori* to assess their effectiveness and to improve and refine the GQM method itself. For instance, the statistical relevance of questions and metrics for each goal must be evaluated. In one project, after it was realized that the number of code elements of a particular kind has no impact on the understandability of a program, the measures were dropped, and others were added and refined in a new definition of the process.

Finally, although definitions of metrics are largely arbitrary (e.g., how do we measure user satisfaction? with a Boolean value? with an integer between 1 and 10?), they must obey some necessary conditions in order to be meaningful; some researchers propose to formalize such conditions as *metrics axioms*, in the same vein as geometric axioms constrain the notion of distance (reflexivity, symmetry). The following are two examples of proposed metrics axioms:

- Whatever complexity function `C(P)` we associate with a program fragment `P`, the complexity of the composition `C(P;Q)` of `P` with another fragment `Q` cannot be less than `C(P)`.

- Any definition of the size of a software system must be such that

  The size of the system is a nonnegative number;
  The size of the system is 0 if and only if the system is empty; and
  The size of the composition of two disjoint systems (two systems that do not share any elements) must be the sum of the sizes of the two components.

Once again, however, despite the intuitive evidence of some properties of any metric definition, we easily run into controversial issues. For instance, a constraint that has been proposed in the literature for a metric of program complexity `C(P)` states that if a program fragment `P` is obtained from another fragment `Q` solely by renaming its identifiers, then `C(P)` must be equal to `C(Q)`. This constraint somehow contradicts some well-accepted style recommendations which claim that better understandability can be achieved through a careful choice of program identifiers.

Some projects have reported positive experiences with the application of GQM. Also, several additions and modifications have been proposed to make the approach more effective. For instance, two suggestions worth reporting are the following:

- The path going from quality goal(s) to metric definition can be enhanced by stressing the key principles (and techniques) influencing the desired quality. For instance, if we want to achieve and measure reusability, we should realize that two key principles affecting good reusability are modularity and abstraction (among others). Good modularity in turn, exhibits low coupling and high cohesion, as we stated in Chapter 3; thus, we should come up with (among other things) a metric that evaluates the level of coupling and cohesion in a modular implementation of our system. In an object-oriented implementation, a possible parameter contributing to such a metric could be the number of public methods used by external modules, as opposed to the number of private ones.

- Besides defining absolute metrics for given quantities (e.g., the ratio between public and private methods in a class), *quality thresholds* should be defined for such values. When a system exhibits measures that exceed such thresholds, warnings should be raised and a deeper investigation should be devoted to understanding whether the irregularity that is found is a symptom of a real problem or of the measurement. Of course, both the metric and the threshold definitions must be subject to careful experimental validation. For instance, a pilot project reported that in an object-oriented system composed of a rich number of classes, the coupling-cohesion ratio among most classes fell within standard ranges; the few exceptions that exhibited unusual deviations turned out be more problematic, required more effort to implement, and were more difficult to reuse. Thus, the experiment validated the metrics that were adopted.

To conclude this section, we present a small summary example derived from an experiment conducted in a real-life project.

### Case Study 6.1

The experiment we describe next was performed to evaluate the effectiveness of the use of a formal specification language, together with a related method, in the context of an industrial environment. The specification language is TRIO+, an object-oriented logic language.

In TRIO+, a system specification is a collection of class definitions, each of which in turn consists of a collection of *items* (functions, predicates, variables, etc.) and logic *axioms*, formalizing the properties of interest. Items may be either private (i.e., not visible outside their class) or public.

The following were two goals, among others, that were defined during the experiment:

Goal 1
*Analyze* TRIO+ specifications
*with the purpose of* improving understanding of
*their* writing effort
*from the point of view of* the project leader
*in the context of* project ELSA (ELSA was the name of the project).

Goal 2
*Analyze* TRIO+ specifications
*with the purpose of* improving understanding of
*their* modifiability
*from the point of view of* the project leader
*in the context of* ELSA.

Suitable and natural questions were formulated and addressed to the designers involved in the project ("How much time did you spend modifying class C to comply with new requirements R?" etc.). The following quantities, among others, were validated against the questions and turned out to be statistically relevant.

the number of axioms in a class
the number of items in a class
the number of public variables in a class
the number of functions in a class
the number of private variables in a class

Notice that even though these quantities are rather simple and intuitive, they showed that a meaningful estimate of the desired qualities could be obtained without resorting to sophisticated measures. More surprisingly, it turned out that *in the given context*, coupling measures such as the number of items shared between different classes were not statistically significant for the two goals pursued.

## 6.10    CONCLUDING REMARKS

This chapter has been devoted to the verification of software qualities, primarily correctness. After reviewing the goals and requirements of verification, we examined major verification techniques. We classified these techniques as analytical versus experimental, or, alternatively, as static versus dynamic. Program testing is experimental. Code inspections, walk-throughs, and correctness proofs are analytic. Symbolic interpretation is a mixture of the two.

This classification is not perfect because it does not always characterize the different techniques clearly (e.g., a walk-through involves manual execution, and symbolic execution is hard to classify). Because, in practice, many verification methods are combinations of static and dynamic techniques, other classifications have been proposed in the literature, with the aim of characterizing such hybrid methods better.

We have covered testing in depth. Starting from the basic terminology and some important theoretical results, we examined several classifications of testing techniques, such as testing in the small versus testing in the large and white-box testing versus black-box testing. We suggested that many different testing criteria can be understood in the light of the *complete-coverage principle*. We examined several such criteria and testing techniques in detail. In general, the different testing techniques have been shown to have complementary features, leading to many hybrid techniques being proposed in the literature.

Many experimental studies have sought to assess the success of various testing techniques. Their results, however, should be examined very carefully, because they depend on many factors that are hard to control. For example, the order in which the tests are applied affects the results: Usually, one applies a simple technique to detect many simple errors and then more sophisticated techniques to detect (fewer) more subtle errors. Also, we should not consider one technique to be more powerful than another just because it seems to detect more errors: We should also take the "difficulty" of the errors into account.

We then reviewed analysis techniques, informal as well as formal. To date, the practical use of formal analysis techniques has been limited, but significant (e.g., in protocol verification, compiler verification, and operating system security). There is still much debate about the practical importance of these techniques, but it should be clear from this chapter that their judicious use can enhance the practice of software engineering.

We discussed debugging as a natural complement to testing and examined its relationship to formal analysis.

Next, we considered the problem of assessing software qualities other than functional correctness. For some qualities, such as performance, well-established models exist. For others, such as reliability, stochastic models that work well in other engineering disciplines are more controversial as far as their applicability to software goes. These models are the subject of active research.

Finally, we introduced the issue of verifying more subjective qualities such as the complexity of understanding and maintaining a program; ease of testing, and a program's abstraction level. We presented some of the most popular approaches to building quantitative models to help carry out such a qualitative evaluation. Although such models are still quite controversial, they are also much needed to help the difficult task of managing the software process and its costs. Chapter 7 contain more discussion of the software process. Much research is ongoing to address the difficulties of measuring software quality.

## FURTHER EXERCISES

**6.39** Consider the following erroneous binary-search procedure:

```
procedure new-binary-search (key: in element; table: in elementTable;
    found: out Boolean, pos: out integer) is
begin
    bottom := table'first; top := table'last;
    middle := (bottom + top) / 2; found := false
    while bottom <= top and not found loop
        if key = table(middle) then
            found:= true;
        else if key < table(middle) then
            top := middle - 1;
        else
            bottom := middle + 1;
        end if;
        middle := (bottom + top) / 2;
    end loop;
end new-binary-search;
```

Show that successfully testing the procedure with arbitrarily large tables does not guarantee correctness; find a testing technique that would detect the error in the procedure.

**6.40** Consider the following program fragment:

```
read(x); read(y);
if x > 0 or y ≤ 0 then
    write("1");
else
    write("2");
end if;
if y > 0 then
    write("3");
else
    write("4");
end if;
```

Discuss how to generate test cases using the statement-coverage criterion.

**6.41** Define how to construct control flow graphs for programs containing structured statements such as **repeat-until, case,** and **if-then-elsif-else-end if**.

**6.42** Give rules for building control flow graphs associated with program fragments containing **goto** statements in addition to structured statements. Also, give rules for transforming a classical flowchart into a control flow graph.

**6.43** Build the control flow graph of the binary search procedure of Example 6.2.

**6.44** Prove that the edge-coverage criterion produces different results from, and is finer than, the statement-coverage criterion.

**6.45** Suppose you reformulate the condition-coverage criterion so that you require, not that all edges, but just that the constituents of compound conditions, of the control flow graph be exercised. Prove why this criterion would not be finer than the edge-coverage criterion.

**6.46** Compute the maximum number of possible execution paths for Euclid's algorithm given in Example 6.5 as a function of the maximum number of input values.

**6.47** Consider the following sorting program fragment:

```
for i in 2 .. n loop
    x := a(i);
    a(0) := x;
    j := i - 1;
    while x < a(j) loop
        a(j + 1) := a(j);
        j := j - 1;
    end loop;
    a(j + 1) := x;
end loop;
```

Select a number of "significant" execution paths, and find values of array a that cause their traversal.

**6.48** In addition to the usual logical operators for composing Boolean expressions, Ada allows operators **or-else** and **and-then**. Give rules for building control flow graphs for statements that use these operators.

**6.49** Build a test set from the specification of procedure search given in item 7 of Section 5.6.2.2. Use the specification to produce not only the test set, but also the corresponding oracle.

**6.50** Black-box techniques do not always solve the oracle problem. Find a case where they are of no help for such a problem among the examples provided in Section 6.3.4.2. Can you explain why this unfortunate circumstance occurs? Could you devise an approach to enrich the technique so that it helps solve the oracle problem?

**6.51** Consider the system described in Figure 6.16. In this system, two modules, $M_1$ and $M_2$, interacting through the operating system OS, must respond to stimuli $I_1$ and $I_2$, for which the maximum rates of occurrence are given. Each stimulus $I_1$ must result in a reply $O_1$ within a given maximum delay time. The same holds for $I_2$, but with a different delay.

**6.52** Use the principle of incrementality to design a test strategy for the system described in the previous exercise. Notice that the two modules could run on different processors or on the same processor, but they share access to OS. Furthermore, the "service" provided by $M_1$ might require some computation by $M_2$, and conversely.

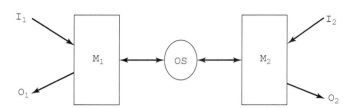

**FIGURE 6.16**

Two modules interacting
through an operating system.

**6.53** Notice the similarity between the syntax-driven testing criterion and the statement-coverage criterion by simply considering syntactic productions instead of statements. In some sense, syntax-driven testing suffers from similar weaknesses as statement coverage. For instance, suppose that a compiler uses at most $k$ temporary cells to evaluate arithmetic expressions. During the compilation, it keeps a counter of the number of cells used, and after using the $k$th cell, it starts again from the first cell, without checking whether the cell is still in use.

**a.** Assume that arithmetic expressions are described by the grammar of Example 6.7.

**b.** For several values of $k$, give examples of expressions satisfying the syntax-directed criterion that fail to expose the error in the compiler.

**c.** Augment the testing criterion by using similar approaches to the way the corresponding white-box criterion has been strengthened in Section 6.3.4.1, in order to allow the detection of erroneous overwriting of a cell and of other errors.

**6.54** Build a program that generates test sentences for any given BNF satisfying the criterion of syntax-driven testing augmented according to point c of Exercise 6.53.

**6.55** The classic approach to testing a compiler is to supply the compiler itself—written in the source language—as the test set. Does this approach satisfy the criterion of syntax-driven testing?

**6.56** (For readers with some familiarity with formal language theory or compiler construction.) Notice that the syntax-driven testing criterion applies to a test domain D consisting of syntactically correct sentences. A compiler, however, should also be tested on incorrect sentences. Try to extend the criterion in order to achieve some completeness even in the compilation of incorrect programs.

**6.57** (For readers with some familiarity with formal language theory or compiler construction.) It is well known that classical BNF defines programming languages only partially. For instance, the usual rule that variable identifiers can be used only if previously declared cannot be expressed by means of the BNF notation. Augment the criterion of syntax-driven testing in such a way that both correct and incorrect sentences with respect to non-BNF rules may be considered possible test cases. Notice that, in practice, such rules are given informally. The reader may refer to the specialized literature to find sample formalizations of these and other aspects of programming language definitions.

**6.58** Try to use the cause-effect graph technique to give a Boolean-function definition of a program that computes the square root of its input value. Why can't you do this?

**6.59** By following the same philosophy we used to reduce the size of the test set for cause-effect graphs, design a criterion that reduces the size of test sets derived by the multiple-condition-coverage criterion given in Exercise 6.6.

**6.60** Systematic test strategies are certainly useful. They should, however, not dissuade us from applying our intuition and empirical knowledge to a problem. Consider the problem of finding the plane in a three-dimensional space in which three given points lie. This can be formally specified as follows:

- For any given three triples $<x_1, y_1, z_1>$ , $<x_2, y_2, z_2>$, and $<x_3, y_3, z_3>$, find values $a, b, c$, and $d$ that satisfy the equations
- $ax_1 + by_1 + cz_1 = d$,
- $ax_2 + by_2 + cz_2 = d$,
- $ax_3 + by_3 + cz_3 = d$.

Which data are most appropriate to check a program implementing this specification?

**6.61** Consider a lock-managing system that services sequences of $lock(f_i)$, $unlock(f_j)$ requests, issued by several users, where $f_i$ and $f_j$ are file names . Clearly, testing such a system should involve submitting several sequences of lock–unlock requests from different users, both acceptable and unacceptable, to check appropriate reactions of the system. For instance, the system should accept the sequence

| | |
|---|---|
| lock($f_1$) | issued by user a |
| lock($f_2$) | issued by user b |
| unlock($f_1$) | issued by user a |
| lock($f_1$) | issued by user b |
| unlock($f_2$) | issued by user b |
| unlock($f_1$) | issued by user b |

but the sequence

| | |
|---|---|
| lock($f_1$) | issued by user a |
| lock($f_2$) | issued by user b |
| lock($f_1$) | issued by user b |
| unlock($f_1$) | issued by user a |
| unlock($f_2$) | issued by user b |
| unlock($f_1$) | issued by user b |

should cause a rejection by the system at the third line.

Figure 6.17 gives a formal definition of acceptable sequences for any file $f_j$, under the simplifying hypothesis that there are only two users. (As a side exercise, you could generalize the definition to the case of any number of files and users by using Petri nets augmented with predicates and actions.)

Use the net of Figure 6.17 to derive test sequences—whether accepted or not—for the system. (For instance, one can derive the second sequence shown by explicitly looking for the firing of a transition that is not enabled in a given PN marking.) Use your intuition and experience on locking policies to rule out some irrelevant sequences from the specified ones in order to limit the amount of testing.

**6.62** Researchers and practitioners have proposed several "mixed testing strategies" intended to combine the advantages of the various techniques discussed in this chapter. Propose your own combination, perhaps also using some kind of random testing at selected points. You may find some suggestions in the specialized literature referenced in the bibliographic notes.

**6.63** List some of the problems that could result from adding debugging statements to code. Discuss possible solutions to these problems. Design an appropriate interface for the assert routine suggested in Section 6.8.

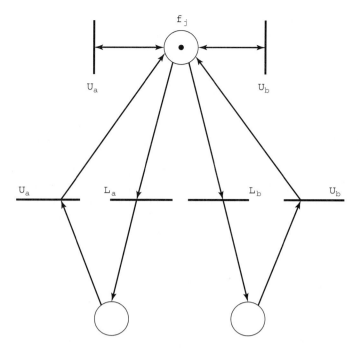

Legend: $L_a$: lock($f_j$) issued by a
$L_b$: lock($f_j$) issued by b
$U_a$: unlock($f_j$) issued by a
$U_b$: unlock($f_j$) issued by b

FIGURE 6.17

A Petri net description of the locking policy of the generic file $f_j$ with
two users.

**6.64** Design testing criteria for the following graph-oriented problems (in some cases, you
may decide to use a formal specification of the problem to gain better insight into it):

**a.** Stating whether a directed graph is connected.

**b.** Finding the number of connected components of an undirected graph.

**c.** Finding maximal cliques in an undirected and in a directed graph. (A clique of a graph
G is a complete subgraph of G; a maximal clique is a clique with the largest number of
nodes.)

**d.** Finding a path, if any, joining any pair of nodes in a graph (whether directed or not).

**6.65** Design a test set for a spell checker. Then run the tests on a word processor having a
spell checker, and report on possible inadequacies with respect to your requirements.

**6.66** Give proof rules for statements not covered in this chapter, such as **for** loops and **case**.

**6.67** Prove the correctness of the sorting program fragment proposed in Exercise 6.47.

**6.68** Design testing criteria for the problem of finding the intersection of two convex polygons
given as sequences of points in the integer Cartesian plane. The program must also be able

to check whether the polygons are convex or not. Take into account the fact that, even if the vertices have integer coordinates, their intersections may not.

**6.69** Design testing criteria for the problem of formatting a text according to the following rules:

The text is a sequence of characters. The special character '\' is used only for specifying commands. \lbreak is the "line break" command; the traditional RETURN, however, may also be used. Commands may be combined with braces { and } to indicate the scope of application of the command. For example, {\b...text...} says to turn the ...text... into boldface. The command for italicizing text is \i. Other formatting commands may be defined by the reader. Formatting commands can be nested. Beginnings and ends must match. Furthermore, two consecutive identical commands negate one another. As an example of the application of these rules, the text

```
yesterday {\b I was {\i in NY, {\b but it was} {\i raining}} a lot}
```

should be printed as

yesterday **I was *in NY,*** *but it was* **raining a lot**

The program must detect and report formatting errors.

You should do a complete and detailed formalization of the specification before designing any tests.

**6.70** Suppose you have a huge database with several millions of records. An error causes a failure whenever the first record of the database is accessed. Discuss how reliable the database appears to its users.

**6.71** Design an integration testing strategy for the module hierarchy of Figure 5.46(b).

**6.72** Write a correct version of the merge algorithm of Example 6.12, and then prove it correct.

**6.73** Consider symbolic execution in the general case of an augmented Petri net (with token values, predicates, and actions), where a place can hold more than one token. Explain why path conditions associated with firing sequences do not necessarily enable a unique firing sequence and why the same firing sequence could be enabled by different path conditions.

**6.74** State other interesting properties of the FSM of Figure 6.13, and investigate their validity.

**6.75** Build an FSM describing the behavior of the PN of Figure 5.28. Which properties hold for such a machine? How do they differ from the properties of the PN of Figure 5.20?

**6.76** In this text, we assume a PN semantics that allows only one transition to fire at each step. Other definitions of the model allow the contemporaneous firing of several transitions (true concurrency semantics of PNs). How does the FSM of Figure 6.13 change if the PN of Figure 5.20 has true concurrency semantics instead of the semantics adopted here? Do the related properties change?

**6.77** Give assertions to help in debugging the programs of Exercise 6.3.

**6.78** Discuss the differences between worst case and average case performance evaluation by means of testing. How can we be sure that the real worst case has actually been observed?

**6.79** Code Euclid's algorithm given in Example 6.5 in Pascal and C. Then compute the quantities $\eta$, $\eta_1$, $\eta_2$, $N$, $N_1$, and $N_2$ for each program. Also, evaluate McCabe's cyclomatic number for the programs.

**6.80**  Show that thanks to the fact that operands and operators tend to alternate in programs (e.g., a + b * c), the following relation on the length of a program holds:

$$N \leq \eta \cdot \eta_1^{\eta_1} \cdot \eta_2^{\eta_2}$$

**6.81**  Critically assess the definition of program level in Halstead's theory.

**6.82**  Suppose you derive the control flow graph for a program $P$ in order to evaluate its cyclomatic complexity. Is the value you obtain affected by the transformation described in Figure 6.2?

**6.83**  While a compiler's functional specification may be easily provided by the official definition of the source language, some other aspects of the compiler are not so easy to specify. For example, how would you specify the requirements for the optimization part of a compiler? How do you specify what code is optimized? Is it possible for a compiler to produce *optimal* code, in the mathematical sense of the word?

**6.84**  How do you test an *optimizing* compiler? How do you distinguish between a normal compiler and an optimizing compiler? Define a plan for testing an optimizing compiler for Ada.

**6.85**  In Section 6.9.3.3, we questioned whether we could be sure that 95% coverage implies more reliability than 90% coverage. Discuss this problem. State a condition under which the answer is yes.

## HINTS AND SKETCHY SOLUTIONS

**6.10**  Inputs to a programs may have a rich structure that can be defined by a BNF grammar. For example, consider a program that uses as input a business form with several (possibly repeated) fields and several options. One can use the input's BNF as a driver to generate test sets.

**6.11**  Certain combinations of inputs may generate an ERROR action.

**6.17**  Top-down integration may anticipate the detection of errors occurring in the early phases of design. The availability of high-level modules, integrated with suitable stubs, may be used as an early prototype of the whole system, perhaps to be demonstrated to the end user.

Top-down testing usually requires testing a subsystem without I/O operations. (In general, these are in lower levels of the hierarchy.) This decreases both the reliability of the testing results (many errors are I/O dependent) and the efficiency of the testing activity, which requires ad hoc procedures for the input of test cases. Observation and evaluation of test results are easier with bottom-up integration.

**6.18**  Policy 1: The error is certainly discovered. In fact, even assuming that, initially, control is given to the consumer, the task will run until the buffer has been emptied. At that point, control will be given to the producer, which will execute four consecutive writes to the buffer (due to the error). This will result in a failure.

Policy 2: Execution is similar to that in policy 1, but starts immediately with the producer.

Policy 3: The failure does not occur, since, whenever there is an item in the buffer and the producer reaches a synchronization point, control is given to the consumer, which empties the buffer. Thus, even a buffer of length 1 would work properly.

**6.19** It is crucial to consider the *times of occurrence* of input events (i.e., when the items are supplied to the producer). Thus, it is reasonable to submit to the system stimuli whose frequency is related to the execution speed of the several processes (e.g., a sequence of stimuli at a rate that is double the execution time of the two processes, a sequence at a greater speed, and a sequence at a lower speed). For each sequence, it should be verified whether some data are lost—that is, whether the sequence of data read by the consumer is the same as the sequence of data input to the system.

**6.25** Part **a**.

Use as part of the invariant $I$: $x = z^{j-1}$ **and** $y \leq j - 1$. The first clause of $I$ formalizes the intuitive notion that, at each loop iteration, $x$ stores the $(j - 1)$th power of $z$, where $j$ is the loop counter. The second clause is used to ensure that $y = j - 1$ at loop exit.

Part **b**.

Suggested invariant: The greatest common divisor of $x$ and $y$ is equal to the greatest common divisor of $input_1$ and $input_2$. (See the exercise for the formal definition of "greatest common divisor.")

**Warning**: To avoid tricky situations, use different identifiers for quantified variables (i.e., variables subject to the **exists** and **for all** operators), on the one hand, and program variables, on the other.

**6.33** Let $p$ be the probability that, during restarting, the initialization failure occurs. Let $\{p_i\}$ be the probabilities of occurrence of all failures that result in restarting the system (including switching off the system by the operator). Then the probability of occurrence of the initialization failure is

$$P = \Sigma_i p_i \cdot p = p \cdot \Sigma_i p_i$$

**6.34** We view an array reference as similar to a function call (i.e., it should be considered an operator applied to a list of operands). The pair " ( , ) " is an operator as well, and the comma, too. In statements of the type $a := b$, where $a$ and $b$ are arrays, $a$ and $b$ should be considered operands.

**6.51** First, provide sequences of $I_1$ stimuli, with no signals of type $I_2$. Then, try the opposite. Finally, try interleaving both types of stimuli with more complex sequences.

**6.55** You may use a "negative" grammar generating the complement of the language. You should integrate systematic approaches to the problem (deterministic context-free languages are closed with respect to the complement operation) with common sense and insight. In fact, the compiler should not only detect errors, but also provide as much guidance as possible to help in correcting them. This is a typical requirement that is almost impossible to formalize completely. All programmers have probably had the experience that a good compiler behaves quite predictably on correct programs and on programs containing "simple" errors, but becomes less and less predictable as it encounters more numerous and more intricate coding errors.

**6.58** Let a condition $C$ be of the type $c_1$ **or** $c_1 \dots$ **or** $c_n$. Instead of trying all possible combinations of input values that make the $c_i$'s true and false, just try the case where they are all false and $n$ cases where just one is true. Repeat similarly for **and** conditions.

**6.59** Some elementary knowledge of Cartesian geometry suggests the following choice:

**a.** three points not on the same straight line.

**b.** three points on the same line.

None of the systematic techniques discussed in this section, however, would have led to this choice.

**6.60** We know that unlock operations preceding lock operations will never be issued. Furthermore, even in the case where the user does so by mistake, they are unlikely to cause trouble. Thus, we can limit, or even avoid completely, the testing of the system with unlock operations corresponding to the firing of transitions $U_a$, $U_b$, with tokens coming from place $f_j$. But note that an unlock by b when a has the lock should be tested.

**6.61** As an example of a mixed testing strategy, you may proceed as follows: Choose a technique that leads to the definition of classes $\{D_i\}$ of the input domain D. Try, by hand, to find an element for each class. Also, try an element for each boundary between different classes. Then, try to achieve more completeness by randomly generating a given number of elements for different classes. (The number of elements to be generated may vary from class to class according to the relevance of the class.)

Writing a random generator for each class can be very hard in some cases. (A "perfect" tool of this type would imply the decidability of the emptiness problem for the class.) Thus, for those cases in which you are unable to randomly generate elements of a given class, you may proceed as follows: Randomly generate elements within D; then decide whether the element generated is in the considered class $D_i$. (This will be decidable in *most* cases.) The failure to generate an element of $D_i$ after a while may suggest a more careful analysis of $D_i$'s properties, regardless of whether you were able to find some of its elements by hand.

The foregoing procedure should be applied to at least one white-box technique and one black-box technique.

**6.62** The debugging code itself may contain errors and need to be verified (e.g., an uninitialized variable may be printed). The new code might also change the behavior of the program (e.g., by causing variables to be allocated to different addresses).

**6.73** With reference to the Petri net of Figure 6.11, the path condition

```
M₁.ok_parity and not M₂.ok_parity and M₃.ok_parity
```

enables both the firing sequence

```
<message_reception, send_ack₂, message_reception,
     send_nack,message_reception, send_ack₃>
```

and the firing sequence

```
<message_reception, message_reception, send_ack₂,
     send_nack, message_reception, send_ack₃>
```

The firing sequence

```
<message_reception, message_reception, send_ack₂,
     send_nack, message_reception, send_ack₃>
```

also is enabled by the path condition

```
(not M₁.ok_parity and M₂.ok_parity and M₂.ok_parity).
```

**6.78** Worst case analysis to verify qualities cannot be done safely on a purely experimental basis. In principle, the only way to achieve results that are absolutely certain is through exhaustive testing. Again, however, some preliminary analysis, to be performed as rigorously as possible, can drive the selection of test cases that are most likely to produce worst case performance. For instance, a simple inspection of the sorting algorithm given in Exercise 6.47 suggests reverse-ordered sequences as test cases to obtain worst case performance. Once again, we have integrated (more or less formal) inspection with experimental evaluation.

**6.80**  The number of different strings of length $k_1 + k_2$ consisting of alternating symbols belonging to $A_1$ of size $k_1$ and $A_2$ of size $k_2$, respectively, is

$$k_1^{k_1} \cdot k_2^{k_2}$$

**6.81**  Is it always true that a smaller volume means more abstraction?

**6.85**  In general, covering more branches in one test set than in another one does not imply more reliability—assuming, of course, that the tests did not produce failures. However, if the larger test set is a superset of the smaller one, we achieve at least as much reliability as in the latter test set, since we exercise the system in all cases of the smaller set, *plus* more.

## BIBLIOGRAPHIC NOTES

The special issues of the *Communications of the ACM* on software testing (CACM [1988]) and of *IEEE Software* on software verification and validation (IEEE Software [1989b]) provide overviews of the field of verification. For the basic terminology, refer to Adrion et al. [1975] and the issue of IEEE Software [1999] on software engineering and standards. The issue of verification versus validation is addressed by Boehm [1984b]. Kemmerer [1985] contains an excellent discussion of why specifications should be tested and also shows how to do this in the context of formal specifications based on logic.

The field of testing is presented by Myers [1979] (who introduces cause-effect graphs and covers code inspections and walk-throughs), Beizer [1983], Hetzel [1984], and Howden [1987]. Black-box testing is covered by Beizer [1995]. Good surveys, classifications, and definitions are also given by Chandrasekaran and Radicchi (eds.) [1981], White [1987], DeMillo et al. [1987], and the seminal paper by Goodenough and Gerhart [1975]. The testing terminology is not always used in the literature in a consistent way. For instance, Goodenough and Gerhart [1975] define a test as being *successful* if the program being tested executes the test successfully. Myers [1979] and others define it in exactly the opposite way: A test is successful if it causes the program to fail. The difference in the two viewpoints is in whether the notion of success is associated with the program succeeding or the test succeeding in discovering an error. Also, Hetzel [1984] and others define a *test case* to be a set of values belonging to the input domain, whereas others define it to be a single value.

Dijkstra's famous sentence on testing being useful to prove the presence, and not the absence, of errors is from Dahl et al. [1972].

Much theoretical and experimental research has addressed the issues of evaluating, comparing, and integrating different testing criteria. Within the rich literature on this topic, we mention Basili and Selby [1987] (who include also code-inspection techniques in their comparison), Duran and Ntafos [1984] (which suggests that random testing has its own advantages), Ntafos [1988] (which compares white-box techniques), and Clarke et al. [1989] (which suggests a systematic approach to the selection of paths in the control flow graph of a program). Zeil [1989] introduces *perturbation testing*, a method that focuses on faults in arithmetic expressions, and describes a method of generating test data.

An important technique is the so-called *mutation analysis*, which may be used to evaluate the thoroughness of a test set T supplied to a given program P. The basic idea is that if T is not able to reveal some difference between P and a suitable variation P' of P, called a *mutant*, then it is unlikely that T can provide evidence of P's correctness. A tutorial presentation of mutation analysis is given by Budd in Chandrasekaran and Radicchi (eds.) [1981].

Jalote [1989] provides a method that can be used both to verify the completeness of specifications of abstract data types (testing specifications) given in an algebraic language and to automatically derive test cases for its implementation in a black-box way. Bouge et al. [1986] also describes the generation of test cases from algebraic specifications. A syntax-driven technique for automatically generating test cases for a compiler is given by Celentano et al. [1980].

Choppy and Kaplan [1990] propose a technique for testing a large system of modules that integrates the execution of implemented and partially specified modules, as is suggested in Example 6.10.

The problem of testing concurrent and real-time systems has not yet been investigated thoroughly. The problem is presented by Brinch Hansen [1978]. Interesting approaches are suggested by Tai and Obaid [1986], with particular reference to the issue of testing repeatability. Mandrioli et al. [1995] present a black-box technique for deriving test cases for real-time systems from specifications coded in the logic language TRIO. They also describe a tool supporting a technique and its application to industrial case studies. San Pietro et al. [2000] address the issue of testing real-time systems in the large.

Informal analysis techniques are described by Fagan [1976, 1986]; Basili and Selby [1987] evaluates those techniques experimentally. A recent and thorough experimental assessment of code inspection techniques is provided by Porter et al. [1997]. Also, Porter and Johnson [1997] argue that meetings are not always cost effective in code inspections.

Formal verification methods obviously require formal specifications. Thus, it is not surprising that the same pioneering papers by McCarthy [1962], Floyd [1967], and Hoare [1969] which laid the foundations of a formal definition of semantics also addressed the issue of formal correctness analysis. Manna [1974] and Mandrioli and Ghezzi [1987], among others, also introduce and discuss formal correctness analysis.

The extension of correctness proof methods to concurrent systems was pioneered by Hoare [1972] and pursued by Owicki and Gries [1976], Lamport [1979, 1989], and Pnueli [1981] (who uses temporal logic), among others. The issue of the correctness of real-time software was discussed by Haase [1981], Fuggetta et al. [1989], and Liu and Shyamasundar [1990]. Heitmeyer and Mandrioli [1996] contains a collection of recent contributions to the field.

Modular correctness proofs are advocated by Coen-Porisini et al. [1994], among others. The B-method (see, e.g., Abrial [1996]) exploits modularization and layering in formal correctness analysis.

The "clean-room" approach to software development has been proposed by Mills et al. [1987b]. The approach is named by analogy with semiconductor production, where defects are prevented by manufacturing in an ultraclean atmosphere. The clean-room approach is based on error prevention, rather than error correction. In particular, modules are formally specified and mathematically proved correct; testing of modules is abolished. Testing is done only at the integration level, by supplying test data that reflect expected usage patterns and by using a reliability model to decide when the system has been tested adequately. Preliminary practical experience with the approach within IBM was encouraging, according to Selby et al. [1987].

Although formal methods are still far from attaining wide application in the industrial world, early significant examples of their application to real cases are reported in Good (ed.) [1977] and Walker et al. [1980]. Crispin [1987] reports on the application of VDM (Vienna Definition Method) to industrial projects. The reader can gain a flavor of the early "formal methods controversy" by looking at essays such as Saeidian et al. [1996] and Gerhart et al. [1993, 1994].

Young and Taylor [1988, 1989] propose a taxonomy for evaluating and possibly integrating different verification techniques, including testing, the static analysis of programs, correctness proofs, and symbolic interpretation.

An introduction to symbolic execution and to its applications to software verification is provided by Clarke and Richardson in Chandrasekaran and Radicchi [1981]. Ghezzi et al. [1989b] show how symbolic interpretation can be extended to the verification of concurrent systems through a suitable extension of Petri nets. Coen-Porisini et al. [2001] discusses how symbolic execution can be applied to safety-critical software.

Seminal papers on model checking are Clarke and Emerson [1981], Clarke et al. [1986] and Queille and Sifakis [1982]. They all exploit temporal logic as an assertion language for expressing the properties of FSMs. Another approach consists of showing the equivalence (or containment) of the behaviors of different machines, one of them being used to specify system requirements, the other one to describe its implementation. Such an approach has been pursued, among others, by Har'El and Kurshan [1990]. After publication of the original papers, much research has been applied to improve model checking, either by augmenting the size of manageable state spaces or by enriching the basic model (e.g., to deal with real-time systems). Among such an abundant literature, we mention Campos et al. [1996], Alur et al. [1990], and Bharadwaj and Heitmeyer [1999]. The book Clark et al. [2000] is a comprehensive treatment of model checking.

The notion of program scaffolding to support debugging is addressed by Bentley [1985]. Brindle and Taylor [1989] address the problem of debugging concurrent Ada programs. A survey of concurrent debugging techniques is given by McDowell and Helmbold [1989]. CACM [1997] provides an updated view of the debugging issue.

Complexity analysis is treated in depth in many texts on algorithm design. A classic is Aho et al. [1974]. For a discussion of performance evaluation, the reader can refer to Ferrari [1978] and Smith [1989].

A complete treatment of software reliability based on the application of statistical methods is presented by Musa et al. [1987]. Musa [1998] represents software reliability as an engineering discipline. Several contributions are also contained in Bittanti [1988]. In particular, the paper by Bittanti et al. provides an overview of the theoretical foundations for the application of statistical models, upon which we have based our discussion. An approach supporting recalibration of the chosen model is described in Brocklehurst et al. [1990].

Knuth [1974] provides an assessment of programming styles with and without **goto** statements and concludes that, in general, the absence of such statements does not unequivocally determine the quality of code.

A general view of several kinds of software metrics, their relations, and their application can be found in Basili [1980], Conte et al. [1986], and Frewin et al. [1985]. The special issue of *IEEE Transactions on Software Engineering* edited by Iyer (TSE [1990]) contains several papers addressing the problem of experimentally validating several subjective software qualities. Fenton and Pfleeger [1998] is a comprehensive treatment of metrics and software measurement in general.

Software science is defined by Halstead [1977]. McCabe [1976, 1983] and McCabe and Butler [1989] presents a measure of complexity and its application to the development of testing strategies. Among the many papers providing critical evaluations, experimental validations, combinations, and variations of different software metrics, we mention Hamer and Frewin [1982] and Shen et al. [1983] (who provide a critical evaluation of Halstead's theory), Albrecht and Gaffney [1983], Basili and Hutchens [1983], Basili et al. [1983], Coulter [1983], Curtis et al. [1979], Henry and Kafura [1981], and Kearney et al. [1986]. The special issue of *IEEE Software* [1990b] provides a view of the state of the art at that time.

The role of measurements in the tailoring of a development support environment is discussed by Basili et al. [1986] and Basili and Rombach [1988]; Basili and Caldiera [1988] suggests how software metrics can be applied to enhance and measure software reusability. Metrics are also applied to software maintainability in Harrison et al. [1982], Kafura and Reddy [1987], and Gibson and Senn [1989].

The GQM methodology is covered in van Solingen and Berghout [1999]. The experiment described in Case Study 6.1 is adapted from Briand and Morasca [1997].

# CHAPTER 7

# The Software Production Process

There are many steps and activities involved in building a software product. We studied software design in Chapter 4, software specification in Chapter 5, and software verification in Chapter 6. How should these activities be organized in relation to each other? The order in which we perform them and other activities defines a life cycle for the software product. More generally, the process we follow to build, deliver, deploy, and evolve the software product, from the inception of an idea all the way to the delivery and final retirement of the system, is called the *software production process*.

Production and manufacturing processes are studied extensively in any discipline whose goal is to produce products. The goal of production processes is to satisfy customers' expectations by delivering quality products on time and within budget, by making products profitable and production reliable, predictable, and efficient. A well-defined production process, such as that used, for example, in automobile production, has many benefits, including supporting automation and the use of standard components and processes.

By defining a model of the software production process, we can reap some of the benefits of standardized processes. But we must also keep two distinguishing characteristics of software in mind: First, software production is largely an intellectual activity, not easily amenable to automation. Second, software is characterized by high instability: requirements change continuously, and, as a consequence, the products themselves must be evolvable.

How, then, should we organize a software production process that will enable us to produce high-quality software products reliably, predictably, and efficiently? In this chapter, we examine different models that attempt to capture this process, also called the "software life cycle." Such models are based on the recognition that software, like any other industrial product, has a life cycle that spans from its initial conception to its retirement and that that life cycle must be anticipated and controlled in order to achieve the desired qualities in the product. We also study how these processes can be more or less automated, or at least made predictable, by the use of standards and methodologies. In our examination, we shall see that blanket prescriptions for the "best methodology for software productivity" do not exist. Accordingly, we examine some development methodologies critically and assess their usefulness in the software process.

In short, while the previous chapters have focused on the software *product*, this chapter focuses on the software development *process*. We shall postpone all management issues to the next chapter, which deals also with the economic aspects of producing software.

Before going deeper into software production process models, we must observe that in many practical cases the software application being developed is a component of a larger system. The software life cycle is therefore a part of a more general system life cycle. For example, the design and development of a distributed system for plant automation deals with both hardware (computing devices, a network, specialized peripherals) and software components. Similarly, the development of an office automation system involves designing workflows based both on manual and automatic procedures. Manual procedures are executed by humans, who interact with software applications, which provide automated support for more standardized tasks.

This chapter is devoted mainly to software development models and only touches the surface of the more general topic of system development. It starts by discussing what a software process model is and why having such a model is important (Sections 7.1 and 7.2). Since a process organizes the flow among activities, Section 7.3 surveys the main development activities involved in software production. Specific process models are then discussed in Section 7.4. After analyzing the traditional waterfall model, we present other models that seek to overcome the weaknesses of the traditional one. In particular, we show that the waterfall model works well when requirements are understood and are not expected to change much; if these conditions are not satisfied, the model is rigid and lacks flexibility.

Most software processes are attempts to control the complexities of the development process. In practice, however, most software activity is devoted to maintaining and enhancing existing legacy software, rather than to the development of new software. Section 7.5 presents and discusses the issues involved in this common situation.

Section 7.6 is devoted to case studies. We first introduce two examples of real software projects and show how their different nature requires the adoption of different process models. We then address two examples of modern industrial processes with contrasting approaches: the "synchronize and stabilize" software development strategy, which has been adopted by the Microsoft Corporation, and the open-source approach, which has been popularized by the Linux operating system development. Section 7.7 deals with organizing and guiding the software production process; we review some important methodologies that are widely adopted in the software industry. We also provide an overview of two traditional approaches: structured analysis/structured design, and Jackson's system development. We then introduce the unified development process, which provides a disciplined development approach in the context of object-oriented development with UML. Section 7.8 deals with the important organizational issue of how to manage all the artifacts produced in the software process, an issue known as "configuration management." Finally, we discuss the need for software standards in Section 7.9.

## 7.1    WHAT IS A SOFTWARE PROCESS MODEL?

As discussed in Chapter 1, in the early days of computing software development was mainly a single-person task. The problem to be solved—very often of a mathematical nature—was well understood, and there was no distinction between the programmer and the end user of the application. The end user—very often a scientist or an engineer—developed the application as a support to his or her own activity. The application, by today's standards, was rather simple. Thus, software development consisted only of coding the application in some low-level language.

The model used in those early days may be called *the code-and-fix model*. Basically, the term denotes a development process that is neither precisely formulated nor carefully controlled; rather, software production consists of the iteration of two steps: (1) write code and (2) fix it to eliminate any errors that have been detected, to enhance existing functionality, or to add new features. The code-and-fix model has been the source of many difficulties and deficiencies. In particular, after a sequence of changes, the structure of the code becomes so messy that subsequent fixes become harder to apply and the results become less reliable. These problems, however, were mitigated by the fact that applications were rather simple and both the application and the software were well understood by the engineer.

As hardware capacity grew, the desire to apply computers in more and more domains, such as business administration and process control, led to software being used in less and less understood environments. A sharp separation arose between software developers and end users. End users with little or no technical background in science and mathematics, such as sales agents and personnel administrators, could not be expected to develop their own applications, due both to the intrinsic complexity of the application's design and implementation and to the users' lack of technical background required to master the complexity of computer systems.

In today's environment, software is developed not for personal use, but for people with little or no background in computers. Sometimes, software is developed in response to a request from a specific customer; increasingly, so-called shrink-wrapped software is developed for the general (consumer) market; sometimes, software is embedded in other consumer products. All three of these situations add new dimensions to the software that were not present in the previous age. Now software is a product that must be marketed, sold, and installed on different machines at different sites. Users must be trained in its use and must be assisted when something unexpected happens.

Thus, economic, as well as organizational and psychological, issues become important. In addition, demand has increased for much higher levels of quality in applications, and reliability requirements have become more stringent. One reason is that end users are not as tolerant of system failures as are system designers. Another reason is that computer-based systems are increasingly applied in areas, such as banking operations and plant control, where system failures may have severe consequences.

Another sharp difference from the previous age is that software development has become a group activity. Group work requires carefully thought-out organizational structures and standard practices, in order to make it possible to predict and control developments. Since labor costs are the dominant cost driver in software development, the selection of appropriate organizational structures to maximize cooperation and minimize interference among team members is crucial to keeping costs under control.

The code-and-fix process model was inadequate to deal with the new software age. First, the increased size of the systems being developed made it difficult to manage their complexity in an unstructured way. The problem was exacerbated by the turnover of software personnel working on projects. Adding new people to an ongoing project was extremely difficult because of the poor (or total lack of) documentation available to guide them in the task of understanding the application properly. Fixing code was difficult because no anticipation of change was taken into account before the start of coding. Similarly, it was difficult to remove errors that required major restructuring of the existing code. These problems underscored the need for a *design phase* prior to coding.

The second reason behind the inadequacy of the code-and-fix model was the frequent discovery, after the system was developed, that the software did not match the user's expectations. So the product either was rejected or had to be redeveloped to achieve the desired goals. Almost inevitably, software development became a sort of never-ending activity. As a result, the development process was unpredictable and uncontrollable, and products were completed over schedule and over budget and did not meet quality expectations. Soon it was realized that a better understanding of the application domain and a more detailed and careful analysis of the requirements were necessary before design and coding could start.

The failure of the code-and-fix model may be attributed to a general phenomenon that we observed in Chapter 2: The fact that software is malleable does not imply that we can mould it to achieve any required behavior, especially when we try to change a piece of code written by someone else. Thus, the apparent ease of change that characterizes software as opposed to other kinds of products is misleading and is a constant source of misconceptions and unrealistic expectations.

As mentioned in Chapter 1, the failure of the code-and-fix process model led to the recognition of the so-called software crisis and, in turn, to the birth of software engineering as a discipline. In particular, the recognition that methods were sorely lacking in the software production process led to the concept of the software life cycle and to structured models for describing it in a precise way in order to make the process predictable and controllable. Boehm [1988] states that the goals of structured process models are to

> determine the *order of stages* involved in software development and evolution, and to establish the *transition criteria* for progressing from one stage to the next. These include completion criteria for the current stage plus choice criteria and entrance criteria for the next stage. Thus a process model addresses the following software project questions:
>
> What shall we do next?
> How long shall we continue to do it?

According to this viewpoint, process models have a twofold effect. On the one hand, they provide guidance to software engineers on the order in which the various technical activities should be carried out within a project; on the other hand, they afford a framework for managing development and maintenance, in that they enable us to estimate resources, define intermediate milestones, monitor progress, etc.

## 7.2    WHY ARE SOFTWARE PROCESS MODELS IMPORTANT?

The concern for quality has been on the increase in most industrial sectors. In addition, awareness of the central importance of the production processes has been increasing. Processes are important because industry cares about their intrinsic qualities, such as uniformity of performance across different projects and productivity, with the aim of improving time to market and reducing production costs. But processes are also important because experience has shown that they have a decisive influence on the quality of products; that is, by controlling processes, we can achieve better control of the required qualities of products.

This relationship between processes and the quality of products holds especially in software production, because of the intrinsic nature of software. If an explicit process is in place, software development proceeds in a predictable and orderly fashion, reducing the chance of introducing faults into the product and providing a means for controlling the quality of what is being developed. If no explicit notion of process is in place, product development can be considered as a black box wherein the only visible flows are at the box's input and output ends. (See Figure 7.1.) At the input side, the flow into the box represents product requirements. At the output end of the box, we hope that the desired product is delivered. Unfortunately, in many real-life cases, the product appears at the output side months or years after the development started and thus after the expenditure of much money. When the product finally does appear, it is often too late and too expensive to care about quality. It is therefore necessary that the concern for quality be present at the beginning, and throughout all stages, of the whole process; it cannot be postponed only to the end of development.

There are some deep reasons that make the approach of Figure 7.1 even worse for software than for other, more traditional kinds of artifacts. The first major difficulty has to do with getting the right product requirements. A product development does not start with precisely stated product requirements, but rather, in most cases, it arises from some informal needs and goals that originate in the customer's business world. The problem is that, in many cases, the customer does not know exactly what he or she wants. The customer has a vague perception of problems to be solved, but is unable to translate this perception into precisely formulated goals, let alone precise requirements that the future system should meet. Furthermore, the software engineer may have little or no previous knowledge of the application domain and thus cannot help much in the process of eliciting the requirements. As a consequence, the input requirements to the process are likely to be informal, fuzzy, largely incomplete, perhaps contradictory, and maybe even not reflecting the user's real needs. If the development process is structured as a black box (see Figure 7.2), its progress (or lack thereof) becomes invisible. Eventually, when the product is delivered, it is very likely that the customer will find it unsatisfactory, at which point post-development modifications, whose cost is high and whose effectiveness is often low, will be required.

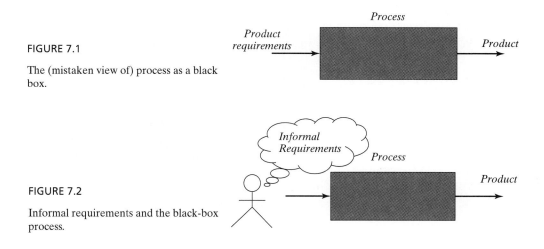

**FIGURE 7.1**

The (mistaken view of) process as a black box.

**FIGURE 7.2**

Informal requirements and the black-box process.

Thus, it is extremely risky to base all design decisions on the assumption that the initial requirements that one is able to elicit and specify capture the customer's expectations precisely. To reduce the risks, it is necessary to open the black box: One must define a suitable process that lends visibility to what is being developed. By seeing inside the black box, one may hope to *gradually* validate what is being developed against the customer's expectations. The process may thus provide continuous feedback to the developers, reducing the time lag between making a decision and discovering that the decision was actually wrong, in turn reducing the costs of developing an acceptable product.

Another difficulty has to do with the inevitable tendency of software requirements to change during the process. As we mentioned, customers often do not know exactly what they want; and even if they do, their requirements keep changing during the process. An increasingly common case of rapidly changing requirements is typical of the development of innovative products, such as many current Internet applications. With these products, the initial requirements are only partially known, and there may not even be any customers "out there" to provide a precise list of features that the application should provide. New demands arise and new potential customers appear as initial implementations are delivered and feedback from initial users plays a role in improving the product.

These concepts suggest an alternative process scheme, which is described pictorially in Figure 7.3. As suggested by the figure, a transparent production process allows the manager and the customer to understand what is going on inside the process. In particular, transparency allows them to observe the artifacts produced during the process. Such artifacts (e.g., use cases, intermediate prototypes, preliminary and incomplete versions, design documentation, test case definition, etc.) may be used to provide some form of validation of the current process. As a result of the validation, it is possible either to decide to proceed to the next step or to reiterate the previous step.

Another fundamental reason that makes the black-box process of Figure 7.1 unacceptable for software is that one cannot expect to assess the quality of the product by simply looking at the product itself. This may differ from the case of other kinds of products. As we observed by way of an example in Section 6.3, we can certify that a bridge can sustain certain load conditions by physically applying those conditions. This ensures that the bridge has an acceptable behavior for all other load conditions that are less stringent than the one used for certification. Thus, a single test verifies the correctness of infinitely many cases. By contrast, in the case of software, a successful test execution, in general, does not tell us much about other possible executions. Testing

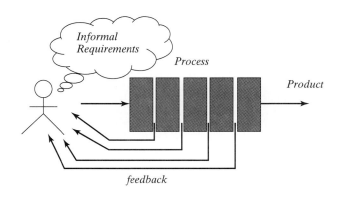

FIGURE 7.3

A transparent process.

and all other kinds of practical analysis techniques have intrinsic weaknesses; they cannot guarantee the absence of defects in software. To achieve higher confidence in the correctness of software, we can structure the process in a way that makes development systematic and therefore less error prone. By combining prevention with continuous verification and validation, an explicitly and clearly defined process may improve our confidence in software qualities.

The descriptions of process models in Sections 7.1 to 7.3 are rather abstract. They are provided here to illustrate the purpose of a software process model and its basic properties. In Section 7.4, we present a number of more concrete process models and discuss how they correspond to the concepts examined in this section.

## 7.3    THE MAIN ACTIVITIES OF SOFTWARE PRODUCTION

Software production can be decomposed into a number of specific activities. The way the activities are organized as steps of a process can vary according to the chosen process model, as we shall see in Section 7.4. No matter how they are organized in a process, however, these activities must be performed for any project. The purpose of this section is to illustrate the activities, their goals, and how they are internally structured. We may think of the steps, roughly, as analysis, design, and implementation, but a careful examination reveals many more steps.

### 7.3.1    Feasibility study

This activity is often performed before the production process actually starts, to support the decision of whether a new development should be started. Its goal is to provide a *feasibility study document*, which presents different scenarios and alternative solutions, along with a discussion of the trade-offs in terms expected costs and benefits. The feasibility study is often used to resolve the build-versus-buy decision for an organization: Should we develop the product ourselves, or can we buy a similar one more economically?

To perform the feasibility study, the software engineer must first analyze the problem, at least at a global level. Indeed, the more the problem is understood, the better alternative solutions, their costs, and their potential benefits for the user can be identified. Therefore, ideally, one should perform as much analysis of the problem as is needed to do a well-founded feasibility study. Unfortunately, this is often highly constrained in practice: The feasibility study is usually done within a limited amount of time and under pressure. Often, the result is an offer to the potential customer, which then leads to a contract that states the conditions under which the software developer will eventually deliver the product. Since software developers cannot be sure that the offer will be accepted, they have a limited incentive for investing resources into analyzing the problem. On the other hand, if the study produces results that are inaccurate, it may underestimate the resources needed to develop the application, and that will result in serious budget problems.

On the basis of the definition of the problem during the preliminary analysis, software developers identify alternative solutions. For each suggested solution, costs and delivery dates are evaluated. Thus, the feasibility study phase does a sort of simulation of the future development process through which it is possible to derive information that helps decide whether development is worthwhile and what the costs are. As we observed, however, the risk is to constrain the future development too early, when the available information is still incomplete, poorly understood, and fuzzy.

In sum, the feasibility study tries to anticipate future scenarios of software development. Its result is a document that should contain at least the following items:

1. A definition of the problem.
2. Alternative solutions and their expected benefits.
3. Required resources, costs, and delivery dates in each proposed alternative solution.

### 7.3.2   Eliciting, understanding, and specifying requirements

There is a consensus, among both software developers and customers, that the activities of eliciting, understanding, and specifying requirements are the most critical aspects of the software engineering process. Indeed, the discipline of *requirements engineering* seeks to develop standard and systematic methods to elicit, document, classify, and analyze requirements. The success of an application depends heavily on the quality of the results of requirements engineering. The ultimate purpose of these requirements-related activities is to understand the goals of the system, to document the requirements to be met, and to specify the qualities required of the software solution, in terms of functionality, performance, ease of use, portability, and so on, such that the overall system requirements are satisfied. The list of software qualities presented in Chapter 2 can serve as a checklist when software requirements are specified. The case study presented toward the end of the current section illustrates in some detail some of the intricacies of requirements definition in real projects.

In specifying requirements, the specifier should describe *what* qualities the application must exhibit, not *how* such qualities are achieved by design and implementation. For example, he or she should define what functions the software must provide, without stating that a certain distributed architecture, module structure, or algorithm should be adopted in the solution. In other words, the specification should not overspecify the system: It should not unduly constrain the design and implementation activity. The engineer should have the freedom—and the responsibility—to select the software architecture, the module structure, and the algorithms best suited to the task of implementing the software.

As we have observed, the software application being developed is often part of a more general system. A crucial requirements activity is deriving software requirements from system requirements. Software requirements are what the software solution should satisfy. They define the responsibilities assigned to the software component within the overall system solution.

The main goal of the requirements activities is to understand precisely the interface between the application to be developed and its external environment. Such an environment can be, say, a physical plant that the application is supposed to monitor and automate, or it can be a library where librarians interact with the system to insert new acquisitions in the catalogue and to lend books to customers, and where customers can browse through the catalogue to find the books they are interested in. To understand the requirements, the software engineer must understand the application domain and must identify the main *stakeholders*—that is, all those who have an interest in the system and who will eventually be responsible for its acceptance. For example, in the case of the library, the software engineers must understand who the expected users of the system are (librarians and customers of the library) and what different access rights to the system they will have. The engineers will need to understand the mechanisms of acquiring books, of borrowing and returning books, etc. The main stakeholders include the librarians and sample customers. Since the library is usually part of a larger system, the individuals responsible for the library in the larger system are also relevant stakeholders. As an example, in the case of the library of a university department, the department head is a stakeholder whose goals and requirements should be properly taken into account. The department head's goal might be to encourage students to borrow both books and journals, in order to stimulate their interest in reading the current scientific literature. Or, alternatively, he or she might require that students borrow only books, while journals can be borrowed only by staff members. The department head may require that staff members should be able to access the catalogue and reserve copies of books and journals through a Web-based interface from their individual workstations, and so on. An important stakeholder is the person or organization who will have the budget to pay for the development—perhaps the dean or the president of the university. Notice that the various stakeholders have different *viewpoints* regarding the system. Each viewpoint provides a partial view of what the system is expected to provide. Sometimes the different viewpoints may even be contradictory. The goal of the software engineer is to integrate and reconcile all the different viewpoints into one coherent view of the system.

The result of the requirements activities is a *requirements specification document*, which describes what the analysis has produced. The purpose of this document is twofold: On the one hand, it must be analyzed and confirmed by the various stakeholders in order to verify whether it captures all of the customers' expectations; on the other hand, it is used by the software engineers to develop a solution that meets the requirements.

The requirements specification document must meet all the specification qualities discussed in Section 5.2. Because many individuals must communicate with each other through it, the document must be *understandable, precise, complete, consistent,* and *unambiguous*. Also, it must be easily *modifiable*, since we know that it must evolve in order to accommodate the evolutionary nature of large systems. These properties were discussed in Chapter 5, especially with reference to functional specifications. We examined several techniques for expressing and documenting system requirements.

As we have observed, the aforesaid properties of a specification are rather difficult to define and achieve independently of their context. For example, "precise" may mean rigorous or even formal to the software engineer. Yet, the end user may be unable to read formal specifications. A way to reconcile the needs of both the customers and the developers may be to transliterate formal specifications into a more palatable form expressed in natural language. One may even go further in this direction and complement the requirements specification document with a preliminary version of the *user manual*, which describes precisely how the user will eventually interact with the system. Such a description can be useful in assessing the results of requirements analysis.

Another possible deliverable of the requirements activities is the definition of the *system test plan*. In fact, during system testing, we must test the system against its requirements. Therefore, the way this will eventually be done may be agreed upon with the customer at the stage of system testing and may be documented along with the requirements specification document.

As can be seen from the previous paragraphs, the requirements activities have multiple goals. To master these goals, as well as the complexity of the application, the software engineer must apply the set of principles discussed in Chapter 3. The crucial issues here are separation of concerns, abstraction, and modularization. The application must be understood and then described at different levels of abstraction, from its overall aspects down to any necessary details. The application must be partitioned into parts that are separately analyzable. It should be possible to view, understand, and describe the application from different viewpoints. As opposed to the usual application of modularity, which may be called *vertical modularity*, wherein each module hides lower level design decisions, viewpoints call for *horizontal modularity*, which structures the system as a collection of views at the same level of abstraction. A typical way to use horizontal modularity is to separate functional requirements into three views: a model of data that are operated upon by the application, a model of the functions performed, and a model of how control structures govern the execution of such functions. In terms of notation, this may be done by using, say, ER diagrams to define the relations among the data, data flow diagrams to define functions, and Petri nets to define control, as we suggested in Section 5.7. Or, using UML, one can use, say, a class diagram to describe the data and the associated operations, use cases to describe functions, and state diagrams to define control.

The way requirements are actually specified is usually subject to standardized procedures in software organizations. Standards may prescribe the form and structure of the requirements specification document, the use of specific analysis methods and notations (e.g., UML), and the kind of reviews and approvals that the document should undergo.

The following is a possible checklist of the contents of the requirements specification document that might guide the software engineer in its production:

1. *The domain*. Brief description of the application domain and of the goals we should fulfill by developing an implementation. This includes a precise documentation of the domain knowledge that is relevant to derive specifications. Who are the stakeholders and what are their goals and expectations? What are the main entities that characterize the domain? What are their main relationships? How are they affected by the system we will develop?

2. *Functional requirements*. These describe what the product does by using informal, semiformal, or formal notations or a suitable mixture of them. Chapter 5 illustrated various kinds of notations and discussed pros and cons of the different approaches. UML is now increasingly used as a practical standard, because it contains different notations for expressing different views of the system.

3. *Nonfunctional requirements*. These may be classified into the following categories: reliability (availability, integrity, security, safety, etc.), accuracy of results, performance, human-computer interface issues, operating constraints, physical constraints, portability issues, and others.

4. *Requirements on the development and maintenance process*. These include quality control procedures (in particular, system test procedures), priorities of the required functions, likely changes to the system maintenance procedures, and other requirements.

### 7.3.2.1 *A case study in requirements engineering*

The case study that follows, derived from a real-life project, illustrates a few typical issues in requirements engineering. We report the study in the style of "how things should be done," rather than telling the whole story.

A railway company decides to introduce a computer-based control system to support the driving of the trains. Certainly, before beginning any design of the system, a deep understanding and specification of its requirements is necessary.

**Identifying stakeholders and their goals**

First, let us analyze who the main stakeholders of such a system are:

- The first obvious stakeholder is the management of the company. But it is also clear that other major stakeholders exist with different—and possibly even conflicting—goals;
- The drivers and their unions, which manage their economic and social interests;
- The passengers, whose requirements are gathered through market studies;
- The companies that will have to implement the system under suitable contracts with the railway company. In fact, as is often the case, the railway company does not itself develop the system. Rather, it contracts for the implementation with several companies, sometimes according to precise bidding rules.

Each one of these stakeholders has different expectations from the new system. Thus, the company must focus on several *goals*, corresponding to the interests of the various stakeholders:

- The company's goal is to improve the quality of service *and* to save costs. One way to decrease costs is to use only one driver per train instead of two, but this would conflict with current safety regulations.
- The drivers want a safe and comfortable job. Thus, they welcome automated support; but they also fear losing their jobs because of the decreased need for drivers. (This is a common trade-off faced in replacing humans with machines.)
- The passengers wish for better service, which, for them, essentially means faster trains that run on-time. But they also want high reliability. There is, in fact, much concern for safety worldwide, due to an increased number of train accidents.
- The producers need a well-defined job assignment (i.e., specifications) so that implementation can proceed smoothly and be coordinated among the several partners. The fact that one organization—the railway company—defines and manages a system which is realized by several independent and competing suppliers has a major impact on requirements definition. In fact, a very precise definition is mandatory not only in the interest of the suppliers, but mainly if the company wants to keep open the option of changing a supplier in the future during system evolution. Furthermore, such a system obviously involves a number of heterogeneous components, both hardware and software, that will be built by several specialized companies. This state of affairs imposes a first overall agreement on system architecture, defining its major components and interactions. (For instance, there will be an onboard subsystem residing on the train and a ground subsystem partially hardwired in the tracks and including antennas.) Only after having decided the overall system architecture and subsystem

responsibilities will it be possible to define precisely not only global system requirements, but also the requirements of the major subsystems, so that such requirements can be the object of suitable contracts among stakeholders.

**Identifying system requirements**

Once the goals of the various stakeholders are understood, we can proceed with a first formulation of global requirements. It is convenient to—roughly—classify them in the following way:

- *Safety requirements.* In principle, accidents should be strictly excluded. In practice, such an absolute requirement is obviously infeasible. Thus, we should resort to a probabilistic requirement such as "the probability of accidents should be less than $10^{-9}$ per year."
- *Utility requirements.* This term denotes requirements defining the level of use-fulness of the system. Such requirements, in turn, are of different types, depending on the points of view of the various stakeholders:
  - The passengers deem the service useful if it is reasonably fast and on time— that is, if there is a low probability of delays (and if the probability of long delays is increasingly low: Small delays are acceptable, but long delays are not tolerated).
  - The company wants to save costs: Furthermore, costs for system implemen-tation, management, and maintenance should be well defined and kept under control.

Clearly, there is a trade-off between such global requirements, not only between safety and utility requirements, but also among utility requirements for different stakeholders.

The foregoing statements only define global strategic requirements: Before the actual project starts, they must be made precise and detailed enough to allow their evaluation, implementation, and validation. However, even without going into a deep analysis, it is immediately clear that some requirements are hard to formalize fully: for instance, what is a "reasonably fast train" and what is a "low probability of delays"? Thus, in some cases, common sense, contracting or negotiating between different stake-holders, or resorting to standards and conventions must be adopted.

Accordingly, as we anticipated, in order to obtain real project requirements, some early organizational and system architectural decisions must be made:

- Safety standards (in terms of failure probabilities) are adopted. Different countries mandate their own standards.
- "Social and organizational decisions" are taken: The unions accept the fact that only one driver exists per train, market analysis and operations research techniques state "reasonable" time schedules, and so on.
- Then, based on the technological state of the art and cost analysis, a basic *system* (not software!) architecture is determined: Essentially, there will be an onboard computerized subsystem and a ground subsystem, suitably com-municating with each other. The task of each subsystem is defined in agree-ment with the companies supplying them. Different suppliers are selected

for different parts of the subsystems. For instance, the ground subsystem consists of sensors, antennas, transmission components, and computing processors.

At this point, a thorough study of the impact of strategic goals on the system architecture is carried out. In some sense, this study is already a "design," but is certainly a required part of requirements engineering. For instance, global safety requirements are translated into specific requirements such as the following:

- The distance between two trains must never be less than $x$ meters.
- Each hardware component must guarantee a mean time to failure greater than 20 years. (We are talking about the overall reliability of the component, which could be achieved by suitable replication if the individual item is not reliable enough.)

Of course, such an analysis "propagates" from the top down, from general requirements to the detailed requirements of any single component, emphasizing once more that (requirement) specification and design are relative concepts. In particular, in this case, there is a long way before coming to real *software* requirements, which apply only to a subset of system components. However, the software engineer should come—and does come—into play much earlier than writing software specifications: Since software typically involves managing and monitoring system components, a global view of system architecture is necessary to design it properly.

A tentative common-sense borderline between requirements engineering and system construction could be the point where the interests of each stakeholder have already been traded off and each further decision can be taken individually by one of them. Without trying to generalize, we simply observe that such a criterion seems to work properly in this case.

Let us now analyze a particular example that illustrates how general goals propagate to detailed requirements and how different viewpoints must be considered when making final decisions about requirements.

The example focuses on system-human (in this case, the driver) interaction and shows how general safety requirements must propagate to this specific part of the system. On the one hand, the driver supplies commands to the system, which is supposed to support him or her: The system activates the brakes and provides power to the engines; it also computes the speed of the train and controls its acceleration. In this case, the driver acts as the "master" and the system is the "slave." On the other hand, the system monitors the driver: For instance, the driver must periodically react to system prompts to guarantee that he or she is at the controls. In this case, instead, the system is the master.

What happens in case of conflicts? Should the system assume that the driver is not able to make correct decisions? Should the system thereafter take control? Or, instead, should the driver be allowed to over-rule the system? For instance, if a train passes a red light despite the driver's having been warned several times that the train was approaching the signal, should the train be stopped independently of any action taken by the driver? Such a decision is justifiable to guarantee a conservative safety requirement.

Notice the similarity between managing possible conflicts between the human driver and the control system and managing the cooperation—but also possible conflicts—between human drivers, whether we are considering train drivers, airplane pilots, and so on.

At the end of the process, a final requirements document is produced that consists of

- An introductory part describing the "mission" of the system.
- An architectural part that details the main structure of the system.
- A collection of specific requirements associated with each subsystem, so that an integrated analysis of the subsystems' requirements will guarantee that the overall goals are indeed achieved. For instance, by conjoining the requirement that brakes are activated if a red signal is passed with other natural requirements on the managing of the signals, it can be proven that no two trains are ever closer than $x$ meters. In some sense, this analysis is already a first *verification* of the system requirements.

At this point, each producer and the company can agree precisely on what each component is supposed to do and how that can be verified—and paid for.

**Final remark about the case study**

We have reported an idealized version of this project. In practice, the real project did not go exactly in the way we described. Not surprisingly, as a postmortem study showed, several problems occurred throughout the process:

- Most of the global high-level requirements and the role played by the several stakeholders were left implicit and were based largely on previous undocumented knowledge of the "experts." Actually, the available "official" documents already described the structure and the behavior of several components without a precise statement of the overall system rationale.
- Attention was focused exclusively on safety requirements, and nothing was explicitly said about utility. Paradoxically, a system that stopped every train forever would have been "correct" with respect to such requirements documents.
- Also implicit was the fact that the requirements themselves depended on the system configuration. Important routes were equipped with more sophisticated and redundant machinery than secondary routes, so that stronger requirements could be guaranteed.
- Almost nothing was said about timing requirements. The implicit assumption was that any computation needed to be done "just in time" in order to be useful. For instance, optimal braking action was computed by exploiting a highly sophisticated mathematical model describing the interaction between the wheel and the rail, but no analysis was performed to verify that such a computation could be completed within a time necessary for the braking to be effective.
- Many other typical defects of poor specifications—inconsistencies, inaccuracies, mixing of "the what and the how"—were uncovered.

As a consequence, some *reengineering* had to be applied, even within the requirements elicitation and specification phase.

Finally, we emphasize that good requirements engineering, as well as maximum care in all of the early life cycle phases, is crucial for the system described in this case study to function as intended. The alternative, experimental testing in the field, can be very expensive and dangerous![1]

### 7.3.3    Definition of the software architecture and detailed design

Design is the activity through which software engineers structure the application at different levels of detail. They might start at a high level by defining the architecture that partitions the functionalities between clients and a server, communicating via synchronous message passing. They might then proceed to a detailed design that involves decomposing clients and server into component modules, defining their interfaces precisely. Each component, in turn, may be decomposed into further lower level subcomponents. The result is a *design specification document*, which contains a description of the software architecture. Besides describing the system in terms of its components, their interfaces, and their interconnections, the design specification document should record both the significant decisions made about the structural elements and their rationale. Such documentation is important to support future inevitable requests for changes that require modifications in the architecture.

The exact format of the design specification document is usually defined as part of companywide standards. The standards may also indicate suggested design methods and practices, along with notations that should be used to document the design. Such notations are similar to TDN or GDN. (See Chapter 4.) UML is now largely adopted as a standard to document the architecture, especially in the case of systems designed according to an object-oriented style.

### 7.3.4    Coding and module testing

Coding and module testing are the activities through which we actually write programs using a programming language. Coding and module testing made up the only recognized development phase in early development processes, but they constitute just one of several phases in any structured development process. These activities result in an implemented and tested collection of modules.

Coding can be subject to companywide standards that may define the entire layout of programs, such as the headers for comments in every unit, naming conventions for variables, classes, and functions, the maximum number of lines in each component, and other aspects that the company deems worthy of standardization.

Module testing is also often subject to company standards, including a precise definition of a test plan, the definition of testing criteria to be followed (e.g., black-box versus white-box testing, or a mixture of the two), the definition of completion criteria

---

[1] Some final experimentation before the system is deployed is indeed scheduled, but, of course, in a very limited way, since it requires that part of the whole system be preempted from receiving normal service.

(e.g., when to stop testing, required coverage criteria), and the management of test cases. Debugging is a related activity performed in this phase.

Module testing is just one of the possible verification activities carried out at the module level. Other such activities include code inspections to check adherence to coding standards and, more generally, to check for a disciplined programming style, as well as checking of software qualities other than functional correctness (e.g., performance).

### 7.3.5   Integration and system testing

Integration amounts to assembling the application from the set of components that were developed and tested separately. Integration is not always recognized as being separate from coding. In fact, incremental developments may progressively integrate and test components as they are developed. (See Section 6.3.5.) Although the two stages may be integrated, they differ conceptually in the scale of the problems that they try to address: The former deals with programming in the small, the latter with programming in the large.

Recall from Section 6.3.5 that integration testing involves testing collections of modules as they are integrated, with each individual module having been tested separately previously. Often, this is done not in a single shot (big-bang testing), but incrementally on progressively larger sets of modules, from small subsystems until the entire system is built.

At the final stage, the development organization performs system testing on the running application. Once the application has undergone system testing, it may be put through "actual" use within the development organization. The purpose of this step is to test the system under realistic conditions, but with understanding and forgiving users. This kind of testing is called *alpha testing*.

Internal standards may be adopted both on the way integration is to be performed, such as top down or bottom up, and on how to design test data and document the testing activity.

### 7.3.6   Delivery, deployment, and maintenance

After the development of an application is completed, a number of post-development activities remain. First, the software must be delivered to the customers. This is often done in two stages. In the first stage, the application is distributed among a selected group of customers prior to its official release. The purpose of this procedure is to perform a kind of controlled experiment to determine, on the basis of feedback from users, whether any changes are necessary before the software is officially released. This kind of system testing done by selected customers is called *beta testing*. Beta testers should be customers who are critical and will actively look for errors in the product. They should be customers who are motivated to have a reliable product at the end of the process. In the second stage, the product is distributed to all customers.

Deployment defines the physical run-time architecture of the system. For example, it consists of allocating server components on certain nodes of a network and client components on others.

Finally, maintenance can be defined as the set of activities that are performed to modify the system after it is delivered to the customer.[2] As we discussed in Chapter 2, maintenance consists of correcting any remaining errors in the system (*corrective maintenance*), adapting the application to changes in the environment (*adaptive maintenance*), and improving, changing, or adding features and qualities to the application (*perfective maintenance*). Recall that the cost of maintenance is often more than 60% of the total cost of software and that about 20% of maintenance costs may be attributed to each of corrective and adaptive maintenance, while over 50% is attributable to perfective maintenance. On the basis of these statistics, *evolution* is probably a better term than maintenance, although the latter is used more widely.

Another type of categorization of maintenance costs was described in an early study conducted by Lientz and Swanson in 1980. The analysis showed that about 42% of costs were attributed to changes in user requirements, about 17% were due to changes in data formats, 12% to emergency fixes, 9% to routine debugging, 6% to hardware changes, 5% to improvements in documentation, 4% to improvements in efficiency, and the rest to other sources.

In general, we can draw the following conclusions regarding maintenance:

- Requirements are a main source of maintenance problems, as we observed earlier, both because requirements are difficult to capture and because they change over time.
- Many errors are not removed until after the system is delivered. This is a serious problem, because the later the errors are found, the more expensive it is to remove them. It is certainly preferable and cheaper to remove a requirements error during analysis than after the system is deployed, because the error has to be repaired in the copies installed at customer sites.
- Change is an intrinsic property of software, but it is difficult to support it in our products.

### 7.3.7    Other activities

All of the activities we have just discussed contain certain kinds of common tasks, such as *documentation, verification*, and *management*.

Documentation is the main result of any activity. For example, a design specification document providing UML diagrams, along with a narrative description that describes the rationale behind certain design decisions, can be the main result of the design activity. As mentioned earlier, companywide standards usually specify the form of documentation required.

As we described in Chapter 6, verification is also part of any software development activity, even though in this Chapter we singled out only two specific cases (module testing and system testing). In most cases, verification is performed as a quality

---

[2] The IEEE Standard (IEEE [1999]) defines maintenance as the "modification of a software product after delivery to correct faults, to improve performance or other attributes, or to adapt the product to a changed environment."

control step via reviews, walk-throughs, and inspections. The goal of verification is to anticipate the discovery and removal of errors as early as possible in order to avoid delivering defective systems.

As we mentioned, some authors distinguish between validation—an assessment of how the product we are building responds to the needs of the customer— and verification—an assessment of the internal correctness of the process (e.g., how a software architecture is correct with respect to the stated requirements). This distinction is motivated by the fact that requirements might not capture exactly what the customer wishes, so that a verified system might still be unacceptable to the customer.

Finally, each activity involves a number of subactivities, and therefore it must be properly managed and controlled. It is also necessary to manage the way activities constitute stages of the development process and the resources involved in the activities— in particular, human resources. We will discuss these issues in Chapter 8.

Another key aspect of the development process is the definition of policies for *product management*: how the deliverables of the various activities are stored, accessed, and modified; how the different versions of the system are built and delpoyed; and what authorizations are necessary for checking software components in and out in a product database. The activities related to controlling the consistency of multiple versions of components and products is called *configuration management*, and is described in Section 7.8.

### Exercise

---

**7.1** Requirements errors may be viewed by customers as errors that need to be repaired by the software producer before the application is formally accepted. They may be viewed by software engineers as incorrectly stated requirements that were accepted by the customer when the requirements specification document was issued and reviewed. Since the customer did not object to the specification at that point, the software engineers reject the arguments of the customer, holding that if the customer wants the application changed, he or she should pay for it. What is your opinion? How can the conflict be solved or alleviated?

---

## 7.4 AN OVERVIEW OF SOFTWARE PROCESS MODELS

In this section, we turn our attention to how the activities of software development can be organized in a process, in order to achieve the results discussed in Section 7.2. We start our discussion with the well-known, traditional waterfall model, which arranges the activities as a linear sequence of steps. We will then discuss the weaknesses of such a model and turn our attention to evolutionary process models, which can more easily accommodate the flexibility required by modern software production.

### 7.4.1 Waterfall Models

The waterfall model was popularized in the 1970s and is still a reference model for most software engineering textbooks and standard industrial practices. Its first appear-

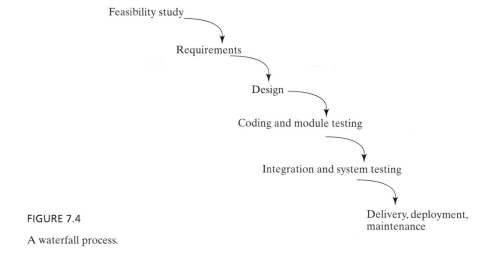

Feasibility study

Requirements

Design

Coding and module testing

Integration and system testing

Delivery, deployment, maintenance

**FIGURE 7.4**

A waterfall process.

ance in the literature dates back to the late 1950s, as the result of experience gained in the development of a large air-defense software system called SAGE (Semi-Automated Ground Environment).

The waterfall model, illustrated in Figure 7.4, is a slight variant of the one presented in Chapter 1. As the figure shows, the process structures the activities we discussed in Section 7.3 as a linear cascade of phases, in which the output of one phase flows as the input to the next one. Each phase, in turn, is structured as a set of subactivities that might be executed by different people concurrently. The following phases are shown in the figure:

- feasibility study
- requirements
- design
- coding and module testing
- integration and system testing
- delivery, deployment, and maintenance

There are many variants of the waterfall model, depending on the organization that uses the model and the specific project; the one we describe here is a representative example. Even though the variants differ in the number and nature of their stages, the underlying philosophy is the same, so that the comments we give here apply to all of them. In particular, all of the variants insist that the requirements phase should be completed for the entire application before one can proceed to the design phase. In turn, the complete design should be specified before starting any implementation.

The choice of a specific waterfall model may be based on the criticality and complexity of the application. Simple and well-understood applications are less demanding in terms of the formal structure of the process by which they are produced; larger and more critical applications may require decomposition of the process into finer grains in order to achieve better control and ensure more rigorous development steps. As an example, consider the development of an application that is expected to be used by nonspecialists, as opposed to experts. In this case, the process should accommodate a phase during which special training material is designed and developed to become part of the product, as well as a delivery phase that includes training for the nonspecialist user. By contrast, for the expert users, there may be no training phase in practice: It is sufficient to provide precise technical manuals. Other details and questions could be answered on the phone by a special customer service representative.

The different roles that customers and developers may play and the different possible relationships between them also affect the structure of the waterfall process and the contents of the individual phases. If we rule out the simple case of the software developer who develops software for personal use, we may observe the following categories:

1. A software company develops a customized application in response to a specific request from a customer, who belongs to a different organization.
2. A software development group develops a customized application for other groups within the same company.
3. A software company develops a generalized application for the marketplace. This kind of software is called *packaged software*.

Clearly, the nature of the feasibility study phase may be different in the three cases. It is crucial in the third case, since it requires estimating the potential market for the application and identifying the features that make it appealing to customers. The application must not be offered on the market too early or too late. In the second case, the feasibility phase may consist of an evaluation of the trade-offs between buying an existing solution (if there is any), developing a solution entirely within the development group, or commissioning (part of) the project to external developers. In the first case, most likely, the alternative between making and buying the application has already been evaluated by the customer, who contracted a software house to develop the new system. In all three cases, the application may be developed entirely from scratch. Or, alternatively, off-the-shelf components may be used to build the application. The latter alternative is becoming increasingly practical, due to the advances in the technology of components and component integration. In all three cases, it is necessary to estimate the resources needed to accomplish the development task. In the second case, however, there is less pressure on the developers, who may take their time analyzing the problem before committing themselves to a certain cost. In fact, in general, this case is characterized by a less risky development process than the first case, which, in turn, is less risky than the third.

Despite all these differences, all waterfall processes are based on the same underlying philosophy and are characterized by three principles: Waterfall models are sequential, phase based, and document driven. They prescribe a sequential, linear flow among phases that may be more or less precisely identified with those described in Figure 7.4. They prescribe that a phase should be completed before the next phases can be started, and each phase results in the preparation of one or more documents that form the input to the next phase.

Organizations that adopt a waterfall model define standards on the way the outputs (*deliverables*) of each stage must be produced. Often, they also prescribe *methods* to be followed in order to produce the desired outputs. These methods are organized in a coherent framework that constitutes the organization's *software development methodology*. The precise definition of the deliverables is important because it gives an unambiguous way of measuring the progress of the project: It is easy to check whether a certain deliverable is delivered exactly on the date when it was expected. If the structure of the deliverable is standardized, one can check not only the delivery date, but also the internal quality of the deliverable in terms of adherence to the specified standard. Even more significant control is possible if the standard also prescribes the method to be followed for producing the deliverable, since one can check whether the result was produced according to the method.

### 7.4.1.1 A waterfall life cycle case study

In this section, we briefly illustrate the military standard MIL-STD-2167 A[3] as a case study of a waterfall software life cycle. This standard contains requirements for the development and acquisition of mission-critical computer systems. Quoting from the standard, "it establishes a uniform software development process which is applicable throughout the system life cycle." The standard is intended to apply to a wide variety of cases, with the exception of simple ones—that is, "small applications which perform a fixed function which is not expected to change for the life of the system."

In what follows, we briefly summarize the main characteristics of the standard. The document that describes the standard is available publicly, and we urge the reader to read it as an example of a standardized waterfall process model. Reading the original document will give a deeper understanding of the evaluation of the waterfall model that we presented in Section 7.4.1.

MIL-STD-2167 A views software development as a phase in the more general system life cycle. The four phases of this life cycle are as follows:

**a.1** concept exploration

**a.2** demonstration and validation

**a.3** full-scale development

**a.4** production and deployment

Quoting from the standard:

The concept exploration phase is the initial planning period when the technical, strategic, and economic bases are established through comprehensive studies, experimental development, and concept evaluation. This initial planning may be directed toward refining proposed solutions or developing alternative concepts to satisfy a required operational capability ...

The demonstration and validation phase is the period when major system characteristics are refined through studies, system engineering, development of preliminary equipment and prototype computer software, and test and evaluation. The objective is to validate the choice of alternatives and to provide the basis for determining whether or not to proceed into the next phase ...

---

[3] This standard has been replaced by MIL-STD-498 (Software Development and Documentation)—see Exercise 7.16.

The full scale development phase is the period when the system, equipment, computer software, facilities, personnel subsystems, training, and the principal equipment and software items necessary for support are designed, fabricated, tested, and evaluated. It includes one or more iterations of the software development cycle. The intended outputs are a system which closely approximates the production item, the documentation necessary to enter the system's production and development phase, and the test results that demonstrate that the system to be produced will meet the stated requirements. During this phase the requirements for additional software items embedded in or associated with the equipment items may be identified. These requirements may encompass firmware, test equipment, environment simulation, mission support, development support, and many other kinds of software. ...

The production and deployment phase is a combination of two overlapping periods. The production period is from production approval until the last system item is delivered and accepted. The objective is to efficiently produce and deliver effective and supported systems to the user(s). The deployment period commences with delivery of the first operational system item and terminates when the last system items are removed from the operational inventory. ...

The software development cycle may span more than one system life cycle phase, or may occur in any one phase. For example, mission simulation software may undergo one iteration of the software development cycle during the concept exploration, while mission application software may undergo many iterations of the software development cycle during the demonstration and validation, full scale development, and production and deployment phases.

The software development cycle consists of six phases:

**b.1** software requirements analysis

**b.2** preliminary design

**b.3** detailed design

**b.4** coding and module testing

**b.5** computer software component integration and testing

**b.6** computer software configuration item testing

These phases map naturally to the stages of the generic waterfall process model illustrated previously. Some comments are necessary, however, on phases b.5 and b.6 Delivered software is designated a *computer software configuration item* (CSCI) by MIL-STD-2167 A; thus, phase b.6 corresponds to system testing in the previous classification. According to the standard, a CSCI consists of one or more *computer software components* (CSCs), which are logical entities composed of one or more *units*.[4] Units are the smallest logical entities; it is they that are implemented in code. Thus, phase b.5 corresponds to what we called integration testing.

An important aspect of MIL-STD-2167 A is that, for each phase of the software life cycle, the standard gives a detailed specification of (a) the activities to be carried out in the phase, (b) the products to be delivered, (c) the reviews to be performed for monitoring, and (d) the structure of the developer's software and associated documentation, as well as the procedures for archiving and accessing the software and its documentation.

---

[4] Actually, we are diverging slightly from MIL-STD-2167A, which distinguishes between top-level CSCs and low-level CSCs, where the latter may recursively contain low-level CSCs as well as units.

### 7.4.1.2  *A critical evaluation of the waterfall model*

The waterfall model has played an important role because it has imposed much-needed discipline on the software development process, thus overcoming unstructured code-and-fix processes. The model has made two fundamental contributions to our understanding of software processes, namely, (1) that the software development process should be subject to discipline, planning, and management, and (2) that implementing the product should be postponed until after the objectives of doing so are well understood.

Because it is an ideal model, the waterfall model can be only approximated in practice. We can characterize it as linear, rigid, and monolithic, as explained next.

The waterfall model is based on the assumption that software development proceeds linearly from analysis down to coding. In practice, this cannot happen, and one should account for disciplined forms of feedback loops. As an example, the purpose of alpha and beta testing is exactly to provide feedback to earlier stages.

To allow explicit and disciplined feedback, a common life cycle model, shown in Figure 7.5, confines the feedback loops to the immediately preceding stages, in order to minimize the amount of rework involved in unconstrained repetition of previous phases. The underlying rationale, however, is that one should strive for linearity of the life cycle, in order to keep the process predictable and easy to monitor. Plans are based on the assumption of linearity, and any deviation from the linear progression through successive stages is discouraged, as it represents a deviation from the original plan and therefore requires replanning.

Another underlying assumption of the waterfall model is phase rigidity—that the results of each phase are frozen before proceeding to the next phase. As a consequence, the model assumes that requirements and design specifications may be frozen at an early stage of development, when our knowledge of the application area and experience in how to deal with it are still rather preliminary and subject to change. This assumption does not recognize the need for customer–developer interaction to evolve the requirements throughout the life cycle.

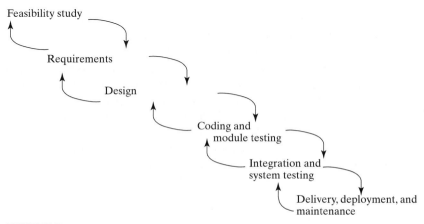

FIGURE 7.5

A waterfall process with explicit feedback loops.

Finally, the waterfall model is monolithic, in the sense that all planning is oriented toward a single delivery date. All analysis is performed before design begins. The product is delivered as a whole, months or even years after the requirements were elicited, analyzed, and specified. If mistakes are made in the requirements stage, and these mistakes are not caught by reviews, we are able to identify the errors only after the system is delivered to the user. But this occurs after much time and effort have been spent, without any possibility of having more immediate forms of feedback. Moreover, since the development process may be long for complex applications—perhaps years—the application may be delivered when the user's needs have changed, and this will require immediate rework.

Referring to the discussion in Section 7.3, we can say that the waterfall model suffers from the weaknesses attributed to all black-box processes: It does not allow enough visibility into the product being developed, until the complete product is completely implemented. Although the waterfall model has introduced discipline into the software development process, this discipline is accomplished through rigidity, which, in turn, introduces new problems into the process, especially when the software is being developed from poorly understood requirements. Among the problems associated with the rigidity of the model are the following:

- It is difficult to estimate resources accurately when only limited information is available. The waterfall model often forces cost estimation and project planning to occur after only a limited amount of analysis has been performed.

- Requirements specification results in a written document that guides and constrains the product to be developed. Still, no matter how precise the description is, it is very difficult for the user to anticipate whether the final system that will be constructed according to the specifications will eventually meet his or her expectations. No matter how readable the textual and graphical description is, it will always be an inanimate document, as opposed to the active tool that will eventually be delivered. The real feedback will always be given after the real system is delivered. Moreover, the customer might approve even very imprecise and incomplete requirements specifications, which turn out not to be a rigorous enough starting point for development. In short, the verification of the requirements specification document performed by the customer may not be very effective, and basing future developments on it may cause serious problems.

- The user often does not know the exact requirements of the application. In some cases, the user *cannot* even know. For example, what were the requirements for a spreadsheet before the first one was ever developed and delivered to users? Thus, the assumption that all requirements should be frozen before any development starts is unrealistic.

- The waterfall model does not stress the need for anticipating changes. Quite the opposite, the model's underlying philosophy is that we should strive for linearity by freezing as much as we can in the early stages. Unfortunately, real life shows that changes occur more frequently than expected. But since the model does not anticipate changes, accommodating them is hard, costly, and unreliable.

- The model enforces standards that are heavily based on the production of given documents at certain specific times. In fact, we have characterized the process as *document driven*. This emphasis may lead to a somewhat bureaucratic style of work, in which many forms are required to be filled out and approved and the software engineer is inclined to pay more attention to the syntax imposed by the standard than to its semantics. Thus, it may happen that fairly elaborate specifications incorporating a variety of diagrams and tables are written for poorly understood user interfaces and functions.

We can indeed trace the reasons for the high maintenance costs of many of today's software systems to the characteristics of the waterfall model. In particular, the difficulty of producing complete and correct requirements specifications results in greater maintenance later. In fact, much of maintenance amounts to eliminating requirements errors (e.g., introducing into the system exactly those functions that the user wants, but that were disregarded or misunderstood in the first place during requirements analysis and specification).

Moreover, since the system that is eventually delivered may not match the user's expectations, maintenance must start immediately. But this poses some serious contractual problems: Who is responsible for the additional costs incurred during maintenance? As we discussed in Exercise 7.1, do we consider such maintenance as repair of errors (and thus payable by the developer) or as meeting new requirements (billable to the customer)? In theory, one should be able to find a precise answer to this question in the requirements specification document.

These points underscore the reasons for high maintenance costs. Software evolution is vital, but it is neither anticipated nor planned. Thus, it is always done under pressure and within a limited budget. In an attempt to minimize the maintenance effort, changes are viewed as "code fixes" and are not documented appropriately. Thus, the implementation soon diverges from the requirements and the design specification.

Of course, not all software is required to evolve. Sometimes, the requirements are well defined from the very beginning and undergo only minor changes, if any. As an example, take the case of a compiler for a given programming language. Unless the language itself is being defined and progressively refined, requirements are frozen when the project starts: The syntax and semantics of the language are known, the target language is also known, and the number and nature of optimizations (if any) are also easy to specify and may be known in advance. In such a case, there are no obstacles in principle to adopting a prespecified and rigid model such as the waterfall process model.

The requirements for a large number of applications, however, are less stable and not perfectly known *a priori*. Even in cases where initial requirements are clear (e.g., in the case of a process control system for which the environment is well known), one should not forget that changes are likely to occur in the future—for example, due to changes in the environment in which the application is embedded or due to changes in technology. Even in the compiler example, one might first deliver a compiler that does a limited number of optimizations and then produce new releases, each providing more and more optimizations. The practical effectiveness of some optimizations may actually be measured only by observing the actual use of the language. (See Case

Study C in the Appendix.) Or one might decide to embed the compiler in a programming environment that provides a progressively richer set of facilities (e.g., in turn, a syntax-directed editor, debugger, static analyzer, and incremental compiler).

The situation, however, is more serious in the case of interactive end-user applications. Most software systems of this kind are dynamic entities that are required to change over time as they acquire more users. To constrain the development of such software in a rigid and monolithic process may be unnatural and counterproductive: Evolution here cannot be kept separate from software development and is an intrinsic part of it.

These deficiencies in the respected and widely adopted waterfall model have led to alternative software production process models, illustrated in Section 7.4.2 through 7.4.4. They also raised the importance of the activities involved in maintaining existing legacy software to the level of those intended to develop applications from scratch, as we will further discuss in Section 7.5.

## 7.4.2    Evolutionary Models

It has been observed that the software engineer should accept the fact that failures in the first version of an application inevitably lead to the need for redoing (part of) the application. "Do it twice" is a principle advocated by Brooks [1995]. According to this approach, the first version of a product is viewed as a trial whose main purpose is to assess the feasibility of the product and to verify the requirements. Then the product is thrown away, and the real development starts on more solid foundations provided by firmly established requirements. Using common terminology, the first version may be viewed as a *throwaway prototype* of the application. In fact, the initial version or prototype is used only temporarily, until it provides enough feedback to the software engineer on the main risks involved in developing the application (i.e., in capturing the exact requirements). The second version is then developed following a waterfall process model. This approach provides a partial solution to some of the problems discussed in the previous section, such as eliminating flaws in the requirements. It does not, however, eliminate the time gap between the definition of the requirements and the delivery of the application. Nor does it stress the need for anticipating changes. It can be viewed, however, as a step in the direction of flexible and nonmonolithic approaches to the software life cycle—also called *evolutionary* or *incremental approaches*—which have been widely advocated in the literature. A rigid and monolithic approach completely details all aspects of a given stage of development before proceeding to the next stage; nothing is working or delivered until the very end of the development cycle. By contrast, an incremental approach consists of stepwise development, in which parts of some stages are postponed in order to produce some useful set of functions earlier in the development of the project.

Boehm [1988] defines the *evolutionary process model* as a "model whose stages consist of expanding increments of an operational software product, with the direction of evolution being determined by operational experience." Increments may be delivered to the customer as they are developed; this is called *evolutionary*, or *incremental, delivery*.

Although incremental delivery is not necessarily implied by an evolutionary model, it adds to the value of the model by getting early user feedback. Obviously, if increments are to be delivered to the customer, they should consist not only of code and internal documentation of the project, but also of user-oriented documentation. In other words, we may define a *delivered increment* to be a self-contained functional unit of software that performs some useful purpose for the customer, along with all supporting material (requirements and design specifications, test plans and test cases, a user manual, and training material).

The development strategy behind an evolutionary process model may be stated in the following simple form (see Gilb [1988]):

1. *Deliver* something to the real user.
2. *Measure* the added value to the user in all critical dimensions.
3. *Adjust* both the design and the objectives based on observed realities.

At first (superficial) sight, an evolutionary process may resemble the old code-and-fix unstructured process. We must, therefore, be careful to retain the discipline introduced by the waterfall model. In particular, the entire process should be kept under control. Software developers should be constantly aware of where they are in the course of actions and what the next steps will be.

The definitions we gave of an evolutionary process are general enough to accommodate a number of specific models. Here, we review the most important ones.

A minimal departure from the waterfall model in the direction of an evolutionary process is represented by what might be called an *incremental implementation* model. The idea is that the waterfall process model is followed down to the design of the whole application; implementation, however, is done incrementally. During requirements analysis and design, special care is placed on the identification of useful subsets of the system that might be delivered to the user and on the definition of interfaces that will later allow new subsystems to be added smoothly. This leads to a plan whereby different parts are implemented, tested, and delivered according to different priorities and at different times. Thus, instead of a single two-step cascade of code-and-test and integration-and-test stages in which the application is developed as a monolith, we have a sequence of code-and-test and integration-and-test stages for the various increments.

Incremental implementation affords only a partial solution to the problems inherent in the waterfall process model. For example, the earliest point at which we can provide the first increment may still be too late. Also, the results of the requirements analysis are still subject to being invalidated later.

The incremental approach may be extended to all stages of the life cycle in order to achieve finer granularity in the process. We call this most general approach an *incremental development-and-delivery model*. Here, we start with a step that covers system objectives, architecture, and planning. The development begins with the analysis of an increment at the requirements level; each increment is then separately designed, coded, tested, integrated, and delivered. In other words, the waterfall model is still followed, but for each separate increment; the overall process model is thus a sequence of miniwaterfall processes. Increments are developed one after the other on the basis of feedback from the customer. In fact, as users actually use the delivered parts, they start to understand better what they actually need. This leads to changes in the requirements for further increments and revisions of the original plan. Viewed from the developer's vantage point, since each increment is simpler than the whole system, it is easier to predict the resources needed to accomplish the development task within acceptable accuracy bounds.

One way to characterize evolutionary models is to say that maintenance disappears as a stage of the life cycle—or, paradoxically, that the life cycle becomes a continuous evolution. In a waterfall model, change—which is discouraged during the development stages—manifests itself as a post-development activity, in the form of maintenance. Since the process does not anticipate change, it is expensive to accommodate such change later. In the incremental development-and-delivery model, by contrast, change may be taken into account easily. In fact, it is so easy that discipline and careful planning are required to prevent useless iteration and never-ending developments, as in the case of the early code-and-fix model.

Prototyping is an evolutionary principle for structuring the life cycle. We have already mentioned the throwaway prototype that follows the do-it-twice rule. We also mentioned the concept of an *evolutionary prototype*. In this case, the prototype is progressively transformed into the final application. An example is a software system in which some parts are deliberately missing and substituted for by a stub. We discussed stubs in the context of testing (Section 6.3.5.2). In such a context, a stub is a prototype that permits some early testing of functions that would otherwise have to be postponed until after the whole system is developed. The concept, however, is more general: The stub can encapsulate a preliminary solution to a given subproblem. If stub interfaces have been designed properly, future development of the real component to replace the prototype will not require any change in the overall structure of the system; that is, the evolution from the prototype to the final system will occur smoothly.

More frequently, prototyping is viewed as a tool to be used in the process of understanding the user's requirements. For example, it is well known that user interfaces are a most critical aspect of interactive end-user applications. Thus, before developing the software that implements the required functionality of an interactive application, the software engineer might wish to define and test alternative user interfaces providing different ways of interacting with the application, in order to show the user how interaction might actually occur in the final application. This may result in several prototypes that do nothing more than display panels on the computer screen and activate dummy functions when specific services are requested by the user through interaction with the application. Different prototypes might differ in the layout of the panels, in the sequences of possible operations, and so on. Some of these will be throwaway prototypes, but one may be chosen to be evolutionary. In fact, the tool used by the software engineer as a prototype of user interfaces may be able to generate the run-time actions that are needed to support input and output in the final application. Once the user has selected the preferred prototype, the task left to the software engineer consists of designing the modules that accomplish what is requested by the various functions that are to be activated as a consequence of interaction. Thus, the prototype gradually evolves into the final system.

This example reveals an important point: Prototyping—and, more generally, evolutionary techniques—may require specific supporting tools. For example, interactive user interfaces are possible because the software engineer can use an appropriate tool for rapid development of these interfaces, such as any of the tools provided by modern user interface management systems. These points will be discussed further in Chapter 9.

In conclusion, with reference to the discussion in Section 7.3, evolutionary process models can be viewed as providing transparent processes that support a form of continuous validation of what is being developed. Evolutionary models help developers understand and analyze the main risks involved in a project, support early identification of requirements errors, and adapt naturally to the evolution of requirements. They match the requirements of the modern software industry, which asks for reduced time to market. For example, a software company may decide to develop an initial version of an innovative product and make it available, free of charge, on the Internet. This is a way to encourage early adopters, who may be the source of useful feedback on enhancements that may be incorporated into the product later. Moreover, early users of the initial version may become captive users when the final product comes to market. This approach may give one software company a competitive advantage over other companies that enter the marketplace later with a similar product. Even if their product is better than the one that was available before, they will have a hard time convincing captive users to change from the product they initially adopted.

### Exercise

---

**7.2**    Suppose you are developing a system composed of six modules A, B, C, D, E, and F, where A USES B, A USES C, C USES D, B USES D, B USES E, E USES F, and C USES F. Define some possible incremental implementation strategies for this system.

---

## 7.4.3    Transformation Model

The transformation model is rooted deeply in theoretical work on formal specifications. The idea is that software development may be viewed as a sequence of steps which gradually transform a specification into an implementation. First, informal requirements are analyzed and functions are specified formally, possibly in an incremental way. Then, the development process takes this formal description and transforms it into a more detailed, less abstract formal description. As we proceed, the description becomes executable by some abstract processor. If we can achieve executability of specifications early in the transformation process, then the executable description may be viewed as an evolutionary prototype that is obtained as a by-product of the transformation process. Further transformations, however, are still necessary to make execution as efficient as is specified in the requirements.

Transformations may be performed manually by the software engineer. In this circumstance, the formal nature of the derivation may provide a kind of mathematical check that a particular step is a correct transformation of the previous one. It is also possible, however, that the support system performs transformations automatically, perhaps under the software engineer's direction. Examples of this kind of transformation are automatic transformation from a recursive to a nonrecursive implementation and other kinds of source-to-source program optimization.

An ideal transformation-based process model is illustrated in Figure 7.6. The process consists of two main stages: *requirements analysis and specification* and *optimization*. The first stage provides a formal specification of requirements, which is fed into the optimization process that does the performance tuning, until a satisfactory, optimized result is produced. The initial specification may not be executable. As it is refined into a more concrete description, it may become executable and increasingly more efficient. The transformation process is controlled by the software engineer and may take advantage of the availability of reusable, off-the-shelf components. Reusable components may take the form of modules to be included in the applications, perhaps after minor modifications, or even derivation steps to be applied as reusable process steps. As the figure shows, new reusable components may be developed during the process and stored in the library.

Before being transformed, specifications are validated against the user's expectations to check whether they capture the real requirements. In the ideal scenario of Figure 7.6, validation of requirements is done in a variety of ways, such as proving formal properties, animating the specification, or executing it.

As shown in the figure, the transformation-based life cycle may be supported by a suitable computer-aided software development environment. The environment provides tools for validating requirements, handling reusable components, performing optimizations (according to some existing catalogue or following directives from the software engineer), and storing the history of the development of the software. Maintaining a history of the development is an important feature for supporting future requests for changes: Any redevelopment will start from the appropriate point in the history of the previous development, in order to accommodate changes in a reliable way and keep the documentation consistent.

The ability of the transformation-based model to support program evolution contrasts with the common practice based on conventional waterfall process models.

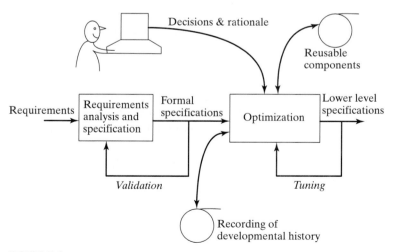

FIGURE 7.6

An ideal transformation-based process model.

As we observed, in a waterfall model, experience has shown that since changes are not anticipated, they are often treated as emergency repairs: They are performed under strong pressure from customers and management and within strict time constraints. As a consequence, programmers tend to make changes only by modifying the code, without propagating the effects of those changes to changes in the specifications. Thus, specification and implementation gradually diverge, making future changes to the application even more difficult to perform. Updating the affected requirements and design specifications is also difficult, because these are usually done manually and changes are difficult to trace back.

The situation is quite different in the transformation-based approach. Since the history of the development of the software—along with the rationale of every transformation step—is recorded by the support environment, the programmer may be forced to forgo changing the code directly and instead start retransforming from the appropriate intermediate step of the history. This is exactly the approach we advocated in Section 4.1.2, which deals with families of programs: Conceptually, each change produces a new family member.

At present, the transformation approach is not a practical paradigm for software production process models. It is still a research-oriented approach, and only experimental environments are available to support it. To become practical, it should scale up from small programs to the development of large and complex systems. Conceptually, however, it enlightens a fundamental point: Programs are formal entities. Specifications, too, may be formal. Thus, the process of deriving an implementation from the specification could be regarded as a rigorous, or even formal, transformation process.

The transformation approach has been studied as a dual method for proving the correctness of small programs. Program correctness proofs represent an *analytic*, mathematically based approach: They provide a formal framework for analyzing program correctness *a posteriori*, after the program is developed. Transformations, instead, are a *constructive*, mathematically based approach: Given a program P and its specification in terms of precondition Pre and postcondition Post, program correctness proofs describe how to verify the truth of {Pre} P {Post}. The transformation approach, by contrast, tries to derive a program P that is guaranteed to be correct *a priori*, given a specification pair <Pre, Post>.

The transformation process, of course, cannot be made entirely mechanical and requires skill and creativity from the programmer. But the programmer is constrained to operate within well-defined formal boundaries, so that his or her confidence in the design process is greatly enhanced and complexity is dominated and kept under control. In addition, the program is derived hand in hand with its correctness proof, so that the result is guaranteed to be correct.

## Exercise

**7.3**   Discuss why one can say that the transformation-based approach, as described in Figure 7.6, favors the reusability of software processes.

### 7.4.4   Spiral Model

The goal of the spiral model of the software production process is to provide a frame-work for designing such processes, guided by the risk levels in the project at hand. As opposed to the previously presented models, the spiral model may be viewed as a *metamodel*, because it can accommodate any process development model. By using it as a reference, one may choose the most appropriate development model (e.g., evolutionary versus waterfall). The guiding principle behind such choice is the level of risk; accordingly, the spiral model provides a view of the production process that supports risk management.

Let us present a few definitions. *Risks* are potentially adverse circumstances that may impair the development process and the quality of products. Boehm [1989] defines *risk management* as a "discipline whose objectives are to identify, address, and eliminate software risk items before they become either threats to successful software operation or a major source of expensive software rework." The spiral model focuses on identifying and eliminating high-risk problems by careful process design, rather than treating both trivial and severe problems uniformly. Software risk management will be discussed further in Chapter 8.

The main characteristic of the spiral model is that it is cyclic and not linear like the waterfall model. (See Figure 7.7.) Each cycle of the spiral consists of four stages, and each stage is represented by one quadrant of the Cartesian diagram. The radius of the spiral represents the cost accumulated so far in the process; the angular dimension represents the progress in the process.

Stage 1 identifies the objectives of the portion of the product under consideration, in terms of qualities to achieve. Furthermore, it identifies alternatives—such as whether to buy, design, or reuse any of the software—and the constraints on the application of the alternatives. The alternatives are then evaluated in stage 2, and potential risk areas are identified and dealt with. Risk assessment may require different kinds of activities to be planned, such as prototyping or simulation. Stage 3 consists of developing and verifying the next-level product; again, the strategy followed by the process is dictated by risk analysis. Finally, stage 4 consists of reviewing the results of the stages traversed so far and planning for the next iteration of the spiral, if any.

If the requirements for the application are understood reasonably well, a conventional waterfall process model may be chosen, which leads to a simple one-turn spiral. In less understood end-user applications, however, the next step may be evolutionary in nature; that is, several spiral turns may be required in order to achieve the desired results. The spiral model can also accommodate any mixture of the previously discussed models, with the appropriate mix chosen so as to minimize the risks involved in development.

The spiral model allows us to restate the issue of robustness versus correctness, discussed in Chapter 2, in a new framework. After one cycle of the spiral, unstated requirements are checked as part of the robustness of the application. As we realize that they should have been specified as requirements, they become part of the specification of the next cycle, if any. Consequently, after each iteration through the cycles, some robustness requirements are transformed into correctness requirements.

### 7.4.5    An Assessment of Process Models

Our description of software process models has followed their actual historical evolution, from the unstructured code-and-fix model, to the waterfall model, to evolutionary models, to transformation-based models. The driving force behind this evolution was the recognition of weaknesses in the extant models and the desire to devise the most effective process to achieve the qualities required for the application at hand.

The code-and fix model can actually be considered no model at all. It consists of following the inspiration and the needs of each particular moment, without carefully thinking and planning out the entire process beforehand. In contrast with the code-and-fix model, the waterfall model falls into the other extreme: It is rigid, prespecified, non-

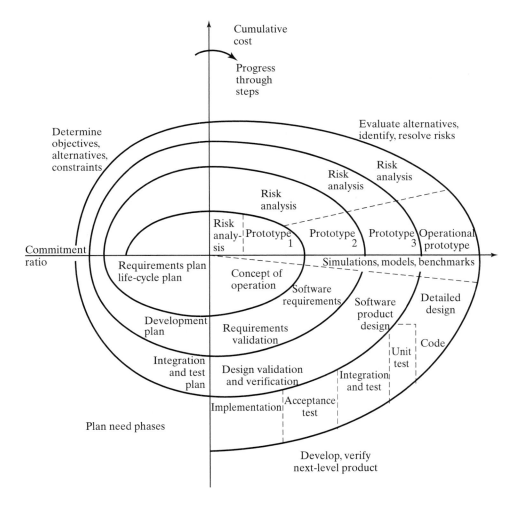

FIGURE 7.7

The spiral software process model.

adaptive, and monolithic. In its practical application, it is usually driven by documentation that measures the progress of the process. Generally, this documentation is voluminous, but totally passive, making changes difficult to apply as the application enters the maintenance stage and causing the documentation to diverge from the implementation.

If the waterfall life cycle is *documentation driven*, we can characterize evolutionary approaches as *increment driven*. In fact, progress through the evolutionary process is marked by the development and possible delivery of increments. The transformation-based approach, instead, can be called *specification driven*, as the development process occurs through iterative refinement of formal specifications. Finally, as we saw, the spiral model is a metamodel that may be called *risk driven*.

So far, there has been little quantitative comparison of the various models. Some initial experiments led by Boehm explored the productivity of a waterfall-based life cycle, compared with that of an evolutionary life cycle based on prototyping and the use of fourth-generation languages in the area of interactive end-user applications. The results showed that the waterfall approach addressed product and process control risks better, whereas the prototyping approach addressed user interfaces better. The prototyping approach also avoided the risks of spending much time on not-so-important aspects of development and helped to concentrate attention on the relevant issues and risks. In addition, both projects had roughly equivalent productivity in terms of their rates of delivered source instructions. They also had comparable performance, but the evolutionary process had 40% less development time and resulted in a product with roughly 40% fewer source instructions. The waterfall-based process had fewer problems in debugging and integration, due to more thought-out design. We shall say more on this point in the bibliographic notes.

Even though comparative studies of the various models are still preliminary and do not support decision making in a quantitative fashion, there is a consensus that in most cases a strictly sequential, monolithic waterfall model should be replaced by more flexible approaches based on evolutionary models. As we observed, this transition is dictated mainly by the need for reducing the risks involved in a new development project. The two chief risks are

- misunderstanding user requirements and basing product development on wrong or partial assumptions; and
- taking a long time to complete the product, which leads to unacceptable time-to-market cycles.

In many practical cases, these are among the most likely risks involved in developing a new product. We discussed the former risk at length earlier in this book. The latter became more and more important as early time to market grew into a crucial competitive factor. The most common approach to reducing time to market is to employ concurrent engineering, which supports the parallel execution of different steps. Concurrent engineering calls for more flexible phasing of activities and more disciplined processes to control the synchronization of parallel activities.

In general, each software project is characterized by its own specific risks, and recognizing them is a necessary initial step to be undertaken by software engineers. According to the spiral model, once the risks are identified, the software engineer is responsible for choosing the life cycle model that best fits the current project. Consequently, there is no unique, perfect, and ready-to-use process model that can be adopted once and for all, in all organizations, for all kinds of products or product families. The myth of the universal model, such as the waterfall life cycle, has been dispelled.

Again, it is important to stress that abandoning the disciplined approach implicit in the waterfall model does not imply falling back to undisciplined practices, such as the code-and-fix model. The development task is still decomposed into activities, such as requirements analysis and specification, design, module implementation, module testing, integration testing, etc. Each of these activities is managed systematically by using the methods and tools we have been discussing throughout the book. What changes is the breakdown of the process into phases in which these activities are performed, the order in which the phases are arranged, and the rules for the transition from one phase to the next. For example, in an incremental development, not all requirements analysis and specification precedes design, and, in turn, not all design precedes implementation. Rather, if the application can be naturally broken down into subsystems, it is possible to arrange the process as a sequence of miniwaterfall processes, each responsible for the development of a subsystem, starting from the subsystem providing the core functionalities and then progressively expanding to the other parts. Other development strategies may also be possible, depending on the nature of the problem being solved. As a final remark, we would discuss a possible use of the waterfall model as a reference model. As Parnas and Clements [1986] pointed out, the waterfall life cycle defines an idealized process, and we will never see a software project that proceeds according to its tenets. The waterfall life cycle can be used, however, to describe the rationale of a project *a posteriori*. The documentation of the project can be structured according to the idealized process, even if the actual process was not performed as a linear sequence of steps. By following the structure of the idealized process, documentation becomes well structured and clearly understandable. According to Parnas and Clements, it is possible to *fake* the real process by producing documents *as if* we were proceeding in the ideal way. The documentation produced in a way that reflects the ideal and purely rational waterfall-based process helps in understanding the system, no matter what process was actually followed to produce the system. In addition, Parnas and Clements observe that some information on the actual production process deserves proper documentation, too: "We make a policy of recording all of the design alternatives that we considered and rejected. For each, we explain why it was considered and why it was finally rejected. Months, weeks, or even hours later, when we wonder why we did what we did, we can find out. Years from now, the maintainer will have many of the same questions and will find his answers in our documents."

## Exercise

**7.4**    Consider the following two examples of software projects: developing a conventional compiler for a known programming language (e.g., C) for a new machine and developing an application to automate a doctor's office. Which of the two is likely to call for a waterfall life cycle development style? Why? What are the likely risks in the two examples, and how can the chosen development life cycle model face the risks?

## 7.5    DEALING WITH LEGACY SOFTWARE

As we discussed in Section 7.4.1 for maintenance, organizations spend a large part of their efforts maintaining existing software, enhancing it, integrating it with new features, and adapting it to the changing environment in which the software is embedded. It is not possible to develop new software from scratch as new requirements arise, because companies make huge investments in developing existing software, in shaping their organizational structure and organizationwide practices around that software, and in training users in the use of the software. The existing software is a legacy asset that organizations need to preserve very carefully before closing it down.

We have discussed the issue of software maintenance at many points in this text. Indeed, because of the social and economic relevance of maintenance, one of our major goals has been to try to teach design principles that would favor software evolution by making it predictable, controllable, and reliable. In particular, the flexible and incremental processes we advocated in this chapter aim at supporting software evolution. Still, our approaches have focused mainly on *forward engineering*—that is, on the software development process in which we move from initial requirements to a product by transforming high-level abstractions and logical designs into a physical implementation of a system. In this section, we instead try to take the legacy software perspective, by briefly outlining a framework in which the various facets of maintenance can be put together in a unified way.

*Reengineering* is the process through which an existing system undergoes an alteration, to be reconstituted in a new form. Usually, the process includes two distinct phases. In one phase, the software engineer proceeds backwards, from the existing system to some abstract representation that allows him or her to understand exactly the structure of the existing system and how to modify it. Such a phase is often called *reverse engineering* (or *refactoring*). In the other phase, the engineer proceeds forward and actually designs and applies the necessary changes. Reverse engineering includes *program understanding*, which means that the software engineer seeks to understand the structure of the program, its main algorithms, and data structures and tries to isolate the main components that need to be restructured. To do so, the engineer has to identify the main system components and their relationships and needs to create abstract representations of the system that aid in understanding it more precisely. This task is, of course, facilitated if the documentation is complete and is consistent with the actual implementation. Very often, however, this is not true, and the engineer needs to go through the painful process of recovering the design from the code and reconstructing abstract representations from low-level implementations.

Lack of documentation and the use of poor development methods in the forward engineering process are the main factors affecting the need for—and the cost of—reverse engineering. In many practical cases, this is exacerbated by a lack of planning and the underestimation of the maintenance phase. In short, maintenance is hindered by previous poorly performed maintenance interventions. In fact, maintenance is often managed as emergency fixes, rather than a planned evolution. Fixes to the system are made without carefully evaluating what their impact is and without carefully documenting them. Therefore, as time goes on, the implementation of the system diverges from its documentation, and this, in turn, makes future changes more and more difficult to apply. It has been proposed that one way to overcome these difficulties would be to introduce one further type of maintenance,[5] called *preventive maintenance*, which consists of planned improvements to the system to prevent future maintenance problems.

These arguments and all we discussed earlier reinforce our view that simply labeling a phase of the development process as maintenance, as the waterfall life cycle model does, does not help, and often misguides, engineers. The process is a continuous evolution, consisting of an iteration of reverse and forward steps (reverse engineering and forward engineering, respectively).

## 7.6    CASE STUDIES

This section is devoted to four case studies. We start with two examples of industrial projects, presented in an anecdotal style to illustrate two quite different situations that resulted in different approaches to software development. The first study exemplifies a complex system with stringent reliability and efficiency requirements whose expected functions were perfectly understood and frozen when the project started. The second typifies a system in which interaction with the end user was the major critical issue and the requirements were largely unknown when the project started and then evolved progressively during development. These two case studies are representative of state-of-the-art applications and practices at the end of the 1980s.

The other two case studies represent larger scale efforts of the next decade. We first illustrate the "synchronize and stabilize" software development process, which became popular in the late 1990s as the way software development is organized within the Microsoft Corporation. Then we illustrate the open-source development, which also became popular in the late 1990s. The two examples are based on different principles and goals, yet they share a highly flexible and evolutionary process approach.

### 7.6.1    Case Study: A Telephone-Switching System

A company had developed one of the first digital switches in the world and had already sold many systems making use of the switches. This initial success had caused a demand for both more features and more powerful switches. The company was ready to invest in a major release to satisfy these demands.

Switching systems are among the most complex embedded, real-time software systems and offer many challenging software engineering problems. The following are their major characteristics:

- They have complex functional specifications.
- There is a need to interface to a large input-output system with tens of thousands of lines and to process thousands of calls in parallel, with response times of well under 1 second.
- They provide uninterrupted service in the presence of intermittent or permanent hardware and software faults.

---

[5] As we mentioned elsewhere, the other kinds are corrective, adaptive, and perfective maintenance.

- There is a need for a large number of instances of the system, with individual variations.
- There is a need to support on-line modification and enhancement over a lifetime of 20 or more years.

The particular development we study here followed the classic waterfall model primarily because the problem was well defined and the company had much experience with the existing system. On the basis of this experience, the people involved felt confident about the accuracy of their estimates.

### 7.6.1.1 *The existing system*

The existing system was primarily the creation of a single (electrical) engineer. It had been written in assembly language for the microprocessor Intel 8080, which was state of the art at the time. The engineer was thoroughly familiar with switching systems, and when microprocessors were introduced, he recognized their potential in telephony. Until that time, special-purpose devices were used for telephone switching. Over several months, the engineer had programmed the major parts of the system to demonstrate the feasibility of his approach. At that time, two other engineers joined him to complete and polish the system.

When first shipped, the system consisted of approximately 50,000 lines of assembly code. By the time a major release was being planned, the system was being "maintained" by a group of approximately 30 software engineers. The original three engineers were still with the company, and they were the main sources of information about the design of the system.

### 7.6.1.2 *Switching systems in general*

A telephone-switching system is responsible for establishing and maintaining connections among telephone lines. The system we are discussing here was a "subscriber" switch. Such a switch is installed in a community and is responsible for connections to and from the actual telephone users in that community. If a call is made from the community to a telephone number in another community that is not served by the same switch, the switch contacts a higher level switch that is responsible for connecting subscriber switches. There are five classes of switches, with the subscriber switch at level 1. The telecommunications network in the world is connected according to a hierarchy. Level 5 switches connect across country boundaries.

The software for a switching system has very stringent real-time, reliability, and fault-tolerance requirements. Because the telephone system is a utility, some of the reliability requirements are even legal requirements. Switching systems use redundant hardware to achieve fault tolerance. Run-time diagnostics attempt to detect failures and automatically configure replacements for failing devices; messages are then sent to the operator to effect the replacement. Such systems are required to work even in the event of major disasters (e.g., earthquakes), and, in general, they do.

### 7.6.1.3 *The architecture of the system*

The architecture of the switching system we are discussing here is shown in Figure 7.8. The subsystems and their functions are as follows:

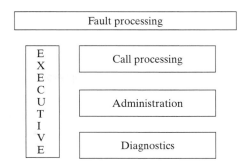

FIGURE 7.8

The architecture of a telephone-switching system.

- *The executive.* This subsystem is the switching system's "operating system." It provides processing, memory, and time management facilities. It performs all the low-level machine operations, such as interrupt processing. The executive allows the system to be used by the different subsystems simultaneously.
- *Call processing.* This subsystem performs the main telephone-switching operations: It supports the placing of a telephone call by detecting the lines going on and off and the numbers being dialed, providing the appropriate dial tones, and connecting to the appropriate lines. Strict real-time requirements are specified for the operation of call processing. For example, the shortest and longest times allowed between two consecutive digits dialed are specified. Different actions must be performed on the basis of the time elapsed between dialed numbers. In general, the response to each particular subscriber action must be limited strictly. For example, if a telephone goes "off hook," its status must be detected—through an interrupt—and a dial tone must be generated. The duration of the interrupt-processing code determines how many off-hook signals can be detected simultaneously and, eventually, how many calls can be processed simultaneously. Thus, adding even a single instruction to the interrupt code could change the system's overall performance. The actual speech path connections are maintained by hardware. Hence, the call-processing software is responsible only for detecting changes in the line signals and establishing the speech paths. Once a path is established, the next action required by the software is only after termination of the call is detected. A finite state machine is a perfectly adequate formalism to precisely specify the operations of the call-processing subsystem.
- *Administration.* This subsystem maintains information on subscribers. It is basically a database that contains information about the numbers supported by the system, the services supported at each number, and which lines can be used to connect to each number. The administration subsystem contains facilities for updating the database either on-line or at regular intervals. It also maintains statistics about traffic patterns in the system.
- *Fault processing.* This subsystem detects malfunctions in the various subsystems and performs the steps necessary to recover from them. For example, it may cause a processor or a memory card to be switched out of service and a replacement to be put into use. Some of the fault-processing function may be performed in hardware.

- *Diagnostics.* This subsystem performs diagnostic operations to locate malfunctioning components and perhaps determine their cause. It may be run manually by technicians, may be automatically invoked by the fault-processing subsystem, or may be run at regular intervals.

The software is, of course, part of a larger system that consists of the processor, hardware devices such as dial-tone generators, and the telephone and trunk lines controlled by the switch. This whole collection must fit in as a node in the country's telephone network.

### 7.6.1.4 The new release

The software development department was already organized according to the structure of the system: There were five groups, each responsible for one of the subsystems. In addition, an integration and testing group performed system testing and released the software. Each group had between four and seven members.

A switch can be characterized by how many lines can be connected to it (i.e., how many subscribers it has), how many calls per hour it can process, and how many calls it can process at a given time. The system under discussion here was capable of handling 10,000 calls per hour. The requirement for the new release was that the system handle 20,000 calls per hour.

The evolution of the new release was planned to follow a systematic life cycle. There was a trivial requirements study phase, specifying the required increase in the capacity of the switch. The three original engineers then did a preliminary feasibility study and design of the system. Not surprisingly, they concluded that the initial system structure had to be preserved. They produced a set of high-level requirements for changes to be made to each existing subsystem. Their thorough familiarity with the existing system made this step possible.

The changes were not confined to the software. For example, the new design required adding more memory to the system. Because the processor was not able to address more than 64K bytes of memory, this required building a special hardware device to allow switching among memory banks. That, in turn, of course necessitated changes in the executive subsystem to support what was essentially a primitive form of virtual memory. The addition of memory banks also required substantial changes to the diagnostics and fault-processing subsystems.

The requirements for each subsystem were then given to the appropriate groups. The design team had built a simulator of the hardware, including the memory banks, during its feasibility study. This simulator was used by all the groups to test their individual subsystems modularly before the actual hardware became available. Once the hardware did become available, people still used the simulator for their initial testing because it was much easier to use. Eventually, when all the subsystems were ready, they were given to the integration-and-testing group, which integrated them and performed extensive functionality and reliability tests. Many defects were found, but they were all local to individual subsystems. Since no major design errors were discovered, the development cycle was fairly linear, requiring iteration only to repair inconsistencies in interfaces between modules. After several months, the system was released and was quite successful in the field.

### 7.6.1.5 An analysis

The software development for the switching system just described is fairly typical of the large class of software engineering projects dealing with legacy software. In many organizations, the major development task is to produce the next release of an existing software system. It is easier to follow the waterfall model for the new release of an existing system than for the initial release, because the application area and the requirements for new releases are relatively well understood. This removes the usual difficulties involved in performing requirements analysis for a new system. Also, the design phase does not suffer from as much uncertainty, because the current design of the system and its limitations are known. It is therefore less likely that the requirements and design phases will have to be repeated, resulting in a linear development cycle exemplified by the waterfall model. In some sense, the previous version of the system behaves like a prototype of the new release.

In this case study, the major difficulties were due to the fact that the implementation language was assembly language. The original reason for using assembly language was that there were no high-level languages at the time. When high-level languages became available, the reason the engineers gave for not using them was the overriding need for efficiency. While it was true that the early compilers for the processor did not generate efficient code, the real reason for not using a high-level language was probably resistance to change. The use of assembly language caused significant technical difficulties. For example, because "clever" pointer arithmetic was used to access the different entries in the subscriber-information database, increasing the number of allowable entries or increasing the size of each entry sometimes required major modifications to the entire software.

The major factor that made the project successful was probably the presence of the original designers of the system. The designers had all the details of the system and all the timings of the different code paths in their heads. Any changes to critical pieces of code were checked first by these "gurus." This continuity also contributed to the linearity of the development cycle, because most defects were detected by the original designers' reviews. Finally, the system was probably also helped along by having to meet very strict reliability requirements. Not only was the initial system, which was the starting point for the new release, reliable, but the culture of the application domain prepared every engineer to accept reliability as a primary requirement. Everyone knew that (partially due to regulatory requirements) the system would not be released before demonstrating the required reliability.

### 7.6.1.6 Footnote

While the release just described was successful, we must add that problems inherent in the system—the unmanageability of large assembly language programs and the lack of any formal or, in any case, adequate specification and documentation—eventually made it impossible for the system to evolve further. One study of the feasibility of redoubling the capacity of the system showed that it could not be done. The only solution was to adopt a new, more powerful processor, but this meant rewriting the software completely, which was not possible in the time frame required to meet the market needs. After searching for solutions, such as automatic translation of the software into the assembly language of the new processor or "decompiling" into a high-level language, it was decided to abandon enhancing the system. By law, the currently installed systems must be maintained for 20 years, but no new versions of the system with any new functionality will be released.

### Exercise

---

**7.5**    It is possible to plan for the retirement of a system during the planning stages of the system. Discuss how such a plan would have applied to the case study just examined. What kinds of information would be included in the plan? What would be the benefits of such a plan?

---

## 7.6.2    Case Study: A Budget Control System

Every company has a budget control activity, devoted to monitoring its financial transactions and ensuring their correspondence with original plans. In general, these transactions and plans are embedded in the company's annual budget. In this section, we present a case study describing the construction and evolution of a system that supports budget control for a small, high-tech company in the consulting and software development business. The description is given in the style of a report on an imaginary software process taking place in an imaginary company where the tool was developed for internal use only. The process, however, is a true account from the real world. We will see that the history of this system development process fits quite well into an evolutionary model.

Section 7.6.2.1 presents the problem and its peculiarities with respect to more conventional problems in business administration, and Sections 7.6.2.2 through 7.6.2.4 present the evolution of the system from a first, rough prototype to a final—but still evolving—system that is integrated with the company's information system. All versions of the system were used in the company (i.e., the initial prototypes were not just throwaway prototypes, but were used as intermediate products).

### 7.6.2.1    *The problem and its peculiarities*

The main goal of budget control is to understand whether the activities performed by a company are proceeding according to the original budget and forecasts, so that appropriate decisions can be taken early if this is not the case. The budget control activity is clearly related to other administrative activities, such as payroll processing, income and expense monitoring, inventory tracking, and tax planning and payment. Just as clear, however, is the fact that budget control is not simply a mechanical activity and cannot be based exclusively on administrative data. The reasons for this are twofold.

First, the information that is relevant to budget control comprises not only objective data, such as time and material costs, prices, and number of items sold, but also more subjective estimates, such as "work in progress" (i.e., an estimate of the value of what was produced so far by the development process while it is still ongoing). It is always difficult to make accurate estimates in the case of software, as we shall see in Chapter 8. We can clearly see the difficulty of estimating the status of work in progress, by comparing the software industry with traditional industries, such as the automobile industry or even the general consumer-product industry, in each of which manufacturing proceeds in a precise, standardized, and often automatic way, so that the status of production may be identified precisely and even measured quantitatively at any point. The company under consideration in this case study had even more difficulties because of its peculiarities. In fact, both the development of new and innovative market products and the consulting activity—consisting mainly of performing feasibility studies and building early research-and-development prototypes—made it difficult to estimate production costs, end-product prices, and the work in progress. Thus, the traditional expertise of professionals skilled in budget control for engineering manufacturing was not applicable to the company in question, whose processes were less formalized and much more flexible.

Second, budget control requires some data that are not usually found in the administrative database. As an example, consider personnel costs. The company's administrative database kept employees separate from external consultants, since different payment procedures were applied to them. Also, the total cost of an employee was partitioned into net salary, tax withheld, health insurance, social security contribution, etc. From the point of view of budget control, however, these distinctions are not relevant: The total cost of a worker is all that matters. Moreover, budget control needs to know how much time a person spends on various projects, in order to determine which projects are doing well and which are in trouble; but this information is irrelevant to conventional administrative procedures. As a result, the information stored in the existing administrative database of the company was not adequate for budget control.

### 7.6.2.2  The first, semiautomated system

When the company realized the need for a well-organized and reliable budget control procedure, the difficulties arising out of its peculiarities soon became apparent. The company realized that the problem was not just choosing a budget control system among those available on the market—assuming, of course, that one could in fact be found; rather, the problem really was to understand exactly what budget control was all about and to develop a mechanized solution hand in hand with the incremental understanding of the problem. Thus, the company decided to form a team composed of a software engineer (with some background in business administration) and an administrative manager, whose joint job was to organize budget control and design an automated system to support the activity.

Initially, the team focused attention on understanding the nature of the problem. This soon confirmed that the existing administrative information system could not be extended to provide the required functionalities. It was also realized that most of the difficulties of the problem were not in the amount of data to be managed (the company consisted of about 30 people and just a few ongoing projects), but rather, lay in the unusual nature of the activities of the company, in the lack of standard production rules, in a fairly hectic rescheduling and rebudgeting of most activities, in personnel turnover, etc. It was therefore clear that documenting a precise statement of the requirements for automating budget control would be possible only after some experience and trial and error. Thus, a major decision was made to apply an evolutionary approach to the development of such a system and to concentrate attention initially more on organizational than on technical aspects of the system, even at the risk of throwing away the first few prototypes.

The first prototype consisted mainly of internal organizational procedures, definitions of logical relations among different pieces of information, and a very limited amount of automatic computation performed through simple productivity tools. Its main features were the following:

- All pieces of information that were relevant to budget control were listed and classified. The sources of information and their relations were defined. Likely future changes to requirements were identified. Examples of expected changes were in the classification of items: Initially, a rough distinction between administrative, production, and distribution expenses was satisfactory, but later, managers would probably ask to distinguish between, say, telephone versus travel expenses. It was also necessary to account for different levels of aggregation of items—for example, travel costs for each project or per project type, or travel costs for the whole company. Other changes were anticipated in the kinds of queries supported by the system. Besides standard queries such as "What is the difference between the estimated and actual revenue of a project?" "What are the total expenses of a given project?" and "How much do we pay for travel?" many unpredictable questions could be raised. Again, the decision was that a first prototype would supply only answers to a fixed and predefined set of questions, but later versions would allow a richer and more flexible set of queries.

- A set of procedures for data collection was defined. Attention was focused on the organizational and logical aspects of the required information, not on its physical format. For instance, every person, whether an employee or an external consultant, was requested to fill out a monthly form stating the time he or she spent on each project and possible expenses, charging them to a given project or activity.[6] Since the first prototype was not supposed to be integrated with the administrative information system, it was decided that data already existing in that system should be duplicated and supplied independently to the budget control system.

At this point, data aggregation was quickly and roughly implemented by a spreadsheet. In the first instantiation, the spreadsheet performed just sums and comparisons, splitting results into major categories. Also, data were manually input into the spreadsheet. Thus, the "budget control database" was just a collection of paper forms, processed through a spreadsheet that produced a report of the type shown in Figure 7.9.

---

[6] Although this procedure is applied widely, it caused organizational problems in the small company we are discussing, since most people worked on several activities in a fairly unstructured way. On the one hand, this lack of structure was a major reason for asking people to fill out such a form; on the other, people who did not fill out the form on a daily basis had problems reconstructing it at the end of the month.

| *month* :                                                  | **March**    |         |
|:-----------------------------------------------------------|:------------:|--------:|
| *project 1*:                          Case study           |              |         |
| ***income*** ( = a + b − c)                                |              | **40,000** |
|     (a) *invoices*                                         |              | 20,000  |
|     (b) *work in progress at the end of the month*        |              | 30,000  |
|     (c) *work in progress at the end of previous month*   |              | 10,000  |
| ***expenses***                                             |              | **25,000** |
|     *manpower in software development*                     |              | 10,000  |
|     *manpower in administrative work*                      |              | 5,000   |
|     *hardware* ∗                                           |              | 500     |
|     . . .                              . . .               |              |         |
| ***earnings***                                             |              | **15,000** |
|         *project 2*:                  UML toolset          |              |         |
|                  ⋮                                         |              |         |
| ***Total income***                                         |              | **150,000** |
| ***Total expenses***                                       |              | **120,000** |
| ***Net earnings***                                         |              | **30,000** |

∗ This means the hardware depreciation cost attributed to the project for the given period.

FIGURE 7.9

A spreadsheet report of an oversimplified budget control.

Clearly, such a procedure involved much manual work, but it was feasible because the amount of data was not so large. In fact, its initial use required much more work in checking the procedure than in data processing. Not only did subjective estimates have to be verified and fixed, but even objective data acquisition required much attention because of consistency requirements. For instance, on the 31st day of a month, an employee could ship an invoice for the delivery of a product, but a different employee could record the removal of the same item from inventory on the 1st day of the following month. This would generate an inconsistency that needed to be reconciled. Thus, the flexibility and simplicity of a spreadsheet far overcompensated for its computational deficiencies. In many cases, the spreadsheet was rearranged "on-line" to supply answers to specific questions from the managers.

In sum, for the first prototype, two months were required to understand the major problems and take organizational decisions, and half a day was needed to set up the first spreadsheet. Furthermore, in the initial three to four months of operation of the software, it was nearly impossible to distinguish between the time needed to perform budget control and the time required to understand the problems of such control and design solutions that would yield better support tools. The development process thus proceeded hand in hand with a deeper understanding of the problem. The spreadsheet used in the fourth month was much richer than the first spreadsheet that was produced. In particular, thanks to using a hierarchical spreadsheet, it was possible to achieve different levels of data aggregation, such as by project, by area (a section of the company devoted to similar projects), and by cost category.

### 7.6.2.3 *A more complete version*

Once the procedures—and risks—related to budget control were better understood, more attention was paid to automating the process. The company decided to develop a new family of prototypes, but to keep the budget control procedure as a stand-alone system, even at the cost of duplication and possible inconsistency of data. A real database was used for storing all information related to budget control. A fourth-generation environment was chosen for its flexibility (many changes in data formats and classification were still anticipated), high-level querying facilities, and support for simple computations.

### 7.6.2.4 *Towards an integrated system*

Eventually, when the problem became fairly well understood, it was decided to integrate the budget control system into the companywide information system. At that point, two independent systems existed: a conventional administrative information system (AIS) and the budget control prototype (BCP), running in a fourth-generation environment on a personal computer. A first major decision was to use the AIS as a source of data for the BCP, but to avoid the opposite, so that the existing and hard-to-modify AIS would not be affected. This required the construction of a batch translator to translate all relevant data already existing in the AIS into the BCP format. The typical output of such a translator was an incomplete form that needed to be filled in during the budget control activity. For instance, all travel expenses were automatically reported from the AIS by the translator, but some information, such as the project to which they referred, had to be added in a later phase. In addition, the final implementation included improvements to the existing database manipulation facilities of the BCP. This was done in an incremental way, simply by adding new functions.

### Exercise

---

**7.6**    Discuss the various prototypes developed in the budget control example as either throwaway or evolutionary prototypes.

---

## 7.6.3    Case Study: The Microsoft Synchronize and Stabilize Process

Most of the initial investigations into software processes originated in the realm of large software systems developed for mainframe-based architectures. Typical examples include applications in the defense or aerospace fields, as well as large management information systems. As mentioned earlier, the rapid growth of personal computer products and, more recently, applications for networked architectures, has changed the approach to building software, to meet with the requirements of higher flexibility, rapid response to changes, and reduced time to market. In this section, we highlight some key aspects of the software process approach followed by a leading software company: Microsoft Corporation.

Microsoft's philosophy for software development is based on decomposing projects into many small teams operating in parallel, but still behaving as a single larger development team. The underlying idea is to obtain the maximum advantage in terms of fast development, but still allow teams and individuals within teams freedom to evolve their designs and operate nearly autonomously. Cusumano and Selby [1995, 1997], who conducted an in-depth study of how Microsoft develops software, called the company's development style *"synchronize and stabilize."* We next describe the essence of this style.

A product development process begins with a *planning phase*, which defines the vision of the product and its specification and schedule. The *vision statement* defines the goals for the new product and prioritizes the features that the product will eventually support. The *specification document* provides a precise description of each foreseen feature, outlines the global architecture of the system, and identifies the main interdependencies among components. On the basis of the specification document, managers define a schedule and organize teams centered around the development of the product features that have been identified. The initial specification does not try to cover and freeze all features and all details within features. Rather, these undergo revision as more is understood of the project as it progresses. Experience indicates that at least 30% of the features listed in the initial specification document change.

Each team is composed of two sets of people: developers and testers, who work in parallel. *Continuous testing* enables the quality of the artifacts to be continuously monitored. The development strategy is highly parallel, both within teams and among teams. Special coordination policies are employed to ensure order in the midst of all the parallel activities. The first is *daily synchronization* through product "builds." By this rule, all team members are requested to enter the results of their daily work into the team's database, after which the product source code is recompiled and a new "build" of the product is transferred to testing. To ensure cross-team coordination, the second key practice is performed: *product stabilization*. This means that suitable milestones are defined which check that the product reaches a stable point in the development (i.e., most of the errors detected in the evolving product are properly fixed). If the milestone is a precondition for shipping the product, its result will be a distributable version of the application.

As Cusumano and Selby [1997] observe, Microsoft's process model (like most highly flexible models) reminds us of the code-and-fix approach ("the hacker software organization," in their words). Cusumano and Selby also observe, however, that Microsoft's approach reveals some insightful ideas on how to combine flexibility (the hacker's culture) in product development with the discipline and structure that mature organizations need to develop successful products. The result is a highly concurrent, incremental development process.

### 7.6.4    Case study: The Open-Source Approach

In recent years, considerable attention has been paid to alternative approaches to software development and even to creating a software business and industry. Practices that were previously dismissed as too *ad hoc* and chaotic for industrial-strength projects proved instead to deliver high-quality products. The success of such products as the Linux operating system, the Apache Web server, the Perl scripting language, and many others, indicated that open-source software can be considered as an alternative approach to the traditional proprietary variety of software development. The example of Linux showed that a single-person operating system kernel developed in 1991 could evolve over the years to a full-featured operating system, as a result of the collective efforts and the continuous changes and improvements made by a globally distributed volunteer developer team. At the end of the 1990s, Linux consisted of more than 1.5 million lines of code, accounted for over 20% of server operating systems, and had 7 million users.

The open-source approach is a policy that regulates licensed software, specifying its use, copy, modification, and distribution rights as follows:

- *Use*. No restriction can limit usage: The software may be used by anybody for any end.
- *Copy*. Any number of copies can be made without any payment.
- *Modification*. Anyone can make derived works from the software. For this to be possible, it is key that "unobfuscated" source code and all the documentation and scaffolding that are needed to produce binary versions accompany distribution of the software.
- *Distribution*. No restrictions can limit the way copies or derived works are distributed. It is always permissible to license derived works under the same terms as the original ones.

Most open-source software licenses specify the *copyleft* condition to prevent the creation of proprietary software derived from open-source products. The copyleft agreement essentially gives people the right to use and copy a product, as opposed to a copy*right* that restricts the copying of a product.

The terms just stated do not prevent open-source software from being sold. However, since copies can be made without limits, the real business cannot derive from selling software, but rather from other, indirect activities (services, accessories, advertisement, etc.). This is just an example of the differences in vision, business model, intellectual property rights, and, more generally, overall philosophy on the nature of software that distinguishes open-source from traditional software development. Dealing with these issues goes beyond the scope of the text. We thus concentrate mainly on he contribution of the open-source approach to alternative, highly distributed process development models characterized by frequent iterations, thanks to the wide availability of the source code and openness to contributions from a large community of developers.

The open-source development model became viable thanks to the widespread availability of the Internet, which enables large-scale and fast collaboration among programmers by providing developers with a virtual-workspace infrastructure. Collaboration on the various directions of evolution of the project is achieved via e-mail and mailing lists. Also available are code repositories wherein all interested parties can find and download the software. Typically, the changes to previous versions are available as patch files that are posted on the mailing lists. In some cases, version and configuration management tools (discussed in Section 7.7) are used to manage code repositories and help manage version control.

The organization of open-source projects is usually based on a small core group of developers and a larger population of contributors. Core developers have long-term involvement with the project and are responsible for receiving contributions, reviewing them, and integrating and accepting those which then enter the code base. Contributors who distinguish themselves in terms of the vision and quality of their contributions may be asked to join the core group. As a result, the structure is highly meritocratic.

Advocates of the open-source approach claim that the products developed according to this style are more reliable than the ones developed conventionally. Linus Torvald, Linux's creator, observed that debugging is highly amenable to parallel work because it requires little coordination. Users become a legion of beta testers that can not only diagnose problems, but also resolve them. Detractors of the open-source approach claim that eventually the conceptual integrity of the products will be broken by ongoing user contributions. The technique, they claim, cannot really scale up to large systems and continuous evolution, due to intrinsic limitations in the loose coordination infrastructure.

## 7.7    ORGANIZING THE PROCESS

Organizing the software process is a critical activity that takes in everything from the management of people to the management of all products produced during the software life cycle. It also involves the definition of appropriate methods and their combination within methodologies. According to Webster's New World Dictionary (1977), a *method* is defined as a way of doing anything, especially an orderly way; a *methodology* is defined as a system of methods. As we already observed, methodologies have frequently been packaged by software organizations into companywide *standards*, in order to make software processes more predictable and reusable.

In this section, we illustrate three widely known methodologies that have found acceptance among software professionals. We start by reviewing structured analysis/structured design (SA/SD) and Jackson's system development (JSD), which were widely used in the past and still are in traditional development environments. We then turn to the Unified Software Development Process, which is becoming an industry standard, in conjunction with the use of UML. Each of these methodologies is representative of either the past or the current state-of-the-art industrial practices and is supported by tools that help develop software according to the methodology. Each aims at complete coverage of the software development process, by providing guidance from the analysis phase down to implementation.

The idea of a methodology that guides programmers in their work in all phases of software development is appealing: It increases people's confidence in what they are doing, it teaches inexperienced people how to solve problems in a systematic way, and it encourages a uniform, standard approach to problem solving.

The main drawback of existing methodologies, however, is that—to a varying degree—they all lack solid formal foundations. They are certainly supported by common sense. They may not, however, be applied mechanically, and they still require the engineer to exercise judgment. Empirical evidence suggests that they are useful in specific application areas. Thus, for engineers specializing in one application area, the adoption of an effective methodology for that area helps shorten development time and facilitates communication among team members.

### 7.7.1    Structured Analysis/Structured Design

Structured analysis/structured design (SA/SD) is a methodology that has evolved through the contribution of several individuals over a number of years. In this section, we provide the main ideas of the methodology, which addresses the two phases of analysis and design.

In the requirements and analysis phase, SA/SD suggests the use of three major conceptual tools for constructing system models: *data flow diagrams* (*DFD*s), a *data dictionary* (*DD*), and *structured English* (*SE*). Data flow diagrams were illustrated in Chapter 5; their main components are shown in Figure 7.10 as a reminder to the reader. A data dictionary is a centralized collection of definitions of all data flowing among functions and to or from data stores. Centralizing all definitions in the dictionary removes the danger of duplications and inconsistencies. Structured English is any highly constrained subset of natural language used to describe the data transformation performed by each elementary bubble (i.e., a bubble that is not refined in terms of another DFD). Obviously, we may replace SE by any other semiformal algorithmic notation. Structured design (SD) will then follow the analysis phase.

The preceding tools may provide system descriptions at various levels of abstraction that may be useful for documenting the results of analysis. First, DFDs may be used both to describe an existing environment in which the automatic procedure to be designed will eventually be embedded and to delineate the logical structure of the application. For example, one may record the workflow in an office with the DFD fragment shown in Figure 7.11. Bubbles are annotated by employee roles, to indicate who is responsible for executing the indicated function. The fragment shows that requests are received and registered by the office concerning, say, the purchase of material. If special authorization is requested, it is handled by a specific person in the office; if special authorization is not requested (or if the authorization is given), the form is stored in a physical file and is then processed by employees 4 through 6. The figure shows the manual operations currently in the system and is the basis for automating them according to SA/SD.

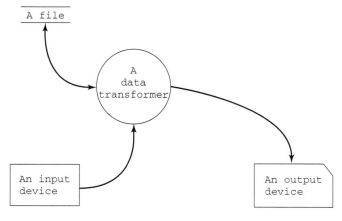

FIGURE 7.10

A simple data flow diagram showing its basic components.

Data flow diagrams allow systems to be described at different levels of abstraction by detailing the behavior of any bubble by a separate diagram. For example, the DFD of Figure 7.11 might be the result of detailing the description of a bubble called "Office XXX" in some higher level DFD that models the flow of information among offices within a company. Indeed, SA/SD suggests that decomposition be done until we reach the point where each transformation is sufficiently simple to allow its behavior to be defined in terms of elementary SE constructs.

SA/SD uses the DFD as a specification of the behavior (i.e., the functional requirements) of the application. The design—the decomposition of the system into modules—is based directly on the DFD and is documented using *structured dia-*

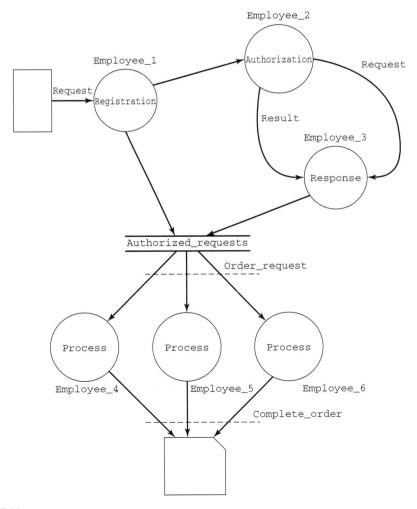

FIGURE 7.11

A data flow description of an office workflow.

*grams* (*SDs*). Figure 7.12 illustrates the behavior of an automated application that will eventually be substituted for employees 4 through 6. The job of design is to convert this DFD into an appropriate hierarchy of modules represented as an SD. As opposed to object-oriented design, SD is function oriented, and its modules represent functional abstractions.

An SD is a directed acyclic graph (DAG)-like structure in which nodes represent modules. By convention, the direction of the arrow is not shown explicitly, and is assumed. Each module represents a functional abstraction, to be implemented later by a subprogram. Thus, in Figure 7.13, if modules $M_1$, $M_2$, and $M_3$ are subordinate to module M, then M calls $M_1$, $M_2$, and $M_3$.

The process from which an SD is derived from a DFD should aim for modules with good coupling and cohesion. For example, the methodology provides suggestions that avoid certain pathological connections such as the following:

- a jump inside a subordinate module, instead of a call to that module;

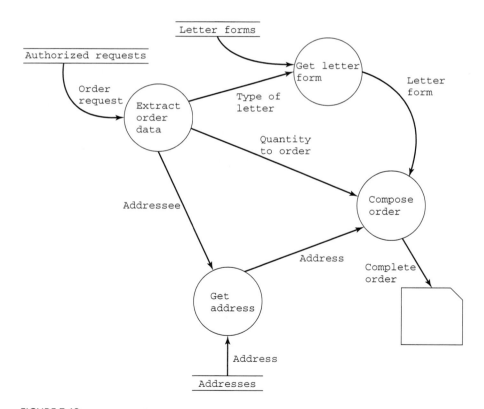

FIGURE 7.12

Automated portion of the office work of Figure 7.11.

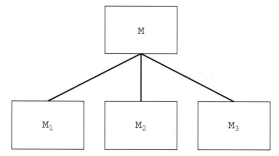

**FIGURE 7.13**

A structured diagram.

- a reference from a module to private data of another module, instead of passing data to the second module via parameters.

As one may notice, the suggestions given by the methodology try to avoid bad programming practices that were common with the use of older, low-level programming languages.

SDs may be made more expressive by decorating the diagrams with additional notations, as shown in Figure 7.14. The figure illustrates which parameters flow between modules: M passes B to $M_1$ and receives A back; M also receives C from $M_2$. The figure also illustrates the control patterns governing the calls of subordinate modules: M either calls $M_1$ or repeatedly calls $M_2$. The diamond symbol represents selection, and the circular arrow represents loops by grouping the modules whose execution is iterated.

DFDs are transformed into SDs manually, but the methodology provides some guidelines to follow. For example, one may arrange the decomposition illustrated in Figure 7.13 in such a way that $M_1$ acts like an abstract input module, $M_3$ acts like an abstract output module, and $M_2$ acts like a transformation module. This arrangement is illustrated by the decorated SD shown in Figure 7.15. The figure also shows that in order to provide the abstract input to M, $M_1$ requests lower level input from $M_{1,1}$ and

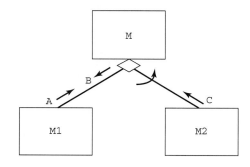

**FIGURE 7.14**

Decorated structured diagram.

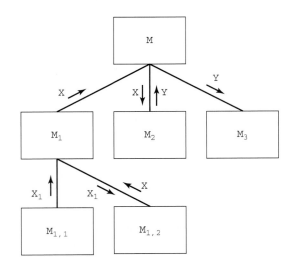

FIGURE 7.15

Typical structure of a decorated SD.

also requests the transformation of such input from $M_{1,2}$. A similar decomposition might occur for $M_2$ and $M_3$.

A possible SD for the DFD of Figure 7.12 is shown in Figure 7.16. SA/SD calls such a decomposition pattern *transform flow centered*. An alternative decomposition pattern, called *transaction flow centered*, is used to describe a module M that may call one of several subordinates, depending on the type of the incoming transaction request.

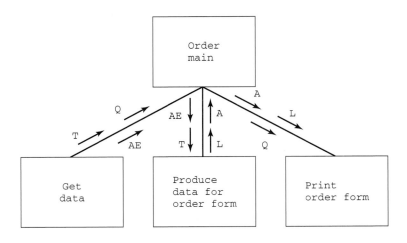

FIGURE 7.16

SD corresponding to DFD of Figure 7.12 (Legend: T = type of letter; Q = quantity; AE = addresses; L = letter form; A = address).

**Exercise**

**7.7**    What are the differences between SDs and GDN?

## 7.7.2    Jackson's System Development and Structured Programming

Jackson's system development (JSD) has been an evolving methodology since its birth in 1983. JSD has grown as a complete life cycle methodology on the foundations provided by Jackson structured programming (JSP), a popular design method adopted in many organizations for business data processing. The concise view of JSD/JSP we give here is not intended to provide a detailed account of the methodology; rather, its purpose is to give a flavor of the concepts upon which it is based.

While SA/SD bases system modeling on DFDs, JSD suggests a technique that represents a mixture of descriptive approaches based on object-oriented design and functional decomposition. Both methodologies address the analysis and implementation aspects of software development.

According to JSD, software development proceeds through a sequence of three stages: the modeling stage, the network stage, and the implementation stage. In the *modeling stage*, the real world is analyzed and represented in terms of *entities*, which model objects in the real world, and *actions* (or *events*) that may affect them. An entity is defined by the actions that model events that may occur in its history. For example, the entity FORM may be composed of the actions GET, to get a form, FILL_IN, to fill the necessary data into the form, and CHECK_IN, to return the filled-in form.

All actions that characterize an entity are ordered in time, thereby providing a process view of the entity, which is described by a *process structure diagram (PSD)*. For example, the entity FORM may be described by the PSD of Figure 7.17(a), where the

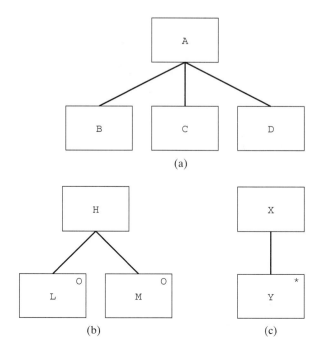

FIGURE 7.17

Process structure diagrams.
(a) Sequences. (b) Selection.
(c) Iteration. (The symbol "*"
in a corner of a box stands for
iteration of the corresponding
function; the symbol "o"
stands for selection.)

left-to-right placement of actions denotes the temporal sequences of the actions. In the diagram, A represents FORM, B denotes the action GET, C designates the action FILL_IN, and D denotes the action CHECK_IN. The ordering represents the fact that first we must GET a form, then we FILL_IN the form, and finally we CHECK_IN the form. In general, PSDs are annotated trees that can describe different orderings of actions—for instance, selection (Figure 7.17(b)) and iteration (Figure 7.17(c)).

In the *network stage*, each entity is modeled as a process, and the entire system is a network of interconnected and communicating processes, described by a *system specification network* (*SSN*). The graphical appearance of SSNs is illustrated in Figure 7.18(a) and Figure 7.18(b). Figure 7.18(a) illustrates the case where the processes P and Q are interconnected by the *data stream* R. A data stream is a FIFO queue of messages; if the queue is empty, then Q waits until P generates a message. Another form of process connection is provided by *state vectors* (Figure 7.18(b)), whereby one process may inspect the state of (i.e., data owned by) another process. The figure shows the case where process Q inspects P's state vector. By inspecting the state vector, a process may access the history of another process, which is recorded in the form of data.

In the *implementation stage*, the network of processes is transformed into an implementation. That is, the concurrent network of processes is transformed into a sequential system that is executable by a conventional machine. This transformation is necessary only if the system is implemented in a traditional programming language, such as COBOL. To effect the transformation, JSD introduces a technique called *process inversion*. Basically, process inversion transforms a pair of communicating sequential processes into a hierarchical structure in which a program invokes a subprogram. More precisely, observe that the case illustrated in Figure 7.18(a) may be made sequential according to one of the following schemes:

- P runs, produces an information item to be consumed by Q, and then transfers control to Q. Q completes its job and then reactivates P.
- Q runs until it needs a datum produced by P. Q then transfers control to P, asking for the datum, and resumes execution upon receipt of the datum.

At this stage, the JSD specifications are nearly complete, so that one may easily implement them in any programming language. To facilitate implementation, further details may be added to PSDs in order to show where some physical operations—such

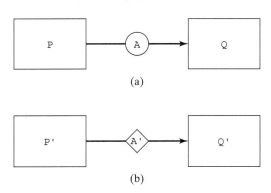

**FIGURE 7.18**

System specification networks (a) Connection by data structure. (b) Connection by state vector.

as opening or closing files, initializing counters, and updating relevant variables—actually occur. Since this final step is exactly the same as a step in the JSP methodology, we explain it shortly in an example of JSP.

JSD supersedes JSP by covering the entire life cycle from requirements to programming, whereas JSP is limited to the programming phase. Another difference between JSD and JSP is that JSP is based on the assumption that the program structure may fall directly out of the modeling of input and output data. By contrast, JSD provides a more general guideline for deriving the program structure systematically from an analysis of the problem specification. Within the JSD methodology, however, it is possible to develop parts of a system using JSP—especially subsystems in which the structure of the process is influenced greatly by the structure of the data. This feature makes JSP particularly suitable for developing the traditional file-processing programs that were typical in the past in the COBOL world.

In JSP, a problem is modeled by specifying the relations among the input and output data using tree-structured diagrams described in the same notation as is used for PSD. Figure 7.19 shows a typical example of the input and output files for an inventory problem. The input file is a sequence of transfer orders, which may be either a receipt or a delivery, grouped by item code; the output is a summary report in which the net transfer is reported for each item.

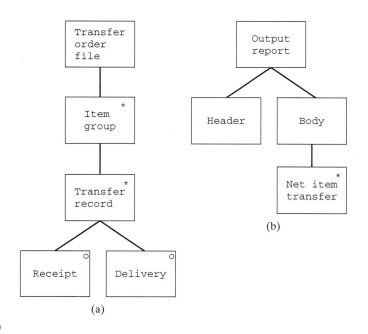

FIGURE 7.19

Input and output processing for an inventory problem.
(a) Input structure. (b) Output structure.

To derive a program that transforms the input file into the output file, JSP suggests that we identify the correspondence between the nodes of the diagrams. In the example, an output report is generated for a transfer order file, and a net item transfer in the output's body corresponds to an item group in the transfer order file. This correspondence is shown in Figure 7.20 by means of the zigzag connections. With these correspondences found, it is fairly straightforward to derive a structure for the required program. We can describe such a program structure by the usual tree-structured diagram as in Figure 7.21(a). Note, however, that it is not always so trivial to establish the correspondence between the input and output data structures and, hence, to derive the program structure. JSP, however, provides specific techniques to solve most practical problems arising in common data-processing situations.

To translate the abstract program structure of Figure 7.21(a) into the desired program, one may proceed by listing all the operations that are needed by the application and then associating them with the program structure by annotating the corresponding diagram. For the example of Figure 7.19, the operations are listed in Figure 7.21(b), and the annotated diagram is shown in Figure 7.21(c). A trivial transformation may translate the annotated diagram into pseudocode or even a programming language.

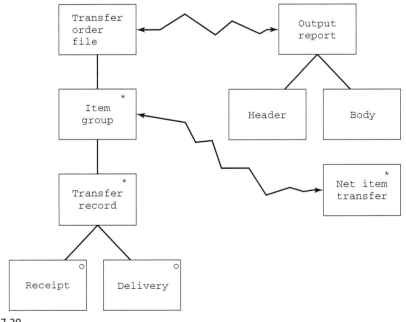

FIGURE 7.20

Matching of input and output structures.

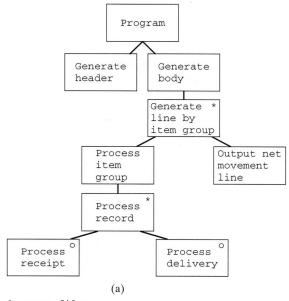

(a)

```
1. open files
2. close files
3. read (item_id, movement)
4. net_item_movement:= 0
5. net_movement_item:= net_movement_item + movement
6. net_movement_item:= net_movement_item - movement
7. write (header)
8. write (net_item_movement_line)
```

(b)

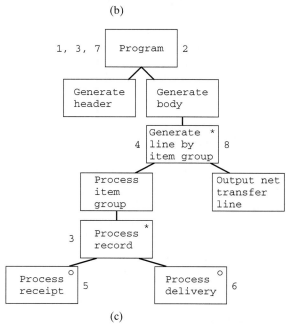

FIGURE 7.21

Deriving a program according to
JSP. (a) Program structure.
(b) Program operations. (c)
Annotated program structure

(c)

**Exercise**

---

**7.8**  Write a program in your favorite language corresponding to the decorated tree of Figure 7.21(c).

---

### 7.7.3    The Unified Software Development Process

The Unified Software Development Process (in short, Unified Process, or UP) has its roots in the industrial experience within Ericsson, a manufacturer of telecommunications equipment, in the late 1960s. Subsequently, that experience led to successor methodologies developed by two other companies: Objectory and Rational. UP has gained the status of a widely adopted industrial standard.

UP uses the Unified Modeling Language (UML) throughout the software life cycle. As we have observed, the rich collection of languages that constitute UML provides specific notations to specify, analyze, visualize, construct, and document the artifacts that are developed in the life cycle of a software system. Software engineers use the notations to produce standardized blueprints that contain a number of different diagrams, each enlightening a certain aspect of the application being developed. As we anticipated in Section 5.7.1, this multiview description of a software system is a distinctive and quite useful feature of the language. UML is not formal in a strict sense. For example, the consistency relations among the different viewpoints provided by different diagrams are not formally defined. UML is, however, an important step in the direction of a standardized language that would allow all software engineers to communicate and interact on rigorous grounds while developing or evolving a given software system.

UP casts the development of an object-oriented system into an *iterative* and *incremental* process model. The underlying principle is that any large software project should be broken into *controlled iterations* (miniprojects) that provide increments of the product. The choice of what should be implemented in an iteration is made by software engineers on the basis of two factors. On the one hand, the iteration should provide an increment which implements use cases that correspond to augmenting the usability of the product developed so far. On the other, the iteration deals with a critical risk identified in the project. Increments can be additive (i.e., they implement new use cases), or perfective (i.e., they improve existing implementations of use cases).

A UP life cycle can be depicted abstractly as a sequence of cycles (see Figure 7.22), from the project's inception to its termination. Each cycle outputs a *product release*—a product ready for delivery. The product is a complete and consistent set of artifacts, including the executable version of the system and all the needed documentation (requirements, design, test cases, etc.), specified in UML. Such documentation is used by developers when they decide to undertake a new cycle. The UML representations available in the release help developers understand exactly the status of the existing implementation from which the new cycle may start.

Each cycle, in turn, is divided into a sequence of *four phases*, as shown in Figure 7.23. Each phase terminates in a *milestone* that may be used for project control. A milestone consists of delivering an intermediate set of artifacts that can be subject to quality control via reviews and inspections. For example, the result of a milestone might be a design model, consisting of a class diagram defining the logical structure of the model, sequence diagrams describing sample run-time scenarios, and state diagrams describing control flows.

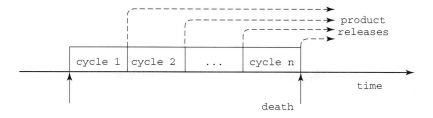

**FIGURE 7.22**

The cycles of a life cycle.

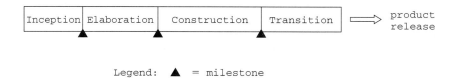

**FIGURE 7.23**

Phases of a UP cycle.

The first phase, called *inception*, roughly corresponds to what we called the feasibility study. Its goal is to document a vision of the product and a business analysis that justifies why the development should be undertaken. The document should address the following questions:

- Who are the expected users of the system, and why should they be willing to use it?
- What is the preliminary, high-level architecture of the system?
- What is the development plan and what are the expected development costs?

In the next phase, called *elaboration*, the use cases that are assumed to become part of the current release are specified in detail, and the software architecture is developed and specified. The expected result of this phase is an architecture model. UP insists that this should constitute a *baseline*. This means that the set of documents describing the architecture must represent an agreed-upon basis for further development within the development team, and therefore, any change is regulated by a formal procedure in order to avoid possible inconsistencies. In the next section, we discuss how the management of a baseline can be accomplished systematically and how software tools may assist in this activity. At the end of the elaboration phase, project managers can refine the development plan and the cost estimations made in the inception phase. It is also possible to reassess how stable the plan is and to verify whether the risks are sufficiently under control to proceed to the next phase.

In the next phase, *construction*, the product is built by enriching the architecture baseline and developing and testing the code. The final milestone of this phase will be a quality check that responds to the following question: Does the product satisfy the user's needs adequately to warrant its delivery?

The *transition* phase corresponds to beta testing. A trusted set of early adopters tries the product and provides reports on possible defects and deficiencies. Some of these will immediately be taken care of by developers; others might be delayed to a subsequent release. The tracking of defects and deficiencies, as well as the policy adopted to handle them, is crucial in this phase. The milestone of the phase is the delivery of the current cycle's product.

No phase of a cycle is monolithic. Rather, each phase is subdivided into a sequence of controlled iterations, as discussed earlier. The iterations are developed according to a plan and yield an increment that is released to be subject to predefined evaluation criteria. An iteration plan must state the expected cost and output artifacts, should allocate human resources, and should define who will do what within each iteration.

One can easily observe that UP achieves the goals of flexibility and incrementality without retreating to unstructured development practices. Rather, its fine-grained iteration steps help in continuous validation and ensure that early changes in the process may be performed to redirect the development if required.

In Section 7.3, we discussed the main activities of software production, and we observed that no matter how the activities are organized in a process, nevertheless they must be performed for any project. In UP, these activities—called workflows—are not organized as sequential phases. Rather, iterations typically go through all main workflows. Figure 7.24 provides a view of how workflows are typically distributed over the four phases of a cycle. For simplicity, we consider the following main workflows: requirements, analysis, design, implementation, and testing. In UP, there is a precise distinction between the requirements and analysis workflows. The requirements workflow deals with capturing requirements and providing a description that can be used as the basis of an agreement between the customer and the developer. The analysis workflow refines and structures the captured requirements, in order to achieve better understanding, improve their maintainability, and help future developments.

Besides being iterative and incremental, UP defines itself as use-case driven and architecture centric. *Use-case driven* means that use cases are employed as the primary means of communicating with stakeholders in the requirements workflow. Furthermore, use cases are the main input to the analysis, design, implementation, and testing workflows. This emphasis on use cases (and on use-case diagrams as a notation) reflects the focus of the methodology on building successful systems for the benefit of their prospective users. Satisfying user needs is in fact the ultimate goal of UP. *Architecture centric* means that the software architecture is the primary artifact used for conceptualizing, constructing, managing, and evolving the system being developed. The term "architecture" is used by UP in a broad sense, as the rationale behind the structural and behavioral organization of an application, how it is composed into progressively larger subsystems, and the style that guides in the organization. The rich set of diagrammatic notations provided by UML allows the architectural description to be expressed by a number of interdependent components.

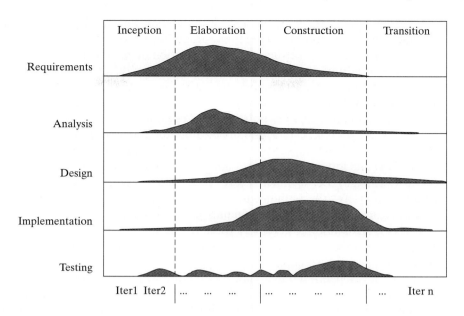

FIGURE 7.24

Activities (workflows), with phases and iterations.

## Exercises

**7.9**  Write a short report illustrating how the different UML notations can be used in the four phases of a UP cycle to describe the artifacts that must be developed in those phases.

**7.10**  UP can be defined as use-case driven, architecture centric, iterative, and incremental. Briefly discuss why.

## 7.8    ORGANIZING ARTIFACTS: CONFIGURATION MANAGEMENT

When software is being developed, several individuals interact and cooperate towards a common goal. These individuals produce several products, some of which are strictly for their own use, such as intermediate versions of modules or test data used during debugging, and others of which become, in one way or another, part of the final products. Individual products are often logically related to one another as components in a collection. For example, a certain use case corresponds to some subsystem; a module interface specification corresponds to a certain delivered source-code module. Finally, products undergo many changes, both during development and in the maintenance phase. There may be hundreds or thousands of components in a collection. How do we keep all this under control, in order to avoid its being lost in an unstructured collection of files, both in the computer and in the drawers of our desks? How do we know which versions of an executable piece of software contain certain versions of source module, so that the elimination of a defect in a module is properly propagated to all affected versions? This is where the need for configuration management arises.

A *configuration* of a product identifies the product's components, and also the specific versions of the components. Configuration management is the discipline of *coordinating software development and controlling the change and evolution of software products and components*. It is an old discipline that has traditionally been studied in the context of systems manufacturing. Its application to software, however, is more recent; in addition, software has special features that make it different from traditional manufacturing. Software adds complexity to configuration management, because changes occur much more frequently than in other kinds of products. Conversely, software configuration management is more amenable to automation, since all items may be stored on media that are accessible by the computer.

Let us examine more closely some of the issues that are addressed by software configuration management. One class of problems has to do with multiple accesses to a common repository of components. Suppose that one of the software engineers on a team has developed a module (say, M) and put it in a centralized database of components for use by other members of the team. For example, M implements some services that are needed by other subsystems, and it might be convenient to use M for developing and testing those subsystems. Suppose also that, for some reason, a member of the team picks up M from the database and modifies it. Finally, suppose that the modification introduces an error and that other members of the team are not notified of the change. Then, when they use M later, it will probably fail to execute properly. To their surprise, the system might crash even if no modification was made to their modules and to the input data. They simply do not know that a change occurred in M!

Another instance of the same problem will occur if two members of the team simultaneously check out the same component and modify it independently. After one checks the component back into the database, there is no guarantee that the same component will be retrieved through a later checkout. In fact, the changes made by one member of the team may be overwritten by another member of the team: Only the latest checked-in copy will be kept.

The foregoing problems are due to *sharing of components*. The simple and natural way to prevent these problems is to give a private copy of M to each of M's potential users. But the difficulty is that each private copy will eventually diverge into a different component.

## Exercise

**7.11** Explain the preceding problems of component sharing by drawing an analogy with shared variables accessed by different tasks in a concurrent programming language like Ada or Java. How can you prevent these problems in the Ada or Java program?

A second class of problems has to do with *handling product families*. The term "product family" is used instead of "program family" to stress the fact that configuration management deals not just with programs, but also with documentation, test data, user manuals, etc. Problems arise because, as a consequence of changes, a component may exist in several versions or a product may exist in several releases. Each member of the product family may consist of different versions of components. Figure 7.25 illustrates this point: Components are grouped together, and different subscripts are used to indicate the various versions of the same component. Three members of the product family F are also indicated.

Even though different members of a product family are indicated by listing the names and versions of components, they are not necessarily stored and kept in that way. An alternative solution might be to have each family member include a copy of all the components. Whatever solution is adopted, however, special care is needed to keep the state of families consistent as changes occur in components that belong to family members.

To proceed in our discussion, we need to refine the concept of a version of a component that we have used so far. First, observe that we may formally define the concept by introducing the relation IS_VERSION_OF among components. IS_VERSION_OF may then be further refined by introducing the two relations IS_REVISION_OF and IS_VARIANT_OF.

According to standard terminology in the field, IS_REVISION_OF defines the concept of a component $C_i$ being a *revision* of another component $C_j$, meaning that $C_i$ is obtained by changing a copy of $C_j$. The version of the component we obtain through revision supersedes the previous version; thus, revisions are created in a linear order.

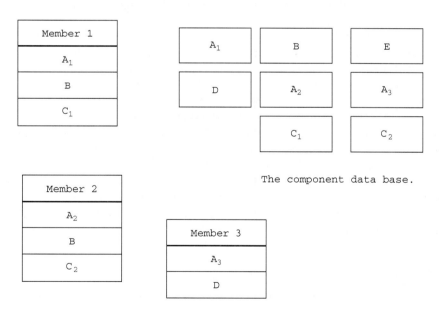

FIGURE 7.25

A family of products using a component database.

There are many reasons one may wish to create a revision of a component, and we might represent this fact by further specializing the relation IS_REVISION_OF. For example, one might wish to specify that one version eliminates a defect from another or that it is the result of a mandatory adaptive maintenance.

Another specialization of IS_VERSION_OF is the relation IS_VARIANT_OF. This relation holds if two components are indistinguishable under some given abstraction. For example, they might be two alternative implementations of the same specification for different machines. Another example is an application whose different variants permit access to different I/O devices (a line printer vs. a laser printer, etc.). Obviously, variants do not supersede the original component and thus are not organized as a linear succession.

In order to handle all products that are generated during the software process, it is necessary to establish projectwide configuration management policies. A typical case may consist of using a *project baseline* in conjunction with a private work space for each member of the development team. As we already mentioned, a project baseline is a central repository of reviewed and approved artifacts that represent a given stable point in the overall system development. The baseline serves as a shared database associated with the project. For example, when programmers are developing their own modules, they use their private work space for storing intermediate versions. The policy that is followed to manage the private work space is left to the individual programmer. When a-module is released to the rest of the team, however, it becomes public and must be stored in the baseline.

Management of the baseline is critical, and therefore, suitable policies must be defined. Such policies may be enforced by configuration management tools. For example, we may specify that revisions should follow a checkout—manipulate—check-in policy. The checkout policy might lock the component, making it inaccessible to other members of the team until a check-in is done to insert a modified version in the baseline.

It is important that the baseline be kept in a consistent state, especially because many of the components of the baseline are actually related to one another. We use the term *derived version* to capture this fact. For example, an object code component is a derived version of a source code component. Similarly, a source code module might be viewed as a derived version of its specification. Note that in the first case the generation of a derived version from the source component may occur automatically, whereas in the second case human intervention is required. In general, care must be taken to ensure that a modification in one component leaves the system in a consistent state with respect to derived versions. Here, too, tools may be used to enforce such policies, as we shall see in Chapter 9. For instance, the tool might ensure that if an object code is used and its corresponding source code was changed, the compiler is automatically invoked to keep the system in a consistent operational state.

## Exercises

**7.12** Provide a detailed description of the two methods for handling product families discussed in Section 7.8 (i.e., defining each family member by references to its components or by copies of the components). Discuss the pros and cons of the methods.

**7.13** Characterize IS_VERSION_OF as a mathematical relation. Is it symmetric? Transitive? What about IS_REVISION_OF? Does it define a hierarchy? Why? Why not?

## 7.9    SOFTWARE STANDARDS

Software standards are needed to achieve acceptable levels of quality in both software products and processes. Standards may be imposed internally or externally. In the first case, the software organization itself decides to adopt standards in order to achieve certain expected benefits. In the latter case, the standard may be mandated to contractors by the customer. For example, MIL-STD-498 (the current successor of MIL-STD 2167A, which was discussed in Section 7.4.1.1) might be imposed on military contractors involved in software development. Other standards are defined by the International Organization for Standardization (ISO) and the Institute of Electrical and Electronics Engineers (IEEE). Of particular importance is ISO 9001, the ISO standard that applies to software development. ISO 9001 is a generic international standard, adopted on a country-by-country basis and written for use by the widest possible audience. As a result, the standard provides requirements (*what* needs to be done), but does not issue specific prescriptive solutions (*how* to do it). Further, being so broadly focused, the ISO 9001 standard does not offer details about its application to specific domains of expertise. To assist in the application of the standard to specific domains, a series of guidelines is available (e.g., ISO 9000-3 is a guideline for the software development industry). We do not describe these standards in this text, but rather, we direct the interested reader to examine them separately as case studies. (see the exercises at the end of the chapter) and refer to the material referenced in the bibliographic notes.

The main benefit of standards is that they enforce a uniform behavior within an organization. This facilitates communication among people, stabilizes the production process, and makes it easier to add new people to ongoing projects. From the point of view of customers, the fact that contractors adhere to certain standards means that it is easier to assess the progress and quality of results. Even more important, standards reduce the strict dependency of customers on specific contractors: Changing contractors is easier if they all follow the same standards.

One must be careful, however, in the enforcement of standards. If a standard is too prescriptive and covers even minor details, then it tends to frustrate progress by constraining creativity within narrow boundaries. In such a case, people tend to adhere to the standard on the surface and may ignore it in substance.

As we have already observed in other cases, it is difficult to define standards that reconcile all the conflicting goals that exist in a project. The following principles should guide the definition of standards:

- Make a clear distinction between mandatory and recommended practices, and then keep the former to a minimum and apply them only to aspects of the system that are understood perfectly. It is discouraging to be forced to follow a standard that is poorly understood.
- View standards as a means of *improving* the professional responsibility of people, not as a substitute for it. Software engineers should decide which additional standards are worth adopting in any specific case.

## 7.10    CONCLUDING REMARKS

The software production process is the set of all activities that must be accomplished in order to produce a software product. As such, it is a glue that amalgamates both technical and managerial issues. Technical issues deal with accomplishing single activities within the process, such as designing the software architecture or deriving test cases for a module. Managerial issues deal with how to organize activities into steps, or phases, of the process and how to handle the resources necessary to produce the product.

In this chapter, we discussed various approaches to organizing the software development process. On the basis of the characteristics of the different approaches, the software engineer should be able to tailor the most appropriate life cycle model to the application under consideration. We also discussed the need for methodologies and standards to guide software development, and we gave examples taken from industrial practice. We concluded that we should not hope for a fixed, standardized set of methods that can guide every practical situation. Methodologies and standards cannot replace the need for creativity or the intellectual responsibility of software engineers. Learning from the various life cycle models presented here and from the principles and methods illustrated in the previous chapters, and taking inspiration from existing methodologies, the software engineer must be able to define the most appropriate process model and choose an effective blend of methods for each specific development process.

## FURTHER EXERCISES

**7.14** Discuss software life cycle models, such as the waterfall model, in light of the principle of separation of concerns.

**7.15** Research the ISO 9001 standard and the 9000-3 guideline. (You may find information by checking the Web page http://www.tantara.ab.ca/iso_list.htm.) Write a short report explaining the role of the standard and of the guideline.

**7.16** Search for information about the MIL-STD-498 standard, and write a short report on it, emphasizing how it differs from MIL-STD-2167 A.

**7.17** If the USES relation is a hierarchy, then incremental implementation is possible. Prove or disprove the truth of this statement.

**7.18** Provide an example, possibly based on your own experience as a software developer, of both a throwaway and an evolutionary prototype.

**7.19** Do you believe that in some near future the transformation-based approach may be totally automated—that is, that software engineers can be left out of the development loop? Why? Why not?

**7.20** For the case study of Section 7.6.2, point out the differences that could occur in the case of a large company, as opposed to the small one examined in the study. How would you change the approach?

**7.21** How would you design the process of developing a budget control product to be sold on the market? Would you try to obtain a unique product that is suitable for any company, or a family of different products for different kinds of companies? How can the target company affect the application?

**7.22** Why is it desirable that the SD is a DAG instead of a tree?

**7.23** Follow SA/SD to model a hotel reception desk. The desk deals with incoming reservations, check-ins, and checkouts. Feel free to deal with all possible details in the operations of the desk. Derive a hierarchical DFD and a first-cut SD.

**7.24** Sketch the elevator problem of Section 5.5.3.1, using JSD.

**7.25** Consider the process inversion step of JSD. Explain why the units in the sequential implementation are actually coroutines.

**7.26** Outline a UP cycle to develop an application automating a hotel reception desk (see Exercise 7.23), and sketch the main UML artifacts.

**7.27** Refer to the activities performed during maintenance, and propose further specializations of IS_REVISION_OF and IS_VARIANT_OF.

**7.28** Characterize IS_VARIANT_OF as a mathematical relation.

**7.29** A module is a variant of another module under a given abstraction. Revise the definition of the relation IS_VARIANT_OF so that you may formally take into account the abstraction under which one module is a variant of another.

**7.30** The software development group of a computer company is involved in producing successive versions of the system software, which consists of the operating system, compilers, databases, and other utilities. To control the management of many source modules, the group adopts a procedure in which a directory, called *public*, contains the sources and executables for all the modules used in the currently released product. Another directory, called *new*, contains the sources and executables for the next release of the software, which is being worked on by the organization. When a new component (e.g., a new compiler or a new editor) is developed and is ready for use by other people in the development organization, the developer moves the component into the directory *new*. Do you see any difficulties with this approach? Are there any advantages to allowing more than one *new* directory? Is it better to have $rel_1, rel_2, ..., rel_N$?

**7.31** Formally define the concept of a derived version in terms of a mathematical relation. Describe how to determine the components that are affected by a modification of a given component.

**7.32** In which phase(s) of the waterfall life cycle would you require tailoring of the process and configuration management policy definitions?

**7.33** Consider the railroad-crossing system introduced in Exercise 3.19. Discuss who the stakeholders are, what their (possibly conflicting) goals are, and what suitable safety and utility requirements they must consider. In order to focus on the interplay among different goals, you may also consider that, in some sense, the system, as described in Exercise 3.19, already includes some "early design decisions." For example, in some cases, railroad crossings are realized not through gates, but with simple traffic signals for the automobile drivers. Which trade-offs occur in such decisions? How do early architectural decisions (signal versus gate) affect later requirements?

## HINTS AND SKETCHY SOLUTIONS

**7.20** If the processes involved in the company and their control procedures are fairly well understood from the beginning (which is more likely to occur in a large company than in a small one), then one could immediately design suitable procedures for data processing, moving closer to a waterfall model. If the same level of uncertainty as in the case study occurs, however, it would probably be wiser to follow an incremental approach. For instance, one could single out a small and significant subsection of the company and produce early prototypes to be applied to it more or less in the same way as in the case study. Only after some experience with early prototypes could one move to the design of a full system for the whole company.

**7.30**  Consider the integration problems faced when, for example, the new release of a compiler requires a new feature in the operating system and the operating system needs to be compiled with the new compiler. Which one is moved into *new* first?

**7.31**  Use the transitive closure of the relation.

## BIBLIOGRAPHIC NOTES

Bennington [1956] and Royce [1970] are among the early proponents of the concept of the software life cycle. Both were influenced by the SAGE project, where development was done in successive stages: an operational plan, operational specifications, coding specifications, coding, parameter testing, assembly testing, shakedown, and system evolution.

The main issues of software engineering, including the process issue, were documented by Boehm [1976]. According to Brooks [1975], the first implementation of every real-life system will always have weaknesses; thus, we should be always plan to throw it away and do every system twice!

The landmark maintenance study that classified types of maintenance activities and their costs was reported by Lientz and Swanson [1980]. Despite its age, it is still quoted as the definitive study of maintenance costs. More recently, Bennett and Rajlich [2000] argue that, since maintenance consumes such a large portion of software costs, labeling the last phase of the development process as maintenance is no longer sufficient. They propose a software life cycle that takes evolution explicitly into account. The life cycle phases are defined to be development, servicing, and phaseout.

A source on various classical paradigms of software processes is the guide to the literature and annotated bibliography by Agresti [1986]. A clear picture emerges of both the conventional, waterfall-based paradigm and the newer approaches. Different life cycle models are compared by Davis et al. [1988], which presents a method of comparing various process models based on an appealing graphical representation. Graham [1989] provides a review of process models, with an emphasis on flexible models. Humphrey [1995] describes a self-improvement strategy to help software developers control, manage, and improve the way they work individually. The strategy is called "the personal software process strategy."

A critical view of the conventional life cycle model is presented by McCracken and Jackson [1982], which advocates evolutionary prototyping. Gilb [1988] discusses software development in the light of a highly flexible life cycle model. Basili and Turner [1975] provide an early report on an evolutionary approach and its success. The benefits of incremental development are discussed by Wong [1984], while Alavi [1984] contrasts a prototyping-based life cycle with a conventional one. Throwaway prototyping is discussed by Gomaa and Scott [1981]. Boehm et al. [1984] report on an experiment that compared the relative benefits of software development based on prototyping with that based on specifications. According to Swartout and Balzer [1982], one of the reasons that the rigid waterfall model fails is that it does not recognizes that specification and implementation are inevitably intertwined. The Extreme Programming approach has been advocated as a radical evolutionary model which focuses the designer's attention on the development of core functionalities and continuous evolution and refactoring (Beck [1999]).

The spiral model is due to Boehm [1988]; the model is motivated by concepts of software costs and risk analysis, discussed by Boehm and Papaccio [1988] and Boehm [1989], respectively.

The transformation-based process model has been advocated by Balzer [1981], Cheatham et al. [1981], Kant and Barstow [1981], Balzer et al. [1983], and Bauer et al. [1989]. Knowledge-based approaches in software engineering are presented in the special issue of *IEEE Transactions on Software Engineering* edited by Mostow (TSE [1985]), in Goldberg [1986] and Rich and Waters [1988], and by some contributions in the special issue of *IEEE Software* [1990a].

Formal approaches to program derivation were pioneered by Dijkstra [1976]; see also Gries [1976], Gries [1981], Linger et al. [1979], and Mills et al. [1987a]. A formal approach to the transformational derivation of software is described in Bauer et al. [1989]; this approach is based on a wide-spectrum language. Partsch and Steinbruggen [1983] reviews early program transformation systems.

Mills et al. [1987b] discusses the so-called cleanroom software development approach, based on formal verification (and no testing) at the unit level and statistical testing at the system level. The emphasis of the approach is on the prevention, rather than the removal, of errors. Selby et al. [1987] provides an empirical evaluation of the approach.

A formal approach to software development based on VDM is described by Bjorner and Jones [1982] and Jones [1986a, 1986b]. The Larch methodology also covers the derivation of programs from their formal specifications. (See Guttag et al. [1985a, 1985b] and Guttag and Horning [1986a, 1986b]).

Osterweil [1987] observed that "software processes are software too." Observing that software development organizations differ in culture, people skills, products delivered, commercial, and development strategies, he concluded that there is no unique, ready-made software development process. Rather, processes must be defined on the basis of the problem to be solved; they must be tailored to the specific development project and should take into account all the particularities of the organization and product being developed. Also, the environments that support software development should be tailored to the specific development process. To satisfy these goals, Osterweil concluded, we need languages to describe software development processes and a process-centered software development environment to support software production. Garg and Jazayeri [1995] is a collection of seminal papers in the area, including the one by Osterweil, focused on software engineering environments. Finkelstein et al. [1994] is a collection of European efforts in this area. Cugola and Ghezzi [1999] is an overview of software process issues.

The issue of defining the appropriate life cycle and factory models to support both application development and software enhancement and reuse is addressed by Basili and Rombach [1988] and Basili and Caldiera [1988]. A discussion of how human factors affect the life cycle is addressed by Mantei and Teorey [1988]. A report on a field study of the software design process on large development projects is given by Curtis et al. [1988]; the study is based on a behavioral process.

The evolution of large systems has been studied by Belady and Lehman [1979] and Lehman and Belady [1985], who derived the following rules:

> **Law of continuing change**. A system undergoes continuing change, until it becomes economical to replace it by a new or a restructured version.
> **Law of increasing entropy**. The entropy of a system increases with time, unless special care is taken to maintain or reduce it.
> **Law of statistically smooth growth**. Attributes that measure the growth of a system are self-regulating and statistically smooth.

Parnas and Clements [1986] provide convincing arguments to show that the waterfall model is an idealized, purely theoretical process and that there is no such thing as a software project that proceeds according to its tenets. Nevertheless, they argue that it is useful to *fake* the real process by producing documents *as if* we were proceeding in the ideal way. They state what each document should contain.

The issue of reengineering existing applications to make them maintainable is addressed in the papers in the special issue of *IEEE Software* [1990a] on maintenance, reverse engineering, and design recovery. Bellay et al. [2000] describes a process for software architecture recovery.

A comparison of software methodologies is described by Bergland [1981]. SA/SD has been advocated by several authors. In particular, DeMarco [1978] illustrates structured analysis, while Yourdon and Constantine [1979] and Myers [1978] illustrate structured design. The methodology has been extended by Ward and Mellor [1985] and Hatley and Pirbhai [1987] to cover the issues of real-time systems.

The Jackson system design methodology—JSD—is presented by Jackson [1983]; Jackson [1975] describes JSP, the earlier methodology addressing the programming phase of software development.

Other traditional methodologies include SADT, presented by Ross [1977], and SREM, presented by Alford [1977]. The former is a structured analysis and design methodology; the latter is a process-based methodology for real-time applications.

The Unified Software Development Process is described by its main designers, Jacobson et al. [1999]. The Microsoft development strategy is analyzed in depth by Cusumano and Selby [1995] and is summarized in Cusumano and Selby [1997]. Cusumano and Yoffie [1999a] discusses more generally the issue of software development on Internet time. In another article, Cusumano and Yoffie [1999b] describe how Netscape had to adapt its development process to cater to cross-platform development requirements for its Internet software. The multiplicity of platforms on which the browser and server have to run places stringent requirements on the process. For a discussion of open-source software development, see Edwards [1998] and Monga [2000]. Raymond [1999] draws a vivid analogy between traditional development approaches and open-source development as the "cathedral" versus "bazaar" mode. Lewis [1999] provides a critical view of the open-source approach and its chance to scale up. The general theme of configuration management, along with a description of support tools, is addressed by Babich [1986] and Tichy [1989]. Conradi and Westfechtel [1998] is a comprehensive survey of version configuration management. Fogel [2000] presents an open-source development process based on the configuration management system CVS, which is discussed in Chapter 9.

There are many originators of software standards, including the IEEE [1999], the International Organization for Standardization (ISO), and the U.S. Department of Defense, which issued the well-known MIL-STD-2167A (DOD [1984]), briefly discussed in this chapter. Other organizations, such as NATO, the European Space Agency(ESA), and even industrial companies, have their own standards, although these are for internal use only.

# Management of Software Engineering

Chapters 4 through 6 dealt with the product of software engineering and the techniques for producing quality products. Chapter 7 discussed the process of software engineering and how to organize it. The current chapter deals with the management of software engineering.

There are many software engineers involved in the development of a software product. Their work must be coordinated and managed. It is a traditional engineering practice to define a project around the product to be developed and to have a manager responsible for the project. Large projects may be composed of several subprojects, each of which may be divided into further subprojects if necessary. The primary job of the project manager is to ensure that the project is completed—that is, that it meets its requirements—within budget and on schedule.

The project manager has many tasks. First comes *planning*: understanding and documenting the goals of the project and developing a schedule, budget, and other resource requirements, all as rigorously as possible. Then comes the acquisition of resources—space, computing resources, materials, and human resources. We shall concentrate on the primary resource used in software engineering: the *human resource*. Acquiring human resources is called *staffing* and involves recruiting, hiring, training, rewarding, retaining, and directing project members. Next comes execution: putting the plan into action. Finally, the progress of the project must be monitored, and actions must be taken to handle both foreseen and unforeseen deviations from the plan. The basic challenge facing the project manager is to make decisions on how best to use limited resources to achieve a set of interdependent and sometimes conflicting goals. A commonly stated summary of the project manager's task is "*plan the work and work the plan.*"

Management decisions have a strong impact on the technical aspects of software engineering. For example, if a software engineer's performance is measured in terms of how many lines of code are produced, the engineer is discouraged from reusing code written by others. If an unrealistically aggressive schedule is imposed on the engineers, they are encouraged to take shortcuts that usually affect the quality of the product and diminish its maintainability. A slack schedule, on the other hand, encourages the engineers either to make grandiose decisions or not to proceed carefully enough, because they depend on having extra time later. Such a schedule could reduce design time and increase debugging time.

The manager faces many decisions that involve complicated trade-offs. What is the benefit of investing in modern software engineering tools? Will investing in such tools shorten the development time, and if so, what is the value of the time saved? How much will the addition of a particular feature cost in terms of development time, and how much benefit will it produce? What will be the impact of using a certain formal method on the development schedule and on the product's quality? Is it possible to shorten the time of the initial delivery of the system at the cost of increased future maintenance? By what factor will maintenance costs increase? What are the costs and benefits of incremental delivery, and which features should be delivered first? If a particular feature is not tested yet, what is the benefit of delivering the product without that feature? What are the trade-offs involved in developing a particular module in-house, compared with modifying a commercially available module? Should an existing software system be modified further, or should an entirely new system be developed from scratch? In an industrial discipline, such questions must be answered through sound and convincing arguments, possibly in a quantitative way. Without a clear cost model that delineates the economic impact of these decisions, there is no good way for a manager and an organization to choose among alternative strategies. The current state of practice in software engineering is to make judgments, check them against expert opinions, try to achieve consensus, and, if possible, calibrate against the data on previous similar projects within the same organization.

To help in resolving software engineering management problems, a number of quantitative approaches to software cost estimation, cost modeling, and cost analysis have been proposed. Many models have been developed, some of which are even available commercially, that allow the manager to develop cost and schedule estimates for a project and perform a sensitivity analysis based on various criteria. Such models are far from perfect; the best that can be said about them is that they are accurate to within 20%, 80% of the time. Even so, they are useful and can complement the manager's judgment and intuition. In this chapter, we study the underlying ideas of these approaches and examine some representative models.

The principles outlined in Chapter 3 apply to the management, as well as technical aspects, of software engineering. For example, the principle of modularity is the underlying motivation for assigning the responsibility for different tasks to different engineers or even groups. By setting up one group to do design, another to develop code, and another to do testing, we are applying modularization to the responsibilities and organization of the project. Hierarchical management organizations apply the principles of abstraction and separation of concerns to allow each tier of management to cope with its own level of abstraction and its own interests.

Much of project planning and scheduling involves estimation—of the complexity of the product, the productivity of individual engineers, the availability of people and other resources, etc. Estimation is always accompanied by the risk of being wrong. Small errors in estimation can usually be tolerated and should not affect the success of a project. Large deviations from the estimates, however, can cause the total failure of a project. Since risk and estimation always go hand in hand, the job of the project manager is to organize a project to minimize risk initially and, when deviations from the original estimates do occur, whether small or large, to detect them and take corrective action. Risk management is thus an important function of the project manager.

Managers in an organization are responsible for more than managing individual projects. Their responsibility spans the overall organization's life cycle. Managers need to evaluate their organization by comparing it with other, competing organizations. They need to assess the capabilities of the organization in order to understand what should be done to improve it. Continuous organizational learning and improvement are key to long-term success. The Capability Maturity Model (CMM) is a well-known and widely adopted software model. Software development organizations use CMM to assess their maturity and to implement an improvement strategy. CMM can also be used to assess software organizations as part of a software acquisition policy and to qualify contractors by requiring them to be certified according to CMM maturity levels.

Following a general discussion of the functions of management in the next section, Sections 8.2 through 8.4 respectively cover the specific management functions of planning, control, and organization. Section 8.5 examines the topic of risk management as applied to software engineering management. Section 8.6 looks at the Capability Maturity Model, and, finally, Section 8.7 summarizes the chapter and also contains some general and concluding remarks on the topic of software engineering management.

## 8.1    MANAGEMENT FUNCTIONS

Management can be defined informally as the art of getting work done through other people. A more classic definition that allows a systematic study of the subject is the following, from Koontz et al. [1980]:

> The creation and maintenance of an internal environment in an enterprise where individuals, working together in groups, can perform efficiently and effectively toward the attainment of group goals.

Thus, the main job of management is to enable a group of people to work towards a common goal. Management is not an exact science, and the many activities involved in it may be classified according to many different schemes. It is standard, however, to consider management as consisting of the following five interrelated activities, the goal of which is to achieve effective group work:

- **Planning**. A manager must decide what objectives are to be achieved, what resources are required to achieve the objectives, how and when the resources are to be acquired, and how the objectives are to be achieved. Planning basically involves determining the flow of information, people, and products within the organization.

- **Organizing**. Organizing involves the establishment of clear lines of authority and responsibility for groups of activities that achieve the goals of the enterprise. Organizing is necessary at the level of a small group, such as a five-person team of software engineers, all the way up to a large corporation composed of several independent divisions. The choice of the organizational structure affects the efficiency of the enterprise. The best organizational structure can be devised only when the goals of the enterprise are clear, and this depends on effective planning.

- **Staffing**. Staffing deals with hiring personnel for the positions that are identified by the organizational structure. Staffing involves defining requirements for personnel; recruiting (identifying, interviewing, and selecting candidates); and compensating, developing, and promoting employees.

- **Directing**. Directing involves leading subordinates. The goal of directing is to guide the subordinates to understand and identify with the organizational structure and the goals of the enterprise. This understanding must be continuously refined by effective and exemplary leadership. Setting examples is especially important in software engineering, where measures of good engineering are lacking. The best training for a beginning engineer is to work alongside a good engineer.

- **Controlling**. Controlling consists of measuring and correcting activities to ensure that goals are achieved. Controlling requires the measurement of performance against plans and taking corrective action when deviations occur.

These general functions of management apply to any management activity, whether in a software engineering organization, an automobile manufacturing plant, or a boy scout group. They also apply at the various levels of an organization, from the first-level manager directing a few engineers to the president of a company directing several vice presidents. A detailed discussion of management principles and techniques is clearly beyond the scope of this book. We have already touched on the subject of organizing the process in Chapter 7. Our discussions of software qualities and objectives in Chapter 2 can form the basis for applying proper planning activities in software engineering. In this chapter, we concentrate on the planning and control of software engineering; we touch on the other management functions only when the nature of software requires the tailoring of general management considerations.

## 8.2   PROJECT PLANNING

The first component of software engineering project management is effective planning of the development of the software. The first step in planning a project is to define and document the assumptions, goals, and constraints of the project. A project needs a clear statement of goals to guide the engineers in their daily decision making. Many engineers on typical projects spend many hours discussing alternatives that are known clearly to the project manager, but that have not been documented or disseminated properly. As an extreme example, if the project is forced to develop software in using a particular methodology because of an explicit requirement from the customer, this requirement must be stated clearly and made known to all the engineers. If the requirement is not universally known and accepted, inevitably the engineers will periodically argue the merits of different methodologies—in the interest of progress, as they see it—and even decide to do some of their work following a different methodology. The goal of the project planning stage is to identify all the external requirements for, and constraints on, the project.

Once the external constraints have been identified, the project manager must come up with a plan for how best to meet the requirements within the given constraints. One of the questions at this stage is what process model will serve the project best. We have discussed the various alternatives in Chapter 7. Another critical decision is to determine the resources required for the project. The resources include the number and skill level of the people, and the amount of computing resources (e.g. workstations, personal computers, and database software).[1] Unlike traditional engineering disciplines, wherein one has to budget for material, the "raw material" used in software is mainly the engineer's brainpower. Thus, the cost of a software project is directly proportional to the number of engineers needed for the project. The problem of predicting how many engineers and other resources are needed for a given software project is known as *software cost estimation*.

Forecasting how many engineers will be needed is a difficult problem that is intimately tied to the problem of how to estimate the productivity of software engineers. There are two parts to the forecasting problem: Estimating the difficulty of the task and estimating how much of the task each engineer can accomplish. Clearly, to estimate the difficulty of the task, one must know what the task is—that is, what the requirements are. As we have seen in previous chapters, however, it is often difficult to specify the software requirements completely *a priori*. It was precisely such difficulties that motivated us to look at the evolutionary process as an alternative to the traditional waterfall model.

Incomplete and imprecise requirements hinder accurate cost estimation. The clearer and more complete the requirements are, the easier it is to determine the resources required. But even when the requirements are clear, estimating the number of engineers needed is a formidable task with inherent difficulties. The best approach is to develop the resource requirements incrementally, revising current estimates as more information becomes available. We have seen that an appropriate adaptation of the spiral model allows one to start with an estimate in the early planning stages and revise the estimate for the remaining tasks at the conclusion of each iteration of the particular phase of the life cycle.

How long it will take a software engineer to accomplish a given task is primarily a function of the complexity of the problem, the engineer's ability, the design of the software, and the tools that are available. For example, adding an undo facility to an editor may require adding a new module or a complete redesign, depending on the current design of the editor. Similarly, writing a front-end parser for a system may be a simple task for an engineer who is familiar with parsing technology, but an extremely difficult task for an engineer who is unaware of, and thus tries to reinvent, the technology. Finally, writing a compiler with compiler development tools is a lot easier than writing it without them.

---

[1] In a more general setting, resources include such things as space and utilities. We concentrate only on software-related issues here. Keep in mind, however, that even the choice of space (e.g., private offices versus shared work areas) has a significant impact on software productivity.

Unlike other engineering disciplines, software engineering is design intensive, as opposed to manufacturing intensive. This means that how long software development will take depends on the intellectual ability of the engineers or, worse yet, on a nonlinear combination of the intellectual abilities of all the engineers.

We have already observed that management decisions have a strong impact on the technical aspects of a project. We can see another example of this in the interplay between management planning and the entire software life cycle. For example, the choice of an evolutionary process model will impose a different kind of resource planning from a waterfall model. While an evolutionary model allows the manager to do resource planning incrementally as more information becomes available, it also requires more flexibility from the manager. Similarly, an incremental model will affect the resource loading for the different phases of the project, such as design and testing, because the phases are iterated incrementally. In general, there is a strong interplay between management functions and the technical aspects of a software engineering project.

## 8.2.1    Software Productivity

One of the basic requirements of management in any engineering discipline is to measure the productivity of the people and processes involved in production. The measurements obtained are used during the planning phase of a project as the basis for estimating resource requirements; they also form the basis for evaluating the performance of individuals, processes, and tools, the benefits of automation, etc. The ability to quantify the impact of various factors on productivity is important if we want to evaluate the many claims made for various "productivity improvement" tools. Indeed, there is an economic need for continued improvements in productivity. Of course, we can be sure that we are making improvements only if we can measure productivity quantitatively. Unfortunately, few, if any, claims made about tools that improve software productivity are based on valid quantitative measurements.

### 8.2.1.1    *Productivity metrics*

We clearly need a metric for measuring software productivity. In manufacturing-dominated disciplines such as automobile or television production, there are simple and obvious metrics to use. For instance, a new manufacturing process that doubles the number of television sets produced per day has doubled the productivity of the factory. By taking into account the costs of the new process, we can determine whether adopting it was cost effective.

The situation is not so simple in a design-dominated discipline like software engineering. To begin with, there is the problem that software does not scale up. For example, the typical productivity figure reported for professional software engineers is a few tens of lines of code per day. If we compare this number with the productivity exhibited on a student project, even beginning students appear to be much more productive than professionals if we simply extrapolate from what they produce on a simple homework project.

There are, however, several obvious reasons that a professional's productivity appears to be less than a student's. Professionals don't spend the majority of their time in strictly engineering activities: Up to half their time may be taken up by meetings, administrative matters, communication with team members, etc. One study showed that as much as 40% of a typical workweek is spent on nontechnical work. This implies that the larger a programming team becomes, the lower the individual productivity figures will be. Moreover, the professional has to satisfy higher quality requirements than the student does: reliability, maintainability, performance, documentation, etc. Further, the inherent complexity of the application affects the programmer's productivity. For example, experience has shown that programmers developing application programs produce as much as three times as many lines per day as programmers working on systems programs. Finally, students' work is mostly a single-person activity, whereas large applications require development teams and a lot of coordination and management.

An ideal productivity metric measures not lines of code, but the amount of value or *functionality* produced per unit time. The problem, however, is that we have no good way of quantifying the concept of functionality. For example, how can we relate the functionality offered by a payroll system to that offered by an air-traffic monitoring system? We need to either find a measure that somehow takes into account the inherent complexities of the different application domains or develop separate metrics for each domain. One such metric, developed for information systems, is called *function points* and is described in the next subsection.

Because of the difficulty of quantifying functionality, the search for a productivity metric has for the most part concentrated on the most tangible product of software engineering: the actual code produced by the engineer. Various metrics based on the size of the code have been developed. We examine these shortly, following our discussion of function points.

Existing metrics, however, are quite controversial, and one must be careful in adopting and using them. This remark holds both for the metrics of product quality that we presented in Chapter 6 and for the metrics of productivity that we illustrate next. Thus, managers should not use their results as objective measures of the ability or the productivity of a software engineer: Inappropriate use of such measures may have large, damaging effects by rewarding poor design and programming practices and demoralizing good engineers.

### 8.2.1.2  *Function points*

Function points attempt to quantify the functionality of a software system. The goal is to arrive at a single number that completely characterizes the system and correlates with observed programmer productivity figures. Actually, the function point characterizes the complexity of the software system and thus can be used to forecast how long it will take to develop the system and how many people will be needed to do it. It can also be used to measure programmer productivity in terms of the number of function points produced per unit time. The function-point method was derived empirically and has been used extensively for business applications and information systems.

According to the method, five items determine the complexity of an application, and the function point of a given software is the weighted sum of these five items. The weights for these items have been derived empirically and validated by observation on many projects. The items and their weights are shown in Table 8.1.

The number of inputs and the number of outputs count the distinct number of items that the user provides to the system and the system provides to user, respectively. In counting the number of outputs, a group of items such as a screen or a file counts as one item; that is, the individual items in the group are not counted separately. The number of inquiries is the number of distinct interactive queries made by the user that require specific action by the system. Files are any group of related information that is maintained by the application on behalf of the user or for organizing the application. Files reveal the bias of the function-point method towards business data processing. Finally, the number of interfaces is the number of external interfaces to other systems (e.g., the number of files to be read or written to disk or the number of files transmitted or received from other systems). Therefore, if the application reads a file that is produced by another application, the file is counted twice, once as input and once as an interface. If a file is maintained by two different applications, it is counted as an interface for each. The focus of function-point analysis is to measure the complexity of an application, based only on the function the application is supposed to provide to users. Therefore, any temporary files produced by the application are not counted in the measure; only those files that are visible or required by the user are so counted.

Once we have a metric, we can use it in many ways. For example, we can compute the productivity of an engineer or a team per month by dividing the function point for an existing piece of software by the number of months it took to develop the software. Or we can divide the amount of money spent to produce the software by the function point to compute how much each function point costs. Or again, we can measure the error rate per function point by dividing the number of errors found by the function point. These function-point-related numbers can be recorded and used as bases for future planning or interproject comparisons. If the function point is an accurate description of the complexity of a product, the numbers should be similar across different projects.

In an interesting experiment, function points were used to measure the relative power of different languages by computing the number of source lines required to code a function point in those languages. The numbers range from around 320 for assembler languages to 128 for C, 91 for Pascal, 71 for Ada 83, 53 for C++ and Java, and 6 for "spreadsheet languages." This experiment is somehow an indication of the utility of function points and a kind of validation of the idea, because the results match our intuitive judgment about the relative expressiveness of the these languages.

**TABLE 8.1**

Function-point items and weights.

| Item | Weight |
| --- | --- |
| Number of inputs | 4 |
| Number of outputs | 5 |
| Number of inquiries | 4 |
| Number of files | 10 |
| Number of interfaces | 7 |

There are obvious weaknesses in the function-point metric, but they do not seem to be insurmountable. For example, it is unlikely that a single weight number is sufficient for all cases. For instance, with regard to counting the number of inputs, some inputs probably require complicated processing and others very simple processing. The same holds for other items. Indeed, a solution to this problem has been to provide a range of weights for each item, basing the particular weight used on a subjective determination of whether the required processing is simple, average, or complex.

Despite these problems, function points have been increasingly adopted by organizations, and experience on their use is continuously growing. A number of extensions have also been proposed, as we shall mention in the bibliographic notes. The major strength of function points is that the metric is not based on the internal structure of the software and thus can be computed once a preliminary design of a system is available.

### Exercises

**8.1**  Compute the function point FP for a payroll program that reads a file of employees and a file of information for the current month and prints checks for all the employees. The program is capable of handling an interactive command to print an individually requested check immediately.

**8.2**  Assume that the payroll program of the previous exercise is expected to read a file containing information about all the checks that have been printed. This file is supposed to be printed and also used by the program the next time it is run, to produce a report that compares payroll expenses of the current month with those of the previous month. Compute the function points for the program. Justify the difference between the function points of this program and those of the previous payroll program by considering how the complexity of the program is affected by adding the requirement of interfacing with another application (in this case, itself).

### 8.2.1.3  *Size of code*

Since software engineers are supposed to produce software, the most tangible product of software engineering is the running software delivered to clients. This has led many people to use the size of the software as a measure of productivity. Of course, the size of the software is not necessarily an indication of how much effort went into producing it, and a programmer who produces twice as many statements as another is not necessarily twice as productive. In general, the size of code is not a measure of *any* quality: A program that is twice as big as another is not necessarily twice as good in any sense. Nevertheless, the most commonly used metrics to measure productivity are based on the size of code, for example, the number of source lines produced per unit of time.

Of course, a code size metric has to be qualified immediately by considering the same issues we did with the software science metric in Chapter 6: Should we count comment lines? Should we count programming language "statements" or simply the number of lines? How many times should we count the lines in a file that is "included" several times? And should we count declarations or just executable statements? By choosing answers to these questions, we arrive at a particular productivity metric based on the size of the code.

Two of the most common code size metrics are delivered source instructions (DSI), in which only lines of code delivered to the customer are counted, and noncommented source statements (NCSS), in which comment lines are not counted. Here, we use the generic unit, KLOC (thousands of lines of code), when we do not want to distinguish between the specific metrics.

Lines of code are used as a productivity metric in many organizations. The acceptance of this metric is due to the ease of measuring it and probably also to the fact that using any metric is better than using nothing at all. At the same time, we must be cognizant of the many problems associated with the measure. At the heart of the problem is that there is no semantic content to the size of code; rather, it is merely a function of the form of software. The observations that follow show some of the deficiencies inherent in the metric.

Consider two programmers faced with the task of programming a module that needs, among many other tasks, to perform a sort operation. One programmer writes his own sort routine, and the other uses her time to find out how to use an existing sort routine in the system library. Even though both accomplish the same task, the engineer who uses the library routine has generally chosen a better approach. Over the life of the software, the library routine has less of a chance of containing errors and is better tested; it allows the programmer to concentrate on the real problems she is trying to solve and perhaps gain better insight into the application rather than code a sorting routine, etc. Yet, the size metric penalizes the use of the library routine, because it recognizes the *other* programmer as more productive! In general, the size-based metric has the unfortunate effect of equating software reuse with lower productivity.

Consider also a programmer who one day discovers a clever abstraction that allows her to replace many special cases in the code she has been developing and replace several specialized procedures with a single general procedure. On this day when she has probably increased the reliability of her software, she can be charged with negative productivity because she has reduced the size of the software. If productivity is measured only in terms of lines of code, she is personally better off not making the improvement in the code.

When lines of code are used as a productivity metric, it is important to know what lines are being counted in order to be able to make accurate comparisons between individuals, projects, or organizations. For example, an organization may produce many software tools to support the development of a particular project. These tools may become useful to many other projects in the organization, but are not delivered to the customer as part of the product. Should these programs be counted in productivity measurements? A commonly adopted convention is to count only the lines of code that are delivered to the customer. To emphasize this decision, the models that use the convention refer to the measure as KDSI—thousands of delivered source instructions.

Using DSI as a measure does not mean that producing internal tools is a worthless activity. In any engineering activity, investments in tools and a support infrastructure are needed to improve productivity. The DSI measure focuses on the objective of the engineering organization and separates the effort involved in building internal tools from that involved in building the product itself. In other engineering disciplines, too, productivity is measured in terms of the final product, not the intermediate "mock-ups."

Another point to consider when comparing the productivity figures reported by different organizations is whether the reported figures include the effect of canceled projects. For various reasons, many projects are canceled before they produce and deliver a product. Whether the numbers of lines of code of these canceled projects are counted in the overall productivity of the organization has a material effect on the productivity figure. Such cancellations also have a secondary impact on the motivation of engineers in the organization and thus affect its overall productivity. Whatever criteria are used for measurement, comparing figures is possible only if the criteria are applied consistently. Since there are no standard metrics, the use and interpretation of available productivity data in the literature must be examined with care.

Another important phenomenon that helps in understanding the problems inherent in using lines of code as a software productivity metric is due to the nature of software evolution. The software evolves according to what can be called "the urban renewal principle" in software maintenance. When a new feature is to be added to the software or an old feature is to be enhanced, the engineer tends to spend as little time as possible understanding what is currently in the software; instead, he or she spends most of the time adding new code to perform the new function. The engineer avoids removing any code that he or she does not understand, even if the code appears to be useless. This behavior causes the code to grow, but renders portions of it useless, a situation contributing to "code decay," which is, not entirely facetiously, analogous to urban decay. Eventually, a brave engineer on some future maintenance assignment will undertake to apply "urban renewal" and remove or replace all the decayed code. At this point, the code will shrink, possibly substantially. More technically, this is what we have previously defined as reverse engineering, or refactoring. Has the engineer suddenly reduced the productivity of the entire organization, or is it that the previous engineers were falsely inflating the productivity figures?

Finally, lines of code are tied to procedural languages and are inherently incapable of dealing with the visual languages in which the programmer uses diagrams or screen panels rather than statements. In general, those measures assume that the lines of code are produced directly by the programmer and therefore do not deal with declarative systems wherein programs are generated automatically.

## Exercises

**8.3**    List the benefits and disadvantages of using library routines rather than writing your own code.

**8.4**    Define a size-based productivity metric that does not penalize the use of library routines.

### 8.2.1.4  *Factors affecting productivity*

Regardless of what metric we use for productivity, even if we simply have an intuitive notion, there are factors that affect engineering productivity. One of the important effects of a productivity metric is that it allows us to measure and quantify the benefits of the various factors. By identifying the major contributors to productivity, organizations can determine quantitatively whether they can afford to change their practices— that is, whether the improvements in productivity are worth the costs associated with the required changes. For example, will changing to a new programming language, adopting a new development process, hiring an efficiency expert, giving the engineers a private office, or allowing them to work at home increase productivity sufficiently to justify the expenses involved?

One study that used lines of code as a metric found that the single most important factor affecting productivity was the capability of the personnel. Half as important, but second on the list, was the complexity of the product, followed by required reliability and timing constraints (e.g., as in real-time software). The least important items on the list were schedule constraints and previous experience with the language used in the project. The effects of these various factors on productivity are reflected in the "cost driver functions" used in cost estimation models, such as the COCOMO model, which we shall examine later.

Many managers believe that an aggressive schedule motivates engineers to do a better, faster job. However, experiments have shown that unrealistically aggressive schedules not only cause the engineers to compromise on intangible aspects of quality, but also cause schedule delays. A surprising finding was that, in a controlled experiment, the subjects who had no schedule at all finished their project first, beating out both the group that had an aggressive schedule and the one that had a relaxed schedule. Experiments have shown that engineers, in general, are good at achieving the one tangible goal that they have been given: If the primary goal is to finish according to a given time schedule, they usually will—but at the cost of other goals, such as clarity of documentation and structure.

A specific example of the effect of overly aggressive scheduling can be seen when design reviews are scheduled far too early in the development cycle. While the manager may want to motivate the engineers to do the job in a shorter time, such premature design reviews force the designer to document only issues that are well understood and deny the reviewers an opportunity to provide useful feedback.

In one project at Hewlett-Packard Company, a group allowed to work at a remote location—a rented house in a small mountainside resort community—achieved productivity figures that were considerably higher than the average numbers for the corporation. The original management fears about leaving the engineers to work by themselves away from the guidance of "headquarters" turned out to be ill-founded. Several explanations have been given for this surprising result. Some have to do with the Hawthorne effect (named after the Hawthorne Works of the Western Electric Co., in Cicero, Illinois, where it was noted that the performance of subjects undergoing an experiment improves simply because the subjects know that they are being observed and thus are somehow being treated as special). Other reasons suggested for the improvement were the much shorter commuting time to work and—perhaps the most important—the isolation of the engineers from the "distractions" provided by the many meetings that they had to attend at their usual place of work. Of course, some of these meetings are meant to inform employees about the company and keep the engineers involved with company goings-on. The trade-off between keeping engineers involved and motivated about the company as a whole and keeping them focused and productive on a particular project is a complicated one. Making such choices between short- and long-term goals is the manager's job and requires careful thought and deliberation.

In addition to the foregoing tangible factors, many intangible factors affect productivity and reduce the credibility of a company's published numbers. Examples of these intangible factors are personnel turnover, canceled projects, reorganizations, and restructuring of systems for better quality.

### 8.2.2   People and Productivity

Because software engineering is predominantly an intellectual activity, the most important ingredient for producing high-quality software efficiently is people. As we mentioned in the last section, experimental evidence shows that the most critical factor of productivity is the capability of the engineers. Despite the intuitive appeal of this notion and strong supporting empirical evidence for it, many managers and organizations consistently behave as if they did not believe it. Considering the great difference in software engineering competence between the best and the worst engineers, and the critical importance of engineering competence in attaining high software productivity, the costs of hiring, retaining, and motivating the best engineers can be justified on economic grounds.

Yet, a common misconception held by managers, as evidenced in their staffing, planning, and scheduling practices, is that software engineers are interchangeable—that is, that one software engineer is as productive as another. In fact, experiments have revealed a large variability in productivity between the best, the average, and the worst engineers. The worst engineers even *reduce* the productivity of the team.

Apart from engineering capability, however, because of the strong amount of interaction required among team members, the personalities of the members also should be taken into account. Some engineers function better on centrally controlled teams, while others are better suited for teams with decentralized control. In short, engineers are simply not interchangeable, due to underlying reasons that have to do with both technical ability and personality.

Another common management practice that fails to recognize the importance of people in the software engineering process is that managers often staff a project with the best available people, rather than attempting to find the best people *per se*. Considering the strong impact of personnel capability on software costs, this is a foolish thing to do. In effect, by assigning ill-prepared engineers to a project, the manager is committing the organization to a training period for those engineers. If this commitment is unintentional and the training haphazard, there is a strong risk that the training will be ineffective and the project unsuccessful or at least late. The way to solve the problem of finding appropriate people must be faced deliberately: One must schedule the training period as a required task, train the people appropriately, hire outside consultants, and control the project closely, perhaps by scheduling frequent incremental deliveries. The point is to recognize the utter importance of key personnel to an intellectual project such as software engineering.

### 8.2.3   Cost Estimation

Cost estimation is part of the planning stage of any engineering activity. Cost estimation in software engineering faces the same challenges as other design-intensive intellectual activities. In such activities, the primary cost is for people. In other engineering disciplines, the cost of materials—chips, bricks, or aluminum, depending on the activity—is a major component of the cost that must be estimated. In software engineering, to estimate the cost, we "only" have to estimate how many engineers are needed.

Software cost estimation has two uses in software project management. First, during the planning stage, one needs to decide how many engineers are needed for the project and develop a schedule accordingly. Second, in monitoring the project's progress, one needs to assess whether the project is progressing according to schedule and, if it is not, take corrective action. In monitoring progress, the manager needs to ascertain how much work has already been accomplished and how much is left to do. Both of these tasks require a metric for measuring "software work accomplishment."

In Section 6.9.3.1, we discussed Halstead's software science as a method of measuring the complexity of a program. Halstead's metric is applied to an existing piece of software and can be used to compare such things as the complexity of two different programs or the relative benefits of two programming languages. By allowing us to compare the inherent complexity of two programs, the software science metric can also be used to measure the productivity of the two programmers who produced those programs. In the planning stages of a project, however, we do not have the program and therefore cannot use Halstead's or any other code-based metric to measure its inherent complexity. Metrics like Halstead's are called *structural* metrics, because they depend on the structure of the software. Instead, we need a *predictive* method to estimate the complexity of software before it has been developed, based on available information, such as the requirements. As we have seen, function points are an example of this class of metrics.

### 8.2.3.1  *Predictive models of software cost*

While lines of code are not an ideal metric for measuring productivity, they have been used as a metric for the total life cycle costs of software. That is, if we could predict how large a software system was going to be before developing it, that size could be used as a basis for determining how much effort would be required, how many engineers would be needed, and how long it would take to develop the software. Furthermore, the size of the software has been used to infer not just the initial development cost, but also the costs associated with the later stages of the life cycle.

The majority of software cost estimation methods thus start by predicting the size of the software and using that as input for deriving the total effort required, the effort required during each phase of the life cycle, personnel requirements, etc. The size estimate drives the entire estimation process. Inferring this initial estimate and assessing its reliability can be considerably simpler if the organization maintains a database of information about past projects.

We can also base the initial estimate on an analytical technique such as function-point analysis. We first compute the function point for the desired software and then divide it by the number FP/LOC (function point divided by number of lines of code) for the project's programming language to arrive at a size estimate.

Besides basing the estimation of effort on the size of code, most cost estimation models share certain other concepts. The purpose of a software cost model is to predict the total development effort required to produce a given piece of software in terms of the number of engineers and the length of time it will take to develop the software. The general formula used to arrive at the *nominal* development effort is

$$PM_{initial} = c\ KLOC^k$$

That is, the nominal number of programmer-months is a function of the number of lines of code. The constants c and k are given by the model. The exponent k is greater than 1, causing the estimated effort to grow nonlinearly with the size of the code. To take into account the many variables that can affect the productivity of the project, so-called cost drivers are used to scale this initial estimate of effort. For example, if modern programming practices are being used, the estimate is scaled downward; if there are real-time reliability requirements, the estimate is scaled upward. The particular cost-driver items are determined and validated empirically. In general, the cost drivers can be classified as being attributes of the following items:

- *Product*. For example, reliability requirements or inherent complexity.
- *Computer*. For example, are there execution time or storage constraints?
- *Personnel*. For example, are the personnel experienced in the application area or the programming language being used?
- *Project*. For example, are sophisticated software tools being used?

The particular attributes in each class differ from model to model. For example, some models use object code for the size estimate, others use source code, and some both object code and source code. Personnel attributes that can be considered include the capability and continuity (absence of turnover) of the personnel. Table 8.2 shows the set of factors considered by different models, classified into five distinct groups of attributes. Size is separated into its own group because of its importance and the different ways in which it is treated in the various models.

The following are the basic steps for arriving at the cost of a proposed software system:

1. Estimate the software's eventual size, and use it in the model's formula to arrive at an initial estimate of effort.
2. Revise the estimate by using the cost driver or other scaling factors given by the model.
3. Apply the model's tools to the estimate derived in step 2 to determine the total effort, activity distribution, etc.

The Constructive Cost Model, known by its acronym COCOMO, is a well-known cost estimation model. The original model, developed in the 1980s, has undergone evolution over time, to become COCOMO II. The original COCOMO was actually a set of three different models of increasing complexity and level of detail. Next, we give an overview of the intermediate model and the steps and details involved in the use of such a model. Then we discuss how COCOMO II differs from the original COCOMO.

### 8.2.3.2  *COCOMO*

The following are some details of how COCOMO applies the general estimation steps:

1. The code size estimate is based on delivered source instructions, KDSI. The initial (nominal) development effort is based on the project's development "mode." COCOMO categorizes the software being developed according to three modes: *organic, semidetached,* and *embedded*. Table 8.3 shows how to

| Group | Factor |
|---|---|
| Size Attributes | Source instructions |
| | Object instructions |
| | Number of routines |
| | Number of data items |
| | Number of output formats |
| | Documentation |
| | Number of personnel |
| Program attributes | Type |
| | Complexity |
| | Language |
| | Reuse |
| | Required reliability |
| | Display requirements |
| Computer attributes | Time constraint |
| | Storage constraint |
| | Hardware configuration |
| | Concurrent h/w developement |
| | Interfacing equipment, s/w |
| Personnel Attributes | Personnel capability |
| | Personnel continuity |
| | Hardware experience |
| | Application experience |
| | Language experience |
| Project attributes | Tools and techniques |
| | Customer interface |
| | Requirements definition |
| | Requirements volatility |
| | Schedule |
| | Security |
| | Computer access |
| | Travel/rehosting/multi-site |
| | Support software maturity |

TABLE 8.2

Factors used in cost estimation models. (Adapted from Table II of Boehm [1984a], ©1984 IEEE, by permission of IEEE.)

determine the mode of a project. The estimator arrives at the development mode by deciding which entries in the table best characterize the project's features, listed in column 1. The heading on the column that best matches the project is the development mode for the project. For example, flight control software for a new airplane falls into the embedded class, and a standard payroll application falls into the organic class. Study the table carefully to see the effect of the various features on the mode and, therefore, on the development effort.

| Feature | Mode | | |
| --- | --- | --- | --- |
| | **Organic** | **Semidetached** | **Embedded** |
| Organizational understanding of product objectives | Thorough | Considerable | General |
| Experience in working with related software systems | Extensive | Considerable | Moderate |
| Need for software conformance with pre-established requirements | Basic | Considerable | Full |
| Need for software conformance with external interface specifications | Basic | Considerable | Full |
| Concurrent development of associated new hardware and operational procedures | Some | Moderate | Extensive |
| Need for innovative data processing architectures, algorithms | Minimal | Some | Considerable |
| Premium on early completion | Low | Medium | High |
| Product size range | <50 KDSI | <300 KDSI | All sizes |
| **Examples** | Batch data reduction | Most transaction processing systems | Large, complex transaction processing systems |
| | Scientific models | New OS, DBMS | Ambitious, very large OS |
| | Busniess models | Ambitious, inventory, production control | Avionics |
| | Familiar OS, compiler | Simple command-control | Ambitious command-control |

TABLE 8.3

COCOMO Software development modes. (From Boehm [1984a], ©1984 IEEE, reprinted by permission of IEEE.)

Each development mode has an associated formula for determining the nominal development effort based on the estimated size of the code. The formulas are shown in Table 8.4. Tables 8.3 and 8.4 together can be considered a quantitative summary of a considerable amount of experimental data collected by Boehm over the years.

**2.** The estimator determines the effort multiplier for the particular project, based on cost-driver attributes. COCOMO uses 15 such attributes to scale the nominal development effort. These attributes are a subset of the general factors listed in Table 8.2 and are given in Table 8.5, along with the multiplier used for each, based on rating the driver for the particular project.

There is a guideline for determining how to rate each attribute for the project at hand. The rating ranges from very low to extra high. The multipliers are

TABLE 8.4

COCOMO Nominal effort and schedule equations. (From Boehm [1984a], ©1984 IEEE, by permission of IEEE.)

| Development mode | Nominal effort | Schedule |
|---|---|---|
| Organic | $(PM)_{NOM} = 3.2(KDSI)^{1.05}$ | $TDEV = 2.5(PM_{DEV})^{0.38}$ |
| Semidetached | $(PM)_{NOM} = 3.0(KDSI)^{1.12}$ | $TDEV = 2.5(PM_{DEV})^{0.35}$ |
| Embedded | $(PM)_{NOM} = 2.8(KDSI)^{1.20}$ | $TDEV = 2.5(PM_{DEV})^{0.32}$ |

multiplied together, and the resulting product is multiplied by the nominal effort derived in step 1 to arrive at the estimate of total effort for the project. Table 8.5 contains a wealth of information. For example, the range of the multipliers for each factor shows the impact of that factor and how much control the manager has over the factor. As an example, the range of analyst capability shows that the difference between using an analyst of very high capability and one of very low capability is a factor of two in the cost estimate. The product attributes, in general, are fixed by the inherent complexity of the product and are not within the control of the manager.

**3.** Given the estimate of the total effort in step 2, COCOMO allows the derivation of various other important numbers and analyses. For example, Table 8.4 (third column) shows the formulas, again based on the development mode, for deriving a recommended length for the project schedule, on the basis of the estimate of the total effort for the project.

The COCOMO model allows sensitivity analyses based on changing the parameters. For example, one can model the change in development time as a function of relaxing the reliability constraints or improving the software development environment. Or one can analyze the cost and impact of unstable hardware on a project's software schedule.

Software cost estimation models such as COCOMO are required for an engineering approach to software management. Without such models, one has only judgment to rely on, which makes decisions hard to trust and justify. Worse, one can never be sure whether improvements are being made to the software. While current models still lack a full scientific justification, they can be used and validated against an organization's project database.

A software development organization should maintain a project database that stores information about the progress of projects. Such a database can be used in many ways: to validate a particular cost estimation model against past projects; to calibrate cost-driver or scaling factors for a model, based on an organization's particular environment; as a basis for arriving at an initial size estimate; or to calibrate estimates of effort that are derived from a model.

The current state of the art of cost estimation modeling makes it hard to have complete trust in the results of the models, but such tools are nevertheless essential for a software development organization as a whole. They can be used to complement expert judgment and intuition.

### 8.2.3.3  *COCOMO II*

Two major issues showed deficiencies in the use of the COCOMO model and motivated a rethinking of the model that eventually led to COCOMO II. The first difficulty

| Cost Drivers | Ratings | | | | | |
| --- | --- | --- | --- | --- | --- | --- |
| | Very low | Low | Nominal | High | Very High | Extra High |
| **Product attributes** | | | | | | |
| Required software reliability | .75 | .88 | 1.00 | 1.15 | 1.40 | |
| Data base size | | .94 | 1.00 | 1.08 | 1.16 | |
| Product complexity | .70 | .85 | 1.00 | 1.15 | 1.30 | 1.65 |
| **Computer attributes** | | | | | | |
| Execution time constraints | | | 1.00 | 1.11 | 1.30 | 1.66 |
| Main storage constraints | | | | | | |
| Platform volatility | | .87 | 1.00 | 1.15 | 1.30 | |
| Computer turn around time | | .87 | 1.00 | 1.07 | 1.15 | |
| **Personnel attributes** | | | | | | |
| Analyst capability | 1.46 | 1.19 | 1.00 | .86 | .71 | |
| Applications experience | 1.29 | 1.13 | 1.00 | .91 | .82 | |
| Programmer capability | 1.42 | 1.17 | 1.00 | .86 | .70 | |
| Virtual machine experience[*] | 1.21 | 1.10 | 1.00 | .90 | | |
| Programming language experience | 1.14 | 1.07 | 1.00 | .95 | | |
| **Project attributes** | | | | | | |
| Use of modern programming practices | 1.24 | 1.10 | 1.00 | .91 | .82 | |
| Use of software tools | 1.24 | 1.10 | 1.00 | .91 | .83 | |
| Required development schedule | 1.23 | 1.08 | 1.00 | 1.04 | 1.10 | |

TABLE 8.5

Effort multipliers used by the COCOMO intermediate model. (From Boehm [1984a], ©1984 IEEE,
reprinted by permission of IEEE.)

was COCOMO's assumption about the process model. The original COCOMO model is strictly geared toward traditional development life cycle models, according to which custom software is built from precisely stated specifications. Its application to newer life cycle approaches—which include nonsequential and rapid-development processes, reuse-driven developments involving off-the-shelf commercial packages, or object-oriented approaches supported by distributed middleware—caused increasing difficulties. The second difficulty was COCOMO's reliance on lines of code as an estimator. It has become increasingly clear that the number of lines of code is hard or even impossible to estimate early in the development cycle.

COCOMO II differs from COCOMO in a number of aspects. First, it is more properly the collection of three different models: the Application Composition Model, the Early Design Model, and the Post-Architecture Model. Second, it uses different models for software size, spanning different ranges of accuracy, from object points to source lines of code.

The *Application Composition Model* is suitable for projects in which software is built around a graphical user interface (GUI) and modern GUI-builder tools are used in the development of the software. The model is often employed during the initial phases of an incrementally developed application, when the prototype of the user interface and of the user-system interaction mechanisms are being developed. This cost prediction model uses a new size metric, called *object points*, which are an extension of function points that is used to indicate the complexity of the application. Object points are a count of the screens, reports, and modules that need to be developed for the application, each weighted by a three-level complexity factor (simple, medium, difficult). The object-point metric is commensurate with the coarse level of detail that is generally available when an Application Composition type of product is in the planning phase (i.e., when cost estimation is to be performed). The *Early Design Model* is used once the requirements are known and alternative software architectures have been explored. According to this model, cost prediction is based on size (given in terms of function points) and a number of coarse-grained cost drivers, which account for such factors as personnel capability and experience. Finally, the *Post-Architecture Model* involves the actual software construction and software maintenance. Here, cost prediction is based on the following items:

- size, expressed either as source instructions or function points (with modifiers to account for reuse);
- 17 multiplicative cost drivers;
- a set of five factors that determine the growth of person-month costs in terms of size.

### Exercises

**8.5** Suppose you are faced with developing a system that you expect will have about 100,000 lines of source instructions. Compute the nominal effort and the development time for each of the three development modes (i.e. organic, semidetached, and embedded).

**8.6** You are the manager of a new project charged with developing a 100,000-line embedded system. You have a choice of hiring from two pools of engineers: highly capable programmers with very little experience in the programming language being used and programmers of low quality, but with a lot of experience with the programming language. What is the impact of hiring all your engineers from one or the other group?

## 8.3 PROJECT CONTROL

As we have said, the purpose of controlling a project is to monitor the progress of the activities against the plans, in order to ensure that the goals are being approached and, eventually, will be achieved. Another aspect of control is to detect, as soon as possible, when deviations from the plan are occurring, so that corrective action may be taken. In software engineering, as in any design-dominated discipline, it is especially important to plan realistically—even conservatively—so as to minimize the need for corrective action. For example, whereas in a manufacturing-dominated discipline it may be justifiable to hire the minimum number of workers necessary and add more employees if production falls below the required level, it has been observed in software engineering that adding people to a project which is late can delay the project even further. This point underscores the importance of not only planning, but also controlling, in software engineering. The sooner deviations from the plan are detected, the more it is possible to cope with them.

### 8.3.1    Work Breakdown Structures

Most project control techniques are based on breaking down the goal of the project into several intermediate goals, each of which can in turn be broken down further. This process can be repeated until each goal is small enough to be well understood. We can then plan for each goal individually—its resource requirements, assignment of responsibility scheduling, etc.

A semiformal way of breaking down the goal is called the *work breakdown structure (WBS)*. With this technique, one builds a tree whose root is labeled by the major activity of the project, such as "build a compiler." Each node of the tree can be broken down into smaller components that are designated the children of the node. This "work breakdown" can be repeated until each leaf in the tree represents a piece of work that the manager feels confident to estimate in terms of size, difficulty, and resource requirements. Figure 8.1 shows the work breakdown structure for a simple compiler development project.

The goal of a work breakdown structure is to identify all the activities that a project must undertake. The tasks can be broken down into as fine a level of detail as is desired or necessary. For example, we might have shown the substructure of a node labeled "design" as consisting of the three different activities of designing the scanner, parser, and code generator. The structure can be used as a basis for estimating the amount of resources necessary for the project as a whole by estimating the resources required for each leaf.

The work breakdown structure is a simple tool that gives the manager a framework for decomposing large tasks into more manageable pieces. Once these pieces have been identified, they can be used as units of work to assign to people. The structure can be refined and extended easily by labeling the nodes with appropriate information, such as the planned length of the activity, the name of the person responsible

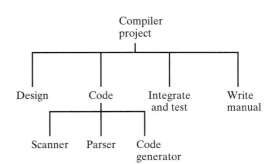

**FIGURE 8.1**

Work breakdown structure for a compiler project.

for the activity, and the starting and ending date of the activity. In this way, the structure can summarize the project plans.

The work breakdown structure can also be used as input into the scheduling process, as we shall see in the subsections that follow. In decomposing the work, we are trying to decide *which* tasks need to be done. In scheduling, we decide the *order* in which to do the tasks. Each work item in the work breakdown structure is associated with an *activity* to perform that item. A schedule tries to order the activities to ensure their timely completion.

Two general notations used for scheduling are Gantt charts and PERT charts. We present these in the next two subsections.

### 8.3.2    Gantt Charts

Gantt charts (developed by Henry L. Gantt) are a project control technique that can be used for several purposes, including scheduling, budgeting, and resource planning. A Gantt chart is a bar chart, with each bar representing an activity. The bars are drawn against a timeline. The length of each bar is proportional to the length of time planned for the activity.

Let us draw a Gantt chart for the tasks identified in the WBS of Figure 8.1. We estimate the number of days required for each of the six tasks as follows: initial design, 45; scanner, 20; parser, 60; code generator, 180; integration and testing, 90; and writing the manual, 90. Using these estimates, we can draw a Gantt chart of the compiler project. (See Figure 8.2.)

A Gantt chart helps in scheduling the activities of a project, but it does not help in identifying them. One can begin with the activities identified in the work breakdown structure, as we did for the compiler example. However, during the scheduling activity, and also during implementation of the project, new activities may be identified that were not envisioned during the initial planning. The manager must then go back and revise the breakdown structure and the schedules to deal with these new activities.

The Gantt chart in Figure 8.2 is actually an enhanced version of standard Gantt charts. The white part of the bar shows the length of time each task is estimated to take. The gray part shows the "slack" time—that is, the latest time by which a task must be finished. One way to view the slack time is that, if necessary, we can slide the white area over the gray area without having to delay the start of the next activity. For example, we have the freedom to delay the start of building the scanner to as late as October 17 and still have it finished in time to avoid delaying the integration and testing activity. The chart shows clearly that the results of the scanner and parser tasks can be used only after the code generator task is completed (in the integration and testing task). A bar that is all white, such as that representing the code generator task, has no slack and must be started and completed on the scheduled dates if the schedule is to be maintained. From the figure, we can see that the tasks "design," "code generator," and "integration and testing" have no slack. It is these tasks, then, that determine the total length of time the project is expected to take.

This example shows that the Gantt chart can be used to allocate resources and plan staffing. For example, from Figure 8.2, we can conclude that the same engineer

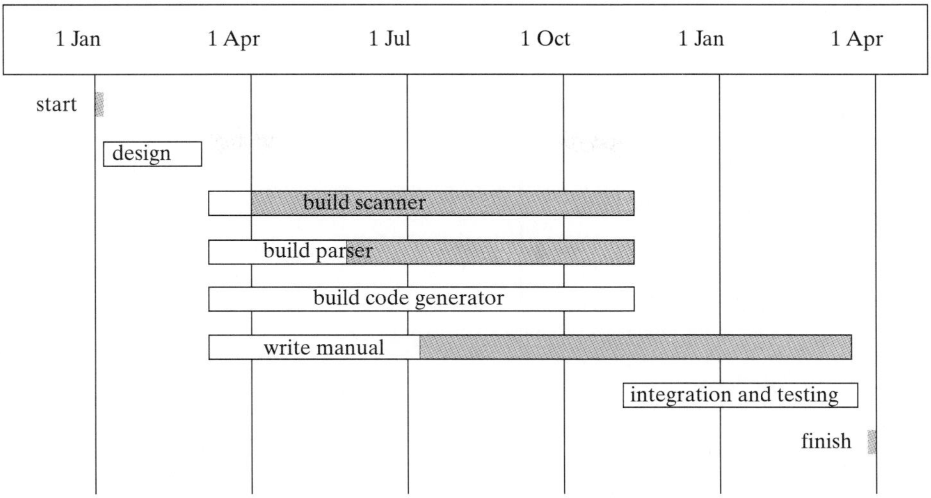

**FIGURE 8.2**

Gantt chart for a simple compiler project.

can be assigned to do the scanner and the parser while another engineer is working on the code generator. Even so, the first engineer will have some slack time that we may plan to use to help the second engineer or to get a head start on the integration and testing activity.

Gantt charts can take different forms, depending on their intended use. They are best used for resource planning and scheduling. For example, if we are trying to schedule the activities of six engineers, we might use a Gantt chart in which each bar represents one of the engineers. In such a chart, the engineers are our resources and the chart shows the *resource loading* during the project. It can help, for example, in scheduling vacation time or in ensuring that the right number of engineers will be available during each desired period. Figure 8.3 shows an example. We could label appropriate sections of the bars to show how much time we expect each engineer to spend on each activity (e.g., designing and building the scanner).

While Gantt charts show each task and its duration clearly, and are therefore useful for resource planning and scheduling, they do not highlight *intertask dependencies*. PERT charts, the subject of the next section, show these dependencies directly.

## 8.3.3 PERT Charts

A PERT (Program Evaluation and Review Technique) chart is a network of boxes (or circles) and arrows. There are different variations of PERT charts. Some use the boxes to represent activities, and some use the arrows to do so. We will use the first approach here. Each box thus represents an activity. Arrows are used to show the dependencies of activities on one another. The activity at the head of an arrow cannot start until the activity at the tail of the arrow is finished. Just as with the nodes in the work break-

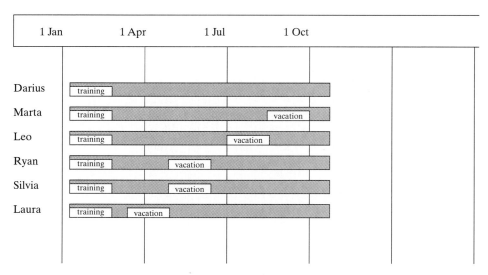

FIGURE 8.3

Gantt chart for scheduling six engineers.

down structure, the boxes in a PERT chart can be decorated with starting and ending dates for activities; the arrows help in computing the earliest possible starting dates for the boxes at their heads. Some boxes can be designated as *milestones*. A milestone is an activity whose completion signals an important accomplishment in the life of the project. By contrast, the failure to make a milestone signals trouble to the manager and requires an explicit action to deal with the deviation from the schedule.

As with Gantt charts, to build a PERT chart for a project, one must first list all the activities required for completion of the project and estimate how long each will take. Then one must determine the dependence of the activities on each other. The PERT chart gives a graphical representation of this information. Clearly, the technique does not help in deciding which activities are necessary or how long each will take, but it does force the manager to take the necessary planning steps to answer these questions.

Figure 8.4 shows a PERT chart for the previous compiler project. The information from the work breakdown structure of Figure 8.1 is used to decide what boxes are needed. The arrows give the new information that was not available in the work breakdown structure. The chart shows clearly that the project consists of the activities of performing the initial design, building a scanner, building a parser, building a code generator, integrating and testing all of these, and writing a manual. Recall that the previous estimates for these six tasks were, respectively, 45, 20, 60, 180, 90, and 90 days.

The figure assumes that the project will start on January 1. Taking holidays (January 1 and 2) into account, we see that the design work will start on January 3. Since the design activity is estimated to take 45 days, any activity that follows the design may start on March 7 at the earliest. The dependency arrows help us compute these earliest start dates on the basis of our estimates of the duration of each activity. These dates are shown in the

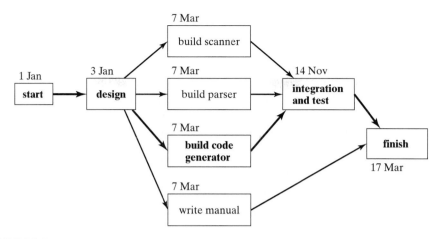

**FIGURE 8.4**

PERT chart for a simple compiler project. Activities on the critical path are shown in boldface type.

figure. We could also compute the earliest finish dates, latest start dates, or latest finish dates, depending on the kind of analysis we want to perform.

The chart shows that the path through the project that consists of the "design," "build code generator," and "integration and testing" activities is the *critical path* for the project. Any delay in any activity in this path will cause a delay in the entire project. The manager must monitor the activities on the critical path much more closely than the other activities.

The following are some of the salient features of a PERT chart:

- It forces and helps the manager to plan.
- It shows the interrelationships among the tasks in the project and, in particular, clearly identifies the critical path of the project, thus helping to focus on it. For example, in the figure, the code generator is clearly the most critical activity in terms of the schedule. The critical path is shown by a dark solid line. We may decide to build a separate subproject for this activity alone, put our best people on the project, or monitor the critical activity more closely. The PERT chart exposes the critical path and allows us the opportunity to consider alternative approaches to cope with a potential problem.
- It exposes all possible parallelism in the activities and thus helps in allocating resources.
- It allows scheduling and simulation of alternative schedules.
- It enables the manager to monitor and control the project.

Despite these advantages, PERT is just a tool, and its use does not automatically guarantee the success of the project. The manager has much latitude in how PERT is used. For example, the granularity of the activities is completely up to the manager. In the compiler example, we could have included such activities as hiring people, purchasing equipment, and securing office space, or we could have added subactivities such as coding, reviewing, and testing for each activity shown. The accuracy of the estimates of the length of time taken by the activities is also an important factor in how well the PERT chart can help in the scheduling activity.

Many variations of PERT charts are possible. For example, we could be interested in the earliest time at which an event can be accomplished or the latest time at which it can be accomplished. In the model presented, there is only one resource associated with each activity: time. We can also incorporate other resources, such as personnel requirements or computer time, to help with budgeting for the project.

For a big project, a PERT chart may contain hundreds of nodes and span many pages. The availability of computer support is essential for managing large PERT networks. Many such tools are available on the market. They support both the initial preparation of the network and the continuous updating of the chart during the project. These tools make it possible to experiment with different scheduling options in order to create different critical paths.

Gantt charts can be derived automatically from PERT charts. Each kind of chart has its own place in the manager's toolbox of control techniques. The Gantt chart helps in planning the utilization of resources, while the PERT chart is better for monitoring the timely progress of activities. If rescheduling becomes necessary—for example, because of a missed milestone—we may want to go back and draw new Gantt charts for replanning the utilization of resources. Again, since these charts are often revised, computer support is essential.

### Exercises

---

**8.7**    In the PERT variation in which activities are associated with arrows, boxes represent the completion of the activities. For example, instead of "build scanner," which is an activity, a box would say "scanner coded," which is an event. Draw a PERT chart with this new convention for the previous example of a compiler.

**8.8**    For the PERT chart of Figure 8.4, decorate the boxes with the following dates that are of interest in different scheduling situations: *earliest start time, earliest finish time, latest allowable start time, latest allowable finish time.*

---

### 8.3.4    Dealing with Deviations from the Plan

Gantt and PERT charts are useful for scheduling the activities and resources of a project. They are also useful for monitoring the progress of the project and detecting deviations from the planned schedule. As each activity is completed, it can be noted in the chart by marking the associated boxes and arrows or bars. Any late completions are easily noticed. Of course, if a delay is associated with a milestone, that is a more serious problem and requires some action on the part of the manager. In addition to checking the chart when activities are completed, the manager should consult the chart at frequent intervals during the project to evaluate its status.

No matter how deviations from the schedule are detected, the manager must decide how to handle them. In activities where production is limited by raw human labor, it is usual to try to get back on schedule by adding people or increasing overtime for existing people. In software engineering and other design activities, however, it is not labor, but intellectual power, that is in short supply. It is much more difficult, therefore, to deal with deviations from the schedule.

The choices of the software engineering manager are rather limited, but there are some options that must be considered carefully. While it is important to recognize that merely adding engineers is not going to help meet the schedule, it is as important to recognize that the right engineering talent *can* help. Thus, temporarily reassigning senior engineers to a part of the project that is suffering or hiring expert troubleshooting consultants are viable options.

Another option is to examine the requirements and remove the ones that are not absolutely necessary. Sometimes, the requirements are "gold plated"; that is, there is too much attempt to provide a shiny veneer that does not add to the substance of the product. Cutting out unnecessary requirements is called *requirements scrubbing*. The success of such a recovery action is directly related to the incrementality principle described in Chapter 3. Even if we are not planning incremental delivery of the product, it is important to design a product that may be divided into subsets. Furthermore, it is key that development proceed incrementally in the order of importance of the requirements. It will not be helpful if we decide that we can scrub some requirements in order to recover from a slip in the schedule, but those requirements have already been implemented. Thus, the incrementality principle must be followed not only during requirements analysis, but also during project planning, scheduling, and implementation.

It is possible that after we consider all options for recovering from a slip in the schedule, we find no appropriate solution. At this point, the best thing to do is to admit the incorrectness of the original plans and schedules and revise the schedule on the basis of new knowledge about the difficulties of the tasks, the capabilities of the engineers, and the availability of the resources. The manager must view a schedule as the best attempt to predict the development cycle. Still, it is merely a prediction, and while it is important to attempt to produce the most accurate prediction possible, it is also important to realize the risks involved with predictions and be prepared to revise the plans if necessary. Clearly, the larger the consequences of a slip in the schedule are, the more important it is to plan and schedule carefully. For example, if a slip will delay the introduction of a product that has been scheduled for months, and invitations have already been sent out to newspaper reporters and security analysts to attend the formal introduction, almost any attempt to recover from such a slip can be justified. In less dramatic cases, accepting a delay may be the right course of action.

## 8.4    ORGANIZATION

The organizing function of management deals with devising roles for individuals and assigning responsibility for accomplishing project goals. Organization is basically motivated by the need for cooperation when the goals are not achievable by a single individual in a reasonable amount of time. The aim of an organizational structure is to facilitate cooperation towards a common goal. An organizational structure is necessary at any level of an enterprise, whether it is to coordinate the efforts of a group of vice presidents who report to the president of the corporation or to orchestrate the interactions among programmers who report to a common project manager.

Management theorists and practitioners have studied the effects of different organizational structures on the productivity and effectiveness of groups. Because the goal of organization is to encourage cooperation, and because cooperation depends substantially on human characteristics, many general organizational rules apply to any endeavor, whether it deals with software production or automobile production.

The nature of software, however, as we discussed in Chapters 1 and 2, distinguishes it from other human artifacts to the extent that it also influences the effectiveness of different organizational structures applied to software development. In this section, we discuss how the unique characteristics of software can guide us in the choice of the appropriate organizational structure and how the right organization can help in achieving software qualities.

The task of organizing can be viewed as building a team: Given a group of people and a common goal, what is the best role for each individual, and how should responsibilities be divided? Analogies with sports teams are illuminating. A basketball team consists of five players on the floor who are playing the game and another perhaps five players who are sitting on the bench as substitutes. Each player knows his or her role. There is one ball, and at any one time, only one player can have it. All other players must know their responsibilities and what to expect from the player with the ball. On well-organized teams, the patterns of cooperation and their effects are clearly visible. In poorly organized teams or teams with novice players, the lack of patterns of cooperation is just as clearly visible: When one player has the ball, the other four scream for it to be passed to them. The player with the ball, of course, shoots the ball instead of passing it to anyone! We observe a similar phenomenon in Case Study A in the appendix of the book.

Some of the considerations that affect the choice of an organizational structure are similar to the factors used in cost estimation models that we have seen earlier. For example, what constitutes an appropriate organization for a project depends on the length of the project. Is it a long-term project or a short, one-shot project? If it is a long-term project, it is important to ensure job satisfaction for individuals, leading to high morale that reduces turnover. Sometimes, the best composition for a team is a mix of junior and senior engineers. This allows the junior engineers to do the less challenging tasks and learn from the senior engineers, who are busy performing the more challenging tasks and overseeing the progress of the junior engineers.

Because of the nature of large software systems, changing requirements, and the difficulties of software specification, it has been observed that adding people to a project late in the development cycle leads to further delays in the schedule. Thus, the issue of personnel turnover is a serious one that must be minimized. On a short-term project, personnel turnover is not as important an issue. On a long-term project, it is essential to allow junior personnel to develop their skills and gain more responsibility as senior personnel move on to other responsibilities. The trade-offs involved in organizing for a short-term or a long-term project are similar to those involved in organizing a basketball team to win a single game, to be a winner over a single season, or to be a consistent winner over many years.

Another issue affecting the appropriate project organization is the nature of the task and how much communication the different team members need to have among themselves. For example, in a well-defined task such as building a payroll system in which modules and their interfaces have been specified clearly, there is not much need for project members to communicate among each other, and excessive communication will probably lead to a delay in accomplishing their individual tasks. On the other hand, in a project where the task is not clearly understood, communication among team members is beneficial and can lead to a better solution. Strictly hierarchical organizations minimize and discourage communication among team members; more democratic organizations encourage it.

One of the general considerations in team organization is the appropriate size for the team. On the one hand, a small team leads to a more cohesive design, less overhead, more unity, and higher morale. On the other hand, some tasks are too complex to be solved by a small team. Since we cannot control the size or the complexity of the tasks we have to solve, we need to match the size and organization of the team to the problem. Too few people cannot solve an inherently large problem, but assigning an inherently small problem to a large team also leads to problems, such as too much overhead, overambitious solutions, and solutions that are too costly.

The direct relationship between program complexity and team size, as we saw in Section 8.2.3.1, is formalized by the COCOMO model, where, given the estimate of the size of the software, we can derive the required number of engineers from a formula. How should these engineers be grouped into teams? In general, a small team suffers less overhead and therefore has more productivity per member. We can summarize the considerations of team size as follows: A team should be large enough, but not too large, and small enough, but not too small. Experimental evidence has shown that the optimal size for programming teams is between three and eight, depending on the task. If more than eight people are needed, one can introduce extra levels of management to keep the span of control of each manager manageable.

The size of a team involved in software development is influenced by the characteristics of the software. If a group of modules exhibits high coupling (as described in Chapter 3), assigning the modules to different people will require too much interaction among the programmers. Thus, an appropriate design must be accompanied by an appropriate assignment of tasks to individuals and an appropriate team organization that makes that assignment possible. Rather than dogmatically dictating a team organization, one must have a flexible approach and choose the organization on the basis of the design of the system. Of course, the design must be produced by a team in the first place, and a good way to approach the task of building the team is incrementally: Start with a small team that produces a first set of the requirements and design, form a larger team and produce a first implementation, and then use the results produced by the team to decide whether an iteration of the whole cycle is required (as in the spiral model), with a possible need for a team reorganization.

Unfortunately, while reorganizing a team might in theory be the best way to accomplish a task, it disrupts people's routines and conflicts with human beings' need for security and inertia. When, why, and how to reorganize a team requires judgment on the part of the manager and cannot be based solely on the design of the software system. As always, the manager must weigh many factors, including the need to complete the project on schedule, to meet budget constraints, to produce a product that meets quality requirements—such as maintainability, which will reduce the project's overall life cycle costs—to keep the engineers motivated and satisfied for future projects, and to allow engineers to both exercise their individuality when desirable and conform to team standards when necessary.

As in any engineering discipline, software engineering requires not only the application of systematic techniques to routine aspects of the software, but also invention and ingenuity when standard techniques are not adequate. Balancing these requirements is one of the most difficult aspects of software engineering management. Clearly, ingenuity and invention cannot be scheduled, but practical software development requires schedules and cost forecasts. Depending on the task, therefore, the organization must allow individual creativity while "legislating" team standards when necessary.

We can categorize software development team organizations according to where decision-making control lies. A team can have centralized control, in which a recognized leader is responsible for and authorized to produce a design and resolve all technical issues. Alternatively, a team's organization can be based on distributing decision-making control and emphasizing consensus. Both of these types of organization, as well as combinations of the two, have been used in practice successfully. The subsections that follow discuss the two kinds of organization in more detail.

### 8.4.1 Centralized-Control Team Organization

Centralized-control team organization is a standard management technique in well-understood disciplines. In this mode of organization, several workers report to a supervisor who directly controls their tasks and is responsible for their performance. Centralized control is based on a hierarchical organizational structure in which a number of supervisors report to a "second-level" manager and so on up the chain, to the president of the enterprise. In general, centralized control works well with tasks which are simple enough that the one person responsible for control of the project can grasp the problem and its solution.

One way to centralize the control of a software development team is through a *chief-programmer team*. In this kind of organization, one engineer, known as the chief programmer, is responsible for the design and all the technical details of the project. The chief programmer reports to a peer project manager who is responsible for the administrative aspects of the project. Other members of the team are a software librarian and programmers who report to the chief programmer and are added to the team on a temporary basis when needed. Specialists may be used as consultants to the team. The need for programmers and consultants, as well as what tasks they perform, is determined by the chief programmer, who initiates and controls all decisions. The software library maintained by the librarian is the central repository for all the software, documentation, and decisions made by the team. Figure 8.5 is a graphical representation of patterns of control and communication supported by this kind of organization.

The chief-programmer team organization has been likened to a surgical team performing an operation. During an operation, one person must be clearly in control, and all other people involved must be in total support of the "chief" surgeon; there is no place or time for individual creativity or group consensus. This analogy highlights the strengths of the chief-programmer team organization, as well as its weaknesses. The chief-programmer team organization works well when the task is well understood, is within the intellectual grasp of one individual, and is such that the importance of fin-

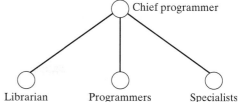

FIGURE 8.5

Patterns of control and communication on a chief-programmer team.

ishing the project outweighs other factors (such as team morale, personnel development, and life cycle costs).

On the negative side, a chief programmer team has a "single point of failure." Since all communication must go through, and all decisions must be made by, the chief programmer, he or she may become overloaded or, indeed, saturated. The success of the chief-programmer team clearly depends on the skill and ability of the chief programmer and the size and complexity of the problem. The choice of chief programmer is the most important determinant of success of the team. Note that, since there is a great variability in people's abilities—as much as a 10-to-1 ratio in productivity—a chief-programmer position may be the best way to exploit the talent of the rare highly proficient engineers.

## 8.4.2  Decentralized-Control Team Organization

In a decentralized-control team organization, decisions are made by consensus, and all work is considered group work. Team members review each other's work and are responsible as a group for what every member produces. Figure 8.6 shows the patterns of control and communication among team members in a decentralized-control organization. The ringlike management structure is intended to show the lack of a hierarchy and that all team members are at the same level.

Such a "democratic" organization leads to higher morale and job satisfaction and, therefore, to less turnover. The engineers feel more ownership of the project and responsibility for the problem, resulting in higher quality in their work. A decentralized-control organization is more suited for long-term projects, because the amount of intragroup communication that it encourages leads to a longer development time, presumably accompanied by lower life cycle costs. The proponents of this kind of team organization claim that it is more appropriate for less understood and more complicated problems, since a group can invent better solutions than a single individual can. Such an organization is based on a technique referred to as "egoless programming," because it encourages programmers to share and review one another's work. Open-source development, discussed in Chapter 7, is the extreme form of egoless programming, with the entire work placed in full view of others, to be examined and improved.

On the negative side, decentralized-control team organization is not appropriate for large teams, where the communication overhead can overwhelm all the engineers, reducing their individual productivity. Decentralized-control team organization also

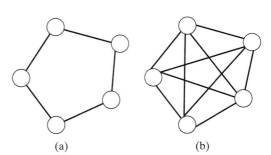

FIGURE 8.6

A decentralized-control team.
**(a)** Management structure. **(b)** Patterns
of communication.

(a)                    (b)

runs the risk of establishing a group that is forever in futile search of a perfect solution that will please everyone.

### 8.4.3  Mixed-Control Team Organization

A mixed-control team organization attempts to combine the benefits of centralized and decentralized control, while minimizing or avoiding their disadvantages. Rather than treating all members the same, as in a decentralized organization, or treating a single individual as the chief, as in a centralized organization, the mixed organization differentiates the engineers into senior and junior engineers. Each senior engineer leads a group of junior engineers and reports, in its turn, to a project manager. Control is vested in the project manager and senior programmers, while communication is decentralized among each set of individuals, peers, and their immediate supervisors. The patterns of control and communication in mixed-control organizations are shown in Figure 8.7.

A mixed-mode organization tries to limit communication to within a small group that is most likely to benefit from it. It also tries to realize the benefits of group decision making by vesting authority in a group of senior programmers or architects. The mixed-control organization is an example of the use of a hierarchy to master the complexity of software development as well as organizational structure.

**Case study 8.1: Open-source development team organization**

The open-source development approach is in some sense not suitable to commercial software development projects because of its reliance on (unpaid) volunteer developers and the lack of an organized schedule, but it is useful as a case study because of its ability to develop reliable and useful products.

The team organization is a mixed mode. Each module has a responsible person. Anyone may review the module and send in corrections and other contributions to the responsible person, who is the ultimate arbiter of what goes into the eventual release of the module.

One of the surprising conclusions of the open-source development organization has been that by increasing the number of people on a project, it is indeed possible to achieve more functionality in the product without overwhelming it with communication overhead. The underlying causes of the success of the approach are difficult to assess,

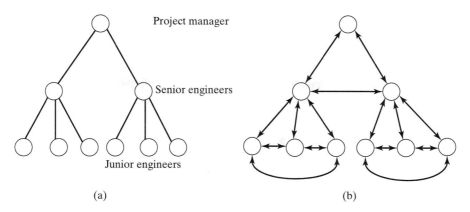

Project manager

Senior engineers

Junior engineers

(a)

(b)

FIGURE 8.7

Mixed-control organizations.
**(a)** Management structure. **(b)** Patterns of communication.

but certainly the combination of a democratic team organization and the appointment of recognized "gurus" to be responsible for key decisions is an essential factor.

### 8.4.4    An Assessment of Team Organizations

In the previous three subsections, we presented different ways of organizing software development teams. Each kind of organization discussed has its proponents and detractors. Each also has its appropriate place.

Experimental assessment of different organizational structures is difficult. It is clearly impractical to run large software development projects using two different types of organization just for the purpose of comparing the effectiveness of the two structures. While cost estimation models can be assessed on the basis of how well they predict actual software costs, an organizational structure cannot be assessed so easily, because one cannot compare the results achieved with those one *would have* achieved with a different organization.

Experiments have been run to measure the effects of such things as the size of the team and the complexity of the task on the effectiveness of development teams. In the choice of team organization, however, it appears that we must be content with the following general considerations:

- Just as no life cycle model is appropriate for all projects, no team organization is appropriate for all tasks.
- Decentralized control is best when communication among engineers is necessary for achieving a good solution.
- Centralized control is best when speed of development is the most important goal and the problem is well understood.
- An appropriate organization limits the amount of communication to what is necessary for achieving the goals of the project—no more and no less.

- An appropriate organization may have to take into account goals other than speed of development, including lower life cycle costs, reduced personnel turnover, repeatability of the process, the development of junior engineers into senior engineers, and widespread dissemination of specialized knowledge and expertise among personnel.

**Case study 8.2: Nokia software factories**

To cope with the huge growth of its business and the increasing importance of software in the development of mobile phones, the Nokia Corporation organizes its software development teams as "software factories." The Nokia software factories are based on four principles:

- *a geographically distributed environment.* A typical project consists of 100 developers dispersed among three to four sites. Working synchronously is not always possible, because of differences in time zones.
- *product family architecture.* An architecture is developed for an entire family, and components are developed to be used in all family members.
- *concurrent engineering.* Components are developed concurrently at different sites. To build a given product, the needed components are retrieved from the various sites and combined in a central location. The parallel development of components shortens the time to market for the product.
- *the use of tools.* The process is supported by the use of tools, especially for requirements engineering, design, coding, version management, configuration management, and testing.

Both the open-source development organization presented in Case Study 8.1 and the Nokia software factories mentioned in this case study are examples of how the Internet has made possible the formation of distributed teams of developers and calls for new models of cooperation and team organization.

## 8.5    RISK MANAGEMENT

An engineering project is expected to produce a reliable product, within a limited time, using limited resources. Any project, however, runs the risk of not producing the desired product, overspending its resource budget, or overrunning its allotted time. Risk accompanies any human activity.

Risk analysis and control is a topic of management theory. Several standard techniques exist for identifying project risks, assessing their impact, and monitoring and controlling them. Knowledge of these techniques allows a project manager to apply them when necessary to increase the chances of success of a project.

We have already seen, in previous chapters, many examples of software development problems that can be viewed from a risk analysis point of view. For example, we have discussed the difficulties of specifying product requirements completely. Given these difficulties, a project runs the risk of producing the wrong product or having the requirements change during development. An effective approach for reducing this risk is prototyping or incremental delivery. A different type of approach to handling the risk of changes in the requirements is to produce a modular design so that such changes can be accommodated by actual changes to the software. Of these approaches, prototyping tries to minimize changes in the requirements, while modular design tries to minimize the *impact* of changes in the requirements. Choosing between the two alternatives, or deciding to use both, should involve a conscious and systematic analysis of the possible risks, their likelihood, and their impact.

An extreme example of poor risk management is given in Case Study A in the appendix. There, improper management of the project caused the entire company to face the risk of bankruptcy. The project was characterized by a total neglect of risk management issues, even though it would have been easy to identify plausible risks and their impact early on and make contingency plans for dealing with them.

At different levels of an organization, different levels of risk can be tolerated. For example, a project manager who is at the beginning of his career may not want to tolerate any delay in the schedule (to minimize risk to his personal career), while his supervisor might be more concerned with the reliability of the product. A project manager might not be willing to tolerate the risk of running over budget by more than 10%, while a higher level manager who is more aware of the value of early time to market, might be willing to overspend the budget by much more if the product can be produced sooner. To complicate matters even more, different people have different tolerances of risk based on their personal nature, as can be evidenced by observing people at a gambling casino.

### Exercise

---

**8.9**    Study Case Study A in the appendix. List three major risks associated with the project described there, and propose a technique for managing each risk.

---

## 8.5.1    Typical Management Risks in Software Engineering

By examining the difficulties that arise in software engineering, we can identify typical areas of risk faced by a software engineering project manager. We have already discussed the example of changes in requirements. Another important risk is not having the right people working on the project. Since there is great variability among the abilities of software engineers, it makes a big difference whether a project is staffed with capable or mediocre engineers. If key positions in a project are staffed with inappropriate people, the project runs the risk of delaying deliveries or producing poor-quality products.

Schedule overrun risks can be reduced by limiting dependencies among tasks. For example, if many tasks cannot be started until a given task is completed, a delay in that one task can delay the entire project. Imagine a computer system project where hardware and software are being developed concurrently. If all software development is scheduled to start after the hardware is completed, any delay in completion of the hardware translates directly into a delay in the entire project. A way to control this scheduling risk is to produce a simulation version of the hardware so that software development can be carried on even if the hardware is delayed. This was done in Case Study C in the appendix.

PERT charts can help a manager identify bottlenecks in the schedule immediately—even mechanically: A node with many outgoing arcs is a sign of trouble, and the manager should try to reschedule activities to avoid it. Such a node should be rescheduled especially if it is on the critical path. One way to reschedule an activity is to break it up into smaller activities such that the arrows going into the original node are distributed among the new (smaller) nodes. Another schedule risk that can be spotted from a PERT chart is a node with many ingoing arcs. This type of node depends on too many activities and often acts as a synchronization point. While such a node may sometimes be necessary, heavy interdependencies should, in general, be avoided.

Table 8.6, from Boehm [1989], can be used as a checklist of common risks and their typical solutions in software engineering management. Examining the risks listed in column 1 of the table, we can see that they overlap the items that are used in software cost estimation models. If a factor has a high multiplier in cost estimation, it represents a risk that must be managed carefully.

## 8.6 CAPABILITY MATURITY MODEL

The Capability Maturity Model (CMM) was developed by the Software Engineering Institute to help both those organizations which develop software to improve their software processes and those organizations which acquire software to assess the quality of their contractors. To fulfill the former goal, CMM provides a guide for software organizations in selecting process improvement strategies by determining the current level of their process maturity and identifying the key factors that would lead to improvement. The underlying assumption, as usual, is that, ultimately, better processes lead to improved quality in the product.

The concept of *maturity* is key in CMM. An immature organization is an organization in which processes are improvised during the course of a project. A process is a sequence of steps that focus on resolving unanticipated crises. Products are often delivered late and their quality is questionable. Conversely, a mature organization has an organizationwide standard approach to software processes that is known and accepted by all engineers. The organization is focused on continuous improvement both in its performance and in the quality of the product. Paulk et al. [1993] states,

> Software process maturity is the extent to which a specific process is explicitly defined, managed, measured, controlled, and effective. Maturity implies a potential for growth in capability and indicates both the richness of an organization's software process and the consistency with which it is applied in projects throughout the organization. As a software organization gains in software maturity, it institutionalizes its software process via policies, standards, and organizational structures. Institutionalization entails building an infrastructure and a corporate culture that supports the methods, practices, and procedures of the business, so that they endure after those who originally defined them have gone.

To capture growth in capability, CMM defines five maturity levels, shown in Figure 8.8, and suggests a number of key practices that help organizations to progress from one level to the next. We briefly review the five levels and discuss the key practices.

| Risk Items | Risk Management Techniques |
|---|---|
| 1. Personnel shortfalls | - Staffing with top talent; job matching; teambuilding; key-personnel agreements; cross training; pre-scheduling key people |
| 2. Unrealistic schedules and budgets | - Detailed multisource cost & schedule estimation; design to cost; incrmental development; software reuse; requirements scrubbing |
| 3. Developing the wrong software functions | - Organization analysis; mission analysis; opsconcept formula-tion; user surveys; prototyping; early user's manuals |
| 4. Developing the wrong user interface | - Prototyping; scenarios; task analysis; user characterization(functionality, style, workload) |
| 5. Gold plating | - Requirments scrubbing; prototyping; cost benefit analysis; design to cost |
| 6. Continuing stream of requirements | - High change threshold; information hiding; incremental development (defer changes to later increments) |
| 7. Shortfalls in externally furnished components | - Benchmarking; inspections; reference checking; compatibility analysis |
| 8. Shortfalls in externally performed tasks | - Refernce checking; pre-award audits; award-fee contracts; competitive design or prototyping; teambuilding |
| 9. Real-time performance shortfalls | - Simulation; benchmarking; modeling; prototyping; instrumentation; tuning |
| 10. Straining computer science capabilities | - Techinal analysis; cost-benefit analysis; prototyping; reference checking |

**TABLE 8.6**

Common risks in software engineering management and techniques for managing them. (From Boehm [1989], reprinted by permission of the author.)

*Level 1* is the *initial* level. Level-1 organizations work on a day-by-day schedule. Their processes are *ad hoc*, often even chaotic. If these organizations succeed in developing quality products, it is only because of the efforts and skills of the individuals involved. In most cases, however, that is not sufficient, especially if projects are complex or if the organization experiences a high turnover in its staffing. Moreover, because of the absence of consolidated knowledge and an organizationwide culture, successful projects can hardly be repeated in other, similar situations.

*Level 2* is the *repeatable* level. At this level, the process does not depend exclusively on individuals, but also on the organization. The required inputs and outputs of the process are clearly identified, the constraints (schedule and budget) are known, and the resources needed to accomplish the goal are carefully evalu-

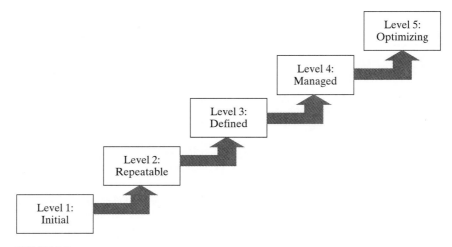

**FIGURE 8.8**

The five levels of CMM and their relationships.

ated and managed. The main focus of a level-2 organization is on management activities. As a consequence of this effort, the process is repeatable, in much the same way as a piece of program with the same inputs and outputs can be executed several times. Each project follows a defined process, but there are no organizationwide, standard processes.

*Level 3* is the *defined* level. At this level, the management and engineering activities that lead to a repeatable process are fully documented, standardized, and integrated. The result is an organizationwide standard process that everyone in the organization knows and follows. Each project may then tailor the standard to develop its own defined process, which accounts for the unique characteristics of the project. Because of the importance of the standard process, a specific group in the organization is often responsible for all the process activities.

*Level 4* is the *managed* level. At this level, the organization sets quantitative goals for both the process and the product. Project and process data are collected and analyzed; then they are used to perform corrective actions and improvements while the project is running.

*Level 5* is the *optimizing* level. At this level, quantitative feedback is incorporated into the process to produce continuous improvement in the organization's processes in general, not just in the currently running process. New technologies and methods that can introduce innovation into the process are carefully evaluated and transferred throughout the organization. Defect analysis is taken seriously. Defects are analyzed carefully in an attempt to uncover their causes, so that steps can be taken to prevent them from recurring.

According to CMM, each maturity level is characterized by some *key process areas* (KPAs). A KPA defines the key practices on which an organization should focus to elevate its process to that maturity level. KPAs are summarized in Table 8.7.

| CMM level | Key process areas |
|-----------|-------------------|
| Initial | None |
| Repeatable | requirements management<br>Software project planning<br>Software project tracking and oversight<br>Software subcontract management<br>Software quality assurance<br>Software configuration management |
| Defined | Organization process focus<br>Organization process definition<br>Training program<br>Intergrated software management<br>Software product engineering<br>Intergroup coordination<br>Peer reviews |
| Managed | Software quality management<br>Quantitive process management |
| Optimizing | Process change management<br>Technology change management<br>Defect prevention |

**TABLE 8.7**

Key process areas for the five levels of CMM.

The intuition behind KPAs is that unless an organization has mastered all the areas in one level of maturity, it is not able to perform at, or even attempt to reach, the next level of maturity. In the table, we can see the importance of configuration management, required at the repeatable level. Peer reviews, such as inspections, are a requirement at the defined level.

## 8.7  CONCLUDING REMARKS

This chapter has presented a concise overview of software engineering management, based on the standard management practice of dividing the management function into planning, organizing, staffing, directing, and controlling. We have discussed the important aspects of software that require special management attention.

While we have talked only about management in the large—that is, management of a group of engineers who must cooperate to produce a common product—many techniques we have discussed can and should be used by the individual engineer as well—that is, in the small. Indeed, each engineer must carefully plan, monitor, and execute the plan for his or her own work. Staffing and directing are the only two management functions that do not apply in the small. In particular, a carefully derived work breakdown structure and PERT chart can help individual engineers on nontrivial activities.

While we have discussed the difficulties in measuring software productivity, we have also stated the importance of defining and collecting such metrics. A software engineering organization must define and adopt metrics, collect measurements on existing projects, and validate the metrics in order to be able to apply management principles to guide the planning, decision making, and monitoring of future projects. In the absence of metrics, there is no way to measure whether progress is being made and, if so, at what rate. In Chapter 6, we studied the goal/question/metric method, which may be used to collect relevant metrics. An active area of research currently is the empirical evaluation of software engineering technologies and processes.

In addition to the technical aspects of management that we have discussed, the manager is involved in resolving conflicts among competing goals. For example,

- In assigning tasks to people, should the experienced engineer be assigned to do all the difficult jobs and get them done fast, or should he or she work with less experienced engineers to train for the future?

- Large software systems exhibit what have been called progressive and antiregressive components in their evolution. A software is evolving progressively when features are being added to it and functionality is increasing. But after adding to the software for a long time, its structure becomes so difficult to deal with, that an effort must be undertaken to restructure the software to make it possible to make further additions later. Reengineering, which does not add any functionality, is an antiregressive component of software, because its goal is to stop the software from regressing beyond hope. The decision that the manager must make is when it is time to undertake antiregressive activities. In its logical extreme, this decision amounts to whether a software system must be retired and a new one developed.

- A common conflict is known as *the mythical man-month conflict*. In some disciplines, people and time are interchangeable; that is, the same task can be accomplished by two people in half the time that it takes a single person. In software engineering, however, adding more people increases the overhead of communication associated with each engineer, preventing a linear increase in productivity with any additional people. In fact, after a certain point in the project, and beyond a certain number of people, adding more people to the project can delay the project rather than speed it up. The difficult task of the manager is to determine when those limits have been reached. The cost estimation models that we have discussed are the beginning of a foundation for allowing such decisions to be made quantitatively.

- Will the approaches that worked on one project work on another project? One of the painfully observed phenomena in software engineering is that many techniques do not scale up; that is, a method that works on smaller projects does not necessarily work on larger projects. Our emphasis throughout the earlier chapters on in-the-small versus in-the-large approaches in, for example, testing or design, was in fact motivated by this inability to scale up in software engineering. A corollary of this observation is that it is not in general possible to derive precise scheduling information from a throwaway prototype. For example, if the prototype demonstrates a tenth of the functionality of the final product, the product will *not* take 10 times the development time that the prototype took. The COCOMO equations reflect this phenomenon.

- Should engineers be encouraged to reuse existing software in order to reduce development time? While software reuse reduces coding time, it may cause difficulties in other phases of the life cycle. If the modules that are reused do not supply the exact interfaces suitable to the design and functionality of the product, they cause the engineer to go through extra effort just to match the interface, and, worse, they lessen the evolvability of the product. Current research is working on discovering ways to decide the costs and benefits of using off-the-shelf components versus in-house development.

Finally, we must recognize that there are no panaceas for software engineering problems. For example, using the latest process—an incremental, prototype-oriented, life cycle model—the latest technology—an advanced tool for configuration management—or the latest methodology—object-oriented analysis and design—will not solve all software production problems. In truth, software engineering is a difficult intellectual activity, and there are no easy solutions to difficult problems. Using the right process, the right technology, the right methodology, and the right tools will certainly help to control the complexities of software engineering, but it will not eliminate them altogether. In practice, because software engineering is such a difficult task at times, and because costs are rising rapidly, managers are tempted to grasp at any believable solution that promises to solve their very real problems.

In sum, a manager has to accept the difficulties of the job and carefully evaluate the impact of any newly proposed panaceas.

## FURTHER EXERCISES

**8.10**  Compare software science measures and function points as measures of complexity. Which do you think is more useful as a predictor of how much a particular software's development will cost?

**8.11**  Consider an application that produces a certain report on a daily, weekly, and monthly basis. Because the focus of function-point analysis is to measure the complexity of an application on the basis of the function it is supposed to provide to users, each report is counted as 1 because it provides a distinct function to the user. Discuss the pros and cons of counting these reports as 3 instead of 1.

**8.12**  Discuss a possible rationale for including, and one for not including, the canceled projects in an organization's productivity measure.

**8.13**  Discuss a possible rationale for including, and one for not including, in an organization's productivity measure, the tools developed in support of a project, but not included in the delivered product.

**8.14**  Discuss the problem of using the lines-of-code productivity metric (DSI) by comparing a programmer who quickly develops a module full of subtle defects that will be discovered after the system is delivered with a programmer who develops a module much more slowly, but without the subtle defects. Discuss possible solutions to this problem.

**8.15**  Some experimental evidence suggests that the initial size estimate for a project affects the nature and results of the project. Consider two different managers charged with developing the same application. One estimates that the size of the application will be

50,000 lines, while the other estimates that it will be 100,000 lines. Discuss how these estimates affect the project throughout its life cycle.

**8.16** Change the WBS of Figure 8.1 to show some subactivities under "design." Modify the Gantt chart of Figure 8.3 and the PERT chart of Figure 8.4 to reflect the change in the WBS.

**8.17** Establishing a chief programmer team is one way of organizing a centralized-control software development team. Describe other ways of organizing a centralized-control team.

**8.18** Argue for or against the following statements:

- A decentralized organization is better than a centralized organization for ill-understood problems.
- For a decentralized organization, a design whereby modules have high coupling is more suited than one whereby modules have low coupling.
- A decentralized organization requires a longer development schedule than does a centralized organization.

**8.19** Suppose you are charged with organizing a team to develop a telephone-switching system that runs on a new processor. (Refer to the case study of Section 7.6.1 for the details associated with a switching system.) Describe a team organization that you would adopt, and justify your choices.

**8.20** Refer to the case study of the budget-control system of Section 7.6.2. Describe how you would organize a chief-programmer team to produce such a system. Describe how you would organize an egoless team to produce the system. Which organization do you think is more appropriate for this kind of system?

**8.21** State the rules for deriving a Gantt chart from a PERT chart, and vice versa. How complete are your rules? As a project, develop a program to do the conversions.

**8.22** Observe that the goal of both Petri nets and PERT charts is to show parallelism and synchronization among activities. State the rules for converting a Petri net to a PERT chart, and vice versa. How complete are your rules? As a project, develop a program to do the conversion.

**8.23** Go back to the case study of Section 7.6.1. Discuss the major risks that were associated with the project and how they were (or could have been) managed.

**8.24** Go back to the case study of Section 7.6.2. Discuss the major risks that were associated with the project and how they were (or could have been) managed.

## HINTS AND SKETCHY SOLUTIONS

**8.4** Find a way to include a count for the library routines that are used.

**8.8** Consider these questions: What if the engineers produce only tools and no product? What if they produce only the product and no tools? What if they produce tools that others can use? What is the behavior that should be rewarded?

**8.10** Consider what the input to each measure is.

**8.15** How many people will be hired? What happens towards the end when one manager discovers that there is a lot more work left to be done, while another might discover that he or she is ahead of schedule?

## BIBLIOGRAPHIC NOTES

Koontz et al. [1980] is a standard textbook on management. Buckle [1977], Bennatan [1992], and Phillips [1998] are more specific to software management. Boehm [1981] is a classic text on understanding and controlling software costs. In another classic, *The Mythical Man-Month*, Brooks [1995] provides many insightful observations on the development of large software systems, including the empirical law that adding people to a project that is late delays the project further. Gilb [1988] discusses software management, with a strong emphasis on the incremental development and delivery approach. DeMarco [1982] is another good book on software management. Boehm [1989] introduces the subject of software risk management and contains many relevant papers. Boehm [1991] is an overview of the subject. De Marco [1995] is an entertaining collection of provocative essays on the problems faced by software engineers and managers.

The influence of human factors in software development is discussed by Weinberg [1971] and Weinberg and Schulman [1974]. The latter is an often-cited source of a study finding that programmers can achieve the primary objective set for them at the cost of short-changing secondary goals. De Marco and Lister [1999] discusses the role of people in software engineering and how to manage them.

Capers Jones [1986] contains a long list of factors and cogent analyses of the different approaches to modeling programming productivity. Curtis et al. [1988] reports on a field study to analyze the factors that affect productivity. "Since large software systems are still generated by humans rather than machines," the authors claim, "their creation must be analyzed as a *behavioral* process." The paper shows that different factors affect software at different layers of an organization. For example, at an individual level, intellectual and technical competence affects the design of the software, whereas at the team level, social processes dominate. Kearney et al. [1986] critically evaluates the role of complexity metrics within an organization. The impact of measurement on management and on the structure of the environment is addressed by Basili and Rombach [1988] and Basili and Caldiera [1988].

Grady and Caswell [1987] report on the history and results of a companywide effort to establish a metrics program at Hewlett-Packard. Grady [1992] presents ways to use metrics to improve project management practices. The "urban decay" analogy is due to M. Mackey (personal communication). The observation that there are progressive and regressive components of software development is due to Belady and Lehman [1979].

Albrecht and Gaffney [1983] introduces function points. (See also Behrens [1983].) Low and Jeffery [1990] compares function points and lines of code and concludes that function points provide a more accurate estimate of a project's size. Matson et al. [1994] describes an assessment of the method. For new initiatives and continuous developments in the area of function points, the reader may refer to the Web page http://www.ifpug.org/.

Section 8.2.3.1 is based on Boehm [1984a], which is an introductory overview of the field of software engineering economics and an update of the state of the art since Boehm's 1981 text. Boehm [1984a] also observes that cost models are far from perfect; they are accurate to within 20%, 80% of the time. The COCOMO II model is described in Boehm et al. [2000]. Boehm and Sullivan [2000] propose an economic basis for software engineering. They argue that, at present, all analysis and estimation concentrates on costs without analyzing the benefit and value to be gained. Yet, today, software adds value to many engineering products, all the way from consumer products, to airplanes, to public transportation systems. Boehm and Sullivan argue that software engineering designs must start with an analysis of the costs as well as the expected value.

The Capability Maturity Model was developed by the Software Engineering Institute in the late 1980s. It was first described in Humphrey [1989]. An overview of the method is presented in Paulk et al. [1993]. CMM has often been criticized for being oriented to large and traditional organizations. Paulk [1998] discusses how the method fits small organizations. SPICE (Software Process Improvement and Capability dEtermination) is an international standard that also deals with process maturity. It is intended both for process improvement and for capability determination (Rout [1995]).

Our discussion of team organizations follows Mantei [1981], which contains a discussion and an evaluation of different team structures in software development. Baker [1972] discusses chief programmer teams.

Abdel-Hamid [1989] and Abdel-Hamid and Madnick [1989] discuss a dynamic model with feedback loops for software project management. The model integrates technical and managerial aspects of software engineering. Abdel-Hamid [1990] discusseses how scheduling decisions affect software development costs. The field of system dynamics has grown in interest and is now actively investigated by the research community. Refer to this book's Website for links to current projects.

For a presentation of PERT, the reader may refer to Wiest and Levy [1977].

The book by DiBona et al.[1990] contains a number of interesting articles on different aspects of open-source development.

# CHAPTER 9

# Software Engineering Tools and Environments

In the previous chapters, we discussed many approaches and principles aimed at building high-quality software by means of an effective development process. In this chapter, we examine various tools and environments for the support of this endeavor. The software engineering activity involves a large number of people engaged in a complex set of activities to produce a large number of artifacts. The purpose of tools and environments is to support the development, verification, maintenance, and evolution of processes and artifacts. As processes and artifacts become more complex, the role of tools becomes more important. Indeed, today's ambitious projects could not succeed without sophisticated tools and environments.

A *tool* supports a particular activity. An *environment* is a collection of related tools. The tools and environments we discuss all aim at automating some of the activities that are involved in software engineering. The generic term for this field of study is *computer-aided software engineering (CASE)*.

Sometimes, tools are strictly necessary to support a given activity. Other times, they simply help make some tasks easier or more efficient. For example, programming languages and their compilers or interpreters are indispensable for executing programs; without them, software would not even exist. On the other hand, one can write specifications manually with paper and pencil, but a word processor is useful in editing the specifications, and it may increase the productivity and reliability of the whole production process. A specialized tool to check the consistency of the specifications as they are entered helps even more.

Section 9.1 begins the chapter with a historical account of software engineering tools. Section 9.2 examines the many dimensions along which we may classify and compare tools. These dimensions provide a systematic way to examine the capabilities of a given tool. Section 9.3 presents the main categories of tools, simply as a list without any attempt at completeness. Because of the rapid developments of tools, exhaustively reviewing and classifying existing tools quickly loses its relevance. Section 9.4 discusses the problem of integrating tools: how tools may communicate and work with each other. Section 9.5 examines the forces that motivate the development of new tools and new categories of tools. This section explains why there is such rapid movement in the software tools area. Finally, Section 9.6 concludes the chapter with a summary.

## 9.1    HISTORICAL EVOLUTION OF TOOLS AND ENVIRONMENTS

The history of tools and environments has been influenced primarily by two factors: technological developments that have made certain tools necessary or possible and a better understanding of software engineering processes. In the early days, when the software engineering activity was limited to programming, the main tools available to the software engineer were programming-related tools such as editors and compilers. Those early tools were viewed as relieving the programmer from clerical activities. The development of file systems enabled programmers to store their programs on-line and, even more important, share them with other programmers. Sharing of files led to the need for configuration and version management tools and other tools to support team-oriented activities.

Advances in graphical displays and user interfaces led to the development of tools that take advantage of the technology. For example, graphical editors help programmers express designs graphically and animate them visually. The area of graphical user interfaces (GUIs) has been an active area of tool development. Visual languages try to make graphics a primary interface to the computer, complementing text input. In modern environments, components of the environment are integrated and composed at the GUI level.

The next technological development that spurred tool development was the movement to distributed platforms. As software teams became distributed and connected over networks, tools were developed to support distributed configuration management and teams. So-called groupware aims at supporting teams so that they can cooperate across distance and time. That is, despite their physical separation, teams can have virtual meetings. Groupware tools also help conduct discussions that go on for a long time, recording the state and content of the discussion so that participants may join and leave it at different times that are convenient to them. Distribution has also led to a number of software distribution and deployment tools.

Looking at the development of software tools over the last several decades, we can identify a number of distinct eras of tool development. At first, individual tools were developed to support single activities such as compilation or debugging. The next wave was to develop *integrated environments* which consist of tools that work together. Typically, such an environment supports one programming language, and the tools are able to invoke one another when necessary. Although the integration of tools is helpful, such environments are often closed and support only tools that are included in the environment. The third era of tool development is focused instead on *open environments*. The idea is that tools have public interfaces which allow them to communicate and cooperate with other tools which respect those interfaces. Open environments allow different groups to build different tools that work together. Current work in open environments is focused on extending their capabilities to distributed environments consisting of heterogeneous machines.

## 9.2    DIMENSIONS FOR COMPARING SOFTWARE TOOLS

Software tools can be compared along many dimensions, such as the level of formality they enforce, the life cycle phase they support, and the interface they provide to the user. In this section, we present several criteria for categorizing and evaluating software tools. When faced with the task of selecting a particular tool, one can use this list of criteria to consider the available alternatives.

### Interaction mode

We may categorize software tools as batch oriented or interactive. Batch-oriented tools support the application of wholesale operations to a collection of documents. For example, batch editing tools such as `grep` and `sed` in the Unix environment enable the programmer to search for all occurrences of a certain keyword or variable name in a set of files. This is usually much more convenient and less prone to error than using an interactive text editor for the same task. Interactive tools are more convenient in other situations, where the immediate feedback from applying changes is helpful. For example, in program debugging, it is useful to make a change and see the result of the change immediately.

It is convenient when tools support both interactive and batch modes of operation. For example, in debugging, sometimes we may want to find an instance when a particular value is assigned to a variable. In this case, interaction with a debugger is useful. Other times, we may want to find all occurrences of an assignment to a variable. In that case, a batch-oriented search is more convenient.

### Exercises

**9.1**    Give examples of batch-oriented and interactive operations in program debugging. Give examples where the use of color would make program browsing easier.

**9.2**    Examine the `emacs` editor available on Unix and personal computers. Does it have batch-oriented commands? Are there advantages to having batch-oriented commands in such an interactive editor?

### Interface format

Computer technology has evolved in the direction of enabling software tools to support increasingly sophisticated formats for human-machine interfaces. Initially, such interfaces were mainly textual. Then, with the advent and prevalence of graphic-oriented interfaces, so-called visual tools and environments with a higher expressive power than the corresponding textual notations became available. Technologies such as multimedia interfaces, color, and hypertext make human-computer interfaces even more sophisticated and productive.

Text-oriented and graphic tools each have their roles. Often, it is useful to support access to both notations for the same underlying model. For instance, consider TDN and GDN, the two design notations introduced in Chapter 4. These are two different external representations of the same design language or model. But GDN may be easier to browse through in order to get a higher level understanding of the design. This is especially true if a tool is available to support browsing through a GDN document in a stepwise fashion, according to the hierarchy defined by the `IS_COMPONENT_OF` relation.

Support for viewing a high-level design and selectively exploding the details of particular modules help in quickly browsing through large designs.

## Exercise

**9.3** Based on your experience with modern interfaces for personal computers, specify the requirements of the interface for a hypothetical tool supporting design specification using TDN or GDN.

### Level of formality

Software developers produce many documents during the software development process. Each document is written in some language whose syntax and semantics can be defined in a more or less formal way. In principle, suitable processors can be associated with any language. The functionality they provide, however, is highly dependent on the level of formality of the language. Typically, a compiler (i.e., a translation algorithm) can be built only for a language whose syntax and semantics are known precisely, while an editor can be built for any language. Similarly, one may build a specialized graphical editor for UML or data flow diagrams, thanks to the fact that their composition rules (their syntax) are defined precisely. On the other hand, we already have observed that data flow diagrams lack a precise semantics; thus, we cannot build an interpreter for executing them. Or, more precisely, if we build an interpreter for data flow diagrams, we would implicitly define a semantics for them.

## Exercise

**9.4** Give some possible execution rules for DFDs.

### Dependency on phase of life cycle

Some tools, such as text editors, may be used in different activities. Other software tools are designed to help in some specific activity that is limited to a certain phase of the software life cycle. We can, therefore, classify tools on the basis of the phase they are intended to support. For example, there are tools for writing requirements specifications, tools for specifying module interfaces, tools for editing code, and tools for debugging. Some environments integrate tools, with the goal of supporting a natural and smooth transition through the software development phases, according to the model that is selected for the software life cycle.

### Degree of standardization

In Chapter 7, we debated the controversial issue of standardizing software construction methods and tools. On the one hand, standardizing an item—say, a life cycle method or a tool—enhances its applicability; on the other hand, it freezes its evolution.

The more a method or a language is standardized, the more software producers are willing to invest in developing support for it. The stability of a method or language guarantees the longevity of its support tools, and this, in turn, guarantees the return on investments in the tools.

Using a standardized tool or method also guarantees a supply of people who are familiar with it and the portability of their knowledge from one project to the next. This is what happens, for example, if we base a development effort on an industrywide operating system or development methodology. Using a proprietary operating system reduces the supply of candidates and adds overhead for training.

In practice, standardization is a matter of degree. Most developers add extensions to a base-level standard.

### Exercises

**9.5**    Discuss the pros and cons of early standardization in the case of programming languages.

**9.6**    Investigate how many versions of the UNIX operating system exist. Are there standards that govern the system? Is Linux a standard operating system?

### Language dependency

Some tools are associated with a particular language, and others are language independent. The former class is called monolingual, the latter polylingual. For instance, a conventional text editor or a word processor can be used as an editor for any programming or specification language, but there are specialized graphical editors for UML diagrams, Petri nets, or DFDs.

Compilers are a typical example of monolingual tools. By contrast, an operating system like UNIX, which provides a large variety of tools in support of software development, may be viewed as a polylingual facility, because it supports program development in different programming languages. Similarly, conventional linkers are polylingual, since they support the linking of object modules derived from the compilation of programs written in different source languages. There are, however, linkers that are specialized to particular programming languages such as Ada or Modula-2. The Smalltalk environment is a good example of a monolingual environment. The Java Development Kit (JDK) is a monolingual tool kit.

In general, monolingual tools provide more specialized help and support, but a polylingual environment is more general and open. A user's experience from a polylingual environment is more portable.

### Static versus dynamic tools

Some tools neither perform nor require execution of the object they operate on, be it a program or a specification document. These tools are applied to such an object to create it, modify it, verify its consistency with respect to some rule, or even measure some static properties, such as length, or detect the presence of certain constructs. We call these tools static. For example, the parser of a programming language, which checks the syntactic correctness of a program, is a static tool. So is a type checker for a typed language: The type checker is a tool that evaluates whether the variables appearing in a program are manipulated consistently with their declared type.

A tool that requires execution of the object it operates on is called *dynamic*. For example, a Perl interpreter, a Petri net simulator, and a statechart simulator are dynamic tools. Static tools support the analysis of models and artifacts; dynamic tools support the simulation of models and artifacts.

### Exercise

**9.7**    Imagine a tool that helps the programmer build correctness proofs. Is this a static or a dynamic tool? What about a symbolic interpreter?

### Development tools versus end-product components

Some tools support the development of end products, but do not become part of them: Once the product is complete, nothing of the tools remains in the application that is released. Other tools are kits of software components that are included in—and become a part of—the end product. These components are usually provided as a run-time support library. The former category includes such tools as project management tools, software specification simulators, test case generators, and debuggers. Examples of the latter category are window managers, which provide run-time libraries to support the human-computer interaction, libraries of mathematical routines to be linked to an application, and a set of macros for the development of specialized spreadsheets.

### Exercise

**9.8**    Discuss compilers and interpreters as development tools versus end-product components. Why is an interpreter useful as a development tool? Why is it more convenient to release a compiled version of an application?

### Single-user versus multiuser tools

Some tools support one user at a time, while others are capable of supporting multiple users at once. Single-user tools are used for personal activities, whereas multiuser tools may be used for groups. Multiuser tools must support the locking of objects to prevent inadvertent interference among multiple users. As the use of networking has increased, with personal computers now shared on networks, even tools on personal computers must be multiuser.

### Single-machine versus network-aware tools

As the Internet entered and then pervaded the computing environment, the sharing of resources has spread from users on a single large machine to users across the network. This means that tools must support the naming and manipulation of objects that do not reside on the user's machine. Of course, some tools are designed specifically to support network operations, such as the distribution of program files to different machines. But even tools such as program editors, which are not specifically used for networking, may need to support the user to access files on the network.

### Exercise

**9.9**    There are two ways to endow tools with network awareness. One is to build such awareness into the operating system in a manner that is transparent to the tools, and the other is to make each tool itself network aware. Discuss the pros and cons of both approaches.

## 9.3   REPRESENTATIVE TOOLS

In this section, we review the most important classes of software production tools. Where appropriate, we analyze a tool with respect to the classification discussed in Section 9.2. The list we produce is necessarily nonexhaustive, as new tools and new types of tools are continuously introduced. The list is just a way for us to talk about some important categories of tools. In the next section, we shall introduce some classifications that help us organize the long list of available tools into a few classes.

### 9.3.1   Editors

Since software is ultimately a more or less complex collection of documents—requirements specifications, descriptions of module architecture, programs, etc.—editors are a fundamental software development tool. Editors support the creation and modification of documents.

With respect to the classification set forth in the previous section, we can place editors in different categories:

- They can be either textual or graphical.
- They can follow a formal syntax, or they can be used for writing informal text or drawing free-form pictures. For instance, a general-purpose graphical editor could be used to produce any kind of diagrams, including formal diagrams such as DFDs, class diagrams, or Petri nets, but such an editor cannot check the syntactic correctness of those diagrams (say, an incorrect Petri net arc connecting two transitions). Similarly, we may use a word processor to write programs in any programming language, but the tool cannot help in finding missing keywords, ill-formed expressions, undeclared variables, etc. To perform such checks, one should use tools that are sensitive to the syntax—and, possibly, the semantics—of the language.
- They can be either monolingual (e.g., an Ada syntax-directed editor) or polylingual (e.g., a generic syntax-directed editor that is driven by the specific syntax of a programming language). A conventional word processor is intrinsically polylingual.

  The Emacs editor is capable of operating in different modes. A mode may be driven by the syntax tables of a particular language, allowing simple checks and standard indentation to be performed by the editor.

- They may be used not only to produce, but also to correct or update, documents. Thus, editors should be flexible (e.g., able to be run interactively or in batch) and easy to integrate with other tools. We have already discussed an example in which an editor was integrated with a debugger, in order to support program correction during debugging.

As another example, consider the integration of a textual and a graphical editor. In fact, even in a graphical editor, there are parts that are more conveniently handled as text—for example, in the case of GDN, the header of an exported subprogram through a module interface or a comment describing a module. In addition, if the GDN and

TDN notations are both provided, it should be possible to enter (or modify) a description using one of these notations and view the resulting design under the other notation. In general, when a tool supports the creation of several views of the same object or phenomenon, it should support links and associations among the views. For example, a UML tools should support navigation among the various UML diagrams.

### 9.3.2 Linkers

Linkers are tools that are used to combine mutually referencing objects into larger objects. Traditional linkers combine object-code fragments into a larger program, but there are also tools for linking modules of a specification document or linking code modules on the basis of their interfaces. Linkers can be both monolingual (when they are language specific) or polylingual (when they can accept modules written in different languages).

Basically, a linker binds names appearing in a module to external names exported by other modules. In the case of language-specific linkers, this may also imply some kind of intermodule type checking, depending on the nature of the language. A polylingual linker may perform only binding resolution, leaving all language-specific activities to other tools.

The concept of a linker has broader applicability than just to programming languages. Typically, if one deals with a modular specification language, a linker for that language would be able to perform checking and binding across various specification modules. For example, for the design illustrated in Figure 4.10, a language-specific linker for TDN/GDN ought to be able to check interfaces according to the USES and IS_COMPONENT_OF relations.

### Exercise

**9.10** Give a list of functions that should be supported by a language-specific linker for TDN.

### 9.3.3 Interpreters

An interpreter executes actions specified in a formal notation: its input code. At one extreme, an interpreter is the hardware that executes machine code. As we mentioned in Chapter 5, however, it is possible to interpret even specifications if they are written in a formal language. In this case, the interpreter behaves as a simulator or a prototype of the end product and can help detect mistakes in the specifications even in the early stages of the software process.

We already have observed that requirements specification often occurs incrementally, hand in hand with the analysis of the application domain. Even in such cases, it would be useful to check the requirements by executing an incompletely specified system. For example, initially one might decide to specify only the sequence of screen panels through which the end user will interact with the system, leaving out the exact specification of the functions that will be invoked in response to the user input. This decision might be dictated by the fact that, in the application under development, user interfaces are the most critical factor affecting the requirements. Thus, we decide to check with the end user whether the interaction style we intend to provide corresponds to his or her expectations, before freezing it in the final implementation. A tool might allow software designers to define screen panels simply by drawing them on the screen. An interpreter would then support the display of screen panels in suitable sequences to demonstrate the interactive sessions with the application. The interpreter should tolerate the incompleteness of specifications (e.g., when no functions are provided in response to the various commands that might be entered in the fields of the screen panels). In essence, the interpreter operates like a *partial prototype*, allowing experimentation with the look and feel of the end product.

In other cases, the results of interpreting the requirements is more properly called *requirements animation*: What we provide on the screen is a view of the dynamic evolution of the model, which corresponds to the physical behavior of the specified system. For example, one might easily animate a finite state machine that is used to model the evolution of a state-changing dynamic system. If the state-changing system is a plant controlled by a computer, and a finite state machine—displayed on the terminal—describes the states entered by the plant as a consequence of commands issued by the computer, we may achieve animation by blinking the states of the finite state machine as the corresponding state of the plant is entered. The control signals may be simulated by pressing any key on the terminal, for example.

Usually, interpreters operate on actual input values. It is possible, however, to design *symbolic interpreters*, which operate on symbolic input values. As we observed in Section 6.5, a symbolic execution corresponds to a whole class of executions on input data. Thus, a symbolic interpreter can be a useful verification tool and can be used as an intermediate step in the derivation of test data that cause execution to follow certain paths.

### Exercise

**9.11**  Give the requirements of a tool for supporting the execution of DFDs, based on the rules you gave in Exercise 9.4. The tool might provide facilities to animate specifications. You may then proceed to design and implement the tool.

## 9.3.4    Code Generators

The software construction process is a sequence of steps that transform a given problem description called a *specification* into another description called an *implementation*. The latter description is more formal, more detailed, and less abstract than the former; it is also more efficiently executable. The transformation process eventually ends in machine-executable code. As mentioned in the previous section, even intermediate steps may be executable. The reason we decide to proceed through additional transformation steps is that interpreters of intermediate steps are, in general, slower than the interpreter of the final product (which in most cases is the computer itself).

Steps in a derivation may require creativity and may be supported by tools to varying degrees. A simple and fully automatic step is the translation from source code into object code. This is performed by one of the oldest and best known software tools, namely, the compiler. Other derivation steps—for example, the decomposition of modules according to the IS_COMPOSED_OF hierarchy—can be only partially supported by tools. The transformation may be recorded, and even controlled, by a suitable tool, but the choice of which lower level modules to use to implement a given higher level module is the designer's responsibility and cannot be automated fully.

With reference to the transformation-based life cycle model illustrated in Chapter 7 (see Figure 7.6), the optimizer tool is essentially a translator supporting the stepwise transformation of specifications into an implementation. As we discussed, the optimizer is only partially automated. The clerical job of recording the transformation steps is automated in order to support later modifications. We also envisioned the case where the optimizer plays the role of an intelligent assistant. The difficult and critical steps, however, cannot be automated; thus, even in this case, most of the creative tasks are the software engineer's responsibility.

Moving from a formal specification of a module to an implementation may also be viewed as a transformation that involves creative activities such as designing data structures or algorithms. Again, automatic tools may support clerical parts of such a transformation. For instance, Java class skeletons can be automatically derived from UML class diagrams. We also saw in Section 5.7.2.1 that the structure of a Larch specification may be automatically mapped into partial Pascal code, leaving the creative part of the transformation to the designer.

Examples of generalized code generators in the business applications world are provided by several so-called *fourth-generation* tools, which automatically generate code from a higher level language (a *fourth-generation language*, or *4GL*). Often, such languages are centered around a database system. Screen panels for human-computer interaction may automatically be generated for inserting or manipulating data in the database and for querying the database. Also, reports may be automatically generated from the database. In this case, the user can choose among several options to define the formats for the report. For instance, given a database of employees, a report on all employees who match certain selection criteria can automatically be generated by specifying simple declarative options, with no need for defining and coding report generation algorithms.

The generation approach to reusing code relies on a generator that generates the application code on the basis of input that specifies the needed components and their integration. In some approaches, the components are also generated automatically on the basis of their specification, while others assume a preexisting set of components that are configured together by the code generator's output.

## 9.3.5   Debuggers

Debuggers may be viewed as special kinds of interpreters. In fact, they execute a program with the purpose of helping to localize and fix errors, by applying the principles described in Chapter 6. Debuggers give the user the following major capabilities:

- to inspect the execution state in a symbolic way. (Here, "symbolic" means "referring to symbolic identifiers of program objects," not that the debugger is a symbolic interpreter.)

- to select the execution mode, such as initiating step-by-step execution or setting breakpoints symbolically.
- to select the portion of the execution state and the execution points that will be inspected, without manually modifying the source code. This not only makes debugging simpler, but also avoids the risk of introducing foreign code that one may forget to remove after debugging.
- to check intermediate assertions, as discussed in Section 6.6.

A debugger can also be used for other reasons than just locating and removing defects from a program. A good symbolic debugger can be employed to observe the dynamic behavior of a program. By *animating* the program in this way, a debugger can be a useful aid in understanding programs written by another programmer, thus supporting program modification and reengineering.

### Exercise

**9.12**  Based on your experience (and frustrations) with existing debuggers, specify the requirements for an ideal debugger for your favorite programming language.

### 9.3.6    Tools Used in Software Testing

There are many tools that support testing in different ways. What follows are the main categories of such tools:

#### Tools for documenting testing

These tools support the bookkeeping of test cases, by providing forms for test case definition, storage, and retrieval. A typical example of a form describing a test case, as provided by a documentation tool, is illustrated in Figure 9.1.

A documentation tool of this type supports testing not only during initial development, but also during maintenance and in regression testing. (See Section 6.3.6.)

| Project Name: | Date of test: |
|---|---|
| Tested function: | |
| Tested module: | |
| Test case description | |
| Description of results: | |
| Comments: | |

FIGURE 9.1

A sample description form for test cases.

**Tools for deriving test cases**

In Chapter 6, we examined several techniques for building test cases. Such techniques can be made more effective by supporting tools, although we know that these tools cannot provide completely mechanical solutions. The main prerequisite for tools that generate test cases is the availability of a formal description. Thus, white-box techniques can be naturally implemented in a (semi)automatic way, since they apply to programs—that is, formal descriptions of algorithms. To apply white-box techniques, we may first use a symbolic interpreter to derive path conditions and then synthesize a set of test values that satisfy those conditions and guarantee traversal of the desired paths. The path might be selected to hit a certain statement or branch, according to a statement or a branch coverage criterion that one wishes to fulfill. In the case of black-box testing, test cases can be automatically derived only if formal specifications are available.

Some tools are intended to aid software engineers in deriving test cases from informal specifications. The engineer follows the structure of the specification document and is helped in the editing of test cases which reflect that structure. For example, the tool allows the engineer to mark up the specification document to isolate individual functions that must be provided by the application. For each marked-up function, the tool presents the engineer with a form to be filled in, of the kind illustrated in Figure 9.1. The "tested function" field of the form may be automatically filled in by the tool, with a reference to the page of the specification document where the function is specified.

**Tools for evaluating testing**

These tools provide various kinds of metrics, such as the number of statements executed, the percentage of paths covered in the control flow graph, and reliability and software science measures. For example, one can decide that module testing is sufficiently complete when a certain path-coverage criterion has been reached.

**Tools for testing other software qualities**

Testing may be used to evaluate qualities such as performance. Performance monitors help keep track of, and verify, execution time, the usage of main memory, and other performance-related parameters.

**Exercise**

**9.13** Given any path condition, can you write an algorithm to synthesize test data that would satisfy the condition? Why? Why not?

### 9.3.7 Static Analyzers

In Chapter 6, we saw that program analysis can be considered a verification technique that complements testing. Similarly, dynamic verification tools such as interpreters and debuggers, as well as other testing-support tools, can be complemented by tools that are devoted to certifying some desired properties without executing the program.

Clearly, the features offered by these tools depend highly on the type of property under consideration. For example, one might desire a deadlock detection tool, to help in designing deadlock-free concurrent systems, or a tool for timing analysis, to prove that a critical real-time system always responds to certain input stimuli within a specified time constraint. For many important properties, tools with industrial applicability are still unavailable. Considerable progress, however, has been made in the recent past with model checkers, such as SPIN.

A particularly relevant and practical case, however, is given by flow-based tools. Several important properties of programs can be classified as *flow properties* (i.e., properties of the variation of some relevant entities—in particular, *data* and *control*) during program execution. Thus, tools for flow analysis are static tools that characterize certain dynamic properties of the flow of data and control.

Data and control flow analyzers can help in the discovery of errors. For instance, data flow analysis can reveal the use of uninitialized variables, and control flow analysis can determine whether there are any unreachable statements in the program. Such properties, however, are undecidable in the general case. Thus, the associated tools may fail to give absolutely precise answers. In that case, one may say that they provide a pessimistic analysis. That is, they point out possible flaws or suspicious-looking statements, which we may later discover to be acceptable. No error, however, remains undetected. For example, a data flow analyzer could report some variable as potentially uninitialized, even if no execution of the program will ever reference the variable before initializing it first.

An oversimplified data flow tool for detecting uninitialized variables could work as follows:

1. Create a list to contain the current status of each program variable.
2. Set the status of every variable to "undefined."
3. Scan the program instructions from the beginning of the program. On encountering a `read` instruction referring to variable x or assignment to variable x, set the status of variable x to "defined." A reference to an undefined variable in an expression is signaled as a potential error.

Of course, in some cases, a variable may be either defined or undefined, depending on program execution (due to the use of conditional statements). Thus, a static analyzer for such an undecidable property can only state weaker properties, such as the *possibility* that some variable is uninitialized when referenced during execution. For instance, in the program fragment

```
begin
        read(x);
        if x > 0 then
        read(y);
        end if;
        z:= y;
        x:= x - w;
        .
        .
        .
end;
```

it is easy to see that x is always initialized. The assignment $x := x - w$ is certainly an error, however, because it will execute with w uninitialized. On the other hand, y may or may not be initialized when $z := y$ is executed.

In a similar manner, control flow analysis may reveal the presence of unreachable statements (unreachable edges in the control flow graph). This is not an error in itself, but certainly shows that the program is coded in a sloppy fashion. Moreover, it is often the symptom of the presence of an error. In the case of concurrent programming, flow analyzers can help detect the risk of deadlocks and other synchronization anomalies.

An interesting use of data flow analysis is to build specialized analyzers for particular applications. For example, in some secure applications, one should prove that no data are transferred from certain modules to other modules. Toward that end, we can use data flow analysis as a substitute for program verification. In this connection, one may think of a tool that allows the user to define a particular flow property of interest and automatically generates an analyzer that checks for the presence of that property.

Flow analyzers can also support program transformation, automatic or not. For instance, many techniques for code optimization are based on data flow analysis.

### Exercise

**9.14**  Consider the following program fragment:

```
read(x);
if x > 0 then
        read(z);
else
        read(y);
end if;
if x > 0 then
        w := z;
else
        w := y;
end if;
```

Is the fragment erroneous or not? Why? Why is it unlikely that an automatic data flow-based tool can provide the exact answer to this question?

## 9.3.8    Graphical User Interface Tools

Due to certain limitations of display devices, the early user interfaces to applications were based on text. After the introduction of graphically powerful display devices, graphical interfaces supplanted textual interfaces in most applications and environments. The design of a friendly user interface is important, because the interface has a significant influence on user satisfaction. Most graphical user interfaces are built from a set of common concepts, such as buttons, dialog boxes, and windows, which have become fairly standard. Most languages have supporting libraries for constructing user interfaces from these basic components. In this regard, we mentioned Swing, the Java library for user interfaces, in Chapter 4.

Graphical user interface components are typically connected through an event-based architecture. All affected components are notified of an event such as a mouse click or the movement of a cursor. More particularly, libraries such as Swing are based on the model view controller architecture described in Chapter 4.

A basic abstraction provided by GUI systems is the window. A *window* is a virtual screen; it provides an interface to the user for an independent activity. Several windows can be active on the screen at the same time, supporting the so-called *desktop metaphor*: the use of the screen in a manner similar to the way a traditional desk is used, with many documents on the top simultaneously. Windows usually are overlapping, as are papers on our desks. Figure 9.2 shows two overlapping windows, displaying two different views of a model of the Tower of Hanoi problem.

**User-interface management systems.** The standardization of user interface concepts such as menus and push buttons has enabled the creation of tools for the generation of user interfaces. A *user-interface management system (UIMS)* provides a set of basic abstractions (windows, menus, scroll bars, etc.) that may be used to customize a variety of interfaces. It also provides a library of run-time routines to be linked to the developed application in order to support input and output. Thus, a UIMS falls both under the category of development tools and under the category of end-product components. This view is summarized graphically in Figure 9.3.

The run-time component of the UIMS manages the bindings between internal data structures of an application and the external view(s) of the application. (See Figure 9.4.) In the model-view-controller terminology, the model is the internal structure of the data, manipulated by the application, and the view is the external structure, visualized on the screen for human-computer interaction. In the example shown in the figure, the controller is the dialog component. It stores the values of the fields of the record entered through the dialog box into the corresponding nodes of the portion of the tree data structure that represents the record internally. UIMSs often have a visual interface themselves, allowing the user to draw the form of the desired interface on the screen, placing the icons in appropriate locations in the window and responding to dialog boxes to fill in the details of each icon in the interface. The UIMS generates the code for the interface automatically.

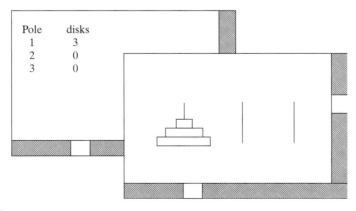

FIGURE 9.2

Two partially overlapping windows containing different views of the same model.

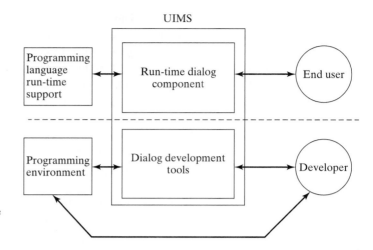

**FIGURE 9.3**

The two-component structure of a user-interface management system.

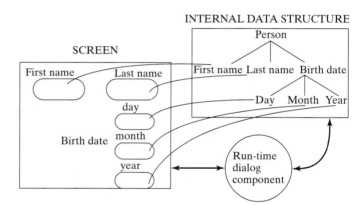

**FIGURE 9.4**

The run-time structure of a UIMS.

### Exercise

**9.15** Graphical interfaces are an improvement over textual interfaces. Some people, however, maintain that graphical interfaces force the user to a very low level of communication by pointing to objects. The answer to graphical interfaces, they claim, is voice communication. What would be the advantages and disadvantages of voice interfaces to applications? In what situations would you prefer to use a voice interface?

### 9.3.9 Configuration Management Tools

We have seen that software construction involves many activities and the production of many types of artifacts. Configuration management systems help in managing changes to artifacts in the presence of the sharing of those artifacts among team members. A configuration management system provides the following basic support:

> **1.** *Repository.* This is a shared database for the storage of artifacts. The repository may be used to store all artifacts produced during a software project. It provides controlled access to the artifacts to prevent accidental overwrites by users.

2. *Version management.* The repository provides the capability of storing different versions of a given artifact. It maintains a history of changes made to each artifact, so that it is possible to see when each version was created and what changes were made from the previous version.

3. *Work-space control.* Each engineer works in a *private* work space. To work on an artifact, the engineer must *check out* the artifact from the repository. This operation gives a copy of the artifact to the engineer in his or her private work space. Changes made in the work space are not visible to other team members. Once the engineer is satisfied with the artifact he or she is working on, the artifact is *checked in*—that is, moved to the repository. At this time, the artifact receives a new version number.

4. *Product modeling and building.* The engineer defines a model or "configuration" of the product. The model is often given in terms of a procedure for building the product from the artifacts stored in the repository. After changes are made to artifacts, a new version of the product may be built on the basis of the defined model.

These functions enable configuration management tools to support controlled change and the evolution of software artifacts. Because of the importance of change and evolution in the development of a project, a configuration management system is an essential support tool in any project. Software development projects use configuration management tools as a way to coordinate the many interrelated activities that take place as a project progresses.

Some configuration management systems extend their basic capabilities. Typical extensions are for the support of concurrent engineering and control of the software process.

Concurrent engineering is supported by relaxing the requirement of exclusive access to artifacts. The private work spaces allow each engineer to work independently. To shorten development time, we may want to have two engineers work on the same artifact concurrently. After their work is finished, their results must be *merged* together. Some configuration management systems provide merging facilities to support concurrent engineering.

The software process can be supported by giving the system more explicit information about the software process. In addition to defining the configuration of a product, some configuration management systems also support the definition of the process for producing the product. In the simplest case, this may involve defining small steps in the process. For example, we might stipulate that if a source code module is checked in, a compilation step should be started immediately and automatically. A further capability would be to define a larger process which indicates that a change in source code must be followed by testing of the affected module before the changed code is checked back in. The system then reminds the engineer to perform the test. With complete process support, the whole process of building the product is defined, and the system monitors the progress of the process and may inform the participants about the current state of the process and their roles in it.

We next examine two common tools that are used in configuration management. CVS is a tool for version management and make is a tool for building products. The combination of the two provides most of the functions we listed earlier for configuration management systems.

**Concurrent Version System.**  The Concurrent Version System (CVS) is a version control system that provides controlled access to files and maintains the history of changes made to them. A public directory contains all the files that constitute the product. Each engineer works in a private directory. The engineer can check out any version of either the entire product or a particular file. Checking out leads to a new revision of the file(s) being copied to the engineer's directory. When the engineer checks in a modified file, he or she can state comments on the reason for the changes. CVS also records a stamp for the time the file was checked in. That way, CVS can provide a record of who changed a file, when the file was changed, why it was modified, and what the actual modifications were. CVS can also provide the actual changes between any two versions.

Each file has a *revision number* consisting of an even number of integers separated by periods. For example, a file starts as 1.1 and may evolve through revisions 1.2, 1.3, and 1.4. (See  Figure 9.5a.) To support parallel development of the evolution of a file, CVS supports a *branching* feature. For example, in Figure 9.5b, we have started a new branch, 1.2.1. The first revision of the file in this branch is called 1.2.1.1. The development of this branch may go on in parallel with the original development, which is called the main *trunk*. At some future time, we may want to join the two branches together. This operation is called a *merge*. For example, we may need to develop two different features for our product, both of which require modifications to the same file. So as not to interfere with the development of those two features, we may create two different branches, one for each feature. After each branch has been developed and tested separately, we could merge the two. We may decide to continue one of the two branches after the merge as well, in which case the main trunk has the combined features, but the other branch contains only one of the two features.

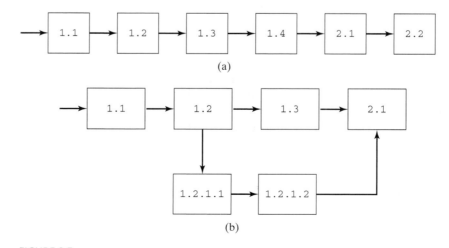

FIGURE 9.5

Versions in CVS. **(a)** A sequence of revisions. **(b)** A branch and a later join.

CVS provides locking to prevent accidental overwrites of files. Since CVS works with any ordinary text file, it may be used not just with source programs, but also for documents, test cases, etc. CVS runs in a client-server environment, so that a central server may be used as the public repository while engineers use remote client machines for their private work spaces.

**make.**    make is a tool that not only aids in building and rebuilding a product, but also helps keep a system in a consistent state after modifications. In general, there are mutual dependencies among the components that constitute a configuration; for example, an object-code module depends on its corresponding source-code module. Once dependencies are specified, invoking make will cause the generation of new versions of any components which depend on components that have been changed.

Consider the following make program:

```
1.      sys : mod1.o mod2.o
2.              ld mod1.o mod2.o -o sys
3.      mod1.o : mod1.c incl.h
4.              cc -c mod1.c
5.      mod2.o : mod2.c incl.h
6.              cc -c mod2.c
```

The program says that the object code of system sys depends on the object code of modules mod1 and mod2 (line 1); specifically, the object code of sys is obtained by linking the object codes of mod1 and mod2 (line 2). In addition, the object code of mod1 depends on its corresponding source-code module and the include file incl (line 3); the object code of mod1 is obtained by compiling the source (line 4). A similar case holds for module mod2 (lines 5 and 6). (For those unfamiliar with UNIX, ld is the invocation of the linker, cc stands for the invocation of the C compiler, .c is a file suffix denoting C program modules, .o is the suffix for object modules, and .h is the suffix for include, or *header*, files.)

Lines 1, 3, and 5 are *dependency* lines. Each dependency line specifies a *target* object that depends on a set of *source* objects (from which the target is built). Each such line in a make file is followed by a set of commands. When invoked, make checks each dependency specification and builds a dependency tree with the target (here, sys) as its root. If a target depends on a source that is newer than it, then the commands associated with the dependency line are executed, presumably to rebuild the target object from the recently modified source objects. The dependency tree is used to determine the minimum number of commands that have to be executed, as well as their order. For example, line 1 says that sys depends on mod1 and mod2. If mod2 is newer than sys, then the linker is invoked to relink mod1 and mod2. By convention, a make program is stored in a makefile.

make uses time stamps (modification times) associated with files to evaluate dependencies. For example, if the time stamp associated with the object code of mod1 has an associated modification date that is older than the date associated with the include file incl.h, then the invocation of make will cause mod1 to be recompiled and relinked to mod2.o.

Many variants of make exist today, but none adds significantly to the capabilities of the original make introduced in the early 1970s.

### Exercises

**9.16** There are two ways for a version control system to store the successive versions of a file (instead of storing complete files for each version). In the first approach, for each new check-in, only the changes are recorded. These are called *deltas*. When a checkout is performed, the original file has to be updated with all the available deltas for the desired revision. In the second approach, the latest revision is stored completely, and "undo" records are maintained in order to be able to revert to old revisions. Discuss the pros and cons of the two approaches. The issues you should consider, among others, are efficiency (disk space and access time) and reliability (the possibility of recovery if a file gets damaged).

**9.17** The dependency statements in a `makefile` may be used to draw a dependency graph for the files named in those statements. The nodes of the graph represent the files named in the `makefile`. We draw an arrow from node a to node b if b depends on a. The `make` tool uses such a graph to decide which actions need to be executed. Draw the dependency graph for the sample `makefile` given in this section. Is the `makefile` allowed to have cycles in this graph? Should the graph be a tree or a forest?

## 9.3.10 Tracking tools

Configuration management tools cut across the phases of the software development process. They are used to support the entire process by controlling access to documents and code that are created and utilized during the different phases of the process. Another class of tools that are used during the entire process is tracking tools, which help maintain information about the process and which track that information. The most important of these are *defect-tracking tools*, which are used to store information about reported defects in the software product and which track that information. Such tracking is important because the defect is typically reported by someone who is not aware of its source. The defect is reviewed and investigated by various people until its probable cause can be identified. Once the cause has been identified, a management decision is made on how to deal with the defect. If the decision is to correct the defect, it is assigned to an engineering team or a particular engineer, who is then responsible for correcting the defect. All information concerning the defect is stored in the tracking system so as to enable the next person in the process to take advantage of the analysis already performed. Further, the tracking system can be used as a valuable history of information about defects found in the system.

An item is usually entered into the defect-tracking tool in response to a *modification request* (MR). An MR may be generated by a customer or internally by the organization. The entries in the defect-tracking tool are classified according to different categories, such as the following:

- By type of MR: defect or enhancement request.
- By source of defect: coding, design, documentation, etc.
- By severity of defect: critical, serious, important, not important.
- By status of MR: entered, in review, assigned for correction, resolved.

Defect-tracking tools are invaluable to both engineers and managers. They help managers monitor the progress of a project and sometimes are used as a basis for deciding when the software is ready for release. For example, a decision could be made to release the software if there are no unresolved critical defects and the only serious defects are well understood and documented.

### Exercises

**9.18** Defect-tracking tools could provide features for deducing some statistical information about defects in a project. Give some examples of statistics that would be useful for a manager.

**9.19** Is it useful for a defect-tracking system to be able to classify defect reports upon the release of a product? If so, give an example of a use for such classification.

### 9.3.11  Reverse and reengineering tools

We have mentioned the importance of the maintenance phase of the software process on a number of occasions. In fact, as the importance of maintenance and, in general, legacy systems have grown, specific methodologies and tools have been developed to help in addressing them. As we discussed, the reengineering process comprises both a backwards (reverse engineering) and a forward phase.

Reverse engineering tools help uncover and, in some general sense, understand an existing system. These tools are sometimes more specifically called program understanding systems. They are aimed at reconstructing the development process in reverse, going back from source code to requirements, by synthesizing suitable abstractions and extracting cross-references and other kinds of documentation material on the product that help make decisions regarding changes to the system. In so doing, they may help create missing documentation for legacy systems that lack proper documentation. For example, such tools may be used to automatically produce control and data flow graphs or use graphs for existing software. Reverse engineering tools also support the process of making the code and other artifacts consistent with each other.

Forward engineering tools help change an existing program by, for example, testing different modifications. These tools have the ability to easily undo those modifications which are not satisfactory. Forward engineering tools could provide support for anything from small unit-level changes all the way to restructuring changes.

One of the important uses for reengineering tools is to help transform legacy systems to newer technologies. For example, a number of tools help transform software written in a procedural language to an object-oriented language. This, of course, requires a redesign of the software in most cases. Some tools have been designed explicitly to do such reengineering of the design.

### Exercises

**9.20** What are the basic steps involved in transforming a program written in a procedural language such as C to an object-oriented language such as C++ or Java?

**9.21** In transforming a procedural code into an object-oriented code, a fundamental step is to identify the "objects" in the procedural code. This is called the *object identification* problem. Suppose you are trying to transform a program written in C. Give some heuristics for identifying objects in C code.

### 9.3.12 Process support tools

In Chapter 7, we saw a variety of software process models. These models differ in the order in which they carry out various activities and in the way they interleave the activities. Process support tools help carry out the software production process. Simple tools can help by maintaining a to-do list for the engineer, reminding him or her of the next possible activities in the process. Such a tool could prevent the engineer from performing some activities if the prerequisite conditions are not met. For example, if "check out, edit, compile, test, check in" has been defined to be an acceptable sequence of process steps, the tool could prevent an attempt to check in until a test has been run. Some simple tools are based on triggers that act as reminders. For instance, as soon as a file has been checked in, notices are sent to those engineers who are dependent on the file. We have already mentioned that some configuration management tools provide features such as these.

A class of tools called *process-centered software engineering environments* (PSEEs) carry the support of the software process to its logical conclusion. These tools provide a process-modeling language for the engineer or manager to define the software production process for the project. To different degrees, process-modeling languages support the definition of the actors in the process, the roles they play, the activities they are allowed or required to perform, the order in which activities are to be carried out, the dependencies of the activities on one another, the inputs and the outputs of activities, and the resources required for each activity. Each engineer is assigned a role, and the PSEE can control, facilitate, or monitor the progress of the activities to different degrees. The challenge in this area has been to find a way to define processes in such that they will combine the rigidity required by the tool and the flexibility required by the human engineer.

The open source process has given rise to its own set of process support tools, the unique characteristic of which is the assumption that the process is open. Usually, the tools run on some application server on the network and all the stored data are open to anyone who subscribes to the service.

#### Exercise

**9.22** Many of the tools we have discussed before support the software production process. Discuss why a configuration management system may be considered a process support tool.

### 9.3.13 Management Tools

Management issues grow more critical as the complexity of a project increases. Thus, the usefulness of management tools becomes more relevant in large, multiperson projects.

As we have observed, most management principles and techniques are quite general and are not specific to software. A few such principles and techniques, however, such as cost estimation techniques, are heavily dependent on software. Accordingly, management activities may be supported by a variety of tools, some devoted to management in general, others specific to software development projects.

General management support facilities include scheduling and control tools based on PERT diagrams and Gantt charts. Among the features typically offered by such tools is the capability of interacting both textually and graphically. For example, the duration of an activity and its precedence relations with other activities may initially be given textually, then visualized graphically, and, finally, updated by direct manipulation of a diagram on the screen. The tool may calculate the starting and ending dates for activities, may balance resource loading, may verify that a resource is not assigned beyond its maximum availability, and so on.

Among software-related management facilities are cost estimation tools based on techniques presented in Chapter 8, such as the COCOMO and COCOMO II models and function-point-based models. In the case of cost estimation, some tools allow the equation underlying the estimation method to be adapted to the specific organization, depending on historical data collected in that organization. Tools supporting source-code metrics can also provide useful information to managers.

### Exercise

---

**9.23**   Study the features provided by a project management tool of your choice, and show how you can use any or all of those features to schedule the activities of a hypothetical software development project of your choice.

---

## 9.4    TOOL INTEGRATION

In the previous section, we discussed some of the main features of software development that may be supported by automated tools. The list we provided is far from exhaustive: A software development organization uses numerous tools. Historically, as the number of tools grew, the problem of dealing with them also grew. In the 1980s, much research and development was devoted to the creation of integrated project support environments, —that is, an integrated collection of tools supporting all phases of the software production process. The PSEEs mentioned in Section 9.3.12 are an example of systems where tools are integrated within a workflow engine that drives the software process.

One ambitious approach attempted to store all artifacts produced in the process in a *repository*, to be accessed by different tools and saved for later use. Such a repository, together with the operations needed to manage it, constitutes the heart of the environment. There were even attempts to define standards for repository-based environments. This approach to an integrated environment aims to have a common data representation for artifacts that different tools can use to communicate with each other. For example, the editor stores a program in such a way that not only can the compiler read and compile it, but also, the debugger can access the program and display it to the debugging engineer, and the defect-tracking tool can refer to the exact module, and the location in it, that has been modified. This approach to tool integration is referred to as *data integration*: The data representation for artifacts is unified so that the different tools work together.

Another approach to integrating tools is referred to as *control integration*: The different tools are able to communicate with each other through control messages. For example, once the engineer closes a program file after modifying it, the editor sends a message to the compiler to compile that file and all other files that depend on it. Control integration is usually implemented through an event-based architecture for tools in which some tools signal events—such as the checking-in of a particular file—and other tools listen for and respond to those events—for example, make automatically runs after a check-in event.

No all-encompassing environment has emerged to support the entire development process. Instead, the concepts of control and data integration have been used to produce integrated environments for given phases of the software process, such as program development or requirements engineering. Modern programming environments now offer a visual development environment in which user-interface development, program development and debugging, and some amount of configuration management are supported.

### Exercise

**9.24** Examine a visual development environment in your facility. Is the environment based on control integration? Data integration? What specific activities does it support besides editing and compiling?

## 9.5    FORCES INFLUENCING THE EVOLUTION OF TOOLS

Software engineering involves a complex set of processes. It is not surprising that tools are constantly being developed to help control the complexity of these processes. But there are other reasons for the rapid development and evolution of software tools. We can classify the forces that direct the development of new tools into three distinct classes.

**To support new technology.**    Any fundamentally new technology requires and motivates the development of a new class of tools. Two good examples of this are graphical user interfaces and networking. The development of GUI terminals has given rise to whole new sets of tools to help in the development of GUI interfaces. The GUI technology not only has spurred the development of tools for GUI development, but also has made the interface to most tools become graphic, to match the terminals.

The emergence of distributed environments in which engineers use individual computers that are connected through a network has also had the same dual effect. First, tools are needed to support distributed environments. For example, tools are needed to support the deployment of software on different computers in a network. On the other hand, software development tools must be enhanced to deal with distributed environments. For example, configuration management systems have to be able to support distributed groups. Accordingly, traditional configuration management systems have been enhanced to allow documents from remote locations on a network to be checked in and checked out.

**To support new software processes.**    A line of research (mentioned in the previous section) has been trying to develop process-centered software engineering environments (PSEEs) in which one can define the process model to be used, and the environment then monitors, controls, and, in general, aids in the execution of the process. The environment could use the information about the process to remind the engineer about the next possible activities—for example, in the form of a to-do list. Such environments have not become widely used. Instead, significantly new software process models seem to initiate the development of their own supporting tools. For example, prototyping tools support a flexible life cycle model based on rapid prototyping. Another example is the open source process, which has given rise to a number of new tools to support the distribution and sharing of source code, merging of modifications, defect-tracking tools, and so on. Application server technology is used to provide the tools to the community of engineers.

**To support a particular method or methodology.**   As new methods or methodologies are introduced, they naturally need their own supporting tools. For example, the emergence of requirements engineering and the better understanding of the activities involved has given rise to tools for eliciting and analyzing requirements. Similarly, the better understanding of maintenance processes has given rise to reverse engineering tools, the acceptance of model checking in testing has been helped by the availability of efficient tools, and the UML-based approaches have given rise to the development of environments based on the UML notation.

## 9.6    CONCLUDING REMARKS

In this chapter, we have given an overview of software engineering tools and environments. We have discussed why the area evolves rapidly and why new kinds of tools are created on a regular basis. It is not possible to survey the field exhaustively, and therefore it is important to have a framework within which we can understand the significance of tools and evaluate their usefulness. To this end, we have given several classification schemes and described the forces that influence the evolution of tools. The classification schemes can be used to critically evaluate and compare software tools. The forces we have discussed may be used to decide when a new tool is needed.

Software engineering is complex. Tools are necessary to help master the field's complexities. Such tools, however, are not panaceas. The software engineer needs mastery of principles and methods, common sense, and good judgment. Those qualities help the engineer choose the right tool and use it appropriately to enhance his or her performance.

## FURTHER EXERCISES

**9.25**  Detail the functions of a language-specific linker for a specification language in which specification modules are developed separately and then integrated. You may choose the language as you prefer. One example might be Larch modules. Another example might be Petri net modules. (Using the latter assumes that you define what an interface is for such modules.)

**9.26**  Given the specification of a module to be implemented, and given a library of pairs `<module_specification, module_implementation>`, specify exactly what kind of logical deductions a tool should be able to perform. Can this be done in a completely mechanical fashion?

**9.27**  Examine one of the existing tools supporting UML. Take a small existing application written in Java or C++ and do a reverse engineering case study by using the tool to provide a high-level description of its module structure using the class diagram.

**9.28** Give the requirements of a tool that supports the execution of finite state machines. The tool must provide facilities to animate specifications. Provide a detailed design of the tool.

**9.29** Give the requirements for a tool that supports the evaluation of the testing activity.

**9.30** Discuss the requirements for a scaffolding tool that supports module testing by generating stubs and drivers. What inputs does the tool need?

## HINTS AND SKETCHY SOLUTIONS

**9.4** You may assume that the data that flow between any two bubbles are typed. Then you must define the language used to specify the function of each bubble and the way bubbles synchronize their access to the data that are produced and consumed.

**9.5** The answer to this question depends on how innovative the language is, although according to Hoare [1973], the job of the language designer is consolidation, not innovation. Extensive experimentation with the language is needed before the language may be frozen. This means that compilers must be available and that people must use them. Otherwise, a premature standard either makes the language useless or does not prevent its later evolution or the spread of dialects.

**9.7** A tool for proving formal correctness is static. A symbolic interpreter is dynamic, although several possible executions are "collapsed" into a single symbolic one. According to some authors, however, this categorization is questionable.

**9.8** An interpreted application is often less efficient. If the compiled version is released, the presence of the interpreter at run time is not needed. Also, the compiled version provides more protection for the developer, since it cannot be easily read or modified by the user.

**9.14** The fragment is erroneous because it depends on the path taken in the first conditional statement, which in turn depends on the value read for variable x. The tool should be able to handle a condition under which variables are either defined or undefined. Furthermore, it should have enough theorem-proving power to state whether such conditions are true, satisfiable, or false.

**9.18** Some useful statistics could be the percentage of defects found during unit testing, integration testing, alpha testing, beta testing, and after release of the system; the percentage of defects attributed to each phase of the process; and the average length of time from reporting of defects to their resolution. One should also monitor the system, for example, to make sure that the number of defects per release goes down, not up.

**9.20** Some important steps are to find objects, find classes, and find inheritance relationships.

## BIBLIOGRAPHIC NOTES

Dart et al. [1987] provides a taxonomy of software development environments, while Osterweil [1981] is an interesting historical reference. The special issue of *IEEE Software* [1990c] presents a view of existing software tools. Tahvanainen and Smolander [1990] offers a rich annotated bibliography. Norman and Nunamaker [1989] provides an assessment of the impact of CASE tools on software engineering productivity.

If we rule out compilers as a special case of code generators, a sampler of tools that support the derivation of code from higher level specifications is given by Lewis in the aforementioned special issue of *IEEE Software* [1990c]. Martin and Leben [1986] presents a comprehensive view of fourth-generation languages. Misra and Jalics [1988] and Verner and Tate [1988] give a critical evaluation of fourth-generation languages and tools. Fuggetta [1993] provides an extensive survey and classification of CASE tools.

Surveys of testing support tools are given by DeMillo et al. [1987] and in the aforementioned special issue of *IEEE Software* [1990c]. Osterweil, in Chandrasekaran and Radicchi [1981], describes both a technique for program verification that integrates testing and analysis strategies and a tool that supports the technique. Kemmerer and Eckmann [1985] describes UNISEX, a symbolic interpreter for Pascal that supports program verification.

For performance monitors, the reader may refer to Ferrari and Minetti (eds.) [1981].

Dittrich et al. [2000] surveys some problems and approaches to software engineering databases. Clemm and Osterweil [1990] describes a persistent object store called Odin, used as the infrastructure for integrating tools into an environment. Thomas and Nejmeh [1992] compares the different forms of tool integration.

Problems, principles, and tools to build user interfaces are described by Coutaz [1985], Schneiderman [1998], Myers [1988], Hartson and Hiix [1989], Young et al. [1988], Linton et al. [1989], and the special issue of *IEEE Software* on user interfaces (IEEE Software [1989a]). For some psychological and ergonomic aspects of the human-computer interaction that have not been discussed in this text, refer to Rubinstein and Hersh [1984] and Guindon [1988].

Tichy [1989], Babich [1986], and Tichy [1994] provide a comprehensive view of configuration management. Conradi and Westfechtel [1998] give a comprehensive survey of the principles of version management. Tichy [1985] describes the design of RCS (Revision Control System), a widely used configuration management system. Horwitz et al. [1989] discusses how consistency among versions is verified on a semantic basis, rather than through a simple textual comparison. The tool make is described by Feldman [1979]. Estublier [2000] reviews the history and the current state of software configuration management. Fogel [2000] describes CVS and also how to develop open source products based on CVS.

The Internet has given rise to a number of tools that support distributed software development and deployment. An interesting system, called the Software Dock, is described in Hall et al. [1999].

Products that support Gantt and PERT scheduling, as well as software cost estimation, exist, and their user manuals can be consulted for specific machines.

Probably the most important tool for software engineering is the programming language. We have not discussed programming languages here. Ghezzi and Jazayeri [1998] give a comprehensive view of programming languages and their role in software engineering.

Some historically important artificial intelligence programming environments are INTERLISP, presented by Teitelman and Masinter [1981], Loops, discussed by Stefik et al. [1983], and KEE, presented by Filman [1988]. Stefik et al. [1986] examine some issues revolving around a multiparadigm environment. Smalltalk80 and its interactive programming environment are described by Goldberg and Robson [1983].

Many tools for software specification are commercially available. Among these, Teamwork supports DFDs and Software Through Pictures provides interesting features for prototyping user interfaces; the tool has an open architecture that lets users extend and customize their work environment (see the special issue of *IEEE Software* [1990c]). Statemate, presented by Harel et al. [1990], is a specification support tool for real-time applications that is based on finite state machines. Rational Rose supports UML notations.

The real-time version of Teamwork is based on the extension of the SA/SD methodology proposed by Ward and Mellor [1985]. Software Through Pictures also extends SA/SD for real-time systems; its extension is based on the notation presented by Hatley and Pirbhai [1987].

Kernighan and Pike [1984] and Schmitt [1989] describe the UNIX and OS/2 environments, respectively. Scheifler et al. [1988], Young [1989], and Stallman [1984] are references for the X Window system, the Xt tool kit, and Emacs, respectively. Boudier et al. [1988] and Thomas [1989] describe PCTE's main features. The "Stoneman" document [DOD, 1980] defined the requirements for Ada programming support environments (known as APSEs); Oberndorf [1988] describes the interface set (CAIS) for an APSE.

The literature contains suggestions, criteria, and proposals for the construction of complete software engineering environments. Of historical interest are Balzer et al. [1983], Stenning [1987], the special section of *IEEE Transactions on Software Engineering* on environment architectures, edited by Penedo and Riddle [TSE, 1988], and the special issue of *IEEE Computer* edited by Henderson and Notkin [Computer, 1987]. Taylor et al. [1988] describes a research effort representative of the 1980s.

Simon [1986] and Tichy [1987] argue about the role of artificial intelligence (AI) in software engineering. Smith et al. and other contributions in the special issue of *IEEE Transactions on Software Engineering* edited by Mostow [TSE, 1985], as well as Goldberg [1986], deal with AI-based environments.

Conklin [1987] surveys hypertext; Bigelow [1988] discusses its role in computer-aided software engineering.

Osterweil [1987] introduced the concept of a "process-centered software engineering environment." Garg and Jazayeri [1995] is a collection of the major papers in this area, including the seminal paper by Osterweil. Cugola and Ghezzi [1999] provides an evaluation of the field.

Bellay and Gall [1998] is a comparison of four commercial reverse engineering tools and a list of criteria for doing such comparisons. Mueller et al. [1992] presents a reverse engineering tool that has been influential in the field. Mueller et al. [2000] reviews software reengineering tools and environments and examines their future prospects.

Gall et al. [1997, 1998, 1999] presents methods for using a history of product releases to discover information about trends in the evolution of the (software) product.

This chapter has presented a long list of tools, in some way based primarily on their functions. It would be useful to have a more structured classification for the area. A number of classification schemes have been proposed in the past. Fuggetta [1993] is one such classification that divides tools into process and metaprocess varieties. The difficulty with these classifications is that they quickly become outdated as new kinds of tools are invented.

# CHAPTER 10

# Epilogue

Our society is growing increasingly dependent on software for its critical functions, from health to defense and from industry to education. Software provides the glue for many services and devices on which we now rely: banking services, home security devices, air-traffic control, airplane navigation, mobile phones, Internet communication, etc. As software is used to provide more functions, our need for larger and more complex software grows. This growth of society's reliance on software both promises exciting opportunities for the software engineering community and, at the same time, places responsibility on the community to find better ways of meeting society's expectations. To meet these expectations, we must be able to produce reliable software at a reasonable cost and within a reasonable amount of time. That is exactly the goal of software engineering.

Throughout this book, we have maintained that the best way to meet software requirements is to apply traditional engineering principles. We started by presenting a set of software qualities (Chapter 2), followed by a set of engineering principles (Chapter 3). In succeeding chapters, we showed how these principles can be applied methodically in different software engineering activities, including software design, specification, verification, process, and management.

In this chapter, we conclude the book by looking to the future of software engineering. We then examine societal and ethical issues that are raised by the increasing use of software in critical applications. Finally, we offer some concluding remarks. As usual, the last section of the chapter contains references to further reading material.

## 10.1   THE FUTURE

In a short time, software technology has developed from infancy to being a dominant force in our society. Indeed, the management and control of most of our society's infrastructure are now entrusted to software. The successful application of software to all areas of society—commerce, business, education, and government—has caused an explosive demand for software in increasingly challenging tasks.

The rapid rise in the demand for software, combined with the effort required to maintain existing software, has created a large and growing backlog of software applications that need to be written. This backlog will not go away easily. There is a critical need for professional software engineers, well trained in principles and theories, to address the backlog.

Successful software engineering requires the application of engineering principles guided by informed management. The principles must themselves be rooted in sound theory. We have emphasized that there are no miracles or panaceas, and there are no "silver bullets." On the other hand, the age-old engineering principles are still valid. We need to critically assess and adapt them to apply to new problems and techniques.

Software engineering is a young discipline, and steady progress is being made. Indeed, the amount of progress from the inception of software engineering is astounding. There are a number of areas that promise to increase software productivity, as well as to help the field mature into a real engineering discipline. In the rest of this section, we take a look at some of these areas.

We have emphasized throughout the book that mathematical, rigorous approaches must be combined with experimentation, intuition, and common sense. For example, the rigor of program verification must be combined with the flexibility of software prototyping. The engineer must be able to follow a highly disciplined process that goes from specification to code, for example, in safety-critical applications. The engineer must also be able to adapt to a process that is highly flexible, for instance, in applications with volatile requirements. The principles we have studied are complementary in many ways. The engineer faces trade-offs in combining them.

Specialization is another sign of a mature engineering profession. Civil engineers, for example, specialize in bridges, in residential houses, and in hotels, restaurants, or hospitals. Years of specialized experience develop the judgment and intuition of a bridge designer to the point where he or she is able to design increasingly more sophisticated bridges. One would not ask an engineer with experience in building apartment complexes to build an important bridge. In the software field, unfortunately, having written a "hello, world" program, a beginning programmer earns the title of programmer and may be asked to program any kind of application. Software engineers will have to specialize in different application domains. We are already seeing some level of specialization—for example, in real-time or database systems or even client-server programming. Specialization will aid in developing common models, notations, and abstractions specific to the different domains. The common abstractions can, in turn, lead to common software components. We are already seeing the development of domain-specific technologies.

Specialization, however, should be built on top of wide-spectrum fundamental education. The education must equip the software engineer with mathematical maturity and the ability to understand and speak the technical language of other fields in which software applications will ultimately be deployed.

An important area of progress is component-based development. The best way to deal with the software backlog is to *avoid* writing new software and use existing components. By building software from preexisting proven parts, we can reduce the time needed to build and verify new software. Many technologies that support component-based development are evolving. Among these technologies are software architectures, particularly for product families and component models and standards.

There are many difficulties, as we have seen, in determining which components should be standard, how to specify the standard components, how to build them, and how to classify and find them. Standard designs and architectures for software products—such as the standard designs for houses—would encourage the development of reusable software components. Standard designs are related to software specialization; this relationship has been exploited for years in the telecommunications industry, where software engineers specialize in different aspects of switching-system software and standard architectures are common-place. We are also seeing standard architectures and component models appear for distributed applications.

These standard architectures and component models aim to allow the use of existing components in new applications. Preexisting components that are already tested and certified can shorten development time significantly. As we have seen, however, it is not easy to specify precisely what these components do. Such component-based software engineering requires progress in many areas, including programming language technology.

Component reuse is sometimes more easily achieved with larger pieces of software. One successful example of software reusability is user-interface management systems. These systems are built on the basis of a standard application design in which the interface component is well isolated from the rest of the system. As we mentioned earlier, a standard application design is a prerequisite for the discovery and use of standard components.

Another example of software reusability is the use of a database system as a component in other applications. The success achieved in reusing a database as a component can also be attributed to the use of a standard architecture that relies on a component for data storage and retrieval. What also helps is the application designer's knowledge of the existence of common database management systems and their interfaces. The well-defined functionality of such systems allows the application designers to tailor their designs to take advantage of, and accept the restrictions on, a database system as a subcomponent.

Reusability can be generalized to apply to all software artifacts, not just lines of code. That is, we need to be able to reuse knowledge, requirements, architecture, design, code, and tests. It is currently difficult to package experience gained from one project to reuse it in other projects.

Again, the reuse of previous knowledge and designs is standard practice in established engineering disciplines such as civil and mechanical engineering. A prerequisite of this reuse is the ability to codify (i.e., specify) existing knowledge. Once such knowledge can be codified, it is provided in handbooks that practicing engineers consult to avoid rederiving knowledge. In a sense, software engineering will be considered to have achieved the status of a true engineering discipline only after we have such handbooks that software engineers can use in their daily work.

The availability of fast communication through the Internet has had profound effects, and caused revolutionary changes in many fields, including software engineering. Distributed virtual teams demand new forms of cooperation, which affect both product technologies and the software process. The distributed environment requires, and has made possible, new user interfaces, new design and review methods, new team organizations, and new tools. As is exemplified by the open-source movement, completely new and surprising alternatives to many traditional approaches are possible. For example, it is possible to coordinate the efforts of very large numbers of software engineers in an apparently arbitrary and democratic way. Also, with regard to application server technologies, we no longer need to develop an application and run it in-house: We can use the functionality on a far-away machine somewhere on the 'Net. New application areas are being dreamed of all the time. Electronic commerce and pervasive computing, for example, hold enough software engineering challenges to keep the field exciting for many years to come.

## 10.2   ETHICS AND SOCIAL RESPONSIBILITY

In this book, we have discussed the technical aspects of software engineering. We have presented principles and methods for producing reliable software. But the growing dependence of society on software also places a tremendous social responsibility on the shoulders of software engineers and their managers. When software is being used to monitor the health of patients, control nuclear power plants, apply the brakes in an automobile, transfer billions of dollars in an instant, launch missiles, or navigate an airplane, it is not simply good engineering to build reliable software; it is also the engineer's ethical responsibility to do so.

There are many reports of software defects that have cost lives or tremendous business losses. One such defect—discovered, fortunately, before the software was put into use—would have caused a fighter airplane to flip each time it crossed the equator. Another software defect was responsible for administering large doses of radiation that caused the deaths of several patients. Yet another, rather famous, defect caused the usually extremely reliable telephone lines to become unavailable for many hours. While not all program defects are as dramatic or as well publicized, all must be treated seriously: Even a seemingly innocuous defect in an electronic game can cause serious stress for a young (or old!) user.

Defects and failures are costly. Unfortunately, they are also unavoidable in any engineering activity. By relying on principles and sound methods, as well as the experiences of the past, we can try to prevent and avoid defects and failures. But when they do occur, we must examine them in order to understand their causes, so that we can avoid such failures in the future. Engineering failures offer valuable information to complement our state of knowledge.

Finally, just as computers and their software have opened up new opportunities for increasing productivity and services, they have also opened up new opportunities for criminal fraud and sabotage. They have provided another way to steal without leaving fingerprints and to shut down or otherwise sabotage businesses without being physically present. While these problems have not been invented by software engineering, and their solutions are not the sole responsibility of software engineers, we are responsible for minimizing, if not eliminating, the new problems that software creates. In particular, it is within the purview of software engineering to build software that resists, as much as possible, unauthorized use, so-called viruses, and serious damage.

Program defects are not merely inconvenient "bugs" or interesting technical puzzles to be captured, but potentially serious business- or life-threatening errors. Building reliable software is a technical objective of the software engineer, but it also has ethical and social implications that must guide the actions of the serious professional. In this light, "hacking"—that is, inserting "playful" bugs into programs, creating viruses, writing quick and dirty code just to meet a schedule or a market window, shipping defective software, and even shipping software that works, but does not meet the agreed-upon specifications—is unethical.

## 10.3    SOFTWARE ENGINEERING CODE OF ETHICS

It is easy, as well as productive, to get lost in the excitement of a project and think of nothing else but the achievement of the project's goals. But because of the importance of software in our society, the work of a software engineer affects more than the immediate project. Sometimes, decisions we make may have far-reaching implications for the public interest. To provide a framework that guides the software engineer in making ethical decisions, the ACM and IEEE Computer Society have developed a "Software engineering code of ethics and professional practices." The "public interest" is central to the code, which emphasizes the professional's obligation to the public at large: The concern for the health, safety, and welfare of the public is primary.

The preamble of the code states that

> Computers have a central and growing role in commerce, industry, government, medicine, education, entertainment, and society at large. Software engineers are those who contribute by direct participation or by teaching, to the analysis, specification, design, development, certification, maintenance, and testing of software systems. Because of their roles in developing software systems, software engineers have significant opportunities to do good or cause harm. To ensure, as much as possible, that their efforts will be used for good, software engineers must commit themselves to making software engineering a beneficial and respected profession. In accordance with that commitment, software engineers shall adhere to the following Code of Ethics and Professional Practice.

The code lists eight principles for the software engineer to follow. These principles divide the code's ethical concerns into different categories and state specific obligations for each category. The eight principles are as follows:

1. **Public**: Software engineers shall act consistently with the public interest.
2. **Client and Employer**: Software engineers shall act in a manner that is in the best interests of their client and employer, consistent with the public interest.

3. **Product**: Software engineers shall ensure that their products and related modifications meet the highest professional standards possible.

4. **Judgment**: Software engineers shall maintain integrity and independence in their professional judgment.

5. **Management**: Software engineering managers and leaders shall subscribe to and promote an ethical approach to the management of software development and maintenance.

6. **Profession**: Software engineers shall advance the integrity and reputation of the profession, consistent with the public interest.

7. **Colleagues**: Software engineers shall be fair to, and supportive of, their colleagues.

8. **Self**: Software engineers shall participate in lifelong learning regarding the practice of their profession and shall promote an ethical approach to the practice of the profession.

For each of the principles, the code gives more detailed recommendations. For example, guideline 2.01 under "Client and Employer" states that software engineers shall "Provide service in their areas of competence, being honest and forthright about any limitation of their experience and education."

While the Code of Ethics does not make it easy for engineers to select among choices that they face in their professional practice, it does provide a framework within which one can think about the issues and apply the best judgment. Such issues are rarely clear cut, and the code does not try to create a straitjacket. Rather, the engineer must adapt the code to the given situation when necessary.

## 10.4 CONCLUDING REMARKS

We have presented many details and principles of software engineering in this book. Successful software engineering requires the integration and use of principles, tools, and methodologies. It requires an understanding of theory and the use of intuition and judgment that is developed only through practice. Textbook knowledge is not enough and does not make one a good software engineer. But practical experience alone, without the textbook knowledge, is not enough either. Both are required. This book provides the necessary textbook knowledge. The application of this knowledge in practice can help make you a successful software engineer.

## BIBLIOGRAPHIC NOTES

Brooks [1987] is a thoughtful piece which argues that there are no "silver bullets" in software engineering. That is, no one solution will address all the challenges in the discipline. Parnas [1985] provides insightful comments on the inherent difficulties of software and addresses the ethical issues raised by mission-critical applications. Parnas [1994b] differentiates among personal, social, and professional responsibility and lists the components of professional responsibility for software engineering. The collection of essays by Parnas are included in the book Hoffman and Weiss [2001].

Neumann [1995] provides an impressive list of software-generated failures and documented risks to the public due to defective software; the list is continuously updated by Neumann's column ("Risks to the Public") in *ACM Software Engineering Notes*.

Denning [1989] is the editor of a special issue of the *Communications of the ACM* that contains a controversial essay by Dijkstra and rebuttals by other prominent educators on the subject of how to teach software engineering. Dijkstra argues for absolute formality. Our viewpoint in this text is that a sound engineering approach must build on formal foundations, but should also integrate empirical knowledge.

The Experience Factory (Basili [1995]) is a model and an approach to running a software development organization so that experience from a project can be packaged and reused in other projects.

CACM [1989] contains several papers dealing with the social responsibility of computing professionals. The topics include the use of computers in law, in the military, and in support of the disabled. The Code of Ethics appears, among other places, in Gottebarn et al. [1999].

Miles [1984] examines the landmark case of *Apple* vs. *Franklin*, which established some of the bases of computer software copyright laws. The open-source movement has uncovered a number issues related to software licensing. Bruce Perens (in an article in Dibona et al. [1999]) discusses the definition of "open-source," as well as various software licensing policies.

The report issued by the Computer Science and Technology Board of the National Research Council of the U.S.A. (CSTB [1989]) proposed a research agenda for software engineering. Ten years later, Basili et al. [1999] assessed some critical issues in software engineering that research must address. The list is the result of a workshop that brought together a panel of experts organized by the National Science Foundation.

Finkelstein [2000] is a collection of articles written by experts in different areas of software engineering. The book presents an outlook of the future in each area for the new millennium.

Having finished this book, you can now follow the current state of the art in several journals. The following are the most important ones for software engineering: *ACM Transactions on Software Engineering and Methodology, IEEE Transactions on Software Engineering, IEEE Software, Communications of the ACM, Software—Practice and Experience*, and *Journal of Systems and Software*. The newsletter *Software Engineering Notes* of the Special Interest Group on Software Engineering of the ACM also contains much useful information.

# Case Studies

Software engineering principles provide a firm foundation upon which to build software systems. Throughout this book, we have presented principles and techniques for a disciplined approach to software engineering. To motivate the need for such a systematic approach, the case studies here offer a close look at the state of practice of software engineering and the problems faced every day by software engineers.

These are case studies of real software engineering projects. We shall review the progress of the projects from their inception to the delivery of the product. We shall see what can go wrong in such projects. We also shall learn that the success or failure of a project depends heavily on technical skills or mistakes, as well as on nontechnical ones, in inseparable ways.

We shall carefully analyze the failures and the successes, trying to relate them to mistakes or deliberate choices that were made in order to highlight the important issues that are often ignored in a software project or in decisions about a software process. A key point is that the people involved in each project were educated and experienced software engineers. Yet, they sometimes repeated the well-known mistakes of many projects that went before them. These projects are fairly typical of industry practices.

As you read through these case studies, contrast the events described with the principles presented in the book. In what ways were the principles followed, and in what ways were they not? Were the reasons for success or failure technical or nontechnical?

## CASE STUDY A: AUTOMATING A LAW OFFICE

A few years ago, the leaders of a software company realized that law offices such as title companies were poorly automated. At most, these offices used general-purpose word processors and, possibly, some package for computing invoices or payroll.

The company felt that an integrated office automation tool, including sophisticated and specialized word-processing features, could lead to more efficiency in law offices. For example, legal documents could be prepared much more efficiently with such a tool because they typically follow some standard rules of composition. Many sales agreements could be expressed using the following pattern:

- Write the standard header of the document (e.g., "This document pertains to the sale of a residence").
- Write the relevant data about the seller. (The typist should have to type only the data necessary to identify the person; all remaining data should be retrieved automatically from the appropriate database.)
- If the seller is married, the data about the spouse should also be included. This action should be done automatically as well.
- The same procedure must be followed for the buyer.
- Then a standard schema of the document should follow. However, some particular data (e.g., dates and payments) should be typed explicitly, some data should be filled in automatically from files, and some data (e.g., taxes) should be computed automatically on the basis of other data.

The analysis of rules of this type, combined with the facts that the company had a strong experience in sophisticated word-processing tools, potential customers were generally wealthy, and no strong competitors existed yet in the market, convinced the leaders of the company that developing a tool for automating law offices could be good business.

The company's first decision was to contact a sample of potential customers to see whether they would be interested in such a product and which features would be desirable. At first, the executives of the firm contacted a few personal acquaintances. Next, they contacted the members of a professional committee on the use of computers in law offices. In both cases, the reaction was enthusiastic, and this led directly to the decision to go ahead with the project.

Thus far, the company's behavior seems quite natural, but it contains a first, serious, mistake: The sample of potential customers that was selected was biased. The people were already familiar with, and fairly supportive of, the benefits of automation, and there was no evidence that this attitude was representative of the whole profession.

Here we see a first example of the interaction between technical and nontechnical knowledge in a feasibility study of software projects. This early analysis of the potential market for the software product was conducted nonscientifically for probably two reasons. On the one hand, market analysis techniques have difficulty dealing with ill-defined markets: It is difficult or even impossible to plan a software product on the basis of the same considerations one uses in examining a project to build a new car or a new washing machine. In this case, the planned software product was intended to create a new market and required analysis of an as-yet nonexistent market. On the other hand, the marketing analysis was performed by "pure software engineers," who had little or no background in the marketing field, but who exhibited a "pioneering" attitude. This attitude overwhelmed the engineering attitude: Innovative software was considered to be the result of a stroke of genius—maybe even luck—more than the result of a structured, tedious, job.

While innovation and pioneering have their places, they cannot form the basis of a discipline and certainly not the basis of a product development schedule.

## A.1 Economic and Financial Planning

Economic and financial planning is another area in which strong interaction between engineering and nonengineering skills is needed in the early planning of a product. Economic and financial planning requires both the ability to forecast future sales—which is influenced by one's knowledge of both the price at which the product can be sold and the number of items sold—and the ability to estimate development costs.

The same market analysis difficulties we discussed before make it difficult to forecast the revenue expected of a new product. The difficulty with estimating software development costs is that software cannot be developed faster simply by adding more people to the project. This distinguishes software from most other engineering products. While the same phenomenon holds during the design phase of any product, what sets software apart is that the "design phase" for software is not a relatively short period at the beginning of development, but seems to go on throughout the entire development process. The person making the cost estimates—who is usually not an engineer—must understand this phenomenon.

In the current case study, the economic analysis, as well as the market analysis, was flawed dramatically. Since the difficulties of making estimates in both areas are well known, the major error—a very common one—was the absence of any risk analysis. No precautions were taken to control what was known to be a critical activity. When it became apparent that all original estimates were terribly wrong, nobody suggested a plan of action of a type that said, "Well, guys, we missed the first deadlines; we are going to spend much more money than originally planned. So let's rethink the whole plan and examine more carefully whether we can still afford to do the project." Instead, only "day-by-day" actions were undertaken, both from a technical and from a financial point of view. The result was that in a short time, the company was in serious financial trouble.

Again, this management mistake is a very common one. It is naturally explained by the fact that short-term decisions overwhelm long-term planning. Too often, the damages of this psychological attitude become apparent when it is too late to recover from them.

## A.2 Technical Planning and Management

At the start of the project, it would have been wise to write clear and precise documents stating the requirements for the new product. These documents should have been based on a careful and organized interaction with potential users, paying close attention to choosing a representative sample of the expected users.

One might argue that it would have been difficult, or even impossible, to write such documents, since the desirable features of the system were not clear in the first place. A possible solution to this problem would have been to put a limited effort into the development of a system that would act as a prototype. The prototype system would then help assess the most critical issues and derive firm requirements by observing users' reactions when they used the system. Unfortunately, the designers did not even realize that a problem existed, and therefore, they did not even consciously choose between the first alternative—specifying requirements carefully—and the second—developing a fast, exploratory prototype.

The lack of a clear understanding of the requirements and of how they would affect costs led the designers to include both questionable features (from the expected user's standpoint) and very expensive features in the system. Everybody was excited with the innovative and challenging features of the product, but nobody paid much attention to fairly obvious, but critical, details. For instance, a sophisticated document specification language was designed to allow users to define their own document composition rules. Very sophisticated—and expensive—word-processing facilities were included without anyone measuring their cost-effectiveness. (They were just "nice to have.") Moreover, for a long time, nobody paid attention to the definition of suitable user interfaces to facilitate the interaction of nontechnical people (e.g., a lawyer or a secretary) with the system. Similarly, sophisticated features for the automatic computation of invoices on the basis of input data (people time, value of services, travel expenses, etc.) were designed, but no attention was paid to standard office operations, such as the filing of large numbers of documents.

From a management point of view, all of the designers of the system were attracted by the most interesting features of the new product, so that a lot of work was done in the early phases to find and compare clever solutions to marginal problems, and no structure was arranged for the design team. Later, someone observed that the design team looked like a soccer team composed of beginning players: Everybody was playing close to where the ball was!

From a technical viewpoint, many typical mistakes were made:

- No analysis was performed to determine whether all the product's features were needed by all users or whether it would be better to restructure the functionality of the product on the basis of different classes of users. More generally, no effort was put into determining which qualities of the product were most critical to its success. For instance, in the choice of the hardware and of the development software (the operating system, programming language, etc.), little or no attention was paid to their evolution, and no effort was made to prepare for possible changes to them.

- No "design for change" was done; that is, no design decision was influenced by any analysis of which parts of the product were likely to change during the product's lifetime (e.g., how might possible changes in the law affect product requirements?).

- Strong pressure was applied to have some (*any*) code running as early as possible.

- No precautions were taken to minimize damages due to personnel turnover.

What is perhaps worth pointing out is that everybody in the company was, of course, aware of such classical mistakes in software engineering. This awareness notwithstanding, the mistakes were made. Thus, knowing the difficulties is not enough: It is also necessary to have the technical and organizational ability and willingness to face them, even at the cost of doing something that does not appear immediately attractive and productive.

## A.3    Project Monitoring

After a while (about six months after the start of development), some mistakes became apparent, both from a technical and from a management point of view. For instance, the lack of a clear definition of the product's functionality caused some initial misunderstandings between the potential users—the ones with whom the early contacts had been established—and the designers. It was realized that some features that had been neglected at the beginning were actually quite important. Also, getting in touch with other potential users showed that not all of them needed the same features. Thus, a modular architecture would have been preferable, even from the user point of view, allowing the product to be customized for different classes of users, just as the same "skeleton" of a car can be sold with different types of engines, with different optional features, etc., or the same personal computer can be sold with many optional features (e.g., a high-resolution video card or a different network adapter). Finally, it became apparent that the original cost estimates were off by an order of magnitude.

This misestimation invalidated the initial economic and financial plans, and the reaction to the situation was even worse than the problem itself: The impact of the mistakes—both technical and nontechnical—was again underestimated. In general, the attitude was of the following type: "OK, we made a few mistakes, but now we are almost done. So let's put in a little more effort, and we'll complete the product soon and will start earning money." That is, no critical and careful analysis of the mistakes was made, nor was a serious replanning and redesign of the whole project attempted. There was only a generic claim of an intuitive confidence in being close to the end.

The consequences of this attitude were disastrous. With the designers under the pressure of "being almost done and close to delivering the product," they focused the design more and more on the very end product—that is, *code*. "Patches" on object code were made wildly, no systematic error and correction logs were kept, and communication among designers occurred almost exclusively orally in an attempt to save time.

The same attitude prevailed on the managerial and financial front: Since "we are almost done," "we just need a little more financing and can accept almost any terms."

## A.4    Initial Delivery

It was decided that income could be generated as soon as the company started delivering the first versions of the product or as soon as new contracts could be signed. In turn, the customers would be good references for the product, resulting in an opportunity both to improve the product and to increase its sales.

This decision, too, turned out to be a big mistake. In fact, a new dimension was added to the already critical technical and management problems. Since the rule was "sign the contract anyway," while the product was not clearly defined and was only partially developed, early customers had many problems with the product. This caused a lot of internal problems also, because it was not clear whether some activity fell under product development or user assistance; nor was it clear who had to do what. After a while, it was realized that almost everybody on the product team had performed some marketing, some development, some user assistance, some hardware acquisition, etc., according to an unpredictable flow of events.

## A.5    Partial Recovery

Eventually, it was realized that the naive way the firm was managing the project was leading to disaster. Thus, a real effort was made, first to define responsibilities clearly (who was responsible for the design, who was responsible for the distribution, etc.),[1] and second, to achieve a clear picture of the state of the product, of its weaknesses, of the effort required to fix them, and so on. This was done even at the expense of slowing down the project, increasing costs, and reducing sales. As a result, people had to resist an initial feeling that the restructuring of the project was impeding "real" progress.

After a while, however, the improvements became apparent, so that, eventually, the product really existed and full documentation was available. The company actually started to ship the product and earn money from it, although far less than expected initially, mainly because the delayed introduction of the product caused it to enter a more competitive market than anticipated.

## CASE STUDY B: BUILDING A FAMILY OF COMPILERS

In contrast to the previous case study, the software engineering project described next was a modest success.

## B.1    Initial Product Planning

The study concerns a project that was conducted in a medium-sized computer company. The goal of the project was to produce a new family of compilers for languages C, FORTRAN, and Pascal for the company's line of computers. The project was undertaken for several reasons:

- The existing compilers were showing their age: They had too many defects that were too hard to fix, and more defects were being reported than could be fixed by the engineers. The existing compilers were written when the company was started, under strict time pressures. The effects of this constraint showed in the quality of the code and the quantity and quality of its documentation. That was the reason the compilers were so hard to repair. It seemed that the compilers had outlived their useful time, and the best thing to do was to retire them.

- There were three different compilers, one each for the three languages C, FORTRAN, and Pascal. Thus, any code generation or optimization essentially had to be applied three different times, and the same defect was reported three different times, once for each language. The technology of compiler writing was now advanced enough that it was possible to write a family of compilers that shared many parts and specialized only in their treatment of language-specific aspects. In particular, the plan called for different parsers for different languages, but a code generator and, as important, a code optimizer to be shared by all the compilers.

---

[1] These roles, of course, existed even before, but they were merely nominal, so that, in practice, everybody was responsible for everything (and nobody was responsible for anything).

- The main attraction of the company's computer was its high performance. Unfortunately, competitors were now introducing new computers with essentially the same hardware performance, but much better compilers. The only way for the company to compete in the performance area was to have the compilers generate much better code. (A new processor was being designed, but it was not expected to be available for several years.) Unfortunately, the current compiler design and code did not allow easy optimization extensions, and the cost of doing three different optimizers seemed prohibitive.

- The combination of all these reasons led the company to the decision that a new family of compilers was needed.

## B.2   Economic and Financial Planning

In established companies, a major product development is preceded by a feasibility study, which, among other things, focuses on economic and financial forecasts. In particular, such a study computes the *return on investment* (ROI), to determine whether the product will produce sufficient profit. In this case, however, the decision to proceed with the development of the compilers was essentially dictated by technical considerations and absolute need.

The only consideration given to economics was a rough calculation of how many people the project would require. Even that analysis was based mostly on how many people were already part of the compiler team, rather than the magnitude of the work to be undertaken.

## B.3   Technical Planning and Management

Early investigation revealed that several software vendors sold compilers that could be used as starting points. Since the company produced a proprietary processor, it would have to write a new code generator (or modify an existing one). There was no reason, however, to rewrite parsers for C, Pascal, and FORTRAN if they could be bought at a reasonable price. The value that the company was going to add to the product was not in parsing technology, but in code generation and optimization.

After careful evaluation of several vendors and their products, one was chosen on the strength of the design of its compilers. The winning compiler satisfied all the requirements: It was constructed from a language-specific parser (C, Pascal, FORTRAN, and others), which translated the source code into a canonic "intermediate code"; an optimizer, which translated from the intermediate code to more optimal intermediate code; and a code generator, which translated from the intermediate code to assembly language. The code generator and optimizer were shared by all compilers for a given machine. The intermediate language was general enough to handle languages that the company was planning to offer later (such as Ada). Finally, and most importantly, the vendor's compilers for existing machines generated very efficient code (benchmarked against other compilers), and the structure of the optimizer allowed the addition of more optimizations.

There was no specific technical or management plan for the project. Since the company was already maintaining a set of compilers, it had a general plan that once the new compilers arrived from the vendor, three engineers would spend "enough" of their time to write a new code generator and a new optimizer. It was vaguely expected that this would take about a year. There was a great reliance on the competence and help of the software vendor. Estimates of time and effort were simply requested from the vendor. This method of software cost estimation is called "expert judgment": Simply ask an expert. It is probably the most commonly practiced method of software cost estimation.

## B.4    Early Development Phases

The requirements and specifications for the project were comparatively easy to produce, as is usual for a compiler project for a standard language. There were some issues that had to be resolved, such as which versions of the languages to accept (for example, there was a FORTRAN standard, but with several popular supersets) and what compiler speed or quality of code was required, but these issues were easily resolved by using the existing set of compilers as a minimum base: The new compilers had to be compatible with the existing ones in terms of *functionality* and had to exceed the existing ones in terms of *quality*. Quality was defined roughly to include the amount of code optimization, the speed of the compiler, the extent of extensions accepted for the standard languages, and the amount of support for source-level debugging (the original compilers did not support this feature).

Once the software became available from the vendor, three engineers were assigned to the project. The senior member of the three was sent to the vendor for one week of training on the software, for which, incidentally, there was not much external documentation: The code was the only source of any information on the software design, assumptions, algorithms, etc. Therefore, the personal training of the engineer was a kind of "oral documentation" on the software.

Once the engineer returned from his training session, the team started working on understanding the existing software and designing their extensions to the "skeleton" code generator that the company had also bought from the vendor. Again relying on the expertise of the vendor, the engineers decided that the design of the code generator skeleton was sufficient, and they did not have to do any major design themselves. They proceeded to the coding phase.

## B.5    Project Monitoring

For a variety of reasons, the project was not monitored very closely or carefully. First, the engineers assigned to the project were already responsible for maintaining the existing compilers. The problems with these compilers always took priority over work on the new compilers, which were not scheduled for release until "sometime later." While the engineers were supposed to spend half of their time on the existing compilers and half on the new ones, in practice the problems with the existing compilers always took precedence and, thus, more of the engineers' time. Second, six months after the vendor software arrived, the project manager decided to leave the company. The second-level manager was assigned as acting manager of the group while a search was initiated for a new manager. The acting manager was, of course, too busy to monitor the compiler project too closely (or at all!). His time was spent looking for a new manager, as well as looking after other groups for which he was responsible.

## B.6 Project Reexamination, Revival, and Goal Setting

Eighteen months after the arrival of the software, 12 months after the departure of the project manager, a new manager was found and hired. The last words of the acting manager before handing over responsibility of the project to the new manager were that the project was in excellent shape and that the release of the new compilers was imminent. What the new manager found, however, was different: There was no explicit schedule, no explicit assignment of responsibility to people, no explicit definition of quality requirements, and no effort being expended toward producing manuals. These factors led to the engineers not having a focused goal, in terms of either time or product.

The new manager had two points in his favor: He was well versed in software engineering, and, more importantly, he did not feel any personal responsibility for the project's late schedule. He could thus draw up a schedule and resource requirements based on his best judgment: Making the current problems in the project visible to company management would not reflect adversely on his abilities as a manager.

The project also had several points in its favor. The most important was that the senior engineer was a very competent software engineer. Second, the base software was indeed well designed, well constructed, and extensible. The extensions made by the engineers all had contributed toward the final goal, and none of them had to be removed.

The first job of the new manager was to quantify the status of the project: how much work was already done, how much work was left to be done, and how much time and effort would be required to get the remaining work done. As a first attempt at estimating the remaining work, the size of the compilers, in terms of number of lines, was measured against the vendor's compilers for other, similar machines. The sizes turned out to be roughly the same. This raised a vague hope that maybe not much more new code was left to be written.

At the time, the engineers had been working on their part of the code, slowly polishing what each was responsible for. For example, one had spent weeks trying to generate the best possible code for Pascal **for** loops. Yet, there was no overall feeling of how much each part that they were working on was contributing to the whole project.

The next step in assessing the current state of the project was to identify a standard test suite for Pascal compilers. The suite would serve several purposes: First, it would document and demonstrate to the management how far the compiler project still had to go; second, it would give the engineers an objective goal; and third, it would establish a basis for regression testing.

Unfortunately, on the first try, of the 350 test cases, the compiler passed fewer than 10! Although this was discouraging to the whole team, a little reflection and some examination of the test results made it clear that the situation was not so bad. Indeed, the situation was a clear example of the difficulty of measuring how much software work is left to do. In this case, a few simple defects in the basic code generation scheme were responsible for all the failures. Fixing those defects, which took less than a day, helped the reputation of the compiler team tremendously: Now, the compiler passed over 100 tests successfully! Disabling the optimizer allowed the compiler to pass another 50 tests. Regardless of how many tests the compiler was still failing—over 200—the foundations were now laid for a way to measure progress. Thus, while the publicly available test suite was initially viewed with skepticism by most of the team as little more than a toy, it now became a challenging goal to be conquered.

The manager informed company executives that the compilers were not even close to being released. The "toy" test suite was proof enough: No matter how much management was interested in shipping the product, it was not interested in shipping a product that clearly did not work. The manager also started working on establishing an agreement between the different departments in the company—marketing, customer service, documentation, and engineering—as to the minimum product that would be shipped. The marketing department was asked to identify 10 beta sites. More importantly, it was asked to locate two existing customers who had the largest applications and had had trouble with the company's first set of compilers. All parties agreed that unless these two customers were happy with the compilers, the compilers would not be released. This agreement established a common goal for the compiler team that was visible to, and understandable by, the whole company.

Once this major agreement had been reached—finally establishing the major project *requirements*—it was possible to make a project plan and schedule various activities. Some activities were external to the compiler team and some were internal. An effort was started to write manuals for the products. The marketing department began producing promotional material (using "carefully tested products" as a marketing slogan).

Soon the team was able to identify some major milestones: passing the standard Pascal test suite completely, self-compilation (being able to compile the family of compilers with the new Pascal compiler), successfully compiling major in-house applications (e.g., editors and simulators), successfully compiling the operating system, successfully compiling typical customer applications (in all three languages), and successfully compiling the two agreed-upon major customer applications. These milestones all assessed functional requirements. Other acceptance milestones were also established. Common industry performance benchmarks were selected to measure the quality of the compilers' code optimization. The minimal goal was established that the code produced by the new compilers had to execute at least 20% faster than the old compilers. Another goal was that the compilation speed had to be no worse than that of the old compilers.

A monthly progress report was established to keep the company management and the team informed of the state of the project.

## B.7    Assignment of Responsibility

It was clear that the abilities of the team members were not uniform and that the members had not been assigned to the most appropriate tasks. For example, it appeared that if the senior engineer had been left alone, he would have been able to produce more than all three engineers combined! The situation called for a reassignment of responsibilities in such a way as to ensure rapid progress, take advantage of all the engineers' strengths, and keep all team members happy and motivated.

The senior engineer was made the lead architect responsible for the overall design and correctness of the software. One junior engineer was assigned to debug the symbolic debugging code under the close supervision of the manager. This was a challenge to the engineer, and the supervision was welcomed. The other junior engineer was assigned to assist the senior engineer and to be responsible for running the tests and summarizing the results. (For example, how many of the 200 test failures were due to the same defect?) Testing is usually not a glamorous activity among software engineers, but in this case, because of the important role that the test suite had played, it was perceived as very important (which it was!).

Finally, one of the company's largest customers, an overseas computer company, was asked to send two compiler testing experts to help in debugging the compilers. The customer was happy to provide this help, because it gave the firm better visibility as to how the project was going and better assurance that it would get a more reliable product.

## B.8    Steady Progress and Release of the Product

Clear goals, clear job assignments, good software design, competent engineering, and concerned supervision led to steady progress. Milestones were met in rapid succession. The testing team was able to identify defects, narrow them down as much as possible, and pass them on to the code experts, who in most cases were able to fix them very quickly. The results of the test suites were routinely "advertising" the amount of progress being made. The new environment created a team out of what used to be individual engineers working on their own code. The team environment reinforced the individual motivations, and the progress reported by the test results added encouragement.

Eight months after the new manager had joined the project and the team had been reorganized, the compilers were released to the manufacturing department. No reports of defects were received for two months after the release of the compilers. (This was in sharp contrast to the experience with the old compilers, which could now be retired.) The careful testing had definitely paid off.

## B.9    Product Distribution

An interesting aside about this case study involves the timing of the release of the product to customers. The manager had been pressed for a release date from the beginning, but he resisted committing the company to a date until after the compilers had passed the first test suite completely. At that time, with some confidence, he gave a release date of October 15. By coincidence (and no doubt, with much luck), the compilers were indeed released to the manufacturing department on October 15. Yet the compilers were not released to customers until six weeks later, meaning that—because of year-end holidays—the customers did not receive the new compilers until January of the following year.

Much of the work needed in manufacturing—bookkeeping, assigning product numbers, updating inventory, etc.—could have been done in anticipation of the October 15 release, so that the product could have been distributed to customers in November. Yet, on the basis of its experience with all previous estimates from the engineering department, the manufacturing department had all the confidence that it would not receive the compilers by October 15. To the manufacturing department, a promise from engineering was sure to be broken!

The monetary effect of the engineering department's promise not being taken seriously was that back orders for the compilers were not filled as early as they could have been, delaying the receipt of important revenue for close to two months. The delay in receiving the sizable revenue in fact made a big difference to the company.

## B.10    Remarks

This case study reveals the following interesting points, which we have examined throughout the book. Let us look at some of them in detail:

**Software reusability.**  Probably the most important factor that led to the success of the project—despite lax initial management—was the fact that the major part of the software and the major design for the rest of it were bought from a vendor who specialized in the product. Reusable parts are crucial to other engineering disciplines, and we have repeatedly emphasized the importance of software reusability. This case study shows that the reusability of both code and design is possible.

**Key personnel.**  There is no doubt that the project would have failed without the lead engineer. In this case, the support of the other two engineers and the project manager allowed the lead engineer to concentrate on the key problems, in a sort of a chief-programmer team style. Highly skilled, highly productive software engineers are rare and hard to replace. Cost estimation models and practical experience show that key personnel are a major determinant of the success or failure of a project.

**Cost estimation.**  If software engineering were truly an engineering discipline, the company's choice of whether to buy software or develop it in-house would have been made on the basis of a cost analysis. Indeed, even the code generator could have been developed through a contract with the vendor of the compiler, but for reasons that are not clear to us, it was not. It would have made a very good case study for a software engineering textbook to say that a cost estimation model (e.g., COCOMO II) was used to decide whether to develop or buy software. Unfortunately, all these decisions were simply based on "expert judgment," with no supporting quantitative assessments. Even the estimate of October 15 for a release date—which turned out to be exact—was based on an intuitive analysis of test results and of the competence of the engineers, rather than a quantitative analysis of how much work was left to do.

**Clear Requirements Priorities.**  While the requirements were not specified formally in one document, the project was helped by having clear, if undocumented, priorities. The existing language standards formed precise functional requirements that had to be met. Further, the company's market dictated that the execution speed of the code to be generated was the most important quality factor. It is interesting that not all compiler projects enjoy the same clarity of goal. Many suffer from unclear requirements: Which standard and which extensions are required, the trade-off between execution speed and usage of memory, how much optimization is desired, and the relative importance of optimization versus the "debuggability" of code or program environment support may all be specified so vaguely that making trade-offs is impossible. The project examined here was also helped by the existence of a base software (the old compilers) against which progress could be measured.

**Testing.**  In many projects, testing is an activity that is done after all the work is finished. In the project we have been looking at, testing had a key role—after the project was revitalized. The tests were used as a means of measuring and communicating the status of the project, as a motivating factor for the engineers, and as a planning tool for what to do next. Again, because the project was a compiler project, many standard test suites could be used. Thus, the project team itself did not have to spend time inventing good test cases. As is common with many other engineering products, standard test suites can be used to certify software products. Of course, this can be done only for standard software products, such as compilers and operating systems, but certification via standard tests can also extend to file systems, sort routines, Web browsers, mathematical libraries, etc. A final point about the role of testing in this project is that enough time was allotted to correct the defects found during testing. That is, testing was performed not merely to prove that the software worked, but instead to find the defects that had to be fixed.

**Visibility.**   Many projects suffer from a lack of visibility or transparency as regards their status, due to psychological and sociological factors, in addition to the technical factors that we have already discussed in relation to estimating the amount of software work that has been accomplished. Individual engineers may not want to admit to themselves or their supervisors that they are behind, or even ahead of, schedule. Their supervisors may not want to admit to themselves or to their managers that they are behind schedule. (They would be jeopardizing their careers.) In turn, the top managers in the company may not want to hear that their projects are behind schedule, and they do not want to admit to the outside world that they are behind schedule. (They would be jeopardizing their company's competitiveness in the marketplace.) In general, the status of a project becomes visible only if the project has truly serious problems from which it may not be able to recover. In the project we have been describing, the new manager had no personal credibility at stake, since he had not drawn up the original schedule and had not made any promises. His not having to be personally accountable for the existing problems allowed him to be able to separate concerns for his career from those for the schedule. He was able to assess the situation and make it known to all the people who were important in making business decisions based on the technical data.

Further, the new visibility of the status of the project to top management was another motivating factor to team members. The standard test suite results served as an impartial, objective, and quantitative way of communicating the status of the project among technical and nontechnical people. The monthly status reports assured managers that progress was being made and gave the engineers a focused goal and motivated them to make progress towards that goal. The first run of the test results dashed all hopes of any miracles. The tendency to hope for miraculously getting back on schedule is common among software engineers because of the absence of objective measures for measuring progress. This has led to the popular saying, "The first 90 percent of the work is done in the first 10 percent of the time; it is the last 10 percent that takes the remaining 90 percent of the time!"

**Life Cycle.**   There certainly was no life cycle planning on the project and no clear life cycle apparent even in hindsight. This situation is probably typical of many medium-sized software projects.

**Compromises Among Goals.**   Technical issues are one of numerous factors involved in making organizational decisions. In fact, the many departments in an organization have different, and sometimes conflicting, goals. For example, the marketing department wants to ship the product as soon as possible, the engineering department wants to delay shipment until the product is perfect, the finance department may want to choose the shipment date on the basis of when it wants the revenue to show on the books, the manufacturing department wants to schedule the shipment of the product to balance the work over the different products, and the customer service department wants to ship a perfect product as soon as possible to resolve all the problems it keeps hearing about regarding the current product, but it wants to make sure that the product is perfect before it is shipped. Reaching a compromise among these goals is often a difficult management task. In the project in question, however, the test results were sufficient to convince all parties that the product was not ready for shipment. Fortunately, the steady progress reported in the monthly status reports allowed the different parties to plan ahead and reach common decisions based on the data. In practice, it is often the absence of objective data that makes group decision making difficult. Psychological and sociological factors are involved here, too, such as the personal ambitions of the decision makers and the friendship or animosity among the different protagonists. These, however, are beyond the scope of this book.

## CASE STUDY C: INCREMENTAL DELIVERY

The following brief case study shows the benefits of incrementality in refining requirements and in delivery of the product:

A computer manufacturer was building a new computer. The hardware people were busy designing and building the hardware. The software groups were busy designing and building the system software. For several reasons, the company had decided to use Pascal for all of its software development. A common goal in these circumstances is to have a compiler ready as early as possible.

The weaknesses of Pascal for systems programming were well known at the time of the project, so it was clear that many extensions were going to be needed. The language group took a poll of all the software engineers on the project to see what extensions would be needed. Every language feature ever discovered was proposed by at least one person as absolutely necessary for the product! It was clear that the compiler, including all the extensions, could not be delivered by the time the other groups were ready to start coding.

The language group decided to use the principle of incrementality. First, the group ranked the needed extensions. It scheduled three releases of the compiler: standard Pascal, Pascal with minimal extensions, and Pascal with all other extensions. The agreement was that after the minimal extensions were used for a while, a more informed decision could be made about what other extensions were actually required.

The extensions were first prototyped by implementing a preprocessor for an existing Pascal compiler. Although the preprocessor was slow and ran only on a host machine (which was not the target machine), it allowed the other engineers to use the extensions and provide feedback to the language group on the usability of the extensions.

Soon after the hardware was available, a Pascal compiler with minimal extensions was ready. This compiler allowed the engineers to start implementing their software (e.g. the operating system and a database). It actually turned out that many people had early versions of their software developed and tested on the host-based version of the prototype. In many cases, all they had to do was recompile their code.

After six months of using the compiler with minimal extensions, the language group took another poll to see whether any other extensions were needed. No other extensions were considered necessary by the users! One new extension (logical operations on integers) made the list nonetheless. This extension was meant to solve some of the efficiency problems with the code generated by the compiler. It is interesting that the original list of user requests did not include any efficiency-related extensions.

Once the language features were stabilized, there were several other compiler releases, each introducing a more sophisticated level of code optimization. Finally, an extension was added to allow bit-level operations, enabling some system code to look clearer and be more efficient.

The incremental delivery of the compiler allowed users to have access to useful functionality and allowed the compiler developers to enhance the compiler on the basis of explicit and definitive user feedback.

## CASE STUDY D: APPLYING FORMAL METHODS IN INDUSTRY

The case study we discuss in this section is an example of a technology transfer project whose main goal was to introduce an innovative approach to formal system specification in industry. In the late 1980s, a major company whose mission is in the field of energy production, transport, and distribution decided to experiment with the use of formal methods in the development of its automation applications. Typical plant automation systems are largely—but not exclusively—computer based. The main motivation for the company's decision was a strong dissatisfaction with its present state of practice. Most of the firm's reasons for its dissatisfaction were fairly standard and have been already discussed in this book: The poor quality of the specification documents in terms of precision, clarity, completeness, and consistency caused several problems during the subsequent phases of implementation and verification. In particular, errors and inadequacies in the specifications were often discovered very late, in the final system-testing stage, with disastrous effects on the budget and the schedule. Such drawbacks were further exacerbated by some peculiar features of the company and of its mission:

- The lifetime of energy production and distribution plants often extends over decades. This requires a clear distinction between their external behavior and the realization of some of their components (typically, computer-based components) whose technology evolves much faster. The situation strongly suggests adaptive maintenance.

- Quite often, the company did not build its own automation systems directly, but commissioned them to external suppliers. This approach further stresses the "what versus how" separation and emphasizes contractual implications of specification documents.

- In most cases, the products are not just single instances of a unique project. Rather, they are *families* of similar, but not identical, products. For instance, hydroelectric power systems have many similarities among each other; however, they differ in terms of several factors, such as environmental context (elevation, size of the reservoir, etc.), amount of power produced, and configuration of the plant. These similarities suggest generality and reusability from the very beginning of the project; that is, those qualities must be present even in the initial specifications, not only in the final product.

To manage the project, a mixed research group was set up with the goal of choosing an existing, or building a new, formal method that matched the needs of the company. The research group included both people from the company and consultants who specialized in formal methods.

Formal methods available at that time were judged inadequate, for two main reasons: They did not address real-time aspects, which were crucial for the application of interest, and they did not stress reusability of the specification and its management and evolution along the life cycle. For these reasons, the research group developed its own formal methods, which consisted essentially of the following features:

- A logic formalism, suitably enriched to deal explicitly with time constraints. A declarative approach based on logic was chosen instead of an operational approach to allow the formulation of more abstract requirements, independently of any implementation choices.

- A fairly standard collection of object-oriented features, such as classes, genericity, and inheritance, to enhance the structuring and evolvability of specifications.

- A set of prototype tools that allowed the editing, validation, and management of specifications, as well as the verification of the implementation, through the semiautomatic generation of test cases.

- A preliminary set of guidelines and methods directing the user during writing, analyzing, and managing specifications and parts of other deliverables (e.g., test plans).

The whole package—language, tools, and methods—was named TRIO.

Soon, engineers tried TRIO on case studies of increasing complexity derived from real-life projects that were ongoing within the company. In all cases, the expected benefits of the approach were confirmed: The specifications produced were unanimously judged to be of better quality compared with previous documents; the formal analysis applied to the specifications was more thorough and almost always either showed subtle problems that were overlooked by informal analysis or provided rigorous evidence of previous intuitions that were not sufficiently evident to all examiners.

On the basis of these first encouraging experiences, the company decided to employ the method on a challenging real-life project, with the goal of gaining a more thorough and complete assessment and of comparing its costs and benefits against those of previous methods. This project is described in the next several sections. We shall also offer a few general conclusions on the exploitation of formal methods in industrial environments.

## D.1    Education and Training

The project was carried out by people from different companies. The specifications were delivered by people from the original company (who were part of the group that developed the TRIO method). The implementation was performed by another company, and verification was carried out jointly by the two companies.

The approach required a preliminary phase of training those people who were unaware of the new method. The training, conducted by TRIO developers, touched all aspects of the method, from the basic logic formalism, to the complete OO specification language, to its tools. Training lasted nearly two months and was quite successful: At the end of this phase, the trainees were sufficiently competent and independent; most important, they became enthusiastic about the new method and were willing to apply it.

It is fair to point out that such a fortunate result has not always been achieved in similar experiences. In general, new methods are more readily accepted by young, recently hired, and highly motivated people, and that was the case in this project. Experience shows that, in general, technology transfer projects require investments in education and training, and their success depends very much on the cooperative attitude of the people involved in the project.

## D.2    Requirements Specification

The types of systems considered by the company have relatively well-established features, and their development follows a fairly standard path. For this reason, the company applied a waterfall life cycle model, with minor adaptations. Thus, attention was initially focused on the specification phase.

The system was a hydroelectric power-generation plant, as sketched in Figure D.1. A pondage power plant is composed of a reservoir where the main water supply accumulates and whose level is regulated by means of a sluice gate. When the sluice gate is open, the water flows through a channel into a tank. From the tank, the water is forced into the power station, where its mechanical energy is converted into electrical energy. The power plant is monitored through a set of sensors and is regulated by means of a set of actuators governed by a central control system.

The formal specification activity did not start completely from scratch, but was preceded by a preparatory activity whose purpose was to produce an overall description of the system structure and an informal specification of the system requirements.

Due to the complexity of the system, the preparatory activity required a significant amount of time and human resources. The activity was conducted by skilled people who were expert in the application domain, although not particularly fluent in, and experienced with, formal methods. The activity resulted in the production of a document 50 pages long, written mainly in an informal, unstructured way: natural language for general descriptions, mixed with simple mathematical and graphical notations describing some quantitative aspects of the system.

The actual formal specification activity was based on this informal specification document. In turn, it led to the production of two different documents. First, a set of notes (about 20 pages long) was produced to update and correct the initial informal specification, mainly to eliminate inconsistencies and incompleteness. These notes were a prerequisite for the formal specification activity. They were prepared by the team of specifiers, including some of the people involved in the preparation of the initial document. It was realized that the same people, when faced with the task of writing the *formal* specification of the system requirements, would be tempted to be more precise and would ask themselves questions they did not ask when they had to provide only an informal system description.

In the second step, a formal specification document was produced. The formal specification focused on the physical components of the system. Thus, it included the declaration of classes such as *reservoir, sluiceGate, channel, powerStation, tank*, and *operator*, which correspond to the components of the hydroelectric power plant shown in Figure D.1. The formal specification document was about 120 pages long, including comments in natural language, added to the logical formulas as a supplement for the

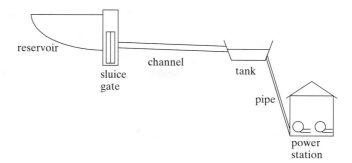

**FIGURE D.1.**

Physical components of the pondage power plant.

reader. It was deliberately decided that comments would be intermixed with formal statements, under the assumption that informal and formal description should *complement*, rather than *replace*, each other.

## D.3    Requirements Validation and Verification Planning

The specification document was used as a source both to validate requirements and to produce a test plan for the system to be implemented. In fact, as we explained in Chapter 5, formal specifications can be used to generate sample system behaviors (as well as check the system for conformance). Such sample behaviors—also called *histories* in our case study—can be utilized to check whether they correspond to the customer's expectations and, therefore, to validate specifications. Furthermore, they can be used to produce test cases that will be supplied to the system, to check whether it behaves according to the specifications. In the next subsections, we briefly report on how this approach was followed in the case study.

### D.3.1    *Validating and Revising the Specification*

The activities of writing the specification and using it to drive the design and validation phases confirmed that the requirements specification is a continuously evolving object that undergoes several modifications, even when a waterfall-like life cycle model is adopted. In this case study,

- During its revision, the specification needed corrections because of remaining incompleteness or inconsistencies. This validation activity was effectively supported by the use of a semantic tool that allowed the specifier to animate and simulate the system's behavior starting from the formal specification. For instance, the inability of the tool to generate some desirable history indicated an incompleteness of the specification. Similarly, an error in the specification could be caught when a desirable behavior contradicted one or more axioms or when a history generated by the tool was considered to be incorrect by the user.

- During the design activity, some requirements, as stated in the formal specification, proved to be infeasible or too expensive to implement. After reaching an agreement with the customer, the requirements were updated, and the formal specification was changed accordingly. This caused a feedback loop from design to specification in the waterfall life cycle.

- The specification needed some adjustments to improve its structure, without really changing the functional requirements expressed therein, but with the purpose of favoring validation and verification.

- The specification needed further changes because of adaptive maintenance, which was necessary not only after the system was implemented, but even while it was being developed. Adaptive maintenance was required due to technological changes in the environment and in the hardware components and peripherals used in the system, which in turn required minor changes in system behavior.

### D.3.2  Test Plan Construction

As we have said, the same techniques and tools that generate system histories for validating specifications can also be applied to support *black-box testing*. As a simple example, suppose that a formula specifies that, as a consequence of a *close* command, a sluice gate must be closed within $\delta_1$ and $\delta_2$ time bounds. The semantic tool could produce the following sample of sequences of events (histories):

```
History 1:
<at time t₀, command close is issued;
    at time t₀ + δ₁, the sluice gate is closed>;
```

$$\text{History 1:}$$
$$<\text{at time } t_0, \text{ command } close \text{ is issued;}$$
$$\text{at time } t_0 + \delta_1, \text{ the sluice gate is closed}>;$$

$$\text{History 2:}$$
$$<\text{at time } t_0, \text{ command } close \text{ is issued;}$$
$$\text{at time } t_0 + \delta_2, \text{ the sluice gate  is closed}>;$$

$$\text{History 3:}$$
$$<\text{at time } t_0, \text{ command } close \text{ is issued;}$$
$$\text{at time } t_0 + \delta_1 + (\delta_2 - \delta_1)/2, \text{ the sluice gate is closed}>;$$

Such histories are then used as test cases by supplying the input *close* at a given time and then verifying whether the corresponding output satisfies the specification. Clearly, in general, there could be many, or even infinite, behaviors that are consistent with a given specification. Thus, the tool must be used interactively to drive the generation of useful behaviors.

In our case study, a complete test set was derived in this way from requirements specifications. This activity required special skills for two main reasons: First, the interactive use of the tool required some nontrivial knowledge of mathematical logic; second, the tool was still in a prototype stage. For this reason, the developers of the method and tool were assigned to it.

Despite all these difficulties, this activity was quite successful both in validating the specification and in generating test cases for the implementation, since several errors, sometimes very subtle, were discovered.

## D.4    Design, Implementation, and Verification

Starting from the formal specification and the test cases, another group performed design, implementation, and testing. The effectiveness of coding was enhanced greatly by the availability of formal specifications; in fact, all the ambiguities and gaps that are typical of informal specifications were already resolved during the validation of specifications. The testing experience was also quite positive. Indeed, since the test cases generated from the formal specification provided a precise trace of the expected behavior, implementation flaws were generally easy to spot.

Nevertheless, a few problems arose during the testing phase, due mostly to the immaturity of the chosen formal method or the supporting tools. For instance, when specifications were nondeterministic (i.e., when they allowed for more than one system reaction to a given stimulus) the output observed in a test could differ from the one derived from the specification. This was not necessarily the symptom of an error, however, and it was necessary to resolve the problem by manually checking the results of testing against the specification. Another difficulty was due to the different time constants in different parts of the system, which could range from milliseconds to minutes. This led to a long cycle of testing for some experiments and to huge report files.

## D.5    Overall Evaluation and Assessment

At the end of the project, the results were analyzed critically to evaluate the methodology of the project and to direct further developments. The analysis focused mainly on technical, business, and organizational aspects of the project.

### D.5.1    Technical Aspects

The adoption of a formal specification technique, together with the related tools to perform validation and verification, certainly increased the cost of the specification.[2] The increased cost, however, was largely justified and was balanced by the better quality of the resulting specification and related documentation and by a significant reduction in the overall costs related to the design, coding, and verification (e.g., testing) of the system that was implemented.

The experience showed that a specification language must support abstraction and modularity. In particular, for a logical language, if the number and length of formulas increase past some thresholds, which, unfortunately, are quite low, the specifier spends most of his or her time simply trying to put the description in a correct syntactic form.

Validation of the specification and verification planning required slightly more resources than expected, but their main objectives were achieved, and the results were considered to be quite satisfactory.

The design activity turned out to be substantially simpler than in similar traditional projects, because of the higher quality of the specification. As a consequence, the need for interaction between the specifiers (i.e., application experts) and implementers (who belonged to a different organization) was significantly reduced. A similar cost reduction was achieved in the coding phase.

---

[2] Cost evaluation did not take the training phase into account.

Testing permitted the discovery of coding errors in a straightforward way. Only few errors were found in the final code. Furthermore, only one error caught in the testing phase was caused by a misinterpretation of the specification, and it was easily identified.

### D.5.2 *Business and Organizational Aspects*

The cost of the project was qualitatively and quantitatively compared with that of an earlier version of a control system of a pondage power plant that was developed according to traditional practice. Specifically, two subsets of the applications whose products (design, code, and documents) had similar complexity and size were identified and compared with respect to cost. Table D.1 and Figure D.2 summarize the result of this analysis, in terms of person-days required for each task in the two subsets. They show unequivocally the benefits of the new method.

It was agreed that the impact of the chosen formal method would have been even greater if

    a. TRIO had been used on a routine basis: Even if training costs were not taken into account, clearly the first application of a new method always requires more learning effort than does an established practice.

    b. TRIO were supported by professional tools with user-friendly interfaces, better performance, more capability to filter the output selectively, and a good level of integration among the different tools.

| EFFORT | *Specification* | *Validation* | *Design* | *Coding* | *Acceptance* | TOTAL |
|---|---|---|---|---|---|---|
| *Old version* | 42 | 11 | 28 | 41 | 133 | 255 |
| *New version* | 72 | 57 | 14.5 | 30 | 37.5 | 211 |

TABLE D.1

Cost comparison between similar project subsets carried over with different methods.

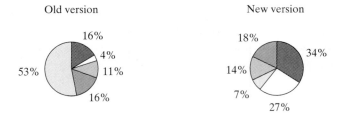

FIGURE D.2.

Comparative pie charts for distribution of effort among the various development phases. The phases are displayed clockwise, beginning with specification, which is the black portion.

    c. The project had gone through the maintenance phase, in which previous methods showed major problems due to poor-quality documentation.

The organizational impact deriving from the adoption of TRIO was very limited, since TRIO easily adjusted to the preexisting development cycle and did not dramatically change the role of the involved personnel. In addition, the TRIO-based approach was appreciated by people involved in the project because it allowed the responsibilities of the customer and the supplier to be precisely described and clearly separated, so that any flaw in the definition, interpretation, or implementation of the specifications could be easily attributed to the right source.

## D.6    The impact of the Project on the Company's Strategy

All in all, the project was successful, and similar successes were obtained in other projects, both within the same company and even outside it. Nevertheless, the new method did not gain widespread use even within the company that originated it. The situation is rather paradoxical, but fairly typical of the realm of formal methods for software engineering. Despite the fact that their advocates have been claiming their value for a long time, and despite the fact that most of the pilot projects in the literature report successes, the acceptance of formal methods in the industrial world is still quite limited, and their usefulness remains rather controversial. An abundant literature contains thorough analyses of this puzzling issue and details proposals that favor the adoption of formal methods by industry. Here, we summarize a few relevant lessons learned, focusing mainly on those which seem to have general applicability, since they agree with the conclusions of similar experiments:

- Formal methods still lack the maturity required for industrial application. It was aptly said that "the problem with formal methods is that they are just *formal, not methods*."[3] This statement emphasizes the fact that research in formal methods has devoted much effort to developing sophisticated formalisms to describe and analyze systems, but little or no effort at all to supporting their use in practical cases.

- Training does not easily scale up: A few motivated teachers (maybe the originators of the new technology) training a few motivated engineers is one thing; gaining wide acceptance among many people with less motivation and different cultural backgrounds is another, entirely different, thing.

- Demo-like tools are not enough to convince the managers of a large company to make a major change towards a new technology. Instead, industrial-strength tools must be available to support software engineers. However, the financial support that is needed to move from early prototypes to well-engineered products can be found only if one can provide some evidence that those products will be accepted in the market. This generates the adverse effect of a circular dependency and the risk of a deadlock.

---

[3] Attributed to John Rushby.

- Incrementality should be exploited. Rather than viewing formal methods as a revolutionary approach or a panacea, they should be proposed as a sequence of small steps starting from existing practices and adding small "amounts of formality" over time. In our case study, it was decided to begin with the existing specification method—an informal one that was fairly widely adopted in the realm of supervision and control systems—and then write fragments of formal specification only to describe critical points. So, initially, the specification could be a mix of informal blueprints, UML-like diagrams, and a few fragments of logical formulas.

- Training people to learn new technologies is a tremendous challenge in large companies, and the problem is exacerbated when such new technologies require a strong background in mathematics. Rather than insisting on retraining designers, who are often resistant to change, it is better to pursue either one or both of the following approaches:

  a) Select as users of the new method only volunteers who are well motivated and perhaps already equipped with an appropriate background in the subject.

  b) Create an environment of close cooperation between specialists in formal methods and application specialists. Experience has shown that by mixing the two, it is possible to understand the requirements of the proposed system and uncover ambiguities and misunderstandings early.

In any case, training and technology transfer must be seen as a long-term goal. The most effective approach is to equip software engineers with proper formal training at the university level.

## CONCLUDING REMARKS

The preceding real-life experiences demonstrate several points. First, the stories are instances of a fairly large class of software projects and related problems. Second, they show that knowing, and even understanding, software development difficulties does not guarantee that mistakes will be avoided. Third, several types of evidence are needed to convince people to change already consolidated development methods; technical success in pilot projects is often not enough to move towards "best practices." This book has tried to provide principles and tools for the production of better software; the responsibility for making appropriate use of them, however, is up to the designer.

The case studies also show that software engineering, as any other engineering field, does not consist of a pure and systematic application of design techniques and tools in a more or less mechanical style, but requires the integration of the techniques and tools with knowledge of several other disciplines and several application areas. No amount of technical competence can replace the need for common sense and ingenuity in the construction of any engineering product. All these skills must be integrated with each other.

It is such integration that allows the software engineer to forecast software development costs, estimate the value of work in progress, etc. Evaluating the percent of the project completed requires technical knowledge and experience in software development, but it also requires the ability to evaluate the economic and financial impact of over- and underestimation.

Finally, technology transfer is perhaps even more difficult in software engineering than in other disciplines and requires explicit and well-thought-out strategies.

## BIBLIOGRAPHIC NOTES

Of the case studies reported here, only case study D is documented in the open literature. The project described is summarized in Basso et al. [1995]. The TRIO formalism was originally defined in Ghezzi et al. [1990]; the main lessons learned from introducing formal methods into industrial environments are reported in Ciapessoni et al. [1999].

# Bibliography

Abdel-Hamid [1989]
  T. K. Abdel-Hamid, "The dynamics of software project staffing: a systems dynamics based simulation approach," *IEEE Transactions on Software Engineering*, 16(2): 109–119, February 1989.

Abdel-Hamid [1990]
  T. K. Abdel-Hamid, "Investigating the cost/schedule trade-off in software development," *IEEE Software*, 7(1): 97–105, January 1990.

Abdel-Hamid and Madnick [1989]
  T. K. Abdel-Hamid and S. E. Madnick, "Lessons learned from modeling the dynamics of software development," *Communications of the ACM*, 32(12): 1426–1438, December 1989.

Abelson et al. [1985]
  H. Abelson, G. J. Sussman, and J. Sussman, *Structure and Interpretation of Computer Programs*, MIT Press, Cambridge, MA, 1985.

Abrial [1996]
  J. R. Abrial, *The B-Book*, Cambridge University Press, Cambridge, U.K., 1996.

ACM [1975]
  *Proceedings of International Conference on Reliable Software* (Los Angeles, Apr. 21–23, 1975), published as *SIGPLAN Notices*, 10(6), June 1975.

Adrion et al. [1975]
  R. W. Adrion, M. A. Branstad, and J. C. Cherniavsky, *Validation, Verification and Testing of Computer Software*, NBS Special Publication 5000–75, National Bureau of Standards, Gaithersburg, MD, 1975.

Agresti [1986]
  W. W. Agresti, "Guide to the literature and annotated bibliography," in W. W. Agresti, editor, *New Paradigms for Software Development*, IEEE Computer Society Press, Los Alamitos, CA, 1986.

Aho et al. [1983]
  A. V. Aho, J. E. Hopcroft, and J. D. Ullman, *The Design and Analysis of Computer Algorithms*, Addison-Wesley, Reading, MA, 1983.

Aho et al. [1988]
  A. V. Aho, R. Sethi, and J. D. Ullman, *Compilers—Principles, Techniques, Tools*, Addison-Wesley, Reading, MA, 1988.

Aho et al. [1988]
  A. V. Aho, B. W. Kernighan, and P. J. Weinberger, *The AWK Programming Language*, Addison-Wesley, Reading, MA, 1988.

Alur et al. [1990]
  R. Alur, C. Courcourbetis, and D. Dill. "Model checking for real-time systems," *Proceedings of 5th Symposium on Logic in Computer Science*, pp. 414–425, 1990.

AjmoneMarsan et al. [1984]
  M. AjmoneMarsan, G. Balbo, and G. Conte, "A class of generalized stochastic Petri nets for the performance evaluation of multiprocessor systems," *ACM Transactions on Computer Systems*, 2(2): 93–122, 1984.

AJPO [1983]

Ada Joint Program Office Military Standard, *Reference Manual for the Ada Programming Language*, MIL-STD-1815A, Washington, DC, 1983.

Alagic and Arbib [1978]

S. Alagic and M. A. Arbib, *The Design of Well-Structured and Correct Programs*, Springer-Verlag, Berlin and New York, 1978.

Alavi [1984]

M. Alavi. "An assessment of the prototyping approach to information systems development," *Communications of the ACM*, 27(6): 556–563, June 1984.

Albrecht and Gaffney [1983]

A. J. Albrecht and J. E. Gaffney, Jr., "Software function, source lines, and development effort prediction: a software science validation," *IEEE Transactions on Software Engineering*, 9(6): 639–647, November 1983.

Alford [1977]

M. W. Alford, "A Requirements engineering methodology for real-time processing requirements," *IEEE Transactions on Software Engineering*, 3(1): 60–69, January 1977.

Ames et al. [1983]

S. R. Ames, Jr., M. Gasser, and R. R. Schell, "Security kernel design and implementation: an introduction," *Computer*, 16(7): 14–22, July 1983.

Ashenhurst [1989]

R. L. Ashenhurst, editor, Forum Letters, *Communications of the ACM*, 32(3): 287–290, March 1989.

Auernheimer and Kemmerer [1985]

B. Auernheimer and R. A. Kemmerer, *ASLAN User's Manual*, Technical Report TR-CS-84-10, Department of Computer Science, University of California at Santa Barbara, March 1985.

Auernheimer and Kemmerer [1986]

B. Auernheimer and R. A. Kemmerer, "RT-ASLAN: a specification language for real-time systems," *IEEE Transactions on Software Engineering*, 12(9): 879–889, September 1986.

Babich [1986]

W. A. Babich, *Software Configuration Management*, Addison-Wesley, Reading MA, 1986.

Baker [1972]

F. T. Baker, "Chief programmer team management of production programming," *IBM Systems Journal*, 11(1): 57–73, 1972.

Balzer [1981]

R. Balzer, "Transformational implementation: an example," *IEEE Transactions on Software Engineering*, 7(1): 3–14, January 1981.

Balzer et al. [1983]

R. Balzer, T. E. Cheatham, Jr., and C. Green, "Software technology in the 1990s: using a new paradigm," *Computer*, 16(11): 39–45, November 1983.

Bartussek and Parnas [1978]

W. Bartussek and D. L. Parnas, "Using assertions about traces to write abstract specifications for software modules," in G. Bracchi and P. C. Lockemann, eds., *Information Systems Methodology*, pp. 211–236, Springer-Verlag, Berlin and New York, October 1978.

Basili [1980]

V. R. Basili, *Tutorial on Models and Metrics for Software Engineering*, IEEE Computer Society Press, Los Alamitos, CA, October 1980.

Basili [1995]

V. R. Basili, "The Experience Factory and Its Relationship to Other Quality Approaches," in *Advances in Computers*, Volume 41, Academic Press, Inc., New York, 1995.

Basili and Caldiera [1988]
V. R. Basili and G. Caldiera, "Reusing existing software," Technical Report, Institute for Advanced Computer Science, Department of Computer Science, University of Maryland at College Park, UMI-ACS-TR-88-72, CS-TR-2116, October 1988.

Basili and Hutchens [1983]
V. R. Basili and D. H. Hutchens, "An empirical study of a syntactic complexity family," *IEEE Transactions on Software Engineering*, 9(6): 664–672, November 1983.

Basili and Rombach [1988]
V. R. Basili and H. D. Rombach, "The TAME project: towards improvement-oriented software environments," *IEEE Transactions on Software Engineering*, 14(6): 758–773, June 1988.

Basili and Selby [1987]
V. R. Basili and R. W. Selby, "Comparing the effectiveness of software testing strategies," *IEEE Transactions on Software Engineering*, 13(12): 1278–1296, December 1987.

Basili and Turner [1975]
V. R. Basili and A. J. Turner, "Iterative enhancement: a practical technique for software development," *IEEE Transactions on Software Engineering*, 1(4): 390–396, December 1975.

Basili et al. [1983]
V. R. Basili, R. W. Selby, Jr., and T.-Y. Phillips, "Metric analysis and data validation across Fortran projects," *IEEE Transactions on Software Engineering*, 9(6): 652–663, November 1983.

Basili et al. [1986]
V. R. Basili, R. W. Selby, and D. H. Hutchens, "Experimentation in software engineering," *IEEE Transactions on Software Engineering*, 12(7): 733–743, July 1986.

Basili et al. [1999]
V. Basili et al., Final Report, NSF Workshop on a Software Research Program for the 21st Century, *Software Engineering Notes* 24(3), May 1999.

Bass et al. [1999]
L. Bass, P. Clements, and R. Kazman. *Software Architecture in Practice*, Addison-Wesley, Reading, MA, 1999.

Basso et al. [1995], M. Basso, E. Ciapessoni E. Crivelli, D. Mandrioli, A. Morzenti, E. Ratto, and P. San Pietro, "A logic-based approach to the specification and design of the control system of a pondage power plant," *Proceedings of the ICSE-17 Workshop on Formal Methods Application in Software Engineering Practice*, 1995, pp. 174–181. Also in C. Tully (ed.), *Improving Software Practice: Case Experience*, John Wiley & Sons, New York, Series in Software Based Systems, pp. 79–96, 1998.

Bauer et al. [1989]
F. L. Bauer, B. Moeller, M. Partsch, and P. Pepper, "Formal program construction by transformations: computer-aided, intuition-guided programming," *IEEE Transactions on Software Engineering*, 15(2): 165–180, February 1989.

Beck [1999]
K. Beck, *Extreme Programming Explained*, Addison-Wesley, Reading, MA, 1999.

Behrens [1983]
C. A. Behrens, "Measuring the productivity of computer systems development activities with function points," *IEEE Transactions on Software Engineering*, 9(6): 648–652, November 1983.

Beizer [1983]
B. Beizer, *Software Testing Techniques*, Van Nostrand Reinhold, New York, 1983.

Beizer [1995]
B. Beizer, *Black-Box Testing Techniques*, John Wiley & Sons, New York, 1995.

Belady and Lehman [1979]
L. A. Belady and M. M. Lehman, "Characteristics of large systems," in *Research Directions in Software Technology*, P. Wegner, ed., MIT Press, Cambridge, MA, 1979.

Bellay and Gall [1998]
  B. Bellay and H. Gall, "An evaluation of reverse engineering tool capabilities," *Journal of Software Maintenance: Research and Practice*, 10(5): 305–32, John Wiley & Sons, New York, September—October 1998.

Bellay et al. [2000]
  B. Bellay, H. Gall, and M. Jazayeri, "Software architecture recovery," in M. Jazayeri, A. Ran, and F. van der Linden, *Software Architecture for Product Families*, Addison-Wesley, Reading, MA, 2000.

Bennatan [1992]
  E. M. Bennatan, *Software Project Management: A Practitioner's Approach*, McGraw-Hill, New York, 1992.

Bennett and Rajlich [2000]
  K. Bennett and V. Rajlich, "A staged model for the software lifecycle," *Computer* 33(7): 66–71, July 2000.

Bennington [1956]
  H. D. Bennington, "Production of large computer programs," *ONR Symposium on Advanced Programming Methods for Digital Computers*, June 1956.

Bentley [1985]
  J. L. Bentley, "Programming pearls: confessions of a coder," *Communications of the ACM*, 28(7): 671–679, July 1985.

Bentley [2000]
  J. L. Bentley, *Programming Pearls*, 2nd ed., Addison-Wesley, Reading, MA, 2000.

Bentley [1988]
  J. L. Bentley, *More Programming Pearls*, Addison-Wesley, Reading, MA, 1988.

Bergland [1981]
  G. D. Bergland, "A guided tour of program design methodologies," *Computer*, 14(10): 13–37, October 1981.

Berry [1987]
  D. M. Berry, "Towards a formal basis for the formal development method and the InaJo specification language," *IEEE Transactions on Software Engineering*, 13(2): 184–201, February 1987.

Bharadwaj and Heitmeyer [1999]
  R. Bharadwaj and C. Heitmeyer, "Model checking complete requirements specifications using abstraction," *Automated Software Engineering* 6(1):37–68, January 1999.

Bidoit et al. [1985]
  M. Bidoit, B. Biebow, M-C. Gaudel, C. Gresse, and G. Guiho, "Exception handling: formal specification and systematic program construction," *IEEE Transactions on Software Engineering*, 11(3): 242–252, March 1985.

Bigelow [1988]
  J. Bigelow, "Hypertext and CASE," *IEEE Software*, 5(2): 23–27, March 1988.

Biggerstaff and Perlis [1989]
  T. Biggerstaff and A. J. Perlis, eds., *Software Reusability*, Volumes 1–2, Addison-Wesley, Reading, MA, 1989.

Bittanti [1988]
  S. Bittanti, ed., *Software Reliability Modelling and Identification*, Lecture Notes in Computer Science, Vol. 341, Springer-Verlag, Berlin and New York, 1988.

Bjorner and Druffel [1990]
  D. Bjorner and L. Druffel, "Position statement: ICSE-12 Workshop on Industrial Experience Using Formal Methods," *Proceedings, 12th International Conference on Software Engineering*, Nice, France, 26–30 March 1990, IEEE Computer Society Press, Los Alamitos, CA, pages 264–266, 1990.

Bjorner and Jones [1982]
  D. Bjorner and C. B. Jones, *Formal Specification and Software Development*, Prentice-Hall International, London, 1982.

Bjorner and Prehn [1983]
D. Bjorner and S. Prehn, "Software engineering aspects of VDM, the Vienna Development Method," in *Theory and Practice of Software Technology*, D. Ferrari et al., eds., pp. 85–134, North-Holland, Amsterdam, 1983.

Boehm [1976]
B. W. Boehm, "Software engineering," *IEEE Transactions on Computers*, 25(12): 1226–1241, December 1976.

Boehm [1981]
B. W. Boehm, *Software Engineering Economics*, Prentice-Hall, Englewood Cliffs, NJ, 1981.

Boehm [1984a]
B. W. Boehm, "Software engineering economics," *IEEE Transactions on Software Engineering*, 10(1): 4–21, January 1984.

Boehm [1984b]
B. W. Boehm, "Verifying and validating software requirements and design specifications," *IEEE Software*, 1(1): 75–88, January 1984.

Boehm [1988]
B. W. Boehm, "A spiral model of software development and enhancement," *Computer*, 21(5): 61–72, May 1988.

Boehm [1989]
B. W. Boehm, *Tutorial on Software Risk Management*, IEEE Computer Society Press, Los Alamitos, CA, 1989.

Boehm [1991]
B. W. Boehm, "Software risk management: principles and practice," *IEEE Software* 8(1): 32–41, January 1991.

Boehm [2000]
B. W. Boehm, "Unifying software engineering and systems engineering," *Computer* 33(3): 114–116, March 2000.

Boehm and Papaccio [1988]
B. W. Boehm and P. N. Papaccio, "Understanding and controlling software costs," *IEEE Transactions on Software Engineering*, 14(10): 1462–1477, October 1988.

Boehm and Sullivan [2000]
B. Boehm and K. Sullivan, "Software Economics: a roadmap," in Finkelstein [2000].

Boehm et al [1978]
B. W. Boehm, J. R. Brown, H. Kaspar, M. Lipow, G. MacLeod, and M. J. Merritt, *Characteristics of Software Quality*, Volume 1 of TRW Series on Software Technology, North-Holland, Amsterdam, 1978.

Boehm et al. [1984]
B. W. Boehm, T. E. Gray, and T. Seewaldt, "Prototyping vs. specifying: a multiproject experiment," *IEEE Transactions on Software Engineering*, 10(3): 133–145, May 1984.

Boehm et al. [2000]
B. W. Boehm, C. Abts, A. W. Brown, S. Chulani, B. K. Clark, E. Horowitz, R. Madachy, D. Reifer, and B. Steece, *Software Cost Estimation with COCOMO II*, Prentice Hall, Englewood Cliffs, 2000.

Bolognesi and Brinksma [1987]
T. Bolognesi and E. Brinksma, "Introduction to the ISO specification language LOTOS," *Computer Networks*, 14(1): 25–59, 1987.

Booch [1986]
G. Booch, "Object-oriented development," *IEEE Transactions on Software Engineering*, 12(12): 211–221, December 1986.

Booch [1987a]
G. Booch, *Software Components with Ada—Structures, Tools, and Subsystems*, Benjamin/Cummings, Menlo Park, CA, 1987.

Booch [1987b]
G. Booch, *Software Engineering with Ada*, 2d ed., Benjamin/Cummings, Menlo Park, CA, 1987.

Booch et al. [1999]
G. Booch, J. Rumbaugh, and I. Jacobson. *The Unified Modeling Language User Guide*, Addison Wesley, Reading, MA, 1999.

Boudier et al. [1988]
G. Boudier, F. Gallo, R. Minot, and I. Thomas, "An overview of PCTE and PCTE$^+$," *Proceedings of Software Development Environments (SDE3)*, Boston, November 28–30, 1988), published as *SIGPLAN Notices*, 24(2): 248–257, February 1989.

Bouge et al. [1986]
L. Bouge, N. Choquet, L. Fribourg, and M. C. Gaudel, "Test sets generation from algebraic specifications using logic programming," *Journal of Systems and Software*, 343–360, November 1986.

Briand and Morasca [1997]
L. Briand and S. Morasca, "Software measurement and formal methods: a case study centered on TRIO+ specifications," IEEE ICFEM'97 (IEEE International Conference on Formal Engineering Methods), Hiroshima, 1997.

Briand et al. [1994]
L. Briand, S. Morasca, and V. R. Basili, "Defining and validating high level design metrics," Technical Report CS-TR-3301. Computer Science Department, University of Maryland, 1994.

Brinch Hansen [1977]
P. Brinch Hansen, *The Architecture of Concurrent Programs*, Prentice-Hall, Englewood Cliffs, NJ., 1977.

Brinch Hansen [1978]
P. Brinch Hansen, "Reproducible testing of monitors," *Software—Practice and Experience*, 8(6): 721–729, 1978.

Brindle and Taylor [1989]
A. Brindle and R. N. Taylor, "A debugger for Ada tasking," *IEEE Transactions on Software Engineering*, 15(3): 293–304, March 1989.

Britton et al. [1981]
K. H. Britton, R. A. Parker, and D. L. Parnas, "A procedure for designing abstract interfaces for device interface modules," *Proceedings, 5th International Conference on Software Engineering*, San Diego, CA, Mar. 9–12, 1981, pp. 195–204, IEEE Computer Society Press, Los Alamitos, CA, 1981.

Brocklehurst et al. [1990]
S. Brocklehurst, P. Y. Chan, B. Littlewood, and J. Snell, "Recalibrating software reliability models," *IEEE Transactions on Software Engineering*, 16(4): 458–470, April 1990.

Brooks [1975, 1995]
F. P. Brooks, Jr., *The Mythical Man-Month: Essays on Software Engineering*, Addison-Wesley, Reading, MA, 1975 (republished in 1995).

Brooks [1987]
F. P. Brooks, Jr., "No silver bullet: essence and accidents of software engineering," *Computer*, 20(4): 10–19, April 1987.

Browne [1980]
J. C. Browne, "The interaction of operating systems and software engineering," *Proceedings of IEEE*, 68(9): 1045–1049, September 1980.

Bruno and Marchetto [1986]
G. Bruno and G. Marchetto, "Process-translatable Petri nets for the rapid prototyping of process control systems," *IEEE Transactions on Software Engineering*, 12(2): 346–357, February 1986.

Buckle [1977]
J. K. Buckle, *Managing Software Projects*, Americal Elsevier, New York, 1977.

Buhr [1984]
R. J. A. Buhr, *System design with Ada*, Prentice-Hall, Englewood Cliffs, NJ, 1984.

Buschmann et al. [1996]
F. Buschmann, R. Meunier, H. Rohnert, P. Sommerlad, and M. Stal, *Pattern Oriented Software Architecture: A System of Patterns*, John Wiley & Sons, New York, 1996.

Bustard et al. [1988]
D. Bustard, J. Elder, and J. Welsh, *Concurrent Program Structures*, Prentice-Hall International, Hemel Hempstead, U.K., 1988.

CACM [1988]
Special issue on Software Testing, published as *Communications of the ACM*, 31(6), June 1988.

CACM [1989]
Special section on Computing and Social Responsibility, published as *Communications of the ACM*, 32(8): 925–956, August 1989.

CACM [1997]
Special issue on Software Debugging, published as *Communications of the ACM*, 40(4), April 1997.

Campos et al. [1996]
S. Campos, E. M. Clarke, and M. Minea, "Analysis of real-time systems using symbolic techniques," in Formal Methods for Real-Time Computing, C. Heitmeyer and D. Mandrioli (eds.), John Wiley, New York, pp. 217–235, 1996.

Capers Jones [1986]
T. C. Jones, *Programming Productivity*, McGraw-Hill, New York, 1986.

Celentano et al. [1980]
A. Celentano, S. Crespi-Reghizzi, P. L. DellaVigna, C. Ghezzi, G. Granata, and F. Savoretti, "Compiler testing using a sentence generator," *Software—Practice and Experience*, 10: 897–918, 1980.

Chandrasekaran and Radicchi [1981]
B. Chandrasekaran and S. Radicchi (eds.), *Computer Program Testing*, North-Holland, Amsterdam, 1981.

Chandy and Misra [1988]
K. M. Chandy and J. Misra, *Parallel Program Design: A Foundation*, Addison-Wesley, Reading, MA, 1988.

Cheatham et al. [1981]
T. E. Cheatham, Jr., G. H. Holloway, and J. A. Townley, "Program refinement by transformation," *Proceedings, 5th International Conference on Software Engineering*, San Diego, Mar. 9–12, 1981, pp. 430–437, IEEE Computer Society Press, Los Alamitos, CA, 1981.

Chen [1976]
P. Chen, "The entity relationship model—towards a unified view of data," *ACM Transactions on Database Systems*, 1(1): 9–36, 1976.

Choppy and Kaplan [1990]
C. Choppy and S. Kaplan, "Mixing abstract and concrete modules: specification, development and prototyping," *Proceedings, 12th International Conference on Software Engineering*, Nice, France, Mar. 26–30, 1990, IEEE Computer Society Press, Los Alamitos, CA, pp. 173–84, 1990.

Ciapessoni et al. [1999]
E. Ciapessoni, A. Coen-Porisini, E. Crivelli, D. Mandrioli, P. Mirandola, and A. Morzenti, "From formal models to formally-based methods: an industrial experience," *ACM Trans. on Software Eng. and Methodologies* 8(1): 79–113, January 1999.

Clarke and Linerson [1981]

E. M. Clarke and E. A. Emerson, "Synthesis of synchronization skeletons for branching time temporal logic," in *Logic for Programs: Workshop*, LNCS Vol. 131, Springer-Verlag, Berlin and New York, 1981.

Clarke et al. [1986]

E. M. Clarke, E. A. Emerson, and A. P. Sistla, "Automatic verification of finite state concurrent systems using temporal logic specifications," *ACM Transactions on Programming Languages and Systems*, 8(2): 244–263, 1986.

Clarke et al. [1989]

L. A. Clarke, A. Podgursky, D. J. Richardson, and S. J. Zeil., "A formal evaluation of data flow path selection criteria," *IEEE Transactions on Software Engineering*, 15(11): 1318–1332, November 1989.

Clarke et al. [2000]

E. M. Clarke, O. Grumberg, and D. Peled, *Model Checking*, MIT Press, Cambridge, MA, 2000.

Clemm and Osterweil [1990]

G. Clemm and L. Osterweil, "A mechanism for environment integration," *ACM Transactions on Programming Languages and Systems*, 12(1): 1–25, January 1990.

Clocksin and Mellish [1984]

W. Clocksin and C. Mellish, *Programming in PROLOG*, 2d ed., Springer-Verlag, Berlin and New York, 1984.

Coen-Porisini et al. [1994]

A. Coen-Porisini, R. Kemmerer, and D. Mandrioli, "A Formal Framework for ASTRAL Intra-level Proof Obligations," *IEEE Trans. on Software Engineering* 20(8): 548–561, August. 1994.

Coen-Porisini et al. [1997]

A. Coen-Porisini, C. Ghezzi, and R. Kemmerer, "Specification of Realtime Systems using ASTRAL," *IEEE Trans. on Software Engineering* 23(9): 572–598, September. 1997.

Coen-Porisini et al. [2001]

A. Coen-Porisini, G. Denaro, M. Pezzé, and C. Ghezzi, "Using Symbolic Execution for Verifying Safety Critical Systems" *Proc. Joint 8th European Software Engineering Conference (ESEC) and 9th ACM SIGSOFT International Symposium on the Foundations of Software Engineering (FSE)*, Vienna, Austria, September 10–14, 2001, ACM Press, New York, 2001.

Cohen et al. [1986]

B. Cohen, W. T. Harwood, and M. I. Jackson, *The Specification of Complex Systems*, Addison-Wesley, Reading, MA, 1986.

Computer [1987]

Special Issue on Seamless Systems, published as *Computer*, 20(11), November 1987.

Computer [1989a]

Special Issue on Rapid Prototyping in Software Development, published as *Computer*, 22(5), May 1989.

Computer [1989b]

Special Issue on Scientific Visualization., published as *Computer*, 22(8), August 1989.

Conklin [1987]

J. Conklin, "Hypertext: an introduction and survey," *Computer*, 20(9): 17–42, September 1987.

Conradi and Westfechtel [1998]

R. Conradi and B. Westfechtel, "Version Models for Software Configuration Management," *ACM Computing Surveys,* 30(2): 232–282, June 1998.

Conte et al. [1986]

S. D. Conte, H. E. Dunsmore, and Y. E. Shen, *Software Engineering Metrics and Models*, Benjamin/Cummings, Menlo Park, CA, 1986.

Coulter [1983]
N. S. Coulter, "Software science and cognitive psychology," *IEEE Transactions on Software Engineering*, 9(2): 166–171, March 1983.

Coutaz [1985]
J. Coutaz, "Abstractions for user interface design," *Computer*, 18(9): 21–34, September 1985.

Crispin [1987]
R. J. Crispin, Experience using VDM in STC, *VDM-Europe Symposium 1987*, Brussels, pp. 19–32, Springer-Verlag, Berlin and New York, March 1987.

CSTB [1989]
Computer Science and Technology Board, National Research Council, *Scaling Up: A Research Agenda for Software Engineering*, National Academy Press, Washington, DC, 1989.

Cugola and Ghezzi [1999]
G. Cugola and C. Ghezzi, "Software processes: a retrospective and a path to the future," *Software Process: Improvement and Practice* 4(3): 101–124, 1999.

Curtis et al. [1979]
B. Curtis, P. Milliman, and S. B. Shepper, "Third time charm: stronger prediction of programmer performance by software complexity metrics," *Proceedings, 4th International Conference on Software Engineering*, Munich, Sept. 17–19, 1979, pp. 356–60, IEEE Computer Society Press, Los Alamitos, CA, 1979.

Curtis et al. [1988]
B. Curtis, H. Krasner, and N. Iscoe, "A field study of the software design process for large systems," *Communications of the ACM*, 31(11): 1268–1287, November 1988.

Cusumano and Selby [1995]
M. A. Cusumano and R. W. Selby, *Microsoft's Secrets: How the World's Most Powerful Software Company Creates Technology, Shapes Markets, and Manages People*, Free Press/Simon & Schuster, New York, 1995.

Cusumano and Selby [1997]
M. A. Cusumano and R. W. Selby, "How Microsoft builds software," *Communications of the ACM*, 40(6): 53-61, June 1997.

Cusumano and Yoffie [1999a]
M. A. Cusumano and D. B. Yoffie, "Software Development on Internet Time," *Computer,* 32(10): 60–69, October 1999.

Cusumano and Yoffie [1999b]
M. A. Cusumano and D. B. Yoffie, "What Netscape learned from cross-platform software development," *Communications of the ACM,* 42(10): 72–78, October 1999.

Dahl et al. [1972]
O. J. Dahl, E. W. Dijkstra, and C. A. R. Hoare, *Structured Programming*, Academic Press, New York, 1972.

Dart et al. [1987]
S. A. Dart, R. L. Ellison, P. H. Feiler, and A. N. Habermann, "Software development environments," *Computer*, 20(11): 18–28, November 1987.

Date [2000]
C. J. Date, *An Introduction to Database Systems*, 7th ed., Addison-Wesley, Reading, MA, 2000.

Davis [1988]
A. M. Davis, "A comparison of techniques for the specification of external system behavior," *Communications of the ACM*, 31(9): 1098–1115, September 1988.

Davis [1990]
A. M. Davis, *Software Requirements: Analysis and Specification*, Prentice Hall, Englewood Cliffs, NJ, 1990.

Davis [1993]
A. M. Davis, *Software Requirements: Objects, Functions, and States*, Prentice Hall, Englewood Cliffs, NJ, 1993.

Davis et al. [1988]
  A. M. Davis, E. H. Bersoff, and E. R. Comer, "A strategy for comparing alternative software development life cycle models," *IEEE Transactions on Software Engineering* 14(10): 1453–1461, October 1988.

DeMarco [1978]
  T. DeMarco, *Structured Analysis and System Specification*, Yourdon Press, New York, 1978.

DeMarco [1982]
  T. DeMarco, *Controlling Software Projects*, Yourdon Press, New York, 1982.

DeMarco [1995]
  T. DeMarco, *Why Does Software Cost So Much?*, Dorset House, New York, 1995.

DeMarco and Lister [1999]
  T. DeMarco, T. R. Lister, *Peopleware: Productive Projects and Teams*, 2nd Ed., Dorset House, New York, 1999.

DeMillo et al. [1979]
  R. D. Millo, R. Lipton, and A. Perlis, "Social processes and proof of theorems and programs," *Communications of the ACM*, 22(5): 271–280, 1979.

DeMillo et al. [1987]
  R. A. DeMillo, M. W. McCracken, R. J. Martin, and J. F. Passafiume, *Software Testing and Evaluation*, Benjamin/Cummings, Menlo Park, CA, 1987.

Denning [1989]
  P. J. Denning, ed., "A debate on teaching computing science," *Communications of the ACM*, 32(12): 1397–1414, December 1989.

DeRemer and Kron [1976]
  F. DeRemer and H. Kron, "Programming-in-the-large versus programming-in-the-small, *IEEE Transactions on Software Engineering* 2(2): 80–86, June 1976.

DiBona et al. [1999]
  C. DiBona, S. Ockman, and M. Stone (eds.), *OPEN SOURCES: Voices from the Open Source Revolution*, O'Reilly and Associates, Sebastopol, CA, 1999.

Dijkstra [1968a]
  E. W. Dijkstra, "Cooperating sequential processes," in F. Genuys, ed., *Programming Languages*, pp. 42–112, Academic Press, New York, 1968.

Dijkstra [1968b]
  E. W. Dijkstra, "The structure of the THE multiprogramming system," *Communications of the ACM*, 11(5): 341–346, May 1968.

Dijkstra [1971]
  E. W. Dijkstra, "Hierachical ordering of sequential processes," *Acta Informatica*, 1(2): 115–138, 1971.

Dijkstra [1976]
  E. W. Dijkstra, *A Discipline of Programming*, Prentice-Hall, Englewood Cliffs, NJ, 1976.

Dijkstra [1989]
  E. W. Dijkstra, "On the cruelty of really teaching computing science," *Communications of the ACM*, 32(12): 1398–1404, December 1989.

Dittrich et al. [2000]
  K. R. Dittrich, D. Tombros, and A. Geppert, "Databases in software engineering: a roadmap," in Finkelstein [2000].

DOD [1980]
  United States Department of Defense, *Stoneman: Requirements for Ada Programming Support Environment*, February 1980.

DOD [1984]
  United States Department of Defense, MIL-STD-2167, March 1984.

Duran and Ntafos [1984]
   J. W. Duran and S. Ntafos, "An evaluation of random testing," *IEEE Transactions on Software Engineering*, 10(4): 438–444, July 1984.

Edwards [1998]
   J. Edwards, "The changing face of freeware, *Computer*, 31(10), October 1998.

Emmerich [2000]
   W. Emmerich, *Engineering Distributed Objects*, John Wiley, Chichester, U.K., 2000.

Engels and Groenwegen [2000]
   G. Engels and Luuk Groenwegen, "Object-oriented modeling: a roadmap," in Finkelstein [2000].

Estublier [2000]
   J. Estublier, "Software configuration management: a roadmap," in Finkelstein [2000].

Fagan [1976]
   M. E. Fagan, "Design and code inspections to reduce errors in program development," *IBM Systems Journal*, 15(3): 182–211, 1976.

Fagan [1986]
   M. E. Fagan, "Advances in software inspection," *IEEE Transactions on Software Engineering*, 12(7): 744–751, July 1986.

Fairley [1985]
   R. Fairley, *Software Engineering Concepts*, McGraw-Hill, New York, 1985.

Fayad and Schmidt [1997]
   M. E. Fayad and D. C. Schmidt, Special issue on application frameworks. *Communications of the ACM* 40(10), October 1997.

Feldman [1979]
   S. I. Feldman, "Make-a program for maintaining computer programs," *Software—Practice and Experience*, 9: 255–265, 1979.

Fenton and Pfleeger [1998]
   N. E. Fenton and S. L. Pfleeger, *Software Metrics: A Rigorous and Practical Approach*, 2d ed., PWS Publishing, Boston, MA, 1998.

Ferrari [1978]
   D. Ferrari, *Computer Systems Performance Evaluation*, Prentice-Hall, Englewood Cliffs, NJ, 1978.

Ferrari and Minetti [1981]
   D. Ferrari and V. Minetti (eds.), *Experimental Computer Performance and Evaluation*, North-Holland, Amsterdam, 1981.

Fetzer [1988]
   J. H. Fetzer, "Program verification: the very idea," *Communications of the ACM*, 31(9): 1048–1063, September 1988.

Filman [1988]
   R. E. Filman, "Reasoning with worlds and truth maintenance in a knowledge-based system shell," *Communications of the ACM*, 31(4): 382–401, April 1988.

Finkelstein [2000]
   A. Finkelstein (ed.), *The Future of Software Engineering*, ACM Press, New York, 2000.

Finkelstein et al. [1994]
   A. Finkelstein, J. Kramer, and B. Nuseibeh (eds.), *Software Process Modelling and Technology*. Research Studies Press Limited (J. Wiley), Chichester, U.K., 1994.

Floyd [1967]
   R. Floyd, "Assigning meanings to programs," *Symposium on Applied Mathematics*, Vol. 19 of Mathematical Aspects of Computer Science, pp. 19–32, J. Schwartz (ed.), American Mathematical Society, New York, 1967.

Fogel [2000]
    K. Fogel, *Open Source Development with CVS*, Coriolis Group, Scottsdale, AZ, Open Press, 2000.
Fowler and Scott [2000]
    M. Fowler (with K. Scott), *UML Distilled*, Second Edition, Addison-Wesley, Reading, MA, 2000.
Freeman [1987a]
    P. Freeman, *Software Perspectives: The System is the Message*, Addison-Wesley, Reading, MA, 1987.
Freeman [1987b]
    P. Freeman, *Tutorial on Resusable Software Engineering*, IEEE Computer Society Press, Los Alamitos, CA, 1987.
Frewin et al. [1985]
    E. Frewin, P. Hamer, B. Kitchenham, N. Ross, and L. Wook, "Quality measurement and modelling—state of the art report," *Technical Report REQUEST/STC ESPRIT*, July 1985.
Fuggetta et al. [1989]
    A. Fuggetta, C. Ghezzi, and D. Mandrioli, "Some considerations on real-time behavior of programs," *IEEE Transactions on Software Engineering*, 15(3): 356–359, March 1989.
Fuggetta [1993]
    A. Fuggetta, "A classification of CASE technology," *Computer*, 26(12), pp. 25–35, December 1993.
Fuggetta et al. [1993]
    A. Fuggetta, C. Ghezzi, D. Mandrioli, and A. Morzenti, "Executable Specifications with Dataflow Diagrams," *Software, Practice and Experience* 23(6): 629–653, June 1993.
Futatsugi et al. [1985]
    K. Futatsugi, J. Goguen, J. Jouannaud, and J. Meseguer, "Principles of OBJ2," *Annual Symposium on Principles of Programming Languages,* New Orleans, pp. 52–66, 1985.
Gall et al. [1997]
    H. Gall, M. Jazayeri, R. Klösch, and G. Trausmuth, "Software Evolution Observations Based on Product Release History," *Proceedings of International Conference on Software Maintenance (ICSM '97)*, pp. 160–167, Bari, Italy, IEEE Computer Society Press, Los Alamitos, CA, September 1997.
Gall et al. [1998]
    H. Gall, K. Hajek, and M. Jazayeri, "Detection of logical coupling based on product release histories," *Proceedings of International Conference on Software Maintenance (ICSM '98)*, pp. 190–197, Washington, DC, IEEE Computer Society Press, Los Alamitos, CA, November 1998.
Gall et al. [1999]
    H. Gall, M. Jazayeri, and C. Riva, "Visualizing software release histories: the use of color and third dimension," *Proceedings of International Conference on Software Maintenance (ICSM '99)*, pp. 99–108, Oxford, UK, IEEE Computer Society Press, Los Alamitos, CA, September 1999.
Gamma et al. [1994]
    E. Gamma, R. Helm, R. Johnson, and J. Vlissides, *Design Patterns: Elements of Object Oriented Software Architecture*, Addison-Wesley, Reading, MA, 1994.
Garg and Jazayeri [1995]
    P. Garg and M. Jazayeri (eds.), *Process-centered software engineering environments*, IEEE Computer Society Press, Los Alamitos, CA, 1995.
Garlan [2000]
    D. Garlan, "Software Architecture: a roadmap," in Finkelstein [2000].
Garzotto et al. [1987]
    F. Garzotto, C. Ghezzi, D. Mandrioli, and A. Morzenti, "On the specification of real-time systems using logic programming," Proceedings, 1st European Software Engineering Conference, *Lecture Notes in Computer Science*, Vol. 289, Springer-Verlag, Berlin and New York, pp. 180–190, 1987.

Gehani and McGettrick [1986]
> N. Gehani and A. McGettrick (eds.), *Software Specification Techniques*, Addison-Wesley, Reading, MA, 1986.

Genrich [1987]
> H. Genrich, "Predicate/transition nets," in *Advances in Petri Nets*, W. Reisig and G. Rozenberg (eds.), Lecture Notes in Computer Science, 254–255, Springer-Verlag, Berlin and New York, 1987.

Gerhart et al. [1993]
> S. Gerhart, D. Craigen, and T. Ralston, "Observations on Industrial Practice Using Formal Methods," *Proc. of 15th International Conference on Software Engineering*, Baltimore, MD, May 1993, pp. 24–33.

Gerhart et al. [1994]
> S. Gerhart, D. Craigen, and T. Ralston, "Experience with Formal Methods in Critical Systems," *IEEE Software*, 11(1): 21–28, January 1994.

Ghezzi and Jazayeri [1998]
> C. Ghezzi and M. Jazayeri, *Programming Language Concepts*, 3d ed., John Wiley and Sons, New York, 1998.

Ghezzi and Mandrioli [1987]
> C. Ghezzi and D. Mandrioli, "On eclecticism in specifications: a case study centered around Petri nets," *Proceedings, 4th International Workshop on Software Specification and Design*, Monterey, CA, pp. 216–225, Apr. 3–4, 1987, IEEE Computer Society Press, Los Alamitos, CA, 1987.

Ghezzi et al. [1989a]
> C. Ghezzi, D. Mandrioli, S. Morasca, and M. Pezzé, "A general way to put time in Petri nets," *Proceedings, 5th International Workshop on Software Specification and Design*, Pittsburgh, May 19–20, 1989, pp. 60–67, IEEE Computer Society Press, Los Alamitos, CA, 1989.

Ghezzi et al. [1989b]
> C. Ghezzi, D. Mandrioli, S. Morasca, and M. Pezzé, "Symbolic execution of concurrent systems using Petri nets," *Computer Languages*, 14(4): 263–281, 1989.

Ghezzi et al. [1990]
> C. Ghezzi, D. Mandrioli, and A. Morzenti, "TRIO: a logic language for executable specifications of real-time systems," *Journal of Systems and Software* 12(2): 107–123, May 1990.

Gibson and Senn [1989]
> V. R. Gibson and J. A. Senn, "System structure and software maintenance performance," *Communications of the ACM* 32(3): 347–358, March 1989.

Gilb [1988]
> T. Gilb, *Principles of Software Engineering Management*, Addison-Wesley, Reading, MA, 1988.

Goguen et al. [1978]
> J. A. Goguen, J. W. Thatcher, and E. G. Wagner, "An initial algebra approach to the specification, correctness, and implementation of abstract data types," in *Current Trends in Programming Methodology*, Vol. 4, R. T. Yeh (ed.), pp. 80–149, Prentice-Hall, Englewood Cliffs, NJ, 1978.

Goldberg [1986]
> A. T. Goldberg, "Knowledge-based programming: a survey of program design and construction techniques," *IEEE Transactions on Software Engineering*, 12(7): 752–768, July 1986.

Goldberg and Robson [1983]
> A. Goldberg and D. Robson, *Smalltalk-80: The Language and Its Implementation*, Addison-Wesley, Reading, MA, 1983.

Gomaa and Scott [1981]
> H. Gomaa and D. Scott, "Prototyping as a tool in the specification of user requirements," *Proceedings, 5th International Conference on Software Engineering*, San Diego, March 9–12, 1981, pp. 333–342.

Good [1977]
    D. Good (ed.), *Constructing Verifiably Reliable and Secure Communications Processing Systems*, Technical Report ICSCA-CMP-6, University of Texas at Austin, January 1977.

Good et al. [1979]
    D. Good, R. Cohen, and J. Keeton-Williams, "Principles of proving concurrent programs in Gypsy," *Proceedings of 6th Annual Symposium on Principles of Programming Languages*, pp. 42–52, January 1979.

Goodenough and Gerhart [1975]
    J. B. Goodenough and S. L. Gerhart, "Toward a theory of test data selection," *IEEE Transactions on Software Engineering*, 1(2): 156–73, June 1975.

Gottebarn et al. [1999]
    D. Gottebarn, K. Miller, and S. Rogerson, "Software Code of Ethics is Approved," *Communications of the ACM,* 42(10): 102–107, October 1999.

Grady [1992]
    R. Grady. *Practical Software Metrics for Project Management and Process Improvement*, Prentice Hall, Englewood Cliffs, NJ, 1992.

Grady and Caswell [1987]
    R. B. Grady and D. L. Caswell, *Software Metrics: Establishing a Company-Wide Program*, Prentice-Hall, Englewood Cliffs, NJ, 1987.

Graham [1989]
    D. R. Graham, "Incremental development: review of monolithic life-cycle development models," *Information and Software Technology*, 31(1): 7–20, 1989.

Gries [1976]
    D. Gries, "An illustration of current ideas on the derivation of correctness proofs and correct programs," *IEEE Transactions on Software Engineering*, 2(4): 238–44, December 1976.

Gries [1981]
    D. Gries, *The Science of Programming*, Springer-Verlag, Berlin and New York, 1981.

Guindon [1988]
    R. Guindon (ed.), *Cognitive Science and Its Application for Human—Computer Interaction*, Lawrence Erlbaum Associates, Hillsdale, NJ, 1988.

Guttag [1977]
    J. Guttag, "Abstract data types and the development of data structures," *Communications of the ACM*, 20(6): 396–404, June 1977.

Guttag and Horning [1983]
    J. V. Guttag and J. J. Horning, "An introduction to the Larch shared language," *Proceedings, 9th IFIP World Computer Congress* (Paris), pp. 809–814, North-Holland, Amsterdam, September 1983.

Guttag and Horning [1986a]
    J. V. Guttag and J. J. Horning, "Report on the Larch Shared Language," *Science of Computer Programming*, 6(2): 103–134, March 1986.

Guttag and Horning [1986b]
    J. V. Guttag and J. J. Horning, "A Larch shared language handbook," *Science of Computer Programming*, 6(2): 135–157, March 1986.

Guttag et al. [1985a]
    J. Guttag, J. Horning, and J. Wing, "The Larch family of specification languages," *IEEE Software*, 2(5): 24–36, September 1985.

Guttag et al. [1985b]
    J. V. Guttag, J. J. Horning, and J. M. Wing, "*Larch in Five Easy Pieces*," Technical Report 5, Digital Systems Research Center, Palo Alto, CA, July 1985.

Haase [1981]
   V. Haase, "Real-time behavior of programs," *IEEE Transactions on Software Engineering* 7(5): 494–501, September 1981.

Hall et al. [1999]
   R. Hall, D. Heimbigner, and A. L. Wolf, "A cooperative approach to support software deployment using the software dock," *Proc. International Conference on Software Engineering (ICSE 99)*, Los Angeles, May 1999, pp. 174–183.

Halstead [1977]
   M. H. Halstead, *Elements of Software Science*, North-Holland, Amsterdam, 1977.

Hamer and Frewin [1982]
   P. G. Hamer and G. D. Frewin, "M. H. Halstead's software science—a critical examination," *Proceedings, 6th International Conference on Software Engineering*, Tokyo, Sept. 13–16, 1982, pp. 197–205, IEEE Computer Society Press, Los Alamitos, CA, September 1982.

Har'El and Kurshan [1990]
   Z. Har'El and R. P. Kurshan, "Software for analytical development of communication protocols," *AT& T Bell Lab. Tech. J.*, Vol. 69, N.1, pp. 45–59, 1990.

Harel [1987]
   D. Harel, "Statecharts: A visual formalism for complex systems," *Science of Computer Programming*, 8(3): 514–530, 1987.

Harel [1988]
   D. Harel, "On visual formalisms," *Communications of the ACM*, 31(5): 514–530, May 1988.

Harel and Naamad [1996]
   D. Harel and A. Namaad, "The STATEMATE semantics of Statecharts," *ACM Transactions on Software Engineering and Management*, 5(4): 293–333, October 1996.

Harel et al. [1990]
   D. Harel, H. Lachover, A. Naamad, A. Pnueli, M. Politi, R. Sherman, A. Shtull-Trauring, and M. Trakhtenbrot, "STATEMATE: a working environment for the development of complex reactive systems," *IEEE Transactions on Software Engineering*, 16(4): 403–414, April 1990.

Harrison et al. [1982]
   W. Harrison, K. Magel, R. Kluczny, and A. DeKock, "Applying software complexity measures to program maintenance," *Computer*, 15(9): 65–79, September 1982.

Hartson and Hiix [1989]
   R. Hartson and D. Hiix, "Human–computer interface development: concepts and systems," *ACM Computing Surveys*, 21(1): 5–92, March 1989.

Hatley and Pirbhai [1987]
   D. Hatley and I. Pirbhai, *Strategies for Real-Time System Specifications*, Dorset House, New York, 1987.

Hauswirth and Jazayeri [1999]
   M. Hauswirth and M. Jazayeri, "A component and communication model for push systems," Proceedings, ESEC/FSE '99, *Lecture Notes in Computer Science*, Vol. 1687, Springer-Verlag, Berlin and New York, pp. 20–38, 1999.

Heitmeyer and Mandrioli [1996]
   C. Heitmeyer and D. Mandrioli (eds.), *Formal methods for real-time computing*, John Wiley, New York, 1996.

Heitmeyer et al. [1996]
   C. Heitmeyer, R. D. Jeffords, and B. G. Labaw, "Automated Consistency Checking of Requirements Specifications," *ACM Transactions on Software Engineering and Methodolgy*, 5(3): 231–261, July 1996.

Heninger [1980]
   K. L. Heninger, "Specifying software requirements for complex systems: new techniques and their application," *IEEE Transactions on Software Engineering*, 6(1): 2–13, January 1980.

Henry and Kafura [1981]
S. Henry and D. Kafura, "Software structure metrics based on information flow," *IEEE Transactions on Software Engineering*, 7(5): 510–518, September 1981.

Hester et al. [1981]
S. D. Hester, D. L. Parnas, and D. F. Utter, "Usign documentation as a software design medium," *Bell Systems Technical Journal*, 60(8): 1941–1977, October 1981.

Hetzel [1984]
W. Hetzel, *The Complete Guide to Software Testing*, QED Information Sciences, Wellesley, MA, 1984.

Hoare [1969]
C. A. R. Hoare, "An axiomatic basis for computer programming," *Communications of the ACM*, 12(10): 576–580, October 1969.

Hoare [1972]
C. A. R. Hoare, "Towards a theory of parallel programming," in C. A. R. Hoare and R. H. Perrott (eds.), *Operating Systems Techniques*, Academic Press, New York, 1972.

Hoare [1973]
C. A. R. Hoare, "Hints on programming language design," *Annual Symposium on Principles of Programming Languages*, Boston, October 1973.

Hoare [1974]
C. A. R. Hoare, "Monitors: an operating system structuring concept," *Communications of the ACM*, 17(10): 549–57, October 1974. (See also Erratum, *Communications of the ACM*, 18(2): 95, February 1975.)

Hoare [1985]
C. A. R. Hoare, *Communicating Sequential Processes*, Prentice-Hall International, Hemel Hempstead, U.K., 1985.

Hoffman [1989]
D. Hoffman, "Practical interface specification," *Software—Practice and Experience*, 19(2): 127–148, February 1989.

Hoffman [1990]
D. Hoffman, "On criteria for module interfaces," *IEEE Transactions on Software Engineering*, 16(5): 537–542, May 1990.

Hoffman and Weiss [2001]
D. M. Hoffman and D. M. Weiss (eds.), *Software Fundamentals—Collected Papers by David L. Parnas*, Addison-Wesley, Reading, MA, 2001.

Hofmeister et al. [1999]
C. Hofmeister, R. Nord, and D. Soni, *Applied Software Architecture*, Addison-Wesley, Reading, MA, 1999.

Holzmann [1997]
G. J. Holzmann, "The model checker Spin," *IEEE Transactions on Software Engineering*, 23(5): 279–295, May 1997.

HOOD [1989]
European Space Agency, Noordwijk, The Netherlands, *HOOD Reference Manual*, Issue 3.0, September 1989.

Horwitz et al. [1989]
S. Horwitz, J. Prins, and T. Reps, "Integrating noninterfering versions of programs," *ACM Transactions on Programming Languages and Systems*, 11(3): 345–387, July 1989.

Howden [1987]
W. E. Howden, *Functional Program Testing*, McGraw-Hill, New York, 1987.

Humphrey [1989]
W. S. Humphrey, *Managing the Software Process*, Addison-Wesley, Reading, MA, 1989.

Humphrey [1995]
W. S. Humphrey, *A Discipline for Software Engineering*, Addison-Wesley, Reading, MA, 1995.

IEEE [1999]
    *Software Engineering Standards*, 1999 Edition, Institute of Electrical and Electronics Engineers, 4 volumes, 1999.

IEEE Software [1989a]
    Special Issue on User Interfaces, published as *IEEE Software*, 6(1), January 1989.

IEEE Software [1989b]
    Special Issue on Software Verification and Validation, published as *IEEE Software*, 6(3), May 1989.

IEEE Software [1990a]
    Special Issue on Maintenance, Reverse Engineering and Design Recovery, published as *IEEE Software*, 7(1), January 1990.

IEEE Software [1990b]
    Special Issue on Metrics, published as *IEEE Software*, 7(2), March 1990.

IEEE Software [1990c]
    Special Issue on Tools Fair (May 1990), published as *IEEE Software*, 7(3). May 1990.

IWSSD [1987]
    *Proceedings of the 4th International Workshop on Software Specification and Design*, Monterey, CA, April 1987, IEEE Computer Society Press, Los Alamitos, CA, 1987.

Jackson [1975]
    M. A. Jackson, *Principles of Program Design*, Academic Press, New York, 1975.

Jackson [1983]
    M. A. Jackson, *System Development*, Prentice-Hall International, London, 1983.

Jackson [1995]
    M. A. Jackson, *Software Requirements and Specifications*, Addison-Wesley, Reading, MA, 1995.

Jackson and Rinard [2000]
    D. Jackson and M. Rinard, "Software Analysis: A Roadmap," in Finkelstein [2000].

Jacobson et al. [1999]
    I. Jacobson, G. Booch, and J. Rumbaugh, *The Unified Software Development Process*, Addison-Wesley, Reading, MA, 1999.

Jalote [1989]
    P. Jalote, "Testing the completeness of specifications," *IEEE Transactions on Software Engineering*, 15(5): 526–531, May 1989.

Jazayeri [1995]
    M. Jazayeri, "Component Programming—A fresh look at software components," Proceedings, 5th European Software Engineering Conference, *Lecture Notes in Computer Science*, Vol. 989, Springer-Verlag, Berlin and New York, pp. 457–474, 1995.

Jazayeri et al. [2000]
    M. Jazayeri, A. Ran, and F. van der Linden, *Software Architecture for Product Families: Principles and Practice*, Addison-Wesley, Reading, 2000.

Jones [1986a]
    C. B. Jones, *Systematic Software Development Using VDM*, Prentice-Hall International, London, 1986.

Jones [1986b]
    C. B. Jones, "Program specification and verification in VDM," *NATO Advanced Study Institute on Logic of Programming and Calculi of Discrete Design* (Marktoberdorf, West Germany), pp. 149–84, Springer-Verlag, Berlin and New York, August 1986.

Kafura and Reddy [1987]
    D. Kafura and G. R. Reddy, "The use of software complexity metrics in software maintenance," *IEEE Transactions on Software Engineering*, 13(3): 335–343, March 1987.

Kant and Barstow [1981]
  E. Kant and D. R. Barstow, "The refinement paradigm: the interaction of coding and efficiency knowledge in program synthesis," *IEEE Transactions on Software Engineering*, 7(5): 458–471, September 1981.

Kearney et al. [1986]
  J. K. Kearney, R. L. Sedlmeyer, W. B. Thompson, M. A. Gray, and M. A. Adler, "Software complexity measurement," *Communications of the ACM*, 29(11): 1044–1050, November 1986.

Kemmerer [1985]
  R. A. Kemmerer, "Testing formal specifications to detect design errors," *IEEE Transactions on Software Engineering*, 11(1): 32–43, January 1985.

Kemmerer and Eckmann [1985]
  R. A. Kemmerer and S. T. Eckmann, "UNISEX: A UNIX based symbolic interpreter for Pascal," *Software–Practice and Experience*, 15(5): 439–458, May 1985.

Kernighan and Pike [1984]
  B. W. Kernighan and R. Pike, *The UNIX Programming Environment*, Prentice-Hall, Englewood Cliffs, NJ, 1984.

Kiczales et al [1997]
  G. Kiczales, J. Lamping, A. Mendhekar, C. Maeda, C. V. Lopes, J-M Loingtier, and J. Irwin, "Aspect-oriented programming," In Proc. European Conference on Object-Oriented Programming (ECOOP), 1997.

Knuth [1974]
  D. E. Knuth, "Structured programming with goto statements," *Computing Surveys*, 6(4): 261–301, December 1974.

Koontz et al. [1980]
  H. Koontz, C. O'Donnell, and H. Weihrich, *Management*, McGraw-Hill, New York, 1980.

Kopetz [1997]
  H. Kopetz, *Real-Time Systems: Design Principles for Distributed Embedded Applications*, Kluwer International Series in Engineering and Computer Science, 395, Dordrecht, Netherlands, April 1997.

Kroeger [1987]
  F. Kroeger, *Temporal Logics of Programs*, EATCS Monographs on Theoretical Computer Science, Springer-Verlag, New York and Berlin, 1987.

Kruchten [1995]
  P. B. Kruchten, "The 4+1 view model of architecture," *IEEE Software*, 29(11): 42–50, November 1995.

Lamport [1979]
  L. Lamport, "A new approach to proving the correctness of multiprocess languages," *ACM Transactions on Programming Languages and Systems*, 1(1): 84–97, July 1979.

Lamport [1989]
  L. Lamport, "A simple approach to specifying concurrent systems," *Communications of the ACM*, 32(1): 32–45, January 1989.

Lehman and Belady [1985]
  M. M. Lehman and L. A. Belady, *Program Evolution*, Academic Press, New York, 1985.

Leveson [1986]
  N. G. Leveson, "Software safety: what, why, and how," *ACM Computing Surveys*, 18(2): 125–164, June 1986.

Leveson [1995]
  N. G. Leveson. *Safeware: System Safety and Computers*. Addison-Wesley, Reading, MA, 1995.

Lewis [1999]
  T. Lewis, "The Open Source Acid Test," *Computer,* 32(2): 125–128, February 1999.

Lientz and Swanson [1980]
  B. P. Lientz and E. B. Swanson, *Software Maintenance Management*, Addison-Wesley, Reading, MA, 1980.

Linger et al. [1979]
    R. C. Linger, H. D. Mills, and B. I. Witt, *Structured Programming: Theory and Practice*, Addison-Wesley, Reading, MA, 1979.

Linton et al. [1989]
    M. A. Linton, J. M. Vlissides, and P. R. Calder, "Composing user interfaces with Inter Views," *IEEE Computer*, 22(2): 8–22, February 1989.

Liskov [1988]
    B. Liskov, "Distributed programming in Argus," *Communications of the ACM*, 31(3): 300–312, March 1988.

Liskov and Guttag [1986]
    B. Liskov and J. Guttag, *Abstraction and Specification in Program Development*, MIT Press, Cambridge, MA, 1986.

Liskov and Guttag [2001]
    B. Liskov and J. Guttag, *Program Development in Java*, Addison-Wesley, Reading, 2001.

Liskov and Zilles [1974]
    B. Liskov and S. N. Zilles, "Programming with abstract data types," *SIGPLAN Notices*, 9(4): 50–60, April 1974.

Liskov and Zilles [1975]
    B. Liskov and S. Zilles, "Specification techniques for data abstraction," *IEEE Transactions on Software Engineering*, 1(1): 7–19, January, 1975.

Liu and Shyamasundar [1990]
    L. Y. Liu and R. K. Shyamasundar, "Static analysis of real-time distributed systems," *IEEE Transactions on Software Engineering*, 16(4): 373–388, April 1990.

Low and Jeffery [1990]
    G. C. Low and R. Jeffery, "Function points in the estimation and evaluation of the software process," *IEEE Transactions on Software Engineering*, 16(1): 64–71 January 1990.

Luqi and Ketabchi [1988]
    Luqi, and M. Ketabchi, "A computer aided prototyping system," *IEEE Software*, 22(3): 66–72, March 1988.

Luqi et al. [1988]
    Luqi, V. V. Berzins, and R. T. Yeh, "A prototyping language for real time software," *IEEE Transactions on Software Engineering*, 14(10): 1409–1423, October 1988.

Mandrioli and Ghezzi [1987]
    D. Mandrioli and C. Ghezzi, *Theoretical Foundations of Computer Science*, John Wiley & Sons, New York, 1987.

Mandrioli et al. [1985]
    D. Mandrioli, R. Zicari, C. Ghezzi, and F. Tisato, "Modeling the Ada task system by Petri Nets," *Computer Languages*, 10(1): 43–61, 1985.

Mandrioli et al.[1995]
    D. Mandrioli, S. Morasca, and A. Morzenti, "Generating Test Cases for Real-Time Systems from Logic Specifications," *ACM Trans. on Computer Systems*, 13(4): 365–398, November 1995.

Manna [1974]
    Z. Manna, *Mathematical Theory of Computation*, McGraw-Hill, New York, 1974.

Manna and Waldinger [1985]
    Z. Manna and R. Waldinger, *The Logical Basis for Computer Programming*, Addison-Wesley, Reading, MA, 1985.

Mantei [1981]
    M. Mantei, "The effect of programming team structures on programming tasks," *Communications of the ACM*, 24(3): 106–113, March 1981.

Mantei and Teorey [1988]
M. M. Mantei and T. J. Teorey, "Cost/benefit analysis for incorporating human factors in the software lifecycle," *Communications of the ACM*, 31(4): 428–439, April 1988.

Martin and Leben [1986]
J. Martin and J. Leben, *Fourth Generation Languages*, Vol. 2, Prentice-Hall, Englewood Cliffs, NJ, 1986.

Matson et al. [1994]
J. Matson, B. Barrett, J. Mellichamp, "Software Development Cost Estimation Using Function Points," *IEEE Transactions on Software Engineering*, 20(4): 275–287, April 1994.

McCabe [1976]
T. J. McCabe, "A complexity measure," *IEEE Transactions on Software Engineering*, 2(4): 308–320, December 1976.

McCabe [1983]
T. J. McCabe, *Tutorial on Structured Testing*, Catalog number EHO 200-6, IEEE Computer Society Press, Los Alamitos, CA, 1983.

McCabe and Butler [1989]
T. J. McCabe and C. W. Butler, "Design complexity measurement and testing," *Communications of the ACM*, 32(12): 1415–1425, December 1989.

McCarthy [1962]
J. McCarthy, "Towards a mathematical science of computation," *Proceeding of IFIP*, pp. 21–28, 1962.

McCracken and Jackson [1982]
D. D. McCracken and M. A. Jackson, "Life-cycle concept considered harmful," *Software Engineering Notes*, pp. 29–32, April 1982.

McDowell and Helmbold [1989]
C. E. McDowell and D.P. Helmbold, "Debugging concurrent programs," *ACM Computing Surveys*, 21(4): 593–622, December 1989.

McLean [1984]
J. McLean, "A formal method for the abstract specification of software," *Journal of the ACM*, 31(3): 600–27, July 1984.

McLean [1990]
J. McLean, "The specification and modeling of computer security," *Computer*, 23(1): 9–16, January 1990.

Merlin and Farber [1976]
P. Merlin and D. Farber, "Recoverability of Communication Protocols," *IEEE Transactions on Communications*, 24(9): 1036–1043, September 1976.

Meyer [2000]
B. Meyer, *Object-Oriented Software Construction*, 2d ed., Prentice-Hall International, Hemel Hempstead, U.K., 2000.

Miles [1984]
D. E. Miles, "Copyrighting computer software after Apple vs. Franklin," *IEEE Software*, 1(2): 84–87, April 1984.

Mills et al. [1987a]
H. D. Mills, V. R. Basili, J. D. Gannon, and R. G. Hamlet, *Principles of Computer Programming: A Mathematical Approach*, Allyn & Bacon, Boston, 1987.

Mills et al. [1987b]
H. D. Mills, M. Dyer, and R. Linger, "Cleanroom software engineering," *IEEE Software*, 4(5): 19–25, September 1987.

Milner [1980]
R. Milner, A *Calculus of Communicating Systems*, Lecture Notes in Computer Science, Vol. 92, Springer-Verlag, Berlin and New York, 1980.

Misra and Jalics [1988]
S. Misra and P. Jalics, "Third-generation versus fourth-generation software development," *IEEE Software*, 5(4): 8–14, July 1988.

Monga [2000]
M. Monga, "A Dynamo for Computers: How Open Source Can Help Software Markets," Politecnico di Milano, Dipartimento di Elettronica e Informazione, Internal Report 2000-28, 2000.

Moriconi and Hare [1986]
M. Moriconi and D. F. Hare, "The PegaSys system: pictures as formal documentation of large programs," *ACM Transactions on Programming Languages and Systems*, 8(4): 524–456, October 1986.

Mueller et al [1992]
H. A. Mueller et al., "A reverse engineering environment based on spatial and visual software interconnection models," *Proc. Fifth ACM SIGSoft Symposium on Software Development Environments*, ACM Press, New York, 1992, pp. 88–98.

Mueller et al [2000]
H. Mueller, J. Jahnke, D. Smith, M.-A. Storey, S. Tilley, and K. Wong, "Reverse engineering: A roadmap," in Finkelstein [2000].

Musa [1999]
J. Musa, *Software Reliability Engineering*, McGraw-Hill, New York, NY, 1999.

Musa and Ackermann [1989]
J. D. Musa and A. F. Ackermann, "Quantifying software validation: when to stop testing?" *IEEE Software*, 6(3): 19–27, May 1989.

Musa et al. [1987]
J. D. Musa, A. Iannino, and K. Okumoto, *Software Reliability: Measurement, Prediction, Application*, McGraw-Hill, New York, 1987.

Musser [1980]
D. Musser, "Abstract data type specification in the AFFIRM system," *IEEE Transactions on Software Engineering*, 6(1): 24–32, January 1981.

Musser and Saini [1996]
D. Musser and A. Saini, *STL Tutorial and Reference Guide*, Prentice Hall, Englewood Cliffs, NJ, 1996.

Myers [1978]
G. J. Myers, *Composite/Structured Design*, Van Nostrand Reinhold, New York, 1978.

Myers [1979]
G. J. Myers, *The Art of Software Testing*, John Wiley & Sons, New York, 1979.

Myers [1988]
B. A. Myers, "A taxonomy of window manager user interfaces," *IEEE Computer Graphics and Applications*, 8(5): 65–84, September 1988.

Nakagawa et al. [1988]
A. T. Nakagawa, K. Futatsugi, S. Tomura, and T. Shimizu, "Algebraic specification of Macintosh's QuickDraw using OBJ2," *Proceedings, 10th International Conference on Software Engineering*, Singapore, April 1988, pp. 334–343, IEEE Computer Society Press, Los Alamitos, CA, April 1988.

Nakajima and Futatsugi [1997]
S. Nakajima and K. Futatsugi, "An object-oriented modeling method for algebraic specifications in CafeOBJ," in *Proceedings of the International Conference on Software Engineering (ICSE '97)*, Boston, May 1997.

Naur et al. [1976]
P. Naur, B. Randell, and J. Buxton (ed.,) *Software Engineering: Concepts & Techniques*, Petrocelli/Charter, New York, 1976.

Neumann [1995]
P. G. Neumann, *Computer-Related Risks*, Addison-Wesley, Reading, MA, 1995.

Norman [1998]
D. A. Norman, *The Invisible Computer*. MIT Press, Cambridge, MA, 1998.

Norman and Draper [1986]
D. A. Norman and S. Draper (eds.), *User Centered System Design: New Perspectives on Human–Computer Interaction*, Laurence Erlbaum Associates, Hillsdale, NJ, 1986.

Norman and Nunamaker [1989]
R. J. Norman and J. F. Nunamaker, Jr., "CASE productivity perceptions of software engineering professionals," *Communications of the ACM*, 32(9): 1102–1108, September 1989.

Ntafos [1988]
S. C. Ntafos, "A comparison of some structural testing strategies," *IEEE Transactions on Software Engineering*, 14(6): 868–874, June 1988.

Nuseibeh and Easterbrook [2000]
B. Nuseibeh and S. Easterbrook, "Requirements engineering: a roadmap," in Finkelstein [2000].

Nuseibeh et al. [1994]
B. Nuseibeh, J. Kramer, and A. Finkelstein, "A Framework for Expressing the Relationships between Multiple Views in Requirements Specification," *IEEE Transactions on Software Engineering*, 20(10): 760–773, October 1994.

Oberndorf [1988]
P. A. Oberndorf, "The common Ada programming support environment (APSE) interface set (CAIS)," *IEEE Transactions on Software Engineering*, 14(6): 742–748, June 1988.

Olender and Osterweil [1990]
K. M. Olender and L. J. Osterweil, "Cecil: a sequencing constraint language for automatic static analysis generation.," *IEEE Transactions on Software Engineering*, 16(3): 268–280, March 1990.

Orfali et al. [1997]
R. Orfali, D. Harkey, and J. Edwards, *Instant CORBA*, John Wiley, New York, 1997.

Osterweil [1981]
L. J. Osterweil, "Software environment research: directions for the next five years," *Computer*, 14(4): 35–43, April 1981.

Osterweil [1987]
L. Osterweil, "Software processes are software too," *Proceedings, 9th International Conference on Software Engineering*, Monterey, CA, March 30-Apr. 2, 1987, pp. 2–13, IEEE Computer Society Press, Los Alamitos, CA, 1987.

Ostroff [1989]
J. S. Ostroff, *Temporal Logic for Real-Time Systems*, John Wiley & Sons, New York, 1989.

Owicki and Gries [1976]
S. Owicki and D. Gries, "Verifying properties of parallel programs: an axiomatic approach," *Communications of the ACM*, 19(5): 279–284, May 1976.

Parnas [1972a]
D. L. Parnas, "A technique for software module specification with examples," *Communications of the ACM*, 15(5): 330–336, May 1972.

Parnas [1972b]
D. L. Parnas, "On the criteria to be used in decomposing systems into modules," *Communications of the ACM*, 15(12): 1053–8, December 1972.

Parnas [1974]
D. L. Parnas, "On a buzzword: hierarchical structure," *Proceedings IFIP Congress* (1974), North-Holland, Amsterdam, 1974.

Parnas [1976]
D. L. Parnas, "On the design and development of program families," *IEEE Transactions on Software Engineering*, 2(2): 1–9, March 1976.

Parnas [1977]
D. L. Parnas, "The use of precise specifications in the development of software," *Proceedings, IFIP*, Toronto, Canada, August 1977, pp. 861–7, B. Gilchrist (ed.), North-Holland, Amsterdam, August 1977.

Parnas [1978]
D. L. Parnas, "Some software engineering principles," in *Structured Analysis and Design*, State of the Art Report, INFOTECH International, pp. 237–247, 1978.

Parnas [1979]
D. L. Parnas, "Designing software for ease of extension and contraction," *IEEE Transactions on Software Engineering*, 5(2): 128–138, March 1979.

Parnas [1985]
D. L. Parnas, "Software aspects of strategic defense systems," *Communications of the ACM*, 28(12): 1326–35, December 1985.

Parnas [1988]
D. L. Parnas, "Why engineers should not use artificial intelligence," *INFOR*, 26(4): 234–246, 1988.

Parnas [1994a]
D. L. Parnas, "Software aging," *Proc. International Conference on Software Engineering (ICSE 94)*, Sorrento, May 1994, pp. 279–287.

Parnas [1994b]
D. L. Parnas, "The professional responsibilities of software engineers," Proc. *of IFIP World Congress, Volume II*, August 1994, pp. 329–339.

Parnas and Clements [1986]
D. L. Parnas and P. C. Clements, "A rational design process: how and why to fake it," *IEEE Transactions on Software Engineering*, 12(2): 251–7, February 1986.

Parnas and Weiss [1987]
D. L. Parnas and D. M. Weiss, "Active design reviews: principles and practices," *Journal of Systems and Software*, 7(4): 259–65, December 1987.

Partsch and Steinbruggen [1983]
H. Partsch and R. Steinbruggen, "Program transformation systems," *ACM Computing Surveys*, 15(3): 199–236, 1983.

Paulk [1998]
M. C. Paulk, "Using the software CMM in small organizations," *Joint 1998 Proceedings of the Pacific Northwest Software Quality Conference and 8th International Conference on Software Quality*, Portland, OR, October 13–14, 1998, pp. 350–361.

Paulk et al. [1993]
M. C. Paulk, B. Curtis, M. B. Chrissis, and C. V. Weber, "The Capability Maturity Model for Software," *IEEE Software*, 10(4): 18–27, June 1993.

Perry and Wolf [1992]
D. E. Perry and A. L. Wolf, "Foundations for the study of software architecture," *ACM SIGSOFT Software Engineering Notes*, 17(4): 40–52, October 1992.

Peterson [1981]
J. L. Peterson, *Petri Net Theory and the Modeling of Systems*, Prentice-Hall, Englewood Cliffs, NJ, 1981.

Petri [1962]

C. A. Petri, *Kommunikationen mit Automaten*, University of Bonn, 1962, PhD dissertation; English translation: Technical Report RADC-TR-65-377, Vol. 1, Suppl 1, Applied Data Research, Princeton, NJ.

Phillips [1998]

D. Phillips, *The Software Project Manager's Handbook*, IEEE Computer Society Press, Los Alamitos, CA, 1998.

Pnueli [1981]

A. Pnueli, "The temporal semantics of computer programs," *Theoretical Computer Science*, 13, 45–60, 1981.

Porter and Johnson [1997], A. Porter and P. M. Johnson, "Assessing Software Review Meetings: Results of a Comparative Analysis of Two Experimental Studies," *IEEE Transactions on Software Engineering*, 23(3): 129–145, March 1997.

Porter et al. [1997]

A. Porter, H. Siy, C. A. Toman, and L. G. Votta, "An experiment to assess the cost–benefits of code inspections in large scale software development," *IEEE Transactions on Software Engineering*, 23(6), June 1997.

Prieto-Diaz and Neighbors [1986]

R. Prieto-Diaz and J. M. Neighbors, "Module interconnection languages," *Journal of Systems and Software*, 6: 307–334, 1986.

Queille and Sifakis [1982]

J-P. Queille and J. Sifakis, "Specification and verification of concurrent systems in CESAR," in *International Symposium on Programming, Lecture Notes in Computer Science*, Vol. 137, Springer-Verlag, Berlin and New York, pp. 337–351, 1982.

Raymond [1999]

E. S. Raymond, "The cathedral and the bazaar," http://www.tuxedo.org/esr/cathedral-bazaar/, November 1998.

Rechtin [1991]

E. Rechtin, *Systems Architecting: Creating and Building Complex Systems*, Prentice Hall, Englewood Cliffs, NJ, 1991.

Reifer [1986]

D. J. Reifer, *Tutorial on Software Management*, IEEE Computer Society Press, Los Alamitos, CA, 1986.

Reisig [1985]

W. Reisig, *Petri Nets: An Introduction*, Springer-Verlag, Berlin and New York, 1985.

Rich and Waters [1988]

C. Rich and R. C. Waters, "The programmer's apprentice: a research overview," *Computer*, 21(11): 10–25, November 1988.

Ringwood [1988]

G. A. Ringwood, "Parlog86 and the dining logicians," *Communications of the ACM*, 31(1): 10–25, January 1988.

Roman and Cox [1989]

G. C. Roman and K. C. Cox, "A declarative approach to visualizing concurrent computations," *Computer*, 22(10): 25–37, October 1989.

Rosenblum and Wolf [1997]

D. Rosenblum and A. Wolf, "A design framework for Internet-scale event observation and notification," Proceedings, ESEC/FSE '97, *Lecture Notes in Computer Science*, Vol. 1301, Springer-Verlag, Berlin and New York, pp. 344–360, 1997.

Ross [1977]

D. Ross, "Structured analysis (SA): a language for communicating ideas," *IEEE Transactions on Software Engineering*, 3(1): 16–34, January 1977.

Rout [1995]
> T. Rout, "SPICE: A Framework for Software Process Assessment," *Software Process: Improvement and Practice 1*(1): 57–66, August 1995.

Royce [1970]
> W. W. Royce, "Managing the development of large software systems: concepts and techniques," *Proceedings WesCon*, August 1970.

Rubinstein and Hersh [1984]
> R. Rubinstein and H. Hersh, *The Human Factor: Designing Computer Systems for People*, Digital Press, Bedford, MA, 1984.

Saiedian et al. [1996]
> H. Saiedian, J. P. Bowen, R. W. Butler, D. L. Dill, R. L. Glass, D. Gries, A. Hall, M. G. Hinchey, C. M. Holloway, D. Jackson, C. B. Jones, M. J. Lutz, D. L. Parnas, J. Rushby, J. Wing, and P. Zave, "An Invitation to Formal Methods," *Computer*, 29(4): 16–30, April 1996.

San Pietro et al. [2000]
> P. San Pietro, A. Morzenti, and S. Morasca, "Generation of execution sequences for modular time critical systems, *IEEE Transactions on Software Engineering*, 26(2): 128–149, Feb. 2000.

Sanden [1989a]
> B. Sanden, "Entity-life modeling and structured analysis in real-time software design—a comparison," *Communications of the ACM*, 32(12): 1458–1466, December 1989.

Sanden [1989b]
> B. Sanden, "The case for eclectic design in real-time software," *IEEE Transactions on Software Engineering*, 15(3): 360–362, March 1989.

Scheifler et al. [1988]
> R. W. Scheifler, J. Gettys, and R. Newman, *X Window System-C Library and Protocol Reference*, Digital Press, Bedford, MA, 1988.

Schmitt [1989]
> D. A. Schmitt, *The OS/2 Programming Environment*, Prentice Hall, Englewood Cliffs, NJ, 1989.

Schneiderman [1998]
> B. Schneiderman, *Designing the User Interface*, 3d ed., Addison-Wesley, Reading, MA, 1998.

Selby et al. [1987]
> R. W. Selby, V. R. Basili, and F. T. Baker, "Cleanroom software development: an empirical evaluation," *IEEE Transactions on Software Engineering*, 13(9): 1027–1037, September 1987.

Shatz and Wang [1989]
> S. M. Shatz and J.-P. Wang, *Tutorial on Distributed-Software Engineering*, IEEE Computer Society Press, Los Alamitos, CA, 1989.

Shaw and Garlan [1996]. M. Shaw and D. Garlan. *Software architecture: perspectives on an emerging discipline*. Prentice Hall, Englewood Cliffs, NJ, 1996.

Shen et al. [1983]
> V. Y. Shen, S. D. Conte, and H. E. Dunsmore, "Software science revisited: a critical analysis of the theory and its empirical support," *IEEE Transactions on Software Engineering*, 9(2): 155–165, March 1983.

Simon [1986]
> H. A. Simon, "Whether software engineering needs to be artificially intelligent," *IEEE Transactions on Software Engineering*, 12(7): 726–732, July 1986.

Skillicorn and Glasgow [1989]
> D. B. Skillicorn and J. I. Glasgow, "Real-time specifications using Lucid," *IEEE Transactions on Software Engineering*, 15(2): 221–229, February 1989.

Smith [1989]
> C. Smith, *Performance Engineering of Software Systems*, Addison-Wesley, Reading, MA, 1989.

Snyder [1986]

A. Snyder, "Encapsulation and inheritance in object-oriented programming languages," *Object-Oriented Programming Systems, Languages and Applications (OOPSLA) Conference* (November 1986), published also as *SIGPLAN Notices*, 21(11): 38–45, November 1986.

Spector and Gifford [1986]

A. Spector and D. Gifford, "A computer science perspective of bridge design," *Communications of the ACM*, 29(4): 268–283, April 1986.

Spivey [1989]

J. Spivey, *The Z Notation—a Reference Manual*, Prentice-Hall, Englewood Cliffs, NJ, 1989.

Spivey [1990]

J. M. Spivey, "Specifying a real-time kernel," *IEEE Software* 7(5): 21–28. Sept. 1990.

SPW [1988]

*Proceedings of the 4th International Software Process Workshop*, C. Tully (ed.), Moretonhampstead, Devon, U.K., May 1988, published as *SIGSOFT Software Engineering Notes*, 14(4), IEEE Computer Society Press, Los Alamitos, CA, June 1989.

Stallman [1984]

R. Stallman, "EMACS: the extensible, customizable, self-documenting display editor," in D. R. Barstow, H. E. Shrobe, and E. Sandewall (eds.), *Interactive Programming Environments*, pp. 300–25, McGraw-Hill, New York, 1984.

Stankovic [1988]

J. A. Stankovic, "Misconceptions about real-time computing: a serious problem for next-generation systems," *Computer*, 21(10): 10–19, October 1988.

Stefik et al. [1983]

M. Stefik, D. Bobrow, S. Mittal, and L. Conway, "Knowledge programming in loops: report on an experimental course," *AI Magazine*, 4(3): 3–13, Fall 1983.

Stefik et al. [1986]

M. Stefik, D. Bobrow, and K. Kahn, "Integrating access-oriented programming into a multiparadigm environment.," *IEEE Software*, 3(1): 10–18, January 1986.

Stenning [1987]

V. Stenning, "On the role of an environment," *Proceedings, 9th International Conference on Software Engineering*, Monterey, Mar. 30-Apr. 2, 1987, pp. 30–34, IEEE Computer Society Press, Los Alamitos, CA, 1987.

Sunshine et al. [1982]

C. Sunshine, D. Thompson, R. Erickson, S. Gerhart, and D. Schwabe, "Specification and verification of communication protocols in AFFIRM using state transition models," *IEEE Transactions on Software Engineering*, 8(5): 460–489 July 1982.

Swartout and Balzer [1982]

W. Swartout and R. Balzer, "On the inevitable intertwining of specification and implementation," *Communications of the ACM*, 25(7): 438–440, July 1982.

Szyperski [1998]

C. Szyperski. *Component Software: Beyond Object-Oriented Programming*, Addison-Wesley, Reading, MA, 1998.

Tahvanainen and Smolander [1990]

V.-P. Tahvanainen and K. Smolander, "An annotated CASE bibliography," *Software Engineering Notes*, 15(1): 79–92, January 1990.

Tai and Obaid [1986]

K. C. Tai and E. E. Obaid, "Reproducible testing of Ada task programs," *2nd IEEE Int. Conference on Ada Applications and Environments*, April 1986.

Tanenbaum [1987]
  A. S. Tanenbaum, *Operating Systems: Design and Implementation*, Prentice-Hall, Englewood Cliffs, NJ, 1987.

Taylor et al. [1988]
  R. N. Taylor, F. C. Belz, L. A. Clark, L. Osterweil, R. W. Selby, J. C. Wileden, A. L. Wolf, and M. Young, "Foundations for the Arcadia Environment Architecture," *Proceedings of Software Development Environments (SDE3)*, Boston, Nov. 28–30, 1988; published as *SIGPLAN Notices*, 24(2): 1–13, February 1989.

Teichrow and Hershey [1977]
  D. Teichrow and E. Hershey, III, "PSL/PSA: a computer aided technique for structured documentation and analysis of information processing systems," *IEEE Transactions on Software Engineering*, 3(1): 41–48, January 1977.

Teitelman and Masinter [1981]
  W. Teitelman and L. Masinter, "The INTERLISP programming environment," *Computer*, 14(4): 25–33, April 1981.

Thomas [1989]
  I. Thomas, "PCTE interfaces: supporting tools in software engineering environments," *IEEE Software*, 6(6): 15–23, November 1989.

Thomas and Nejmeh [1992]
  I. Thomas and B. A. Nejmeh, "Definition of tool integration for environments," *IEEE Software* 9(2), Mar. 1992, pp. 29–35.

Tichy [1985]
  W. F. Tichy, "RCS—a system for version control," *Software—Practice and Experience*, 15(7): 637–654, July 1985.

Tichy [1987]
  W. F. Tichy, "What can software engineers learn from AI?" *Computer*, 20(11): 43–54, November 1987.

Tichy [1989]
  W. F. Tichy, "Software configuration management," IEEE Computer Society Press, Los Alamitos, CA, *Tutorial notes of 11th ICSE*, May 1989.

Tichy [1994]
  W. F. Tichy (ed.), "Configuration management," in *Trends in Software*, vol. 2, John Wiley & Sons, New York, 1994.

TSE [1985]
  Special issue on Artifical Intelligence and Software Engineering, published as *IEEE Transactions on Software Engineering*, 11(11), Nov. 1985.

TSE [1988]
  Special issue on Software Engineering Environment Architectures, published as *IEEE Transactions on Software Engineering*, 14(6), June 1988.

TSE [1990]
  Special issue on Experimental Computer Science, published as *IEEE Transactions on Software Engineering*, 16(2), February 1990.

Ullman and Widom [1997]
  J. D. Ullman and J. Widom, *A First Course on Database Systems*, Prentice Hall, Englewood Cliffs, NJ, 1997.

van Lamsweerde [2000a]
  A. van Lamsweerde, "Requirements Engineering in the Year 2000," *Proceedings of the International Conference on Software Engineering (ICSE 2000)*, Limerick, Ireland, IEEE Computer Society Press, Los Alamitos, CA, June 2000.

van Lamsweerde [2000b]
  A. van Lamsweerde, "Formal Specification: A Roadmap," in Finkelstein [2000].

van Solingen and Berghout [1999]
R. van Solingen and E. Berghout. *The Goal/Question/Metric Method*. McGraw-Hill Publishing Co., New York, 1999.

Verner and Tate [1988]
J. Verner and G. Tate, "Estimating size and effort in fourth generation development," *IEEE Software*, 5(4): 15–22, July 1988.

Walker et al. [1980]
B. Walker, R. A. Kemmerer, and G. Popek, "Specification and verification of the UCLA Unix security kernel," *Communications of the ACM*, 23(2): 118–131, February 1980.

Ward and Mellor [1985]
P. T. Ward and S. J. Mellor, *Structured Development for Real-Time Systems*, Yourdon Press, New York, 1985.

Wasserman et al. [1990]
A. I. Wasserman, P. A. Pircher, and R. J. Muller, "The object-oriented structured design notation for software design representation," *Computer*, 23(3): 50–63, March 1990.

Wegner [1984]
P. Wegner, "Capital-intensive software technology," *IEEE Software*, 1(3): 7–46, July 1984.

Wegner [1987]
P. Wegner, "Dimensions of object-based language design," *Object-Oriented Programming Systems, Languages and Applications (OOPSLA) Conference*; published as *SIGPLAN Notices*, 22(12): 168–82, December 1987.

Weihl [1989]
W. E. Weihl, "Local atomicity properties: modular concurrency control for abstract data types," *ACM Transactions on Programming Languages and Systems*, 11(2): 249–282, April 1989.

Weinberg [1971]
G. M. Weinberg, *The Psychology of Computer Programming*, Van Nostrand Reinhold, New York, 1971.

Weinberg and Schulman [1974]
G. M. Weinberg and E. L. Schulman, "Goals and performance in computer programming," *Human Factors*, 16(1): 70–77, 1974.

White [1987]
L. J. White, "Software testing and verification," in M. C. Yovits (ed.), *Advances in Computers*, pp. 337–91, Academic Press, New York, 1987.

Wiest and Levy [1977]
J. D. Wiest and F. K. Levy, *A Management Guide to PERT/CPM*, Prentice-Hall, Englewood Cliffs, NJ, 1977.

Wilkstrom [1987]
A. Wilkstrom, *Functional Programming Using Standard ML*, Prentice-Hall International, Hemel Hempstead, U.K., 1987.

Wing and Nixon [1989]
J. M. Wing and M. R. Nixon, "Extending Ina Jo with temporal logic," *IEEE Transactions on Software Engineering*, 15(2): 181–97, February 1989.

Wirth [1971]
N. Wirth, "Program development by stepwise refinement," *Communications of the ACM*, 14(4): 221–227, April 1971.

Wirth [1977]
N. Wirth, "Towards a discipline of real-time programming," *Communications of the ACM*, 20(8): 577–583, August 1977.

Wirth [1983]
> N. Wirth, *Programming in Modula-2*, 2d ed., Springer-Verlag, Berlin and New York, 1983.

Wong [1984]
> C. Wong, "A successful software development," *IEEE Transactions on Software Engineering*, 10(6): 714–727, November 1984.

Woodcock and Davies [1996]
> J. Woodcock and J. Davies, *Using Z: Specification, Refinement, and Proof*. Prentice Hall, Englewood Cliffs, NJ, 1996.

Wordsworth [1990]
> J. B. Wordsworth, "The CICS application programming interface definition," in *Proceedings of Z User Workshop*, Oxford, U.K., 1990, pp. 285–294.

Yadav et al. [1988]
> S. B. Yadav, R. R. Bravocco, A. T. Chatfield, and T. M. Rajkumar, "Comparison of analysis techniques for information requirement determination," *Communications of the ACM*, 31(9): 1090–1097, September 1988.

Yau and Tsai [1986]
> S. S. Yau and J. J. P. Tsai., "A survey of software design techniques," *IEEE Transactions on Software Engineering*, 12(6): 713–721, June 1986.

Young [1989]
> D. A. Young, *X Window Systems—Programming and Applications with Xt*, Prentice-Hall, Englewood Cliffs, NJ, 1989.

Young and Taylor [1988]
> M. Young and R. M. Taylor, "Combining static analysis with symbolic execution," *IEEE Transactions on Software Engineering*, 14(10): 1499–1511, October 1988.

Young and Taylor [1989]
> M. Young and R. N. Taylor, "Rethinking the taxonomy of fault detection techniques," *Proceedings, 11th International Conference on Software Engineering*, Pittsburgh, May 15–18, 1989, pp. 53–63, IEEE Computer Society Press, Los Alamitos, CA, 1989.

Young et al. [1988]
> M. Young, R. N. Taylor, and D. B. Troup, "Software environment architectures and user interface facilities," *IEEE Transactions on Software Engineering*, 14(6): 697–708, June 1988.

Yourdon and Constantine [1979]
> E. Yourdon and L. Constantine, *Structural Design*, Prentice-Hall, Englewood Cliffs, NJ, 1979.

Zave [1982]
> P. Zave, "An operational approach to requirements specification for embedded systems," *IEEE Transactions on Software Engineering*, 18(3): 250–269, May 1982.

Zave [1984]
> P. Zave, "The operational versus the conventional approach to software development," *Communications of the ACM*, 27(2): 104–118, February 1984.

Zave and Schell [1986]
> P. Zave and W. Schell, "Salient features of an executable specification language and its environment," *IEEE Transactions on Software Engineering*, 12(2): 312–325, February 1986.

Zeil [1989]
> S. J. Zeil, "Perturbation techniques for detecting domain errors," *IEEE Transactions on Software Engineering*, 15(6): 737–746, June 1989.

# Index